SHORT STORIES: A CRITICAL ANTHOLOGY

ENSAF THUNE
Hofstra University

RUTH PRIGOZY
Hofstra University

The Macmillan Company, New York

To

Arne and Steve

Printed in the United States of America

The Macmillan Company
866 Third Avenue, New York, New York 10022

Library of Congress catalog card number: 72-80182

Printing: 1 2 3 4 5 6 7 8 Year: 3 4 5 6 7 8 9

Acknowledgments

Alain Robbe-Grillet, from "The Secret Room," in *Snapshots.* Translated by Bruce Morrissette. Copyright © 1968 by Grove Press, Inc.

Anton Chekhov, "Gusev." Reprinted with permission of The Macmillan Company from *The Witch and Other Stories* by Anton Chekhov, translated by Constance Garnett. Copyright 1918 by The Macmillan Company, renewed 1946 by Constance Garnett.

Joseph Conrad, "Il Conde." Reprinted with the permission of J. M. Dent & Sons, Ltd., and the Trustees of the Joseph Conrad Estate.

Thomas Mann, "Little Herr Friedemann." From *Tonio Kroger and Other Stories* translated by David Luke. Copyright © 1970 by Bantam Books, Inc.

James Joyce, "Counterparts." From *Dubliners* by James Joyce. Originally published by B. W. Huebsch in 1916. Copyright © 1967 by The Estate of James Joyce. All Rights Reserved. Reprinted by permission of The Viking Press, Inc.

Katherine Mansfield, "A Dill Pickle." Copyright 1920 by Alfred A. Knopf, Inc. and renewed 1948 by J. Middleton Murry. Reprinted from *The Short Stories of Katherine Mansfield* by permission of Alfred A. Knopf, Inc.

Sherwood Anderson, "The Egg." Reprinted by permission of Harold Ober Associates, Inc. Copyright © 1921 by B. W. Huebsch, Inc. Renewed 1948 by Eleanor C. Anderson.

Italo Svevo, "Traitorously," translated by Ben Johnson; "The Mother," translated by L. Collison-Morley, from Italo Svevo's *Short Sentimental Journey and Other Stories,* 1967. Originally published by the University of California Press; reprinted by permission of The Regents of the University of California.

Franz Kafka, "A Country Doctor," and "A Fable." Reprinted by permission of Schocken Books Inc. from *The Penal Colony* and *The Great Wall of China,* by Franz Kafka. Copyright © 1948, 1946 by Schocken Books Inc.

Rudyard Kipling, "The Gardener." Copyright 1926 by Rudyard Kipling. From the book *Debits and Credits* by Rudyard Kipling. Reprinted by permission of Mrs. George Bambridge and Doubleday and Company, Inc.

F. Scott Fitzgerald, "Dalyrimple Goes Wrong." "Dalyrimple Goes Wrong" is reprinted by permission of Charles Scribner's Sons from *Flappers and Philosophers* by F. Scott Fitzgerald. Copyright 1920 Charles Scribner's Sons; renewal copyright 1948 Zelda Fitzgerald.

Ernest Hemingway, "Soldier's Home." "Soldier's Home" is reprinted by permission of Charles Scribner's Sons from *In Our Time* by Ernest Hemingway. Copyright 1925 Charles Scribner's Sons; renewal copyright 1953 Ernest Hemingway.

D. H. Lawrence, "The Man Who Loved Islands." From *The Woman Who Rode Away and Other Stories,* by D. H. Lawrence. Copyright 1928 by D. H. Lawrence and renewed 1956 by Frieda Lawrence Ravagli. Reprinted by permission of Alfred A. Knopf, Inc.

Sigrid Undset, "Simonsen." From *Told in Norway.* Reprinted by permission of The American-Scandinavian Foundation.

William Faulkner, "Death Drag." Copyright 1931 by Charles Scribner's Sons; assigned to Random House, Inc.; renewed 1959 by William Faulkner. Reprinted from *Collected Stories of William Faulkner* by permission of Random House, Inc.

Richard Wright, "Bright and Morning Star." From *Uncle Tom's Children* by Richard Wright. Copyright, 1938, by Richard Wright; renewed 1966 by Ellen Wright. Reprinted by permission of Harper & Row, Publishers, Inc.

Katherine Anne Porter, "The Downward Path to Wisdom." Copyright, 1939, 1967, by Katherine Anne Porter. Reprinted from her volume, *The Leaning Tower and Other Stories* by permission of Harcourt Brace Jovanovich, Inc.

Eudora Welty, "Death of a Traveling Salesman." From *A Curtain of Green and Other Stories,* copyright 1941, 1969, by Eudora Welty. Reprinted by permission of Harcourt Brace Jovanovich, Inc.

Jean-Paul Sartre, "The Wall." Translated by Lloyd Alexander. Copyright 1948 by New Directions Publishing Corporation. Reprinted by permission of New Directions Publishing Corporation.

J. F. Powers, "The Forks." Copyright 1947 by J. F. Powers. From *Prince of Darkness and Other Stories* by J. F. Powers. Reprinted by permission of Doubleday & Company, Inc.

Saul Bellow, "Looking for Mr. Green." From *Mosby's Memoirs and Other Stories* by Saul Bellow. Copyright 1951 by Saul Bellow. Reprinted by permission of The Viking Press, Inc.

John Cheever, "The Enormous Radio." From *The Enormous Radio and Other Stories* by John Cheever. Copyright 1953 by John Cheever. With permission of Funk & Wagnalls, Publisher.

Elizabeth Taylor, "Spry Old Character." From *Hester Lily and 12 Short Stories* by Elizabeth Taylor. Copyright © 1953 by Elizabeth Taylor. Originally appeared in *The New Yorker*. Reprinted by permission of The Viking Press, Inc.

Flannery O'Connor, "Good Country People." From *A Good Man Is Hard to Find and Other Stories*, © copyright, 1955, by Flannery O'Connor. Reprinted by permission of Harcourt Brace Jovanovich, Inc.

Bernard Malamud, "The Last Mohican." Reprinted with the permission of Farrar, Straus & Giroux, Inc. From *Pictures of Fidelman* by Bernard Malamud, copyright © 1958, 1969 by Bernard Malamud.

Heinrich Böll, "Christmas Every Day." Reprinted by permission of Joan Daves. Copyright © 1957 by Heinrich Böll.

Philip Roth, "Defender of the Faith." From *Goodbye Columbus*. Copyright © 1959 by Philip Roth. Reprinted by permission of the publisher, Houghton Mifflin Company.

Muriel Spark, "Bang-Bang You're Dead." From the book *Voices at Play* by Muriel Spark. Copyright © 1961 by Muriel Spark. Reprinted by permission of J. B. Lippincott Company.

Jorge Luis Borges, "Deutsches Requiem." Translated by Julian Palley. Jorge Luis Borges, *Labyrinths*. Copyright © 1962 by New Directions Publishing Corporation. Reprinted by permission of New Directions Publishing Corporation.

Alberto Moravia, "He and I." Reprinted with the permission of Farrar, Straus & Giroux, Inc. From *More Roman Tales* by Alberto Moravia, copyright © 1963 by Martin Secker & Warburg Ltd.

Yukio Mishima, "The Pearl." Translated by Geoffrey W. Sargent. From Yukio Mishima, *Death in Midsummer*. Copyright © 1966 by New Directions Publishing Corporation. Reprinted by permission of New Directions Publishing Corporation.

LeRoi Jones, "The Screamers." Copyright © 1967 by LeRoi Jones. Reprinted by permission of The Sterling Lord Agency, Inc.

Abram Tertz, "Pkhentz." Reprinted by permission of *Encounter*.

Donald Barthelme, "Report." Reprinted with the permission of Farrar, Straus & Giroux, Inc. From *Unspeakable Practices, Unnatural Acts* by Donald Barthelme, copyright © 1967, 1968 by Donald Barthelme.

Preface

In this anthology, the editors have tried to present the short story in its historical, critical, and cultural contexts. Previous critical investigations of the short story have generally treated these three areas individually, or with primary emphasis on one aspect. Whereas the theory and criticism of drama and of the novel have been recognized as forces shaping those two genres, the critical theory of the short story has, by comparison, received only a casual glance. Yet there is no question that short-story criticism has helped form and shape its own branch of fiction.

Our aim has been to remedy the situation and, through systematic analysis, to place the short story in a serious perspective. By briefly tracing the history of the short story, by surveying the development of its critical theory, by examining the terminology used to describe fictional elements, and finally, in the introductory essay to the stories that make up the bulk of this book, by discussing the social and moral significance of more than forty works, we hope to furnish a total framework for the study and enjoyment of the short story.

We have selected those stories we believe to be of the highest quality and greatest diversity, those that seem to us most likely to appeal to both student and teacher. At the same time, we have chosen stories that are most representative of the developing genre. One third of the stories have not been previously anthologized. Of the rest, a small number are staples of short-story collections, while the others are less familiar stories by acknowledged masters of the form. Writers of many nationalities are represented. Almost half are American or English, for two reasons: first, because we believe that, although it is imperative that we be acquainted with foreign literature, many artistic values are lost in translation; and second, because America, particularly in the last fifty years, has produced more than her share of able short-story writers.

In our discussion of the stories, we have avoided condensed or exhaustive interpretations. Our purpose is to initiate the student's response by providing him with a meaningful social or moral framework for each story. Through brief example and suggestion, we hope to encourage the student to formulate his own critical judgments. In the critical section, in all but a very few instances, references are confined to the stories in this volume.

We wish to acknowledge gratefully the help of our friends and colleagues: Professor Leo Gurko of Hunter College, and members of the English and Comparative Literature departments at Hofstra University; Mrs. L. D. Smits of the New Canaan, Connecticut, Public Library for her help in locating hard-to-find material; Great Neck, New York, Public Library; the Yale University and Hofstra University libraries; Mrs. Louisa Ayoub and Miss Barbara Stroh of Hofstra University for their invaluable help in the preparation of the manuscript.

E. T.
R. P.

Contents

HISTORY AND THEORY OF THE SHORT STORY

SHORT STORIES

History and Theory of the Short Story

PART I

The Historical-Critical Context of the Short Story

In 1968 and 1969, a small-circulation literary magazine, the *Kenyon Review*, published an international symposium on the short story. Contributors included writers, critics, and literary agents. One question dominated every discussion: Is there a future for the short story, or is the brief flowering of the newest form of fiction already over? The popularity of television and films, along with rising magazine production costs, have caused many established journals to fold. *The Saturday Evening Post*, *Collier's*, and *The Woman's Home Companion* were three of the mass-circulation magazines that once printed hundreds of new short stories every year. In the twenties and thirties, a successful writer like F. Scott Fitzgerald could earn a handsome income from his magazine fiction. Today, even the surviving mass-circulation magazines print fewer stories; most, like *McCall's*, *Redbook*, and *Ladies' Home Journal*, are chiefly devoted to feature articles and columns that focus on contemporary issues.

The blame for the decline of the short story's popularity cannot be attributed only to TV and rising costs. The modern reading public has long been surfeited by a steady diet of sentimental, wish-fulfillment formula stories. Our age has witnessed several wars, rapid technological change, and widened contact among diverse cultures. The reading public has grown more sophisticated, more sensitive to the falsehoods of the old-style commercial fiction. Television has heightened public awareness of the problems that face contemporary societies. The reader's desire for "facts" reflects his anxiety to keep pace with the speed at which news is currently made. Truman Capote's *In Cold Blood* and Tom Wolfe's *The Kandy Kolored, Tangerine-Flake Streamline Baby* are both "non-fiction novels," whose popularity reflects the new mood of the public. Nevertheless, the form of the short story still attracts writers. Every short-story writer participating in the symposium indicated his faith in the short story as a living form of fiction. But the question of public lack of receptiveness remains.

History clearly shows that the short story has never held a secure position in the literary hierarchy. Many of the critics and commentators who shaped and molded it regarded the short story as a stepchild in the family of prose fiction, outshone by its older and weightier relative, the novel. Since the first appearance of the short story in the form we currently recognize, early in the nineteenth century, critics have pondered exactly what this undoubtedly commercial, but artistically questionable hybrid was. By reviewing the attitudes and exploring the theories that have developed around the short story, we hope not only to sketch the outlines of its past life, but to illuminate its future direction as well.

THE HISTORICAL BACKGROUND

A brief historical review of short narrative will throw light on the theory and practice of the modern short story.

Short narrative has been part of man's cultural heritage as far back as history records. First in verse and then in prose, stories representing the ideals, aspirations, and customs of societies were collected in the ancient world and passed down to future generations. Evidence dating from as early as 3000 B.C. shows that the Egyptians inscribed little tales on papyrus and stored them in their tombs. Written stories were the results of centuries of oral narrative tradition. The storyteller was an important figure in ancient society; he traveled from community to community singing or reciting local tales which he constantly augmented with contributions gleaned on his travels. Folk tales, in Germany called *märchen,* were anonymous prose stories with a long oral history behind them. They were the sources of the fairy tales that are familiar today to every child. The *Iliad,* Homer's epic account (recorded about the ninth century B.C.) of the feats of gods and heroes in the much earlier Trojan War, had its origins in oral tradition. The Greek myths were originally oral narratives, later written down and preserved for their cultural value (see Hesiod's *Theogony, ca.* eighth century B.C.).

The earliest written collections of stories came from ancient India. The *Jatakas,* or teachings of Buddha, and the *Panchatantra,* or Hindu beast fables, both date from about 500 B.C. The *fable* was a brief narrative in prose or verse, illustrating a moral point. The characters were animals who talked like human beings. The most famous group of animal fables is attributed to Aesop, a Greek slave who lived during the sixth century B.C. Written versions of Aesop's fables date from the first and second centuries A.D. By the Middle Ages, the animal fable, like *The Owl and the Nightingale* (1225), had become very popular in Western Europe. Two modern examples of the fable in this volume are Svevo's "The Mother" and Kafka's "A Fable." The *apologue* was another form of the fable, using human characters, but with a similar didactic purpose. It became popular in later religious literature.

The Old Testament Bible abounds in short narratives: the historical-legendary accounts of Esther, Ruth, and David and Goliath are examples. In the New Testament, we find Christ's *parables,* brief narratives presenting a clear parallel between the elements in the story and the intended moral. Examples of the parable are the Good Samaritan story and the story of the prodigal son.

Several types of short fiction that were popular throughout the Middle Ages, until about 1600, also contributed to the development of the short story. First, there was the *conte dévot,* which appeared in France in the twelfth and thirteenth centuries. These *contes dévots* were short religious verse tales recounting miracles performed by saints, and intended for pious instruction. They were extremely popular and circulated widely, particularly the group known as the Miracles of Mary. These narratives glorified chivalrous devotion to ideal womanhood, as represented by the figure of the Virgin Mary. In their emphasis on courtly standards of conduct, they resemble the *prose romances* of twelfth- and thirteenth-century France and fourteenth-century England. The prose romance related a series of incidents loosely held together by biographical details. The hero was generally an ideal knight, like Sir Lancelot in the Arthurian romances.

Another forerunner of the short story was the *fabliau,* which developed in thirteenth-century France and survived for more than a century. Fabliaux were short, humorous narratives, usually in verse, designed primarily for entertainment rather than instruction. They exposed human weaknesses, frequently those of women or clergymen. The subject matter of the fabliaux was often bawdy and the language coarse. They were written about and for the middle and lower classes, using realistic details and more sophisticated storytelling techniques than most short narratives of the period. A fine specimen of the fabliau in English is Chaucer's "Miller's Tale" from *The Canterbury Tales* (1387–1395). The fabliau was also an influence on Boccaccio's prose *novellas.*

The *lai* was a secular short verse tale of romance and chivalric adventure, circulated by troubadours in the thirteenth and fourteenth centuries. The best French lais were written by Marie de France as early as 1200. Several English versions of the lai are noteworthy, such as *Sir Orfeo* (*ca.* 1320), which retells, with alterations to suit the era, the Greek legend of Orpheus and Eurydice.

The *exemplum* was a very compressed story told in medieval times to illustrate a moral point. The moral was often suggested at the beginning rather than at the end of the tale. Exempla were commonly used in sermons. They provided Chaucer with models for the brief instructive passages preceding the stories in *The Canterbury Tales.* "The Pardoner's Tale" is a brilliant specimen of the exemplum. Any of the short narrative types described earlier, if used for illustrative purposes, may be regarded as exempla, even the ancient *Jatakas.* Church literature of the Middle Ages converted hundreds of secular stories into religious exempla. Their sources were varied, including mythology, history, contes, fables, and folk tales. The thirteenth-century *Gesta Romanorum* was a famous collection of exempla in Latin, telling of the deeds of Roman emperors and heroes. Translated into English in the fifteenth century, it became an important sourcebook for later writers. *A Mirror for Magistrates* (1559) was a verse collection of historical exempla that used the decline of persons of high estate to point morals about human frailty, vice, and the instability of fame.

By the early sixteenth century, prose narrative had begun to replace verse, partly as a result of the introduction of printing, which stimulated silent reading, partly because the coming of the Renaissance brought a shift in values. The popularity of the overtly moral tale lessened somewhat, and jest books, like the *Hundred Mery Talys* (1526), with short, humorous anecdotes ranging from jokes and puns to sketches and tales, caught the fancy of the public.

A more important form of short narrative popular in the Renaissance was the *novella.* These short prose tales were in vogue as early as the fourteenth century in Italy, where Boccaccio's *Decameron* was widely read and copied. In England, William Painter's *Palace of Pleasure* (1566) was a compilation of the best-known French and Latin stories about Italian life. It appeared at a time when interest in anything Italian was high. The Italian novellas were of two kinds: legitimate romantic prose tales, expressing courtly ideals, and satirical burlesques or parodies of romantic attitudes. Painter's collection included many tales with a didactic purpose.

In Spain, the *picaresque* tale developed during the sixteenth century. The *picaro,* Spanish for "rogue," was a rascal whose escapades provided the basis for a series of realistic and satiric adventures in which, by his wit, the *picaro* usually managed to triumph over folly and vice. *Don Quixote* (1605), the most famous predecessor of the novel as we know it, typifies the use of the picaresque story within a long narrative framework. A widely circulated collection of picaresque stories, published in France a century later, is Le Sage's *Gil Blas* (1715).

Another important precursor of the modern short story, the prose sketch, originated in the Renaissance. Sketches circulated first in pamphlets and periodicals, later in newspapers. These brief and realistic narratives about the life of the middle class were overshadowed in the Renaissance by the more popular entertainment form, drama; in the eighteenth century, however, they were to become a staple of popular literature. Renaissance examples of the short periodical sketch are Thomas Deloney's *The Gentle Craft* (1597), which celebrated the guild of shoemakers, and Thomas Dekker's pamphlet stories, *The Raven's Almanacke* (1609).

The periodical sketch survived well into the nineteenth and even the twentieth centuries. It first achieved genuine success, however, in the early eighteenth century in *The Tatler* (1709), written by Richard Steele (1672–1729), and *The Spectator* (1711–1714), written by Joseph Addison (1672–1719) and Steele. The periodical sketch was essentially a product of city life. It was stimulated by the growth of a reading public interested in town manners and customs. The epistolary or letter form was often used in these sketches to add a personal touch and greater complexity to the characters. (Samuel Richardson's long novel, *Clarissa,* 1747–48, was written solely in the form of letters between characters.) Most of these sketches focused on character rather than plot, although *The Spectator* occasionally printed a melodramatic tale of passion. Generally, they combined characteristics of the formal essay with fictional narrative. The most famous group of *Spectator* papers concerned a central figure, Sir Roger de Coverley, in whom we have a realistic, often humorous, and decidedly human portrait of an English gentleman of the period. The *Tatler* and *Spectator* sketches often ran to as many as four or five thousand words.

The typical eighteenth-century novel used much of the material and many of the techniques originally employed in the periodical sketch. Dr. Samuel Johnson's periodical, *The Rambler* (1750), developed the form further, giving serious attention to narrative structure. The results were fewer character sketches and more stories with recognizable plots. Dickens's "Horatio Sparkins"—from *Sketches by Boz* (1836)—is a fine example of the humorous sketch still popular in the nineteenth century.

Daniel Defoe (1660?–1731) wrote a number of short fictional works in which he applied realistic details to supernatural or extraordinary events. In his "True Relation of the Apparition of One Mrs. Veal," Defoe's rambling narrative and minute rendering of surface realism never flag; they effectively deflect the reader from considering the implausibility of the idea. Like other narratives of the period, it is not a short story in the modern sense; there is no climax, no finished development of plot. The author simply leaves off when he has decided he is finished, without formally concluding the situation.

Oriental stories, exemplified by The Arabian Nights, dating back to the eighth century and first published in Europe in French in 1704, were another important contribution to the background of the short story. Either purely romantic or overlaid with morality, they were exciting adventure tales. Many of them used allegory, a narrative technique whereby the characters and sometimes the setting as well are made to represent abstract ideas and symbolic or moral concepts. The Arabian Nights were widely circulated and satisfied the reading public's taste for exotic fiction.

By the end of the eighteenth century, the overtly moral story had died out, although, as the next section will show, the moral intent of fiction was an important issue for later critics of the short story. With the growth of a mass market and the rise of commercial magazine fiction in the nineteenth century, the era of the modern short story really begins.

THE MODERN SHORT STORY

Washington Irving (1783–1859), the American writer who is regarded as the originator of the short story, once explained why the form appealed to him, as a writer, more than the novel. First, the short story liberated him from dependence on the conventions of long fiction. Second, and as a corollary, it allowed him the freedom to pursue originality and artistic excellence. Irving believed that novel-writing inevitably results in long dull patches of narrative. The success of a work, he held, hinges on the telling rather than the tale. The anecdote, or plot, for him is merely "a frame on which to stretch my materials." If the faults of a brief work are immediately obvious, so, too, are its merits. The audience will quickly appreciate the artistry of short fiction and will return to it with ever-renewed pleasure. The primary purpose of fiction, which is to entertain, will then be fulfilled. In his own work, notably "Rip Van Winkle" and "The Legend of Sleepy Hollow," Irving combined American and European history and folklore, contemporary social observation, and humor, to create stories that have enduring appeal.

In America, the short story was quickly accepted by a reading public eager to fill its leisure hours with light diversion. Lavishly decorated annuals or monthly gift-books filled with sentimental romances were prominently displayed on parlor tables. Adapted from German models, with names like *The Atlantic Souvenir* (1826–1832), *The Token* (1828–1842), and *Godey's Lady's Book* (1830–1898), they appealed to young girls and women with a taste for pretty, banal accounts of unrequited love and Gothic melodramas filled with ghosts, devils, mad queens, and haunted mansions.

Many of the stories were written by women, but regardless of the sex of the contributor, the quality of the popular fiction in the 1820s and 1830s was generally low. On rare occasions stories by Poe, Hawthorne, and other serious writers found their way into the *Lady's Book* or an annual. In their way, these early periodicals did encourage the growth of a native literature at a time when uncopyrighted English works were being pirated and disseminated in America.

In England, in the early years of the nineteenth century, the short story was not as widely accepted as it was in America. The taste for three-volume novels led to the magazine serialization of all fiction, even shorter works. *Blackwood's Magazine* (1817) provided leading writers with their first important outlet for short works. It was followed in the next two decades by several others, including *The Keepsake* (1827) and *Heath's Book of Beauty* (1833). In addition to sentimental stories of the type that filled American magazines, the English periodicals carried many moral tales—instructive and frequently skillful retellings of old legends—and short fictional works masquerading as fact. In Ireland, which like America had a rich tradition of folk narrative, the short story developed more freely and with more variation than it did in England.[1]

The stories of this era in all countries were uniformly rambling and episodic. In an installment of his *Autocrat at the Breakfast Table* (1832), Oliver Wendell Holmes made a plea for the brief, compressed narrative that was to become the modern short story. However, it was not until Edgar Allan Poe (1809–1848) set an example, both through his own superb stories and his penetrating criticism of those by other writers, that the short story became a fixture of modern literature.

For twenty years, in an era of rampant commercialism, Poe waged a fierce, lonely, and often fruitless battle on behalf of literary excellence

[1] See Wendell V. Harris, "English Short Fiction in the Nineteenth Century," *Studies in Short Fiction,* 6 (Fall 1968), pp. 1–93, for an excellent historical review of the English short story.

and critical independence. His critical theory was to become a major force in the development of the short story.

To begin with, merely by discussing the craft of the short story seriously, Poe raised it to the level of an important and independent literary art. By accompanying his principles with brilliant examples from his own pen, he secured for the short story the attention of both general reading public and men of letters.

The heart of Poe's theory of the short story is contained in a passage from his review of Hawthorne's *Twice-Told Tales* (1842):

> A skilful literary artist has constructed a tale. If wise, he has not fashioned his thoughts to accommodate his incidents; but having conceived, with deliberate care, a certain unique or single *effect* to be wrought out, he then invents such incidents—he then combines such events as may best aid him in establishing this preconceived effect. If his very initial sentence tend not to the outbringing of this effect, then he has failed in his first step. In the whole composition there should be no word written, of which the tendency, direct or indirect, is not to the one pre-established design.

Because unity of effect cannot be achieved in a work that requires of the reader more than one sitting, Poe established the proper reading time for a short story as from half an hour to one or two hours. Among the effects a tale might create are "terror, passion or horror or a multitude of other such points." In *The Philosophy of Composition* (1846), Poe expanded his conception of the highest aim of the short story to include not only Truth—the satisfaction of the intellect—but Passion, the excitement of the heart.

In his theory, Poe left little to chance or accident. To achieve a logical sequence of action that will result in unity of effect, the writer must work out, with mathematical precision, the details of his plot up to the denouement (the high point and subsequent unraveling of a plot) before he begins to write. The rigidity of Poe's statements enabled later writers to use them as rationales for their own tightly plotted, "well-made" stories.

Poe's theories did not succeed in improving the quality of the popular story, but they brought a response from contemporary writers, among them Nathaniel Hawthorne (1804–1864). Poe had criticized Hawthorne's *Twice-Told Tales* for being too filled with allegory to convey passion, too shadowy and pallid to develop unity of effect adequately. Hawthorne admitted (in the *Democratic Review*, December, 1844) that his love of allegory brought a meditative chill to his sketches. He suggested that they be read in "the clear brown twilight atmosphere" in which they were written. Allegory, he argued, while not adding profundity, might enlarge the scope of the story beyond the individual's private sensibility. Hawthorne's remarks suggest that his stories have a wider applicability than those that seek only a single effect. Through allegory, the short story might embrace broader concerns of mankind.

Both Poe and Hawthorne reflected in their writing and criticism the romantics' belief in the primacy of the artist's imagination in artistic creation. By the middle of the nineteenth century, however, as social and philosophical interests changed, a shift began from romantic to realistic theories of perception and creativity.

To the romantic writer, the imagination of the artist is the starting point of creation. The mind is the ultimate reality because it is in touch with the infinite (divinity) through an intuitive sense, the imagination. The artist's highest achievement is his faithful reproduction of his own imaginative conception of the world. In "Roger Malvin's Burial," Hawthorne states that the imagination alters the outer world "by casting certain circumstances into the shade." In his Preface to *The House of the Seven Gables,* Hawthorne explains the difference between the romance and the novel. His remarks also suggest some differences between romanticism and realism:

> When a writer calls his work a Romance, it need hardly be observed that he wishes to claim a certain latitude, both as to its fashion and material, which he would not have felt himself entitled to assume, had he professed to be writing a Novel. The latter form of composition is presumed to aim at a very minute fidelity, not merely to the possible, but to the probable and ordinary course of man's experience. The former—while, as a work of art, it must rigidly subject itself to laws, and while it sins unpardonably, so far as it may swerve aside from the truth of the human heart—has fairly a right to present that truth under circumstances, to a great extent, of the writer's own choosing or creation. If he think fit, also, he may so manage his atmospherical medium as to bring out or mellow the lights and deepen and enrich the shadows of the picture. He will be wise, no doubt, to make a very moderate use of the privileges here stated, and, especially, to mingle the Marvellous rather as a slight, delicate, and evanescent flavor, than as any portion of the actual substance of the dish offered to the Public.

The view of artistic creation described by Hawthorne had developed over many years and under many influences. Philosophers like John Locke (1632–1704), Bishop George Berkeley (1685–1753), and David Hume (1711–1776) had begun, more than a century earlier, to explore the workings of the human mind. John Stuart Mill (1806–1873) in England and William James (1842–1910) in America continued the studies of their predecessors, focusing on the nature of individual feeling. The English poets William Wordsworth (1770–1850) and Samuel Taylor Coleridge (1772–1834) stressed the expression of feeling and imagination, both sources of artistic inspiration. In their poetic theories, they defined the poet's feeling as the primary element in the creative process. Coleridge maintained that there were no fixed rules for composition. Each poem worked according to its own law and evolved naturally into its own unique form.[2]

[2] In this one respect, Poe's critical theories were rationalistic in the extreme, even antiromantic, and quite prescriptive.

Romantic theories of artistic creation carried over from poetry into prose fiction. Romantic fiction in general tended to present life as magnified, more heroic, more picturesque and exciting than it really was. Realism attempted to faithfully recapture the outer world in fiction. The starting point for the realist, in fact, is the outer world, from which his imagination selects and shapes details of plot and character so as to convey a sense of actuality. He will normally choose characters and incidents that tend to reflect the average or ordinary in human experience, as Hawthorne noted. The manner of writing is as important to the realist as the matter. The subject must be rendered so carefully as to create an illusion of reality, for no realist wholly believed he could reproduce external experience with total fidelity. Insofar as the imagination transforms the objective world, it is as important to the realistic writer as it is to the romantic.

Most writers were neither totally romantic nor totally realistic. The predominating attitude of many merely shifted in the nineteenth century from one approach to the other. Romanticism has been vigorously alive in the twentieth century, as stories like Fitzgerald's "Dalyrimple Goes Wrong" and Conrad's "Il Conde" attest. Many writers, indeed, from the nineteenth century to the present, have maintained that man's natural appetite demands unusual incidents in fiction. A story may employ realistic details freely so long as it satisfies the reader's longings and daydreams.

In France, Guy de Maupassant (1850–1893), whose short stories earned him a world-wide reputation, was a leading advocate of fictional realism. In the introduction to his novel *Pierre et Jean* (1888), Maupassant made it clear that realism was much more than the transcription of commonplace events. Truth, he believed, was the presentation of scenes and incidents more striking and cogent than reality itself, arranged so as to produce the illusion of reality. How to convey the illusion of reality was a central concern of realistic theory; it virtually dominated the critical writings of Henry James (1843–1916).

James, the great American novelist and short-story writer, was a steady admirer of Maupassant's unerring instinct for selecting details that capture the essence of a scene. James's own criticism was an important contribution to discussions of literary realism in his day. His influence on the teaching and appreciation of literature in the twentieth century has been equally impressive. He believed that the writer must take his craft seriously before the public would do so. Critical theory, for James, was the writer's "core of conviction," evidence of his seriousness of purpose. James devoted himself to the task of setting down in prefaces, letters, notebooks, and formal essays (notably, "The Art of Fiction," 1884), his observations on his problems and those of other writers.

Behind everything he wrote was his belief that the "air of reality" (he also called it "solidity of specification") was the supreme virtue of fiction. It might be achieved by conveying to the reader an intense impression of "felt life." The successful rendering of felt life depended chiefly on the "point of view" (see Part II, *Elements,* pages 37–48) through which details of the objective world are intelligently and intensely filtered. The writer should select a fictional counterpart for himself (James called it a "central consciousness") whose fine perceptions would render reality scrupulously. In this connection, his famous remark from "The Art of Fiction" bears repeating: "The deepest quality of a work of art will always be the quality of mind of the producer."

In his story in this volume, "Four Meetings," James gives a full picture of Caroline Spencer's pathetic life by selecting only a few details that poignantly contrast her dingy surroundings with her gallant efforts to beautify them. The narrator's perceptions and observations provide the intensity of vision through which James brings the reader into close contact with the pathos of her wasted life.

Even though he wrote more than eighty stories, James never found it easy to compress his material into the length he desired. His critical writings detail a lifelong struggle to "squeeze" an idea into five or seven thousand words; he rarely wrote stories of fewer than ten thousand. Despite his difficulties, he paid tribute late in life to the form he had named "short story": "The wish and dream have lately grown stronger than ever in me . . . the desire that the literary heritage . . . that I may leave, shall consist of a large number of perfect *short* things" (Preface to *Roderick Hudson*, 1906).

Most nineteenth-century writers faced, directly or indirectly, the question of morality in fiction. The problem was particularly acute in connection with the short story, which had begun its existence as purely commercial entertainment without a serious or uplifting purpose. To avoid the label of immorality, the earliest short-story writers frequently added passages of overt moralizing to tales of love, mystery, or adventure. Washington Irving had conceded that the short story must have a moral, but he preferred it disguised with "sweets and spices" so as not to spoil the reader's enjoyment. Poe's definition of the aims of the short story was implicitly, although not conventionally, moral. In "William Wilson," the narrator's sins—drinking, gambling—were recognizably moral offenses to Poe's readers. Hawthorne, we have already noted, suggested that his tales embraced the most important moral issues facing an individual. In "Roger Malvin's Burial," Reuben Bourne's trouble is rooted in the conflict between his private needs and the moral ideas of his society. For Hawthorne, the exploration of moral principles was itself a moral foundation of fiction. James, like many realists, believed that the writer's devotion to his craft constituted the highest morality. In "The Art of Fiction," he stated that the artist must be perfectly free; his primary obligation to his work is that it be interesting. It is moral to the extent that it fulfills the aim of the realist—to render reality faithfully.

James's criticism of Maupassant (1888, essay reprinted in *The House of Fiction*) specifically linked the issues of morality and craftsmanship. Because Maupassant stressed one aspect of life—the senses, chiefly sex—James could say that the picture of human life reflected in Maupassant's stories was distorted, hence unrealistic. (In "Useless Beauty," the conflict between the husband and wife is presented in explicitly sexual terms.) Like other nineteenth-century critics, James thus broached the issue of morality in fiction. Although he treated the problem obliquely, he nonetheless illustrated how significant an issue morality was in the theory and practice of the nineteenth-century short story.

Anton Chekhov, the great Russian short-story writer and dramatist (1860–1904), shared James's conviction that the writer's responsibility was not to resolve moral questions, but simply to practice his craft. Unlike James, Chekhov did not write formal criticism, but his critical remarks, as well as his own stories, were as important to later generations of writers as James's were. Chekhov's intentions in writing short stories paralleled those of James: simplicity, brevity, objectivity, and selectivity. He, too, valued the dramatized over the narrated incident, as more clearly conveying a sense of living experience. Chekhov's own stories, however, are totally unlike James's. Influenced by *A Sportman's Sketches*, which was published in 1852 by his fellow Russian, Ivan Turgenev (1818–1883), Chekhov's stories are brief ("Gusev," included here, is a longer one), and deceptively simple and aimless; they resemble episodes rather than fully plotted works. There are no real central complications, denouements, or dramatic endings. Chekhov once advocated, where necessary, eliminating the beginnings and endings of stories. He constantly reiterated his view of the discipline that the short story demanded of the writer. Every unnecessary word, he maintained, must be carefully cut. Chekhov's advice to writers often seems as firm and prescriptive as Poe's and that of Poe's disciples. His purpose was totally unlike theirs, however, for he disliked the "well-made" story. Because Chekhov's work was not available in English until the Constance Garnett translations began to appear toward the end of the nineteenth century, his influence on writers and critics was not apparent in England and America until the second decade of the twentieth century.

In 1899, the American short-story writer Bret Harte (1836–1902) reviewed half a century of the American short story. He emphasized the unique contributions of American culture, particularly its extravagant, irreverent folk humor, and praised a small group of realists, the "local color" school, for discovering the richness of the American language. Harte felt that the secret of the successful American short story was its treatment of native American life with all its variety, speed, and vitality. His own sentimental Western adventure stories created stereotyped characters—the gallant gambler, the prostitute with a heart of gold—who were to become stock figures in popular Western fiction and films of a later era. Stephen Crane, who is frequently described as a naturalist,[3] combined the mythology of the American West with his own unique brand of irony to create, in "The Blue Hotel," a bitter version of the popular American "Western."

[3] The naturalists were a group of writers, many of whom started their careers as newspapermen, who tried to present a truthful picture of the realities of existence as they saw them. Based on the biological theories of fiction with Darwinian implications as expounded by Emile Zola (1840–1902), naturalism's major theses were that man lacks free will, that he is conditioned by his heredity and environment, and that he is adrift in an indifferent universe. Morality, to the naturalist, is a set of socially conditioned responses that thwart an individual's free growth and expression. Frank Norris (1870–1902) and Theodore Dreiser (1871–1945) were other major American naturalists.

While Crane and other rebellious young writers were breaking new ground for the short story, Brander Matthews (1852–1929), himself a writer and critic, and professor of English at Columbia University, was clarifying theory and technique according to the rules advanced by Poe half a century earlier. In two essays (1884, 1885), which were later circulated as a book, *The Philosophy of the Short Story* (1906), Matthews offered a definitive outline of the short story as a separate, unique literary form with its own set of conventions. The (hyphenated) "short-story," Matthews said, must have unity, compression, fantasy, and originality. Unity of effect derived from the story's plot, around which all other fictional elements should be organized. Matthews' formulations were based on his survey of fifty years of the American short story which, since Poe, had been notable for its strong central plot.

In England, Matthews' articles stimulated discussion of the British short story. Unlike the American form, this was characteristically a long and rambling structure much like the English novel, which relied on extended passages of narrative that summarized rather than dramatized action. In addition to Matthews' articles, the most important influences on the English short story were Henry James, Robert Louis Stevenson (1850–1894), and Rudyard Kipling (1865–1936). Both Stevenson and Kipling employed realistic details, strong plots, rapid sequences of action, and exciting, often melodramatic episodes; the results were concise and striking stories with strong romantic overtones. With brilliant irony, Kipling frequently satirized the conventional moral codes of the British upper classes (see, for example, "The Gardener" in this volume).

The strong-plot, or well-made story was a staple of popular fiction well into the twentieth century. The successes of Harte, Stevenson, and Kipling were exceptions to the profusion of mediocre, predictable formula stories that were inundating the market. In response to a seemingly inexhaustible demand, and with respect for the financial rewards of commercial fiction, a new publishing enterprise was launched in America. Dozens of writers' handbooks were published in the first two decades of the twentieth century. Based on the typically American assumption that application, energy, and moderate skill were all that were necessary to succeed, the handbooks offered strict rules for aspiring writers. Their model was the plot story, epitomized by the breezy, colloquial stories of O. Henry (William Sydney Porter, 1862–1910), with their inevitable surprise endings. The handbooks simplified some rules, for example, by suggesting that only one major character appear in a story, and complicated others, as when they recommended an intricate ordering of episodes, which Matthews had considered unnecessary. The American short-story writer Jack London (1876–1916) revealed the extent of commercial magazine dictatorship: "Put a snapper at the end, so if they are crowded for space they can cut off your contents anywhere, re-attach the snapper, and the story will still retain form."[4] He admitted, however, that had the short-story market

[4] Quoted by E. J. O'Brien, *The Dance of the Machines* (New York: The Macauley Company, 1929), pp. 131–132.

been less rigid, he would have written many stories quite different from those he had produced.

By 1915, when the stories of Turgenev and Chekhov had become available to a wide English-speaking audience, a chorus of protest began to mount against the American plot story. Critics felt that the bloom was gone, that the American writers were pandering to the lowest tastes of their readers by following stale literary conventions. The Russians, they felt, were genuinely writing about life. In England, too, the reading public's new demand for any short fiction, regardless of its quality, was criticized by novelists who had long depended for their livelihood on the three-volume novel (see George Gissing's description of this development on the English literary scene some years earlier in his novel *New Grub Street,* 1891).

The severest attack on the popular American short story came from Edward J. O'Brien (1890–1941), a journalist and poet, who, each year from 1915 to 1940, edited a collection of the best American short stories. In the twenty-six years that he served as editor, *Best Stories* sold more than a quarter of a million copies. O'Brien's intention in putting together his annual collections was to introduce the American public to short stories as unlike the popular magazine monstrosities as possible. In doing so, he hoped to stimulate the reading public's taste for higher quality fare, to provide a market for new and unusual fiction, and to encourage young writers to follow their natural artistic inclinations. Unalterably opposed to rules for writing, O'Brien looked for and found new writers. He published Sherwood Anderson, Ernest Hemingway, F. Scott Fitzgerald, and Katherine Anne Porter, whose experiments with form and style in unknown magazines were leading the short story away from the mechanization of the past fifty years. O'Brien incorporated his attacks on the popular short story in two critical books, *The Advance of the American Short Story* (1923) and *The Dance of the Machines* (1929). His most serious charge was that the short story had abdicated the primary responsibility of fiction: to portray real people in recognizably human situations. He felt that the short story, like the machine, manufactured "types." He attributed the lifelessness of the American short story to the standardization of American life. Because it seemed to reflect the haste, restlessness, and rootlessness of our culture, the short story became, for O'Brien and other critics, a symbol of the American's pathological mania for quick results. Ring Lardner's clever, mock-illiterate parody of a short-story handbook (*How to Write Short Stories*, 1924) epitomized the serious writer's disgust with the popular formula story:

> But a little group of our deeper drinkers has suggested that maybe boys and gals who wants to take up writing as their life work would be benefited if some person like I was to give them a few hints in regards to the technic of the short story, how to go about planning it and writing it, when and where to plant the love interest and climax, and finally how to market the finished product without leaving no bad taste in the mouth.

Other young writers shared O'Brien's aversion to fixed rules for writing short stories. Sherwood Anderson (1876–1941), whose collection of stories, *Winesburg, Ohio* (1919), heralded a new era in the American short story, rejected the standard view of plot. He saw the conventional plot as a framework on which the author would develop his idea into a salable product (*A Story-Teller's Story,* 1924). For Anderson, a story simply grew out of the author's mind. It took shape as he responded to life, which was his raw material. A writer could not fit his impressions of life into a ready-made structure. Anderson's contemporary, Katherine Anne Porter (1894–), best summed up the artist's dislike of formula writing: "The short story is a special and difficult medium, and contrary to a widely spread popular superstition, it has no formula that can be taught by correspondence school." [5] She went on to dismiss classifications of fiction that the handbooks had made ridiculous: "Please call my works by their right names: we have four that cover any division, short stories, long stories, short novels, novels." [6]

The widespread refusal to define literary form was more than just a response to commercialism. It reflected a growing philosophical awareness that there was an indefinable element in life itself. Reality seemed more fluid than it had ever been; a general mood of uncertainty made it seem merely foolish to impose fixed rules on the elusive process of artistic creation. (See Stories, *Introduction: The Short Story in the Modern World.*) Psychological theory and psychoanalysis generated new interest in the individual mind and the complexity of individual personality. Writers began to feel that the inner lives of their characters were more real than their observable actions. (The drama in Katherine Mansfield's "A Dill Pickle" derives from the thoughts and feelings of the two main characters.) Henri Bergson (1859–1941) had proposed that the individual's psychological time (*la durée*), which represented the intensity of his inner experience, was a more accurate measure of reality than chronological time. The moment in which a character acutely feels an experience may seem to him of much longer duration than the actual time that has elapsed. Conventional division into minutes, hours, and days is unrelated to the duration of experience within the individual. For literature, Bergson's concept meant that the writer had to reveal the endless flux of feeling and thought within his characters. Clearly, the short-story writer would need new techniques to render the new view of reality.

French symbolism was one of the major influences on the formation of new fictional techniques in the twentieth century. Through the poetry of Baudelaire, Rimbaud, Mallarmé, and Verlaine, the American short story again felt the effects of Edgar Allan Poe. Paradoxically, Poe, whose criticism inspired the well-made story, was also an indirect source of the loose, formless works perfected by Anderson, James Joyce (1882–1941), and Katherine Mansfield (1888–1923). In Poe's poetry and even in many

[5] Quoted in Georgianne Trask and Charles Burkhart, eds., *Storytellers and Their Art* (Garden City, N.Y.: Doubleday & Company (Anchor Books), 1963), p. 372.

[6] Quoted in Whit and Hallie Burnett, eds., *The Modern Short Story in the Making* (New York: Hawthorn Books, 1964), p. 404.

of his short stories, emphasis on the self and the soul, revelation through symbols and metaphors of nuances of feeling, sense imagery, particularly synesthesia (the exchange of sensory faculties, e.g., "an orange sound"), musicality, and suggestiveness, provided the symbolists with a key to unlock the poetic imagination. The symbolists felt that the writer must invent a new language capable of expressing the uniqueness of his personality.

James Joyce's short stories, collected in *Dubliners* (1914), and his artistic theory, as he set it down in his novel *Portrait of the Artist As a Young Man* (1916), gave the new writers an important aesthetic term, "epiphany," to describe the effects they were trying to achieve in their stories. The epiphany is the story's moment of revelation; a veil is raised and the previously hidden meaning is suddenly illuminated. Although Joyce brought the term into general critical usage, the literary effect it described had already been achieved in stories by Chekhov and Mansfield. It has become a major characteristic of the contemporary story. Sherwood Anderson's remark, "The true history of life was but a history of moments," expresses the underlying premise governing the writer's use of epiphany. A good example of Anderson's use of epiphany is the moment in "The Egg" when the son gets a sudden insight into the tragedy of his father's life as the older man, humiliated, lies weeping. (Other technical changes in the form of the short story during this period are described in Part II, *Elements of the Short Story.*)

Critics and many readers in the United States and abroad gradually accepted the new short story, but the debate about form did not end. Those who admired Maupassant, Stevenson, Kipling, and other masters of strong-plot stories were united in deploring the formlessness of new fiction. Their adversaries celebrated Chekhov's deceptively casual stories as models of a new art form that could express universal meanings. W. Somerset Maugham (1874–1965), the popular English novelist and short-story writer, wrote many essays on the short story in the course of a long lifetime of literary activity. Maugham admitted that he liked best the kinds of stories he wrote himself, stories that could hold the listener's attention over the dinner table or in a ship's smoking-room. Critics frequently derided Maugham's own stories, although entertaining and beautifully crafted, as superficial. His defense of his practice was also a defense of other well-made stories which, because of their structural similarities to mediocre magazine fiction, seemed lacking in seriousness and artistry. All well-made, strong-plot stories were certainly not trivial or unstimulating, but the emphasis on ambiguity, nuance, and symbol in the new stories made the old plot-story seem overly simple and obvious by comparison.

Opposition to the well-made story was solidified by the influential "New Critics." The New Criticism, a literary movement that developed in the forties and fifties, was started by a group of Southern intellectuals, among them poets and critics John Crowe Ransom (1888–), Allen Tate (1899–), and Robert Penn Warren (1905–). In their manifesto, *I'll Take My Stand* (1930), they attacked modern industrial society for pursuing scientific progress at the expense of art. The essays of their fellow poet T. S. Eliot (1888–1965) noted the loss of religious tradition, and Allen Tate analyzed the disappearance of aesthetic order. The central critical principle of the New Critics was clearly stated: "Pure criticism would be divorced from history, biography, sociology or psychology and would confine itself to explaining the intrinsic qualities of a work of art." [7] "Autonomy" and "intrinsic" were key words in the New Critics' doctrine. Autonomy meant that the literary work must be studied independently of external standards, author's opinions, or social-historical contexts. Intrinsic referred to their conviction that the literary work was valid in terms of its internal structure; the critic should focus his attention on the arrangement of elements within the work. The New Critics admired the lyric poem, with which they often compared the short story. They frequently seemed to equate the degree of complexity in a literary work with its artistic value. They admired the loosely plotted, symbolic, and psychological story. New Criticism is important in the history and theory of the short story because of its pervasive influence in universities for over twenty years. It helped form tastes and set standards both for college audiences and for those who would continue in academic life. Their close attention to the text of a story added an important dimension to a growing body of short-story theory. Although many writers rejected the detailed scrutiny to which the New Critics subjected their stories, the movement helped to heighten the reader's sensitivity to the aims and effects of the serious short-story writer.

Several other critical schools have been born in the last two or three decades—in part as reactions against the orthodoxies of the New Criticism. They reflect the currently complicated, but lively critical scene. Many of them have, directly or indirectly, affected the study of the short story.[8]

[7] Rene Wellek and Austin Warren, *Theory of Literature* (New York: Harcourt Brace Jovanovich, Inc., 1949).

[8] The original impulse for "myth critics" of the middle 1950s came from psychoanalyst C. G. Jung (1875–1961), who theorized that we find in literature repeated patterns of behavior ("archetypes") that conform to patterns of thought and feeling: society's "collective unconscious." Essentially ahistorical, the myth critics elaborated on the discoveries in anthropology, folklore, and psychology, of ritualistic patterns of behavior in primitive societies, which recur throughout history as basic expressions of subconscious drives of social groups. The myth critics created a new vogue in critical terminology: "initiation," "archetypal," "allegorical," "mythic." In terms of the short story, the myth critics traced recurring archetypal patterns of escape ("Rip Van Winkle" was a model), the theme of double identity or dual consciousness (see "William Wilson" and "He and I" in this volume), initiation and/or nature-myth (Faulkner's "The Bear").

Canadian critic Northrop Frye's (1912–   ) *Anatomy of Criticism* (1957) incorporates myth criticism into a generic approach to prose fiction. Frye's criticism grows out of his conviction that recent literary critics have examined all forms of prose fiction according to formulations about the realistic novel. To Frye, each form of fiction should be studied in terms of its own conventions, the form the writer has elected to pursue.

An extension and addition to Frye's method is Robert Scholes' and Robert Kellogg's *The Nature of Narrative* (1966), which insists that by studying the continuity of each type of narrative within a five-thousand-year-old tradition we may discover the continuous or recurrent elements in narrative art. Study of the short story would inevitably include Ovid's contributions to the short tale, and continue with close analyses of a variety of short narrative forms. The short story, ideally, would be studied as short narrative form, not, as has generally been the case, along with the novel.

A fairly recent development in the theory of the novel has influenced many contemporary short-story writers. In the 1950s, supporters of the "new novel" in France and elsewhere were saying that past literary theories are irrelevant in the modern era, an "age of suspicion."[9] They decided that the old novel form was now dead because the novelist no longer believes in his characters or plot. The public, too, has lost its taste for fiction; it trusts only the pure fact, which needs no interpreter. They called for a "new novel" to answer the needs of the suspicious reader. Alain Robbe-Grillet's *For a New Novel* (1965) is a major theoretical statement of the French movement. His position is that the writer must discard all literary traditions which falsify reality by assuming that man exists in a stable, coherent universe. Because no one object has more significance than another, the writer must seize equally upon all details. The "new novel" must be a precise record of the sensations stimulated by surface experience. Robbe-Grillet's theories have proved more effective in short stories and very short novels than in lengthier fiction. His own short story, "The Secret Room," is a very brief, but minutely detailed description of a victim and her murderer. It opens:

> The first thing to be seen is a red stain, of a deep, dark shining red, with almost black shadows. It is in the form of an irregular rosette, sharply outlined, extending in several directions in wide outflows of unequal length, dividing and dwindling afterward into single sinuous streaks.

The rest of the story continues in the same vein, detail piled upon detail. The total effect is one of cumulative horror. There is no interruption in the emotionless narrative to deflect the reader from the graphic picture of a violent, sexually suggestive scene. In its intensity of visual impression, coupled with shifting viewpoints and ambiguities, the new fiction resembles many recent films, like Robbe-Grillet's own "Last Year At Marienbad." Although LeRoi Jones is not part of the "new novel" group, his story, "The Screamers," presents a somewhat similar succession of striking visual and auditory images.

Looking back over the short story as it has developed from the nineteenth century to the present, one is struck by the enormous range and

---

The Chicago critics, led by Ronald Crane, moved away from New Critical textual analysis to categorizing fiction according to Aristotelian rules, by the kinds of feelings aroused in the reader. Austin McGiffert Wright, in his study *The American Short Story In the Twenties* (1961), thus classifies a story in terms of its purpose—rhetorical or didactic—and its arousal of a specific emotion in the reader.

The "mimetic" school of criticism (notably Erich Auerbach in *Mimesis*, 1953, and Ian Watt in *The Rise of the Novel*, 1957) regards prose fiction technique as formed by the artist's view of society, which is itself a development out of his particular era. Discussion of a story would focus on a writer's conception of the real world and the formal method by which he seeks to render it. In an extension of the mimetic approach, Marshall McLuhan locates the sources of contemporary style in technological advances in communications media—radio and television primarily. Recent attempts to compare the techniques of short story and film are typical of McLuhan's technological-mimetic approach.

[9] Nathalie Sarraute, *The Age of Suspicion* (New York: Grove Press, 1963).

variety of its forms. For the past seventy-five years, critics and commentators have been impressed with its unmistakable vitality. Many of them have recorded in books, articles, and even brief notes their impressions and theories about the short story—what it is, what it does, what makes it a special and unique form. We have already summarized the major movements in critical theory. Actually, very little formal criticism has developed around the short story. Most short-story criticism is scattered, discursive, and unsystematized. Before we consider the future of the short story, therefore, it may be helpful to review the main lines of discussion not mentioned previously. The following has been culled from innumerable sources, which are cited in the *Bibliography* following Part II.

The Short Story and the Novel

The first consideration here has been: Can the short story be defined as an independent genre, or must it be measured against the conventions of the novel? In the nineteenth century, critics fought to establish it as more than merely a short, trivial novel. Today, most would agree that the short story in form and purpose is unlike the novel. Some critics maintain that it was born late because it had to wait until the novel had explored and located its boundaries. Although it may be an outgrowth and continuation of the novel (a theory belied by the long tradition of short-fiction narrative), its survival has depended less than that of the novel on the presence of leisure and money, classic conditions of middle-class society. It could thus appeal to a consistently wider audience.

Flexibility. The short story is often regarded as more flexible, more open to a writer's experiments than the novel. For example, it can free the writer from the use of chronological time and allow him wider latitude in choosing characters. A character need not age in a short story; it is even possible to write a short story without any characters at all. A novel, on the other hand, depends on both time and character. The implicit assumption of this argument is that by "novel" we mean only the realistic novel perfected in the eighteenth and nineteenth centuries.

Range. Many critics have argued about the comparative scope or range of the short story and the novel. Early critics frequently felt that the short story was a surface work, leaving no room for the subjectivity and depth of a novel. Chekhov regarded writing a novel as a serious step which he was unready to take. He would confine himself to "short, unpretentious stories . . . and not climb mountains." [10] The novel can render successive states of feeling, and thus convey a wider range of human experience. The short story, however, frequently achieves a more immediate and more intense impression. The difference between the two has been compared to the difference between a love affair and a marriage. In the latter, the responsibility is total.

[10] Anton Chekhov, *Life and Letters of Anton Chekhov*, ed. S. S. Koteliansky and Philip Tomlinson (New York: Benjamin Blom, 1965), p. 119.

Characterization. What differences exist in characterization in the two forms? Critics have often conceded that the situation is the principal concern of the short story, characterization that of the novel. The Irish short-story writer Frank O'Connor (1903–1966) finds that the major difference between the two is the difference between characters regarded as representative figures in the novel and characters regarded as lonely outcasts in the short story. Characters in the novel must be accurate reflections of society; in the short story, they may be strange, anomalous, unique [11] (see Part II, *Elements of the Short Story*).

Structure. Statements about narrative structure in novel and short story have been particularly contradictory and uncertain. Generally, however, there is agreement that the short story presents a simpler action with less narration, greater unity, and more immediate impact on the reader (see Part II, *Elements of the Short Story*).

Language. Are there differences between the short story and the novel in the use of language? There has been little extended discussion of this problem, although a few commentators have contended that the short-story writer must devote greater attention to the sentence and the word than the novelist, whose primary considerations are paragraphs and even chapters. Critics stress verbal virtuosity as the distinguishing feature of the short story.

Purpose. Finally, many critics have compared the ultimate purpose or meaning of the two forms. Here opinion is clearly divided. On the one hand, because the short story is exempt from the novel's conclusiveness, it may be closer to aesthetic and moral truth, which is tentative at best. On the other hand, the novel is said to resemble a philosophical treatise on life, making it a *less* absolute statement than the short story. Both forms are regarded as capable of reflecting contemporary life. The novel probes the unknown depths of the mind, whereas the short story, accommodating itself readily to formlessness, can more accurately reflect the fragmentation, restlessness, and uncertainty of modern consciousness. One is impressed, after reading arguments on both sides, by the individual writer's bias for the form at which he has been most successful.

The Short Story and Lyric Poetry

The argument introduced by Poe, that the short story is the nearest prose equivalent of the lyric poem, gained renewed currency in this century shortly after stories by James Joyce and Katherine Mansfield appeared. Critics often applied the criteria for lyric poetry to the modern short story. The short story, like the lyric poem, can be "an intense expression of one quality of mind and soul . . . isolated from the rest of human experience." [12] Both forms are more highly regarded now than they were

[11] Frank O'Connor (pseudonym for Michael O'Donovan), *The Lonely Voice: A Study of the Short Story* (Cleveland: World Publishing Company, 1963).

[12] Wayne Booth, *The Rhetoric of Fiction* (Chicago: University of Chicago Press, 1961), p. 63.

in the nineteenth century; comparing one to the other today is to praise both forms.

The Short Story, Drama, and Films

Because the short story has often seemed to offer the writer imaginative possibilities beyond those of the novel, attempts have been made to demonstrate its resemblance to drama and film. Chekhov believed the requirements of the short story to be similar to Aristotle's rules for the drama. Critics often cite immediacy and unified action as characteristics of both forms.

Recent critical works have tried to find parallels in the development of short stories and films in the twentieth century. The story, like the film, moves through a series of "subtly implied gestures and swift shots . . . the two arts, rendering life largely by suggestion, brief episodes, picture sequences, indirect narration and . . . symbolism, developed together.[13]

Descriptive Definitions of the Short Story

Length and Unity. It is assumed that the principal feature of a short story is its shortness; it must "pack in" what it has to say. "Packing in," however, is not simple. Kipling says, "A tale from which pieces have been raked out is like a fire that has been poked. One does not know that the operation has been performed, but everyone feels the effect." [14] The problem is to condense and compress without producing a synopsis. There is little disagreement that despite its shortness, a story must be complete in itself. To most critics, unity or wholeness is best effected by limiting the story to a single impression, as Poe advised. To some, it means working toward a climax or crisis, or using one situation that represents a quintessential human experience.

The problem of a story's wholeness is related to its treatment of time. The short story may treat an event from a point in time, which then becomes the crisis of the story; one moment can quickly place past and future into their proper perspectives. Another device through which the short story may achieve unity and immediacy is the use of a single point of view, as originally proposed by Henry James.

Characterization. Although few dispute that the short story can convey complex emotional and psychological states, most writers and critics agree that genuinely complex characterization is not possible in so short a form. Character in a short story is at best a hieroglyphic or a caricature, and the reader accepts it as such. The writer's skill can create the illusion of complexity in a short-story character, but close examination will reveal the illusion. Because there is so little room for gradual development in a short story, the writer is forced to portray character through a few quick strokes. A character's development is revealed through a series of actions that offer

[13] H. E. Bates, *The Modern Short Story* (London: Thomas Nelson & Sons, Ltd., 1945), p. 207.
[14] Rudyard Kipling, *Something of Myself,* quoted in Trask and Burkhart, p. 47.

him opportunities to make significant choices. There is little room in the short story for many such choices; hence characterization cannot achieve its fullest dimension.

Personality of the Writer

Finally, abandoning comparative and descriptive criteria altogether, writers and critics have for years attempted to study the short story solely in terms of the personality of the author. It is the last, indefinable, and indispensable element in literature; it explains the inexplicable. As Eudora Welty puts it, "The value of a story is the thing nearest dependent upon the individual and personal factor involved, the writer behind the writing." [15]

To return to the original question, Has the short story a future? On the basis of current evidence, no one should confidently predict its demise. If critical interest is any measurement of its health, the short story, as the preceding essay demonstrates, is thriving. Just a few years ago, a new scholarly publication, *Studies in Short Fiction*, was born; it is devoted to serious study of the short story.

The market for the short story is admittedly a reduced one, but new publishing fields, like original paperback collections,[16] are still opening. *The New Yorker, Esquire,* and *Playboy* continue to reach a mass market, limited though it may be when compared to the magazine audience of the twenties and thirties. Several anthologies of contemporary fiction originally published in small-circulation literary journals have been published by major companies. They are intended for the general reader as well as for the college student.[17] Although sales are notoriously poor, new collections of stories by successful contemporary novelists appear regularly in bookstores. The short story is certainly not dead; it may even face the prospect of a healthy survival in a much less commercial form than in the past. Undoubtedly the market for mediocre-to-poor stories has dried up, however.

We may conclude that the future is not altogether bleak for the serious young short-story writer. Limited channels should remain open, and may even expand. The college audience has been growing steadily in recent years, particularly in community colleges. The student who acquires a taste for short stories in college represents the reading public of tomorrow; he may insure the future of the short story.

[15] Eudora Welty, *Short Stories* (New York: Harcourt Brace Jovanovich, 1949).

[16] *New American Review* (New York: The New American Library, 1967–); *New American Story* (New York: Grove Press, 1965); a twenty-four-page tabloid newspaper of short stories, *Fiction*, made its first appearance in 1972.

[17] *Fiction of the Sixties*, ed. Stanley Elkin (Garden City, N.Y.: Doubleday & Company (Anchor Books), 1971).

Elements of the Short Story

PART II

Elements of the Short Story

"Everything is technique which is not the lump of experience."
(Mark Schorer, "Technique as Discovery")

INTRODUCTION

The beginning of criticism, writes one critic, is to read aright. He goes on to say, however, that where fiction is concerned, attempts at right reading generally result in varying degrees of "unsuccess." First, it is difficult to grasp the form of a story in a single unified impression, as one can with a painting or a piece of sculpture. The second reason, with which we are presently concerned, is that many of the critical terms which the reader uses to describe his fictional experience have rarely been given lucid and consistent definition.

Drama, poetry, and the visual arts have an established history of theory and criticism, whereas fictional theory in general, and the short story in particular, is of comparatively recent origin, and as the preceding section shows, of a rather controversial or uncertain nature. As a result, fictional critical terminology has borrowed freely from the jargon of other literary art forms. Its critical language is far more extensive, but at the same time it is less unified and organized. One could probably fill several pages with terms currently used in novel and short-story critiques, many of which are varied names for the same thing. The following randomly selected list of a few of these terms and coinages gives an indication of the amorphousness, and for the reader, confusion, that exists in this sphere of fictional study: authority, eye, mind, eyewitness, observer, point of view, center of vision, angle of vision, first-person narrator, omniscient narrator, concealed narrator, method of central intelligence, psychic distance, third person omniscient, third person limited, third person objective, limited focus, credibility, closeup, scenic, effect, atmosphere, panorama, mise-en-scène, description, background, setting, distance, immediacy, scale, pace, rhythm,

[1] For dates of authors and critics cited in this chapter, and for further publishing information, please consult either Part I, or the Bibliography.

cutback, flashback, tone, style, imagery, foreshadowing, implication, suggestion, symbolism, action, conflict, discovery, complication, resolution, peripety, enveloping action, specific action, plot, theme, donnée, climax, denouement, beginning, ending, exposition, trap, situation, key moment, suspense, episode, episodic, length, brevity, restraint, compression, economy, selection, light and loose structures, total unity, organic structure, total meaning, pattern, design, form, etc.

In an attempt to impose a measure of order on this vast unruly area, the following section will trace the development of attitudes toward the major fictional elements both by leading critics and by writers on their craft. The aim is to enable the reader to see how a growing sophistication in the handling of fictional art forms, as well as the changing concerns of different periods, affect definitions of such basic terms as "plot" or "moral idea." He can then better understand why a post-Jungian-Freudian era would regard "point of view"—with its psychological implications—as more important than "plot"; or why in our present self-critical climate we are returning to an emphasis on "moral" or "human" concern in fiction.

The technical structure of a story is an essential aspect of its meaning. The short story, like the novel, tries to suggest reasons and explanations for what seems mysterious and confusing in the human condition: in relations between people, and in the subtle workings of the human psyche. It is able to do this partially through the "form" of a story. As a writer selects and arranges the hard facts—actions and events—of his material, he is consciously or unconsciously trying to impose some degree of order upon the seeming irrationality of the physical world of experience. The recognition of the fact that a story has organic unity—i.e., its meaning is inseparable from its form—is the first step toward an intelligent and sensitive reading of the short story.

There are three main technical areas in fiction around which a large body of critical and aesthetic theory has accumulated:

a) *Action* in its double pattern of external movement of incident, and inner movement of idea. Action is the starting point of fiction. The question, however, of whether it is better to stress the pattern of events, or the pattern of ideas, has been and still is a matter for open discussion.

b) *Point of view,* which can be described as the distance established between narrator and subject matter. This was one of Henry James's major concerns when he was grappling with the question of form in fiction. It was not until later that James's concepts were developed and formalized to show the relationship of "distance" and "angle of vision" to such matters as narrative method, narrator, characterization, and setting. Since then, much theoretical data has accumulated on the significance of point of view "not only as a mode of dramatic delimitation, but more particularly, of thematic definition." [2]

c) *Language,* which involves all conscious use of poetical and linguistic devices for the purpose of meaning and effect. Recently, as we noted in

[2] Mark Schorer, "Technique as Discovery," *Hudson Review,* I (1948).

Part I, the approach to the meaning of a story through its language has been gradually gaining support among critics.[3]

In the pages that follow, where these categories will be discussed in detail, every effort will be made to state the changing tide of opinion and definition as objectively as possible. The order in which the elements are discussed is intended to reflect generally the history of shifting focus of attention in the writing and criticism of fiction. Critical data has been gathered with a view to making the reader aware of the range of aesthetic possibilities in fiction. It will then be left up to him to determine where to place an emphasis in the assessment of a particular story. For an approach to be effective, it must be suitable not only to the kind of story, but also to the reader's sensibility, knowledge, and experience of literature. It must be remembered that although categorical divisions and generalizations are necessary for the purpose of study and analysis, the moment they begin to suggest a closed method they are a threat to right reading. As T. S. Eliot once remarked, the only method a reader should properly develop is "to be very intelligent."

It is impossible for a reader to say that the meaning of a story is to be found mainly in its theme, or in its characters, or in its imagery, or that any of these features has a significance that can be isolated from that of the others. The meaning of a story, as of a novel or a poem, lies in its totality, in the unique and complete sum of its parts. Every story carries within it its own form, and cannot therefore be measured or tested against an "ideal" concept outside itself.

ACTION

a) Plot: External, Internal

A definition of action as plot in any literary fiction must begin with Aristotle, who was the first to use and define the term in his *Poetics*. Plot (*mythos*), says Aristotle, is made through the imitation or representation (*mimesis*) of action (*praxis*). *Mythos* and *praxis*, i.e., plot and action, are described as being very closely associated, and it is not always clear from Aristotle's essay just what the distinction between them is. A plot has a beginning, middle, and end, and should preferably be complex, which means that it should contain a crisis in the form either of reversal (*peripeteia*) or recognition (*anagnorisis*). In drama, to which Aristotle is specifically referring, the crisis marks the high point between the development or complication of the problem, and its denouement, i.e., its unravelling and resolution. A general outline of a plot, he states, should be carefully planned beforehand, and then the particulars and details filled in afterward. Of the six elements that he lists as making up a tragedy—

[3] Ably summed up in David Lodge's *The Language of Fiction,* which owes much to the influence of such works as E. K. Wimsatt's *The Verbal Icon,* and Wayne Booth's *The Rhetoric of Fiction.*

plot, character, diction, thought, spectacle, and song—Aristotle considers plot the most important, although he makes the reservation that character and thought determine its success or failure.

The history of plot in the last two centuries is the history of the expansion and transformation in fictional aesthetic theory of Aristotle's original term, from its simple interpretation as a relatively mechanical shape—the arrangement of events advancing through time—to its complex possibilities as the energizing and informing agent in the movement of ideas. In its broadest sense, plot comprehends everything that goes toward progression in a fiction, and Aristotle must have had something of this in mind when he defined plot as the "soul" of a tragedy.

One of the first critical stances to be taken in modern times on the role of plot, as a series of incidents or events, in the short story was that of Edgar Allan Poe in 1842 (see Part I).

Poe's statement suggests that the skill of a short-story writer lies in his ability to weld—without the reader's catching sight of the joints and seams—the event on the one hand, and the effect and idea on the other. He is therefore, unintentionally perhaps, implying a lack of organic unity in a work of fiction. Elsewhere in his writing, however, he stresses the essential unity in a story, and the necessity that no word be written, direct or indirect, that does not tend to the one pre-established design. He states, furthermore, that the effect of a well-written story upon the reader is a "sense of the fullest satisfaction" because "the idea of the tale has been presented unblemished . . . and undisturbed."

Toward the end of the nineteenth century fictional criticism begins to sound a note of mistrust in incident as a focal point in a story. The old mechanical plot with a structured beginning, middle, and end is judged as untrue to life, and extremists begin to question the necessity of any incident at all in a story. As early as the middle of the nineteenth century, the French novelist Flaubert, a lone voice at that time, had written that the perfect story he envisaged would have "nothing" happening in it. Much later, E. M. Forster, whose influence on fictional theory was great in the 1920s, goes still further and defines incident, which he calls the "story" aspect of fiction, as "low, atavistic . . . appealing only to the childish and primitive in us." Henry James's critical essays also express a suspicion of incident for its own sake. But James feels, as Aristotle had pointed out, that in reality incident and character are inseparable: "What is character but the determination of incident? What is incident but the illustration of character?"

The writing practices of such great short-story writers as Chekhov and Katherine Mansfield seemed to prove the insignificance of action as a series of incidents in a short story, as both "Gusev" and "A Dill Pickle" show. Their stories were called, to use a worn-out phrase, "slices of life," a term intended to denote their concern with isolated moments rather than with complete actions in the lives of their characters. Edith Wharton's assertion in the early twentieth century seems to have clinched the matter once and for all. If plot is that elaborate puzzle into which characters have to be squeezed and fitted, then, she writes, it has gone "to the lumber-room of discarded conventions."

With the rejection of the inherited idea of plot in the early twentieth century, conventional beginnings, or the preambles so popular in nineteenth-century fiction, all but disappeared (compare Poe's or Melville's beginnings with those of James, for instance, or of any of the contemporary writers). "Beginnings are ridiculous affairs," writes Franz Kafka, describing them as newborn creatures that can only be partially formed yet must carry within them the organization of the whole. Chekhov advises young writers to fold in two and tear up the first half of a story, which is generally superfluous. Dramatic openings that "situated" the story at a stroke became popular, but were not always effective because sometimes what followed was inevitably anticlimactic.

Poe had emphasized the importance of a foreknown denouement. But with the new concepts endings, like beginnings, underwent a change. The "closed" form began to give way to an open-endedness suggesting the continuous process of life ("Looking for Mr. Green," "Counterparts," and "Simonsen" may be regarded as different examples of the open-ended short story). The popular trick ending described by Frank Norris as "withholding the real point and meaning until the last sentence or paragraph . . . then suddenly unfolding it in a few brief words" was also discarded because of its "sense of bump." Of the primary shape of plot laid down by Aristotle only "middle" seems to have survived.

The strongest blow against conventional plotting came in the early decades of this century with the growth of time theories. If the measurability and predictability of time is denied,[4] it follows that conventional forms, e.g., plot in its primary sense of events in time sequence, are also denied. Such a concept of time was, of course, not entirely new, as Laurence Sterne, the eighteenth-century British novelist, had shown more than one hundred and fifty years earlier in *Tristram Shandy*. However, its development in a number of philosophical works, as well as in Marcel Proust's monumental and influential *A la Recherche du Temps Perdu*, helped to destroy the belief that literary theories and rules can determine the shape and form of movement in fiction.

Critics and writers alike are generally in agreement that there are "happenings" in the modern short story, even when it appears to be standing still. However, the nature of event here is changed from what it was in older stories, being now more intellectual and emotional than physical. Drama in the modern short story, as Edith Wharton so succinctly described it, has moved from the street to the soul of man, thus providing much less surface furor. What the disciples and emulators of Chekhov may sometimes have mistaken for no movement or happening in his stories is actually submerged movement. Chekhov, in fact, as his letters betray, frequently criticizes attempts at story writing as producing a multitude of details that merely pile up into a heap without "movement"

[4] For a more detailed discussion of time in fiction, see Part I.

or "occurrence." More recently, Alberto Moravia, writing of the development of fictional technique, speaks of the "new" kind of plot and character found in twentieth-century fiction, which differ from the "well-assembled machine kind" of the nineteenth century. Plot in modern fiction, he explains, is the "dialectical struggle" between the themes of psychology and of action in which the twentieth-century fictional hero finds his expression and articulation. "He and I" is a perfect example of such a view.

There are indications in recent times of a counter line of thought concerning the value and function of plot in fiction. Aristotle's original term is reinterpreted and expanded in order to comprehend—as Northrop Frye persuasively shows in *Anatomy of Criticism* and *Fables of Identity*—both form and substance, *mythos* and myth, the external story and the informing idea. Plot as conceived of by its new advocates is a measure of the writer's intellectual and aesthetic power to convey the truth behind the seeming irrelevancy and waste of life's "stories."

Plot, writes R. S. Crane in his article "The Concept of the Plot and the Plot of Tom Jones," [5] is a first principle, not merely a "mechanical" framework for an idea, "but rather . . . the final end which everything in the work, if that is to be felt as a whole, must be made, directly or indirectly to serve." Crane, amplifying the Aristotelian definition, sees plot as a synthetic term made up of three elements or causes. Its meaning may vary according to which of the three elements is used as the synthesizing principle. First, there is the plot of action, where the emphasis is placed on a change in the situation of the protagonist, brought about by character and thought [e.g., "The Blue Hotel"]. Second, there is the plot of character, where the emphasis falls on a change in the protagonist's moral character, evidenced in action, thought, and feeling [e.g., "Bright and Morning Star"]. Finally, there is the plot of thought, and this stresses "a completed process of change in the thought of the protagonist and consequently in his feelings, conditioned and directed by character and action [e.g., "The Wall"].

The short story as a fluid form made up of a series of loose impressions, in the manner of many of Katherine Mansfield's stories, is not as popular today as it once was. Plot is regarded by many contemporary writers as the necessary "bones" of a story, "not interesting like expression, or signs of experience, but the support of the whole." [6] A good plot, writes Stephen Vincent Benét, in advice to a young writer, does not grow haphazardly, but must be carefully constructed spatially and temporally. Elizabeth Bowen even suggests that a writer can learn much about form from storytelling to children and from the detective story. Indications show that some modern short-story writers are not averse to using features of the well-made plot, which devotees of Henry James had strongly objected to. "The Enormous Radio" is built around a contrived situation, and in

[5] R. S. Crane, "The Concept of Plot and the Plot of Tom Jones," in *Critics and Criticism, Ancient and Modern,* ed. R. S. Crane (Chicago: University of Chicago Press, 1952).

[6] Ivy Compton-Burnett, from "A Conversation Between I. Compton-Burnett and M. Jourdain," *Orion* (1945), quoted in Miriam Allott, *Novelists on the Novel.*

"Traitorously," a melodramatic ending acts as an external symbol of the underlying idea. The best stories, writes one critic, are those that suggest through the artistic framework the disorder and quality of wonderment of life, "the visible form should be loose . . . causal underneath, casual or seemingly accidental above. Plot below, story above, with the plot part hidden." [7]

In a recent account of the history of the term *plot,* in *The Critical Idiom: Plot* (1970), the author, Elizabeth Dipple, opens with the statement: "Plot currently has no strong place in the pantheon of acceptable literary terms." As her introduction goes on to show, what she is specifically referring to in that statement is the school of "new novelists" (see Part I).

The "new novelists" turn away from plot on the plea that it has an "adjectival" stress. In their view, it controls and manipulates the reader's response, which should evolve freely as the whole object or action unfolds before him. Their aim is to create a narrative art form which eliminates narrator as far as possible, and which stresses the object or thing (as they prefer to call action). There is no need here to go into the question of whether or not the kind of uncompromising neutrality they aim for is possible in fiction. It is important, however, to note, as Miss Dipple points out, that Robbe-Grillet himself, spokesman for that school of writers, "at one point breaks down and asserts that he does indeed have a plot, had his critics eyes to see it."

To sum up: In the technical development of the short story the initial stress on mechanical plotting and external incident shifts toward the end of the nineteenth century to an involvement with character and an internal more complex movement within a story. Critics and writers like James and Forster describe "story" as the confused expression of life, and "plot" as the discriminating expression of art. Modern critical theory, though by no means giving plot importance for its own sake, sees it as an inextricable and necessary part of idea and the total structure of story, regarded not as an end in itself, but as a composite unit in a complex structure. R. P. Blackmur (1904–1965), contemporary American writer and critic, recalls Aristotle's words that plot "is the foundation, or as it were the soul of the tragic art, with character portrayal second." He goes further to state that in the artist's rubric it is right to put character second to plot, because plot as *mythos* reaches "into the driving psyche . . . which endures and even outlives human behaviour." [8]

One of the means frequently used to distinguish different kinds of plotting in terms of structure or of ideological reference is through geometric forms. The linear plot is causal and simple in structure, and is sometimes described by parallel lines when there is a double plot. As plot becomes infused with moral content colored by Judeo-Christian implications, it is often described as a circle, although the principle underlying

[7] Leon Surmelian, *Techniques of Fiction Writing: Measure and Madness* (Garden City, N.Y.: Doubleday & Company, 1968).

[8] R. P. Blackmur, Prefatory Note to *Eleven Essays in the European Novel* (New York: Harcourt Brace Jovanovich, 1943).

this circle, i.e., man returning to his point of origin, is distinct from the pagan idea inherent in the wheel of fortune, which stresses the rise and fall of man's lot. The modern story sometimes finds its corresponding shape in the chain or hourglass, indicative presumably of the complex movement through time that the mind must undergo in order to understand the meaning of human nature and of existence. These two shapes perhaps also suggest the intricate unity of design, where elements combine in patterns and rhythms to form a single but complex structure.

b) Idea, Theme

One of the unfortunate commonplaces of classroom interpretation of fiction is the attempt to extricate a meaning, or worse still a moral (in its narrow sense as a set of rules tending toward good behavior), from a story—as if the idea, as distinct from topic or subject matter, existed independently of plot instead of being a substantial aspect of it. Because of what Northrop Frye calls "our primitive literary vocabulary," theoretical criticism, in an attempt to rediscover basic unities and interrelationships in critical concepts, frequently turns to a re-examination of Aristotelian vocabulary. According to Frye, "theme" is the closest modern word to Aristotle's *dianoia,* or "thought," which has a threefold meaning: a) the conventional or apparent subject or topic of a story, which may be easily summarized or paraphrased; b) "the sententious reflexion that the [fiction] suggests to the meditative reader," i.e., its moral, in the broad sense, or human concern, or "idea"; c) the concept of the whole, including both form and content: "the theme, so considered, differs appreciably from the moving plot: it is the same in substance, but we are now concerned with the details in relation to a unity." In their highest sense, then, *dianoia* and *mythos,* theme and plot, become a simultaneous unity, like Aristotle's "complete action," conveying what Poe had previously described as a "single effect."

The shift of interest from plot to idea reflects in part the storyteller's attempt to understand himself and his environment, and the ways in which character and situation in everyday life comment on human nature. "While the novelist of yesterday preferred to relate the crises of life, the acute phases of the mind and heart, "writes Maupassant in the Preface to his famous novel *Pierre et Jean* (1888), "the novelist of today writes the history of the heart, soul and intellect in their normal condition." The function of the modern story is to establish a connection and relationship between the fictional and real worlds through the "inner world of longings and illusions, habits and frustrations, which [a fictional 'self'] tries to work into the outer world." [9]

It is not the storyteller's business, however, as Chekhov points out, to solve the questions that his vision of life raises, but rather to probe the mystery of such questions. Nor should it be the writer's concern to advocate ideas, but to initiate attitudes toward ideas. Although the fictional

[9] Albert Cook, *The Meaning of Fiction* (Detroit: Wayne State University Press, 1960).

world may carry an illusion of reality, it is still a fictional world. "A writer does not wish to reconcile existence with his vision," says Katherine Mansfield; his aim is "to create his own world *in* this world."

A story's effectiveness is measured as much by the quality of the writer's vision as by his artistic sensibility and skill as a maker of plots. One of the dangers of creative writing classes, says Flannery O'Connor, in an address to a writers' workshop, is to encourage bad writers by providing them with easy formulas for story writing. Today, she says, there are so many competent writers who lack vision that "the short story as a medium is in danger of dying of competence." The moral idea is "the light by which a writer sees," the inspiration without which a story cannot properly grow.

The majority of themes in the modern short story revolve around the human personality, and the conduct of human beings in given milieus. We are likely to remember a character from the best stories we have read without necessarily remembering the specific things that happened to him. According to Northrop Frye, different kinds of plottings in fiction can be most accurately classified in terms of their heroes, and how these heroes are related to their environments. Professor Frye bases his theory on a little-known passage in Aristotle's *Poetics*, which states that differences in fiction are the result of different "elevations" of characters in them. He develops Aristotle's ideas into a schematic classification of fictional characters:

(1) Those superior in *kind* to both men and environment, and found in myths.

(2) Those superior in *degree* to men and environment, and found in romances.

(3) Those superior to men but not to environment, and they are the heroes of the high mimetic mode of tragedy and epic.

(4) Those like the average man, superior neither to others nor to environment, and these belong to the low mimetic mode of comedy and to realistic fiction.

(5) Those inferior in power of intelligence to the average man, who create the atmosphere of frustration and absurdity of the ironic mode. These last are the heroes, or antiheroes, of most recent serious fiction.

In his book *Some Principles of Fiction*, Robert Liddell, contemporary British critic, speaks of the modern novelist's difficulty in choosing themes, because of the death of the organic community and the disorientation and depersonalization of life. However, those factors in our keyed-up modern system that may create a problem for the novelist actually prove advantageous for the short-story writer. For if the novel, as Liddell says, gets better effects from portraying "people" rather than isolated individuals, the short story, being much more personal, tends to deal, as Frank O'Connor points out, "with the outlawed figures wandering about the fringes of society." [10] The most characteristic kind of modern short story,

[10] Frank O'Connor, pseudonym for Michael O'Donovan, *The Lonely Voice* (Cleveland: World Publishing Company, 1963).

according to him, shows what the novel does only occasionally: "an intense awareness of human loneliness," which is illustrated in such stories as "Little Herr Friedemann," "Good Country People," "The Egg," and "The Wall," to name only a few.

Concerned with the moral and human content in fiction, Alan Friedman in *The Turn of the Novel* describes incident as the thread on which hangs the "ethical form—that is, the stream of moral outcomes—a stream of conscience," which in his view flows from innocence to experience. Anticipating critical accusations of verbal gimmickry, Friedman explains his rationale for making the distinction between the current term "stream of consciousness" and his variation of it (and although he speaks of the novel what he says is applicable also to the short story): "Whereas evidently novels can exist without rendering a stream of consciousness, no novel can exist without rendering a stream of conscience. The latter is the moral *movement* of fiction itself. . . . The stream of events in a novel is the flux of experience viewed from the outside. . . . The stream (or flux) of conscience is an inside view: it is the flux of experience viewed morally."

Henry James's assertion that the more he worked the more it came home to him that "solidity and importance of subject" in fiction, together with the emotional capacity engendered, are really what count the most, remains basically unchallenged today, in spite of occasional reservations by aestheticians [11] or by avant-garde writers that modern fiction tends to eliminate the human element. As Chekhov states, when a writer observes, selects, guesses, and combines, he is pressing forward toward meaning, otherwise: "There would be nothing to conjecture and nothing to select."

Writing of the range of possible fictional topics, Elizabeth Bowen says that great stories deal with a handful of recurring basic themes, which remain true over the years, but which appear in different guises from storyteller to storyteller. Among such constants she lists: "conflicts or rivalries and their resolution, pride or its fate, estrangement and reconciliation, revenge or forgiveness, quests and searches rewarded or unrewarded, abidingness versus change, love and its proof." [12] Many short-story themes stem from the basic human need for such things as recognition (e.g., "The Downward Path to Wisdom"), simple human dignity (e.g., "A Simple Soul"), love and security (e.g., "The Gardner"), and spiritual fulfillment (e.g., "The Last Mohican").

Although conflict is not always apparent, most short stories do in fact contain some degree of conflict. This may take the form of a simple contest between man and external forces, or a more complex struggle between human beings. The most sophisticated form, found in the majority of modern short stories, is that between opposing impulses and desires within a character, of which "William Wilson" is an obvious example, and "Soldier's Home" a more subtle one. The short story, by its very nature

[11] There are thinkers like Ortega y Gasset who complain that human content in fiction "is in principle incompatible with aesthetic enjoyment proper." But even he recognizes that fiction, by its very nature, is conducive to "contemplation."

[12] Elizabeth Bowen, "Rx for a Story Worth Telling," quoted in Trask, *Storytellers and Their Art* (Garden City, N.Y.: Doubleday & Company, 1963).

"catching pieces of life as they fly by," reflects life's impermanence and mutability. Most stories deal with some form of change or discovery either in the visible behavior of characters, or in their inner awareness of themselves and of their world. The latter may be redemptive awareness, such as Fidelman's ("The Last Mohican"), or a despairing knowledge such as Irene's ("The Enormous Radio").

The choice of subject for the short-story writer is in a sense more of a personal matter than it is for the novelist. According to the evidence of writers themselves, although a novelist may dispense with personality, the storyteller can do well only in the knowledge that he is "putting on a personal individual act." Sean O'Faolain, the Irish writer and critic, even goes so far as to say that a short story is "an immense confidence trick" aimed at communicating personality under the guise of telling a story.

To sum up what has been said so far: The history of the short story shows a shift from Poe's early stress on a "tight" plot, where the denouement is known beforehand, to a "loose" plot, where theme and idea take over the dynamics of a story, and the direction of an action is not always known, but as Hemingway says of his stories, everything changes as it moves. The controlling force in this type of fiction is the writer's perception of life and his attempt to establish a connection and meaning between the fictional and real worlds.

It is by no means easy to trace and define meaning in fiction, and it certainly cannot be "pulled out" of a story in the old worn-out manner of classroom discussion, particularly with modern fiction where meaning is generally hidden in symbol, and cannot be separated from the total movement of character and event. A story is an experience, not an abstraction, and its meaning, therefore, can be found only in its entirety.

One of the obvious reasons for the difficulty in this aspect of fictional analysis is the reader's constant need to evaluate the work against his own knowledge of the physical world of experience. It is easy for a reader to be overly intelligent, and to read thematic questions into a story rather than out of it. To prevent such a possibility, a reader must constantly keep the total work in sight.

POINT OF VIEW

A story is dominated by three or possibly four points of view: those of the narrator; of one or more of its characters; and of the reader. If the narrator's point of view is distinct from that of the author, then a fourth point of view may be added. Frequently a reader will identify himself with either a character or the narrator and his view will naturally develop from theirs.

One of the significant functions of point of view in the short story is the control of irony.[13] Disparity of understanding among people results in

[13] For further detail see Scholes and Kellogg, *The Nature of Narrative.*

ironic situations, which may enforce a point with greater economy and incisiveness than direct statement. Most stories contain some degree of irony, which arises from inevitable differences between the levels of point of view. In many modern stories irony is a controlling factor in the delineation of idea or character. Two notable examples of how idea is woven into an ironic framework may be found in "Report" and "Pkhentz."

Many aspects in a story assume shape and perspective in relation to the "post of observation," Henry James's term for point of view, just as different views in film are obtained through the sweep of the camera eye in close-ups, side views, flashbacks, etc. One of the storyteller's primary concerns, therefore, is the choice of a narrator who establishes best distance and focus for the realization of the author's idea. Ideal distance, by means of which the most effective view of the story as a whole and of its parts is obtained, also controls the choice of narrative method. Likewise how much or how little, in what vivid or ambiguous light, is shown of the characters, and of their background and setting, is in great measure determined by the nature and angle of the seeing eye.

a) Narrator

The progress of narrator from the simple authoritative eyewitness of the early Greek and Hebrew stories to the highly polished and subtle reflector of the human soul in modern fiction forms one of the most fascinating chapters in the development of fictional techniques. Generally speaking, there are three or four basic angles, though, of course, many more variations, from which an account of a story may be given.

The first of these to be considered is the oldest and simplest—the first-person "I" narrator, where the writer tells the story from his own point of view and on his own authority. As fictional techniques develop, the first-person narrator changes from being the writer himself to one of the characters, either in the role of observer, or as the story moves closer to the drama, in the role of an actor. The first-person narrator is the "readiest means of dramatically heightening impression," [14] because it suggests the precise definite edge of a personal, intimate tone, and because, being a single view, it makes for unity and economy of attention.

The greatest drawback of this point of view is the narrator's limited awareness of the scene around him. Henry James called it a "barbarous" method, and discounted it as a valuable point of view. In analytical stories particularly, where penetrating insight and consciousness are necessary, the "I" narrator is handicapped because he cannot legitimately get behind and within himself and other characters, but can only report and describe. First-person point of view is retrospective rather than immediate and dramatic. It is therefore unsuitable for much modern fiction, which aims at a "presentness" free from emotional and moral evaluation.

From the limitations of first-person narrator, it is a natural step to omniscient narrator, of whom there are several varieties, and whose effectiveness as the central eye has been, and still is, the subject of lively

[14] Percy Lubbock, *The Craft of Fiction* (New York: The Viking Press, 1921).

debate. The omniscient author-narrator can be, as one critic points out, personal subjective and intrusive, or impersonal objective and self-effaced.[15] The tendency has been to move away from the former, characterized strongly in nineteenth-century fiction, toward a "masked" narrator with a less obtrusive omniscience. One of the outspoken defenders of the rightness and validity of narrator omniscience among contemporary writers is Elizabeth Bowen. The storyteller, she says, should have "right of entry into memories, sensation and thought processes" of any or all of his characters. Omniscience, though it may appear naive, is best for the writer, she feels, and its appropriate use need only be controlled by the demands of plot. Thus plot may necessitate at times that some characters be seen from the outside only, and that others be bathed in ambiguity. In such stories as "A Simple Soul" and "Gusev," where the main characters are deficient in self-awareness, an omniscient narrator is necessary if the author's purpose is to show them in a sympathetic rather than an ironic light. Omniscience in the hands of a great master, writes the contemporary American critic and author Allen Tate, suggests the broad scope and complexity of life through the continual juxtaposition of overall view and closeups.

The attack against omniscience among some critics and writers turns out on close examination to be an attack against *discernible* omniscience. Flaubert's insistence that the writer be impersonal and scientific does not imply limitation upon his free movement in time and space, but rather that he must not intrude his person and views upon the reader. Henry James's concept of the indirect approach, defined by R. P. Blackmur as "the existence of a definite created sensibility interposed between the reader and the felt experience," explains the objection to omniscience. The writer, James says, cannot put the reader in direct contact with any subject or happening, because only an omniscient God can tell what "is." The writer can only represent a happening through someone's concept or feeling of it. James's concept developed for him into the method of the "central intelligence," which will be discussed later, and which, in a sense, is a sophisticated compromise between the limited autobiographical "I" and the omniscient storyteller. Talking about a subject instead of artistically presenting it "destroys illusion of fictive present." [16] In order to preserve this illusion it seems necessary to silence the author-narrator and, as in realistic drama with its stress on scene, pretend in a sense that he does not even exist.

Such writers as Katherine Mansfield and Chekhov repeatedly stress the importance of author effacement, and boast of the fact that their private philosophies cannot be perceived in their stories. Katherine Mansfield writes that any story she attempts when in a self-conscious mood "will be full of sediment. . . . One must learn, one must practice to forget oneself." Chekhov, likewise, writing about the ideas of a character in one of his short stories, says to a friend: "Trust me, and do not search in them

[15] Leon Surmelian, *Techniques of Fiction Writing.*

[16] A. A. Mendilow, *Time and the Novel* (London: British Book Center, 1952).

for Chekhov's ideas. . . . One must regard them as material things, as symptoms, entirely from an objective standpoint, trying not to agree or disagree with them." In another letter he advises a young writer to be cold when describing grief, because such a detached attitude provides a background against which the grief stands in sharper outline. "You may weep and moan over your stories . . . but I consider that one must do this so that the reader does not notice it." Maupassant sees a further advantage in a narrator's objectivity and detachment, namely, the freedom to attack.

Recently, however, there have been signs of a re-evaluation of attitudes toward author-narrator omniscience and intrusion, of which Wayne Booth's *The Rhetoric of Fiction*[17] is one example. Booth bases his argument on the notion that the impact of a story cannot be measured by the degree of an author's personality or impersonality, by whether he shows or tells. In support of his argument he refers to such writers as Fielding, Smollett, and Boccaccio, among others, "whose splendid and complex skill" behind the seemingly simple effects of intrusive, all-knowing authors, gives the reader far greater delight than do the stories of many an imitator of James or Hemingway. Boccaccio's artistry, states Booth, lies "in his ability to order various forms of telling in the service of various forms of showing."

Booth denounces the fallacy that it is possible for a writer to efface himself and become wholly detached and impersonal. What the "expulsion of author" actually means is the "expulsion of direct address," because everything in a story is in one way or another the result of authorial intervention and choice. According to him, the roving internal view discussed later, for instance, although it claims the height of effacement on the part of the author, is "omniscience with teeth in it." A close analysis of so-called objective noncommittal stories usually turns up some unusual, and not easily detectable commitment. There can be no such thing as ideal distance in practical terms, because a writer sometimes establishes one kind of distance on a specific axis (e.g., the emotional) so as to increase the reader's involvement on another (e.g., the social). If this is the case, then the call for objectivity, he concludes, is really a "call for unconventionality," and although an author may choose his mask or disguise, he cannot choose to disappear.

In every story, and this is the important theory Booth is leading up to, there is what he calls an "implied author" or second self, whether dramatized or not. A writer "creates not simply an ideal impersonal 'man in general' but an implied version of himself," which is intensified if the author is the first-person narrator. He may have as many second selves, or implied authors, as he has stories, and it is the sense of this implied self that ties the form and content of a story into an artistic whole.

Modern experimentations with shifts in distance between implied author, whose standard of judgment is usually adopted by the reader, and

[17] Wayne Booth, *The Rhetoric of Fiction* (Chicago: University of Chicago Press, 1961), specifically Parts I and III.

an unreliable narrator confirm the significance of author omniscience. If the view of the narrator is open to question, says Booth, the total effect of a story and its degree of irony is precariously suspended. In some cases, where it is impossible to establish the proper distance, straight description of dramatic irony may be best. Misconceptions between characters, that only an omniscient narrator would know of, are sometimes more effective if given by a reliable narrator independent of a subjective vision. (The validity of this theory could perhaps be tested against Mishima's "The Pearl.") As Booth points out, even the most impersonal of authors has at his disposal many means by which he can direct a reader toward his intended meaning. (In "Deutsches Requiem" Borges makes use of explanatory footnotes, which are part of the total structure of his story.) The contemporary author usually tries for the more subtle forms of reader manipulation, though he is not entirely above the more obvious forms also, as the existence of stories in the allegorical and satirical modes show.

Wayne Booth is by no means alone in his recognition of the significance of the authorial voice and his attempt to reinstate it. In his introduction to a collection of the short novels of Dostoevsky, Thomas Mann, who in his own writing aimed at neutrality and a "cool fastidious attitude toward humanity," underscores the artistic advantage of Dostoevsky's "'appearance' of addressing himself to a reader." Mann finds that through his authorial intervention, Dostoevsky actually creates a highly dramatic "fiction within fiction." "No story writer," says Sean O'Faolain, "so fully betrays himself [i.e., surrenders to himself] in practice, as the man who cultivates complete impersonality." The Jamesian concept, that although a writer is ultimately all-knowing, his story looks poor and thin if his omniscience is openly claimed by him, is not perhaps as convincing as it once was.

The need for a deeper penetration into character, combined with the desire to establish and maintain an illusion of reality, was responsible in part for the development of the indirect "central intelligence" view. This view, brilliantly and movingly handled by James, came in time to be adopted as the standard view of most modern short stories. In his Preface to *The Golden Bowl* James comments on his preference for this indirect, oblique view:

> Again and again, on review, the shorter things in especial that I have gathered into this Series have ranged themselves not as my own impersonal account of the affair in hand, but as my account of somebody's impression of it—the terms of this person's access to it and estimate of it contributing thus by some fine little law to intensification of interest. The somebody is often, among my shorter tales I recognise, but an unnamed, unintroduced and (save by right of intrinsic wit) unwarranted participant, the impersonal author's concrete deputy or delegate, a convenient substitute or apologist for the creative power otherwise so veiled and disembodied.

In this mode of narration there is a return to the third-person view, but instead of being the author's, it is the inward consciousness of one of the characters. Drama and action move to the plane of interior life as the character converts the outward scene into his most private thought and feeling. If the central eye is not merely that of an impersonal onlooker but of the main character himself, then there is a shift of weight from scene to speaker. Although this view is fixed in space like first-person view, it has the advantage of greater freedom in time through the use of flashbacks and foreshadowing. The effective combination of author's and character's views creates a richer, more complex representation of life than that of first-person narrator. It is the combination of this double view that results in the subtle texture of such stories as "Four Meetings," "Traitorously," "Deutsches Requiem," and "Bang-Bang You're Dead."

One problem arises from this central angle of vision, but as Percy Lubbock points out,[18] James's delicate handling of it in his own stories establishes a useful precedent. The single seeing eye is never objectively "seen," and therefore is likely to remain vague and shadowy. If the viewer is merely an observer, then there is not much harm done, for the reader will still get a full picture of the main actors through his eyes. But if the hero is himself the seeing eye, it is necessary that he be made partially visible to the reader. James is able to do this effectively, Lubbock states, by occasionally closing his hero's consciousness, "letting his vision lapse for a while," thereby placing him for the reader at the same distance as the other characters. The result is a clearer, more comprehensive glimpse of scene and characters. The central character still never sees himself objectively, yet by indirection the reader has a more precise view of him. A new dimension is, as it were, added, freeing the central figure briefly, and enabling him "to cast his own shadow upon the scene."

The central intelligence, because it is a single point of view that yet allows penetration and depth, is particularly well suited to the modern short story, which frequently portrays an individual consciousness in conflict with itself, or its environment. It is the method of subjective fiction, anticipating interior monologue, and providing the most effective mode of expression for the isolated, withdrawn man, the hero of the modern short story, struggling to preserve his mind and individuality in a dehumanized society.

Although central-intelligence view is single, it is by no means simple. As Sean O'Faolain points out, it is a mobile view, like the camera eye, which has one general main direction of which closeups, distances, etc., are only variations. It makes use of the best features of both first-person and omniscient narrator without the rigidity of either. The depth and width of perspective it allows achieves immediacy and easy identification, because it suggests an awareness "of the complex shifting equilibrium of contrary forces in the course of the struggle." [19]

The central-intelligence view, sometimes called limited intelligence because it is single, may be extended to a succession of characters in a story. The result is a complex, multidimensional view of the subject, more

[18] Lubbock, *Craft of Fiction.*
[19] A. A. Mendilow, *Time and the Novel.*

suitable to the scope of the novel than the short story. Wayne Booth calls this form of it "roving internal view" and counts sixteen such points of vision in Faulkner's *As I Lay Dying.* If the short story makes use of this type of view, it generally limits the angles of vision to two main characters.

As the analytic method of the modern psychological story developed, writers were not satisfied with merely following the conscious thoughts of characters, and a new point of view came into being with "stream-of-consciousness" fiction. Although this term is more applicable to the novel than the short story, it is so frequently referred to in fictional criticism that a brief word of explanation is necessary.

According to psychologists, the average person has a fuzzy notion of what "consciousness" means. Technically speaking, as Robert Humphrey explains it in *Stream of Consciousness in the Modern Novel,* consciousness covers the entire area of mental activity ranging from incoherent pre- or subconscious levels, called also "prespeech" levels because they do not involve communication, to the rational "speech levels" which exist on the margins of mental awareness. Prespeech levels of consciousness, he continues, are "not censored, rationally controlled or logically ordered," and it is with the attempt to capture and register them, and thereby in some measure to understand them, that stream-of-consciousness fiction is concerned. As defined by Humphrey, stream of consciousness is not a technique but a type of fiction whose primary aim is to reveal the psychic being of characters. A number of different techniques may be used to achieve that aim.

One of these techniques which concerns us most in terms of the short story is interior monologue. It is written in the first person, but is different from the traditional account of first-person narrator, discussed earlier, in that it is supposedly not addressed to a reader, but is caught, as it were, "in the original raw stage before its rhetorical organization." [20] The advantage of the interior monologue over the traditional first-person view is that it penetrates far deeper into the springs of motivation and feeling as it follows the mind's free association of thought.

The primary object of interior monologue, according to Dujardin,[21] who first defined the term in *Le monologue intérieur,* is the complete suppression and effacement of author, although in actual fact the association of thought is by no means altogether free but is subject to careful control. As the monologue develops, secret unconfessed longings are interwoven in a "dream wish-fulfillment" line with the character's conscious experience. Lapses from the character's present thoughts are frequently marked by disordered speech and syntax: unfinished, broken-up sentences, repetitions of words or phrases that have acquired emotional overtones for the character, changes in punctuation, and so on, that gradually form recognizable motifs and designs. These lapses into reveries or hallucinations are usually evoked by some word or happening in the present situation. In-

[20] Surmelian, *Techniques of Fiction Writing.*

[21] Edouard Dujardin, nineteenth-century French author and pioneer in stream-of-consciousness fiction.

terior monologue is frequently used in the short story, because, unlike some of the other more complex techniques in stream-of-consciousness fiction, it remains closer to coherent levels of consciousness and is therefore more easily contained and communicated within the design of the short story. An unusual fusion of this form and conventional first-person account is found in Alberto Moravia's "He and I," and another variation of it in Donald Barthelme's "Report."

b) Narrative Method

There are two ways of telling a story: through scene or through summary, both of which are controlled by the distance and angle of vision the writer wishes to establish between teller, tale, and reader. Scene is the dramatic method of "rendering," to use Henry James's term, or of showing rather than reporting. It is the readiest means of objective narration because it detaches itself from surrounding features and from the presence or voice of the narrator, thereby gaining in emphasis and relief. The novel, of course, can only make occasional use of scene, whereas many short stories, like Hemingway's "The Killers," can be strictly scene from start to finish. Henry James was among the first to emphasize the vital role of scene in fiction, as the "condition to which narrative seems always to aspire."

In addition to its presentness and immediacy, scene provides the necessary framework for conflict, an essential aspect of the modern short story as it moves toward drama and its related genres. In recent years, as noted in Part I, the short story has drawn closer to film, exploiting its scenic techniques, which rely on suggestion and fast movement rather than discursiveness and unnecessary detail.

The scenic method, however, cannot perform everything in fiction, and that is why, even in the short story, it must be supplemented by summary. Its greatest limitation is that it does not allow deeper analysis of the mind and feelings than can be suggested in a character's words and gestures. It cannot be the sole method, therefore, of the psychological story, which necessitates excursions into aspects of character beyond visible and audible signs. Scene can also prove uneconomical, because, unless action has been prepared for in advance through summary, it must waste a portion of its strength in exposition.

Summary, defined by James as the "pictorial" or "panoramic" method, is more appropriate to the tempo of a novel than a short story. Like the chorus in a Greek play, it voices the general rather than the individual view. It allows for a slower pace, generally accompanied by greater reflection, and consequently depth, as the high pitch of scene is lowered. Russian writers of the nineteenth century, like Tolstoy, used it very effectively. The pictorial or summary method conveys experience at second hand, and, unlike scenes, underscores the narrator's view. It may be narrative, descriptive, or discursive.

The merit of the short story cannot be measured in terms of the extent to which it uses the dramatic scenic method, or the more expansive pictorial. The real question is whether the use of either method contributes to the total realization of a writer's idea. Most short stories achieve their effect through the subtle fusion of both methods.

c) Character and Characterization

Characters in fiction may carry an illusion of reality. They are generally surrounded by the familiar details of life. The thoughts and feelings they express are, for the most part, within the range of our imaginative, if not our actual experience. In our attempt to search out their meaning and assess the truth of their world, we apply to them the narrow tests and rules of our own manners and mores. It is easy to forget that characters in fiction, although lifelike, are not real people. Even if they pre-exist within a sociological, historical, or clinical context, they must be put, in Henry James's words, "through the crucible of the artist's imagination," before they can be transmuted into art.

A character in a story is a composite copy, made up of a fusion of traits, frequently drawn from widely separate experiences. Most writers are in agreement that people in real life lack the coherence and unity, or the clarity and intensity, necessary to a fictional character. Although real people may suggest types and individuals to a writer, they provide only a "tiny fertile substratum." [22] Their speech, actions, and thoughts have to be tensed and heightened, which may explain why some characters in fiction appear more convincing than people in real life.

A fictional character may be a familiar figure in a domestic or social set-up but his meaning often reaches beyond the limitations of his recognizable scene. He is both an individual as well as a social or moral type. We remember him both for his idiosyncracies, as well as for what he represents outside of himself—perhaps a class, profession, ethnic group, ideology, or morality for which he is a spokesman, or maybe a mythical or archetypal pattern on which he is modeled. The impulse to typify is as strong in the short story as it is in the novel (see Dickens' "Horatio Sparkins"). Such richly connotative titles as "Good Country People" and "The Last Mohican" reflect the larger patterns of values that the individuals in the stories partially portray. There are many modern stories that even go so far as to deny their characters any conventional mark of individuality, such as name, speech, or physical features. Such characters stand for the faceless, nameless beings of an impersonal and mechanical world.

The necessity for compactness in a short story limits the number of characters. Chekhov repeatedly warns young writers against the effect of overcrowding. "There are a great many acting persons in your story . . . they dissipate the attention of the reader and fail to make a clear impression. . . . There are two courses open to you: fewer characters, or—write a novel." In another letter he suggests that the center of gravity in a short story should never be in more than two people. Secondary characters, like

[22] Somerset Maugham, quoted in Trask, *Storytellers.*

the groom in Kafka's "A Country Doctor," may function significantly by providing contrasts to the main characters. They may also motivate change and development in the protagonist through their reactions and responses, as the sheriff and his men do in "Bright and Morning Star."

The short story, because of aesthetic necessity, cannot give an extended development of character. Time here has to be foreshortened, although the illusion of continuity may still be preserved. A character in a short story is not likely to undergo a complex dynamic change before our eyes, but some degree of actual, or imminent, change in him is frequently the basis of plot in modern stories.

In order to trace the pattern of change in a fictional character it may be useful, according to some critics, to analyze plot in terms of the stages that contribute to such a change. Norman Friedman, in his essay "What Makes a Short Story Short," lists five such possible stages in the action: 1) "precipitating cause," which brings a character in his initial state; 2) "counterplot action," reflecting the outcome of that state; 3) "inciting cause," leading out of the counterplot and toward a reversal; 4) "progressive action," describing the process of change in him; 5) "culmination," reflecting the catastrophe or resolution after the completion of the process. Although such a neat formula may be helpful in the analysis of some stories, it should by no means be allowed to lead to a closed method of approach.

Character change in most modern short stories is internal, from ignorance to awareness, rather than circumstantial. Sometimes a writer will use a static character—i.e., one who does not undergo obvious change in personality or awareness, in contrast to a dynamic character—to bring about a change in the reader's own perceptions and attitudes. Many of Chekhov's stories fall in this category.

According to the degree of their development, fictional characters are sometimes labelled "flat" or "round" for convenience. E. M. Forster, the first to popularize the terms, defines the *flat* character as a type, a caricature seen from one angle and built around a single idea. The *round* character, conversely, moves before the reader in a variety of lights, frequently taking him by surprise. Gradually the unpredictable in his behavior gives way, in the course of a story, to the inevitable, as potential becomes actual in the face of pressure. Flat characters, though generally regarded as requiring less skill, are nevertheless necessary to convey one kind of vision. They dramatize the average man reacting in terms of habit and reflex responses. If the main characters in a story are flat, the narrative is then moving toward the form of parable or fable.

There are many ways by which a character may evolve physically and psychologically in fiction. The most obvious method of representation is through categorical statements by author or narrator, as in "The Pearl" and "A Simple Soul." This is the method of summary, and has tended to fall into disfavor, particularly in the short story. Most short-story writers prefer to let their characters materialize within the dramatic context of a story. This is the scenic method, whose advantages have already been discussed. The analytical method of the psychological story, through direct analysis, interior monologue, or central-intelligence view has likewise been discussed earlier.

Another means by which character in fiction may be revealed is through dialogue, which solidifies relationships between characters, and also reveals the temperament and rhythm of the speakers. According to many writers dialogue requires more art, perhaps, than any other element. It should sound realistic and true to life, giving the flavor of a speaker's idiom and dialect, without being commonplace. The tendency in modern fiction has been toward a selective use of dialogue, set in relief against the narrative. Only the most vital portions of speech are recorded, and a more subtle effect is built up from suspended or unspoken words. In "Death of a Traveling Salesman" there is a minimal exchange of words between the characters, yet the reader has a sense of a rich and full silent communication between them. Maupassant, on the other hand, uses dialogue as a means of providing a philosophical basis for his story "Useless Beauty." The use of speech can be a valuable source of dramatic presentation, but may weaken the effect of a story if abused.

The variations inherent in the different means of characterization are infinite. Some knowledge of psychology on the part of the storyteller may be useful, but not indispensable. Perhaps what counts most of all in effective characterization is an intense human awareness, and the ability to recreate it imaginatively. This is why the point of view of a child, like Stephen in "The Downward Path to Wisdom," or of an unsophisticated adult, like Félicité in "A Simple Soul" and Gusev in "Gusev," because it is spontaneous and uncluttered, can be a very effective means of commenting on life.

Great characters in fiction are a measure, most readers will agree, of the unconscious greatness within a writer's own soul, and the same ego generally runs through all of an author's characters. Perhaps the most important test of the greatness of a fictional character, particularly in the short story, is that he go on existing for the reader beyond the limits of the story itself. If the author's artistic execution is right, the meaning of his characters goes well beyond the situation he has envisioned for them in the story.

d) Setting

Everything must happen somewhere, even if that "where" is not fixed spatially or temporally. In order for a setting to be effective and valid it should provide a frame, or a point of view, through which the characters and action can be seen. A sense of locale, writes Eudora Welty, gives equilibrium and direction to a story by establishing a plausible world of appearances for the "made" characters and action, thus intensifying the illusion of life and reality. Place, however, she suggests, does not have to be strictly regional, as in real life. It may be necessary for the details of a short-story setting to convey the multiformity of abstract form. In her story "Death of a Traveling Salesman," she demonstrates very ably how background details may be both real and symbolic, natural, yet sufficiently distorted to convey the emotional and physical stress of the dying salesman. A setting's vividness and solidity of texture is derived from the intensity of an author's vision rather than from its correspondence to an actual place.

As with a character's physique, setting is generally a composite copy made up of scattered images, recollections, and dreams, not necessarily connected, but all drawn from life. And because its primary function, at least in most modern short stories, is not to reproduce the external world accurately, but to serve the development of character and action, most place details drawn from life, says Elizabeth Bowen, require some degree of distortion. The most useful kind of details therefore, in her view, are those which have mellowed through time and imagination in the memory, or else those associated with once-seen and not so familiar places.

How setting is handled depends on what it means to the writer and how he wants to relate it to his theme. Henry James considered it important, but in a typical rather than specific sense. In the modern realistic short story it is viewed as an active molding force on character and action. In many stories it is a necessary part of theme, corresponding to, or perhaps contrasting with, character and action. The rugged settings in many of Hemingway's stories are related to the exacting, implacable values that govern the action of many of his heroes. Faulkner, on the other hand, gains his effect in "Death Drag" through the ironic, perhaps even tragic, contrast between the patched and shabby visible world, and the indomitable "outraged" spark of life within the little stunt man.

LANGUAGE

Turning from an emphasis on point of view as "the most useful distinction available to the student of fiction," [23] today's critics tend to regard the study of language as the first step toward understanding the form and meaning of a story. Story writers in the last two centuries have almost uniformly fought for the recognition that, in fiction as well as in poetry, idea is inseparable from expression. Flaubert describes style as penetrating an idea like a dagger thrust. It is "the lifeblood of thought . . . an absolute way of looking at things," he writes. Thus every story necessitates a fresh approach by the reader. "Truth" in fiction, as novelist Graham Greene says, is equivalent to style, and it was with the aim of making this equivalence absolute and complete that James Joyce experimented with fictional language.

Critical theory, however, has lagged behind the practice of writers, and the attempt to provide a methodology for the explication and evaluation of fictional language is of recent origin, and still in the process of formulation, as David Lodge's discussion of it in *The Language of Fiction* shows. There are still many critics today, however, who tend to avoid close con-

[23] Norman Friedman, "Point of View in Fiction: The Development of a Critical Concept," *Publications of the Modern Language Association,* Vol. LXX, no. 5 (1955).

cern with the language of fiction, believing it to lack intrinsic value. Albert Cook, in *The Meaning of Fiction*, sums up this view in his claim that if there is fidelity to life, and depth of observation in a story, fictional style may be "clumsy," "blundering," "tasteless," or "flat"; "a good novel may be ill written, a poor one well written." Such a view is generally supported by the argument that fiction, unlike poetry, is comparatively easy to translate.

The real test of the intrinsic value of the language of fiction, however, according to Lodge, is not whether a work is translatable, but whether it resists paraphrase. Can the same idea or story be communicated in a different set of words and still arouse exactly the same kind of response in the reader? In point of fact, linguistic form in both poetry and prose is a single continuum, because both are involved with the same activity—"the making of fictions," writes Lodge. The truth of scientific or historic facts can be measured or controlled by what is prior or independent of them. But fictions have no alternative equal. They exist as certain words in a certain order, and therefore cannot be paraphrased. Words are not a virgin medium, like the media of other arts; they are already impressed with a complexity of meanings before a writer can make his individual creative use of them. The reader tends to forget this fact, particularly in fiction, and to regard words as if they were merely informative, rather than creative. But the language of fiction, in spite of its being closer to that of common experience, is no more neutral than that of poetry. It determines at every point the tone and direction of all the elements we have so far discussed in the making of a story.

The storyteller, like the poet, faces innumerable linguistic possibilities and his choice is motivated in large part by his aesthetic logic. His ideas and interpretation of life are valuable in direct relation to their effectiveness in communication. Although some novelists may write, or pretend to write, as if they do not intend to be published, the short story, as its history shows, is written strictly with an audience in mind, and is therefore inescapably rhetorical, i.e., the writer will use every possible stylistic means by which to control and motivate a reader's response. Such means in the best stories are subtly integrated, and discerned only upon close textual analysis. They fulfill according to Wayne Booth, one, or all, of three functions: (a) to heighten the reader's response, because his natural response is unreliable, as experience of everyday life proves; (b) to give direction to the values and point of view underlying meaning in a story. This is necessary because values and attitudes are in constant flux; (c) to motivate unconventional responses, such as sympathy for a villain. Joseph Conrad explains the significance of style in fiction most succinctly when he says that his task as a story writer is to make the reader hear, feel, and, above all, see "by the power of the written word."

In the course of selecting the most useful method of approach to the study of the language of fiction, Lodge explains why he rejects the two main existing approaches of (a) stylistics and (b) linguistics, preferring instead the more flexible method of literary criticism. The method of "New Stylistics" advocates the replacement of impressionistic generalization in the appreciation of literature by the close study and explanation of particular examples. From these specifics the critic makes generalizations, then goes back to the specifics to test his generalizations, and so on. This method can be very useful if its approach is to the text as a whole. The tendency of the method, however, as Lodge explains, is to draw general hypotheses about the culture and age of the author. The continental school of stylistics, in particular, stresses the study of stylistic deviations from general use, because these mark significant "shifts in the soul of an epoch."

The discipline of linguistics is also unsatisfactory, according to Lodge, first, because it is a controversial area of study, and second, because its method is too strictly scientific to suit the study of literature, which of necessity carries an element of subjectivism. Literary criticism, on the other hand, has an advantage over these two methods. Unlike stylistics, its concern is not the language as a whole, but the literary text as a whole, and unlike linguistics, it takes into consideration the personal element underlying critical explanation and appreciation. The literary critic, however, uses some of the elements of both stylistic and linguistic disciplines to enrich his approach to language.

The most useful approach to the study of style in fiction, according to Lodge, is the "structural." This method traces significant threads through the language of a story. "By tracing a linguistic thread or threads—a cluster of images, or value-words, or grammatical constructions— . . . we produce a kind of spatial diagram of the accumulative and temporally-extended reading experience."

The first and main step toward the recognition of such threads is the perception of repetitive patterns. The significance of repetition need not be determined by whether all readers easily recognize it. Repetition cannot be measured statistically, and the degree to which it may throw light on meaning and value in a story depends upon the critical use made of it, for repetition of any kind does not in itself carry value or explanation.

Wayne Booth has a word of caution at this point. Although style, he writes, is one of the main sources of insight into an author's "norms," too much emphasis upon the merely verbal can exclude a proper estimate of his skill in other areas—his choice of character, episode, scene, and idea. It would appear, therefore, that although good criticism should begin, as Lodge says, with a sensitive response to the creative use of language, it must continually test the validity of its linguistic findings in terms of all the other elements in a story. There is a great deal, particularly in a short story, that is not stated in actual words, but that derives its impact from the author's awareness of life and his ability to suggest his perceptions through contrasts, juxtapositions, and timing, all of which involve judgment and choice, which are not necessarily related to linguistic skill.

a) Compression and Selection

The first need to be considered in the language of a short story, perhaps because it is most frequently alluded to, concerns its economy and compression (discussed also in Part I). The short story is compelled by its very nature to give, as Henry James says in his discussion on foreshortening, "all the sense . . . without all the substance." The most successful short-story writers of the nineteenth century, a period much given to "weighty words" and sermonizing, were writers who deviated from tradition, like Maupassant and Chekhov, masters in the art of distillation and understatement.

Long works require a different kind of execution, Chekhov remarks in a letter, "but in short stories it is better to say not enough than to say too much . . . only compactness makes short things live." A sculptor about to carve a face from marble, he tells another friend, must work to remove from the slab "everything that is not face. . . . When someone spends the least possible number of movements on an act, that is grace," he writes.

Like Chekhov, Katherine Mansfield also felt that effectiveness in a short story was achieved as much by what was left out as what was put in. Commenting on a doubt that sometimes plagued Chekhov that perhaps he left too much out of his stories, she says, "The truth is, one can get only *so much* into a story; there is always a sacrifice. One has to leave out what one knows and longs to use. . . . It is always a kind of race to get in as much as one can before it disappears." Dostoevsky, whose stories were always written under great economic and emotional pressure, felt that a writer needs time to do the work of pruning. When young ideas rush crowding into an author's head, he should not hurry to express them all, but "await the synthesis." The great figures of literature "created by the great writers have generally grown out of long and stubborn labor," he writes. "The attempts and sketches, however, that have gone to the making of the picture should not be displayed at all to the reader."

In order to achieve compression without losing substance, a writer must select his details and words with great skill, for although compression is needful, yet enough specific details in a story are necessary to give the texture of life and make a story interesting and convincing. The form of a story lies in its particulars—as much as in its larger elements and moral categories.

How to strike a happy mean between too much and not enough detail has been the concern of most short-story writers. Naturalistic description for its own sake can be disconcerting, particularly in the short story. And yet a dearth of detail, or the wrong kind of detail, which fails to suggest richer and deeper meaning, can be equally damaging, resulting sometimes in mere synopsis writing. In order to avoid thinness of texture, the short-story writer has learned to develop and refine for his own purposes the poetic devices of suggestion, which enable him to give to his characters and action an illusion of completeness and continuity. The advantage of such devices is that they allow the writer to achieve the necessary concentration of meaning, and at the same time intensify a reader's pleasure by involving him in the explication of meaning.

b) Poetical Effects

Literal meanings of words are inadequate to convey the complexity of human thought and emotions. Consequently, fictional language is rich in figurative devices that add both beauty and depth to style. Symbol, metaphor, simile, analogy, hyperbole, allegory, and periphrasis are all included in the wide range of poetical means available to the writer of fiction. The most popular of these devices in the modern short story, perhaps because of its greater sophistication, as well as its capacity for a richer concentration of meaning, is the symbol or metaphorical image.

In his essay "Fiction and the 'Analogical Matrix,'"[24] Mark Schorer defines the merits of metaphorical language: (1) It gives each style its individual quality and tone, e.g., dryness, heaviness, and so on; (2) It "expresses, defines and evaluates theme," thus demonstrating the directions and limits of meaning contained in a story; (3) Metaphor and symbol convey the underthought running counter to a story's paraphrasable over-thought. In this capacity, metaphorical language is the basis of structure in fiction, as it is in poetry; (4) Metaphorical language is a measure of a writer's vision and his imaginative power to express it.

Symbol adds dimension through the counterposing of different ideas and levels of meaning. It extends the line of meaning, which though unspecified, is directed and controlled by an author. There are various kinds of symbols: (a) those that refer to an isolated object or event, and may carry a conventional meaning (e.g., "rose" for beauty), or a private meaning, which may change with each author—like snow and rain symbolizing the destructive forces of nature in "The Man Who Loved Islands," whereas rain is a life-giving force in "Pkhentz"; (b) recurring thematic symbols, or series of symbols, richer and more subtle than those just described, which act as unifying links in the total design of a story, or which relate the specific local happening to the broad scope of life. Such stories as those of Poe, Anderson, Conrad, and Lawrence use clusters of images as a means of defining theme.

The most useful symbols grow naturally out of the design of a story, although, as Katherine Mansfield confesses, symbol is sometimes used unwarrantably "to round off something." An example of how details gradually accumulate meaning, and consequently symbolic effect, in the course of a story, can be found in Heinrich Böll's "Christmas Every Day."

c) Grammar and Syntax

Maupassant writes that it is preferable, although more difficult, to bend accepted language and syntax to one's will, making them express everything, even what they do not say, than to coin new expressions or revive archaisms. He defines "truly admirable" style as that which works with the common forms of language, infusing them with new life and meaning through ingenious reshaping and variation in structure.

No aspect of grammar or syntax is too small for the imagination of the storyteller who, because of the matter of space, works with words and sentences. Rearrangement of normal prose syntax and repetitive use of unusual grammatical forms are means by which modern psychological fiction expresses complex workings of mind and emotions. Our increased knowledge in the areas of psychology and anthropology has taught us, as Proust so aptly says, that human beings are "giants immersed in im-

[24] Mark Schorer, "Fiction and the 'Analogical Matrix'," *Kenyon Review,* XI (1949).

measurable time." Therefore, the writer who wishes to penetrate the depths of personality must somehow reflect this durational flux in his writing. A writer may suggest a character's uninterrupted flow of consciousness through unexpected shifts in verb tense; the running together of sentences and units of meaning, even perhaps avoiding paragraph divisions altogether; and the use of coordinate conjunctions in the beginnings of sentences or paragraphs.

A writer's skill in the aesthetic rearrangement of language is frequently put to the test in the matter of dialogue, especially in modern fiction, because our public language is relatively unimaginative. Spoken words in a story must convey the shape and flavor of the speaker's language without its poverty. Conversations whose aim is to crystallize character confrontations must be rich in symbolic and metaphoric suggestion. Unless a story writer has a fine ear for words, Mark Twain wrote some half a century ago, his conversations are going to be "full of flats and sharps."

The possibilities of giving fictional language a greater fluidity through changes or dislocations of normal word order are infinite, as the experimentation of such writers as James Joyce, William Faulkner, and Franz Kafka suggests. Repetition of unusual linguistic forms, however, does not always further a writer's intended meaning, as we noted earlier. It is important that the reader examine and assess all linguistic patterns in terms of the context as a whole, in order to be able to distinguish what is functional and significant from mere gimmickry and verbal acrobatics.

d) Titles

The choice of a short-story title is often a measure of a writer's sensitivity to, and skill with, words, although rarely do two writers follow the same principles of title selection. Faulkner, for instance, says that the best and most relevant titles should come to the writer suddenly and effortlessly from the welter of his personal experience. He relates that the only time he was forced to hunt for a title, it turned out to be bad. Hemingway, on the other hand, would make a list of sometimes a hundred possible titles. He would then, he explains, begin eliminating perhaps all of them, to start all over again.

Titles generally provide important clues to meaning, and in the modern short story, where meaning is frequently couched in symbol and metaphorical language, this can be of significance to the reader. For instance titles like "A Dill Pickle" or "The Downward Path to Wisdom" may direct a reader's thought by emphasizing particular elements in a story, thereby providing a good starting point for the exploration of its meaning.

CONCLUSION

The only possible conclusion to a discussion of this nature is to restress the limitations of most statements on method and craft in fiction. However useful, they must always be somewhat arbitrary. Authority and credibility in fiction are not altogether matters of technique. As Allen Tate puts it, "Method is the result of a moral and philosophical attitude . . . as the author begins to understand what it is in life that interests him most, he also becomes aware of the methods which will enable him to create in language his fullest sense of that interest."

A reader can become so doctrinaire about the kind of critical approach that reaffirms his concept and experience of literature as to forget that the house of fiction has, as James said, "not one window, but a million." Writers, recording their impressions of life, are all united in their involvement with the human scene, and it would be pointless to argue that one view, or one method of watching life, is truer or more significant than another.

Each impression of life conveyed through the house of fiction is unique, and should not be measured in terms of rules or standards outside itself. Yet the ultimate worth and meaning of a story must emerge from its coherence, although by no means correspondence, with the human scene. There are many stories that make no attempt at copying reality—stories like "Pkhentz," of a hunchback who is really a flower lost in our disoriented world, or like "The Enormous Radio," of a radio that tunes one into the reality behind the masks and disguises of people's lives. These stories satisfy us no less than the realistic "slices of life" because, in their symbolic imagistic way, they also enrich our knowledge of human beings and of the meaning of existence.

The "truth" of a story resides in many things: the quality of a writer's vision, his ability to keep this vision undistorted by personal or cultural bias, the balance he establishes between his vision and the spectrum of human life, and his skill in using the resources of his art to achieve the maximum effect in unity, credibility, and persuasion.

Bibliography

Aldridge, John W. (ed.), *Critiques and Essays on Modern Fiction: 1920–1951.* New York: The Ronald Press Company, 1952.

Allott, Miriam. *Novelists on the Novel.* New York: Columbia University Press, 1959.

Altenbernd, Lynn, and Leslie L. Lewis. *A Handbook for the Study of Fiction.* New York: The Macmillan Company, 1966.

Alter, Robert. *Rogue's Progress: Studies in the Picaresque Novel.* Cambridge, Mass.: Harvard University Press, 1964.

Anderson, David M. "Isaac Bashevis Singer: Conversations in California," *Modern Fiction Studies,* **XVI** (1970–71), 423–39.

Anderson, Sherwood. *Winesburg, Ohio.* Ed. by John H. Ferres. New York: The Viking Press, Inc. (Critical Edition), 1966.

Aristotle. *Poetics.* Chapel Hill, N.C.: University of North Carolina Press, 1942.

Auerbach, Eric. *Mimesis.* Princeton, N.J.: Princeton University Press, 1953.

Baldeshwiler, Eileen, "The Lyric Short Story: The Sketch of a History," *Studies in Short Fiction,* **VI** (1969), 443–53.

Bates, H. E. *The Modern Short Story: A Critical Survey.* London: Thomas Nelson & Sons, Ltd., 1945.

Beach, J. W. *The Twentieth Century Novel: Studies in Technique.* New York: Appleton-Century-Crofts, 1932.

Beachcroft, Thomas O. *The Modest Art: A Survey of the Short Story in English.* New York: Oxford University Press, 1968.

Benét, Stephen Vincent. *On Writing.* Vermont: The Stephen Greene Press, 1964.

Bentley, Phyllis. *Some Observations on the Art of Narrative.* New York: The Macmillan Company, 1947.

Blackmur, R. P. *Eleven Essays in the European Novel.* New York: Harcourt Brace Jovanovich, Inc., 1943.

Booth, Wayne. *The Rhetoric of Fiction.* Chicago: University of Chicago Press, 1961.

Bowen, Elizabeth. *How Do I Write My Novels.* (B.B.C. Interview) London: P. Marshall, 1948.

Boynton, R. W., and M. Mack. *Introduction to the Short Story.* New York: Hayden Book Company, Inc., 1965.

Bradbury, Malcolm. "Towards a Poetics of Fiction: 1) An Approach Through Structure," *Novel,* **I** (1967), 45–52.

Bromberg, Bertil. *Studies in the Narrative Technique of First Person Novel.* Trans. by Michael Taylor and Harold H. Borland. Stockholm: Almgrist & W. Rsell, 1962.

Brooks, Cleanth, and R. P. Warren. *Understanding Fiction.* New York: Appleton-Century-Crofts, 1959.

Buckler, William. *Novels in the Making.* Boston: Houghton Mifflin Company, 1961.

Burgum, Edwin Berry. *The Novel and the World's Dilemma.* New York: Oxford University Press, 1947.

Burnett, Whit, and Hallie Burnett (eds.). *The Modern Short Story in the Making.* New York and London: Hawthorn Books, Inc., 1964.

Canby, Henry Seidel. *The Short Story in English.* New York: Holt, Rinehart and Winston, Inc., 1909; reprinted 1932.

Cather, Willa. *On Writing: Critical Studies on Writing as an Art.* New York: Alfred A. Knopf, Inc., 1949.

Chekhov, Anton. *Letters on the Short Story, Drama and Other Literary Topics.* Ed. by Louis S. Friedland. New York: Dover Publications, Inc., 1961.

———. *Life and Letters of Anton Chekhov.* Ed. by S. S. Koteliansky and Philip Tomlinson. New York: Benjamin Blom, 1965; first published London: Cassell & Co., Ltd., 1925.

———. *Literary and Theatrical Reminiscences.* Ed. by S. S. Koteliansky. London: Routledge & Kegan Paul Ltd., 1927.

Comfort, Alex. *The Novel and Our Time.* London: Phoenix House, 1948.

Conrad, Joseph. *Joseph Conrad on Fiction.* Ed. by Walter F. Wright. Lincoln, Neb.: University of Nebraska Press, 1964.

Cook, Albert. *The Meaning of Fiction.* Detroit: Wayne State University Press, 1960.

Cowley, Malcolm. *The Literary Situation.* New York: The Viking Press, Inc., 1954.

Crane, R. S. "The Concept of Plot and the Plot of Tom Jones," reprinted in *Approaches to the Novel.* Ed. by Robert Scholes. San Francisco: Chandler Publishing Company, 1961.

Creeley, Robert. Preface to *The Gold Diggers,* reprinted in *New American Story.* New York: Grove Press, Inc., 1965.

Current-Garcia, Eugene, and Walton R. Patrick. *What Is the Short Story?* Chicago: Scott, Foresman and Company, 1961.

Daiches, David. *The Novel and the Modern World.* Chicago: University of Chicago Press, 1960.

Davis, Robert Murray. *The Novel: Modern Essays in Criticism.* Englewood Cliffs, N.J.: Prentice-Hall, Inc., 1969.

Dipple, Elizabeth. *The Critical Idiom: Plot.* London: Methuen & Co., Ltd., 1970.

Dostoevsky, Fyodor. *Letters*. Trans. by Ethel Coburn Mayne. New York: McGraw-Hill Book Company, 1964.

Dunlop, J. C. *History of Prose Fiction*. Bohn's Library, 1888.

Edel, Leon. *The Modern Psychological Novel*. New York: Grove Press, Inc., 1959.

Edgar, Pelham. *The Art of the Novel*. New York: The Macmillan Company, 1933.

Felheim, Marvin. "Recent Anthologies of the Novella," *Genre*, **II** (1969), 21–27.

Forster, E. M. *Aspects of the Novel*. New York: Harcourt Brace Jovanovich, Inc., 1927.

Friedman, Alan. *The Turn of the Novel*. New York: Oxford University Press, 1966.

Friedman, Norman. "Point of View in Fiction: The Development of a Critical Concept," *Publications of the Modern Language Association*, **LXX** (1955), 1160–84.

———. "What Makes a Short Story Short," *Modern Fiction Studies*, **IV** (1958), 103–17.

Frye, Northrop. *The Anatomy of Criticism*. Princeton, N.J.: Princeton University Press, 1957.

———. *Fables of Identity*. New York: Harcourt Brace Jovanovich, Inc., 1963.

Galsworthy, John. *The Creation of Character in Literature*. London: Clarendon Press, 1931.

Glasgow, Ellen. *A Certain Measure*. New York: Harcourt Brace Jovanovich, Inc., 1943.

Gold, Herbert. *Fiction of the Fifties*. Garden City, N.Y.: Doubleday & Company, Inc., 1959.

———. *The Age of Happy Problems*. New York: The Dial Press, 1962.

Hardy, Barbara. *The Appropriate Form*. London: University of London Press, 1964.

Hart, W. M. *The Short Story, Medieval and Modern*. Berkeley, Calif.: University of California Press, 1917.

Harvey, W. J. *Character and the Novel*. Ithaca, N.Y.: Cornell University Press, 1965.

Heydrick, Benjamin A. *Types of the Short Story*. Chicago: Scott, Foresman and Company, 1913.

Humphrey, Robert. *Stream of Consciousness in the Modern Novel*. Berkeley, Calif.: University of California Press, 1962.

"International Symposium on the Short Story," *Kenyon Review*, Part I, **XXX** (1968), 443–90; Part II, **XXXI** (1969), 57–94.

James, Henry. *The Art of the Novel*. Ed. and Introduction by R. P. Blackmur. New York: Charles Scribner's Sons, 1934; 1950.

———. *The House of Fiction: Essays on the Novel*. Ed. by Leon Edel. London: R. Hart-Davis, 1957.

———. *The Notebooks of Henry James*. Ed. by F. O. Matthiessen and Kenneth Murdock. New York: George Braziller, Inc., 1955.

Joyce, James. *Letters*, Vol. I. Ed. by S. Gilbert; Vol. II, III. Ed. by R. Ellmann. New York: The Viking Press, Inc., 1966.

Kempton, K. P. *The Short Story*. Cambridge, Mass.: Harvard University Press, 1947.

Kermode, Frank. *The Sense of an Ending*. London: Oxford University Press, 1967.

Kumar, Shiv K. *Bergson and the Stream of Consciousness Novel*. London and Glasgow: Blackie and Son Limited, 1962.

Langer, Suzanne. *Feeling and Form*. New York: Charles Scribner's Sons, 1953.

Lardner, Ring. *How to Write Short Stories*. New York: Charles Scribner's Sons, 1924.

Lesser, Simon O. *Fiction and the Unconscious*. Boston: Beacon Press, 1957.

Liddell, Robert. *Some Principles of Fiction*. Indianapolis: Indiana University Press, 1954.

———. *A Treatise on the Novel*. London: Jonathan Cape Limited, 1947.

Lodge, David. *The Language of Fiction*. New York: Columbia University Press, 1966.

Loomis, Roger Sherman (ed.). Introduction to *Medieval Romances*. New York: Random House, Inc., Modern Library, 1957.

Lubbock, Percy. *The Craft of Fiction*. New York: The Viking Press, Inc., 1921; 1957.

Macauley, Robie, and George Lanning. *Technique in Fiction*. New York: Harper & Row, Inc., 1964.

Mailer, Norman. "Some Children of the Goddess," *Esquire*, July 1963; reprinted in *Contemporary American Novelists*. Ed. by Harry T. Moore. Carbondale, Ill.: Southern Illinois University Press, 1964.

Mansfield, Katherine. *Novels and Novelists*. New York: Alfred A. Knopf, Inc., 1930.

———. *Journal of Katherine Mansfield*. Ed. by J. Middleton Murry. New York: Alfred A. Knopf, Inc., 1964.

———. *The Scrapbook of Katherine Mansfield*. Ed. by J. Middleton Murry. New York: Alfred A. Knopf, Inc., 1940.

Maugham, W. Somerset. *Points of View*. Garden City, N.Y.: Doubleday & Company, Inc., 1958.

———. *Selected Prefaces and Introductions*. Garden City, N.Y.: Doubleday & Company, Inc., 1963.

———. *A Writer's Notebook*. Garden City, N.Y.: Doubleday & Company, Inc., 1949.

Maupassant, Guy de. Introduction to *Pierre et Jean*. Paris: Ollendorff, 1888.

Mendilow, A. A. *Time and the Novel*. London: British Book Center, 1952.

Miller, James. *Myth and Method: Modern Theories of Fiction*. Lincoln, Neb.: University of Nebraska Press, 1960.

Moravia, Alberto. *Man As an End*. New York: Farrar, Straus & Giroux, Inc., 1965.

Mudrick, Marvin. "Character & Event in Fiction," *Yale Review*, **L** (1961), 202–18.

Muir, Edwin. *The Structure of the Novel.* New York: Harcourt Brace Jovanovich, Inc., 1929.

Norris, Frank. "The Modern Short Story," *The Literary Criticism of Frank Norris.* Ed. by Donald Pizer. Austin, Tex.: University of Texas Press, 1964.

O'Brien, Edward J. *The Advance of the American Short Story.* New York: Dodd, Mead & Co., 1923.

———. *The Dance of the Machines: The American Short Story in the Industrial Age.* New York: The Macauley Company, 1929.

O'Connor, Flannery. *Mystery and Manners.* Ed. by Sally and Robert Fitzgerald. New York: Farrar, Straus & Giroux, Inc., 1969.

O'Connor, W. V. *Forms of Modern Fiction.* Minneapolis, Minn.: University of Minnesota Press, 1948.

O'Connor, Frank (pseudonym for Michael O'Donovan). *The Lonely Voice: A Study of the Short Story.* Cleveland: World Publishing Company, 1963.

O'Faolain, Sean. *The Short Story.* New York:The Devin-Adair Company, 1951.

Ortega y Gasset, José. *The Dehumanization of Art and Notes on the Novel.* Princeton, N.J.: Princeton University Press, 1948.

Pattee, Fred L. *The Development of the American Short Story.* New York: Harper & Row, Inc., 1923.

Peden, William. *The American Short Story: Front Line in the National Defense of Literature.* Boston: Houghton Mifflin Company, 1964.

Peyre, Henri. *Fiction in Several Languages.* Boston: Houghton Mifflin Company, 1968.

Poirier, Richard. *The Performing Self: Compositions and Decompositions in the Languages of Contemporary Life.* New York: Oxford University Press, 1971.

Porter, Katherine Anne. *The Collected Essays and Occasional Writings of Katherine Anne Porter.* New York: Delacorte Press, 1970.

Pritchett, V. S. *The Living Novel and Later Appreciations.* New York: Random House, Inc., 1964.

Read, Herbert. *English Prose Style.* Boston: Beacon Press, 1952.

Robbe-Grillet, Alain. *For a New Novel.* New York: Grove Press, Inc., 1965.

Sarraute, Nathalie. *The Age of Suspicion.* New York: Grove Press, Inc., 1963.

Scholes, Robert. *Approaches to the Novel.* San Francisco: Chandler Publishing Company, 1961.

———. *Elements of Fiction.* New York: Oxford University Press, 1968.

Scholes, Robert, and Robert Kellogg. *The Nature of Narrative.* New York: Oxford University Press, 1966.

Schorer, Mark. *The World We Imagine.* New York: Noonday Press, 1968.

———. "Fiction and the 'Analogical Matrix'," *Kenyon Review,* **XI** (1949), 549–60.

Stang, Richard. *The Theory of the Novel in England, 1850–1870.* New York: Columbia University Press, 1959.

Stevick, Philip, ed. *The Theory of the Novel.* New York: The Free Press, 1967.

Stroud, Theodore A. "A Critical Approach to the Short Story," *Journal of General Education,* **IX** (1956), 91–100.

Studies in Short Fiction. Newberry, S.C.: Newberry College, **I–IX** (1963–current).

Surmelian, Leon. *Techniques of Fiction Writing: Measure and Madness.* Garden City, N.Y.: Doubleday & Company, 1968.

Tate, Allen, and Caroline Gordon. *The House of Fiction.* New York: Charles Scribner's Sons, 1960.

Tolstoy, Leo. *What Is Art, and Essays on Art.* New York: Oxford University Press, 1930.

Trask, Georgianne, and Charles Burkhart (eds.) *Storytellers and Their Art.* Garden City, N.Y.: Doubleday & Company (Anchor Books), 1963.

Unterecker, J. E., (ed.) *Approaches to the Twentieth Century Novel.* New York: Thomas Y. Crowell Company, 1967.

Van Ghent, Dorothy. *The English Novel: Form and Function.* New York: Harper & Row, Publishers, Inc., 1953.

Walcutt, Charles C. *Man's Changing Mask: Modes and Methods of Characterization in Fiction.* Minneapolis, Minn.: University of Minnesota Press, 1966.

Ward, A. C. *Aspects of the Modern Short Story in English and American.* London: London University Press, 1924.

Watt, Ian. *The Rise of the Novel.* Berkeley, Calif.: University of California Press, 1957.

Wellek, René, and Austin Warren. *Theory of Literature.* New York: Harcourt Brace Jovanovich, Inc., 1949.

Welty, Eudora. *Short Stories.* New York: Harcourt Brace Jovanovich, Inc., 1949.

West, Ray B., Jr., and R. W. Stallman. *The Art of Modern Fiction.* New York: Holt, Rinehart and Winston, Inc., 1949.

West, Ray B., Jr., *The Short Story in America: 1900–1950.* Chicago: Henry Regnery Company, 1952.

———. *The Writer in the Room.* Lansing, Mich.: Michigan State University Press, 1968.

Wharton, Edith. *The Writing of Fiction.* New York: Charles Scribner's Sons, 1925.

Williams, Blanche Colton. *Our Short Story Writers.* New York: Moffat, Yard & Company, 1922.

Williams, William Carlos. *A Beginning on the Short Story.* Yonkers, N. Y.: Alicat Bookshop Press, 1950.

Wilson, Angus. *The Wild Garden.* Berkeley, Calif.: University of California Press, 1963.

Woolf, Virginia. *Granite and Rainbow.* New York: Harcourt Brace Jovanovich, Inc., 1958.

Wright, Austin McGiffert. *The American Short Story in the Twenties.* Chicago: University of Chicago Press, 1961.

Writers at Work: The Paris Review Interviews. Ed. by Malcolm Cowley. New York: The Viking Press, 1958.

Writers at Work: The Paris Review Interviews, 2nd Series. Introduction by Van Wyck Brooks. New York: The Viking Press, 1963.

Writers at Work: The Paris Review Interviews, 3rd Series. Introduction by Alfred Kazin. New York: The Viking Press, 1967.

Zabel, Morton D. *Craft and Character in Modern Fiction.* New York: The Viking Press, 1957.

Zola, Emile. *The Experimental Novel,* originally published 1893. In George Becker (ed.), *Documents of Modern Literary Realism.* Princeton, N.J.: Princeton University Press, 1963.

Short Stories

Introduction: The Short Story in the Modern World

The preceding essay is concerned with the theory and technique of the short story. No story, however, is interesting solely on theoretical or technical grounds. It must possess a special quality that renders it vital, or to use that abused word, "relevant" for other ages. It must enlarge the reader's vision, heighten his perception, and without necessarily duplicating his experience, touch him in areas that immediately concern him. That is the meaning of relevance as it expresses the individual's genuine need to find connections between past and present. The short story of enduring vitality reflects, illuminates, or explores significant aspects of human experience. In doing so, it enables the reader, in the truest sense, to share in the creative act.

The short story, as the most recent form of fiction, almost from its birth began to feel the pressures of the modern world. The British poet and critic Matthew Arnold (1822–1888), in describing his age "with its sick hurry, its divided aims," isolated the problem that was to engage the major writers from the late nineteenth century to the present. What do the words "divided aims" mean with respect to the short-story writer and his subjects?

In the relatively stable middle-class society of the eighteenth century, writer and reader generally shared a common set of values.[1] They tended to agree about what were the important or significant experiences in human life. The early novel examined but did not really challenge widely accepted principles. Much of the fiction of the late eighteenth and early nineteenth centuries was concerned with the relation between individual happiness and moral conduct. England's Jane Austen (1775–1817) portrayed characters who waver and stray from the moral norms of their class. The delightful complications in her novels lie in the individual's struggle to follow paths of conduct that ultimately insure private happiness and public good.

[1] What was true for England was also true in broad outline for other countries where the short story developed. In England, however, the situation was not complicated by the violent upheavals that shook other Western nations during this period of social change. The short story and novel, which developed along with the rise to power of the middle class, can be said to follow—with inevitable differences within each country—a general pattern.

Nineteenth-century society began to change under the pressures of industrialism and the accompanying complexity of social institutions. Private lives within all classes grew more complicated and fragmented. Differences between social groups were more noticeable. Influenced by the new science of psychology, individuals even within the same group no longer necessarily believed that what was important or valuable for one person was equally so for another, or for society at large. They began to examine the values long revered by the middle class—economic success and social position. It had become apparent to many that the visible signs of worldly achievement often bore little relation to a person's moral worth.

The central concerns of late nineteenth and early twentieth-century writers were sharpened by a series of crises that created a wide cleavage between the aims expressed by societies and the practices in which they privately engaged. The writer was moved not only to question the dominant values, but to challenge them, and particularly to explode the myths of gentility that often masked ugly and violent truths. Large-scale wars intensified the individual's quest for meaning; a mood of crisis began to prevail in a world that seemed marked by irrationality. Writers were disenchanted with pre-existing beliefs in what constituted happiness: family life, romantic love, personal success, religious faith, community well-being, and national pre-eminence. In discarding the old truths, their search frequently carried them into re-examinations of national goals and practices: power politics, conquest, paternalism, and imperialism. They began to explore patiently and minutely the crisis of belief that threatened the old order. Their writings touched on every aspect of life in modern Western society, for only by removing their masks and holding their actions up to a fresh scrutiny might individuals and nations recover health and sanity. Fiction, to the extent that it penetrated the crust of hypocrisy, was enlisted in the struggle for human survival. The search for new values, begun in the last century, is still a major subject of fiction in the 1970's.

A number of the stories in this volume explore values in terms of their implications for the individual placed in a situation that forces him to redefine his aims and expectations of life.

Both **Dalyrimple Goes Wrong** and **Soldier's Home** were written shortly after World War I, which began, as Dalton Trumbo says, "like a summer festival" and ended "nine million corpses later." [2] Both deal with the postwar sensibility, the community's fickle adulation of the war hero, and the effects of youthful disillusionment with American values on the lives of returned soldiers. Both are stories of initiation and disenchantment, yet the differences between the two are as striking as the similarities.

"Dalyrimple Goes Wrong" ironically reverses the Horatio Alger success myth: hard work is neither edifying nor character-building, but dehumanizing and devitalizing. Young war hero Bryan Dalyrimple shrewdly recognizes that "cutting corners"—rejecting childhood notions of the morality of hard work and faithfulness to duty—offers the poor but bright young man the best opportunity for happiness. He learns that money *can*

[2] Dalton Trumbo, Introduction to *Johnny Got His Gun* (New York: Bantam Books, 1970).

buy at least the materials of happiness, and in true American style, applies his new knowledge to the task of rising in the world. Morality, he discovers, is simply a description of our actions; evil means being found out. Bryan's new morality works; he will remain on the "right side of the fence," and the possibilities for his future are limitless.

Dalyrimple is not broken by his new knowledge. Unlike Krebs in "Soldier's Home," he is the kind of American who is destined to survive, for he has a ready substitute for conventional morality: romantic heroism. Dalyrimple imagines himself the descendant of legendary rebels of the past, the "new psychological rebel of his own century—defying the sentimental a priori forms of his own mind." He regards his actions as automatically invested with heroism. The Bryan Dalyrimples, likable, but fundamentally shallow, will always have a handy rationale for their decisions. They are precursors of the new "heroes" of twentieth-century business and politics.

F. Scott Fitzgerald himself did not see action in World War I; Ernest Hemingway did, and was psychologically and physically wounded on the battlefield. The differences in their experiences certainly help to account for the dissimilarities in outlook in the two stories and in the two heroes. Dalyrimple's war was a "nine-day romp"; it never touched him. In Krebs, an average young man before the war, the battlefield experience caused traumatic shock. He has returned too late for the celebration that greeted the conquering hero. The war is still painfully alive for him; for those around him at home, it exists only as a set of stale romantic clichés. They want to be titillated by tales of wartime atrocities, filled with sensationalism and violence. They do not want to be told the truth: that war is not glamorous, or beautiful, or exotic, or ennobling. The two words that pervade the story are "lies" and "nausea." Krebs is sickened by the gulf that exists between the truth, the validity of his actual experience, and the lies with which society clothes it. The rightness of his wartime actions is lost amid the hypocrisy that corrupts the meaning of any action. Because life is a lie for Krebs, he withdraws into drowsy games at the pool hall or simply into sleep. He awakens only for the maps and history books that symbolize the authenticity of his own experiences. Like ball games and hardening bacon fat, they are real things and are thus trustworthy.

Involvement with others, with women, with his parents, means overwhelming complications—playing the game of life according to falsehoods about love, religion, family loyalty, and diligent work. For Krebs, the road ahead leads not to certain success as it does for Dalyrimple, but to escape and total disengagement. In the eyes of society, Krebs is the failure, a drifter on the periphery of life. Hemingway soberly, seriously, with controlled economy of language, and Fitzgerald with wit, satire, and humor, provide glimpses into the postwar disillusion that stimulated a crisis in contemporary values.

In Kipling's **The Gardener,** war also underscores the chaos and destructiveness of modern life, where the soldiers' graveyard symbolizes our spiritual wilderness. But the emphasis in this story is on the atrophy of feeling that results from an individual's—here, Helen Turrell's—rigid adherence to narrow and stultifying social conventions. In the modern world, Kipling suggests, we manufacture human responses much as we do material goods, thus depriving ourselves finally not only of human love, but of spiritual insight as well.

"The Gardener" explores values on three levels: individual (Helen), worldly (the village), and spiritual (Christian belief). Helen is a limited woman; her social and moral boundaries are defined by the village, whose snobbery she shares and limitations she respects. She lives by appearances and denies her deepest needs. Through Helen, Kipling criticizes the immorality that accepts waging war for financial gain, the innocence that speaks of the slaughter of human life as a "show," the dehumanization that evades facing death. Helen's mourning is automatic; she has no outlet for her grief. She rejects even the consolation of religion, confessing, "I haven't dared to think much about that sort of thing." At the end of the story, in a reminder—with Biblical echoes—of man's dependency on transcendent values, Kipling looks to the eternal source of grace which even the unaware, like Helen Turrell, are freely given.

To many writers, the spurious values society offers the individual deny him his elementary human need: to feel for others and through feeling to communicate with them. Flannery O'Connor, in **Good Country People,** finds that not only sentimental falsifications and mechanical gestures, but hyperintellectual abstractions, too, are responsible for emotional death. As Kipling does in "The Gardener," she establishes the connection between feeling and faith, suggesting that the absence of religious belief deprives man of the ability to sympathize and identify with the suffering of others.

Hulga-Joy has placed a wall of abstraction between herself and her world. She is blind to her buried life, and believes that her mind totally controls her body. Actually, she is trapped by and completely dependent upon her physical being, symbolized by her artificial leg, without which she is physically and intellectually helpless. Her illusions about herself are as blinding as Mrs. Hopewell's sentimental optimism, Mrs. Freeman's mechanical materialism, and Manley Pointer's relentless pessimism. Each of the major characters recites a painful litany of spiritual blight. Mrs. Freeman's clinical specifications of secret diseases, Mrs. Hopewell's defensively cheerful clichés, Manley Pointer's stock of hard-boiled wisdom, and Hulga-Joy's proud philosophical nihilism reflect the emptiness of their individual visions. To the extent that the individual denies feeling and rejects faith, he becomes spiritually grotesque. Hulga-Joy is not the only cripple among the good country people.

Like Hulga-Joy, Johannes Friedemann, in Thomas Mann's **Little Herr Friedemann,** believes that there are substitutes for the normal pleasures of love and marriage, from which his physical deformity excludes him. To compensate for the deprivations in his life, he, too, has overcultivated one part of himself, expressed in his taste for poetry, music, and epicurean delights. An embodiment of the humanist outlook, he would like to believe that life itself is a "thing of goodness," and that the absence of the greatest happiness need not scar one's existence. He thinks that he accepts his narrowly respectable bourgeois world, and, indeed, he does become one of its staunchest citizens. Johannes Friedemann, however, is as self-delusive as Hulga-Joy, as susceptible as she to the romantic illusions they have both firmly rejected.

The sexual passions that Friedemann has long suppressed rise suddenly to mock his serenity. Unwilling to admit his physical need, he cloaks it in dreams of romantic love. Forced to face the reality of a brutal rejection, he finally sees himself as a weak, despised creature in an indifferent universe, at the mercy of his own violent, uncontrollable, and irrational impulses. His faith in the power of reason and the individual will crumbles.

Rage at himself, at his world, at the blinding truth of his whole life, leaves him without motive or desire to live. For Thomas Mann, total dedication to any single value can turn even a positive principle into a destructive myth. Humanism and the delicate refinements of taste may prove as restrictive as a conventional middle-class code of morality. To preserve a bland, passionless existence is to deny the source of life, and ultimately to annihilate life itself.

Bernard Malamud and Philip Roth return to the past, hoping to discover in old communal values and traditions new sources of strength for modern man. Recent memories of the Nazi holocaust and the everlasting shame of the concentration camps weigh heavily on the heroes of **The Last Mohican** and **Defender of the Faith.** Both Fidelman and Marx go back to the moral heritage of Judaism in their attempt to reconcile the conflicting claims of the individual and the community in an age where "responsibility" has become a meaningless abstraction.

Fidelman, "The Last Mohican," is a new-world Jew returning to the old world—Rome, the Eternal City—prepared for every contingency save one: he has no moral preparation for life. Like so many of the characters in stories of this era, Fidelman touches only the surface of life. He tries to live dispassionately, attending only to his physical well-being, covering moral and spiritual questions with a veneer of clever words and untested ideas. A failure as a painter, Fidelman becomes a critic, an observer rather than a participant in life. He even avoids visiting the noblest treasures of Rome lest they unduly excite him.

Susskind, the archetypal *schnorrer* (in Yiddish, a beggar or sponger), also acts as the Virgil leading Fidelman-Dante [3] through the catacombs and "mazed streets" of his moral by-ways. In the "cemeterial dark" of the past, Fidelman discovers, through art and religion, the message at the heart of the teachings of Judaism and Christianity: responsibility, compassion, and love even for the most despised remnant of mortality. Susskind, the ultimate wandering Jew, refugee even from Israel and symbol of all the dispossessed victims of twentieth-century madness, recovers for Fidelman the values of his past. Susskind's last message thus completes Fidelman's journey to triumphant rebirth.

Whereas Malamud's Fidelman gives aid and finds redemption through giving, Roth's Nathan Marx finds redemption through refusal; help may

[3] In Dante's *Divine Comedy* (ca. 1307–21), the poet Virgil conducts Dante through Hell and Purgatory.

sometimes be merely the quick route to an easy conscience. Grossbart, an even more outrageous *schnorrer* than Susskind, awakens Marx to the meanings that the surface rituals of Judaism often obscure. Like Fidelman, Marx returns to the synagogue to find a way out of his moral dilemma: should Jews "stick together" in the aftermath of Nazism? Should group values—in this case "mercy" and "loyalty"—guide the individual even when he finds them morally questionable?

Marx learns not only that he has not "lost his feelings," but that they actually dominate him. Soft, self-indulgent sentimentality, his grandmother's comfortable interpretation of Judaism, blurs his judgment and leads him to a moral compromise. Marx ultimately discovers, as Fidelman does, that the individual must pursue more than his own physical and psychological satisfaction. The discovery that his responsibility extends to justice for *all* the men in his unit confirms the highest moral law of Judaism. Man must reject the pressures of conformity and place his faith in himself as guardian of the precious old values that can add meaning to a new age.

Richard Wright traces a similar conflict between old and new values within the consciousness of the mother in **Bright and Morning Star.** As a child, she had sought refuge in Jesus, the "Bright n Mawnin Star" of the soft, warm past that blanketed her from a threatening white world. Later, she replaced undemanding faith with blind suspicion of all whiteness. Unlike the simple soul of Flaubert's story, who retreats further and further into an uncomplicated world, the old mother gradually sheds the blindfolds that have proved inadequate shields against the harsh realities of her violent universe. Her social vision gradually enlarges; no longer "mired between two abandoned worlds," she renounces both individual heroism and unquestioning party loyalty. Her recognition that the new brotherhood must be conceived in love lends her the strength to perform the deed that unites her with her bright and morning star.

Pervading many of the stories, as we have seen, is the suspicion that Christian values have been irrevocably subverted by a wave of materialism accompanying technological progress. Nowhere is that suspicion more apparent than in J. F. Powers' **The Forks,** where even a member of the clergy suffers from the same spiritual impoverishment as the laity. Through the conflict between young, evangelical Father Eudex and the petty bureaucratic Monsignor, Powers casts a cold eye on religious leaders who follow the same false gods as their straying parishioners.

Monsignor, consumed with ambition, rigid, concerned only with form and surface, takes loving care of his chromium-trimmed car and plans a formal garden lavish enough to rival the setting of a Borgia palace. Utterly sure of the rightness of his judgments, he deplores any deviation from his prescribed rules. Were he bishop, "the dark forest of decisions would not exist."

Father Eudex, for whom the priesthood has always symbolized care of the poor, the lepers, and even striking pickets, is a constant outrage to Monsignor's sense of propriety. Through the witty and often humorous sparring match that culminates at the dinner table, Powers hints that the teachings of Jesus are in danger of vanishing from the Church, their rightful earthly residence.

The Egg and **Death of a Traveling Salesman** describe the failure of American men trapped by our deceptive social values. Each narrative, however, accrues rich, symbolic overtones that finally transcend the individual case and the particular society.

"The Egg" is, as Irving Howe notes, a "parable of human defeat" [4] that details man's struggle against the pitiless forces of an arbitrary universe. Beginning with his entrapment by the alluring mythology of success, "the American passion for getting up in the world," the father's career provides the son with a lesson in failure. His wry pessimism as he narrates the story reveals how thoroughly the son has absorbed his father's despair, and how clouded, as a result, is his own view of human possibility. His grim recitation of the chicken's struggle for survival etches with bleak clarity the misery any creature must endure, from birth, through disease and disaster, to death. The grotesque mutations in the jars are shocking reminders of the intervention of chance in the mysterious cycle of life.

There is a tragic intensity in the story of the egg. It derives from the father's frustration as he channels his compulsive energies into the chicken farm, and from the son's awe at the sheer power a delicate, thin-shelled egg can wield over a human life. We are left with the paradoxical message that the egg, the origin of life, may also symbolize a destructive element at the very heart of creation.

The traveling salesman has long been a comic figure in the folklore of American business. A hearty, jovial raconteur, he tries to ingratiate himself to prospective customers with a ready stock of jokes for the men and sly seductions for the women. Rootless and alone, his home a series of drab hotel rooms, he is a mythic embodiment of human isolation, and a tragic outgrowth of a stock figure of early American folk humor, the shrewd Yankee peddler.[5]

Eudora Welty's salesman has reached the end of his route. His "customary enthusiasm," his projecting voice, his false heartiness, no longer protect him from the growing emptiness that signals his approaching death. Weak and debilitated after his illness, he has no support against the cold, silent desolation of his last trip.

The trip itself resembles a dream or reverie; by faint clues and indirection, Welty suggests that the salesman's last journey is psychological and spiritual. On the brink of death, he stumbles on the revelation that gives meaning to the confused welter of his experience. Lost, estranged from himself, society, and nature, he absorbs the healing message of the country couple.

His trip to Beulah, the Biblical "Happy Land" (*Isaiah,* lxii:4), is a journey of spiritual discovery. Like Nathan Marx, Fidelman, and the old mother of Wright's story, he turns back to his childhood, and in the warm

[4] Irving Howe, *Sherwood Anderson* (New York: William Sloane Associates, 1951), p. 170.

[5] Arthur Miller's play, *Death of a Salesman,* 1949, is a classic dramatization of salesman Willy Loman's life as an embodiment of the American tragedy.

memory of his grandmother rediscovers the human values he had long ago discarded. In a moment of supreme pathos, he realizes the simplicity, yet enormity, of the life he has rejected. Oppressed by his knowledge, sensing that he has indeed been on a dangerous journey, he flees toward the only refuge that will accept him. In the moonlight, his car sits "like a boat," waiting for the passenger to embark on his final voyage.

Another group of stories explores values primarily as they operate within the context of society. Whereas the previous group focused on the individual and then by extension on his world, these stories consider somewhat more abstractly the values that characterize communities and nations; the individuals in them are, to a considerable extent, embodiments of philosophical and moral attitudes, less important in themselves than in what they illustrate about their world.

The Enormous Radio is a modern morality tale that looks beneath the surface lives of a statistically representative couple, Jim and Irene Westcott. Typical of affluent, college-bred urbanites, surrounded by appliances and gadgets in a luxury high-rise apartment, the Westcotts have, at first glance, everything. The arrival of the new radio, with its "malevolent green light" (a reversal of F. Scott Fitzgerald's symbolic green light of hope in *The Great Gatsby*), shatters Irene's innocence and Jim's complacency. Tearing aside the Westcotts' comforting illusions, the radio sounds a discordant concert of human confusion. It finally bares the ugliness of their own marriage, a tenuous structure built on money, anxiety, and greed. As a footnote to the preceding events, the radio announcer blandly recites the violent occurrences of an ordinary day. His words are the hollow echoes of a world that trivializes self-discovery, neutralizes horror, and denies the individual the dignity of tragedy.

The Pearl, too, is about keeping up appearances and conforming to social conventions. A genuinely funny story, it exposes the ridiculous deceptions of people trapped by their determination to save face and preserve dignity.

Mishima's group of ladies—idle, vain, and sentimental—are caught in an intricate web of petty falsehood that serves as a satiric commentary on the utter triviality of the initial complication. In an effort to avoid the delicate problem posed by the human digestive system, the women become prisoners of their limited sense of propriety. The straightforward narrative, maintaining the pretense that the matter is entirely serious, merely heightens the comedy. The reader is left to speculate that the story may be a parody of the complicated machinations in which institutions and governments regularly engage.

Like "The Pearl" and "The Enormous Radio," **The Blue Hotel** is set in a community of pretenders. Residents and guests of Fort Romper's Palace Hotel laugh at the Swede's timorous entrance and ridicule his illusions about the raw, uncivilized West. Scully hastily reassures the Swede, boasting about the new line of "ilictric street cars" that will be the conclusive testimonial to the civilization of Fort Romper.

But Scully himself is a pretender; acting the role of hospitable innkeeper, he is revealed under stress as weak, trivial, and bloodthirsty. Similarly, all of the figures in the story (Johnnie, the Easterner, the cowboy, and the Swede) reveal weaknesses—either cowardice, dishonesty, stupidity, or bestiality—that puncture their civilized pretensions. As if commenting on the paltriness of man's struggle to maintain his illusions, Nature is thoroughly indifferent; as the blizzard whirls about them, the wind tears the words from Scully's lips and scatters them.

The Easterner's final speech raises the question of moral responsibility, the basis of genuine civilization, and perhaps the foundation of our whole system of values. The problem—and it has been raised with special urgency in recent years at war-crimes tribunals—is this: does the proven guilt of one offender exonerate others who, like the Cowboy, "didn't do anythin'," and thereby passively collaborated in an immoral act?

In several stories, the decay of values marks the end of an era, the passing of one world and the confusion that heralds the birth of another. Although there are other equally important themes in the story, Conrad's **Il Conde** clearly traces the last days of a representative of an effete aristocracy. The narrator and Il Conde share the sensibilities of a class that respects those gestures associated with refinement and taste. Beauty and art shield the old man from involvement with a changing society. But the encroaching barbarians are waiting in the wings, as Il Conde discovers in his humiliating encounter with the rude young man. The lush beauty of Naples and the romantic, orchestrated background are ironic counterpoints to his defeat. Never questioning the essence of his code and robbed of his dignity, Il Conde surrenders a life that contained the seeds of its own destruction.

Two stories, **Christmas Every Day** and **Deutsches Requiem,** return to the tragedy of twentieth-century Germany for its revelations about the nature of man and the moral life of society. Like "Il Conde," but with broader implications, "Christmas Every Day" uncovers the insularity underlying a parable of modern history. From the opening statement, "Symptoms of decline have become evident in our family," Böll forces the reader into a symbolic interpretation of ensuing events. The narrator's neutral monotone and moral obliquity are themselves signs of social disintegration. His narrative traces a series of bizarre circumstances that comment tellingly on the moral indifference of a group of Germans who might have saved themselves and their nation from Nazism had they been less intent on preserving moribund values and readier to acknowledge social change. Focusing on empty rituals and forsaking the spirit of Christianity which the rituals originally embodied, the family withdraws, as Il Conde did, and allows barbarism to supplant its civilization.

Böll suggests that those who survived Nazism tainted postwar Germany with their guilt and caused a spiritual malaise that took expression in frantic pursuit of passing salvations: communism, existentialism, religious fanaticism. The final image of the old aunt, the senile prelate, and the avaricious actors is a haunting evocation of contemporary social disorder. In an age filled with "piles of ruins" and "untended parks," even the grotesque Christmas celebration satisfies the narrator's nostalgia for a lost world. In an uncertain present, the dark past merges with a dim and unknown future.

"Though he slay me, yet will I trust in him." (*Job*). With these words, which convey the essence of the Judeo-Christian tradition, Jorge Luis Borges begins the autobiographical statement of Otto Dietrich zur Linde, former subdirector of a Nazi concentration camp. In zur Linde's ancestry the polarities of German history conjoin: Prussian army officer and humanistic theologian. The narrator's childhood, too, was molded by opposites: first, by Shakespeare and Brahms; later, by the German philosophers Schopenhauer, Nietzsche, and Spengler.[6]

The story recreates zur Linde's reflections on the eve of his execution as murderer and torturer. It reveals the clash between the amoral intellectualism nurtured by his German upbringing and human feeling—abstract and particular—as exemplified by the American poet Walt Whitman and the Jewish musician, David Jerusalem, whose death zur Linde has engineered. Zur Linde's thoughts epitomize the dedication of the committed idealist, the man to whom feeling is anathema and in whom the will is triumphant. The irrefutable logic of his final assertion of the morality of violence is a paradoxical outgrowth of excessive idealism. Through the symbols of Germany, representing any civilization that has pursued an idea, and Jerusalem, which stands for the city where feeling is ardently celebrated. Borges bares a central conflict of the modern age. Western culture, for him, is a labyrinth in which we may trace the sequential logic that resulted in Germany's defeat and may portend the immolation of our whole civilization.[7]

Donald Barthelme projects his fear of the decline of American civilization into a futuristic society that carries grim reminders of Stanley Kubrick's powerful science-fiction film, "2001: A Space Odyssey." In the depersonalized world of **Report**, communication has been replaced by the

[6] As this story depends for its full effect on the reader's familiarity with the work of several philosophers, it may be helpful to summarize briefly some of their major theories. Arthur Schopenhauer (1788–1860), strongly influenced by his predecessor, Immanuel Kant (1724–1804), formulated the idea of the will, which is superior to knowledge and ethically evil. Individual will is part of the vast will which permeates all of nature. Friedrich Wilhelm Nietzsche (1844–1900), influenced by Schopenhauer, admired, above all, strength of will and endurance as well as the ability to inflict pain for important ends. Compassion, he believed, was a weakness to be resisted. Nietzsche prophesied an era of great wars. An individualist himself, he was a believer in the hero as the savior of civilization. He had no particular admiration for Germany, preferring an international ruling race. He criticized Christianity bitterly. For Nietzsche, the noble man is in himself a will-to-power, and is capable of cruelty and crime to further his designs. Opposed to both redemption and repentance, he denounced sympathy as an eradicable weakness. Oswald Spengler (1880–1936) theorized that every culture passes through a life cycle from youth through maturity through old age to death. He described Western civilization as being in its decline and prophesied its conquest by the "yellow race." Although he believed in the individual's subservience to the state and supported German influence over European nations, he did not support Nazi theories of racial superiority.

[7] See Carter Wheelock, *The Mythmaker: A Study of Motif and Symbol in the Short Stories of Jorge Luis Borges* (Austin, Texas: University of Texas Press, 1969), pp. 160–64, for a discussion of "Deutsches Requiem" as a study of ways of perceiving reality according to the Alephic and Zahiristic world views.

language of technocracy. The truest expression of the society is a parody of a famous humanistic statement. "Nothing mechanical is alien to me" is the motto of a civilization that has achieved the final absurdity: a moral sense on punched cards. Brief impressionistic details at the beginning and end of the story reflect a vision of natural beauty that the machine can neither see nor duplicate. They remind us that the human element, however feeble, will survive even in a world totally stripped of values.

With the collapse of a belief in an accepted universal order, and the subsequent disintegration of values, modern man suddenly finds himself terrifyingly free and alone, with nothing fixed in his inner or outer worlds to cling to for support or defense—"in the bright realm of values, we have no excuse behind us, nor justification before us. We are alone . . ." [8] The necessity for modern man to take a new view of himself and of his universe, to reidentify and reorient himself, is obvious if he is to continue to exist meaningfully. This has become the subject of much contemporary philosophical study. Failing to find the meaning and cohesion he is desperately searching for in a fragmented world, modern man may at least learn through introspection how to endure his condition with dignity.

A great deal of the fiction of the last half century is as much preoccupied with redefining the meaning of existence as it is with reevaluating values. Although relatively few stories that address themselves to problems of being (i.e., to the question: Who or what am I?) are "existential" in the strict sense of the word, a great number deal with issues and arguments that are basic to existential thought: the break between mind and world, and man's resulting confusion as to where he most nearly belongs, if at all, in the animal, social, or intellectual kingdoms; his search for a lost or new identity; suspicion of collective societies, which tend to set boundaries to man's thought and action according to dubious systems of value; the alienation and isolation of the individual; his rebellion and protest against a seemingly "absurd" universe. A brief explanation of existential thought, without necessarily categorizing the group of stories we are about to discuss, may provide a useful point of reference for them.

It has frequently been said that no two existentialists are likely to have the same vision of the human dilemma, because the contemplation of existence, i.e., the act of living, is bound to be subjective, unlike other more objective philosophies which study the nature and essence of things. Jean Paul Sartre, the leading contemporary French exponent of existentialism, complains, in fact, that the term has become so "stretched" and broad that it has lost all meaning.

There are two broad areas of existential thought, the Christian or theistic, and the atheistic. Both approaches begin with a belief in the worth and dignity of man, and in his inalienable right to develop himself as a free human being. This freedom, instead of relaxing man's obligation toward others, actually heightens his sense of moral responsibility both toward himself and toward all of humanity. "Humanization" comes about

[8] Jean Paul Sartre, *Existentialism*, trans. by Bernard Frechtman (New York: Philosophical Library, 1947).

through awareness. Man must be totally conscious of the incongruous in life, for only then can he transcend it, and perhaps even find joy or elation in his struggle and endurance, as Grebe does in Bellow's story **Looking for Mr. Green.**

The strict existentialist has an abhorrence of collectivism, whether communistic, totalitarian, or democratic. He believes that societies promote belief in a happy, rational, progressive universe, thereby anesthetizing man's moral and questioning faculties. Societies encourage man to evade the reality of death, for instance, because of the contradictions it poses to their "happiness" credos. But to the existential thinker, death is the one clear certainty of each individual life. It can neither be outstripped nor shared. And it is only in man's calm and dignified acceptance of that fact that he finds his crowning fulfillment. Thus one of the recurring motifs in existential fiction concerns the drama of man's "humanization" through his confrontation with death. Naked and alone, like Kafka's doctor, and stripped of all the protective camouflages of civilization, man is forced to come to terms with his mortality. Kafka's mouse in the fable learns that there is *no* other direction for him, even though the cat may mockingly delude him before it swallows him up.

It is at this point that the humanistic existentialist parts ways with the theistic existentialist. The former accepts the fact of man's ultimate alienation from and irreconcilability to the world. He does so rebelliously, but he endures, and continues to assert himself in the face of futility, just as Sisyphus continues to roll uphill the rock that simply rolls down again. Driven to the extremity, the theistic existentialist makes a "leap of faith," as Abraham and Job once did. He believes in the existence of a God, who is rationally incomprehensible, but who will give order and coherence to the world. Evil and death within this "redemptive resolution" are viewed as necessary aspects of a larger pattern that will some day reconcile man to his universe.

Of the stories to be discussed below, only one, or perhaps two, may be classified formally as existential stories. However, each one of them touches upon some aspect or another that lies at the heart of existential thought, bringing new insights and depths to the paramount question of the meaning of life and of man's position in a hostile universe.

Saul Bellow's richly detailed story **Looking for Mr. Green** traces an agonizing day's experience in the life of a civil servant, a representative of the bureaucratic system, whose task is to track down a crippled Negro in the ghettos of Chicago, in order to deliver to him a welfare check. In spite of the complications that hamper his search, Grebe, the protagonist, never gives up. That he has a personal stake in this tortuous and seemingly impossible assignment is made clear in his relationship to the scene. He is a native Chicagoan, and reproaches himself for not knowing this ghetto area better. Like Mr. Green, the subject of his search, he, too, is something of a marginal figure, and the possible play on their names, Grebe/Green, might even suggest a closer relationship between them.

The philosophical question relentlessly pursued throughout the nuances and symbolic situations of the story may be stated in some such words as these: Where can man find his true identity, that condition of life where "being" and "seeming" are one, where the name (the external mark of identification) fits the "real" man? Grebe, in his intellectual and cultural isolation, is particularly well qualified for such a mission. He has tested and rejected one kind of intellectual order—symbolized in his now useless college education—because of its failure, during the crisis of the Depression, to cope with the realities of life. When the story begins, he is in the process of searching out the truth and validity of another form of order—that of the labels and identifications conferred by the great social machine.

Unlike Raynor, his supervisor at the relief agency, who has rejected the higher forms of intellection in favor of pragmatism, Grebe never really loses faith in the ultimate power and necessity of "idea." Man's true identity is not just a matter of externals. He keeps reminding himself "there must be a way to find a person," if man can only discover the right point of contact. His encounter with Mr. Fields may be regarded as the climactic moment in which all of the conflicting elements converge. Mr. Fields's status as welfare recipient gently mocks his great dream of creating sixty Negro millionaires in five years. At the same time Mr. Fields derives a special kind of exultation in assuming the identity granted him by the social order. Grebe is aware of the incongruity of the whole situation, but is sufficiently inspired by it to resume the search he was about to give up.

At the end Grebe turns up a drunken naked woman, in an embarrassingly incriminating situation, to say the least, who hints at the possibility of a real Mr. Green existing somewhere in the shadows. Face to face with a squalid and incoherent physical reality, Grebe feels ashamed and humiliated at the discovery, but nevertheless experiences a sense of elation. The dignity and worth of life are affirmed for him in the struggle. The story has an open end, a typical characteristic of Bellow's fiction. Although Grebe never actually finds Mr. Green, he continues to cherish a hope: "For after all, he *could* be found." One can compare this story's openendedness with the positive resolution of "The Last Mohican" or with the equally clear, but more pessimistic note of "Death of a Traveling Salesman," two other quest stories involving the search for lost or forgotten values.

The individual in conflict with an impersonal, disinterested collective machine is the subject of Sartre's **The Wall.** Within a vast totalitarian mechanism, whose primary concern is its own efficient functioning, the fate of single men is regarded indifferently. This is reflected in the officers' perfunctory questioning of the prisoners' names and occupations, "they [the officers] didn't listen to the answers, or at least didn't seem to," and in the Belgian doctor's clinical, rather than humanitarian, interest in the prisoners. Meaning is frequently couched in symbol and evocative imagery. The men find the prison cell "terrifically cold"—clothes are frequently a symbol of man's protective illusions or beliefs—and dark, yet Ibbetia prefers it to his previous solitary confinement in a monastery cell. As the hour of his death approaches, Ibbetia undergoes a process of spiritual and emotional stripping. Impulses, feelings, desires, in fact, all that gives meaning and value to experience, gradually fall away from him.

He is not only repelled by things he has customarily disliked—the cowardliness of Juan, or the inhumanity of the doctor—but becomes indifferent even to the comradeliness of Tom and the memory of Concha's love.

Sartre suggests—and this is the controversial premise of the story—that Ibbetia gains human stature at the moment when he becomes free of all motivations and values that exist outside of him. This happens when he discovers that he can supply neither moral nor emotional reasons why he should die for Ramon Gris or any other person. Having passed the high mark when "the illusion of being eternal" is irrevocably lost, Ibbetia is left with a single impulse: his own *will* to die "cleanly." The rat which at that point runs out from under his feet suggests his relationship to the petty little men around him. Unlike Grebe's elation, Ibbetia's gaiety as he sees the absurdity of his situation is hysterical, changing from laughter to weeping at the end.

The attempt to get at the root of society's moral sickness and decay is the burden of Kafka's **A Country Doctor.** The story, which is framed within the bewildering disoriented atmosphere of a nightmare, is, like most dream literature, rich in symbols that admit multilevel interpretations. The hero is a country doctor, who has led an overly ordered neat life, doing, in his words, "my duty to the uttermost, to the point where it became almost too much." Confronted with an unexpected crisis, he suddenly discovers his spiritual, intellectual, and emotional bankruptcy. No help can come from religion, for "the parson sits at home and unravels his vestments." Traditional answers are sterile and meaningless. The sick boy's family is hostile, but pleading, and he feels old and impotent in the knowledge that the little faith they still have in him is unjustified. Kafka's doctor, like Ibbetia, comes to an impasse—there is no cure for the boy's wound, his servant-girl Rose is being mauled at home, and even the comfort of a coat is denied him on the cold and lonely trip home. But, like Ibbetia, he also achieves some degree of awareness. After some effort he sees the wound, which by implication becomes his own. He is vaguely conscious that his neglect of Rose (the life of simple love—compare with the treatment of a similar concept in Welty's "Death of a Traveling Salesman") is related to his present crisis. His formulistic, overly disciplined life as a country doctor provides him with no means in dealing with "false" night alarms. Symbolic associations here operate on a variety of levels, psychoanalytical, social, or metaphysical. The groom, for instance, may be considered as a male potency figure, suggested in the horses "buttocking" out of the dark pigsty and in his potential rape of Rose, thus providing a contrast to the doctor's impotence, anxiety, and guilt. But he could also represent brute physical reality at odds with the world of idea and intellect.

The break between the private world of idea and the public world of physical experience is satirically dramatized in the science-fiction setting of Abram Tertz's **Pkhentz.** The hunchback disguise which the hero is forced to assume in order to survive in a hostile, and in his view uncivilized world, is symptomatic of the deformed condition of public life (compare to the use of deformity in "Little Herr Friedemann" and "Good

Country People.") The demands of daily existence in a world deprived of ideals and of faith turn its creatures into schizophrenics. This is the leitmotif that runs through the nightmarish and often ludicrous entanglements between the protagonist, a creature accidentally fallen from another planet, and the caricatured human beings he encounters. The opening scene at the laundry establishes the symbolic framework and sets the tone of the story, as the narrator itemizes the dirty clothing of the "real" hunchback with frank brutality. The ineffectual use of water at the laundry is in contrast to what rain—symbolic of a life-giving heavenly force—can do for the narrator. Deprived of real water, in a debased world where all human relationships and activities are stripped of beauty and idealism, Tertz's lonely hero begins to wither away. There is a scene of supreme comedy when the disguised hunchback confronts the real one, and the underlying grotesqueness of human life is revealed. Tertz's story, like Bellow's, is open-ended. The hero prefers death to the possibility of his some day assuming crippled and deformed humanity. But instead of surrendering immediately, he retreats for a period into a symbolic state of grace, where "There will be many warm and pleasant nights. And many stars . . ." and he can dream of his native land.

The intellectual's self-exile from the human scene, which he finds incompatible with the needs of his mind, does not necessarily result in satisfaction or fulfillment. On the contrary, it can, and often does, carry with it its own form of distemper and death. This is the controlling theme in two stories whose settings and techniques are totally different: D. H. Lawrence's **The Man Who Loved Islands**, and Muriel Spark's **Bang-bang You're Dead.**

Lawrence's story, a wonderful *tour-de-force,* in his best incantatory style, builds up its meaning through the sensuous suggestion and evocation established between landscape and states of mind. His hero, a cultured man of discriminate taste and much learning—perhaps a more youthful, positive version of Conrad's Il Conde—believes at first that it is possible for the human intellect to create a utopian island community. He tries to revive the style of an old-world aristocratic charm, but is quickly robbed of all illusion when he discovers the mocking disparity between his stated goal of a happy community and the farcical nature of the islanders' pretense of contentment. His subsequent systematic withdrawal from a world that he believes to be ruled by contradictory and even malevolent forces reflects his own gradual inner ossification as a human being. The pulsating rhythms of nature begin to "bore" him, as the brilliant and exotic colors of Africa do Sybil in Muriel Spark's story. His botanical research becomes meaningless, divorced from the context of life, symbolized perhaps in his rejection of the living "Flora." The malevolence of nature, which seems to intensify for him in direct proportion to his withdrawal, projects the growing terror and loneliness within him caused by the death of his "passional" self. Lawrence himself believed that the way to man's salvation lay through the feelings and passions. The last section is full of images denoting guilt, fear, and death: *foul, unclean, repulsion, guilt, nerve-wracked, torture, horror,* and *darkness,* culminating in a barren landscape of deathly enveloping snow.

Quite unlike Lawrence's panoramic story is Muriel Spark's highly dramatic virtuoso piece. The structure of this story resembles—or parodies—that of a Greek tragedy. It is built up of five choric passages, counterpointed by five episodic flashbacks followed by a finale, like the five choral *stasimons* alternating with five *epeisodions* and climaxed by a dirge, which weave the thread of a Greek tragedy.[9] The choric passages in the story, made up of the commonplaces and clichés of the guests' running commentary, provide an ironic framework for the episodes recalled in Sybil's memory as the films unroll. Their mock character reaches its peak in the conclusive "anti-dirge" that places human tragedy and death on the same level as tropical plants and nature-study shots. The author's caustic wit touches everyone in the story, even the protagonist, who questions whether she is a woman or an "intellectual monster," and through whose mind the drama of past and present unfolds. Like Lawrence's islander, she also suffers guilt and anxiety over her inability to reconcile the worlds of physical and intellectual experience. Unlike him, however, she feels that some form of expiation is necessary to justify her existence, hence her abortive attempts at love making. The accidental death of Desirée, who is clearly intended as a surrogate for Sybil, is ambiguous, suggesting both expiation and judgment. This story, rich in comic undertones of the bitter kind, achieves its effect frequently through the juxtaposition of contradictory elements: Sybil's logic against Desireé's illogic—which is yet the logic of instinct—in dealing Sybil "premature death" at every game; the simultaneous blossoming and decline of Sybil's love affairs, ironically suggested at one point in her sipping "bitter" lemon juice, while the passion-fruit bottles lie unopened by her side.

If the intellectual view of life, with its agonizing awareness of the complications and contradictions inherent in man's world, does not always provide a happy answer to his dilemma, can the "simple" view achieve that end? This is the main question underlying Flaubert's **A Simple Soul** and Chekhov's **Gusev.** Félicité's and Gusev's homogeneous and uncluttered vision of life provides them with a sense of inner harmony that enables them to confront life's adversities and frustrations with dignity and calm. They are ignorant, superstitious, and simple-minded, but these qualities are glossed over with a kindly sympathy. Whatever their shortcomings, Félicité and Gusev stand in favorable contrast to the narrow bourgeois world of Madame Aubain on the one hand, who is vividly portrayed with Flaubert's unfaltering eye for detail, and the wearying, vicious intellectualism of Pavel Ivanitch on the other. Their secret lies perhaps in their childlike ability to transform and harmonize the chaos of

[9] *Choric* refers to the function of a chorus in Greek *tragedy,* which provides a background of moral commentary and evaluation. *Stasimon* is a "stationary" song by the chorus, which always stood in the same place. *Epeisodions* are the dramatic episodes and incidents that make up the plot. A dirge is a short poem lamenting someone's death.

external reality through a creative imaginative act. When outer forces become unbearably oppressive, Gusev, even at the point of death, continues to believe in his world because he "dreams" of a beautiful past rooted in tradition and faith. Félicité's inner "dream" world, likewise, not only gives her the strength to function more effectively than any other person in the community but also enables her to apprehend the highest mystical truth yearned for by the religious devotee—a vision of the "Holy Ghost." Some critics claim that Flaubert's tone is mocking, yet he makes it clear that Félicité's love and unbelievable capacity for renunciation have qualified her for that moment of insight. Gusev's and Félicité's lives are affirmed by the beauty and harmony of their deaths. In Gusev's case, nature joins in a kind of cosmic dance as his body is cast into the waters, and Félicité is exalted in her dying moments as a "vision" of caroling angels gently guides her soul into heaven.

That man may be betrayed by inherited reality as well as ideals is the brooding theme of Svevo's fable **The Mother,** which was written in 1910, in anticipation perhaps of the horror that was to overtake Europe a few years later. One of the earliest and most popular forms of short narrative (see Part 1), the animal fable is still a viable form of narration, although in its modern dress it combines elements of both fable and parable. It is an extremely economic and concentrated form that suggests meaning on a variety of levels. Come-Come's rejection by the Mother may convey on one level Svevo's personal bitterness and disillusionment with a literary establishment (the chicks are a particularly articulate group) that blocked him out. But it also relates to the larger motif of man's ultimate alienation. The tone of the fable is dark and pessimistic. Svevo suggests sardonically that not only is man's physical environment limited but his visions and dreams are earthbound and deluding. Come-Come's bitter experience results in the substitution of one illusion for another: the image of a perfect, ideal, utopian Mother is replaced by an equally unreal image of her as a "horrible monster."

One of the most moving and forceful expressions of the initiation/rejection theme is to be found in Katherine Anne Porter's **The Downward Path to Wisdom.** This story, told from the child's point of view, portrays with sensitive mastery an oblique adult world. It traces the bitter, relentless course of a four-year-old's initiation into the ugly realities of his little world, the knowledge of his rejection, and finally the shattering birth of rebellion and hatred in his spirit. Like the young chick Come-Come, Stephen works desperately but helplessly to create an identity for himself in a world of love. But the facts of his environment, like the clay he plays with at school, refuse to cooperate. Evidence piles up heavily against a discordant, ineffectual adult world that makes unnatural demands of Stephen, such as Uncle David's smug hypocritical notions of good behavior and honesty, or the women's confused attitudes toward sex, which breed guilt feelings in him. At the end, "howling" and "bleating," like a little animal he is witness to the triumph of a reality that denies him his small share of humanity.

The dehumanization process, unless arrested, must result in the final supremacy of brute force. Richard Wright's "Bright and Morning Star," which we discussed earlier, traces with a fine balance of vision the unbearably painful discovery of the protagonist's identity, both as a black woman and as a human being in a violent world. Sue learns that the process of affirming her existence entails pushing her opponents to their evil extremity. Forced to perform a hateful and violent act, she learns how her limited physical being has driven her into a corner from which the only way out is violence, and, secondly, that the real affirmation of her existence demands the expansion of her view from its narrow context of black versus white to victim versus victimizer.

The Screamers, a totally different story, although it, too, deals with the cult of isolation and protest, attempts to state in poetic, emotive language the ethic of the black American concerned with the assertion of his existence. Jones's story, a poem in prose, is an example of how effect can be achieved through a purely metaphorical and poetic use of language. The controlling metaphor revolves around the sounds of black music, specifically the honk of horns, an impassioned chronicle of black identity, with its pulsating rhythms growing out of the "diphthong culture" and "black cults of emotion." In an essay entitled "The Myth of 'Negro Literature,'" Jones says that Negro music alone, particularly blues and jazz, remains the only "consistent exhibitor of 'Negritude' in formal American culture simply because the bearers of its tradition maintained their essential identities as Negroes." In "The Screamers," he gives aesthetic treatment to that belief by infusing the images conjured from the sounds and rhythms of the horn with the story of the black man's struggle for survival.

So far we have followed the theme of disorder and violence within the framework of changing values in a dehumanized world. Three stories which deal with this theme within the psychological framework are **Counterparts, William Wilson,** and **He and I.** Here the emphasis shifts perceptibly from the external scene—which still plays an important role at least in Poe's and Joyce's stories—to an analysis of the inner self. The theme of the "double" is by no means new. As long ago as the fourth century B.C., the Greek dramatist Sophocles, in his Oedipus plays, had expressed an awareness that even the wisest and calmest of natures may harbor a dark self with criminal or violent potential. Literature is full of stories of the *doppelgänger,* (German for "double") stories of dual personalities, good and evil, involved in a power struggle (for instance, R. L. Stevenson's *The Strange Case of Dr. Jekyll and Mr. Hyde,* and Oscar Wilde's *The Picture of Dorian Gray*).

The analogy suggested in the title of Joyce's story **Counterparts** has often been taken to refer to symmetry of theme and structure, "Mr. Alleyne is to dirty-eyed Farrington as he is to his son." The title, however, could also refer to the ironic contrast between Farrington's inflated image of himself and the reality of his laziness, debauchery, and utter lack of moral fiber. The extent to which the external scene, with its complex pressures, brings out the depravity and viciousness in Farrington is made quite clear through a series of vivid naturalistic details, as Farrington makes the rounds of Dublin pubs. It is easy to escape from the frustrations and humiliations of life in the twilight state of mental torpor induced by drink, when the boastful exchange of imagined and exaggerated experiences creates false illusions of grandeur. The mock heroics of the test of strength between Farrington and Weathers anticipates the former's brutal confrontation with his son. And yet the ending raises a significant question. Farrington returns to a home from which the mother is missing, and the little boy trying to save himself from his father's blind wrath promises him an appeal—in the form of a "Hail Mary"—to the figure of perfect and eternal motherhood.

Moravia's "He and I" is a dramatic monologue, with comic and tragic overtones, of the gradual split between the rational conscious and irrational subconscious self. The external scene, which is vividly outlined in Joyce's story, here is muted and distorted as it filters through the sick mind of the narrator. The cause of the protagonist's neurosis is suggested only slightly in the opening lines: an inadequate and frustrating sex relationship, a favorite Moravian theme. Actual schizophrenia develops gradually, for at first Guglielmo recognizes the voice echoing through the deserted rooms as his own. Then, imperceptibly, the voice takes on a new personality, as well as hostile attitudes that are different from Guglielmo's conscious ones. The other self is seen as a "cunning devil" thrusting Guglielmo towards a violent act which his conscious self shrinks from, and struggles to avert. Guglielmo's world at the end is dismal and forlorn, being both prison and madhouse at the same time.

Of the two stories that treat the theme of the double, Poe's "William Wilson" is the more complex and provocative. Except for the emotionally charged opening and closing sections with their dashes, rhetorical questions, inversions and archaisms, the tone and style of the protagonist's account of the terrible experience that has cut through his life is rational and analytical. In the attempt to answer the shattering questions he raises in the opening paragraph, he goes over his past life methodically and carefully, starting with his first awareness of an inherited family weakness, an "imaginative and easily excitable temperament." Details of his school life are vividly etched upon his memory, reflecting Poe's belief in the vital influence of childhood impressions upon later life. William Wilson struggles to discover the truth of his childhood experiences in the prisonlike schoolhouse, whose principal is also the pastor of the church, a symbol of the repressive forces of both church and school on an impressionable child. The schoolhouse—in Poe's work, a house is frequently a symbol of the mind—is labyrinthine, with narrow winding passages and dark recesses. Oppressed by its "prohibitive" atmosphere, William Wilson, an unusual child, first becomes aware of his double. Unlike Moravia's Guglielmo, who achieves no awareness whatsoever, Poe's protagonist is a complex figure. Within the realm of insanity, he is yet sane enough to try to unravel the mystery of the perverse self which destroys his double, his better self. Language and syntax in Poe are used not only to heighten mood, but as means of characterization (for example, the excessive number of parentheses in this story indicate the narrator's carefully reflective habits, and his feverish struggle to arrive at the truth). The force of the story lies in Poe's power to evoke through language and symbol the protagonist's different states of mind.

Although it does not deal with the psychological double, **Roger Malvin's Burial** is also a brilliant psychological study, in this case, of guilt and compulsion. It begins with a conflict between private need and public morality. Reuben Bourne's conventional conception of chivalry and heroism causes him to tell the lie that results in psychological torment for him and inevitable tragedy for his family.

The story gradually discloses the repressed motives that force Reuben to return to the forest where, actually and metaphorically, lie the "secret places" of his soul. The landscape through which he journeys toward expiation is a psychic projection of his internal confusion, a notable example of the power of the imagination to distort outer reality. As he approaches the site of Roger Malvin's death, Reuben's feelings, seeking release from the chains of lifelong concealment, surge to the surface. Ironically, the act that "cures" his illness also solidifies his despair. Through a suggestive, sometimes ambiguous narrative, "Roger Malvin's Burial" is a frightening study of the blind forces that can dwell unconsciously within man and drive him beyond the limits of rationality.

Although the emphasis in this discussion has been on the larger moral implications of fiction, short stories are, of course, rich in other qualities: characterization, dramatic intensity, humor, symbolism. There are several, however, in which the portrayal of the human personality in all its mystery and complexity, is so vivid that it subsumes other considerations.

In Faulkner's **Death Drag,** the airplane stunt-man brings to an ordinary small town a glimpse into a personality so extraordinary, so far beyond the range of normal experience, that the residents are left awed and uncomprehending. An alien, an outcast, a physical grotesque, the stunt-man swoops down on the quiet town in an airplane as patched, shabby, and indomitably courageous as he. With a narrative drive paralleling the suspense before the flight, the story moves in a straight line to its incongruous concluding image: the puny, twisted, "froglike" creature in a daring tilt with death. In the strange little man with his implacable stubbornness and outraged humanity, the impulse to survive is so powerful that even Providence seems to bend to his will. In "Death Drag," Faulkner has created a figure whose ferocious energy seems to transcend the printed page.

Miss Caroline Spencer, heroine of Henry James's **Four Meetings,** is as unlike the Jewish stunt-man of Faulkner's story as anyone could be, yet she shares with him an extraordinary tenacity and an iron will. She, too, is incongruous, a delicate, pretty young woman whose single-minded intensity is a vast reserve of strength that enables her to survive "the stricken field of her life." Miss Spencer's determination, however, destroys as well as preserves her. Her romantic illusions are a protective screen against the life that she passionately desires and immeasurably fears. Europe, she believes, would make her live, yet it is her avoidance of life that results in the supreme folly of meaningless renunciation. The narrator is angry and disgusted at a pathetic picture of human waste: his "thin-stemmed . . . flower of Puritanism," blinded by a peculiarly American innocence. Yet he dimly perceives that Miss Spencer has followed a course for which she has been truly prepared.

Another area of interest in the short story concerns the complexity of human impulses as they affect people's relationships with each other. Maupassant's little-known story **Useless Beauty,** in its study of a wife's struggle to assert her individuality, has a timely interest for the reader today. The domestic drama, which structurally provides a frame for the main idea, raises the question: What are the grounds of a wife's relationship to her husband in a modern age? This question is amplified during the interpolated philosophical discussion. It becomes part of the larger issue of nature's wasteful and destructive ways, and the necessity of man's mind controlling matter. The ending is perhaps a little ambiguous. It is not altogether clear whether nature needs to be controlled or transcended.[10]

The man in Maupassant's story leaves the scene excited by the awakening of new feelings for his wife, "more formidable than antique and simple love." Katherine Mansfield's story **A Dill Pickle** picks up the situation from the other end, as it were, and shows us what happens to a man and woman, who, intent upon promoting the "formidable" kinship of souls, neglect to work out the more basic "antique and simple" matters. When they meet after a separation of six years the woman recalls moments when in their exciting exchange of ideas and aspirations "their souls had, as it were, put their arms around each other and dropped into the same sea." But she also remembers his petty, irritating bourgeois habits, that repelled her as a woman, and drove her to write a cruel but "so clever" farewell letter to him. The story suggests that the blame for the failure of the affair is to be shared by both, for though sensitive and imaginative, each is enclosed within a private shell of self-deception and egocentricity. The title in this story is a leading one, suggesting the missing element in their relationship. The dill pickle is symbolic, and when the woman tries to recreate in her imagination the event in which it is featured, its taste for her is "terribly sour."

The problems of old age in a fast-moving materialistic world that worships the cult of youth and success are a shameful witness to society's dehumanization. In an age that works hard and creatively to anesthetize the fact of death to the point where people, particularly if they are rich, can pretend it does not exist, Svevo's story **Traitorously** may appear unnecessarily melodramatic. Yet the ending, with its romantic suggestion of poetic justice, does not really mar the effect of the story. For death has already been anticipated in the delicate exposure of the old men's lives: their selfish and narrow aims in youth, the values they had betrayed, and

[10] As, for instance, G. B. Shaw advocates in *Back to Methuselah,* where he portrays the evolution of the man/woman relationship from what he calls the "tom-cat" stage, lasting six or seven years, into the impersonal, sexless love of the He-Ancient and She-Ancient.

the opportunities for good they had allowed to go by. The narrator, through whose eyes we see the fragments of their lives fall into place, has an advantage over his friend. He at least gains awareness, which is the first step toward restitution, if that is not too late. The story is a marvelous example of economy and concentration in its subtle handling of character relationship and mood.

The lonely plight of the aged, if they happen also to be poor and handicapped, is the subject of Elizabeth Taylor's **Spry Old Character,** a moving story, not without its moments of wry, kindly humor. The author sets her tone immediately. The Home for the Blind absorbs the surplus of society's charity, its "vitiated" left-overs, and its weekly rituals of "dispiriting jollity." These are the customary methods by which society dispenses with its obligations toward the aged. As long as the old folks play their role, in keeping with society's accepted image for them, then everything works out and everyone can be "happy." Everyone, that is, except the spry old Harrys of the world, who are doomed to remain as lonely marginal figures, belonging neither in the suffocating, joyless atmosphere of a home, nor in the outer world, where they are too old to join the scramble for survival. Harry discovers, despairingly, that his brief escape from the Home has not resolved his anomaly. The details of the fair, graphically outlined through the narrator's seeing eye, and sensuously through Harry's inner perceptiveness, reflect the course of his spirit's emasculation: physically tired, with the "braying music cuffing his ears," like an animal who has to fawn for "the scraps and shreds" they throw to him, he desperately fears the moment when "his act" will be over and he may remain unclaimed.

Sigrid Undset's **Simonsen** shows another side of the problem of old age, faltering and helpless before a cold indifferent world of changing values. Simonsen has never amounted to much in his youth. A man of average qualifications, the most that can be said in his favor—and this the author allows Olga Martinsen to give eloquent witness to—is that he is a loving, kindly soul. But simple kindliness alone cannot justify his existence to a generation that measures virtue and merit by signs of outward rank, respectability, and the size of a bank account. Sigrid Undset sees Simonsen with a clear and steady eye. She is fully aware of his lackadaisical easy-going morality, and his unwillingness to take life too seriously. But at the same time she also questions whether life as it is lived by his son and daughter-in-law is worth taking seriously. The Christmas setting with its rich reminder of humane and brotherly ideals stands in sharp relief to the cruelties of the actual scene: little Svanhild's sled, not worth much, stolen by a gang of hoodlums, who may remind the reader of the young man in "Il Conde"; and Simonsen himself edged out to the cold, lonely north, away from the one home he has known in his old age. In a series of character confrontations, Sigrid Undset's penetrating and sympathetic insight into human nature allows each one to reveal the truth of what he stands for through his speech, gestures, reactions, and tone of voice. Her vision of life is akin to that of the Christian existentialist. As Simonsen wipes away his tears of frustration at an inhumane and irrational world, he consoles himself "with the thought that there was after all a higher destiny that ruled everything."

Daniel Defoe

Daniel Defoe (1660?–1731), English novelist and political pamphleteer, grew up in London in a middle-class nonconformist family. At twenty-three he decided against entering the Presbyterian ministry, and instead became a merchant, traveling widely throughout England and abroad. He led an active public life, both as an economic theorist and as a radical, outspoken dissenter. As a result of his political involvements, he was brought to trial, placed in the stocks, and later imprisoned. Of his many business ventures, he once wrote, "Thirteen times I have been rich and poor." He went bankrupt in 1692, but managed during the next ten years to pay off most of his debts. Until his death, however, he was haunted by creditors. His most famous political pamphlet, "The Shortest Way with the Dissenters" (1702), which seems on the surface to support the Tory view, is actually a devastating reductio ad absurdum *of Tory arguments. In his fiction, Defoe observed human behavior with a keen eye, and reflected with powerful fidelity the relationships between individuals and their environment. His best-known novels are* Robinson Crusoe *(1719) and* Moll Flanders *(1722).*

TRUE RELATION OF THE APPARITION OF ONE MRS. VEAL

This thing is so rare in all its circumstances and on so good authority, that my reading and conversation have not given me anything like it. It is fit to gratify the most ingenious and serious inquirer. Mrs. Bargrave is the person to whom Mrs. Veal appeared after her death; she is my intimate friend, and I can avouch for her reputation for these fifteen or sixteen years, on my own knowledge; and I can affirm the good character she had from her youth to the time of my acquaintance. Though, since this relation, she is calumniated by some people that are friends to the brother of Mrs. Veal who appeared to think the relation of this appearance to be a reflection, and endeavour what they can to blast Mrs. Bargrave's reputation and to laugh the story out of countenance. But by the circumstances thereof, and the cheerful disposition of Mrs. Bargrave, notwithstanding the ill usage of a very wicked husband, there is not yet the least sign of dejection in her face; nor did I ever hear her let fall a desponding or murmuring expression; nay, not when actually under her husband's barbarity, which I have been a witness to, and several other persons of undoubted reputation

Now you must know Mrs. Veal was a maiden gentlewoman of about thirty years of age, and for some years past had been troubled with fits, which were perceived coming on her by her going off from her discourse very abruptly to some impertinence. She was maintained by an only brother, and kept his house in Dover. She was a very pious woman, and her brother a very sober man, to all appearance; but now he does all he can to null and quash the story. Mrs. Veal was intimately acquainted with Mrs. Bargrave from her childhood. Mrs. Veal's circumstances were then mean; her father did not take care of his children as he ought, so that they were exposed to hardships. And Mrs. Bargrave in those days had as unkind a father, though she wanted neither for food nor clothing; while Mrs. Veal wanted for both, insomuch that she would often say, "Mrs. Bargrave, you are not only the best, but the only friend I have in the world; and no circumstance of life shall ever dissolve my friendship." They would often condole each other's adverse fortunes, and read together *Drelincourt upon Death,* and other books; and so, like two Christian friends, they comforted each other under their sorrow.

Some time after, Mr. Veal's friends got him a place in the custom-house at Dover, which occasioned Mrs. Veal, by little and little, to fall off from her intimacy with Mrs. Bargrave, though there was never any such thing as a quarrel; but an indifferency came on by degrees, till at last Mrs. Bargrave had not seen her in two years and a half, though above a twelve-month of the time Mrs. Bargrave hath been absent from Dover, and this last half-year has been in Canterbury about two months of the time, dwelling in a house of her own.

In this house, on the eighth of September, one thousand seven hundred and five, she was sitting alone in the forenoon, thinking over her unfortunate life, and arguing herself into a due resignation to Providence, though her condition seemed hard. "And," said she, "I have been provided for hitherto, and doubt not but I shall be still, and am well satisfied that my afflictions shall end when it is most fit for me." And then took up her sewing work, which she had no sooner done but she hears knocking at the door; she went to see who was there, and this proved to be Mrs. Veal, her old friend, who was in a riding habit. At that moment of time the clock struck twelve at noon.

"Madam," says Mrs. Bargrave, "I am surprised to see you, you who have been so long a stranger"; but told her she was glad to see her, and offered to salute her, which Mrs. Veal complied with, till their lips almost touched, and then Mrs. Veal drew her hand across her own eyes, and said, "I am not very well," and so waived it. She told Mrs. Bargrave she was going a journey, and had a great mind to see her first. "But," says Mrs. Bargrave, "how can you take a journey alone? I am amazed at it, because I know you have a fond brother." "Oh," says Mrs. Veal, "I gave my brother the slip, and came away, because I had so great a desire to see you before I took my journey." So Mrs. Bargrave went in with her into another room within the first, and Mrs. Veal sat her down in an elbow-chair, in which Mrs. Bargrave was sitting when she heard Mrs. Veal knock. "Then," says Mrs. Veal, "my dear friend, I am come to renew our old friendship again, and beg your pardon for my breach of it; and if you can forgive me, you are the best of women." "Oh," says Mrs. Bargrave, "do not mention such a thing; I have not had an uneasy thought about it." "What did you think of me?" says Mrs. Veal. Says Mrs. Bargrave, "I thought you were like the rest of the world, and that prosperity had made you forget yourself and me." Then Mrs. Veal reminded Mrs. Bargrave of the many friendly offices she did her in former days, and much of the conversation they had with each other in the times of their adversity; what books they read, and what comfort in particular they received from Drelincourt's *Book of Death,* which was the best, she said, on the subject ever wrote. She also mentioned Dr. Sherlock, and two Dutch books which were translated, wrote upon death, and several others. But Drelincourt, she said, had the clearest notions of death and of the future state of any who had handled that subject. Then she asked Mrs. Bargrave whether she had Drelincourt. She said, "Yes." Says Mrs. Veal, "Fetch it." And so Mrs. Bargrave goes upstairs and brings it down. Says Mrs. Veal, "Dear Mrs. Bargrave, if the eyes of our faith were as open as the eyes of our body, we should see numbers of angels about us for our guard. The notions we have of Heaven now are nothing like what it is, as Drelincourt says; therefore be comforted under your afflictions, and believe that the Almighty has a particular regard to you, and that your afflictions are marks of God's favour; and when they have done the business they are sent for, they shall be removed from you. And believe me, my dear friend, believe what I say to you, one minute of future happiness will infinitely reward you for all your sufferings. For I can never believe" (and clasps her hand upon her knee with great earnestness, which, indeed, ran through most of her discourse) "that ever God will suffer you to spend all your days in this afflicted state. But be assured that your afflictions shall leave you, or you them, in a short time." She spake in that pathetical and heavenly manner that Mrs. Bargrave wept several times, she was so deeply affected with it.

Then Mrs. Veal mentioned Doctor Kendrick's *Ascetic,* at the end of which he gives an account of the lives of the primitive Christians. Their pattern she recommended to our imitation, and she said, "their conversation was not like this of our age. For now," says she, "there is nothing but vain, frothy discourse, which is far different from theirs. Theirs was to edification, and to build one another up in faith, so that they were not as we are, nor are we as they were. But," said she, "we ought to do as they did; there was a hearty friendship among them; but where is it now to be found?" Says Mrs. Bargrave, "It is hard indeed to find a true friend in these days." Says Mrs. Veal, "Mr. Norris has a fine copy of verses, called *Friendship in Perfection,* which I wonderfully admire. Have you seen the book?" says Mrs. Veal. "No," says Mrs. Bargrave, "but I have the verses of my own writing out." "Have you?" says Mrs. Veal; "then fetch them"; which she did from above stairs, and offered them to Mrs. Veal to read, who refused, and waived the thing, saying, "holding down her head would make it ache"; and then desiring Mrs. Bargrave to read them to her, which she did. As they were admiring *Friendship,* Mrs. Veal said, "Dear Mrs. Bargrave, I shall love you forever." In these verses there is twice used the word Elysian. "Ah!" says Mrs. Veal, "these poets have such names for

Heaven." She would often draw her hand across her own eyes, and say, "Mrs. Bargrave, do not you think I am mightily impaired by my fits?" "No," says Mrs. Bargrave; "I think you look as well as ever I knew you."

After this discourse, which the apparition put in much finer words than Mrs. Bargrave said she could pretend to, and as much more as she can remember—for it cannot be thought that an hour and three quarters' conversation could all be retained, though the main of it she thinks she does—she said to Mrs. Bargrave she would have her write a letter to her brother and tell him she would have him give rings to such and such; and that there was a purse of gold in her cabinet, and that she would have two broad pieces given to her cousin Watson.

Talking at this rate, Mrs. Bargrave thought that a fit was coming upon her, and so placed herself on a chair just before her knees, to keep her from falling to the ground, if her fits should occasion it; for the elbow-chair, she thought, would keep her from falling on either side. And to divert Mrs. Veal, as she thought, took hold of her gown-sleeve several times, and commended it. Mrs. Veal told her it was a scoured silk, and newly made up. But, for all this, Mrs. Veal persisted in her request, and told Mrs. Bargrave she must not deny her. And she would have her tell her brother all their conversation when she had the opportunity. "Dear Mrs. Veal," says Mrs. Bargrave, "it is much better, methinks, to do it yourself." "No," says Mrs. Veal, "though it seems impertinent to you now, you will see more reasons for it hereafter." Mrs. Bargrave, then, to satisfy her importunity, was going to fetch a pen and ink, but Mrs. Veal said, "Let it alone now, but do it when I am gone; but you must be sure to do it"; which was one of the last things she enjoined her at parting, and so she promised her.

Then Mrs. Veal asked for Mrs. Bargrave's daughter. She said she was not at home. "But if you have a mind to see her," says Mrs. Bargrave, "I'll send for her." "Do," says Mrs. Veal; on which she left her, and went to a neighbour's to see her; and by the time Mrs. Bargrave was returning, Mrs. Veal was without the door in the street, in the face of the beast-market, on a Saturday (which is market-day), and stood ready to part as soon as Mrs. Bargrave came to her. She asked her why she was in such haste. She said she must be going, though perhaps she might journey till Monday; and told Mrs. Bargrave she hoped she should see her again at her cousin Watson's house before she went whither she was going. Then she said she would take her leave of her, and walked from Mrs. Bargrave, in her view, till a turning interrupted the sight of her, which was three-quarters after one in the afternoon.

Mrs. Veal died the seventh of September, at twelve o'clock at noon, of her fits, and had not above four hours' senses before her death, in which time she received the sacrament. The next day after Mrs. Veal's appearance, being Sunday, Mrs. Bargrave was mightily indisposed with a cold and sore throat, that she could not go out that day; but on Monday morning she sends a person to Captain Watson's to know if Mrs. Veal was there. They wondered at Mrs. Bargrave's inquiry, and sent her word she was not there, nor was expected. At this answer, Mrs. Bargrave told the maid she had certainly mistook the name or made some blunder. And though she was ill, she put on her hood and went herself to Captain Watson's, though she knew none of the family, to see if Mrs. Veal was there or not. They said they wondered at her asking, for that she had not been in town; they were sure, if she had, she would have been there. Says Mrs. Bargrave, "I am sure she was with me on Saturday almost two hours." They said it was impossible, for they must have seen her if she had. In comes Captain Watson, while they were in dispute, and said that Mrs. Veal was certainly dead, and the escutcheons were making. This strangely surprised Mrs. Bargrave, when she sent to the person immediately who had the care of them, and found it true. Then she related the whole story to Captain Watson's family; and what gown she had on, and how striped; and that Mrs. Veal told her that it was scoured. Then Mrs. Watson cried out, "You have seen her indeed, for none knew but Mrs. Veal and myself that the gown was scoured." And Mrs. Watson owned that she described the gown exactly; "for," said she, "I helped her to make it up." This Mrs. Watson blazed all about the town, and avouched the demonstration of truth of Mrs. Bargrave's seeing Mrs. Veal's apparition. And Captain Watson carried two gentlemen immediately to Mrs. Bargrave's house to hear the relation from her own mouth. And when it spread so fast that gentlemen and persons of quality, the judicious and skeptical part of the world, flocked in upon her, it at last became such a task that she was forced to go out of the way; for they were in general extremely satisfied of the truth of the thing, and plainly saw that Mrs. Bargrave was no hypochondriac, for she always appears with such a cheerful air and pleasing mien that she has gained the favour and esteem of all the gentry, and it is thought a great favour if they can but get the relation from her own mouth. I should have told you before that Mrs. Veal told Mrs. Bargrave that her sister and brother-in-law were just come down from London to see her. Says Mrs. Bargrave, "How came you to order matters so strangely?" "It could not be helped," said Mrs. Veal. And her brother and sister did come to see her, and entered the town of Dover just as Mrs. Veal was expiring. Mrs. Bargrave asked her whether she would drink some tea. Says Mrs. Veal, "I do not care if I do; but I'll warrant you this mad fellow"—meaning Mrs. Bargrave's husband—"has broke all your trinkets." "But," says Mrs. Bargrave, "I'll get something to drink in for all that"; but Mrs. Veal waived it, and said, "It is no matter; let it alone," and so it passed.

All the time I sat with Mrs. Bargrave, which was some hours, she recollected fresh saying of Mrs. Veal. And one material thing more she told Mrs. Bargrave, that old Mr. Bretton allowed Mrs. Veal ten pounds a year, which was a secret, and unknown to Mrs. Bargrave till Mrs. Veal told her.

Mrs. Bargrave never varies in her story, which puzzles those who doubt of the truth, or are unwilling to believe it. A servant in the neighbour's yard adjoining to Mrs. Bargrave's house heard her talking to somebody an hour of the time Mrs. Veal was with her. Mrs. Bargrave went out to her next neighbour's the very moment she parted with Mrs. Veal, and told her what ravishing conversation she had had with an old friend, and told the whole of it. Drelincourt's *Book of Death* is, since this happened, bought up strangely. And it is to be observed that, notwithstanding all the trouble and fatigue Mrs. Bargrave has undergone upon this account, she never took the value of a farthing, nor suffered her daughter to take anything of anybody, and therefore can have no interest in telling the story.

But Mr. Veal does what he can to stifle the matter, and said he would see Mrs. Bargrave; but yet it is certain matter of fact that he has been at Captain Watson's since the death of his sister, and yet never went near Mrs. Bargrave; and some of his friends report her to be a liar, and that she knew of Mr. Bretton's ten pounds a year. But the person who pretends to say so has the reputation to be a notorious liar among persons whom I know to be of undoubted credit. Now, Mr. Veal is more of a gentleman than to say she lies, but says a bad husband has crazed her; but she needs only present herself, and it will effectually confute that pretense. Mr. Veal says he asked his sister on her death-bed whether she had a mind to dispose of anything. And she said no. Now the things which Mrs. Veal's apparition would have disposed of were so trifling, and nothing of justice aimed at in her disposal, that the design of it appears to me to be only in order to make Mrs. Bargrave satisfy the world of the reality thereof as to what she had seen and heard, and to secure her reputation among the reasonable and understanding part of mankind. And then again, Mr. Veal owns that there was a purse of gold; but it was not found in her cabinet, but in a comb-box. This looks improbable; for that Mrs. Watson owned that Mrs. Veal was so very careful of the key of her cabinet that she would trust nobody with it. And Mrs. Veal's often drawing her hands over her eyes, and asking Mrs. Bargrave whether her fits had not impaired her, looks to me as if she did it on purpose to remind Mrs. Bargrave of her fits, to prepare her not to think it strange that she should put her upon writing to her brother, to dispose of rings and gold, which looks so much like a dying person's bequest; and it took accordingly with Mrs. Bargrave as the effect of her fits coming upon her, and was one of the many instances of her wonderful love to her and care of her, that she should not be affrighted, which, indeed, appears in her whole management, particularly in her coming to her in the daytime, waiving the salutation, and when she was alone; and then the manner of her parting, to prevent a second attempt to salute her.

Now, why Mr. Veal should think this relation a reflection—as it is plain he does, by his endeavouring to stifle it—I cannot imagine; because the generality believe her to be a good spirit, her discourse was so heavenly. Her two great errands were, to comfort Mrs. Bargrave in her affliction, and to ask her forgiveness for breach of friendship, and with a pious discourse to encourage her. So that, after all, to suppose that Mrs. Bargrave could hatch such an invention as this, from Friday noon to Saturday noon—supposing that she knew of Mrs. Veal's death the very first moment—without jumbling circumstances, and without any interest, too, she must be more witty, fortunate, and wicked, too, than any indifferent person,

I dare say, will allow. I asked Mrs. Bargrave several times if she was sure she felt the gown. She answered modestly, "If my senses be to be relied on, I am sure of it." I asked her if she heard a sound when she clapped her hand upon her knee. She said she did not remember she did, but said she appeared to be as much a substance as I did who talked with her. "And I may," said she, "be as soon persuaded that your apparition is talking to me now as that I did not really see her; for I was under no manner of fear, and received her as a friend, and parted with her as such. I would not," says she, "give one farthing to make any one believe it; I have no interest in it; nothing but trouble is entailed upon me for a long time, for aught I know; and, had it not come to light by accident, it would never have been made public." But now she says she will make her own private use of it, and keep herself out of the way as much as she can; and so she has done since. She says she had a gentleman who came thirty miles to her to hear the relation; and that she had told it to a room full of people at the time. Several particular gentlemen have had the story from Mrs. Bargrave's own mouth.

This thing has very much affected me, and I am as well satisfied as I am of the best-grounded matter of fact. And why we should dispute matter of fact, because we cannot solve things of which we can have no certain or demonstrative notions, seems strange to me; Mrs. Bargrave's authority and sincerity alone would have been undoubted in any other case.

Edgar Allan Poe

Edgar Allan Poe (1809–1849), American poet, short-story writer and critic, was born in Boston to actors Elizabeth and David Poe. Orphaned at the age of two, Poe spent his early years with his uncle, John Allan, in Richmond, Virginia. He attended schools in England and Richmond, enrolled at the University of Virginia, but completed only one semester. Estranged from his uncle, unemployed, and in serious financial difficulty, Poe joined the Army, eventually attending West Point, from which he was (willingly) expelled. His first volume of poetry was published in 1827 and he followed it with short stories and critical essays for several magazines which he also served as editor. In 1835, he married his thirteen-year-old cousin, Virginia Clemm, who died in 1847. Two years later, Poe attended a party in Baltimore, after which he disappeared for three days, was discovered by friends lying unconscious on a street, and died shortly thereafter without regaining consciousness. His high-strung personality and erratic behavior led critics and biographers to distort his life. Exaggerated stories still circulate about his drinking. He is remembered for his lyric poetry, his tales of the "grotesque and arabesque," his invention of the detective story, and his enormous influence on subsequent writers. His best-known stories are probably "The Fall of the House of Usher" and "The Purloined Letter." *(See pages 80–81 of Introduction.)*

WILLIAM WILSON

What say of it? what say CONSCIENCE grim,
That spectre in my path?
CHAMBERLAIN'S *Pharronida*

Let me call myself, for the present, William Wilson. The fair page now lying before me need not be sullied with my real appellation. This has been already too much an object for the scorn—for the horror—for the detestation of my race. To the uttermost regions of the globe have not the indignant winds bruited its unparalleled infamy? Oh, outcast of all outcasts most abandoned!—to the earth art thou not for ever dead? to its honors, to its flowers, to its golden aspirations?—and a cloud, dense, dismal, and limitless, does it not hang eternally between thy hopes and heaven?

I would not, if I could, here or to-day, embody a record of my later years of unspeakable misery, and unpardonable crime. This epoch—these later years—took unto themselves a sudden elevation in turpitude, whose origin alone it is my present purpose to assign. Men usually grow base by degrees. From me, in an instant, all virtue dropped bodily as a mantle. From comparatively trivial wickedness I passed, with the stride of a giant, into more than the enormities of an Elah-Gabalus. What chance—what one event brought this evil thing to pass, bear with me while I relate. Death approaches; and the shadow which foreruns him has thrown a softening influence over my spirit. I long, in passing through the dim valley, for the sympathy—I had nearly said for the pity—of my fellow men. I would fain have them believe that I have been, in some measure, the slave of circumstances beyond human control. I would wish them to seek out for me, in the details I am about to give, some little oasis of *fatality* amid a wilderness of error. I would have them allow—what they cannot refrain from allowing—that, although temptation may have erewhile existed as great, man was never *thus*, at least, tempted before—certainly, never *thus* fell. And is it therefore that he had never thus suffered? Have I not indeed been living in a dream? And am I not now dying a victim to the horror and the mystery of the wildest of all sublunary visions?

I am the descendant of a race whose imaginative and easily excitable temperament has at all times rendered them remarkable; and, in my earliest infancy, I gave evidence of having fully inherited the family character. As I advanced in years it was more strongly developed; becoming, for many reasons, a cause of serious disquietude to my friends, and of positive injury to myself. I grew self-willed, addicted to the wildest caprices, and a prey to the most ungovernable passions. Weak-minded, and beset with constitutional infirmities akin to my own, my parents could do but little to check the evil propensities which distinguished me. Some feeble and ill-directed efforts resulted in complete failure on their part, and, of course, in total triumph on mine. Thenceforward my voice was a household law; and at an age when few children have abandoned their leading-strings, I was left to the guidance of my own will, and became, in all but name, the master of my own actions.

My earliest recollections of a school-life are connected with a large, rambling, Elizabethan house, in a misty-looking village of England, where were a vast number of gigantic and gnarled trees, and where all the houses were excessively ancient. In truth, it was a dream-like and spirit-soothing place, that venerable old town. At this moment, in fancy, I feel the refreshing chilliness of its deeply-shadowed avenues, inhale the fragrance of its thousand shrubberies, and thrill anew with undefinable delight, at the deep hollow note of the church-bell, breaking, each hour, with sullen and sudden roar, upon the stillness of the dusky atmosphere in which the fretted Gothic steeple lay imbedded and asleep.

It gives me, perhaps, as much of pleasure as I can now in any manner experience, to dwell upon minute recollections of the school and its concerns. Steeped in misery as I am—misery, alas! only too real—I shall be pardoned for seeking relief, however slight and temporary, in the weakness of a few rambling details. These, moreover, utterly trivial, and even ridiculous in themselves, assume, to my fancy, adventitious importance, as connected with a period and a locality when and where I recognize the first ambiguous monitions of the destiny which afterward so fully overshadowed me. Let me then remember.

The house, I have said, was old and irregular. The grounds were extensive, and a high and solid brick wall, topped with a bed of mortar and broken glass, encompassed the whole. This prison-like rampart formed the limit of our domain; beyond it we saw but thrice a week—once every Saturday afternoon, when, attended by two ushers, we were permitted to take brief walks in a body through some of the neighboring fields—and twice during Sunday, when we were paraded in the same formal manner to the morning and evening service in the one church of the village. Of this church the principal of our school was pastor. With how deep a spirit of wonder and perplexity was I wont to regard him from our remote pew in the gallery, as, with step solemn and slow, he ascended the pulpit! This reverend man, with countenance so demurely benign, with robes so glossy and so clerically flowing, with wig so minutely powdered, so rigid and so vast,—could this be he who, of late, with sour visage, and in snuffy habiliments, administered, ferule in hand, the Draconian Laws of the academy? Oh, gigantic paradox, too utterly monstrous for solution!

At an angle of the ponderous wall frowned a more ponderous gate. It was riveted and studded with iron bolts, and surmounted with jagged iron spikes. What impressions of deep awe did it inspire! It was never opened save for the three periodical egressions and ingressions already mentioned; then, in every creak of its mighty hinges, we found a plenitude of mystery—a world of matter for solemn remark, or for more solemn meditation.

The extensive enclosure was irregular in form, having many capacious recesses. Of these, three or four of the largest constituted the play-ground. It was level, and covered with fine hard gravel. I well remember it had no trees, nor benches, nor any thing similar within it. Of course it was in the rear of the house. In front lay a small parterre, planted with box and other shrubs, but through this sacred division we passed only upon rare occasions indeed—such as a first advent to school or final departure thence, or perhaps, when a parent or friend having called for us, we joyfully took our way home for the Christmas or Midsummer holidays.

But the house!—how quaint an old building was this!—to me how veritably a palace of enchantment! There was really no end to its windings—to its incomprehensible subdivisions. It was difficult, at any given time, to say with certainty upon which of its two stories one happened to be. From each room to every other there were sure to be found three or four steps either in ascent or descent. Then the lateral branches were innumerable—inconceivable—and so returning in upon themselves, that our most exact ideas in regard to the whole mansion were not very far different from those with which we pondered upon infinity. During the five years of my residence here, I was never able to ascertain with precision, in what remote locality lay the little sleeping apartment assigned to myself and some eighteen or twenty other scholars.

The school-room was the largest in the house—I could not help thinking, in the world. It was very long, narrow, and dismally low, with pointed Gothic windows and a ceiling of oak. In a remote and terror-inspiring angle was a square enclosure of eight or ten feet, comprising the *sanctum,* "during hours," of our principal, the Reverend Dr. Bransby. It was a solid structure, with massy door, sooner than open which in the absence of the "Dominie," we would all have willingly perished by the *peine forte et dure.* In other angles were two other similar boxes, far less reverenced, indeed, but still greatly matters of awe. One of these was the pulpit of the "classical" usher, one of the "English and mathematical." Interspersed about the room, crossing and recrossing in endless irregularity, were innumerable benches and desks, black, ancient, and time-worn, piled desperately with much bethumbed books, and so beseamed with initial letters, names at full length, grotesque figures, and other multiplied efforts of the knife, as to have entirely lost what little of original form might have been their portion in days long departed. A huge bucket with water stood at one extremity of the room, and a clock of stupendous dimensions at the other.

Encompassed by the massy walls of this venerable academy, I passed, yet not in tedium or disgust, the years of the third lustrum of my life. The teeming brain of childhood requires no external world of incident to occupy or amuse it; and the apparently dismal monotony of a school was replete with more intense excitement than my riper youth has derived from luxury, or my full manhood from crime. Yet I must believe that my first mental development had in it much of the uncommon—even much of the *outré.* Upon mankind at large the events of very early existence rarely leave in mature age any definite impression. All is gray shadow—a weak and irregular remembrance—an indistinct regathering of feeble pleasures and phantasmagoric pains. With me this is not so. In childhood I must have felt with the energy of a man what I now find stamped upon memory in lines as vivid, as deep, and as durable as the *exergues* of the Carthaginian medals.

Yet in fact—in the fact of the world's view—how little was there to remember! The morning's awakening, the nightly summons to bed; the connings, the recitations; the periodical half-holidays, and perambulations; the play-ground, with its broils, its pastimes, its intrigues—these, by a mental sorcery long forgotten, were made to involve a wilderness of sensation, a world of rich incident, an universe of varied emotion, of excitement the most passionate and spirit-stirring. *"Oh, le bon temps, que ce siècle de fer!"*

In truth, the ardor, the enthusiasm, and the imperiousness of my disposition, soon rendered me a marked character among my schoolmates, and by slow, but natural gradations, gave me an ascendancy over all not greatly older than myself—over all with a single exception. This exception was found in the person of a scholar, who, although no relation, bore the same Christian and surname as myself—a circumstance, in fact, little remarkable; for, notwithstanding a noble descent, mine was one of those everyday appellations which seem, by prescriptive right, to have been, time out of mind, the common property of the mob. In this narrative I have therefore designated myself as William Wilson—a fictitious title not very dissimilar to the real. My namesake alone, of those who in school phraseology constituted "our set," presumed to compete with me in the studies of the class—in the sports and broils of the play-ground—to refuse implicit belief in my assertions, and submission to my will—indeed, to interfere with my arbitrary dictation in any respect whatsoever. If there is on earth a supreme and unqualified despotism, it is the depotism of a mastermind in boyhood over the less energetic spirits of its companions.

Wilson's rebellion was to me a source of the greatest embarrassment; the more so as, in spite of the bravado with which in public I made a point of treating him and his pretensions, I secretly felt that I feared him, and could not help thinking the equality which he maintained so easily with myself, a proof of his true superiority; since not to be overcome, cost me a perpetual struggle. Yet this superiority—even this equality—was in truth acknowledged by no one but myself; our associates, by some unaccountable blindness, seemed not even to suspect it. Indeed, his competition, his resistance, and especially his impertinent and dogged interference with my purposes, were not more pointed than private. He appeared to be destitute alike of the ambition which urged, and of the passionate energy of mind which enabled me to excel. In his rivalry he might have been supposed actuated solely by a whimsical desire to thwart, astonish, or mortify myself; although there were times when I could not help observing, with a feeling made up of wonder, abasement, and pique, that he mingled with his injuries, his insults, or his contradictions, a certain most inappropriate, and assuredly most unwelcome *affectionateness* of manner. I could only conceive this singular behavior to arise from a consummate self-conceit assuming the vulgar airs of patronage and protection.

Perhaps it was this latter trait in Wilson's conduct, conjoined with our identity of name, and the mere accident of our having entered the school upon the same day, which set afloat the notion that we were brothers, among the senior classes in the academy. These do not usually inquire with much strictness into the affairs of their juniors. I have before said, or should have said, that Wilson was not, in a most remote degree, connected with my family. But assuredly if we *had* been brothers we must have been twins; for, after leaving Dr. Bransby's, I casually learned that my namesake was born on the nineteenth of January, 1813—and this is a somewhat remarkable coincidence; for the day is precisely that of my own nativity.

It may seem strange that in spite of the continual anxiety occasioned me by the rivalry of Wilson, and his intolerable spirit of contradiction, I could not bring myself to hate him altogether. We had, to be sure, nearly every day a quarrel in which, yielding me publicly the palm of victory, he, in some manner, contrived to make me feel that it was he who had deserved it; yet a sense of pride on my part, and a veritable dignity on his own, kept us always upon what are called "speaking terms," while there were many points of strong congeniality in our tempers, operating to awake in me a sentiment which our position alone, perhaps, prevented from ripening into friendship. It is difficult, indeed, to define, or even to describe, my real feelings toward him. They formed a motley and heterogeneous admixture—some petulant animosity, which was not yet hatred, some esteem, more respect, much fear, with a world of uneasy curiosity. To the moralist it will be necessary to say, in addition, that Wilson and myself were the most inseparable of companions.

It was no doubt the anomalous state of affairs existing between us, which turned all my attacks upon him (and there were many, either open or covert) into the channel of banter or practical joke (giving pain while assuming the aspect of mere fun) rather than into a more serious and determined hostility. But my endeavors on this head were by no means uniformly successful, even when my plans were the most wittily concocted; for my namesake had much about him, in character, of that unassuming and quiet austerity which, while enjoying the poignancy of its own jokes, has no heel of Achilles in itself, and absolutely refuses to be laughed at. I could find, indeed, but one vulnerable point, and that, lying in a personal peculiarity, arising, perhaps, from constitutional disease, would have been spared by any antagonist less at his wit's end than myself—my rival had a weakness in the faucial or guttural organs, which precluded him from raising his voice at any time *above a very low whisper*. Of this defect I did not fail to take what poor advantage lay in my power.

Wilson's retaliations in kind were many; and there was one form of his practical wit that disturbed me beyond measure. How his sagacity first discovered at all that so petty a thing would vex me, is a question I never could solve; but having discovered, he habitually practised the annoyance. I had always felt aversion to my uncourtly patronymic, and its very common, if not plebeian praenomen. The words were venom in my ears; and when, upon the day of my arrival, a second William Wilson came also to the academy, I felt angry with him for bearing the name, and doubly disgusted with the name because a stranger bore it, who would be the cause of its twofold repetition, who would be constantly in my presence, and whose concerns, in the ordinary routine of the school business, must inevitably, on account of the detestable coincidence, be often confounded with my own.

The feeling of vexation thus engendered grew stronger with every circumstance tending to show resemblance, moral or physical, between my rival and myself. I had not then discovered the remarkable fact that we were of the same age; but I saw that we were of the same height, and I perceived that we were even singularly alike in general contour of person and outline of feature. I was galled, too, by the rumor touching a relationship, which had grown current in the upper forms. In a word, nothing could more seriously disturb me (although I scrupulously concealed such disturbance) than any allusion to a similarity of mind, person, or condition existing between us. But, in truth, I had no reason to believe that (with the exception of the matter of relationship, and in the case of Wilson himself) this similarity had ever been made a subject of comment, or even observed at all by our schoolfellows. That *he* observed it in all its bearings, and as fixedly as I, was apparent; but that he could discover in such circumstances so fruitful a field of annoyance, can only be attributed, as I said before, to his more than ordinary penetration.

His cue, which was to perfect an imitation of myself, lay both in words and in actions; and most admirably did he play his part. My dress it was an easy matter to copy; my gait and general manner were without difficulty, appropriated; in spite of his constitutional defect, even my voice did not escape him. My louder tones were, of course, unattempted, but then the key—it was identical; *and his singular whisper, it grew the very echo of my own.*

How greatly this most exquisite portraiture harassed me (for it could not justly be termed a caricature), I will not now venture to describe. I had but one consolation—in the fact that the imitation, apparently, was noticed by myself alone, and that I had to endure only the knowing and strangely sarcastic smiles of my namesake himself. Satisfied with having produced in my bosom the intended effect, he seemed to chuckle in secret over the sting he had inflicted, and was characteristically disregardful of the public applause which the success of his witty endeavors might have so easily elicited. That the school, indeed, did not feel his design, perceive its accomplishment, and participate in his sneer, was, for many anxious months, a riddle I could not resolve. Perhaps the *gradation* of his copy rendered it not readily perceptible; or, more possibly, I owed my security to the masterly air of the copyist, who, disdaining the letter (which in a painting is all the obtuse can see), gave but the full spirit of his original for my individual contemplation and chagrin.

I have already more than once spoken of the disgusting air of patronage which he assumed toward me, and of his frequent officious interference with my will. This interference often took the ungracious character of advice; advice not openly given, but hinted or insinuated. I received it with a repugnance which gained strength as I grew in years. Yet, at this distant day, let me do him the simple justice to acknowledge that I can recall no occasion when the suggestions of my rival were on the side of those errors or follies so usual to his immature age and seeming inexperience; that his moral sense, at least, if not his general talents and worldly wisdom, was far keener than my own; and that I might, to-day, have been a better and thus a happier man, had I less frequently rejected the counsels embodied in those meaning whispers which I then but too cordially hated and too bitterly despised.

As it was I at length grew restive in the extreme under his distasteful supervision, and daily resented more and more openly, what I considered his intolerable arrogance. I have said that, in the first years of our connection as schoolmates, my feelings in regard to him might have been easily ripened into friendship; but, in the latter months of my residence at the academy, although the intrusion of his ordinary manner had, beyond doubt, in some measure, abated, my sentiments, in nearly similar proportion, partook very much of positive hatred. Upon one occasion he saw this, I think, and afterward avoided, or made a show of avoiding me.

It was about the same period, if I remember aright, that, in an altercation of violence with him, in which he was more than usually thrown off his guard, and spoke and acted with an openness of demeanor rather foreign to his nature, I discovered, or fancied I discovered, in his accent, in his air, and general appearance, a something which first startled, and then deeply interested me, by bringing to mind dim visions of my earliest infancy—wild, confused, and thronging memories of a time when memory herself was yet unborn. I cannot better describe the sensation which oppressed me, than by saying that I could with difficulty shake off the belief of my having been acquainted with the being who stood before me, at some epoch very long ago—some point of the past even infinitely remote. The delusion, however, faded rapidly as it came; and I mention it at all but to define the day of the last conversation I there held with my singular namesake.

The huge old house, with its countless subdivisions, had several large chambers communicating with each other, where slept the greater number of the students. There were, however (as must necessarily happen in a building so awkwardly planned), many little nooks or recesses, the odds and ends of the structure; and these the economic ingenuity of Dr. Bransby had also fitted up as dormitories; although, being the merest closets, they were capable of accommodating but a single individual. One of these small apartments was occupied by Wilson.

One night, about the close of my fifth year at the school, and immediately after the altercation just mentioned, finding everyone wrapped in sleep, I arose from bed, and, lamp in hand, stole through a wilderness of narrow passages, from my own bedroom to that of my rival. I had long been plotting one of those ill-natured pieces of practical wit at his expense in which I had hitherto been so uniformly unsuccessful. It was my intention, now, to put my scheme in operation and I resolved to make him feel the whole extent of the malice with which I was imbued. Having reached his closet, I noiselessly entered, leaving the lamp, with a shade over it, on the outside. I advanced a step and listened to the sound of his tranquil breathing. Assured of his being asleep, I returned, took the light, and with it again approached the bed. Close curtains were around it, which, in the prosecution of my plan, I slowly and quietly withdrew, when the bright rays fell vividly upon the sleeper, and my eyes at the same moment, upon his countenance. I looked—and a numbness, an iciness of feeling instantly pervaded my frame. My breast heaved, my knees tottered, my whole spirit became possessed with an objectless yet intolerable horror. Gasping for breath, I lowered the lamp in still nearer proximity to the face. Were these—*these* the lineaments of William Wilson? I saw, indeed, that they were his, but I shook as if with a fit of the ague, in fancying they were not. What *was* there about them to confound me in this manner? I gazed—while my brain reeled with a multitude of incoherent thoughts. Not thus he appeared—assuredly not *thus*—in the vivacity of his waking hours. The same name! the same contour of person! the same day of arrival at the academy! And then his dogged and meaningless imitation of my gait, my voice, my habits, and my manner! Was it, in truth, within the bounds of human possibility, that *what I now saw* was the result, merely, of the habitual practice of this sarcastic imitation? Awe-stricken, and with a creeping shudder, I extinguished the lamp, passed silently from the chamber, and left, at once, the halls of that old academy, never to enter them again.

After a lapse of some months, spent at home in mere idleness, I found myself a student at Eton. The brief interval had been sufficient to enfeeble my remembrance of the events at Dr. Bransby's, or at least to effect a material change in the nature of the feelings with which I remembered them. The truth—the tragedy—of the drama was no more. I could now find room to doubt the evidence of my senses; and seldom called up the subject at all but with wonder at the extent of human credulity, and a smile at the vivid force of the imagination which I hereditarily possessed. Neither was this species of skepticism likely to be diminished by the character of the life I led at Eton. The vortex of thoughtless folly into which I there so immediately and so recklessly plunged, washed away all but the froth of my past hours, engulfed at once every solid or serious impression, and left to memory only the veriest levities of a former existence.

I do not wish, however, to trace the course of my miserable profligacy here—a profligacy which set at defiance the laws, while it eluded the vigilance of the institution. Three years of folly, passed without profit, had but given me rooted habits of vice, and added, in a somewhat unusual degree, to my bodily stature, when, after a week of soulless dissipation, I invited a small party of the most dissolute students to a secret carousal in my chambers. We met at a late hour of the night; for our debaucheries were to be faithfully protracted until morning. The wine flowed freely, and there were not wanting other and perhaps more dangerous seductions; so that the gray dawn had already faintly appeared in the east while our delirious extravagance was at its height. Madly flushed with cards and intoxication, I was in the act of insisting upon a toast of more than wonted profanity, when my attention was suddenly diverted by the violent, although partial, unclosing of the door of the apartment, and by the eager voice of a servant from without. He said that some person, apparently in great haste, demanded to speak with me in the hall.

Wildly excited with wine, the unexpected interruption rather delighted than surprised me. I staggered forward at once, and a few steps brought me to the vestibule of the building. In this low and small room there hung no lamp; and now no light at all was admitted, save that of the exceedingly feeble dawn which made its way through the semi-circular window. As I put my foot over the threshold, I became aware of the figure of a youth about my own height, and habited in a white kerseymere morning frock, cut in the novel fashion of the one I myself wore at the moment. This the faint light enabled me to perceive; but the features of his face I could not distinguish. Upon my entering, he strode hurriedly up to me, and, seizing me by the arm with a gesture of petulant impatience, whispered the words "William Wilson" in my ear.

I grew perfectly sober in an instant.

There was that in the manner of the stranger, and in the tremulous shake of his uplifted finger, as he held it between my eyes and the light, which filled me with unqualified amazement; but it was not this which had so violently moved me. It was the pregnancy of solemn admonition in the singular, low, hissing utterance; and, above all, it was the character, the tone, *the key,* of those few, simple, and familiar, yet *whispered* syllables, which came with a thousand thronging memories of by-gone days, and struck upon my soul with the shock of a galvanic battery. Ere I could recover the use of my senses he was gone.

Although this event failed not of a vivid effect upon my disordered imagination, yet was it evanescent as vivid. For some weeks, indeed, I busied myself in earnest enquiry, or was wrapped in a cloud of morbid speculation. I did not pretend to disguise from my perception the identity of the singular individual who thus perseveringly interfered with my affairs, and harassed me with his insinuated counsel. But who and what was this Wilson?—and whence came he?—and what were his purposes? Upon neither of these points could I be satisfied—merely ascertaining, in regard to him, that a sudden accident in his family had caused his removal from Dr. Bransby's academy on the afternoon of the day in which I myself had eloped. But in a brief period I ceased to think upon the subject, my attention being all absorbed in a contemplated departure for Oxford. Thither I soon went, the uncalculating vanity of my parents furnishing me with an outfit and annual establishment, which would enable me to indulge at will in the luxury already so dear to my heart—to vie in profuseness of expenditure with the haughtiest heirs of the wealthiest earldoms in Great Britain.

Excited by such appliances to vice, my constitutional temperament broke forth with redoubled ardor, and I spurned even the common restraints of decency in the mad infatuation of my revels. But it were absurd to pause in the detail of my extravagance. Let it suffice, that among spendthrifts I out-Heroded Herod, and that, giving name to a multitude of novel follies, I added no brief appendix to the long catalogue of vices then usual in the most dissolute university of Europe.

It could hardly be credited, however, that I had, even here, so utterly fallen from the gentlemanly estate, as to seek acquaintance with the vilest arts of the gambler by profession, and, having become an adept in his despicable science, to practice it habitually as a means of increasing my already enormous income at the expense of the weak-minded among my fellow-collegians. Such, nevertheless, was the fact. And the very enormity of this offense against all manly and honorable sentiment proved, beyond doubt, the main if not the sole reason of the impunity with which it was committed. Who, indeed, among my most abandoned associates, would not rather have disputed the clearest evidence of his senses, than have suspected of such courses, the gay, the frank, the generous William Wilson—the noblest and most liberal commoner at Oxford—him whose follies (said his parasites) were but the follies of youth and unbridled fancy—whose errors but inimitable whim—whose darkest vice but a careless and dashing extravagance?

I had been now two years successfully busied in this way, when there came to the university a young *parvenu* nobleman, Glendinning—rich, said report, as Herodes Atticus—his riches, too, as easily acquired. I soon found him of weak intellect, and, of course, marked him as a fitting subject for my skill. I frequently engaged him in play, and contrived, with the gambler's usual art, to let him win considerable sums, the more effectually to entangle him in my snares. At length, my schemes being ripe, I met him (with the full intention that this meeting should be final and decisive) at the chambers of a fellow-commoner (Mr. Preston), equally intimate with both, but who, to do him justice, entertained not even a remote suspicion of my design. To give to this a better coloring, I had contrived to have assembled a party of some eight or ten, and was solicitously careful that the introduction of cards should appear accidental, and originate in the proposal of my contemplated dupe himself. To be brief upon a vile topic, none of the low finesse was omitted, so customary upon similar occasions, that it is a just matter for wonder how any are still found so besotted as to fall its victim.

We had protracted our sitting far into the night, and I had at length effected the manœuvre of getting Glendinning as my sole antagonist. The game, too, was my favorite *écarté*. The rest of the company, interested in the extent of our play, had abandoned their own cards, and were standing around us as spectators. The *parvenu,* who had been induced by my artifices in the early part of the evening, to drink deeply, now shuffled, dealt, or played, with a wild nervousness of manner for which his intoxication, I thought, might partially, but could not altogether account. In a very short period he had become my debtor to a large amount, when, having taken a long draught of port, he did precisely what I had been coolly anticipating—he proposed to double our already extravagant stakes. With a well-feigned show of reluctance, and not until after my repeated refusal had seduced him into some angry words which gave a color of *pique* to my compliance, did I finally comply. The result, of course, did but prove how entirely the prey was in my toils: in less than an hour he had quadrupled his debt. For some time his countenance had been losing the florid tingle lent it by the wine; but now, to my astonishment, I perceived that it had grown to a pallor truly fearful. I say, to my astonishment. Glendinning had been represented to my eager inquires as immeasurably wealthy; and the sums which he had as yet lost, although in themselves vast, could not, I supposed, very seriously annoy, much less so violently affect him. That he was overcome by the wine just swallowed, was the idea which most readily presented itself; and, rather with a view to the preservation of my own character in the eyes of my associates, than from any less interested motive, I was about to insist, peremptorily, upon a discontinuance of the play, when some expressions at my elbow from among the company, and an ejaculation evincing utter despair on the part of Glendinning, gave me to understand that I had effected his total ruin under circumstances which, rendering him an object for the pity of all, should have protected him from the ill offices even of a fiend.

What now might have been my conduct it is difficult to say. The pitiable condition of my dupe had thrown an air of embarrassed gloom over all; and, for some moments, a profound silence was maintained, during which I could not help feeling my cheeks tingle with the many burning glances of scorn or reproach cast upon me by the less abandoned of the party. I will even own that an intolerable weight of anxiety was for a brief instant lifted from my bosom by the sudden and extraordinary interruption which ensued. The wide, heavy folding doors of the apartment were all at once thrown open, to their full extent, with a vigorous and rushing impetuosity that extinguished, as if by magic, every candle in the room. Their light, in dying, enabled us just to perceive that a stranger had entered, about my own height, and closely muffled in a cloak. The darkness, however, was not total; and we could only *feel* that he was standing in our midst. Before any one of us could recover from the extreme astonishment into which this rudeness had thrown all, we heard the voice of the intruder.

"Gentlemen," he said, in a low, distinct, and never-to-be-forgotten *whisper* which thrilled to the very marrow of my bones, "Gentlemen, I make an apology for this behavior, because in thus behaving, I am fulfilling a duty. You are, beyond doubt, uninformed of the true character of the person who has to-night won at *écarté* a large sum of money from Lord Glendinning. I will therefore put you upon an expeditious and decisive plan of obtaining this very necessary information. Please to examine, at your leisure, the inner linings of the cuff of his left sleeve, and the several little packages which may be found in the somewhat capacious pockets of his embroidered morning wrapper."

While he spoke, so profound was the stillness that one might have heard a pin drop upon the floor. In ceasing, he departed at once, and as abruptly as he had entered. Can I—shall I describe my sensations? Must I say that I felt all the horrors of the damned? Most assuredly I had little time for reflection. Many hands roughly seized me upon the spot, and lights were immediately reprocured. A search ensued. In the lining of my sleeve were found all the court cards essential in *écarté,* and, in the pockets of my wrapper, a number of packs, fac-similes of those used at our sittings, with the single exception that mine were of the species called, technically, *arrondées;* the honors being slightly convex at the ends, the lower cards slightly convex at the sides. In this disposition, the dupe who cuts, as customary, at the length of the pack, will invariably find that he cuts his antagonist an honor; while the gambler, cutting at the breadth, will, as certainly, cut nothing for his victim which may count in the records of the game.

Any burst of indignation upon this discovery would have affected me less than the silent contempt, or the sarcastic composure, with which it was received.

"Mr. Wilson," said our host, stooping to remove from beneath his feet an exceedingly luxurious cloak of rare furs, "Mr. Wilson, this is your property." (The weather was cold; and, upon quitting my own room, I had thrown a cloak over my dressing wrapper, putting it off upon reaching the scene of play.) "I presume it is supererogatory to seek here (eyeing the folds of the garment with a bitter smile) for any farther evidence of your skill. Indeed, we have had enough. You will see the necessity, I hope, of quitting Oxford—at all events, of quitting instantly my chambers."

Abased, humbled to the dust as I then was, it is probable that I should have resented this galling language by immediate personal violence, had not my whole attention been at the moment arrested by a fact of the most startling character. The cloak which I had worn was of a rare description of fur; how rare, how extravagantly costly, I shall not venture to say. Its fashion, too, was of my own fantastic invention; for I was fastidious to an absurd degree of coxcombry, in matters of this frivolous nature. When, therefore, Mr. Preston reached me that which he had picked up upon the floor, and near the folding-doors of the apartment, it was with an astonishment nearly bordering upon terror, that I perceived my own already hanging on my arm (where I had no doubt unwittingly placed it), and that the one presented me was but its exact counterpart in every, in even the minutest possible particular. The singular being who had so disastrously exposed me, had been muffled, I remembered, in a cloak; and none had been worn at all by any of the members of our party, with the exception of myself. Retaining some presence of mind, I took the one offered me by Preston; placed it, unnoticed, over my own; left the apartment with a resolute scowl of defiance; and, next morning ere dawn of day, commenced a hurried journey from Oxford to the continent, in a perfect agony of horror and of shame.

I fled in vain. My evil destiny pursued me as if in exultation, and proved, indeed, that the exercise of its mysterious dominion had as yet only begun. Scarcely had I set foot in Paris, ere I had fresh evidence of the detestable interest taken by this Wilson in my concerns. Years flew, while I experienced no relief. Villain!—at Rome, with how untimely, yet with how spectral an officiousness, stepped he in between me and my ambition! At Vienna, too—at Berlin—and at Moscow! Where, in truth, had I *not* bitter cause to curse him within my heart? From his inscrutable tyranny did I at length flee, panic-stricken, as from a pestilence; and to the very ends of the earth *I fled in vain.*

And again, and again, in secret communion with my own spirit, would I demand the questions "Who is he?—whence came he?—and what are his objects?" But no answer was there found. And now I scrutinized, with a minute scrutiny, the forms, and the methods, and the leading traits of his impertinent supervision. But even here there was very little upon which to base a conjecture. It was noticeable, indeed, that, in no one of the multiplied instances in which he had of late crossed my path, had he so crossed it except to frustrate those schemes, or to disturb those actions, which, if fully carried out, might have resulted in bitter mischief. Poor justification this, in truth, for an authority so imperiously assumed! Poor indemnity for natural rights of self-agency so pertinaciously, so insultingly denied!

I had also been forced to notice that my tormentor, for a very long period of time (while scrupulously and with miraculous dexterity maintaining his whim of an identity of apparel with myself) had so contrived it, in the execution of his varied interference with my will, that I saw not, at any moment, the features of his face. Be Wilson what he might, *this,* at least, was but the veriest of affectation, or of folly. Could he, for an instant, have supposed that, in my admonisher at Eton—in the destroyer of my honor at Oxford—in him who thwarted my ambition at Rome, my revenge at Paris, my passionate love at Naples, or what he falsely termed my avarice in Egypt—that in this, my arch-enemy and evil genius, I could fail to recognize the William Wilson of my school-boy days—the namesake, the companion, the rival—the hated and dreaded rival at Dr. Bransby's? Impossible!—but let me hasten to the last eventful scene of the drama.

Thus far I had succumbed supinely to this imperious domination. The sentiment of deep awe with which I habitually regarded the elevated character, the majestic wisdom, the apparent omnipresence and omnipotence of Wilson, added to a feeling of even terror, with which certain other traits in his nature and assumptions inspired me, had operated, hitherto, to impress me with an idea of my own utter weakness and helplessness, and to suggest an implicit, although bitterly reluctant submission to his arbitrary will. But, of late days, I had given myself up entirely to wine; and its maddening influence upon my hereditary temper rendered me more and more impatient of control. I began to murmur—to hesitate—to resist. And was it only fancy which induced me to believe that, with the increase of my own firmness, that of my tormentor underwent a proportional diminution? Be this as it may, I now began to feel the inspiration of a burning hope, and at length nurtured in my secret thoughts a stern and desperate resolution that I would submit no longer to be enslaved.

It was at Rome, during the Carnival of 18—, that I attended a masquerade in the palazzo of the Neapolitan Duke Di Broglio. I had indulged more freely than usual in the excesses of the wine-table; and now the suffocating atmosphere of the crowded rooms irritated me beyond endurance. The difficulty, too, of forcing my way through the mazes of the company contributed not a little to the ruffling of my temper; for I was anxiously seeking (let me not say with what unworthy motive) the young, the gay, the beautiful wife of the aged and doting Di Broglio. With a too unscrupulous confidence she had previously communicated to me the secret of the costume in which she would be habited, and now, having caught a glimpse of her person, I was hurrying to make my way into her presence. At this moment I felt a light hand placed upon my shoulder, and that ever-remembered, low, damnable *whisper* within my ear.

In an absolute frenzy of wrath, I turned at once upon him who had thus interrupted me, and seized him violently by the collar. He was attired, as I had expected, in a costume altogether similar to my own; wearing a Spanish cloak of blue velvet, begirt about the waist with a crimson belt sustaining a rapier. A mask of black silk entirely covered his face.

"Scoundrel!" I said, in a voice husky with rage, while every syllable I uttered seemed as new fuel to my fury; "scoundrel! impostor! accursed villain! you shall not—you *shall not* dog me unto death! Follow me, or I stab you where you stand!"—and I broke my way from the ballroom into a small antechamber adjoining, dragging him unresistingly with me as I went.

Upon entering, I thrust him furiously from me. He staggered against the wall, while I closed the door with an oath, and commanded him to draw. He hesitated but for an instant; then, with a slight sigh, drew in silence, and put himself upon his defence.

The contest was brief indeed. I was frantic with every species of wild excitement, and felt within my single arm the energy and power of a multitude. In a few seconds I forced him by sheer strength against the wainscotting, and thus, getting him at mercy, plunged my sword, with brute ferocity, repeatedly through and through his bosom.

At that instant some person tried the latch of the door. I hastened to prevent an intrusion, and then immediately returned to my dying antagonist. But what human language can adequately portray *that* astonishment, *that* horror which possessed me at the spectacle then presented to view? The brief moment in which I averted my eyes had been sufficient to produce, apparently, a material change in the arrangements at the upper or farther end of the room. A large mirror—so at first it seemed to me in my confusion—now stood where none had been perceptible before; and as I stepped up to it in extremity of terror, mine own image, but with features all pale and dabbled in blood, advanced to meet me with a feeble and tottering gait.

Thus it appeared, I say, but was not. It was my antagonist—it was Wilson, who then stood before me in the agonies of his dissolution. His mask and cloak lay, where he had thrown them, upon the floor. Not a thread in all his raiment—not a line in all the marked and singular lineaments of his face which was not, even in the most absolute identity, *mine own!*

It was Wilson; but he spoke no longer in a whisper, and I could have fancied that I myself was speaking while he said:

"You have conquered, and I yield. Yet henceforth art thou also dead—dead to the World, to Heaven, and to Hope! In me didst thou exist—and, in my death, see by this image, which is thine own, how utterly thou hast murdered thyself."

Nathaniel Hawthorne

*Nathaniel Hawthorne (1804–1864) was born in Salem, Massachusetts, the son of Capt. Nathaniel Hawthorne and Elizabeth Manning Hawthorne. His father died when he was four, and the family moved to Maine. Hawthorne graduated from Bowdoin College in 1825, and spent the subsequent twelve years in Salem, Massachusetts, where he lived almost as a recluse, preparing himself for a writing career. He lived briefly at Brook Farm, the experimental community founded by transcendentalists; later, he wrote a novel about his experiences there—*The Blithedale Romance *(1852). In 1842, Hawthorne married Sophia Peabody. His first volume of short stories,* Twice-Told Tales, *had been published in 1837. His second,* Mosses from an Old Manse *(1846) was written in Concord, Massachusetts, where he spent the early years of his marriage. He later moved back to Salem, where he served as surveyor of the Customs House. He continued to write on a regular basis, however, and published his famous* The Scarlet Letter *in 1850. While at Bowdoin, Hawthorne had become a close friend of Franklin Pierce and, when Pierce was elected President in 1852 (Hawthorne had written his campaign biography), he appointed Hawthorne consul at Liverpool and Manchester, in England. Hawthorne returned from Europe in 1860. His health declined and he died four years later. Hawthorne's works often deal symbolically with the social, moral, and psychological consequences of sin. His interest in this theme was stimulated in part by his own ancestor who had participated in the Salem witchcraft trials in the seventeenth century.* *(See page 81 of Introduction.)*

ROGER MALVIN'S BURIAL

One of the few incidents of Indian warfare naturally susceptible of the moonlight of romance was that expedition undertaken for the defence of the frontiers in the year 1725, which resulted in the well-remembered "Lovell's Fight." Imagination, by casting certain circumstances judicially into the shade, may see much to admire in the heroism of a little band who gave battle to twice their number in the heart of the enemy's country. The open bravery displayed by both parties was in accordance with civilized ideas of valor; and chivalry itself might not blush to record the deeds of one or two individuals. The battle, though so fatal to those who fought, was not unfortunate in its consequences to the country; for it broke the strength of a tribe and conduced to the peace which subsisted during several ensuing years. History and tradition are unusually minute in their memorials of their affair; and the captain of a scouting party of frontier men has acquired as actual a military renown as many a victorious leader of thousands. Some of the incidents contained in the following pages will be recognized, notwithstanding the substitution of fictitious names, by such as have heard, from old men's lips, the fate of the few combatants who were in a condition to retreat after "Lovell's Fight."

. . . . . .

The early sunbeams hovered cheerfully upon the tree-tops, beneath which two weary and wounded men had stretched their limbs the night before. Their bed of withered oak leaves was strewn upon the small level space, at the foot of a rock, situated near the summit of one of the gentle swells by which the face of the country is there diversified. The mass of granite, rearing its smooth, flat surface fifteen or twenty feet above their heads, was not unlike a gigantic gravestone, upon which the veins seemed to form an inscription in forgotten characters. On a tract of several acres around this rock, oaks and other hard-wood trees had supplied the place of the pines, which were the usual growth of the land; and a young and vigorous sapling stood close beside the travellers.

The severe wound of the elder man had probably deprived him of sleep; for, so soon as the first ray of sunshine rested on the top of the highest tree, he reared himself painfully from his recumbent posture and sat erect. The deep lines of his countenance and the scattered gray of his hair marked him as past the middle age; but his muscular frame would, but for the effect of his wound, have been as capable of sustaining fatigue as in the early vigor of life. Languor and exhaustion now sat upon his haggard features; and the despairing glance which he sent forward through the depths of the forest proved his own conviction that his pilgrimage was at an end. He next turned his eyes to the companion who reclined by his side. The youth—for he had scarcely attained the years of manhood—lay, with his head upon his arm, in the embrace of an unquiet sleep, which a thrill of pain from his wounds seemed each moment on the point of breaking. His right hand grasped a musket; and, to judge from the violent action of his features, his slumbers were bringing back a vision of the conflict of which he was one of the few survivors. A shout—deep and loud in his dreaming fancy—found its way in an imperfect murmur to his lips; and, starting even at the slight sound of his own voice, he suddenly awoke. The first act of reviving recollection was to make anxious inquiries respecting the condition of his wounded fellow-traveller. The latter shook his head.

"Reuben, my boy," said he, "this rock beneath which we sit will serve for an old hunter's gravestone. There is many and many a long mile of howling wilderness before us yet; nor would it avail me anything if the smoke of my own chimney were but on the other side of that swell of land. The Indian bullet was deadlier than I thought."

"You are weary with our three days' travel," replied the youth, "and a little longer rest will recruit you. Sit you here while I search the woods for the herbs and roots that must be our sustenance; and, having eaten, you shall lean on me, and we will turn our faces homeward. I doubt not that, with my help, you can attain to some one of the frontier garrisons."

"There is not two days' life in me, Reuben," said the other, calmly, "and I will no longer burden you with my useless body, when you can scarcely support your own. Your wounds are deep and your strength is failing fast; yet, if you hasten onward alone, you may be preserved. For me there is no hope, and I will await death here."

"If it must be so, I will remain and watch by you," said Reuben, resolutely.

"No, my son, no," rejoined his companion. "Let the wish of a dying man have weight with you; give me one grasp of your hand and get you hence. Think you that my last moments will be eased by the thought that I leave you to die a more lingering death? I have loved you like a father, Reuben; and at a time like this I should have something of a father's authority. I charge you to begone that I may die in peace."

"And because you have been a father to me, should I therefore leave you to perish and to lie unburied in the wilderness?" exclaimed the youth. "No; if your end be in truth approaching, I will watch by you and receive your parting words. I will dig a grave here by the rock, in which, if my weakness overcome me, we will rest together; or, if Heaven gives me strength, I will seek my way home."

"In the cities and wherever men dwell," replied the other, "they bury their dead in the earth; they hide them from the sight of the living; but here, where no step may pass perhaps for a hundred years, wherefore should I not rest beneath the open sky, covered only by the oak leaves when the autumn winds shall strew them? And for a monument, here is this gray rock, on which my dying hand shall carve the name of Roger Malvin; and the traveller in days to come will know that here sleeps a hunter and a warrior. Tarry not, then, for a folly like this, but hasten away, if not for your own sake, for hers who will else be desolate."

Malvin spoke the last few words in a faltering voice, and their effect upon his companion was strongly visible. They reminded him that there were other and less questionable duties than that of sharing the fate of a man whom his death could not benefit. Nor can it be affirmed that no selfish feeling strove to enter Reuben's heart, though the consciousness made him more earnestly resist his companion's entreaties.

"How terrible to wait the slow approach of death in this solitude!" exclaimed he. "A brave man does not shrink in the battle; and, when friends stand round the bed, even women may die composedly; but here—"

"I shall not shrink even here, Reuben Bourne," interrupted Malvin. "I am a man of no weak heart, and, if I were, there is a surer support than that of earthly friends. You are young, and life is dear to you. Your last moments will need comfort far more than mine; and when you have laid me in the earth, and are alone, and night is settling on the forest, you will feel all the bitterness of the death that may now be escaped. But I will urge no selfish motive to your generous nature. Leave me for my sake, that, having said a prayer for your safety, I may have space to settle my account undisturbed by worldly sorrows."

"And your daughter,—how shall I dare to meet her eye?" exclaimed Reuben. "She will ask the fate of her father, whose life I vowed to defend with my own. Must I tell her that he travelled three days' march with me from the field of battle and that then I left him to perish in the wilderness? Were it not better to lie down and die by your side than to return safe and say this to Dorcas?"

"Tell my daughter," said Roger Malvin, "that, though yourself sore wounded, and weak, and weary, you led my tottering footsteps many a mile, and left me only at my earnest entreaty, because I would not have your blood upon my soul. Tell her that through pain and danger you were faithful, and that, if your lifeblood could have saved me, it would have flowed to its last drop; and tell her that you will be something dearer than a father, and that my blessing is with you both, and that my dying eyes can see a long and pleasant path in which you will journey together."

As Malvin spoke he almost raised himself from the ground, and the energy of his concluding words seemed to fill the wild and lonely forest with a vision of happiness; but, when he sank exhausted upon his bed of oak leaves, the light which had kindled in Reuben's eye was quenched. He felt as if it were both sin and folly to think of happiness at such a moment. His companion watched his changing countenance, and sought with generous art to wile him to his own good.

"Perhaps I deceive myself in regard to the time I have to live," he resumed. "It may be that, with speedy assistance, I might recover of my wound. The foremost fugitives must, ere this, have carried tidings of our fatal battle to the frontiers, and parties will be out to succor those in like condition with ourselves. Should you meet one of these and guide them hither, who can tell but that I may sit by my own fireside again?"

A mournful smile strayed across the features of the dying man as he insinuated that unfounded hope,—which, however, was not without its effect on Reuben. No merely selfish motive, nor even the desolate condition of Dorcas, could have induced him to desert his companion at such a moment—but his wishes seized on the thought that Malvin's life might be preserved, and his sanguine nature heightened almost to certainty the remote possibility of procuring human aid.

"Surely there is reason, weighty reason, to hope that friends are not far distant," he said, half aloud. "There fled one coward, unwounded, in the beginning of the fight, and most probably he made good speed. Every true man on the frontier would shoulder his musket at the news; and, though no party may range so far into the woods as this, I shall perhaps encounter them in one day's march. Counsel me faithfully," he added, turning to Malvin, in distrust of his own motives. "Were your situation mine, would you desert me while life remained?"

"It is now twenty years," replied Roger Malvin,—sighing, however, as he secretly acknowledged the wide dissimilarity between the two cases,—"it is now twenty years since I escaped with one dear friend from Indian captivity near Montreal. We journeyed many days through the woods, till at length overcome with hunger and weariness, my friend lay down and besought me to leave him; for he knew that, if I remained, we both must perish; and, with but little hope of obtaining succor, I heaped a pillow of dry leaves beneath his head and hastened on."

"And did you return in time to save him?" asked Reuben, hanging on Malvin's words as if they were to be prophetic of his own success.

"I did," answered the other. "I came upon the camp of a hunting party before sunset of the same day. I guided them to the spot where my comrade was expecting death; and he is now a hale and hearty man upon his own farm, far within the frontiers, while I lie wounded here in the depths of the wilderness."

This example, powerful in affecting Reuben's decision, was aided, unconsciously to himself, by the hidden strength of many another motive. Roger Malvin perceived that the victory was nearly won.

"Now, go, my son, and Heaven prosper you!" he said. "Turn not back with your friends when you meet them, lest your wounds and weariness overcome you; but send hitherward two or three, that may be spared, to search for me; and believe me, Reuben, my heart will be lighter with every step you take towards home." Yet there was, perhaps, a change both in his countenance and voice as he spoke thus; for, after all, it was a ghastly fate to be left expiring in the wilderness.

Reuben Bourne, but half convinced that he was acting rightly, at length raised himself from the ground and prepared himself for his departure. And first, though contrary to Malvin's wishes, he collected a stock of roots and herbs, which had been their only food during the last two days. This useless supply he placed within reach of the dying man, for whom, also, he swept together a bed of dry oak leaves. Then climbing to the summit of the rock, which on one side was rough and broken, he bent the oak sapling downward, and bound his handkerchief to the topmost branch. This precaution was not unnecessary to direct any who might come in search of Malvin; for every part of the rock, except its broad, smooth front, was concealed at a little distance by the dense undergrowth of the forest. The handkerchief had been the bandage of a wound upon Reuben's arm; and, as he bound it to the tree, he vowed by the blood that stained it that he would return, either to save his companion's life or to lay his body in the grave. He then descended, and stood, with downcast eyes, to receive Roger Malvin's parting words.

The experience of the latter suggested much and minute advice respecting the youth's journey through the trackless forest. Upon this subject he spoke with calm earnestness, as if he were sending Reuben to the battle or the chase while he himself remained secure at home, and not as if the human countenance that was about to leave him were the last he would ever behold. But his firmness was shaken before he concluded.

"Carry my blessing to Dorcas, and say that my last prayer shall be for her and you. Bid her to have no hard thoughts because you left me here,"—Reuben's heart smote him,—"for that your life would not have weighed with you if its sacrifice could have done me good. She will marry you after she has mourned a little while for her father; and Heaven grant you long and happy days, and may your children's children stand round your death bed! And, Reuben," added he, as the weakness of mortality made its way at last, "return, when your wounds are healed and your weariness refreshed,—return to this wild rock, and lay my bones in the grave, and say a prayer over them."

An almost superstitious regard, arising perhaps from the customs of the Indians, whose war was with the dead as well as the living, was paid by the frontier inhabitants to the rites of sepulture; and there are many instances of the sacrifice of life in the attempt to bury those who had fallen by the "sword of the wilderness." Reuben, therefore, felt the full importance of the promise which he most solemnly made to return and perform Roger Malvin's obsequies. It was remarkable that the latter, speaking his whole heart in his parting words, no longer endeavored to persuade the youth that even the speediest succor might avail to the preservation of his life. Reuben was internally convinced that he should see Malvin's living face no more. His generous nature would fain have delayed him, at whatever risk, till the dying scene were past; but the desire of existence and the hope of happiness had strengthened in his heart, and he was unable to resist them.

"It is enough," said Roger Malvin, having listened to Reuben's promise. "Go, and God speed you!"

The youth pressed his hand in silence, turned, and was departing. His slow and faltering steps, however, had borne him but a little way before Malvin's voice recalled him.

"Reuben, Reuben," said he, faintly; and Reuben returned and knelt down by the dying man.

"Raise me, and let me lean against the rock," was his last request. "My face will be turned towards home, and I shall see you a moment longer as you pass among the trees."

Reuben, having made the desired alteration in his companion's posture, again began his solitary pilgrimage. He walked more hastily at first than was consistent with his strength; for a sort of guilty feeling, which sometimes torments men in their most justifiable acts, caused him to seek concealment from Malvin's eyes; but after he had trodden far upon the rustling forest leaves he crept back, impelled by a wild and painful curiosity, and, sheltered by the earthy roots of an uptorn tree, gazed earnestly at the desolate man. The morning sun was unclouded, and the trees and shrubs imbibed the sweet air of the month of May; yet there seemed a gloom on Nature's face, as if she sympathized with mortal pain and sorrow. Roger Malvin's hands were uplifted in a fervent prayer, some of the words of which stole through the stillness of the woods and entered Reuben's heart, torturing it with an unutterable pang. They were the broken accents of a petition for his own happiness and that of Dorcas; and, as the youth listened, conscience, or something in its similitude, pleaded strongly with him to return and lie down again by the rock. He felt how hard was the doom of the kind and generous being whom he had deserted in his extremity. Death would come like the slow approach of a corpse, stealing gradually towards him through the forest, and showing its ghastly and motionless features from behind a nearer and yet a nearer tree. But such must have been Reuben's own fate had he tarried another sunset; and who shall impute blame to him if he shrink from so useless a sacrifice? As he gave a parting look, a breeze waved the little banner upon the sapling oak and reminded Reuben of his vow.

. . . . . .

Many circumstances combined to retard the wounded traveller in his way to the frontiers. On the second day the clouds, gathering densely over the sky, precluded the possibility of regulating his course by the position of the sun; and he knew not but that every effort of his almost exhausted strength was removing him farther from the home he sought. His scanty sustenance was supplied by the berries and other spontaneous products of the forest. Herds of deer, it is true, sometimes bounded past him, and partridges frequently whirred up before his footsteps; but his ammunition had been expended in the fight, and he had no means of slaying them. His wounds, irritated by the constant exertion in which lay the only hope of life, wore away his strength and at intervals confused his reason. But, even in the wanderings of intellect, Reuben's young heart clung strongly to existence; and it was only through absolute incapacity of motion that he at last sank down beneath a tree, compelled there to await death.

In this situation he was discovered by a party who, upon the first intelligence of the fight, had been despatched to the relief of the survivors. They conveyed him to the nearest settlement, which chanced to be that of his own residence.

Dorcas, in the simplicity of the olden time, watched by the bedside of her wounded lover, and administered all those comforts that are in the sole gift of woman's heart and hand. During several days Reuben's recollection strayed drowsily among the perils and hardships through which he had passed, and he was incapable of returning definite answers to the inquiries with which many were eager to harass him. No authentic particulars of the battle had yet been circulated; nor could mothers, wives, and children tell whether their loved ones were detained by captivity or by the stronger chain of death. Dorcas nourished her apprehensions in silence till one afternoon when Reuben awoke from an unquiet sleep, and seemed to recognize her more perfectly than at any previous time. She saw that his intellect had become composed, and she could no longer restrain her filial anxiety.

"My father, Reuben?" she began; but the change in her lover's countenance made her pause.

The youth shrank as if with a bitter pain, and the blood gushed vividly into his wan and hollow cheeks. His first impulse was to cover his face; but, apparently with a desperate effort, he half raised himself and spoke vehemently, defending himself against an imaginary accusation.

"Your father was sore wounded in the battle, Dorcas; and he bade me not burden myself with him, but only to lead him to the lakeside, that he might quench his thirst and die. But I would not desert the old man in his extremity, and, though bleeding myself, I supported him; I gave him half my strength, and led him away with me. For three days we journeyed on together, and your father was sustained beyond my hopes, but, awaking at sunrise on the fourth day, I found him faint and exhausted; he was unable to proceed; his life had ebbed away fast; and—"

"He died!" exclaimed Dorcas, faintly.

Reuben felt it impossible to acknowledge that his selfish love of life had hurried him away before her father's fate was decided. He spoke not; he only bowed his head; and between shame and exhaustion, sank back and hid his face in the pillow. Dorcas wept when her fears were thus confirmed; but the shock, as it had been long anticipated, was on that account the less violent.

"You dug a grave for my poor father in the wilderness, Reuben?" was the question by which her filial piety manifested itself.

"My hands were weak; but I did what I could," replied the youth in a smothered tone. "There stands a noble tombstone above his head; and I would to Heaven I slept as soundly as he!"

Dorcas, perceiving the wildness of his latter words, inquired no further at the time; but her heart found ease in the thought that Roger Malvin had not lacked such funeral rites as it was possible to bestow. The tale of Reuben's courage and fidelity lost nothing when she communicated it to her friends; and the poor youth, tottering from his sick chamber to breathe the sunny air, experienced from every tongue the miserable and humiliating torture of unmerited praise. All acknowledged that he might worthily demand the hand of the fair maiden to whose father he had been "faithful unto death"; and, as my tale is not of love, it shall suffice to say that in the space of a few months Reuben became the husband of Dorcas Malvin. During the marriage ceremony the bride was covered with blushes, but the bridegroom's face was pale.

There was now in the breast of Reuben Bourne an incommunicable thought—something which he was to conceal most heedfully from her whom he most loved and trusted. He regretted, deeply and bitterly, the moral cowardice that had restrained his words when he was about to disclose the truth to Dorcas; but pride, the fear of losing her affection, the dread of universal scorn, forbade him to rectify this falsehood. He felt that for leaving Roger Malvin he deserved no censure. His presence, the gratuitous sacrifice of his own life, would have added only another and a needless agony to the last moments of the dying man; but concealment had imparted to a justifiable act much of the secret effect of guilt; and Reuben, while reason told him that he had done right, experienced in no small degree the mental horrors which punish the perpetrator of undiscovered crime. By a certain association of ideas, he at times almost imagined himself a murderer. For years, also, a thought would occasionally recur, which, though he perceived all its folly and extravagance, he had not power to banish from his mind. It was a haunting and torturing fancy that his father-in-law was yet sitting at the foot of the rock, on the withered forest leaves, alive, and awaiting his pledged assistance. These mental deceptions, however, came and went, nor did he ever mistake them for realities, but in the calmest and clearest moods of his mind he was conscious that he had a deep vow unredeemed, and that an unburied corpse was calling to him out of the wilderness. Yet such was the consequence of his prevarication that he could not obey the call. It was now too late to require the assistance of Roger Malvin's friends in performing his long-deferred sepulture; and superstitious fears, of which none were more susceptible than the people of the outward settlements, forbade Reuben to go alone. Neither did he know where in the pathless and illimitable forest to seek that smooth and lettered rock at the base of which the body lay: his remembrance of every portion of his travel thence was indistinct, and the latter part had left no impression upon his mind. There was, however, a continual impulse, a voice audible only to himself, commanding him to go forth and redeem his vow; and he had a strange impression that, were he to make the trial, he would be led straight to Malvin's bones. But year after year that summons, unheard but felt, was disobeyed. His one secret thought became like a chain binding down his spirit and like a serpent gnawing into his heart; and he was transformed into a sad and downcast yet irritable man.

In the course of a few years after their marriage changes began to be visible in the external prosperity of Reuben and Dorcas. The only riches of the former had been his stout heart and strong arm; but the latter, her father's sole heiress, had made her husband master of a farm, under older cultivation, larger, and better stocked than most of the frontier establishments. Reuben Bourne, however, was a neglectful husbandman; and, while the lands of the other settlers became annually more fruitful, his deteriorated in the same proportion. The discouragements to agriculture were greatly lessened by the cessation of Indian war, during which men held the plough in one hand and the musket in the other, and were fortunate if the products of their dangerous labor were not destroyed, either in the field or in the barn, by the savage enemy. But Reuben did not profit by the altered condition of the country; nor can it be denied that his intervals of industrious attention to his affairs were but scantily rewarded with success. The irritability by which he had recently become distinguished was another cause of his declining prosperity, as it occasioned frequent quarrels in his unavoidable intercourse with the neighboring settlers. The results of these were innumerable lawsuits; for the people of New England, in the earliest stages and wildest circumstances of the country, adopted, whenever attainable, the legal mode of deciding their differences. To be brief, the world did not go well with Reuben Bourne; and, though not till many years after his marriage, he was finally a ruined man, with but one remaining expedient against the evil fate that had pursued him. He was to throw sunlight into some deep recess of the forest, and seek subsistence from the virgin bosom of the wilderness.

The only child of Reuben and Dorcas was a son, now arrived at the age of fifteen years, beautiful in youth, and giving promise of a glorious manhood. He was peculiarly qualified for, and already began to excel in, the wild accomplishments of frontier life. His foot was fleet, his aim true, his apprehension quick, his heart glad and high; and all who anticipated the return of Indian war spoke of Cyrus Bourne as a future leader in the land. The boy was loved by his father with a deep and silent strength, as if whatever was good and happy in his own nature had been transferred to his child, carrying his affections with it. Even Dorcas, though loving and beloved, was far less dear to him; for Reuben's secret thoughts and insulated emotions had gradually made him a selfish man, and he could no longer love deeply except where he saw or imagined some reflection or likeness of his own mind. In Cyrus he recognized what he had himself been in other days; and at intervals he seemed to partake of the boy's spirit, and to be revived with a fresh and happy life. Reuben was accompanied by his son in the expedition, for the purpose of selecting a tract of land and felling and burning the timber, which necessarily preceded the removal of the household goods. Two months of autumn were thus occupied, after which Reuben Bourne and his young hunter returned to spend their last winter in the settlements.

. . . . . .

It was early in the month of May that the little family snapped asunder whatever tendrils of affections had clung to inanimate objects, and bade farewell to the few who, in the blight of fortune, called themselves their friends. The sadness of the parting moment had, to each of the pilgrims, its peculiar alleviations. Reuben, a moody man, and misanthropic because unhappy, strode onward with his usual stern brow and downcast eye, feeling few regrets and disdaining to acknowledge any. Dorcas, while she wept abundantly over the broken ties by which her simple and affectionate nature had bound itself to everything, felt that the inhabitants of her inmost heart moved on with her, and that all else would be supplied wherever she might go. And the boy dashed one teardrop from his eye, and thought of the adventurous pleasures of the untrodden forest.

Oh, who, in the enthusiasm of a daydream, has not wished that he were a wanderer in a world of summer wilderness, with one fair and gentle being hanging lightly on his arm? In youth his free and exulting step would know no barrier but the rolling ocean or the snow-topped mountains; calmer manhood would choose a home where Nature had strewn a double wealth in the vale of some transparent stream; and when hoary age, after long, long years of that pure life, stole on and found him there, it would find him the father of a race, the patriarch of a people, the founder of a mighty nation yet to be. When death, like the sweet sleep which we welcome after a day of happiness, came over him, his far descendants would mourn over the venerated dust. Enveloped by tradition in mysterious attributes, the men of future generations would call him godlike; and remote posterity would see him standing, dimly glorious, far up the valley of a hundred centuries.

The tangled and gloomy forest through which the personages of my tale were wandering differed widely from the dreamer's land of fantasy; yet there was something in their way of life that Nature asserted as her own, and the gnawing cares which went with them from the world were all that now obstructed their happiness. One stout and shaggy steed, the bearer of all their wealth, did not shrink from the added weight of Dorcas; although her hardy breeding sustained her, during the latter part of each day's journey, by her husband's side. Reuben and his son, their muskets on their shoulders and their axes slung behind them, kept an unwearied pace, each watching with a hunter's eye for the game that supplied their food. When hunger bade, they halted and prepared their meal on the bank of some unpolluted forest brook, which, as they knelt down with thirsty lips to drink, murmured a sweet unwillingness, like a maiden at love's first kiss. They slept beneath a hut of branches, and awoke at peep of light refreshed for the toils of another day. Dorcas and the boy went on joyously, and even Reuben's spirit shone at intervals with an outward gladness; but inwardly there was a cold, cold sorrow, which he compared to the snowdrifts lying deep in the glens and hollows of the rivulets while the leaves were brightly green above.

Cyrus Bourne was sufficiently skilled in the travel of the woods to observe that his father did not adhere to the course they had pursued in their expedition of the preceding autumn. They were now keeping farther to the north, striking out more directly from the settlements, and into a region of which savage beasts and savage men were as yet the sole possessors. The boy sometimes hinted his opinions upon the subject, and Reuben listened attentively, and once or twice altered the direction of their march in accordance with his son's counsel; but, having so done, he seemed ill at ease. His quick and wandering glances were sent forward, apparently in search of enemies lurking behind the tree trunks; and, seeing nothing there, he would cast his eyes backwards as if in fear of some pursuer. Cyrus, perceiving that his father gradually resumed the old direction, forbore to interfere; nor, though something began to weigh upon his heart, did his adventurous nature permit him to regret the increased length and the mystery of their way.

On the afternoon of the fifth day they halted, and made their simple encampment nearly an hour before sunset. The face of the country, for the last few miles, had been diversified by swells of land resembling huge waves of a petrified sea; and in one of the corresponding hollows, a wild and romantic spot, had the family reared their hut and kindled their fire. There is something chilling, and yet heart-warming, in the thought of these three, united by strong bands of love and insulated from all that breathe beside. The dark and gloomy pines looked down upon them, and, as the wind swept through their tops, a pitying sound was heard in the forest; or did those old trees groan in fear that men were come to lay the axe to their roots at last? Reuben and his son, while Dorcas made ready their meal, proposed to wander out in search of game, of which that day's march had afforded no supply. The boy, promising not to quit the vicinity of the encampment, bounded off with a step as light and elastic as that of the deer he hoped to slay; while his father, feeling a transient happiness as he gazed after him, was about to pursue an opposite direction. Dorcas, in the meanwhile, had seated herself near their fire of fallen branches, upon the moss-grown and mouldering trunk of a tree uprooted years before. Her employment, diversified by an occasional glance at the pot, now beginning to simmer over the blaze, was the perusal of the current year's Massachusetts Almanac, which, with the exception of an old black-letter Bible, comprised all the literary wealth of the family. None pay a greater regard to arbitrary divisions of time than those who are excluded from society; and Dorcas mentioned, as if the information were of importance, that it was now the twelfth of May. Her husband started.

"The twelfth of May! I should remember it well," muttered he, while many thoughts occasioned a momentary confusion in his mind. "Where am I? Whither am I wandering? Where did I leave him?"

Dorcas, too well accustomed to her husband's wayward moods to note any peculiarity of demeanor, now laid aside the almanac and addressed him in that mournful tone which the tender-hearted appropriate to griefs long cold and dead.

"It was near this time of the month, eighteen years ago, that my poor father left this world for a better. He had a kind arm to hold his head and a kind voice to cheer him, Reuben, in his last moments; and the thought of the faithful care you took of him has comforted me many a time since. Oh, death would have been awful to a solitary man in a wild place like this!"

"Pray Heaven, Dorcas," said Reuben, in a broken voice,—"pray Heaven that neither of us three dies solitary and lies unburied in this howling wilderness!" And he hastened away, leaving her to watch the fire beneath the gloomy pines.

Reuben Bourne's rapid pace gradually slackened as the pang, unintentionally inflicted by the words of Dorcas, became less acute. Many strange reflections, however, thronged upon him; and, straying onward rather like a sleep walker than a hunter, it was attributable to no care of his own that his devious course kept him in the vicinity of the encampment. His steps were imperceptibly led almost in a circle; nor did he observe that he was on the verge of a tract of land heavily timbered, but not with pine trees. The place of the latter was here supplied by oaks and other of the harder woods; and around their roots clustered a dense and bushy under-growth, leaving, however, barren spaces between the trees, thick strewn with withered leaves. Whenever the rustling of the branches or the creaking of the trunks made a sound, as if the forest were waking from slumber, Reuben instinctively raised the musket that rested on his arm, and cast a quick, sharp glance on every side; but, convinced by a partial observation that no animal was near, he would again give himself up to his thoughts. He was musing on the strange influence that had led him away from his premeditated course, and so far into the depths of the wilderness. Unable to penetrate to the secret place of his soul where his motives lay hidden, he believed that a supernatural voice had called him onward, and that a supernatural power had obstructed his retreat. He trusted that it was Heaven's intent to afford him an opportunity of expiating his sin; he hoped that he might find the bones so long unburied; and that, having laid the earth over them, peace would throw its sunlight into the sepulchre of his heart. From these thoughts he was aroused by a rustling in the forest at some distance from the spot to which he had wandered. Perceiving the motion of some object behind a thick veil of undergrowth, he fired, with the instinct of a hunter and the aim of a practised marksman. A low moan, which told his success, and by which even animals can express their dying agony, was unheeded by Reuben Bourne. What were the recollections now breaking upon him?

The thicket into which Reuben had fired was near the summit of a swell of land, and was clustered around the base of a rock, which, in the shape and smoothness of one of its surfaces, was not unlike a gigantic gravestone. As if reflected in a mirror, its likeness was in Reuben's memory. He even recognized the veins which seemed to form an inscription in forgotten characters: everything remained the same, except that a thick covert of bushes shrouded the lower part of the rock, and would have hidden Roger Malvin had he still been sitting there. Yet in the next moment Reuben's eye was caught by another change that time had effected since he last stood where he was now standing again behind the earthy roots of the uptorn tree. The sapling to which he had bound the bloodstained symbol of his vow had increased and strengthened into an oak, far indeed from its maturity, but with no mean spread of shadowy branches. There was one singularity observable in this tree which made Reuben tremble. The middle and lower branches were in luxuriant life, and an excess of vegetation had fringed the trunk almost to the ground; but a blight had apparently stricken the upper part of the oak, and the very topmost bough was withered, sapless, and utterly dead. Reuben remembered how the little banner had fluttered on that topmost bough, when it was green and lovely, eighteen years before. Whose guilt had blasted it?

. . . . . .

Dorcas, after the departure of the two hunters, continued her preparations for their evening repast. Her sylvan table was the moss-covered trunk of a large fallen tree, on the broadest part of which she had spread a snow-white cloth and arranged what were left of the bright pewter vessels that had been her pride in the settlements. It had a strange aspect, that one little spot of homely comfort in the desolate heart of Nature. The sunshine yet lingered upon the higher branches of the trees that grew on rising ground; but the shadows of evening had deepened into the hollow where the encampment was made, and the firelight began to redden as it gleamed up the tall trunks of the pines or hovered on the dense and obscure mass of foliage that circled round the spot. The heart of Dorcas was not sad; for she felt that it was better to journey in the wilderness with two whom she loved than to be a lonely woman in a crowd that cared not for her. As she busied herself in arranging seats of mouldering wood, covered with leaves, for Reuben and her son, her voice danced through the gloomy forest in the measure of a song that she had learned in youth. The rude melody, the production of a bard who won no name, was descriptive of a winter evening in a frontier cottage, when, secured from savage inroad by the high piled snow-drifts, the family rejoiced by their own fireside. The whole song possessed the nameless charm peculiar to unborrowed thought, but four continually-recurring lines shone out from the rest like the blaze of the hearth whose joys they celebrated. Into them, working magic with a few simple words, the poet had instilled the very essence of domestic love and household happiness, and they were poetry and picture joined in one. As Dorcas sang, the walls of her forsaken home seemed to encircle her; she no longer saw the gloomy pines, nor heard the wind which still, as she began each verse, sent a heavy breath through the branches, and died away in a hollow moan from the burden of the song. She was aroused by the report of a gun in the vicinity of the encampment; and either the sudden sound, or her loneliness by the glowing fire, caused her to tremble violently. The next moment she laughed in the pride of a mother's heart.

"My beautiful young hunter! My boy has slain a deer!" she exclaimed, recollecting that in the direction whence the shot proceeded Cyrus had gone to the chase.

She waited a reasonable time to hear her son's light step bounding over the rustling leaves to tell of his success. But he did not immediately appear; and she sent her cheerful voice among the trees in search of him.

"Cyrus! Cyrus!"

His coming was still delayed; and she determined, as the report had apparently been very near, to seek for him in person. Her assistance, also, might be necessary in bringing home the venison which she flattered herself he had obtained. She therefore set forward, directing her steps by the long-past sound, and singing as she went, in order that the boy might be aware of her approach and run to meet her. From behind the trunk of every tree, and from every hiding-place in the thick foliage of the undergrowth, she hoped to discover the countenance of her son, laughing with the sportive mischief that is born of affection. The sun was now beneath the horizon, and the light that came down among the leaves was sufficiently dim to create many illusions in her expecting fancy. Several times she seemed indistinctly to see his face gazing out from among the leaves; and once she imagined that he stood beckoning to her at the base of a craggy rock. Keeping her eyes on this object, however, it proved to be no more than the trunk of an oak fringed to the very ground with little branches, one of which, thrust out farther than the rest, was shaken by the breeze. Making her way round the foot of the rock, she suddenly found herself close to her husband, who had approached in another direction. Leaning upon the butt of his gun, the muzzle of which rested upon the withered leaves, he was apparently absorbed in the contemplation of some object at his feet.

"How is this, Reuben? Have you slain the deer and fallen asleep over him?" exclaimed Dorcas, laughing cheerfully, on her first slight observation of his posture and appearance.

He stirred not, neither did he turn his eyes towards her; and a cold, shuddering fear, indefinite in its source and object, began to creep into her blood. She now perceived that her husband's face was ghastly pale, and his features were rigid, as if incapable of assuming any other expression than the strong despair which had hardened upon them. He gave not the slightest evidence that he was aware of her approach.

"For the love of Heaven, Reuben, speak to me!" cried Dorcas; and the strange sound of her own voice affrighted her even more than the dead silence.

Her husband started, stared into her face, drew her to the front of the rock, and pointed with his finger.

Oh, there lay the boy, asleep, but dreamless, upon the fallen forest leaves! His cheek rested upon his arm—his curled locks were thrown back from his brow—his limbs were slightly relaxed. Had a sudden weariness overcome the youthful hunter? Would his mother's voice arouse him? She knew that it was death.

"This broad rock is the gravestone of your near kindred, Dorcas," said her husband. "Your tears will fall at once over your father and your son."

She heard him not. With one wild shriek, that seemed to force its way from the sufferer's inmost soul, she sank insensible by the side of her dead boy. At that moment the withered topmost bough of the oak loosened itself in the stilly air, and fell in soft, light fragments upon the rock, upon the leaves, upon Reuben, upon his wife and child, and upon Roger Malvin's bones. Then Reuben's heart was stricken, and the tears gushed out like water from a rock. The vow that the wounded youth had made the blighted man had come to redeem. His sin was expiated,—the curse was gone from him; and in the hour when he had shed blood dearer to him than his own, a prayer, the first for years, went up to Heaven from the lips of Reuben Bourne.

Charles Dickens

Charles Dickens (1812–1870), one of the most popular English novelists, was the second of eight children. An unstable father and a somewhat ineffectual mother contributed to a childhood of humiliation and deprivation. His darkest childhood memory, which he treated semiautobiographically in David Copperfield *(1849–50), was of working in a blacking factory, sticking labels on bottles, while his family was living miserably in debtors' prison. When his father came into a small inheritance, Dickens was able to return to school, for a couple of years. He then took a job as a clerk in an attorney's office, and struggled to educate himself. He became a reporter, wrote sketches for his paper, and later produced many long serialized novels that were to bring him international fame. Dickens's championing of the cause of the underpriviliged contributed to national reforms of factory and prison conditions. He created a vast gallery of unforgettable characters whose names have become household words, among them Mr. Pickwick, Mr. Micawber, Fagin, and Uriah Heep. His literary output was large, and includes such classics as* Oliver Twist *(1838),* A Christmas Carol *(1843), and* Great Expectations *(1860–61).*

HORATIO SPARKINS

"Indeed, my love, he paid Teresa very great attention on the last assembly night," said Mrs. Malderton, addressing her spouse, who after the fatigues of the day in the City, was sitting with a silk handkerchief over his head, and his feet on the fender, drinking his port;—"very great attention; and I say again, every possible encouragement ought to be given him. He positively must be asked down here to dine."

"Who must?" inquired Mr. Malderton.

"Why, you know whom I mean, my dear—the young man with the black whiskers and the white cravat, who has just come out at our assembly, and whom all the girls are talking about. Young—dear me! what's his name?—Marianne, what *is* his name?" continued Mrs. Malderton, addressing her youngest daughter, who was engaged in netting a purse, and looking sentimental.

"Mr. Horatio Sparkins, ma," replied Miss Marianne, with a sigh.

"Oh! yes, to be sure—Horatio Sparkins," said Mrs. Malderton. "Decidedly the most gentleman-like young man I ever saw. I am sure in the beautifully-made coat he wore the other night, he looked like—like—"

"Like Prince Leopold, ma—so noble, so full of sentiment!" suggested Marianne, in a tone of enthusiastic admiration.

"You should recollect, my dear," resumed Mrs. Malderton, "that Teresa is now eight-and-twenty; and that it really is very important that something should be done."

Miss Teresa Malderton was a very little girl, rather fat, with vermilion cheeks, but good-humoured, and still disengaged, although, to do her justice, the misfortune arose from no lack of perseverance on her part. In vain had she flirted for ten years; in vain had Mr. and Mrs. Malderton assiduously kept up an extensive acquaintance among the young eligible bachelors of Camberwell, and even of Wandsworth and Brixton; to say nothing of those who "dropped in" from town. Miss Malderton was as well known as the lion on the top of Northumberland House, and had an equal chance of "going off."

"I am quite sure you 'd like him," continued Mrs. Malderton, "he is so gentlemanly!"

"So clever!" said Miss Marianne.

"And has such a flow of language!" added Miss Teresa.

"He has a great respect for you, my dear," said Mrs. Malderton to her husband. Mr. Malderton coughed, and looked at the fire.

"Yes, I 'm sure he 's very much attached to pa's society," said Miss Marianne.

"No doubt of it," echoed Miss Teresa.

"Indeed, he said as much to me in confidence," observed Mrs. Malderton.

"Well, well," returned Mr. Malderton, somewhat flattered; "if I see him at the assembly to-morrow, perhaps I 'll ask him down. I hope he knows we live at Oak Lodge, Camberwell, my dear?"

"Of course—and that you keep a one-horse carriage."

"I 'll see about it," said Mr. Malderton, composing himself for a nap; "I 'll see about it."

Mr. Malderton was a man whose whole scope of ideas was limited to Lloyd's, the Exchange, the India House, and the Bank. A few successful speculations had raised him from a situation of obscurity and comparative poverty, to a state of affluence. As frequently happens in such cases, the ideas of himself and his family became elevated to an extraordinary pitch as their means increased; they affected fashion, taste, and many other fooleries, in imitation of their betters, and had a very decided and becoming horror of anything which could, by possibility, be considered *low*. He was hospitable from ostentation, illiberal from ignorance, and prejudiced from conceit. Egotism and the love of display induced him to keep an excellent table: convenience, and a love of good things of this life, ensured him plenty of guests. He liked to have clever men, or what he considered such, at his table, because it was a great thing to talk about; but he never could endure what he called "sharp fellows." Probably, he cherished this feeling out of compliment to his two sons, who gave their respected parent no uneasiness in that particular. The family were ambitious of forming acquaintances and connections in some sphere of society superior to that in which they themselves moved; and one of the necessary consequences of this desire, added to their utter ignorance of the world beyond their own small circle, was that any one who could lay claim to an acquaintance with people of rank and title, had a sure passport to the table at Oak Lodge, Camberwell.

The appearance of Mr. Horatio Sparkins at the assembly had excited no small degree of surprise and curiosity among its regular frequenters. Who could he be? He was evidently reserved, and apparently melancholy. Was he a clergyman?—He danced too well. A barrister?—He said he was not called. He used very fine words, and talked a great deal. Could he be a distinguished foreigner, come to England for the purpose of describing the country, its manners and customs; and frequenting public balls and public dinners, with the view of becoming acquainted with high life, polished etiquette, and English refinement?—No, he had not a foreign accent. Was he a surgeon, a contributor to the magazines, a writer of fashionable novels, or an artist?—No; to each and all of these surmises, there existed some valid objection.—"Then," said everybody, "he must be *somebody*."—"I should think he must be," reasoned Mr. Malderton, within himself, "because he perceives our superiority, and pays us so much attention."

The night succeeding the conversation we have just recorded, was "assembly night." The double-fly was ordered to be at the door of Oak Lodge at nine o'clock precisely. The Miss Maldertons were dressed in sky-blue satin trimmed with artificial flowers; and Mrs. M. (who was a little fat woman), in ditto ditto, looked like her eldest daughter multiplied by two.

Mr. Frederick Malderton, the eldest son, in full-dress costume, was the very *beau ideal* of a smart waiter; and Mr. Thomas Malderton, the youngest, with his white dress-stock, blue coat, bright buttons, and red watch-ribbon, strongly resembled the portrait of that interesting, but rash young gentleman, George Barnwell. Every member of the party had made up his or her mind to cultivate the acquaintance of Mr. Horatio Sparkins. Miss Teresa, of course, was to be as amiable and interesting as ladies of eight-and-twenty on the look-out for a husband usually are. Mrs. Malderton would be all smiles and graces. Miss Marianne would request the favour of some verses for her album. Mr. Malderton would patronise the great unknown by asking him to dinner. Tom intended to ascertain the extent of his information on the interesting topic of snuff and cigars. Even Mr. Frederick Malderton himself, the family authority on all points of taste, dress, and fashionable arrangement; who had lodgings of his own in town; who had a free admission to Covent Garden Theatre; who always dressed according to the fashions of the months; who went up the water twice a week in the season; and who actually had an intimate friend who once knew a gentleman who formerly lived in the Albany,—even he had determined that Mr. Horatio Sparkins must be a devilish good fellow, and that he would do him the honour of challenging him to a game of billiards.

The first object that met the anxious eyes of the expectant family on their entrance into the ball-room, was the interesting Horatio, with his hair brushed off his forehead, and his eyes fixed on the ceiling, reclining in a contemplative attitude on one of the seats.

"There he is, my dear," whispered Mrs. Malderton to Mr. Malderton.

"How like Lord Byron!" murmured Miss Teresa.

"Or Montgomery!" whispered Miss Marianne.

"Or the portraits of Captain Cook!" suggested Tom.

"Tom—don't be an ass!" said his father, who checked him on all occasions, probably with a view to prevent his becoming "sharp"—which was very unnecessary.

The elegant Sparkins attitudinised with admirable effect, until the family had crossed the room. He then started up, with the most natural appearance of surprise and delight; accosted Mrs. Malderton with the utmost cordiality; saluted the young ladies in the most enchanting manner; bowed to, and shook hands with, Mr. Malderton, with a degree of respect amounting almost to veneration; and returned the greetings of the two young men in a half-gratified, half-patronising manner, which fully convinced them that he must be an important, and, at the same time, condescending personage.

"Miss Malderton," said Horatio, after the ordinary salutations, and bowing very low, "may I be permitted to presume to hope that you will allow me to have the pleasure—"

"I don't *think* I am engaged," said Miss Teresa, with a dreadful affectation of indifference—"but, really—so many—"

Horatio looked handsomely miserable.

"I shall be most happy," simpered the interesting Teresa, at last. Horatio's countenance brightened up, like an old hat in a shower of rain.

"A very genteel young man, certainly!" said the gratified Mr. Malderton, as the obsequious Sparkins and his partner joined the quadrille which was just forming.

"He has a remarkably good address," said Mr. Frederick.

"Yes, he is a prime fellow," interposed Tom, who always managed to put his foot in it—"he talks just like an auctioneer."

"Tom!" said his father solemnly, "I think I desired you, before, not to be a fool." Tom looked as happy as a cock on a drizzly morning.

"How delightful!" said the interesting Horatio to his partner, as they promenaded the room at the conclusion of the set—"how delightful, how refreshing it is, to retire from the cloudy storms, the vicissitudes, and the troubles, of life, even if it be but for a few short fleeting moments: and to spend those moments, fading and evanescent though they be, in the delightful, the blessed society of one individual—whose frowns would be death, whose coldness would be madness, whose falsehood would be ruin, whose constancy would be bliss; the possession of whose affection would be the brightest and best reward that Heaven could bestow on man?"

"What feeling! what sentiment!" thought Miss Teresa, as she leaned more heavily on her companion's arm.

"But enough—enough!" resumed the elegant Sparkins, with a theatrical air. "What have I said? what have I—I—to do with sentiments like these! Miss Malderton"—here he stopped short—"may I hope to be permitted to offer the humble tribute of—"

"Really, Mr. Sparkins," returned the enraptured Teresa, blushing in the sweetest confusion, "I must refer you to papa. I never can, without his consent, venture to—"

"Surely he cannot object—"

"Oh, yes. Indeed, indeed, you know him not!" interrupted Miss Teresa, well knowing there was nothing to fear, but wishing to make the interview resemble a scene in some romantic novel.

"He cannot object to my offering you a glass of negus," returned the adorable Sparkins, with some surprise.

"Is that all?" thought the disappointed Teresa. "What a fuss about nothing!"

"It will give me the greatest pleasure, sir, to see you to dinner at Oak Lodge, Camberwell, on Sunday next at five o'clock, if you have no better engagement," said Mr. Malderton, at the conclusion of the evening, as he and his sons were standing in conversation with Mr. Horatio Sparkins.

Horatio bowed his acknowledgments, and accepted the flattering invitation.

"I must confess," continued the father, offering his snuffbox to his new acquaintance, "that I don't enjoy these assemblies half so much as the comfort—I had almost said the luxury—of Oak Lodge. They have no great charms for an elderly man."

"And after all, sir, what is man?" said the metaphysical Sparkins. "I say, what is man?"

"Ah! very true," said Mr. Malderton; "very true."

"We know that we live and breathe," continued Horatio; "that we have wants and wishes, desires and appetites—"

"Certainly," said Mr. Frederick Malderton, looking profound.

"I say, we know that we exist," repeated Horatio, raising his voice, "but there we stop; there, is an end to our knowledge; there, is the summit of our attainments; there, is the termination of our ends. What more do we know?"

"Nothing," replied Mr. Frederick—than whom no one was more capable of answering for himself in that particular. Tom was about to hazard something, but, fortunately for his reputation, he caught his father's angry eye, and slunk off like a puppy convicted of petty larceny.

"Upon my word," said Mr. Malderton the elder, as they were returning home in the fly, "that Mr. Sparkins is a wonderful young man. Such surprising knowledge! such extraordinary information! and such a splendid mode of expressing himself!"

"I think he must be somebody in disguise," said Miss Marianne. "How charmingly romantic!"

"He talks very loud and nicely," timidly observed Tom, "but I don't exactly understand what he means."

"I almost begin to despair of *your* understanding anything, Tom," said his father, who, of course, had been much enlightened by Mr. Horatio Sparkins's conversation.

"It strikes me, Tom," said Miss Teresa, "that you have made yourself very ridiculous this evening."

"No doubt of it," cried everybody—and the unfortunate Tom reduced himself into the least possible space. That night, Mr. and Mrs. Malderton had a long conversation respecting their daughter's prospects and future arrangements. Miss Teresa went to bed, considering whether, in the event of her marrying a title, she could conscientiously encourage the visits of her present associates; and dreamed, all night, of disguised noblemen, large routs, ostrich plumes, bridal favours, and Horatio Sparkins.

Various surmises were hazarded on the Sunday morning, as to the mode of conveyance which the anxiously-expected Horatio would adopt. Did he keep a gig?—was it possible he could come on horseback?—or would he patronise the stage? These, and other various conjectures of equal importance, engrossed the attention of Mrs. Malderton and her daughters during the whole morning after church.

"Upon my word, my dear, it's a most annoying thing that that vulgar brother of yours should have invited himself to dine here to-day," said Mr. Malderton to his wife. "On account of Mr. Sparkins's coming down, I purposely abstained from asking any one but Flamwell. And then to think of your brother—a tradesman—it's insufferable! I declare I wouldn't have him mention his shop, before our new guest—no, not for a thousand pounds! I wouldn't care if he had the good sense to conceal the disgrace he is to the family; but he's so fond of his horrible business, that he *will* let people know what he is."

Mr. Jacob Barton, the individual alluded to, was a large grocer; so vulgar, and so lost to all sense of feeling, that he actually never scrupled to avow that he wasn't above his business: "he 'd made his money by it, and he didn't care who know'd it."

"Ah! Flamwell, my dear fellow, how d 'ye do?" said Mr. Malderton, as a little spoffish man, with green spectacles, entered the room. "You got my note?"

"Yes, I did; and here I am in consequence."

"You don't happen to know this Mr. Sparkins by name? You know everybody?"

Mr. Flamwell was one of those gentlemen of remarkably extensive information whom one occasionally meets in society, who pretend to know everybody, but in reality know nobody. At Malderton's, where any stories about great people were received with a greedy ear, he was an especial favourite; and, knowing the kind of people he had to deal with, he carried his passion of claiming acquaintance with everybody, to the most immoderate length. He had rather a singular way of telling his greatest lies in a parenthesis, and with an air of self-denial, as if he feared being thought egotistical.

"Why, no, I don't know him by that name," returned Flamwell in a low tone, and with an air of immense importance. "I have no doubt I know him, though. Is he tall?"

"Middle-sized," said Miss Teresa.

"With black hair?" inquired Flamwell, hazarding a bold guess.

"Yes," returned Miss Teresa, eagerly.

"Rather a snub nose?"

"No," said the disappointed Teresa, "he has a Roman nose."

"I said a Roman nose, didn't I?" inquired Flamwell. "He 's an elegant young man?"

"Oh, certainly."

"With remarkably prepossessing manners?"

"Oh, yes!" said all the family together. "You must know him."

"Yes, I thought you knew him, if he was anybody," triumphantly exclaimed Mr. Malderton. "Who d' ye think he is?"

"Why, from your description," said Flamwell, ruminating, and sinking his voice, almost to a whisper, "he bears a strong resemblance to the Honourable Augustus Fitz-Edward Fitz-John Fitz-Osborne. He 's a very talented young man, and rather eccentric. It 's extremely probable he may have changed his name for some temporary purpose."

Teresa's heart beat high. Could he be the Honourable Augustus Fitz-Edward Fitz-John Fitz-Osborne. What a name to be elegantly engraved upon two glazed cards, tied together with a piece of white satin ribbon! "The Honourable Mrs. Augustus Fitz-Edward Fitz-John Fitz-Osborne!" The thought was transport.

"It 's five minutes to five," said Mr. Malderton, looking at his watch: "I hope he 's not going to disappoint us."

"There he is!" exclaimed Miss Teresa, as a loud double-knock was heard at the door. Everybody endeavoured to look—as people when they particularly expect a visitor always do—as if they were perfectly unsuspicious of the approach of anybody.

The room-door opened—"Mr. Barton!" said the servant.

"Confound the man!" murmured Malderton. "Ah! my dear sir, how d' ye do! Any news?"

"Why, no," returned the grocer, in his usual bluff manner. "No, none partickler. None that I am much aware of. How d' ye do, gals and boys? Mr. Flamwell, sir—glad to see you."

"Here 's Mr. Sparkins!" said Tom, who had been looking out at the window, "on *such* a black horse!" There was Horatio, sure enough, on a large black horse, curvetting and prancing along, like an Astley's supernumerary. After a great deal of reining in, and pulling up, with the accompaniments of snorting, rearing, and kicking, the animal consented to stop at about a hundred yards from the gate, where Mr. Sparkins dismounted, and confided him to the care of Mr. Malderton's groom. The ceremony of introduction was gone through, in all due form. Mr. Flamwell looked from behind his green spectacles at Horatio with an air of mysterious importance; and the gallant Horatio looked unutterable things at Teresa.

"Is he the Honourable Mr. Augustus what 's his name?" whispered Mrs. Malderton to Flamwell, as he was escorting her to the dining-room.

"Why, no—at least not exactly," returned that great authority—"not exactly."

"Who *is* he then?"

"Hush!" said Flamwell, nodding his head with a grave air, importing that he knew very well; but was prevented, by some grave reasons of state, from disclosing the important secret. It might be one of the ministers making himself acquainted with the views of the people.

"Mr. Sparkins," said the delighted Mrs. Malderton, "pray divide the ladies. John, put a chair for the gentleman between Miss Teresa and Miss Marianne." This was addressed to a man who, on ordinary occasions, acted as half-groom, half-gardener; but who, as it was important to make an impression on Mr. Sparkins, had been forced into a white neckerchief and shoes, and touched up, and brushed, to look like a second footman.

The dinner was excellent; Horatio was most attentive to Miss Teresa, and every one felt in high spirits, except Mr. Malderton, who knowing the propensity of his brother-in-law, Mr. Barton, endured that sort of agony which the newspapers inform us is experienced by the surrounding neighbourhood when a pot-boy hangs himself in a hay-loft, and which is "much easier to be imagined than described."

"Have you seen your friend, Sir Thomas Noland, lately, Flamwell?" inquired Mr. Malderton, casting a sidelong look at Horatio, to see what effect the mention of so great a man had upon him.

"Why, no—not very lately. I saw Lord Gubbleton the day before yesterday."

"Ah! I hope his lordship is very well?" said Malderton, in a tone of the greatest interest. It is scarcely necessary to say that, until that moment, he had been quite innocent of the existence of such a person.

"Why, yes; he was very well—very well indeed. He 's a devilish good fellow. I met him in the City, and had a long chat with him. Indeed, I 'm rather intimate with him. I couldn't stop to talk to him as long as I could wish, though, because I was on my way to a banker's, a very rich man, and a Member of Parliament, with whom I am also rather, indeed I may say very, intimate."

"I know whom you mean," returned the host, consequentially—in reality knowing as much about the matter as Flamwell himself. "He has a capital business."

This was touching on a dangerous topic.

"Talking of business," interposed Mr. Barton, from the centre of the table. "A gentleman whom you knew very well, Malderton, before you made that first lucky spec of yours, called at our shop the other day, and—"

"Barton, may I trouble you for a potato?" interrupted the wretched master of the house, hoping to nip the story in the bud.

"Certainly," returned the grocer, quite insensible of his brother-in-law's object—"and he said in a very plain manner—"

"*Floury*, if you please," interrupted Malderton again; dreading the termination of the anecdote, and fearing a repetition of the word "shop."

"He said, says he," continued the culprit, after despatching the potato; "says he, how goes on your business? So I said, jokingly—you know my way—says I, I 'm never above my business, and I hope my business will never be above me. Ha, ha!"

"Mr. Sparkins," said the host, vainly endeavouring to conceal his dismay, "a glass of wine?"

"With the utmost pleasure, sir."

"Happy to see you."

"Thank you."

"We were talking the other evening," resumed the host, addressing Horatio, partly with the view of displaying the conversational powers of his new acquaintance, and partly in the hope of drowning the grocer's stories—"we were talking the other night about the nature of man. Your argument struck me very forcibly."

"And me," said Mr. Frederick. Horatio made a graceful inclination of the head.

"Pray, what is your opinion of woman, Mr. Sparkins?" inquired Mrs. Malderton. The young ladies simpered.

"Man," replied Horatio, "man, whether he ranged the bright, gay, flowery plains of a second Eden, or the more sterile, barren, and I may say, commonplace regions, to which we are compelled to accustom ourselves, in times such as these, man under any circumstances, or in any place—whether he were bending beneath the withering blasts of the frigid zone, or scorching under the rays of a vertical sun—man, without woman, would be—alone."

"I am very happy to find you entertain such honourable opinions, Mr. Sparkins," said Mrs. Malderton.

"And I," added Miss Teresa. Horatio looked his delight, and the young lady blushed.

"Now, it 's my opinion," said Mr. Barton—

"I know what you're going to say," interposed Malderton, determined not to give his relation another opportunity, "and I don't agree with you."

"What?" inquired the astonished grocer.

"I am sorry to differ from you, Barton," said the host, in as positive a manner as if he really were contradicting a position which the other had laid down, "but I cannot give my assent to what I consider a very monstrous proposition."

"But I meant to say—"

"You never can convince me," said Malderton, with an air of obstinate determination. "Never."

"And I," said Mr. Frederick, following up his father's attack, "cannot entirely agree in Mr. Sparkins's argument."

"What?" said Horatio, who became more metaphysical, and more argumentative, as he saw the female part of the family listening in wondering delight—"what? Is effect the consequence of cause? Is cause the precursor of effect?"

"That 's the point," said Flamwell.

"To be sure," said Mr. Malderton.

"Because, if effect is the consequence of cause, and if cause does precede effect, I apprehend you are wrong," added Horatio.

"Decidedly," said the toad-eating Flamwell.

"At least, I apprehend that to be the just and logical deduction?" said Sparkins, in a tone of interrogation.

"No doubt of it," chimed in Flamwell again. "It settles the point."

"Well, perhaps it does," said Mr. Frederick; "I didn't see it before."

"I don't exactly see it now," thought the grocer; "but I suppose it 's all right."

"How wonderfully clever he is!" whispered Mrs. Malderton to her daughters, as they retired to the drawing-room.

"Oh, he 's quite a love!" said both the young ladies together; "he talks like an oracle. He must have seen a great deal of life."

The gentlemen being left to themselves, a pause ensued, during which everybody looked very grave, as if they were quite overcome by the profound nature of the previous discussion. Flamwell, who had made up his mind to find out who and what Mr. Horatio Sparkins really was, first broke silence.

"Excuse me, sir," said that distinguished personage, "I presume you have studied for the bar? I thought of entering once, myself—indeed, I'm rather intimate with some of the highest ornaments of that distinguished profession."

"N-no!" said Horatio, with a little hesitation; "not exactly."

"But you have been much among the silk gowns, or I mistake?" inquired Flamwell, deferentially.

"Nearly all my life," returned Sparkins.

The question was thus pretty well settled in the mind of Mr. Flamwell. He was a young gentleman "about to be called."

"I shouldn't like to be a barrister," said Tom, speaking for the first time, and looking round the table to find somebody who would notice the remark.

No one made any reply.

"I shouldn't like to wear a wig," said Tom, hazarding another observation.

"Tom, I beg you will not make yourself ridiculous," said his father. "Pray listen, and improve yourself by the conversation you hear, and don't be constantly making these absurd remarks."

"Very well, father," replied the unfortunate Tom, who had not spoken a word since he had asked for another slice of beef at a quarter-past five o'clock, P. M., and it was then eight.

"Well, Tom," observed his good-natured uncle, "never mind! *I* think with you. *I* shouldn't like to wear a wig. I 'd rather wear an apron."

Mr. Malderton coughed violently. Mr. Barton resumed—"For if a man's above his business—"

The cough returned with tenfold violence, and did not cease until the unfortunate cause of it, in his alarm, had quite forgotten what he intended to say.

"Mr. Sparkins," said Flamwell, returning to the charge, "do you happen to know Mr. Delafontaine, of Bedford Square?"

"I have exchanged cards with him; since which, indeed, I have had an opportunity of serving him considerably," replied Horatio, slightly colouring; no doubt, at having been betrayed into making the acknowledgment.

"You are very lucky, if you have had an opportunity of obliging that great man," observed Flamwell, with an air of profound respect.

"I don't know who he is," he whispered to Mr. Malderton, confidentially, as they followed Horatio up to the drawing-room. "It 's quite clear, however, that he belongs to the law, and that he is somebody of great importance, and very highly connected."

"No doubt, no doubt," returned his companion.

The remainder of the evening passed away most delightfully. Mr. Malderton, relieved from his apprehensions by the circumstances of Mr. Barton's falling into a profound sleep, was as affable and gracious as possible. Miss Teresa played the "Fall of Paris," as Mr. Sparkins declared, in a most masterly manner, and both of them, assisted by Mr. Frederick, tried over glees and trios without number; they having made the pleasing discovery that their voices harmonised beautifully. To be sure, they all sang the first part; and Horatio, in addition to the slight drawback of having no ear, was perfectly innocent of knowing a note of music; still, they passed the time very agreeably, and it was past twelve o'clock before Mr. Sparkins ordered the mourning-coach-looking steed to be brought out—an order which was only complied with, on the distinct understanding that he was to repeat his visit on the following Sunday.

"But, perhaps, Mr. Sparkins will form one of our party tomorrow evening?" suggested Mrs. M. "Mr. Malderton intends taking the girls to see the pantomime." Mr. Sparkins bowed, and promised to join the party in box 48, in the course of the evening.

"We will not tax you for the morning," said Miss Teresa, bewitchingly; "for ma is going to take us to all sorts of places, shopping. I know that gentlemen have a great horror of that employment." Mr. Sparkins bowed again, and declared that he should be delighted, but business of importance occupied him in the morning. Flamwell looked at Malderton significantly.—"It 's term time!" he whispered.

At twelve o'clock on the following morning, the "fly" was at the door of Oak Lodge, to convey Mrs. Malderton and her daughters on their expedition for the day. They were to dine and dress for the play at a friend's house. First, driving thither with their band-boxes, they departed on their first errand to make some purchases at Messrs. Jones, Spruggins, and Smith's, of Tottenham-court Road; after which, they were to go to Redmayne's in Bond Street; thence, to innumerable places that no one ever heard of. The young ladies beguiled the tediousness of the ride by eulogising Mr. Horatio Sparkins, scolding their mamma for taking them so far to save a shilling, and wondering whether they should ever reach their destination. At length, the vehicle stopped before a dirty-looking ticketed linendraper's shop, with goods of all kinds, and labels of all sorts and sizes, in the window. There were dropsical figures of seven with a little three-farthings in the corner, "perfectly invisible to the naked eye"; three hundred and fifty thousand ladies' boas, *from* one shilling and a penny halfpenny; real French kid shoes, at two and ninepence per pair; green parasols, at an equally cheap rate; and "every description of goods," as the proprietors said—and they must know best—"fifty per cent. under cost price."

"Lor! ma, what a place you have brought us to!" said Miss Teresa; "what *would* Mr. Sparkins say if he could see us!"

"Ah! what, indeed!" said Miss Marianne, horrified at the idea.

"Pray be seated, ladies. What is the first article?" inquired the obsequious master of the ceremonies of the establishment, who, in his large white neckcloth and formal tie, looked like a bad "portrait of a gentleman" in the Somerset House exhibition.

"I want to see some silks," answered Mrs. Malderton.

"Directly, ma'am.—Mr. Smith! Where *is* Mr. Smith?"

"Here, sir," cried a voice at the back of the shop.

"Pray make haste, Mr. Smith," said the M.C. "You never are to be found when you 're wanted, sir."

Mr. Smith, thus enjoined to use all possible despatch, leaped over the counter with great agility, and placed himself before the newly-arrived customers. Mrs. Malderton uttered a faint scream; Miss Teresa, who had been stooping down to talk to her sister, raised her head, and beheld—Horatio Sparkins!

We will draw a veil, as novel-writers say, over the scene that ensued. The mysterious, philosophical, romantic, metaphysical Sparkins—he who, to the interesting Teresa, seemed like the embodied idea of the young dukes and poetical exquisites in blue silk dressing-gowns, and ditto ditto slippers, of whom she had read and dreamed, but had never expected to behold, was suddenly converted into Mr. Samuel Smith, the assistant at a "cheap shop"; the junior partner in a slippery firm of some three weeks' existence. The dignified evanishment of the hero of Oak Lodge, on this unexpected recognition, could only be equalled by that of a furtive dog with a considerable kettle at his tail. All the hopes of the Maldertons were destined at once to melt away, like the lemon ices at a Company's dinner; Almack's was still to them as distant as the North Pole; and Miss Teresa had as much chance of a husband as Captain Ross had of the northwest passage.

Years have elapsed since the occurrence of this dreadful morning. The daisies have thrice bloomed on Camberwell Green; the sparrows have thrice repeated their vernal chirps in Camberwell Grove; but the Miss Maldertons are still unmated. Miss Teresa's case is more desperate than ever; but Flamwell is yet in the zenith of his reputation; and the family have the same predilection for aristocratic personages, with an increased aversion to anything *low*.

Gustave Flaubert

The French novelist Gustave Flaubert (1821–1880) was born in Rouen. He began writing early, gathering impressions, particularly from his contact with hospitals, operating theaters, and anatomy classes through his father, a successful surgeon. Because of a nervous disorder, thought to be epilepsy, he gave up law study and devoted himself to writing. A perfectionist, who disliked "accepted ideas," he worked to achieve a style "as rhythmical as verse and as precise as the language of science." His works include Madame Bovary *(1856) and* L'Education Sentimentale *(1874).* *(See page 77–78 of Introduction.)*

A SIMPLE SOUL

I

For half a century the housewives of Pont-l'Evêque had envied Madame Aubain her servant Félicité.

For a hundred francs a year, she cooked and did the housework, washed, ironed, mended, harnessed the horse, fattened the poultry, made the butter and remained faithful to her mistress—although the latter was by no means an agreeable person.

Madame Aubain had married a gay rake without any money, who died at the beginning of 1809, leaving her with two young children and a number of debts. She sold all her property excepting the farm of Toucques and the farm of Geffosses, the income of which barely amounted to 5,000 francs; then she left her house in Saint-Melaine, and moved into a less pretentious one which had belonged to her ancestors and stood back of the market-place. This house, with its slate-covered roof, was built between a passage-way and a narrow street that led to the river. The interior was so unevenly graded that it caused people to stumble. A narrow hall separated the kitchen from the parlour, where Madame Aubain sat all day in a wicker armchair near the window. Eight mahogany chairs stood in a row against the white wainscoting. An old piano, standing beneath a barometer, was covered with a pyramid of old books and boxes. On either side of the yellow marble mantelpiece, in Louis XV style, stood a tapestry armchair. The clock represented a temple of Vesta; and the whole room smelled musty, as it was on a lower level than the garden.

On the first floor was Madame's bed-chamber, a large room papered in a flowered design and containing the portrait of Monsieur dressed in the costume of a dandy. It communicated with a smaller room, in which there were two little cribs, without any mattresses. Next came the parlour (always closed), filled with furniture covered with sheets. Then a hall, which led to the study, where books and papers were piled on the shelves of a book-case that enclosed three quarters of the big black desk. Two panels were entirely hidden under pen-and-ink sketches, water-colour landscapes and Audran engravings, relics of better times and vanished luxury. On the second floor, a garret-window lighted Félicité's room, which looked out upon the meadows.

She rose at daybreak, in order to attend mass, and she worked without interruption until night; then, when dinner was over, the dishes cleared away and the door securely locked, she would bury the log under the ashes and fall asleep in front of the hearth with a rosary in her hand. Nobody could bargain with greater obstinacy, and as for cleanliness, the lustre on her brass sauce-pans was the envy and despair of other servants. She was most economical, and when she ate she would gather up crumbs with the tip of her finger, so that nothing should be wasted of the loaf of bread weighing twelve pounds which was baked especially for her and lasted three weeks.

Summer and winter she wore a checkered small scarf fastened in the back with a pin, a cap which concealed her hair, a red skirt, grey stockings, and an apron with a bib like those worn by hospital nurses.

Her face was thin and her voice shrill. When she was twenty-five, she looked forty. After she had passed fifty, nobody could tell her age; erect and silent always, she resembled a wooden figure working automatically.

II

Like every other woman, she had had an affair of the heart. Her father, who was a mason, was killed by falling from a scaffolding. Then her mother died and her sisters went their different ways; a farmer took her in, and while she was quite small, let her keep cows in the fields. She was clad in miserable rags, beaten for the slightest offence and finally dismissed for a theft of thirty sous which she did not commit. She took service on another farm where she tended the poultry; and as she was well thought of by her master, her fellow-workers soon grew jealous.

One evening in August (she was then eighteen years old), they persuaded her to accompany them to the fair at Colleville. She was immediately dazzled by the noise, the lights in the trees, the brightness of the dresses, the laces and gold crosses, and the crowd of people all capering at the same time. She was standing modestly at a distance, when presently a young man of well-to-do appearance, who had been leaning on the pole of a wagon and smoking his pipe, approached her, and asked her for a dance. He treated her to cider and cake, bought her a silk shawl, and then, thinking she had guessed his purpose, offered to see her home. When they came to the end of a field he threw her down brutally. But she grew frightened and screamed, and he walked off.

One evening, on the road leading to Beaumont, she came upon a wagon loaded with hay, and when she overtook it, she recognized Théodore. He greeted her calmly, and asked her to forget what had happened between them, as it "was all the fault of the drink."

She did not know what to reply and wished to run away.

Presently he began to speak of the harvest and of the notables of the village; his father had left Colleville and bought the farm of Les Écots, so that now they would be neighbors. "Ah!" she exclaimed. He then added that his parents were looking around for a wife for him, but that he himself was not so anxious and preferred to wait for a girl who suited him. She hung her head. He then asked her whether she had ever thought of marrying. She replied, smilingly, that it was wrong of him to make fun of her. "Oh! no, I am in earnest," he said, and put his left arm around her waist while they sauntered along. The air was soft, the stars were bright, and the huge load of hay oscillated in front of them, drawn by four horses whose ponderous hoofs raised clouds of dust. Without a word from their driver they turned to the right. He kissed her again and she went home. The following week, Théodore obtained meetings.

They met in yards, behind walls or under isolated trees. She was not ignorant, as girls of well-to-do families are—for the animals had instructed her;—but her reason and her instinct of honour kept her from falling. Her resistance exasperated Théodore's love and so in order to satisfy it (or perhaps unconsciously), he offered to marry her. She would not believe him at first, so he made solemn promises. But in a short time he mentioned a difficulty; the previous year, his parents had purchased a substitute for him; but any day he might be drafted and the prospect of serving in the army alarmed him greatly. To Félicité his cowardice appeared a proof of his love for her, and her devotion to him grew stronger. When she met him, he would torture her with his fears and his entreaties. At last, he announced that he was going to the prefecture himself for information, and would let her know everything on the following Sunday, between eleven o'clock and midnight.

When the time drew near, she ran to meet her lover. But instead of Théodore, one of his friends was at the meeting-place. He informed her that she would never see her sweetheart again, for, in order to escape the conscription, he had married a rich old woman, Madame Lehoussais, of Toucques.

The poor girl's sorrow was frightful. She threw herself on the ground, she cried and called on the Lord, and wandered around desolately until sunrise. Then she went back to the farm, declared her intention of leaving, and at the end of the month, after she had received her wages, she packed all her belongings in a handkerchief and started for Pont-l'Evêque.

In front of the inn, she met a woman wearing widow's weeds, and upon questioning her, learned that she was looking for a cook. The girl did not know very much, but appeared so willing and so modest in her requirements, that Madame Aubain finally said:

"Very well, I will give you a trial."

And half an hour later Félicité was installed in her house.

At first she lived in a constant anxiety that was caused by "the style of the household" and the memory of "Monsieur," that hovered over everything. Paul and Virginie, the one aged seven, and the other barely four, seemed made of some precious material; she carried them on her back, and was greatly mortified when Madame Aubain forbade her to kiss them every other minute.

But in spite of all this, she was happy. The comfort of her new surroundings had obliterated her sadness.

Every Thursday, friends of Madame Aubain dropped in for a game of cards, and it was Félicité's duty to prepare the table and heat the foot-warmers. They arrived at exactly eight o'clock and departed before eleven.

Every Monday morning, the dealer in second-hand goods, who lived under the alley-way, spread out his wares on the sidewalk. Then the city would be filled with a buzzing of voices in which the neighing of horses, the bleating of lambs, the grunting of pigs, could be distinguished, mingled with the sharp sound of wheels on the cobble-stones. About twelve o'clock, when the market was in full swing, there appeared at the front door a tall, middle-aged peasant, with a hooked nose and a cap on the back of his head; it was Robelin, the farmer of Geffosses. Shortly afterwards came Liébard, the farmer of Toucques, short, round and ruddy, wearing a grey jacket and spurred boots.

Both men brought their landlady either chickens or cheese. Félicité would invariably thwart their ruses and they held her in great respect.

At various times, Madame Aubain received a visit from the Marquis de Grémanville, one of her uncles, who was ruined and lived at Falaise on the remainder of his estates. He always came at dinner-time and brought an ugly poodle with him, whose paws soiled the furniture. In spite of his efforts to appear a man of breeding (he even went so far as to raise his hat every time he said "My deceased father"), his habits got the better of him, and he would fill his glass a little too often and relate broad stories. Félicité would show him out very politely and say: "You have had enough for this time, Monsieur de Grémanville! Hoping to see you again!" and would close the door.

She opened it gladly for Monsieur Bourais, a retired lawyer. His bald head and white cravat, the ruffling of his shirt, his flowing brown coat, the manner in which he took snuff, his whole person, in fact, produced in her the kind of awe which we feel when we see extraordinary persons. As he managed Madame's estates, he spent hours with her in Monsieur's study; he was in constant fear of being compromised, had a great regard for the magistracy and some pretensions to learning.

In order to facilitate the children's studies, he presented them with an engraved geography book which represented various scenes of the world: cannibals with feather head-dresses, a gorilla kidnapping a young girl, Arabs in the desert, a whale being harpooned, etc.

Paul explained the pictures to Félicité. And, in fact, this was her only literary education.

The children's studies were under the direction of a poor devil employed at the town-hall, who sharpened his pocket-knife on his boots and was famous for his penmanship.

When the weather was fine, they went to Geffosses. The house was built in the centre of the sloping yard; and the sea looked like a grey spot in the distance. Félicité would take slices of cold meat from the lunch basket and they would sit down and eat in a room next to the dairy. This room was all that remained of a cottage that had been torn down. The dilapidated wall-paper trembled in the drafts. Madame Aubain, overwhelmed by recollections, would hang her head, while the children were afraid to open their mouths. Then, "Why don't you go and play?" Their mother would say; and they would scamper off.

Paul would go to the old barn, catch birds, throw stones into the pond, or pound the trunks of the trees with a stick till they resounded like drums. Virginie would feed the rabbits and run to pick the wild flowers in the fields, and her flying legs would disclose her little embroidered pantalettes. One autumn evening, they struck out for home through the meadows. The new moon illumined part of the sky and a mist hovered like a veil over the windings of the river. Oxen, lying in the pastures, gazed mildly at the passing persons. In the third field, however, several of them got up and surrounded them. "Don't be afraid," cried Félicité; and murmuring a sort of lament, she passed her hand over the back of the nearest ox; he turned away and the others followed. But when they came to the next pasture, they heard frightful bellowing.

It was a bull which was hidden from them by the fog. He advanced towards the two women, and Madame Aubain prepared to flee for her life. "No, no! not so fast," warned Félicité. Still they hurried on, for they could hear the noisy breathing of the bull close behind them. His hoofs pounded the grass like hammers, and presently he began to gallop! Félicité turned around and threw handfuls of grass in his eyes. He hung his head, shook his horns and bellowed with fury. Madame Aubain and the children, huddled at the end of the field, were trying to jump over the ditch. Félicité continued to back before the bull, blinding him with dirt, while she shouted to them to make haste.

Madame Aubain finally slid into the ditch, after shoving first Virginie and then Paul into it, and though she stumbled several times she managed, by dint of courage, to climb the other side of it.

The bull had driven Félicité up against a fence; the foam from his muzzle flew into her face and in another minute he would have disembowelled her. She had just time to slip between two bars and the huge animal, thwarted, paused.

For years, this occurrence was a topic of conversation in Pont-l'Evêque.

But Félicité took no credit to herself, and probably never knew that she had been heroic.

Virginie occupied her thoughts solely, for the shock she had sustained gave her a nervous affection, and the physician, Monsieur Poupart, prescribed the salt-water bathing at Trouville. In those days, Trouville was not greatly patronised. Madame Aubain gathered information, consulted Bourais, and made preparations as if they were going on an extended trip.

The baggage was sent the day before on Liébard's cart. On the following morning, he brought around two horses, one of which had a woman's saddle with a velveteen back to it, while on the crupper of the other was a rolled shawl that was to be used for a seat. Madame Aubain mounted the second horse, behind Liébard. Félicité took charge of the little girl, and Paul rode Monsieur Lechaptois' donkey, which had been lent for the occasion on the condition that they should be careful of it.

The road was so bad that it took two hours to cover the eight miles. The two horses sank knee-deep into the mud and stumbled into ditches; sometimes they had to jump over them. In certain places, Liébard's mare stopped abruptly. He waited patiently till she started again, and talked of the people whose estates bordered the road, adding his own moral reflections to the outline of their histories. Thus, when they were passing through Toucques, and came to some windows draped with nasturtiums, he shrugged his shoulders and said: "There's a woman, Madame Lehoussais, who, instead of taking a young man—." Félicité could not catch what followed; the horses began to trot, the donkey to gallop, and they turned into a lane; then a gate swung open, two farm-hands appeared and they all dismounted at the very threshold of the farm-house.

Mother Liébard, when she caught sight of her mistress, was lavish with joyful demonstrations. She got up a lunch which comprised a leg of mutton, tripe, sausages, a chicken fricassée, sweet cider, a fruit tart and some preserved prunes; then to all this the good woman added polite remarks about Madame, who appeared to be in better health, Mademoiselle, who had grown to be "superb," and Paul, who had become singularly sturdy; she spoke also of their deceased grandparents, whom the Liébards had known, for they had been in the service of the family for several generations.

Like its owners, the farm had an ancient appearance. The beams of the ceiling were mouldy, the walls black with smoke and the windows grey with dust. The oak sideboard was filled with all sorts of utensils, plates, pitchers, tin bowls, wolf-traps. The children laughed when they saw a huge syringe. There was not a tree in the yard that did not have mushrooms growing around its foot, or a bunch of mistletoe hanging in its branches. Several of the trees had been blown down, but they had started to grow in the middle and all were laden with quantities of apples. The thatched roofs, which were of unequal thickness, looked like brown velvet and could resist the fiercest gales. But the wagon-shed was fast crumbling to ruins. Madame Aubain said that she would attend to it, and then gave orders to have the horses saddled.

It took another thirty minutes to reach Trouville. The little caravan dismounted in order to pass Les Ecores, a cliff that overhangs the bay, and a few minutes later, at the end of the dock, they entered the yard of the Golden Lamb, an inn kept by Mother David.

During the first few days, Virginie felt stronger, owing to the change of air and the action of the sea-baths. She took them in her little chemise, as she had no bathing suit, and afterwards her nurse dressed her in the cabin of a customs officer, which was used for that purpose by the bathers.

In the afternoon, they would take the donkey and go to the Roches-Noires, near Hennequeville. The path led at first through undulating grounds, and then to a plateau, where pastures and tilled fields alternated. At the edge of the road, mingling with the brambles, grew holly bushes, and here and there stood large dead trees whose branches traced zigzags upon the blue sky.

Ordinarily, they rested in a field facing the ocean, with Deauville on their left, and Havre on their right. The sea glittered brightly in the sun and was as smooth as a mirror, and so calm that they could scarcely distinguish its murmur; sparrows chirped joyfully and the immense canopy of heaven spread over it all. Madame Aubain brought out her sewing, and Virginie amused herself by braiding reeds; Félicité wove lavender blossoms, while Paul was bored and wished to go home.

Sometimes they crossed the Toucques River in a boat, and started to hunt for sea-shells. The outgoing tide exposed star-fish and sea-urchins, and the children tried to catch the flakes of foam which the wind blew away. The sleepy waves lapping the sand unfurled themselves along the shore that extended as far as the eye could see, bounded on the land side by the dunes, which separated it from the "Swamp," a large meadow shaped like a hippodrome. When they went home that way, Trouville, on the slope of a hill below, grew larger and larger as they advanced, and, with all its houses of unequal height, seemed to spread out before them in a sort of giddy confusion.

When the heat was too oppressive, they remained in their rooms. The dazzling sunlight cast bars of light between the shutters. Not a sound in the village, not a soul on the sidewalk. This silence intensified the tranquility of everything. In the distance, the hammers of some calkers pounded the hull of a ship, and the sultry breeze brought them an odour of tar.

The principal diversion consisted in watching the return of the fishing-boats. As soon as they passed the beacons, they began to ply to windward. The sails were lowered to one third of the masts, and with their fore-sails swelled up like balloons they glided over the waves and anchored in the middle of the harbour. Then they crept up alongside of the dock and the sailors threw the quivering fish over the side of the boat; a line of carts was waiting for them, and women with white caps sprang forward to receive the baskets and embrace their men-folk.

One day, one of them spoke to Félicité, who, after a little while, returned to the house gleefully. She had found one of her sisters, and presently Nastasie Barette, wife of Léroux, made her appearance, holding an infant in her arms, another child by the hand, while on her left was a little cabin-boy with his hands in his pockets and his cap on his ear.

At the end of fifteen minutes, Madame Aubain bade her go.

They always hung around the kitchen, or approached Félicité when she and the children were out walking. The husband, however, did not show himself.

Félicité developed a great fondness for them; she bought them a stove, some shirts and a blanket; it was evident that they exploited her. Her foolishness annoyed Madame Aubain, who, moreover did not like the nephew's familiarity, for he called her son "thou";—and, as Virginie began to cough and the season was over, she decided to return to Pont-l'Evêque.

Monsieur Bourais assisted her in the choice of a college. The one at Caen was considered the best. So Paul was sent away and bravely said good-bye to them all, for he was glad to go to live in a house where he would have boy companions.

Madame Aubain resigned herself to the separation from her son because it was unavoidable. Virginie brooded less and less over it. Félicité missed the noise he made, but soon a new occupation diverted her mind. Beginning from Christmas, she accompanied the little girl to her catechism lesson every day.

III

After she had made a curtsey at the threshold, she would walk up the aisle between the double lines of chairs, open Madame Aubain's pew, sit down and look around.

Girls and boys, the former on the right, the latter on the left-hand side of the church, filled the stalls of the choir; the priest stood beside the reading-desk; on one stained window of the side aisle, the Holy Ghost hovered over the Virgin; on another one, Mary knelt before the Child Jesus, and behind the altar, a wooden group represented Saint Michael felling the dragon.

The priest first read a condensed lesson of sacred history. Félicité visualized in her imagination Paradise, the Flood, the Tower of Babel, blazing cities, dying nations, and shattered idols; and out of this she developed a great respect for the Almighty and a great fear of His wrath. Then, when she listened to the story of the Passion, she wept. Why had they crucified Him who loved little children, nourished the people, made the blind see, and who, out of humility, had wished to be born among the poor, in a stable? The sowings, the harvests, the wine-presses, all those familiar things which the Scriptures mention, formed a part of her life; the word of God sanctified them; and she loved the lambs with increased tenderness for the sake of the Lamb, and the doves because of the Holy Ghost.

She found it hard, however, to think of the latter as a person, for was it not a bird, a flame, and sometimes only a breath? Perhaps it is its light that at night hovers over swamps, its breath that propels the clouds, its voice that renders church-bells harmonious. And Félicité worshipped devoutly, while enjoying the coolness and the stillness of the church.

As for the dogma, she could not understand it and did not even try. The priest discoursed, the children recited, and she went to sleep, only to awaken with a start when they were leaving the church and their wooden shoes clattered on the stone pavement.

In this way, she learned her catechism, her religious education having been neglected in her youth; and thenceforth she imitated all Virginie's religious practices, fasted when she did, and went to confession with her. At the Corpus-Christi Day they both decorated an altar.

She worried in advance over Virginie's first communion. She fussed about the shoes, the rosary, the book and the gloves. With what nervousness she helped the mother dress the child!

During the entire ceremony, she felt anguished. Monsieur Bourais hid part of the choir from view, but directly in front of her, the flock of maidens, wearing white wreaths over their lowered veils, formed a snow-white field, and she recognized her darling by the slenderness of her neck and her devout attitude. The bell tinkled. All the heads bent and there was a silence. Then, at the peals of the organ the singers and the worshippers struck up the Agnus Dei; the boys' procession began; behind them came the girls. With clasped hands, they advanced step by step to the lighted altar, knelt at the first step, received one by one the Host, and returned to their seats in the same order. When Virginie's turn came, Félicité leaned forward to watch her, and through that imagination which springs from true affection, she at once became the child, whose face and dress became hers, whose heart beat in her bosom, and when Virginie opened her mouth and closed her eyes, she did likewise and came very near fainting.

The following day, she presented herself early at the church so as to receive communion from the curé. She took it with the proper feeling, but did not experience the same delight as on the previous day.

Madame Aubain wished to make an accomplished girl out of her daughter; and as Guyot could not teach English or music, she decided to send her to the Ursulines at Honfleur.

The child made no objection, but Félicité sighed and thought Madame was heartless. Then, she thought that perhaps her mistress was right, as these things were beyond her understanding. Finally, one day, an old *fiacre* stopped in front of the door and a nun stepped out. Félicité put Virginie's luggage on top of the carriage, gave the coachman some instructions, and smuggled six jars of jam, a dozen pears and a bunch of violets under the seat.

At the last minute, Virginie had a fit of sobbing; she embraced her mother again and again, while the latter kissed her on her forehead, and said: "Now, be brave, be brave!" The step was pulled up and the carriage drove off.

Then Madame Aubain had a fainting spell, and that evening all her friends, including the two Lormeaus, Madame Lechaptois, the ladies

Rochefeuille, Messieurs de Houppeville and Bourais, called on her and tendered their sympathy.

At first the separation proved very painful to her. But her daughter wrote her three times a week and the other days she herself wrote to Virginie. Then she walked in the garden, read a little, and in this way managed to fill out the emptiness of the hours.

Each morning, out of habit, Félicité entered Virginie's room and gazed at the walls. She missed combing her hair, lacing her shoes, tucking her in her bed, and the bright face and little hand when they used to go out for a walk. In order to occupy herself she tried to make lace. But her clumsy fingers broke the threads; she had no heart for anything, lost her sleep and "wasted away," as she put it.

In order to have some distraction, she asked leave to have visits from her nephew Victor.

He would come on Sunday, after church, with ruddy cheeks and bared chest, bringing with him the scent of the country. She would set the table and they would sit down opposite each other, and eat their dinner; she ate as little as possible, herself, to avoid any extra expense, but would stuff him so with food that he would finally go to sleep. At the first stroke of vespers, she would wake him up, brush his trousers, tie his cravat and walk to church with him, leaning on his arm with maternal pride.

His parents always told him to get something out of her, either a package of brown sugar, or soap, or brandy, and sometimes even money. He brought her his clothes to mend, and she accepted the task gladly, because it meant another visit from him.

In August, his father took him on a coasting-vessel.

It was vacation time and the arrival of the children consoled Félicité. But Paul was capricious, and Virginie was growing too old to be thee'd-and-thou'd, a fact which seemed to produce a sort of embarrassment in their relations.

Victor went successively to Morlaix, to Dunkirk, and to Brighton; whenever he returned from a trip he would bring her a present. The first time it was a box of shells; the second, a coffee-cup; the third, a big doll of ginger-bread. He was growing handsome, had a good figure, a tiny moustache, kind eyes, and a little leather cap that sat jauntily on the back of his head. He amused his aunt by telling her stories mingled with nautical expressions.

One Monday, the 14th of July, 1819 (she never forgot the date), Victor announced that he had been engaged on a merchant-vessel and that in two days he would take the steamer at Honfleur and join his boat, which was going to start from Havre very soon. Perhaps he might be away two years.

The prospect of his departure filled Félicité with despair, and in order to bid him farewell, on Wednesday night, after Madame's dinner, she put on her pattens and trudged the four miles that separated Pont-l'Evêque from Honfleur.

When she reached the Calvary, instead of turning to the right, she turned to the left and lost herself in coal-yards; she had to retrace her steps; some people she spoke to advised her to hasten. She walked helplessly around the harbour filled with vessels, and knocked against hawsers. Presently the ground sloped abruptly, lights flitted to and fro, and she thought all at once that she had gone mad when she saw some horses in the sky.

Others, on the edge of the dock, neighed at the sight of the ocean. A derrick pulled them up in the air and dumped them into a boat, where passengers were bustling about among barrels of cider, baskets of cheese and bags of meal; chickens cackled, the captain swore and a cabin-boy rested on the railing, apparently indifferent to his surroundings. Félicité, who did not recognise him, kept shouting: "Victor!" He suddenly raised his eyes, but while she was preparing to rush up to him, they withdrew the gangplank.

The packet, towed by singing women, glided out of the harbour. Her hull squeaked and the heavy waves beat up against her sides. The sail had turned and nobody was visible;—and on the ocean, silvered by the light of the moon, the vessel formed a black spot that grew dimmer and dimmer, and finally disappeared.

When Félicité passed the Calvary again, she felt as if she must entrust that which was dearest to her to the Lord; and for a long while she prayed, with uplifted eyes and a face wet with tears. The city was sleeping; some customs officials were strolling in the fresh air; and the water kept pouring through the holes of the dam with a deafening roar. The town clock struck two.

The parlour of the convent would not open until morning, and surely a delay would annoy Madame; so, in spite of her desire to see the other child, she went home. The maids of the inn were just arising when she reached Pont-l'Evêque.

So the poor boy would be on the ocean for months! His previous trips had not alarmed her. One can come back from England and Brittany; but America, the colonies, the islands, were all lost in an uncertain region at the very end of the world.

From that time on, Félicité thought solely of her nephew. On warm days she feared he would suffer from thirst, and when it stormed, she was afraid he would be struck by lightning. When she harkened to the wind that rattled in the chimney and dislodged the tiles on the roof, she imagined that he was being buffeted by the same storm, perched on top of a shattered mast, with his whole body bent backward and covered with sea-foam; or—these were recollections of the engraved geography book—he was being devoured by savages, or captured in a forest by apes, or dying on some lonely coast. She never mentioned her anxieties, however.

Madame Aubain worried about her daughter.

The sisters thought that Virginie was affectionate but delicate. The slightest emotion enervated her. She had to give up her piano lessons. Her mother insisted upon regular letters from the convent. One morning, when the postman failed to come, she grew impatient and began to pace to and fro, from her chair to the window. It was really extraordinary! No news for four days.

In order to console her mistress by her own example, Félicité said:

"Why, Madame, I haven't had any news since six months."—

"From whom?"—

The servant replied gently:

"Why—from my nephew."

"Oh, yes, your nephew!" And shrugging her shoulders, Madame Aubain continued to pace the floor as if to say: "I did not think of it.—Besides, I do not care, a cabin-boy, a pauper!—but my daughter—what a difference! just think of it!—"

Félicité, although she had been reared roughly, was very indignant. Then she forgot about it .

It appeared quite natural to her that one should lose one's head about Virginie.

To her the two children were of equal importance; they were united in her heart and their fate was to be the same.

The chemist informed her that Victor's vessel had reached Havana. He had read the information in a newspaper.

Félicité imagined that Havana was a place where people did nothing but smoke, and that Victor walked around among Negroes in a cloud of tobacco. Could a person, in case of need, return by land? How far was it from Pont-l'Evêque? In order to learn these things, she questioned Monsieur Bourais. He reached for his map and began some explanations concerning longitudes, and smiled with superiority at Félicité's bewilderment. At last, he took his pencil and pointed out an imperceptible black point in the scallops of an oval blotch, adding: "There it is." She bent over the map; the maze of coloured lines hurt her eyes without enlightening her; and when Bourais asked her what puzzled her, she requested him to show her the house Victor lived in. Bourais threw up his hands, sneezed, and then laughed uproariously; such ignorance delighted his soul; but Félicité failed to understand the cause of his mirth, she whose intelligence was so limited that she perhaps expected to see even the picture of her nephew!

It was two weeks later that Liébard came into the kitchen at market-time, and handed her a letter from her brother-in-law. As neither of them could read, she called upon her mistress.

Madame Aubain, who was counting the stitches of her knitting, laid her work down beside her, opened the letter, started, and in a low tone and with a searching look said: "They tell you of a—misfortune. Your nephew—."

He had died. The letter told nothing more.

Félicité dropped on a chair, leaned her head against the back and closed her eyelids; presently they grew pink. Then, with drooping head, inert hands and staring eyes she repeated at intervals:

"Poor little chap! poor little chap!" Liébard watched her and sighed. Madame Aubain was trembling. She suggested to Félicité that she go to see her sister in Trouville. With a gesture, Félicité replied that it was not necessary.

There was a silence. Old Liébard thought it about time for him to take leave.

Then Félicité said:

"They have no sympathy, they do not care!"

Her head fell forward again, and from time to time, mechanically, she toyed with the long knitting-needles on the work-table.

Some women passed through the yard with a basket of wet clothes. When she saw them through the window, she suddenly remembered her own wash; as she had soaked it the day before, she must go and rinse it now. So she rose and left the room.

Her tub and her board were on the bank of the Toucques. She threw a heap of clothes on the ground, rolled up her sleeves and with her wooden beater, made loud pounding which could be heard in the neighbouring gardens. The meadows were empty, the breeze wrinkled the stream, at the bottom of which were long grasses that looked like the hair of corpses floating in the water. She restrained her sorrow and was very brave until night; but, when she had gone to her own room, she gave way to it, burying her face in the pillow and pressing her two fists against her temples.

A long while afterward, she learned through Victor's captain the circumstances which surrounded his death. At the hospital they had bled him too much, treating him for yellow fever. Four doctors held him at one time. He died almost instantly, and the chief surgeon had said:

"Here goes another one!"

His parents had always treated him barbarously; she preferred not to see them again, and they made no advances, either from forgetfulness or out of innate hardness.

Virginie was growing weaker.

A cough, continual fever, oppressive breathing and spots on her cheeks indicated some serious trouble. Monsieur Poupart had advised a sojourn in Provence. Madame Aubain decided that they would go, and she would have had her daughter come home at once, had it not been for the climate of Pont-l'Evêque.

She made an arrangement with a livery-stable man who drove her over to the convent every Tuesday. In the garden there was a terrace, from which the view extended to the Seine. Virginie walked in it, leaning on her mother's arm and treading the dead vine leaves. Sometimes the sun, shining through the clouds, made her blink her lids, when she gazed at the sails in the distance, and let her eyes roam over the horizon from the château of Tancarville to the lighthouses of Havre. Then they rested in the arbour. Her mother had brought a little cask of fine Malaga wine, and Virginie, laughing at the idea of becoming intoxicated, would drink a few drops of it, but never more.

Her strength returned. Autumn passed. Félicité began to reassure Madame Aubain. But, one evening, when she returned home after an errand, she met Monsieur Poupart's coach in front of the door; Monsieur

Poupart himself was standing in the vestibule and Madame Aubain was tying the strings of her bonnet. "Give me my foot-warmer, my purse and my gloves; and be quick about it," she said.

Virginie had congestion of the lungs; perhaps it was desperate.

"Not yet," said the physician, and both got into the carriage, while the snow fell in thick flakes. It was almost night and very cold.

Félicité rushed to the church to light a candle. Then she ran after the coach, which she overtook after an hour's chase, sprang up behind and held onto the straps. But suddenly a thought crossed her mind: "The yard had been left open; supposing that burglars got in!" And down she jumped.

The next morning, at daybreak, she called at the doctor's. He had been home, but had left again. Then she waited at the inn, thinking that strangers might bring her a letter. At last, at daylight she took the diligence for Lisieux.

The convent was at the end of a steep and narrow street. When she arrived about half way, she heard strange noises, a funeral knell. "It must be for some one else," thought she; and she pulled the knocker violently.

After several minutes had elapsed, she heard footsteps, the door was half opened, and a nun appeared. The good sister, with an air of compunction, told her that "she had just passed away." And at the same time the tolling of Saint-Léonard's increased.

Félicité reached the second floor. Already at the threshold, she caught sight of Virginie lying on her back, with clasped hands, her mouth open and her head thrown back, beneath a black crucifix inclined toward her, and stiff curtains which were less white than her face. Madame Aubain lay at the foot of the couch, clasping it with her arms and uttering groans of agony. The Mother Superior was standing on the right side of the bed. The three candles on the bureau made red blurs, and the windows were dimmed by the fog outside. The nuns carried Madame Aubain from the room.

For two nights, Félicité never left the corpse. She would repeat the same prayers, sprinkle holy water over the sheets, get up, come back to the bed and contemplate the body. At the end of the first vigil, she noticed that the face had taken on a yellow tinge, the lips grew blue, the nose grew pinched, the eyes were sunken. She kissed them several times and would not have been greatly astonished had Virginie opened them; to souls like these the supernatural is always quite simple. She washed her, wrapped her in a shroud, put her into the casket, laid a wreath of flowers on her head and arranged her curls. They were blonde and of an extraordinary length for her age. Félicité cut off a big lock and put half of it into her bosom, resolving never to part with it.

The body was taken to Pont-l'Evêque, according to Madame Aubain's wishes; she followed the hearse in a closed carriage.

After the ceremony it took three quarters of an hour to reach the cemetery. Paul, sobbing, headed the procession; Monsieur Bourais followed, and then came the principal inhabitants of the town, the women covered with black capes, and Félicité. The memory of her nephew, and the thought that she had not been able to render him these honours, made her doubly unhappy, and she felt as if he were being buried with Virginie.

Madame Aubain's grief was uncontrollable. At first she rebelled against God, thinking that he was unjust to have taken away her child—she who had never done anything wrong, and whose conscience was so pure! But no! she ought to have taken her South. Other doctors would have saved her. She accused herself, prayed to be able to join her child, and cried in the midst of her dreams. Of the latter, one more especially haunted her. Her husband, dressed like a sailor, had come back from a long voyage, and with tears in his eyes told her that he had received the order to take Virginie away. Then they both consulted about a hiding-place.

Once she came in from the garden, all upset. A moment before (and she showed the place), the father and daughter had appeared to her, one after the other; they did nothing but look at her.

During several months she remained inert in her room. Félicité scolded her gently; she must keep up for her son and also for the other one, for "her memory."

"Her memory!" replied Madame Aubain, as if she were just awakening, "Oh! yes, yes, you do not forget her!" This was an allusion to the cemetery where she had been expressly forbidden to go.

But Félicité went there every day. At four o'clock exactly, she would go through the town, climb the hill, open the gate and arrive at Virginie's tomb. It was a small column of pink marble with a flat stone at its base, and it was surrounded by a little plot enclosed by chains. The flower-beds were bright with blossoms. Félicité watered their leaves, renewed the gravel, and knelt on the ground in order to till the earth properly. When Madame Aubain was able to visit the cemetery she felt very much relieved and consoled.

Years passed, all alike and marked by no other events than the return of the great church holidays: Easter, Assumption, All Saints' Day. Household happenings constituted the only data to which in later years they often referred. Thus, in 1825, workmen painted the vestibule; in 1827, a portion of the roof almost killed a man by falling into the yard. In the summer of 1828, it was Madame's turn to offer the hallowed bread; at that time, Bourais disappeared mysteriously; and the old acquaintances, Guyot, Liébard, Madame Lechaptois, Robelin, old Grémanville, paralysed for a long time, passed away one by one. One night, the driver of the mail in Pont-l'Evêque announced the Revolution of July. A few days afterward a new sub-prefect was nominated, the Baron de Larsonnière, ex-consul in America, who, besides his wife, had his sister-in-law and her three grown daughters with him. They were often seen on their lawn, dressed in loose blouses, and they had a parrot and a Negro servant. Madame Aubain received a call, which she returned promptly. As soon as she caught sight of them, Félicité would run and notify her mistress. But only one thing was capable of arousing her: a letter from her son.

He could not follow any profession as he was absorbed in drinking. His mother paid his debts and he made fresh ones; and the sighs that she heaved while she knitted at the window reached the ears of Félicité who was spinning in the kitchen.

They walked in the garden together, always speaking of Virginie, and asking each other if such and such a thing would have pleased her, and what she would probably have said on this or that occasion.

All her little belongings were put away in a closet of the room which held the two little beds. But Madame Aubain looked them over as little as possible. One summer day, however, she resigned herself to the task, and when she opened the closet the moths flew out.

Virginie's frocks were hung under a shelf where there were three dolls, some hoops, a doll-house, and a basin which she had used. Félicité and Madame Aubain also took out the skirts, the handkerchiefs, and the stockings and spread them on the beds, before putting them away again. The sun fell on the piteous things, disclosing their spots and the creases formed by the motions of the body. The air was warm and the sky blue, and blackbirds trilled in the garden; everything seemed bathed in happiness. They found a little hat of soft brown plush, but it was entirely moth-eaten. Félicité asked for it. Their eyes met and filled with tears; at last the mistress opened her arms and the servant threw herself against her breast and they hugged each other, giving vent to their grief in a kiss which equalized them for a moment.

It was the first time that this had ever happened, for Madame Aubain was not of an expansive nature. Félicité was as grateful for it as if it had been some favour, and thenceforth loved her with animal-like devotion and a religious veneration.

Her kind-heartedness increased. When she heard the drums of a marching regiment passing through the street, she would stand in the doorway with a jug of cider and give the soldiers a drink. She nursed cholera victims. She protected Polish refugees, and one of them even declared that he wished to marry her. But they quarrelled, for one morning when she returned from the Angelus she found him in the kitchen coolly eating a dish which he had prepared for himself during her absence.

After the Polish refugees, came Colmiche, an old man who was credited with having committed frightful misdeeds in '93. He lived near the river in the ruins of a pig-sty. The children watched him through the cracks in the walls and threw stones that fell on his miserable bed, where he lay gasping with catarrh, with long hair, inflamed eyelids, and a tumour as big as his head on one arm.

She got him some linen, tried to clean his hovel and dreamed of installing him in the bake-house without his being in Madame's way. When the cancer broke, she dressed it every day; sometimes she brought him some cake and placed him in the sun on a bundle of hay; and the poor old creature, trembling and drooling, would thank her in his broken voice, and put out his hands whenever she left him. Finally he died; and she had a mass said for the repose of his soul.

That day a great joy came to her: at dinner-time, Madame de Larsonnière's servant called with the parrot, its cage, and perch, chain, and lock. A note from the baroness told Madame Aubain that as her husband had been promoted to a prefecture, they were leaving that night, and she begged her to accept the bird as a remembrance and a token of her esteem.

For a long time the parrot had been on Félicité's mind, because he came from America, which reminded her of Victor, and she had approached the Negro on the subject.

Once even, she had said:

"How glad Madame would be to have him!"

The man had repeated this remark to his mistress who, not being able to keep the bird, took this means of getting rid of it.

IV

He was called Loulou. His body was green, his head blue, the tips of his wings were pink and his breast was golden.

But he had the tiresome tricks of biting his perch, pulling his feathers out, scattering refuse and spilling the water of his bath. Madame Aubain grew tired of him and gave him to Félicité for good.

She undertook his education, and soon he was able to repeat: "Pretty boy! Your servant, sir! I salute you, Marie!" His perch was placed near the door and several persons were astonished that he did not answer to the name of "Jacquot," for every parrot is called Jacquot. They called him a goose and a log, and these taunts were like so many dagger thrusts to Félicité. Strange stubbornness on Loulou's part, who would not talk when people watched him!

Nevertheless, he liked society; for on Sunday, when the ladies Rochefeuille, Monsieur de Houppeville and the new habitués, Onfroy, the chemist, Monsieur Varin and Captain Mathieu, dropped in for their game of cards, he struck the window-panes with his wings and made such a racket that it was impossible to talk.

Bourais' face must have appeared very funny to Loulou. As soon as he saw him he would begin to roar. His voice re-echoed in the yard, and the neighbors would come to the windows and begin to laugh, too; and in order that the parrot might not see him, Monsieur Bourais edged along the wall, pushed his hat over his eyes to hide his profile, and entered by the garden door; the looks he gave the bird lacked affection.

Loulou, having once thrust his head into the butcher-boy's basket, received a slap, and from that time he always tried to nip his enemy. Fabu threatened to wring his neck, although he was not cruelly inclined, notwithstanding his big whiskers and tattooings. On the contrary, he rather liked the bird and, out of deviltry, tried to teach him to swear. Félicité, alarmed by these proceedings, put Loulou in the kitchen, took off his chain and let him walk all over the house.

When he went downstairs, he rested his beak on the steps, lifted his right foot and then his left one; but his mistress feared that such feats would make him dizzy. He became ill and was unable to eat. There was a small growth under his tongue like those chickens are afflicted with. Félicité pulled it off with her nails and cured him. One day, Paul was imprudent enough to blow the smoke of his cigar in his face; another time,

Madame Lormeau was teasing him with the tip of her umbrella and he swallowed the tip. Finally he got lost.

She had put him on the grass to cool him and went away only for a second; when she returned, she found no parrot! She hunted among the bushes, on the bank of the river, and on the roofs, without paying any attention to Madame Aubain, who screamed at her: "Take care! You must be insane!" Then she searched every garden in Pont-l'Evêque and stopped the passers-by to inquire of them: "Haven't you perhaps seen my parrot?" To those who had never seen the parrot, she described him minutely. Suddenly she thought she saw something green fluttering behind the mills at the foot of the hill. But when she was at the top of the hill she could not see it. A hawker told her that he had just seen the bird in Saint-Melaine, in Mother Simon's store. Félicité rushed to the place. The people did not know what she was talking about. At last she came home, exhausted, with her slippers worn to shreds, and despair in her heart. She sat down on the bench near Madame and was telling of her search when presently a light weight dropped on her shoulder—Loulou! What the deuce had he been doing? Perhaps he had just taken a little walk around the town!

She did not easily forget her scare; in fact, she never got over it. In consequence of a cold, she developed a sore throat; and some time afterward she had an earache. Three years later she was stone deaf, and spoke in a very loud voice even in church. Although her sins might have been proclaimed throughout the diocese without any shame to herself, or ill effects to the community, the curé thought it advisable to receive her confession in the vestry-room.

Imaginary buzzings also added to her bewilderment. Her mistress often said to her: "My goodness, how stupid you are!" and she would answer: "Yes, Madame," and look for something.

The narrow circle of her ideas grew more restricted than it already was; the bellowing of the oxen, the chime of the bells no longer reached her intelligence. All things moved silently, like ghosts. Only one noise penetrated her ears; the parrot's voice.

As if to divert her mind, he reproduced for her the tick-tack of the spit in the kitchen, the shrill cry of the fish-vendors, the saw of the carpenter who had a shop opposite, and when the door-bell rang, he would imitate Madame Aubain: "Félicité! go to the front door."

They held conversations together, Loulou repeating the three phrases of his repertory over and over, Félicité replying by words that had no greater meaning, but in which she poured out her feelings. In her isolation, the parrot was almost a son, a lover. He climbed upon her fingers, pecked at her lips, clung to her shawl, and when she rocked her head to and fro like a nurse, the big wings of her cap and the wings of the bird flapped in unison. When clouds gathered on the horizon and the thunder rumbled, Loulou would scream, perhaps because he remembered the storms in his native forests. The dripping of the rain would excite him to frenzy; he flapped around, struck the ceiling with his wings, upset everything, and would finally fly into the garden to play. Then he would come back into the room, light on one of the andirons, and hop around in order to get dry.

One morning during the terrible winter of 1837, when she had put him in front of the fire-place on account of the cold, she found him dead in his cage, hanging to the wire bars with his head down. He had probably died of congestion. But she believed that he had been poisoned, and although she had no proof whatever, her suspicion rested on Fabu.

She wept so sorely that her mistress said: "Why don't you have him stuffed?"

She asked the advice of the chemist, who had always been kind to the bird.

He wrote to Havre for her. A certain man named Fellacher consented to do the work. But, as the coach driver often lost parcels entrusted to him, Félicité resolved to take him to Honfleur herself.

Leafless apple-trees lined the edges of the road. The ditches were covered with ice. The dogs on the neighboring farms barked; and Félicité, with her hands beneath her cape, her little black sabots and her basket, trotted along nimbly in the middle of the road. She crossed the forest, passed by the Haut-Chêne and reached Saint-Gatien.

Behind her, in a cloud of dust and impelled by the steep incline, a mail-coach drawn by galloping horses advanced like a whirlwind. When he saw a woman in the middle of the road, who did not get out of the way, the driver stood up in his seat and shouted to her and so did the postilion, while the four horses, which he could not hold back, accelerated their pace; the two leaders were almost upon her; with a jerk of the reins he threw them to one side, but, furious at the incident, he lifted his big whip and lashed her from her head to her feet with such violence that she fell to the ground unconscious.

Her first thought, when she recovered consciousness, was to open the basket. Loulou was unharmed. She felt a sting on her right cheek; when she took her hand away it was red, for the blood was flowing.

She sat down on a pile of stones, and dried her cheek with her handkerchief; then she ate a crust of bread she had put in her basket, and consoled herself by looking at the bird.

Arriving at the top of Ecquemanville, she saw the lights of Honfleur shining in the distance like so many stars; further on, the ocean spread out in a confused mass. Then a weakness came over her; the misery of her childhood, the disappointment of her first love, the departure of her nephew, the death of Virginie; all these things came back to her at once, and, rising like a swelling tide in her throat, almost choked her.

Then she wished to speak to the captain of the vessel, and without stating what she was sending, she gave him some instructions.

Fellacher kept the parrot a long time. He always promised that it would be ready for the following week; after six months he announced the shipment of a case, and that was the end of it. Really, it seemed as if Loulou would never come back to his home. "They have stolen him," thought Félicité.

Finally he arrived, sitting bolt upright on a branch which could be screwed into a mahogany pedestal, with his foot in the air, his head on one side, and in his beak a nut which the taxidermist, with a taste for show, had gilded. She put him in her room.

This place, to which only a chosen few were admitted, looked like a chapel and a second-hand shop, so filled was it with devotional and heterogeneous things. The door could not be opened easily on account of the presence of a large wardrobe. Opposite the window that looked out into the garden, a small round window opened on the yard; a table was placed by the cot and held a wash-basin, two combs, and a piece of blue soap in a broken saucer. On the walls were rosaries, medals, a number of Holy Virgins, and a holy-water basin made out of a coconut; on the bureau, which was covered with a napkin like an altar, stood the box of shells that Victor had given her; also a watering-can and a balloon, writing books, the engraved geography book and a pair of shoes; on the nail which held the mirror hung Virginie's little plush hat! Félicité carried this sort of respect so far that she even kept one of Monsieur's old coats. All the things which Madame Aubain discarded, Félicité begged for her own room. Thus, she had artificial flowers on the edge of the bureau, and the picture of the Comte d'Artois in the recess of the window. By means of a board, Loulou was set on a portion of the chimney which advanced into the room. Every morning when she awoke, she saw him in the dim light of dawn and recalled bygone days and the smallest details of insignificant actions, without any sense of bitterness or grief.

As she was unable to communicate with people, she lived in a sort of somnambulistic torpor. The processions of Corpus-Christi Day seemed to wake her up. She visited the neighbours to beg for candlesticks and mats so as to adorn the temporary altars in the street.

In church, she always gazed at the Holy Ghost, and noticed that there was something about it that resembled a parrot. The likeness appeared even more striking on an Epinal color-print, representing the baptism of our Saviour. With his scarlet wings and emerald body, it was really the image of Loulou. Having bought the picture, she hung it instead of that of the Comte d'Artois next to Loulou so that she could take them in at one glance.

They were associated in her mind, the parrot becoming sanctified through the neighborhood of the Holy Ghost, and the latter becoming more lifelike in her eyes, and more comprehensible. In all probability our Father had never chosen to express himself through a dove, as the latter cannot speak; it must have surely been one of Loulou's ancestors. And Félicité said her prayers in front of the colored picture, though from time to time she turned slightly toward the bird.

She desired very much to enter in the ranks of the "Daughters of the Virgin." But Madame Aubain dissuaded her from it.

A most important event occurred: Paul's marriage.

After being first a notary's clerk, then in business, then in the customs, and a tax collector, and having even applied for a position in the administration of woods and forests, he had at last, when he was thirty-six years old, by a divine inspiration, found his vocation: the Registrar's

Office! and he displayed such a high ability that an inspector had offered him his daughter's hand and promised him his influence.

Paul, who had become quite settled, brought his bride to visit his mother.

But she looked down upon the customs of Pont-l'Evêque, put on airs, and hurt Félicité's feelings. Madame Aubain felt relieved when she left.

The following week they learned of Monsieur Bourais' death in an inn. There were rumours of suicide, which were confirmed; doubts concerning his integrity arose. Madame Aubain looked over her accounts and soon discovered his numerous embezzlements; sales of wood which had been concealed from her, false receipts, etc. Furthermore, he had an illegitimate child, and entertained a friendship for "a person in Dozulé."

These base actions affected her very much. In March, 1853, she developed a pain in her chest; her tongue looked as if it were coated with smoke, and the leeches they applied did not relieve her oppression; and on the ninth evening she died, being just seventy-two years old.

People thought that she was younger, because her hair, which she wore in bands framing her pale face, was brown. Few friends regretted her loss, for her stiffness had kept people at a distance. Félicité mourned for her as servants seldom mourn for their masters. The fact that Madame should die before her perplexed her mind and seemed contrary to the order of things, and absolutely monstrous and inadmissible. Ten days later (the time to journey from Besançon), the heirs arrived. Her daughter-in-law ransacked the drawers, kept some of the furniture, and sold the rest; then they went back to their own home.

Madame's armchair, foot-warmer, work-table, the eight chairs, everything was gone! The places occupied by the pictures formed yellow squares on the walls. They had taken the two little beds, and the wardrobe had been emptied of Virginie's belongings! Félicité went upstairs, overcome with grief.

The following day a sign was posted on the door; the chemist screamed in her ear that the house was for sale.

For a moment she tottered, and had to sit down.

What hurt her most was to give up her room,—so nice for poor Loulou! She would glance at him in despair as she implored the Holy Ghost, and it was this way that she contracted the idolatrous habit of saying her prayers kneeling in front of the bird. Sometimes the sun fell through the window on his glass eye, and lighted a great spark in it which sent Félicité into ecstasy.

Her mistress had left her an income of three hundred and eighty francs. The garden supplied her with vegetables. As for clothes, she had enough to last her till the end of her days, and she economised on the light by going to bed at dusk.

She rarely went out, in order to avoid passing in front of the second-hand dealer's shop where there was some of the old furniture. Since her fainting spell, she dragged her leg, and as her strength was failing rapidly, old Mother Simon, who had lost her money in the grocery business, came every morning to chop the wood and pump the water.

Her eyesight grew dim. She did not open the shutters after that. Many years passed. But the house did not sell or rent. Fearing that she would be put out, Félicité did not ask for repairs. The laths of the roof were rotting away, and during one whole winter her bolster was wet. After Easter she spit blood.

Then Mother Simon went for a doctor. Félicité wished to know what her complaint was. But, being too deaf to hear, she caught only one word: "Pneumonia." She was familiar with it and gently answered:—"Ah! like Madame," thinking it quite natural that she should follow her mistress.

The time for the festal shrines in the street drew near.

The first one was always erected at the foot of the hill, the second in front of the post-office, and the third in the middle of the street. This last position occasioned some rivalry, and the parish ended by choosing Madame Aubain's yard.

Félicité's fever grew worse. She was sorry that she could not do anything for the altar. If she could, at least, have contributed something toward it! Then she thought of the parrot. Her neighbors objected that it would not be proper. But the curé gave his consent and she was so grateful for it that she begged him to accept after her death, her only treasure, Loulou. From Tuesday until Saturday, the day before the event, she coughed more frequently. In the evening her face was contracted, her lips stuck to her gums and she began to vomit; and on the following day, she felt so low that she called for a priest.

Three neighbors surrounded her when the dominie administered the extreme unction. Afterwards she said that she wished to speak to Fabu.

He arrived in his Sunday clothes, very ill at ease among the funeral surroundings.

"Forgive me," she said, making an effort to extend her arm, "I believed it was you who killed him!"

What did such accusations mean? Suspect a man like him of murder! And Fabu became excited and was about to make trouble.

"Don't you see she is not in her right mind?"

From time to time Félicité spoke to shadows. The women left her and Mother Simon sat down to breakfast.

A little later, she took Loulou and holding him up to Félicité:

"Say good-bye to him, now!" she commanded.

Although he was not a corpse, he was eaten up by worms; one of his wings was broken and the wadding was coming out of his body. But Félicité was blind now, and she took him and laid him against her cheek. Then Mother Simon removed him in order to set him on the altar.

V

The grass exhaled an odour of summer; flies buzzed in the air, the sun shone on the river and warmed the slated roof. Old Mother Simon had returned to Félicité and was peacefully falling asleep.

The ringing of bells woke her; the people were coming out of church. Félicité's delirium subsided. By thinking of the procession, she was able to see it as if she had taken part in it. All the school-children, the singers and the firemen walked on the sidewalks, while in the middle of the street came first the custodian of the church with his halberd, then the beadle with a large cross, the teacher in charge of the boys and a sister escorting the little girls; three of the smallest ones, with curly heads, threw rose leaves into the air; the deacon with outstretched arms conducted the music; and two incense-bearers turned with each step they took toward the Holy Sacrament, which was carried by Monsieur le Curé, attired in his handsome chasuble and walking under a canopy of red velvet supported by four men. A crowd of people followed, jammed between the walls of the houses hung with white sheets; at last the procession arrived at the foot of the hill.

A cold sweat broke out on Félicité's forehead. Mother Simon wiped it away with a cloth, saying inwardly that some day she would have to go through the same thing herself.

The murmur of the crowd grew louder, was very distinct for a moment and then died away. A volley of musketry shook the window-panes. It was the postilions saluting the Sacrament. Félicité rolled her eyes and said as loudly as she could:

"Is he all right?" meaning the parrot.

Her death agony began. A rattle that grew more and more rapid shook her body. Froth appeared at the corners of her mouth, and her whole frame trembled. In a little while could be heard the music of the bass horns, the clear voices of the children and the men's deeper notes. At intervals all was still, and their shoes sounded like a herd of cattle passing over the grass.

The clergy appeared in the yard. Mother Simon climbed on a chair to reach the attic window, and in this manner could see the altar. It was covered with a lace cloth and draped with green wreaths. In the middle stood a little frame containing relics; at the corners were two little orange-trees, and all along the edge were silver candlesticks, porcelain vases containing sun-flowers, lilies, peonies, and tufts of hydrangeas. This mound of bright colours descended diagonally from the first floor to the carpet that covered the sidewalk. Rare objects arrested one's eye. A golden sugar-bowl was crowned with violets, earrings set with Alençon stones were displayed on green moss, and two Chinese screens with their bright landscapes were near by. Loulou, hidden beneath roses, showed nothing but his blue head which looked like a piece of lapis-lazuli.

The singers, the canopy-bearers and the children lined up against the side of the yard. Slowly the priest ascended the steps and placed his radiant shining sun on the lace cloth. Everybody knelt. There was deep silence; and the censers slipping on their chains were swung high in the air. A blue vapour rose in Félicité's room. She opened her nostrils and inhaled it with a mystic sensuousness; then she closed her lids. Her lips smiled. The beats of the heart grew fainter and fainter, and vaguer, like a fountain giving out, like an echo dying away;—and when she exhaled her last breath, she thought she saw in the half-opened heavens a gigantic parrot hovering above her head.

Guy de Maupassant

Guy de Maupassant (1850–1893) was born near Dieppe. He studied briefly for the law, and after serving in the Franco-Prussian War, accepted an administrative government post. Gustave Flaubert, then a leading French novelist, and a friend of Maupassant's family, undertook the younger man's training as a writer, but barely lived to see Maupassant's story, "Boule de Suif," unanimously acclaimed a masterpiece (1880). Maupassant's writing career was brief, but he produced several collections of short stories and novels, best known among them, La Maison Tellier *(1881),* Mademoiselle Fifi *(1883), and the novel* Pierre et Jean *(1880). "'Useless Beauty'" he noted, "is the finest story I ever wrote. It is nothing but a symbol." It was published shortly before he suffered a complete mental collapse in 1891.* *(See page 82 of Introduction.)*

USELESS BEAUTY

I

A very elegant victoria, with two beautiful black horses, was drawn up in front of the mansion. It was a day in the latter end of June, about half past five in the afternoon, and the sun shone warm and bright into the large courtyard.

The Countess de Mascaret came down just as her husband, who was coming home, appeared in the carriage entrance. He stopped for a few moments to look at his wife and grew rather pale. She was very beautiful, graceful, and distinguished-looking, with her long oval face, her complexion like gilt ivory, her large gray eyes, and her black hair; and she got into her carriage without looking at him, without even seeming to have noticed him, with such a particularly high-bred air, that the furious jealousy by which he had been devoured for so long again gnawed at his heart. He went up to her and said: "You are going for a drive?"

She merely replied disdainfully: "You see I am!"

"In the Bois de Boulogne?"

"Most probably."

"May I come with you?"

"The carriage belongs to you."

Without being surprised at the tone of voice in which she answered him, he got in and sat down by his wife's side, and said: "Bois de Boulogne." The footman jumped up by the coachman's side, and the horses as usual pawed the ground and shook their heads until they were in the street. Husband and wife sat side by side, without speaking. He was thinking how to begin a conversation, but she maintained such an obstinately hard look, that he did not venture to make the attempt. At last, however, he cunningly, accidentally as it were, touched the Countess's gloved hand with his own, but she drew her arm away, with a movement which was so expressive of disgust, that he remained thoughtful, in spite of his usual authoritative and despotic character. "Gabrielle!" said he at last.

"What do you want?"

"I think you are looking adorable."

She did not reply, but remained lying back in the carriage, looking like an irritated queen. By that time they were driving up the Champs-Elysées, toward the Arc de Triomphe. That immense monument, at the end of the long avenue, raised its colossal arch against the red sky, and the sun seemed to be sinking on to it, showering fiery dust on it from the sky.

The streams of carriages, with the sun reflecting from the bright, plated harness and the shining lamps, were like a double current flowing, one toward the town and one toward the wood, and the Count de Mascaret continued: "My dear Gabrielle!"

Then, unable to bear it any longer, she replied in an exasperated voice: "Oh! do leave me in peace, pray; I am not even at liberty to have my carriage to myself, now." He, however, pretended not to hear her, and continued: "You have never looked so pretty as you do to-day."

Her patience was decidedly at an end, and she replied with irrepressible anger: "You are wrong to notice it, for I swear to you that I will never have anything to do with you in that way again." He was stupefied and agitated, and his violent nature gaining the upper hand, he exclaimed: "What do you mean by that?" in such a manner as revealed rather the brutal master than the amorous man. But she replied in a low voice, so that the servants might not hear, amid the deafening noise of the wheels:

"Ah! What do I mean by that? What do I mean by that? Now I recognize you again! Do you want me to tell everything?"

"Yes."

"Everything that has been on my heart, since I have been the victim of your terrible selfishness?"

He had grown red with surprise and anger, and he growled between his closed teeth: "Yes, tell me everything."

He was a tall, broad-shouldered man, with a big, red beard, a handsome man, a nobleman, a man of the world, who passed as a perfect husband and an excellent father, and now for the first time since they had started she turned toward him, and looked him full in the face: "Ah! You will hear some disagreeable things, but you must know that I am prepared for everything, that I fear nothing, and you less than anyone, to-day."

He also was looking into her eyes, and already was shaking with passion; then he said in a low voice: "You are mad."

"No, but I will no longer be the victim of the hateful penalty of maternity, which you have inflicted on me for eleven years! I wish to live like a woman of the world, as I have the right to do, as all women have the right to do."

He suddenly grew pale again, and stammered: "I do not understand you."

"Oh! yes; you understand me well enough. It is now three months since I had my last child, and as I am still very beautiful, and as, in spite of all your efforts you cannot spoil my figure, as you just now perceived, when you saw me on the outside flight of steps, you think it is time that I should become *enceinte* again."

"But you are talking nonsense!"

"No, I am not; I am thirty, and I have had seven children, and we have been married eleven years, and you hope that this will go on for ten years longer, after which you will leave off being jealous."

He seized her arm and squeezed it, saying: "I will not allow you to talk to me like that, for long."

"And I shall talk to you till the end until I have finished all I have to say to you, and if you try to prevent me, I shall raise my voice so that the two servants, who are on the box, may hear. I only allowed you to come with me for that object, for I have these witnesses, who will oblige you to listen to me, and to contain yourself; so now, pay attention to what I say. I have always felt an antipathy for you, and I have always let you see it, for I have never lied, Monsieur. You married me in spite of myself; you forced my parents, who were in embarrassed circumstances, to give me to you, because you were rich, and they obliged me to marry you, in spite of my tears.

"So you bought me, and as soon as I was in your power, as soon as I had become your companion, ready to attach myself to you, to forget your coercive and threatening proceedings, in order that I might only remember that I ought to be a devoted wife and to love you as much as it might be possible for me to love you, you became jealous—you—as no man has ever been before, with the base, ignoble jealousy of a spy, which was as degrading for you as it was for me. I had not been married eight months, when you suspected me of every perfidiousness, and you even told me so. What a disgrace! And as you could not prevent me from being beautiful, and from pleasing people, from being called in drawing-rooms, and also in the newspapers, one of the most beautiful women in Paris, you tried everything you could think of to keep admirers from me, and you hit upon the abominable idea of making me spend my life in a constant state of motherhood, until the time when I should disgust every man. Oh! do not deny it! I did not understand it for some time, but then I guessed it. You even boasted about it to your sister, who told me of it, for she is fond of men and was disgusted at your boorish coarseness.

"Ah! Remember our struggles, doors smashed in, and locks forced! For eleven years you have condemned me to the existence of a brood mare. Then as soon as I was pregnant, you grew disgusted with me, and I saw nothing of you for months, and I was sent into the country, to the family mansion, among fields and meadows, to bring forth my child. And when I reappeared, fresh, pretty, and indestructible, still seductive and constantly surrounded by admirers, hoping that at last I should live a little like a young rich woman who belongs to society, you were seized by jealousy again, and you recommenced to persecute me with that infamous and hateful desire from which you are suffering at this moment, by my side.

And it is not the desire of possessing me—for I should never have refused myself to you—but it is the wish to make me unsightly.

"Besides this, that abominable and mysterious circumstance took place, which I was a long time in penetrating (for I grew sharp by dint of watching your thoughts and actions). You attached yourself to your children with all the security which they gave you while I bore them in my womb. You felt affection for them, with all your aversion for me, and in spite of your ignoble fears, which were momentarily allayed by your pleasure in seeing me a mother.

"Oh! how often have I noticed that joy in you! I have seen it in your eyes and guessed it. You loved your children as victories, and not because they were of your own blood. They were victories over me, over my youth, over my beauty, over my charms, over the compliments which were paid me, and over those who whispered round me, without paying them to me. And you are proud of them, you make a parade of them, you take them out for drives in your coach in the Bois de Boulogne, and you give them donkey rides at Montmorency. You take them to theatrical matinées so that you may be seen in the midst of them, and that people may say: 'What a kind father!' and that it may be repeated."

He had seized her wrist with savage brutality, and squeezed it so violently that she was quiet, though she nearly cried out with the pain. Then he said to her in a whisper:

"I love my children, do you hear? What you have just told me is disgraceful in a mother. But you belong to me; I am master—your master. I can exact from you what I like and when I like—and I have the law on my side."

He was trying to crush her fingers in the strong grip of his large muscular hand, and she, livid with pain, tried in vain to free them from that vise which was crushing them; the agony made her pant, and the tears came into her eyes. "You see that I am the master, and the stronger," he said. And when he somewhat loosened his grip, she asked him: "Do you think, that I am a religious woman?"

He was surprised and stammered: "Yes."

"Do you think that I could lie, if I swore to the truth of anything to you, before an altar on which Christ's body is?"

"No."

"Will you go with me to some church?"

"What for?"

"You shall see. Will you?"

"If you absolutely wish it, yes."

She raised her voice and said: "Philip!" And the coachman, bending down a little, without taking his eyes from his horses, seemed to turn his ear alone toward his mistress, who said: "Drive to St. Philip-du-Roule's." And the carriage, which had reached the entrance of the Bois de Boulogne, returned to Paris.

Husband and wife did not exchange a word during the drive. When the carriage stopped before the church, Madame de Mascaret jumped out, and entered it, followed by the Count, a few yards behind her. She went, without stopping, as far as the choir-screen, and falling on her knees at a chair, she buried her face in her hand. She prayed for a long time, and he, standing behind her, could see that she was crying. She wept noiselessly, as women do weep when they are in great and poignant grief. There was a kind of undulation in her body, which ended in a little sob, hidden and stifled by her fingers.

But Count de Mascaret thought that the situation was long drawn out, and he touched her on the shoulder. That contact recalled her to herself, as if she had been burned, and getting up, she looked straight into his eyes.

"This is what I have to say to you. I am afraid of nothing, whatever you may do to me. You may kill me if you like. One of your children is not yours, and one only; that I swear to you before God, who hears me here. That is the only revenge which was possible for me, in return for all your abominable male tyrannies, in return for the penal servitude of child-bearing to which you have condemned me. Who was my lover? That you will never know! You may suspect everyone, but you will never find out. I gave myself up to him, without love and without pleasure, only for the sake of betraying you, and he made me a mother. Which is his child? That also you will never know. I have seven; try and find out! I intended to tell you this later, for one cannot completely avenge oneself on a man by deceiving him, unless he knows it. You have driven me to confess it to-day; now I have finished."

She hurried through the church, toward the open door, expecting to hear behind her the quick steps of her husband whom she had defied, and to be knocked to the ground by a blow of his fist, but she heard nothing, and reached her carriage. She jumped into it at a bound, overwhelmed with anguish, and breathless with fear; she called out to the coachman, "Home!" and the horses set off at a quick trot.

II

The Countess de Mascaret was waiting in her room for dinner time, as a criminal sentenced to death awaits the hour of his execution. What was he going to do? Had he come home? Despotic, passionate, ready for any violence as he was, what was he meditating, what had he made up his mind to do? There was no sound in the house, and every moment she looked at the clock. Her maid had come and dressed her for the evening, and had then left the room again. Eight o'clock struck; almost at the same moment there were two knocks at the door, and the butler came in and told her that dinner was ready.

"Has the Count come in?"

"Yes, Madame la Comtesse; he is in the dining-room."

For a moment she felt inclined to arm herself with a small revolver, which she had bought some weeks before, foreseeing the tragedy which was being rehearsed in her heart. But she remembered that all the children would be there, and she took nothing except a smelling-bottle. He rose somewhat ceremoniously from his chair. They exchanged a slight bow, and sat down. The three boys, with their tutor, Abbé Martin, were on her right, and the three girls, with Miss Smith, their English governess, were on her left. The youngest child, who was only three months old, remained upstairs with his nurse.

The Abbé said grace, as was usual when there was no company, for the children did not come down to dinner when there were guests present; then they began dinner. The Countess, suffering from emotion which she had not at all calculated upon, remained with her eyes cast down, while the Count scrutinized, now the three boys, and now the three girls with uncertain, unhappy looks, which traveled from one to the other. Suddenly, pushing his wineglass from him, it broke, and the wine was spilt on the tablecloth, and at the slight noise caused by this little accident, the Countess started up from her chair, and for the first time they looked at each other. Then, almost every moment, in spite of themselves, in spite of the irritation of their nerves caused by every glance, they did not cease to exchange looks, rapid as pistol shots.

The Abbé, who felt that there was some cause for embarrassment which he could not divine, tried to get up a conversation, and started various subjects, but his useless efforts gave rise to no ideas and did not bring out a word. The Countess, with feminine tact and obeying the instincts of a woman of the world, tried to answer him two or three times, but in vain. She could not find words, in the perplexity of her mind, and her own voice almost frightened her in the silence of the large room, where nothing else was heard except the slight sound of plates and knives and forks.

Suddenly, her husband said to her, bending forward: "Here, amid your children, will you swear to me that what you told me just now is true?"

The hatred which was fermenting in her veins suddenly roused her, and replying to that question with the same firmness with which she had replied to his looks, she raised both her hands, the right pointing toward the boys and the left toward the girls, and said in a firm, resolute voice, and without any hesitation: "On the heads of my children, I swear that I have told you the truth."

He got up, and throwing his table napkin on to the table with an exasperated movement, turned round and flung his chair against the wall. Then he went out without another word, while she, uttering a deep sigh, as if after a first victory, went on in a calm voice: "You must not pay any attention to what your father has just said, my darlings; he was very much upset a short time ago, but he will be all right again, in a few days."

Then she talked with the Abbé and with Miss Smith, and had tender, pretty words for all her children; those sweet, spoiling mothers' ways which unlock little hearts.

When dinner was over, she went into the drawing-room with all her little following. She made the elder ones chatter, and when their bedtime came she kissed them for a long time, and then went alone into her room.

She waited, for she had no doubt that he would come, and she made up her mind then, as her children were not with her, to defend her human flesh, as she defended her life as a woman of the world; and in the pocket of her dress she put the little loaded revolver which she had bought a few weeks before. The hours went by, the hours struck, and every sound was hushed in the house. Only the cabs continued to rumble through the streets, but their noise was only heard vaguely through the shuttered and curtained windows.

She waited, energetic and nervous, without any fear of him now, ready for anything, and almost triumphant, for she had found means of torturing him continually, during every moment of his life.

But the first gleams of dawn came in through the fringe at the bottom of her curtains, without his having come into her room, and then she awoke to the fact, much to her surprise that he was not coming. Having locked and bolted her door, for greater security, she went to bed at last, and remained there, with her eyes open, thinking, and barely understanding it all, without being able to guess what he was going to do.

When her maid brought her tea, she at the same time gave her a letter from her husband. He told her that he was going to undertake a longish journey, and in a postscript he added that his lawyer would provide her with such money as she might require for her expenses.

III

It was at the opera, between two of the acts in *Robert the Devil.* In the stalls, the men were standing up, with their hats on, their waistcoats cut very low so as to show a large amount of white shirt front, in which the gold and precious stones of their studs glistened. They were looking at the boxes crowded with ladies in low-cut dresses, covered with diamonds and pearls, women who seemed to expand like flowers in that illuminated hothouse, where the beauty of their faces and the whiteness of their shoulders seemed to bloom for inspection, in the midst of the music and of human voices.

Two friends, with their backs to the orchestra, were scanning those parterres of elegance, that exhibition of real or false charms, of jewels, of luxury, and of pretension which showed itself off all round the Grand Theater. One of them, Roger de Salnis, said to his companion, Bernard Grandin: "Just look how beautiful Countess de Mascaret still is."

Then the elder, in turn, looked through his opera glasses at a tall lady in a box opposite, who appeared to be still very young, and whose striking beauty seemed to appeal to men's eyes in every corner of the house. Her pale complexion, of an ivory tint, gave her the appearance of a statue, while a small, diamond coronet glistened on her black hair like a cluster of stars.

When he had looked at her for some time, Bernard Grandin replied with a jocular accent of sincere conviction: "You may well call her beautiful!"

"How old do you think she is?"

"Wait a moment. I can tell you exactly, for I have known her since she was a child, and I saw her make her *début* into society when she was quite a girl. She is—she is—thirty—thirty-six."

"Impossible!"

"I am sure of it."

"She looks twenty-five."

"She has had seven children."

"It is incredible."

"And what is more, they are all seven alive, as she is a very good mother. I go to the house, which is a very quiet and pleasant one, occasionally. Her respect for family life is made quite clear."

"How very strange! And have there never been any reports about her?"

"Never."

"But what about her husband? He is peculiar, is he not?"

"Yes and no. Very likely there has been a little drama between them, one of those little domestic dramas which one suspects, which one never finds out exactly, but which one guesses pretty nearly."

"What is it?"

"I do not know anything about it. Mascaret leads a very fast life now, after having been a model husband. As long as he remained a good spouse, he had a shocking temper and was crabbed and easily took offense, but since he has been leading his present, rackety life, he has become quite indifferent; but one would guess that he has some trouble, a worm gnawing somewhere, for he has aged very much."

Thereupon the two friends talked philosophically for some minutes about the secret, unknowable troubles, which differences of character, or perhaps physical antipathies, which were not perceived at first, give rise to in families. Then Roger de Salnis, who was still looking at Madame de Mascaret through his opera-glasses, said:

"It is almost incredible that that woman has had seven children!"

"Yes, in eleven years; after which, when she was thirty, she put a stop to her period of production in order to enter into the brilliant period of entertaining, which does not seem near coming to an end."

"Poor women!"

"Why do you pity them?"

"Why? Ah! my dear fellow, just consider! Eleven years of maternity, for such a woman! What a hell! All her youth, all her beauty, every hope of success, every poetical ideal of a bright life, sacrificed to that abominable law of reproduction which turns the normal woman into a mere machine for maternity."

"What would you have? It is only Nature!"

"Yes, but I say that Nature is our enemy, that we must always fight against Nature, for she is continually bringing us back to an animal state. You may be sure that God has not put anything on this earth that is clean, pretty, elegant, or accessory to our ideal, but the human brain has done it. It is we who have introduced a little grace, beauty, unknown charm, and mystery into creation by singing about it, interpreting it, by admiring it as poets, idealizing it as artists, and by explaining it as learned men who make mistakes, but who find ingenious reasons, some grace and beauty, some unknown charm and mystery in the various phenomena of Nature.

"God only created coarse beings, full of the germs of disease, and who, after a few years of bestial enjoyment, grow old and infirm, with all the ugliness and all the want of power of human decrepitude. He only seems to have made them in order that they may reproduce their species in a repulsive manner, and then die like ephemeral insects. I said, *reproduce their species in a repulsive manner,* and I adhere to that expression. What is there as a matter of fact, more ignoble and more repugnant than that ridiculous act of the reproduction of living beings, against which all delicate minds always have revolted, and always will revolt? Since all the organs which have been invented by this economical and malicious Creator serve two purposes, why did he not choose those that were unsullied, in order to intrust them with that sacred mission, which is the noblest and the most exalted of all human functions? The mouth which nourishes the body by means of material food, also diffuses abroad speech and thought. Our flesh revives itself by means of itself, and at the same time, ideas are communicated by it. The sense of smell, which gives the vital air to the lungs, imparts all the perfumes of the world to the brain: the smell of flowers, of woods, of trees, of the sea. The ear, which enables us to communicate with our fellow-men, has also allowed us to invent music, to create dreams, happiness, the infinite, and even physical pleasure, by means of sounds!

"But one might say that the Creator wished to prohibit man from ever ennobling and idealizing his commerce with women. Nevertheless, man has found love, which is not a bad reply to that sly Deity, and he has ornamented it so much with literary poetry, that woman often forgets the contact she is obliged to submit to. Those among us who are powerless to deceive themselves have invented vice and refined debauchery, which is another way of laughing at God, and of paying homage, immodest homage, to beauty.

"But the normal man makes children; just a beast that is coupled with another by law.

"Look at that woman! Is it not abominable to think that such a jewel, such a pearl, born to be beautiful, admired, fêted, and adored, has spent eleven years of her life in providing heirs for the Count de Mascaret?"

Bernard Grandin replied with a laugh: "There is a great deal of truth in all that, but very few people would understand you."

Salnis got more and more animated. "Do you know how I picture God myself?" he said. "As an enormous, creative organ unknown to us, who scatters millions of worlds into space, just as one single fish would deposit its spawn in the sea. He creates, because it is His function as God to do so, but He does not know what He is doing, and is stupidly prolific in His work, and is ignorant of the combinations of all kinds which are produced by His scattered germs. Human thought is a lucky little local, passing accident, which was totally unforeseen, and is condemned to disappear with this earth, and to recommence perhaps here or elsewhere, the same or different, with fresh combinations of eternally new beginnings. We owe it to this slight accident which has happened to His intellect, that we are very uncomfortable in this world which was not made for us, which had not been prepared to receive us, to lodge and feed us, or to satisfy reflecting beings, and we owe it to Him also that we have to struggle without ceasing against what are still called the designs of Providence, when we are really refined and civilized beings."

Grandin, who was listening to him attentively, as he had long known the surprising outbursts of his fancy, asked him: "Then you believe that human thought is the spontaneous product of blind, divine reproduction?"

"Naturally? A fortuitous function of the nerve-centers of our brain, like some unforeseen chemical action which is due to new mixtures, and which also resembles a product of electricity, caused by friction or the unexpected proximity of some substance, and which, lastly, resembles the phenomena caused by the infinite and fruitful fermentations of living matter.

"But, my dear fellow, the truth of this must be evident to anyone who looks about him. If human thought, ordained by an omniscient Creator, had been intended to be what it has become, altogether different from mechanical thoughts and resignation, so exacting, inquiring, agitated, tormented, would the world which was created to receive the beings which we now are have been this unpleasant little dwelling place for poor fools, this salad plot, this rocky, wooded, and spherical kitchen garden where your improvident Providence has destined us to live naked, in caves or under trees, nourished on the flesh of slaughtered animals, our brethren, or on raw vegetables nourished by the sun and the rain.

"But it is sufficient to reflect for a moment, in order to understand that this world was not made for such creatures as we are. Thought, which is developed by a miracle in the nerves of the cells in our brain, powerless, ignorant, and confused as it is, and as it will always remain, makes all of us who are intellectual beings eternal and wretched exiles on earth.

"Look at this earth, as God has given it to those who inhabit it. Is it not visibly and solely made, planted and covered with forests, for the sake of animals? What is there for us? Nothing. And for them? Everything. They have nothing to do but to eat, or go hunting and eat each other, according to their instincts, for God never foresaw gentleness and peaceable manners; He only foresaw the death of creatures which were bent on destroying and devouring each other. Are not the quail, the pigeon, and the partridge the natural prey of the hawk? The sheep, the stag, and the ox that of the great flesh-eating animals, rather than meat that has been fattened to be served up to us with truffles, which have been unearthed by pigs, for our special benefit?

"As to ourselves, the more civilized, intellectual, and refined we are, the more we ought to conquer and subdue that animal instinct, which represents the will of God in us. And so, in order to mitigate our lot as brutes, we have discovered and made everything, beginning with houses, then exquisite food, sauces, sweetmeats, pastry, drink, stuffs, clothes, ornaments, beds, mattresses, carriages, railways, and innumerable machines, besides arts and sciences, writing and poetry. Every ideal comes from us as well as the amenities of life, in order to make our existence as simple reproducers, for which divine Providence solely intended us, less monotonous and less hard.

"Look at this theater. Is there not here a human world created by us, unforeseen and unknown by Eternal destinies, comprehensible by our minds alone, a sensual and intellectual distraction, which has been invented solely by and for that discontented and restless little animal that we are?

"Look at that woman, Madame de Mascaret. God intended her to live in a cave naked, or wrapped up in the skins of wild animals, but is she not better as she is? But, speaking of her, does anyone know why and how her brute of a husband, having such a companion by his side, and especially after having been boorish enough to make her a mother seven times, has suddenly left her, to run after loose women?"

Grandin replied: "Oh! my dear fellow, this is probably the only reason. He found that always living with her was becoming too expensive in the end, and from reasons of domestic economy, he has arrived at the same principles which you lay down as a philosopher."

Just then the curtain rose for the third act, and they turned round, took off their hats, and sat down.

IV

The Count and Countess de Mascaret were sitting side by side in the carriage which was taking them home from the opera, without speaking. But suddenly the husband said to his wife: "Gabrielle!"

"What do you want?"

"Don't you think that this has lasted long enough?"

"What?"

"The horrible punishment to which you have condemned me for the last six years."

"What do you want? I cannot help it."

"Then tell me which of them it is?"

"Never."

"Think that I can no longer see my children or feel them round me, without having my heart burdened with this doubt. Tell me which of them it is, and I swear that I will forgive you, and treat it like the others."

"I have not the right to."

"You do not see that I can no longer endure this life, this thought which is wearing me out, or this question which I am constantly asking myself, this question which tortures me each time I look at them. It is driving me mad."

"Then you have suffered a great deal?" she said.

"Terribly. Should I, without that, have accepted the horror of living by your side, and the still greater horror of feeling and knowing that there is one among them whom I cannot recognize, and who prevents me from loving the others?"

She repeated: "Then you have really suffered very much?" And he replied in a constrained and sorrowful voice:

"Yes, for do I not tell you every day that it is intolerable torture to me? Should I have remained in that house, near you and them, if I did not love them? Oh! You have behaved abominably toward me. All the affection of my heart I have bestowed upon my children, and that you know. I am for them a father of the olden time, as I was for you a husband of one of the families of old, for by instinct I have remained a natural man, a man of former days. Yes, I will, confess it, you have made me terribly jealous, because you are a woman of another race, of another soul, with other requirements. Oh! I shall never forget the things that you told me, but from that day, I troubled myself no more about you. I did not kill you, because then I should have had no means on earth of ever discovering which of our—of your children is not mine. I have waited, but I have suffered more than you would believe, for I can no longer venture to love them, except, perhaps, the two eldest; I no longer venture to look at them, to call them to me, to kiss them; I cannot take them on to my knee without asking myself: 'Can it be this one?' I have been correct in my behavior toward you for six years, and even kind and complaisant; tell me the truth, and I swear that I will do nothing unkind."

He thought, in spite of the darkness of the carriage, that he could perceive that she was moved, and feeling certain that she was going to speak at last, he said: "I beg you, I beseech you to tell me."

"I have been more guilty than you think, perhaps," she replied; "but I could no longer endure that life of continual pregnancy, and I had only one means of driving you from my bed. I lied before God, and I lied, with my hand raised to my children's heads, for I have never wronged you."

He seized her arm in the darkness, and squeezing it as he had done on that terrible day of their drive in the Bois de Boulogne, he stammered: "Is that true?"

"It is true."

But he in terrible grief said with a groan: "I shall have fresh doubts that will never end! When did you lie, the last time or now? How am I to believe you at present? How can one believe a woman after that? I shall never again know what I am to think. I would rather you had said to me: 'It is Jacques, or, it is Jeanne.' "

The carriage drove them into the courtyard of their mansion, and when it had drawn up in front of the steps, the Count got down first as usual, and offered his wife his arm, to help her up. And then, as soon as they had reached the first floor he said: "May I speak to you for a few moments longer?"

And she replied: "I am quite willing."

They went into a small drawing-room, while a footman in some surprise, lit the wax candles. As soon as he had left the room and they were alone, he continued: "How am I to know the truth? I have begged you a thousand times to speak, but you have remained dumb, impenetrable, inflexible, inexorable, and now to-day, you tell me that you have been lying. For six years you have actually allowed me to believe such a thing! No, you are lying now, I do not know why, but out of pity for me, perhaps?"

She replied in a sincere and convincing manner: "If I had not done so, I should have had four more children in the last six years!"

And he exclaimed: "Can a mother speak like that?"

"Oh!" she replied, "I do not at all feel that I am the mother of children who have never been born; it is enough for me to be the mother of those that I have, and to love them with all my heart. I am—we are—women who belong to the civilized world, Monsieur, and we are no longer, and we refuse to be, mere females who restock the earth."

She got up, but he seized her hands. "Only one word, Gabrielle. Tell me the truth!"

"I have just told you. I have never dishonored you."

He looked her full in the face, and how beautiful she was, with her gray eyes, like the cold sky. In her dark hair dress, on that opaque night of black hair, there shone the diamond coronet, like a cluster of stars. Then he suddenly felt, felt by a kind of intuition, that this grand creature was not merely a being destined to perpetuate his race, but the strange and mysterious product of all the complicated desires which have been accumulating in us for centuries but which have been turned aside from their primitive and divine object, and which have wandered after a mystic, imperfectly seen, and intangible beauty. There are some women like that, women who blossom only for our dreams, adorned with every poetical attribute of civilization, with that ideal luxury, coquetry, and æsthetic charm which should surround the living statue who brightens our life.

Her husband remained standing before her, stupefied at the tardy and obscure discovery, confusedly hitting on the cause of his former jealousy, and understanding it all very imperfectly. At last he said: "I believe you, for I feel at this moment that you are not lying, and formerly, I really thought that you were."

She put out her hand to him: "We are friends then?"

He took her hand and kissed it, and replied: "We are friends. Thank you, Gabrielle."

Then he went out, still looking at her, and surprised that she was still so beautiful, and feeling a strange emotion arising in him, which was, perhaps, more formidable than antique and simple love.

Henry James

Henry James (1843–1916) was born to a wealthy, intellectual New York family. His father was a notable theologian and philosopher; his older brother, William, was also a famous philosopher and psychologist. The James family traveled extensively abroad, where the young Henry James was privately educated. He decided early in life to become a writer; a trip to Europe led him to choose the European scene as a more suitable permanent residence for a writer than America. In 1876, he settled in England, where he was to spend most of the rest of his life. When World War I broke out, James declared his devotion to his adopted country by becoming a naturalized British subject. For forty years, James produced an enormous number of novels and stories of technical brilliance and subtlety. One of his favorite themes was the comparison of Europeans and Americans. His literary philosophy is best summed up in advice to the young writer: "Try to be one of the people on whom nothing is lost." James's most famous works include The Portrait of a Lady *(1881)* The Turn of the Screw *(1898), and* The Ambassadors *(1903).* *(See page 81 of Introduction.)*

FOUR MEETINGS

I saw her but four times, though I remember them vividly; she made her impression on me. I thought her very pretty and very interesting—a touching specimen of a type with which I had had other and perhaps less charming associations. I'm sorry to hear of her death, and yet when I think of it why *should* I be? The last time I saw her she was certainly not—! But it will be of interest to take our meetings in order.

I

The first was in the country, at a small tea-party, one snowy night some seventeen years ago. My friend Latouche, going to spend Christmas with his mother, had insisted on my company, and the good lady had given in our honour the entertainment of which I speak. To me it was really full of savour—it had all the right marks: I had never been in the depths of New England at that season. It had been snowing all day and the drifts were knee-high. I wondered how the ladies had made their way to the house; but I inferred that just those general rigours rendered any assembly offering the attraction of two gentlemen from New York worth a desperate effort.

Mrs. Latouche in the course of the evening asked me if I "didn't want to" show the photographs to some of the young ladies. The photographs were in a couple of great portfolios, and had been brought home by her son, who, like myself, was lately returned from Europe. I looked round and was struck with the fact that most of the young ladies were provided with an object of interest more absorbing than the most vivid sun-picture. But there was a person alone near the mantelshelf who looked round the room with a small vague smile, a discreet, a disguised yearning, which seemed somehow at odds with her isolation. I looked at her a moment and then chose. "I should like to show them to that young lady."

"Oh yes," said Mrs. Latouche, "she's just the person. She doesn't care for flirting—I'll speak to her." I replied that if she didn't care for flirting she wasn't perhaps just the person; but Mrs. Latouche had already, with a few steps, appealed to her participation. "She's delighted," my hostess came back to report; "and she's just the person—so quiet and so bright." And she told me the young lady was by name Miss Caroline Spencer—with which she introduced me.

Miss Caroline Spencer was not quite a beauty, but was none the less, in her small odd way, formed to please. Close upon thirty, by every presumption, she was made almost like a little girl and had the complexion of a child. She had also the prettiest head, on which her hair was arranged as nearly as possible like the hair of a Greek bust, though indeed it was to be doubted if she had ever seen a Greek bust. She was "artistic," I suspected, so far as the polar influences of North Verona could allow for such yearnings or could minister to them. Her eyes were perhaps just too round and too inveterately surprised, but her lips had a certain mild decision and her teeth, when she showed them, were charming. About her neck she wore what ladies call, I believe, a "ruche" fastened with a very small pin of pink coral, and in her hand she carried a fan made of plaited straw and adorned with pink ribbon. She wore a scanty black silk dress. She spoke with slow soft neatness, even without smiles showing the prettiness of her teeth, and she seemed extremely pleased, in fact quite fluttered, at the prospect of my demonstrations. These went forward very smoothly after I had moved the portfolios out of their corner and placed a couple of chairs near a lamp. The photographs were usually things I knew—large views of Switzerland, Italy and Spain, landscapes, reproductions of famous buildings, pictures and statues. I said what I could for them, and my companion, looking at them as I held them up, sat perfectly still, her straw fan raised to her under-lip and gently, yet, as I could feel, almost excitedly, rubbing it. Occasionally, as I laid one of the pictures down, she said without confidence, which would have been too much: "Have you seen that place?" I usually answered that I had seen it several times—I had been a great traveller, though I was somehow particularly admonished not to swagger—and then I felt her look at me askance for a moment with her pretty eyes. I had asked her at the outset whether she had been to Europe; to this she had answered "No, no, no"—almost as much below her breath as if the image of such an event scarce, for solemnity, brooked phrasing. But after that, though she never took her eyes off the pictures, she said so little that I feared she was at last bored. Accordingly when we had finished one portfolio I offered, if she desired it, to desist. I rather guessed the exhibition really held her, but her reticence puzzled me and I wanted to make her speak. I turned round to judge better and then saw a faint flush in each of her cheeks. She kept waving her little fan to and fro. Instead of looking at me she fixed her eyes on the remainder of the collection, which leaned, in its receptacle, against the table.

"Won't you show me that?" she quavered, drawing the long breath of a person launched and afloat but conscious of rocking a little.

"With pleasure," I answered, "if you're really not tired."

"Oh I'm not tired a bit. I'm just fascinated." With which as I took up the other portfolio she laid her hand on it, rubbing it softly. "And have you been here too?'

On my opening the portfolio it appeared I had indeed been there. One of the first photographs was a large view of the Castle of Chillon by the Lake of Geneva. "Here," I said, "I've been many a time. Isn't it beautiful?" And I pointed to the perfect reflexion of the rugged rocks and pointed towers in the clear still water. She didn't say "Oh, enchanting!" and push it away to see the next picture. She looked a while and then asked if it weren't where Bonnivard, about whom Byron wrote, had been confined. I assented, trying to quote Byron's verses, but not quite bringing it off.

She fanned herself a moment and then repeated the lines correctly, in a soft flat voice but with charming conviction. By the time she had finished, she was nevertheless blushing. I complimented her and assured her she was perfectly equipped for visiting Switzerland and Italy. She looked at me askance again, to see if I might be serious, and I added that if she wished to recognise Byron's descriptions she must go abroad speedily—Europe was getting sadly dis-Byronised. "How soon must I go?" she thereupon enquired.

"Oh I'll give you ten years."

"Well, I guess I can go in *that* time," she answered as if measuring her words.

"Then you'll enjoy it immensely," I said; "you'll find it of the highest interest." Just then I came upon a photograph of some nook in a foreign city which I had been very fond of and which recalled tender memories. I discoursed (as I suppose) with considerable spirit; my companion sat listening breathless.

"Have you been *very* long over there?" she asked some time after I had ceased.

"Well, it mounts up, put all the times together."

"And have you travelled everywhere?"

"I've travelled a good deal. I'm very fond of it and happily have been able."

Again she turned on me her slow shy scrutiny. "Do you know the foreign languages?"

"After a fashion."

"Is it hard to speak them?"

"I don't imagine you'd find it so," I gallantly answered.

"Oh I shouldn't want to speak—I should only want to listen." Then on a pause she added: "They say the French theatre's so beautiful."

"Ah the best in the world."

"Did you go there very often?"

"When I was first in Paris I went every night."

"Every night!" And she opened her clear eyes very wide. "That to me is"—and her expression hovered—"as if you tell me a fairy-tale." A few minutes later she put to me: "And which country do you prefer?"

"There's one I love beyond any. I think you'd do the same."

Her gaze rested as on a dim revelation and then she breathed "Italy?"

"Italy," I answered softly too; and for a moment we communed over it. She looked as pretty as if instead of showing her photographs I had been making love to her. To increase the resemblance she turned off blushing. It made a pause which she broke at last by saying: "That's the place which—in particular—I thought of going to."

"Oh that's the place—that's the place!" I laughed.

She looked at two or three more views in silence. "They say it's not very dear."

"As some other countries? Well, one gets back there one's money. That's not the least of the charms."

"But it's *all* very expensive, isn't it?"

"Europe, you mean?"

"Going there and travelling. That has been the trouble. I've very little money. I teach, you know," said Miss Caroline Spencer.

"Oh of course one must have money," I allowed; "but one can manage with a moderate amount judiciously spent."

"I think I should manage. I've saved and saved up, and I'm always adding a little to it. It's all for that." She paused a moment, and then went on with suppressed eagerness, as if telling me the story were a rare, but possibly an impure satisfaction. "You see it hasn't been only the money—it has been everything. Everything has acted against it. I've waited and waited. It has been my castle in the air. I'm almost afraid to talk about it. Two or three times it has come a little nearer, and then I've talked about it and it has melted away. I've talked about it too much," she said hypocritically—for I saw such talk was now a small tremulous ecstasy. "There's a lady who's a great friend of mine—she doesn't want to go, but I'm always at her about it. I think I must tire her dreadfully. She told me just the other day she didn't know what would become of me. She guessed I'd go crazy if I didn't sail, and yet certainly I'd go crazy if I did."

"Well," I laughed, "you haven't sailed up to now—so I suppose you *are* crazy."

She took everything with the same seriousness. "Well, I guess I must be. It seems as if I couldn't think of anything else—and I don't require photographs to work me up! I'm always right *on* it. It kills any interest in things nearer home—things I ought to attend to. That's a kind of craziness."

"Well then the cure for it's just to go," I smiled—"I mean the cure for this kind. Of course you may have the other kind worse," I added—"the kind you get over there."

"Well, I've a faith that I'll go *some* time all right!" she quite elatedly cried. "I've a relative right there on the spot," she went on, "and I guess he'll know how to control me." I expressed the hope that he would, and I forget whether we turned over more photographs; but when I asked her if she had always lived just where I found her, "Oh no sir," she quite eagerly replied; "I've spent twenty-two months and a half in Boston." I met it with the inevitable joke that in this case foreign lands might prove a disappointment to her, but I quite failed to alarm her. "I know more about them than you might think"—her earnestness resisted even that. "I mean by reading—for I've really read considerable. In fact I guess I've prepared my mind about as much as you *can*—in advance. I've not only read Byron—I've read histories and guide-books and articles and lots of things. I know I shall rave about everything."

" 'Everything' is saying much, but I understand your case," I returned. "You've the great American disease, and you've got it 'bad'—the appetite, morbid and monstrous, for colour and form, for the picturesque and the romantic at any price. I don't know whether we come into the world with it—with the germs implanted and antecedent to experience; rather perhaps we catch it early, almost before developed consciousness—we *feel*, as we look about, that we're going (to save our souls, or at least our senses) to be thrown back on it hard. We're like travellers in the desert—deprived of water and subject to the terrible mirage, the torment of illusion, of the thirst-fever. They hear the plash of fountains, they see green gardens and orchards that are hundreds of miles away. So we with *our* thirst—except that with us it's *more* wonderful: we have before us the beautiful old things we've never seen at all, and when we do at last see them—if we're lucky!—we simply recognise them. What experience does is merely to confirm and consecrate our confident dream."

She listened with her rounded eyes. "The way you express it's too lovely, and I'm sure it will be just like that. I've dreamt of everything—I'll know it all!"

"I'm afraid," I pretended for harmless comedy, "that you've wasted a great deal of time."

"Oh yes, that has been my great wickedness!" The people about us had begun to scatter; they were taking their leave. She got up and put out her hand to me, timidly, but as if quite shining and throbbing.

"I'm going back there—one *has* to," I said as I shook hands with her. "I shall look out for you."

Yes, she fairly glittered with her fever of excited faith. "Well, I'll tell you if I'm disappointed." And she left me, fluttering all expressively her little straw fan.

II

A few months after this I crossed the sea eastward again and some three years elapsed. I had been living in Paris and, toward the end of October, went from that city to the Havre, to meet a pair of relatives who had written me they were about to arrive there. On reaching the Havre I found the steamer already docked—I was two or three hours late. I repaired directly to the hotel, where my travellers were duly established. My sister had gone to bed, exhausted and disabled by her voyage; she was the unsteadiest of sailors and her sufferings on this occasion had been extreme. She desired for the moment undisturbed rest and was able to see me but five minutes—long enough for us to agree to stop over, restoratively, till the morrow. My brother-in-law, anxious about his wife, was unwilling to leave her room; but she insisted on my taking him a walk for aid to recovery of his spirits and his land-legs.

The early autumn day was warm and charming, and our stroll through the bright-coloured busy streets of the old French seaport beguiling enough. We walked along the sunny noisy quays and then turned into a wide pleasant street which lay half in sun and half in shade—a French provincial street that resembled an old water-colour drawing: tall grey steep-roofed red-gabled many-storied houses; green shutters on windows and old scroll-work above them; flower-pots in balconies and white-capped women in doorways. We walked in the shade; all this stretched away on the sunny side of the vista and made a picture. We looked at it as we passed along; then suddenly my companion stopped—pressing my arm and staring. I followed his gaze and saw that we had paused just before reaching a café where, under an awning, several tables and chairs were disposed upon the pavement. The windows were open behind; half a dozen plants in tubs were ranged beside the door; the pavement was besprinkled with clean bran. It was a dear little quiet old-world café; inside, in the comparative dusk, I saw a stout handsome woman, who had pink ribbons in her cap, perched up with a mirror behind her back and smiling at some one placed out of sight. This, to be exact, I noted afterwards; what I first observed was a lady seated alone, outside, at one of the little marble-topped tables. My brother-in-law had stopped to look at her. Something had been put before her, but she only leaned back, motionless and with her hands folded, looking down the street and away from us. I saw her but in diminished profile; nevertheless I was sure I knew on the spot that we must already have met.

"The little lady of the steamer!" my companion cried.

"Was she on your steamer?" I asked with interest.

"From morning till night. She was never sick. She used to sit perpetually at the side of the vessel with her hands crossed that way, looking at the eastward horizon."

"And are you going to speak to her?"

"I don't know her. I never made acquaintance with her. I wasn't in form to make up to ladies. But I used to watch her and—I don't know why—to be interested in her. She's a dear little Yankee woman. I've an idea she's a school-mistress taking a holiday—for which her scholars have made up a purse."

She had now turned her face a little more into profile, looking at the steep grey house-fronts opposite. On this I decided. "I shall speak to her myself."

"I wouldn't—she's very shy," said my brother-in-law.

"My dear fellow, I know her. I once showed her photographs at a tea-party." With which I went up to her, making her, as she turned to look at me, leave me in no doubt of her identity. Miss Caroline Spencer had achieved her dream. But she was less quick to recognise me and showed a slight bewilderment. I pushed a chair to the table and sat down. "Well," I said, "I hope you're not disappointed!"

She stared, blushing a little—then gave a small jump and placed me. "It was you who showed me the photographs—at North Verona."

"Yes, it was I. This happens very charmingly, for isn't it quite proper for me to give you a formal reception here—the official welcome? I talked to you so much about Europe."

"You didn't say too much. I'm so intensely happy!" she declared.

Very happy indeed she looked. There was no sign of her being older; she was as gravely, decently, demurely pretty as before. If she had struck me then as a thin-stemmed, mild-hued flower of Puritanism it may be imagined whether in her present situation this clear bloom was less appealing. Beside her an old gentleman was drinking absinthe; behind her the *dame de comptoir* in the pink ribbons called "Alcibiade, Alcibiade!" to the long-aproned waiter. I explained to Miss Spencer that the gentleman with me had lately been her shipmate, and my brother-in-law came up and was introduced to her. But she looked at him as if she had never so much as seen him, and I remembered he had told me her eyes were always fixed on the eastward horizon. She had evidently not noticed him, and, still timidly smiling, made no attempt whatever to pretend the contrary. I stayed with her on the little terrace of the café while he went back to the hotel and to his wife. I remarked to my friend that this meeting of ours at the first hour of her landing partook, among all chances, of the miraculous, but that I was delighted to be there and receive her first impressions.

"Oh I can't tell you," she said—"I feel so much in a dream. I've been sitting here an hour and I don't want to move. Everything's so delicious and romantic. I don't know whether the coffee has gone to my head—it's *so* unlike the coffee of my dead past."

"Really," I made answer, "if you're so pleased with this poor prosaic Havre you'll have no admiration left for better things. Don't spend your appreciation all the first day—remember it's your intellectual letter of credit. Remember all the beautiful places and things that are waiting for you. Remember that lovely Italy we talked about."

"I'm not afraid of running short," she said gaily, still looking at the opposite houses. "I could sit here all day—just saying to myself that here I am at last. It's so dark and strange—so old and different."

"By the way then," I asked, "how come you to be encamped in this odd place? Haven't you gone to one of the inns?" For I was half-amused, half-alarmed at the good conscience with which this delicately pretty woman had stationed herself in conspicuous isolation on the edge of the sidewalk.

"My cousin brought me here and—a little while ago—left me," she returned. "You know I told you I had a relation over here. He's still here—a real cousin. Well," she pursued with unclouded candour, "he met me at the steamer this morning."

It was absurd—and the case moreover none of my business; but I felt somehow disconcerted. "It was hardly worth his while to meet you if he was to desert you so soon."

"Oh he has only left me for half an hour," said Caroline Spencer. "He has gone to get my money."

I continued to wonder. "Where *is* your money?"

She appeared seldom to laugh, but she laughed for the joy of this. "It makes me feel very fine to tell you! It's in circular notes."

"And where are your circular notes?"

"In my cousin's pocket."

This statement was uttered with such clearness of candour that—I can hardly say why—it gave me a sensible chill. I couldn't at all at the moment have justified my lapse from ease, for I knew nothing of Miss Spencer's cousin. Since he stood in that relation to her—dear respectable little person—the presumption was in his favour. But I found myself wincing at the thought that half an hour after her landing her scanty funds should have passed into his hands. "Is he to travel with you?" I asked.

"Only as far as Paris. He's an art-student in Paris—I've always thought that so splendid. I wrote to him that I was coming, but I never expected him to come off to the ship. I supposed he'd only just meet me at the train in Paris. It's very kind of him. But he *is,*" said Caroline Spencer, "very kind—and very bright."

I felt at once a strange eagerness to see this bright kind cousin who was an art-student. "He's gone to the banker's?" I enquired.

"Yes, to the banker's. He took me to an hotel—such a queer quaint cunning little place, with a court in the middle and a gallery all round, and a lovely landlady in such a beautifully fluted cap and such a perfectly fitting dress! After a while we came out to walk to the banker's, for I hadn't any French money. But I was very dizzy from the motion of the vessel and I thought I had better sit down. He found this place for me here—then he went off to the banker's himself. I'm to wait here till he comes back."

Her story was wholly lucid and my impression perfectly wanton, but it passed through my mind that the gentleman would never come back. I settled myself in a chair beside my friend and determined to await the event. She was lost in the vision and the imagination of everything near us and about us—she observed, she recognised and admired, with a touching intensity. She noticed everything that was brought before us by the movement of the street—the peculiarities of costume, the shapes of vehicles, the big Norman horses, the fat priests, the shaven poodles. We talked of these things, and there was something charming in her freshness of perception and the way her book-nourished fancy sallied forth for the revel.

"And when your cousin comes back what are you going to do?" I went on.

For this she had, a little oddly, to think. "We don't quite know."

"When do you go to Paris? If you go by the four o'clock train I may have the pleasure of making the journey with you."

"I don't think we shall do that." So far she was prepared. "My cousin thinks I had better stay here a few days."

"Oh!" said I—and for five minutes had nothing to add. I was wondering what our absentee was, in vulgar parlance, "up to." I looked up and down the street, but saw nothing that looked like a bright and kind American art-student. At last I took the liberty of observing that the Havre was hardly a place to choose as one of the æsthetic stations of a European tour. It was a place of convenience, nothing more; a place of transit, through which transit should be rapid. I recommended her to go to Paris by the afternoon train and meanwhile to amuse herself by driving to the ancient fortress at the mouth of the harbour—that remarkable circular structure which bore the name of Francis the First and figured a sort of small Castle of Saint Angelo. (I might really have foreknown that it was to be demolished.)

She listened with much interest—then for a moment looked grave. "My cousin told me that when he returned he should have something particular to say to me, and that we could do nothing or decide nothing till I should have heard it. But I'll make him tell me right off, and then we'll go to the ancient fortress. Francis the First, did you say? Why, that's lovely. There's no hurry to get to Paris; there's plenty of time."

She smiled with her softly severe little lips as she spoke those last words, yet, looking at her with a purpose, I made out in her eyes, I thought, a tiny gleam of apprehension. "Don't tell me," I said, "that this wretched man's going to give you bad news!"

She coloured as if convicted of a hidden perversity, but she was soaring too high to drop. "Well I guess it's a *little* bad, but I don't believe it's *very* bad. At any rate I must listen to it."

I usurped an unscrupulous authority. "Look here; you didn't come to Europe to listen—you came to *see!*" But now I was sure her cousin would come back; since he had something disagreeable to say to her he'd infallibly turn up. We sat a while longer and I asked her about her plans of travel. She had them on her fingers' ends and told over the names as solemnly as a daughter of another faith might have told over the beads of a rosary: from Paris to Dijon and to Avignon, from Avignon to Marseilles and the Cornice road; thence to Genoa, to Spezia, to Pisa, to Florence, to Rome. It apparently had never occurred to her that there could be the least incommodity in her travelling alone; and since she was unprovided with a companion I of course civilly abstained from disturbing her sense of security.

At last her cousin came back. I saw him turn toward us out of a side-street, and from the moment my eyes rested on him I knew he could but be the bright, if not the kind, American art-student. He wore a slouch hat and a rusty black velvet jacket, such as I had often encountered in the Rue Bonaparte. His shirt-collar displayed a stretch of throat that at a distance wasn't strikingly statuesque. He was tall and lean, he had red hair and freckles. These items I had time to take in while he approached the café, staring at me with natural surprise from under his romantic brim. When he came up to us I immediately introduced myself as an old acquaintance of Miss Spencer's, a character she serenely permitted me to claim. He looked at me hard with a pair of small sharp eyes, then he gave me a solemn wave, in the "European" fashion, of his rather rusty sombrero.

"You weren't on the ship?" he asked.

"No, I wasn't on the ship. I've been in Europe these several years."

He bowed once more, portentously, and motioned me to be seated again. I sat down, but only for the purpose of observing him an instant—I saw it was time I should return to my sister. Miss Spencer's European protector was, by my measure, a very queer quantity. Nature hadn't shaped him for a Raphaelesque or Byronic attire, and his velvet doublet and exhibited though not columnar throat weren't in harmony with his facial attributes. His hair was cropped close to his head; his ears were large and ill-adjusted to the same. He had a lackadaisical carriage and a sentimental droop which were peculiarly at variance with his keen conscious strange-coloured eyes—of a brown that was almost red. Perhaps I was prejudiced, but I thought his eyes too shifty. He said nothing for some time; he leaned his hands on his stick and looked up and down the street. Then at last, slowly lifting the stick and pointing with it, "That's a very nice bit," he dropped with a certain flatness. He had his head to one side—he narrowed his ugly lids. I followed the direction of his stick; the object it indicated was a red cloth hung out of an old window. "Nice bit of colour," he continued; and without moving his head transferred his half-closed gaze to me. "Composes well. Fine old tone. Make a nice thing." He spoke in a charmless vulgar voice.

"I see you've a great deal of eye," I replied. "Your cousin tells me you're studying art." He looked at me in the same way, without answering, and I went on with deliberate urbanity: "I suppose you're at the studio of one of those great men." Still on this he continued to fix me, and then he named one of the greatest of that day; which led me to ask him if he liked his master.

"Do you understand French?" he returned.

"Some kinds."

He kept his little eyes on me; with which he remarked: "Je suis fou de la peinture!"

"Oh I understand that kind!" I replied. Our companion laid her hand on his arm with a small pleased and fluttered movement; it was delightful to be among people who were on such easy terms with foreign tongues. I got up to take leave and asked her where, in Paris, I might have the honour of waiting on her. To what hotel would she go?

She turned to her cousin enquiringly and he favoured me again with his little languid leer. "Do you know the Hôtel des Princes?"

"I know where it is."

"Well, that's the shop."

"I congratulate you," I said to Miss Spencer. "I believe it's the best inn in the world; but, in case I should still have a moment to call on you here, where are you lodged?"

"Oh it's such a pretty name," she returned gleefully. "À la Belle Normande."

"I guess I know my way round!" her kinsman threw in; and as I left them he gave me with his swaggering head-cover a great flourish that was like the wave of a banner over a conquered field.

III

My relative, as it proved, was not sufficiently restored to leave the place by the afternoon train; so that as the autumn dusk began to fall I found myself at liberty to call at the establishment named to me by my friends. I must confess that I had spent much of the interval in wondering what the disagreeable thing was that the less attractive of these had been telling the other. The *auberge* of the Belle Normande proved an hostelry in a shady by-street, where it gave me satisfaction to think Miss Spencer must have encountered local colour in abundance. There was a crooked little court, where much of the hospitality of the house was carried on; there was a staircase climbing to bedrooms on the outer side of the wall; there was a small trickling fountain with a stucco statuette set in the midst of it; there was a little boy in a white cap and apron cleaning copper vessels at a conspicuous kitchen door; there was a chattering landlady, neatly laced, arranging apricots and grapes into an artistic pyramid upon a pink plate. I looked about, and on a green bench outside of an open door labelled Salle-à-Manger, I distinguished Caroline Spencer. No sooner had I looked at her than I was sure something had happened since the morning. Supported by the back of her bench, with her hands clasped in her lap, she kept her eyes on the other side of the court, where the landlady manipulated the apricots.

But I saw that, poor dear, she wasn't thinking of apricots or even of landladies. She was staring absently, thoughtfully; on a nearer view I could have certified she had been crying. I had seated myself beside her before she was aware; then, when she had done so, she simply turned round without surprise and showed me her sad face. Something very bad indeed had happened; she was completely changed, and I immediately charged her with it. "Your cousin has been giving you bad news. You've had a horrid time."

For a moment she said nothing, and I supposed her afraid to speak lest her tears should again rise. Then it came to me that even in the few hours since my leaving her she had shed them all—which made her now intensely, stoically composed. "My poor cousin has been having one," she replied at last. "He has had great worries. His news was bad." Then after a dismally conscious wait: "He was in dreadful want of money."

"In want of yours, you mean?"

"Of any he could get—honourably of course. Mine *is* all—well, that's available."

Ah it was as if I had been sure from the first! "And he has taken it from you?"

Again she hung fire, but her face meanwhile was pleading. "I gave him what I had."

I recall the accent of those words as the most angelic human sound I had ever listened to—which is exactly why I jumped up almost with a sense of personal outrage. "Gracious goodness, madam, do you call that his getting it 'honourably'?"

I had gone too far—she coloured to her eyes. "We won't speak of it."

"We *must* speak of it," I declared as I dropped beside her again. "I'm your friend—upon my word I'm your protector; it seems to me you need one. What's the matter with this extraordinary person?"

She was perfectly able to say. "He's just badly in debt."

"No doubt he is! But what's the special propriety of your—in such tearing haste!—paying for that?"

"Well, he has told me all his story. I *feel* for him so much."

"So do I, if you come to that! But I hope," I roundly added, "he'll give you straight back your money."

As to this she was prompt. "Certainly he will—as soon as ever he can."

"And when the deuce will that be?"

Her lucidity maintained itself. "When he has finished his great picture."

It took me full in the face. "My dear young lady, damn his great picture! Where is this voracious man?"

It was as if she must let me feel a moment that I did push her!—though indeed, as appeared, he was just where he'd naturally be. "He's having his dinner."

I turned about and looked through the open door into the salle-à-manger. There, sure enough, alone at the end of a long table, was the object of my friend's compassion—the bright, the kind young art-student. He was dining too attentively to notice me at first, but in the act of setting down a well-emptied wineglass he caught sight of my air of observation. He paused in his repast and, with his head on one side and his meagre jaws slowly moving, fixedly returned my gaze. Then the landlady came brushing lightly by with her pyramid of apricots.

"And that nice little plate of fruit is for him?" I wailed.

Miss Spencer glanced at it tenderly. "They seem to arrange everything so nicely!" she simply sighed.

I felt helpless and irritated. "Come now, really," I said; "do you think it right, do you think it decent, that that long strong fellow should collar your funds?" She looked away from me—I was evidently giving her pain. The case was hopeless; the long strong fellow had "interested" her.

"Pardon me if I speak of him so unceremoniously," I said. "But you're really too generous, and he hasn't, clearly, the rudiments of delicacy. He made his debts himself—he ought to pay them himself."

"He has been foolish," she obstinately said—"of course I know that. He has told me everything. We had a long talk this morning—the poor fellow threw himself on my charity. He has signed notes to a large amount."

"The more fool he!"

"He's in real distress—and it's not only himself. It's his poor young wife."

"Ah he has a poor young wife?"

"I didn't know—but he made a clean breast of it. He married two years since—secretly."

"Why secretly?"

My informant took precautions as if she feared listeners. Then with low impressiveness: "She was a Countess!"

"Are you very sure of that?"

"She has written me the most beautiful letter."

"Asking you—whom she has never seen—for money?"

"Asking me for confidence and sympathy"—Miss Spencer spoke now with spirit. "She has been cruelly treated by her family—in consequence of what she has done for him. My cousin has told me every particular, and she appeals to me in her own lovely way in the letter, which I've here in my pocket. It's such a wonderful old-world romance," said my prodigious friend. "She was a beautiful young widow—her first husband was a Count, tremendously high-born, but really most wicked, with whom she hadn't been happy and whose death had left her ruined after he had deceived her in all sorts of ways. My poor cousin, meeting her in that situation and perhaps a little too recklessly pitying her and charmed with her, found her, don't you see?"—Caroline's appeal on this head was amazing!—"but too ready to trust a better man after all she had been through. Only when her 'people,' as he says—and I do like the word!—understood she *would* have him, poor gifted young American art-student though he simply was, because she just adored him, her great-aunt, the old Marquise, from whom she had expectations of wealth which she could yet sacrifice for her love, utterly cast her off and wouldn't so much as speak to her, much less to *him*, in their dreadful haughtiness and pride. They *can* be haughty over here, it seems," she ineffably developed—"there's no mistake about that! It's like something in some famous old book. The family, my cousin's wife's," she by this time almost complacently wound up, "are of the oldest Provençal noblesse."

I listened half-bewildered. The poor woman positively found it so interesting to be swindled by a flower of that stock—if stock or flower or solitary grain of truth was really concerned in the matter—as practically to have lost the sense of what the forfeiture of her hoard meant for her. "My dear young lady," I groaned, "you don't want to be stripped of every dollar for such a rigmarole!"

She asserted, at this, her dignity—much as a small pink shorn lamb might have done. "It isn't a rigmarole, and I shan't be stripped. I shan't live any worse than I *have* lived, don't you see? And I'll come back before long to stay with them. The Countess—he still gives her, he says, her title, as they do to noble widows, that is to 'dowagers,' don't you know? in England—insists on a visit from me *some* time. So I guess for *that* I can start afresh—and meanwhile I'll have recovered my money."

It was all too heart-breaking. "You're going home then at once?"

I felt the faint tremor of voice she heroically tried to stifle. "I've nothing left for a tour."

"You gave it *all* up?"

"I've kept enough to take me back."

I uttered, I think, a positive howl, and at this juncture the hero of the situation, the happy proprietor of my little friend's sacred savings and of the infatuated *grande dame* just sketched for me, reappeared with the clear consciousness of a repast bravely earned and consistently enjoyed. He stood on the threshold an instant, extracting the stone from a plump apricot he had fondly retained; then he put the apricot into his mouth and, while he let it gratefully dissolve there, stood looking at us with his long legs apart and his hands thrust into the pockets of his velvet coat. My companion got up, giving him a thin glance that I caught in its passage and which expressed at once resignation and fascination—the last dregs of her sacrifice and with it an anguish of upliftedness. Ugly vulgar pretentious dishonest as I thought him, and destitute of every grace of plausibility, he had yet appealed successfully to her eager and tender imagination. I was deeply disgusted, but I had no warrant to interfere, and at any rate felt that it would be vain. He waved his hand meanwhile with a breadth of appreciation. "Nice old court. Nice mellow old place. Nice crooked old staircase. Several pretty things."

Decidedly I couldn't stand it, and without responding I gave my hand to my friend. She looked at me an instant with her little white face and rounded eyes, and as she showed her pretty teeth I suppose she meant to smile. "Don't be sorry for me," she sublimely pleaded; "I'm very sure I shall see something of this dear old Europe yet."

I refused however to take literal leave of her—I should find a moment to come back next morning. Her awful kinsman, who had put on his sombrero again, flourished it off at me by way of a bow—on which I hurried away.

On the morrow early I did return, and in the court of the inn met the landlady, more loosely laced than in the evening. On my asking for Miss Spencer, "*Partie,* monsieur," the good woman said. "She went away last night at ten o'clock, with her—her—not her husband, eh?—in fine her Monsieur. They went down to the American ship." I turned off—I felt the tears in my eyes. The poor girl had been some thirteen hours in Europe.

IV

I myself, more fortunate, continued to sacrifice to opportunity as I myself met it. During this period—of some five years—I lost my friend Latouche, who died of a malarious fever during a tour in the Levant. One of the first things I did on my return to America was to go up to North Verona on a consolatory visit to his poor mother. I found her in deep affliction and sat with her the whole of the morning that followed my arrival—I had come in late at night—listening to her tearful descant and singing the praises of my friend. We talked of nothing else, and our conversation ended only with the arrival of a quick little woman who drove herself up to the door in a "carry-all" and whom I saw toss the reins to the horse's back with the briskness of a startled sleeper throwing off the bedclothes. She jumped out of the carry-all and she jumped into the room. She proved to be the minister's wife and the great town-gossip, and she had evidently, in the latter capacity, a choice morsel to communicate. I was as sure of this as I was that poor Mrs. Latouche was not absolutely too bereaved to listen to her. It seemed to me discreet to retire, and I described myself as anxious for a walk before dinner.

"And by the way," I added, "if you'll tell me where my old friend Miss Spencer lives, I think I'll call on her."

The minister's wife immediately responded. Miss Spencer lived in the fourth house beyond the Baptist church; the Baptist church was the one on the right, with that queer green thing over the door; they called it a portico, but it looked more like an old-fashioned bedstead swung in the air. "Yes, do look up poor Caroline," Mrs. Latouche further enjoined. "It will refresh her to see a strange face."

"I should think she had had enough of strange faces!" cried the minister's wife.

"To see, I mean, a charming visitor"—Mrs. Latouche amended her phrase.

"I should think she had had enough of charming visitors!" her companion returned. "But *you* don't mean to stay ten years," she added with significant eyes on me.

"Has she a visitor of that sort?" I asked in my ignorance.

"You'll make out the sort!" said the minister's wife. "She's easily seen; she generally sits in the front yard. Only take care what you say to her, and be very sure you're polite."

"Ah she's so sensitive?"

The minister's wife jumped up and dropped me a curtsey—a most sarcastic curtsey. "That's what she is, if you please. 'Madame la Comtesse'!"

And pronouncing these titular words with the most scathing accent, the little woman seemed fairly to laugh in the face of the lady they designated. I stood staring, wondering, remembering.

"Oh I shall be very polite!" I cried; and, grasping my hat and stick, I went on my way.

I found Miss Spencer's residence without difficulty. The Baptist church was easily identified, and the small dwelling near it, of a rusty white, with a large central chimney-stack and a Virginia creeper, seemed naturally and properly the abode of a withdrawn old maid with a taste for striking effects inexpensively obtained. As I approached I slackened my pace, for I had heard that some one was always sitting in the front yard, and I wished to reconnoitre. I looked cautiously over the low white fence that separated the small garden-space from the unpaved street, but I descried nothing in the shape of a Comtesse. A small straight path led up to the crooked door-step, on either side of which was a little grass-plot fringed with currant-bushes. In the middle of the grass, right and left, was a large quince-tree, full of antiquity and contortions, and beneath one of the quince-trees were placed a small table and a couple of light chairs. On the table lay a piece of unfinished embroidery and two or three books in bright-coloured paper covers. I went in at the gate and paused halfway along the path, scanning the place for some further token of its occupant, before whom—I could hardly have said why—I hesitated abruptly to present myself. Then I saw the poor little house to be of the shabbiest and felt a sudden doubt of my right to penetrate, since curiosity had been my motive and curiosity here failed of confidence. While I demurred a figure appeared in the open doorway and stood there looking at me. I immediately recognised Miss Spencer, but she faced me as if we had never met. Gently, but gravely and timidly, I advanced to the door-step, where I spoke with an attempt at friendly banter.

"I waited for you over there to come back, but you never came."

"Waited where, sir?" she quavered, her innocent eyes rounding themselves as of old. She was much older; she looked tired and wasted.

"Well," I said, "I waited at the old French port."

She stared harder, then recognised me, smiling, flushing, clasping her two hands together. "I remember you now—I remember that day." But she stood there, neither coming out nor asking me to come in. She was embarrassed.

I too felt a little awkward while I poked at the path with my stick. "I kept looking out for you year after year."

"You mean in Europe?" she ruefully breathed.

"In Europe of course! Here apparently you're easy enough to find."

She leaned her hand against the unpainted door-post and her head fell a little to one side. She looked at me thus without speaking, and I caught the expression visible in women's eyes when tears are rising. Suddenly she stepped out on the cracked slab of stone before her threshold and closed the door. Then her strained smile prevailed and I saw her teeth were as pretty as ever. But there had been tears too. "Have you been there ever since?" she lowered her voice to ask.

"Until three weeks ago. And you—you never came back?"

Still shining at me as she could, she put her hand behind her and reopened the door. "I'm not very polite," she said. "Won't you come in?"

"I'm afraid I incommode you."

"Oh no!"—she wouldn't hear of it now. And she pushed back the door with a sign that I should enter.

I followed her in. She led the way to a small room on the left of the narrow hall, which I supposed to be her parlour, though it was at the back of the house, and we passed the closed door of another apartment which apparently enjoyed a view of the quince-trees. This one looked out upon a small wood-shed and two clucking hens. But I thought it pretty until I saw its elegance to be of the most frugal kind; after which, presently, I thought it prettier still, for I had never seen faded chintz and old mezzotint engravings, framed in varnished autumn leaves, disposed with so touching a grace. Miss Spencer sat down on a very small section of the sofa, her hands tightly clasped in her lap. She looked ten years older, and I needn't now have felt called to insist on the facts of her person. But I still thought them interesting, and at any rate I was moved by them. She was peculiarly agitated. I tried to appear not to notice it; but suddenly, in the most inconsequent fashion—it was an irresistible echo of our concentrated passage in the old French port—I said to her: "I do incommode you. Again you're in distress."

She raised her two hands to her face and for a moment kept it buried in them. Then taking them away, "It's because you remind me," she said.

"I remind you, you mean, of that miserable day at the Havre?"

She wonderfully shook her head. "It wasn't miserable. It was delightful."

Ah was it? my manner of receiving this must have commented. "I never was so shocked as when, on going back to your inn the next morning, I found you had wretchedly retreated."

She waited an instant, after which she said: "Please let us not speak of that."

"Did you come straight back here?" I nevertheless went on.

"I was back here just thirty days after my first start."

"And here you've remained ever since?"

"Every minute of the time."

I took it in; I didn't know what to say, and what I presently said had almost the sound of mockery. "When then are you going to make that tour?" It might be practically aggressive; but there was something that irritated me in her depths of resignation, and I wished to extort from her some expression of impatience.

She attached her eyes a moment to a small sun-spot on the carpet; then she got up and lowered the window-blind a little to obliterate it. I waited, watching her with interest—as if she had still something more to give me. Well, presently, in answer to my last question, she gave it. "Never!"

"I hope at least your cousin repaid you that money," I said.

At this again she looked away from me. "I don't care for it now."

"You don't care for your money?"

"For ever going to Europe."

"Do you mean you wouldn't go if you could?"

"I can't—I can't," said Caroline Spencer. "It's all over. Everything's different. I never think of it."

"The scoundrel never repaid you then!" I cried.

"Please, please—!" she began.

But she had stopped—she was looking toward the door. There had been a rustle and a sound of steps in the hall.

I also looked toward the door, which was open and now admitted another person—a lady who paused just within the threshold. Behind her came a young man. The lady looked at me with a good deal of fixedness—long enough for me to rise to a vivid impression of herself. Then she turned to Caroline Spencer and, with a smile and a strong foreign accent, "*Pardon, ma chère!* I didn't know you had company," she said. "The gentleman came in so quietly." With which she again gave me the benefit of her attention. She was very strange, yet I was at once sure I had seen her before. Afterwards I rather put it that I had only seen ladies remarkably like her. But I had seen them very far away from North Verona, and it was the oddest of all things to meet one of them in that frame. To what quite other scene did the sight of her transport me? To some dusky landing before a shabby Parisian *quatrième*—to an open door revealing a greasy ante-chamber and to Madame leaning over the banisters while she holds a faded wrapper together and bawls down to the portress to bring up her coffee. My friend's guest was a very large lady, of middle age, with a plump dead-white face and hair drawn back *à la chinoise*. She had a small penetrating eye and what is called in French *le sourire agréable*. She wore an old pink cashmere dressing-gown covered with white embroideries, and, like the figure in my momentary vision, she confined it in front with a bare and rounded arm and a plump and deeply-dimpled hand.

"It's only to spick about my café," she said to her hostess with her *sourire agréable*. "I should like it served in the garden under the leetle tree."

The young man behind her had now stepped into the room, where he also stood revealed, though with rather less of a challenge. He was a gentleman of few inches but a vague importance, perhaps the leading man of the world of North Verona. He had a small pointed nose and a small pointed chin; also, as I observed, the most diminutive feet and a manner of no point at all. He looked at me foolishly and with his mouth open.

"You shall have your coffee," said Miss Spencer as if an army of cooks had been engaged in the preparation of it.

"C'est bien!" said her massive inmate. "Find your bouk"—and this personage turned to the gaping youth.

He gaped now at each quarter of the room. "My grammar, d' ye mean?"

The large lady however could but face her friend's visitor while persistently engaged with a certain laxity in the flow of her wrapper. "Find your bouk," she more absently repeated.

"My poetry, d' ye mean?" said the young man, who also couldn't take his eyes off me.

"Never mind your bouk"—his companion reconsidered. "To-day we'll just talk. We'll make some conversation. But we mustn't interrupt Mademoiselle's. Come, come"—and she moved off a step. "Under the leetle tree," she added for the benefit of Mademoiselle. After which she gave me a thin salutation, jerked a measured "Monsieur!" and swept away again with her swain following.

I looked at Miss Spencer, whose eyes never moved from the carpet, and I spoke, I fear, without grace. "Who in the world's that?"

"The Comtesse—that *was:* my *cousine* as they call it in French."

"And who's the young man?"

"The Countess's pupil, Mr. Mixter." This description of the tie uniting the two persons who had just quitted us must certainly have upset my gravity; for I recall the marked increase of my friend's own as she continued to explain. "She gives lessons in French and music, the simpler sorts—"

"The simpler sorts of French?" I fear I broke in.

But she was still impenetrable, and in fact had now an intonation that put me vulgarly in the wrong. "She has had the worst reverses—with no one to look to. She's prepared for any exertion—and she takes her misfortunes with gaiety."

"Ah well," I returned—no doubt a little ruefully, "that's all I myself am pretending to do. If she's determined to be a burden to nobody, nothing could be more right and proper."

My hostess looked vaguely, though I thought quite wearily enough, about: she met this proposition in no other way. "I must go and get the coffee," she simply said.

"Has the lady many pupils?" I none the less persisted.

"She has only Mr. Mixter. She gives him all her time." It might have set me off again, but something in my whole impression of my friend's sensibility urged me to keep strictly decent. "He pays very well," she at all events inscrutably went on. "He's not very bright—as a pupil; but he's very rich and he's very kind. He has a buggy—with a back, and he takes the Countess to drive."

"For good long spells I hope," I couldn't help interjecting—even at the cost of her so taking it that she had still to avoid my eyes. "Well, the country's beautiful for miles," I went on. And then as she was turning away: "You're going for the Countess's coffee?"

"If you'll excuse me a few moments."

"Is there no one else to do it?"

She seemed to wonder who there should be. "I keep no servants."

"Then can't I help?" After which, as she but looked at me, I bettered it. "Can't she wait on herself?"

Miss Spencer had a slow headshake—as if that too had been a strange idea. "She isn't used to *manual* labour."

The discrimination was a treat, but I cultivated decorum. "I see—and you *are*." But at the same time I couldn't abjure curiosity. "Before you go, at any rate, please tell me this: who *is* this wonderful lady?"

"I told you just who in France—that extraordinary day. She's the wife of my cousin, whom you saw there."

"The lady disowned by her family in consequence of her marriage?"

"Yes; they've never seen her again. They've completely broken with her."

"And where's her husband?"

"My poor cousin's dead."

I pulled up, but only a moment. "And where's your money?"

The poor thing flinched—I kept her on the rack. "I don't know," she woefully said.

I scarce know what it didn't prompt me to—but I went step by step. "On her husband's death this lady at once came to you?"

It was as if she had had too often to describe it. "Yes, she arrived one day."

"How long ago?"

"Two years and four months."

"And has been here ever since?"

"Ever since."

I took it all in. "And how does she like it?"

"Well, not *very* much," said Miss Spencer divinely.

That too I took in. "And how do *you*—?"

She laid her face in her two hands an instant as she had done ten minutes before. Then, quickly, she went to get the Countess's coffee.

Left alone in the little parlour I found myself divided between the perfection of my disgust and a contrary wish to see, to learn more. At the end of a few minutes the young man in attendance on the lady in question reappeared as for a fresh gape at me. He was inordinately grave—to be dressed in such parti-coloured flannels; and he produced with no great confidence on his own side the message with which he had been charged. "She wants to know if you won't come right out."

"Who wants to know?"

"The Countess. That French lady."

"She has asked you to bring me?"

"Yes sir," said the young man feebly—for I may claim to have surpassed him in stature and weight.

I went out with him, and we found his instructress seated under one of the small quince-trees in front of the house; where she was engaged in drawing a fine needle with a very fat hand through a piece of embroidery not remarkable for freshness. She pointed graciously to the chair beside her and I sat down. Mr. Mixter glanced about him and then accommodated himself on the grass at her feet; whence he gazed upward more gapingly than ever and as if convinced that between us something wonderful would now occur.

"I'm sure you spick French," said the Countess, whose eyes were singularly protuberant as she played over me her agreeable smile.

"I do, madam—*tant bien que mal*," I replied, I fear, more dryly.

"Ah *voilà!*" she cried as with delight. "I knew it as soon as I looked at you. You've been in my poor dear country."

"A considerable time."

"You love it then, *mon pays de France?*"

"Oh it's an old affection." But I wasn't exuberant.

"And you know Paris well?"

"Yes, *sans me vanter,* madam, I think I really do." And with a certain conscious purpose I let my eyes meet her own.

She presently, hereupon, moved her own and glanced down at Mr. Mixter. "What are we talking about?" she demanded of her attentive pupil.

He pulled his knees up, plucked at the grass, stared, blushed a little. "You're talking French," said Mr. Mixter.

"*La belle découverte!*" mocked the Countess. "It's going on ten months," she explained to me, "since I took him in hand. Don't put yourself out not to say he's *la bêtise même,*" she added in fine style. "He won't in the least understand you."

A moment's consideration of Mr. Mixter, awkwardly sporting at our feet, quite assured me that he wouldn't. "I hope your other pupils do you more honour," I then remarked to my entertainer.

"I have no others. They don't know what French—or what anything else—is in this place; they don't want to know. You may therefore imagine the pleasure it is to me to meet a person who speaks it like yourself." I could but reply that my own pleasure wasn't less, and she continued to draw the stitches through her embroidery with an elegant curl of her little finger. Every few moments she put her eyes, near-sightedly, closer to her work—this as if for elegance too. She inspired me with no more confidence than her late husband, if husband he was, had done, years before, on the occasion with which this one so detestably matched: she was coarse, common, affected, dishonest—no more a Countess than I was a Caliph. She had an assurance—based clearly on experience; but this couldn't have been the experience of "race." Whatever it was indeed it did now, in a yearning fashion, flare out of her. "Talk to me of Paris, *mon beau Paris* that I'd give my eyes to see. The very name of it *me fait languir*. How long since you were there?"

"A couple of months ago."

"*Vous avez de la chance!* Tell me something about it. What were they doing? Oh for an hour of the Boulevard!"

"They were doing about what they're always doing—amusing themselves a good deal."

"At the theatres, *hein?*" sighed the Countess. "At the cafés-concerts? *sous ce beau ciel*—at the little tables before the doors? *Quelle existence!* You know I'm a Parisienne, monsieur," she added, "to my finger-tips."

"Miss Spencer was mistaken then," I ventured to return, "in telling me you're a Provençale."

She stared a moment, then put her nose to her embroidery, which struck me as having acquired even while we sat a dingier and more desultory air. "Ah I'm a Provençale by birth, but a Parisienne by—inclination." After which she pursued: "And by the saddest events of my life—as well as by some of the happiest, *hélas!*"

"In other words by a varied experience!" I now at last smiled.

She questioned me over it with her hard little salient eyes. "Oh experience!—I could talk of that, no doubt, if I wished. *On en a de toutes les sortes*—and I never dreamed that mine, for example, would ever have *this* in store for me." And she indicated with her large bare elbow and with a jerk of her head all surrounding objects; the little white house, the pair of quince-trees, the rickety paling, even the rapt Mr. Mixter.

I took them all bravely in. "Ah if you mean you're decidedly in exile—!"

"You may imagine what it is. These two years of my *épreuve—elles m'en ont données, des heures, des heures!* One gets used to things"—and she raised her shoulders to the highest shrug ever accomplished at North Verona; "so that I sometimes think I've got used to this. But there are some things that are always beginning again. For example my coffee."

I so far again lent myself. "Do you always have coffee at this hour?"

Her eyebrows went up as high as her shoulders had done. "At what hour would you propose to me to have it? I must have my little cup after breakfast."

"Ah you breakfast at this hour?"

"At mid-day—*comme cela se fait.* Here they breakfast at a quarter past seven. That 'quarter past' is charming!"

"But you were telling me about your coffee," I observed sympathetically.

"My *cousine* can't believe in it; she can't understand it. *C'est une fille charmante,* but that little cup of black coffee with a drop of '*fine,*' served at this hour—they exceed her comprehension. So I have to break the ice each day, and it takes the coffee the time you see to arrive. And when it does arrive, monsieur—! If I don't press it on *you*—though monsieur here sometimes joins me!—it's because you've drunk it on the Boulevard."

I resented extremely so critical a view of my poor friend's exertions, but I said nothing at all—the only way to be sure of my civility. I dropped my eyes on Mr. Mixter, who, sitting cross-legged and nursing his knees, watched my companion's foreign graces with an interest that familiarity had apparently done little to restrict. She became aware, naturally, of my mystified view of him and faced the question with all her boldness. "He adores me, you know," she murmured with her nose again in her tapestry —"he dreams of becoming *mon amoureux*. Yes, *il me fait un cour acharnée* —such as you see him. That's what we've come to. He has read some French novel—it took him six months. But ever since that he has thought himself a hero and me—such as I am, monsieur—*je ne sais quelle dévergondée!*"

Mr. Mixter may have inferred that he was to that extent the object of our reference; but of the manner in which he was handled he must have had small suspicion—preoccupied as he was, as to my companion, with the ecstasy of contemplation. Our hostess moreover at this moment came out of the house, bearing a coffee-pot and three cups on a neat little tray. I took from her eyes, as she approached us, a brief but intense appeal—the mute expression as I felt, conveyed in the hardest little look she had yet addressed me, of her longing to know what, as a man of the world in general and of the French world in particular, I thought of these allied forces now so encamped on the stricken field of her life. I could only "act" however, as they said at North Verona, quite impenetrably—only make no answering sign. I couldn't intimate, much less could I frankly utter, my inward sense of the Countess's probable past, with its measure of her virtue, value and accomplishments, and of the limits of the consideration to which she could properly pretend. I couldn't give my friend a hint of how I myself personally "saw" her interesting pensioner—whether as the runaway wife of a too-jealous hair-dresser or of a too-morose pastry-cook, say; whether as a very small bourgeoise, in fine, who had vitiated her case beyond patching up, or even as some character, of the nomadic sort, less edifying still. I couldn't let in, by the jog of a shutter, as it were, a hard informing ray and then, washing my hands of the business, turn my back for ever. I could on the contrary but save the situation, my own at least, for the moment, by pulling myself together with a master hand and appearing to ignore everything but that the dreadful person between us *was* a "grande dame." This effort was possible indeed but as a retreat in good order and with all the forms of courtesy. If I couldn't speak, still less could I stay, and I think I must, in spite of everything, have turned black with disgust to see Caroline Spencer stand there like a waiting-maid. I therefore won't answer for the shade of success that may have attended my saying to the Countess, on my feet and as to leave her: "You expect to remain some time in these *parages?*"

What passed between us, as from face to face, while she looked up at me, *that* at least our companion may have caught, that at least may have sown, for the aftertime, some seed of revelation. The Countess repeated her terrible shrug. "Who knows? I don't see my way—! It isn't an existence, but when one's in misery—! *Chère belle,*" she added as an appeal to Miss Spencer, "you've gone and forgotten the *'fine'!*"

I detained that lady as, after considering a moment in silence the small array, she was about to turn off in quest of this article. I held out my hand in silence—I had to go. Her wan set little face, severely mild and with the question of a moment before now quite cold in it, spoke of extreme fatigue, but also of something else strange and conceived—whether a desperate patience still, or at last some other desperation, being more than I can say. What was clearest on the whole was that she was glad I was going. Mr. Mixter had risen to his feet and was pouring out the Countess's coffee. As I went back past the Baptist church I could feel how right my poor friend had been in her conviction at the other, the still intenser, the now historic crisis, that she should still see something of that dear old Europe.

Anton Chekhov

Anton Chekhov (1860–1904) was born at Taganrog, Russia, the son of a tradesman and grandson of a liberated serf. During the years he spent as a medical student in Moscow, from 1879 to 1884, he wrote hundreds of humorous potboilers to help support his family. Soon after his graduation he began to develop the "Chekhovian" style. His ardent humanitarianism and social spirit involved him in such things as the study of prison conditions, making protestations about the Dreyfus case, and resignation from the Russian Academy when Maxim Gorky was refused a seat as Academician. In 1897 he developed tuberculosis, from which he died in 1904. Chekhov believed that "the aim of fiction is absolute and honest truth"; hence spring his stories about isolated human beings who are unable to communicate with each other. His many volumes of short stories significantly influenced the form. Today he is perhaps better known for his plays The Seagull *(1896),* The Three Sisters, *(1901), and* The Cherry Orchard *(1904).* *(See page 77 of Introduction.)*

GUSEV

I

It was getting dark; it would soon be night.

Gusev, a discharged soldier, sat up in his hammock and said in an undertone:

"I say, Pavel Ivanitch. A soldier at Sutchan told me: while they were sailing a big fish came into collision with their ship and stove a hole in it."

The nondescript individual whom he was addressing, and whom everyone in the ship's hospital called Pavel Ivanitch, was silent, as though he had not heard.

And again a stillness followed. . . . The wind frolicked with the rigging, the screw throbbed, the waves lashed, the hammocks creaked, but the ear had long ago become accustomed to these sounds, and it seemed that everything around was asleep and silent. It was dreary. The three invalids—two soldiers and a sailor—who had been playing cards all the day were asleep and talking in their dreams.

It seemed as though the ship were beginning to rock. The hammock slowly rose and fell under Gusev, as though it were heaving a sigh, and this was repeated once, twice, three times. . . . Something crashed on to the floor with a clang: it must have been a jug falling down.

"The wind has broken loose from its chain . . ." said Gusev, listening.

This time Pavel Ivanitch cleared his throat and answered irritably:

"One minute a vessel's running into a fish, the next, the wind's breaking loose from its chain. . . . Is the wind a beast that it can break loose from its chain?"

"That's how christened folk talk."

"They are as ignorant as you are then. . . . They say all sorts of things. One must keep a head on one's shoulders and use one's reason. You are a senseless creature."

Pavel Ivanitch was subject to sea-sickness. When the sea was rough he was usually ill-humoured, and the merest trifle would make him irritable. And in Gusev's opinion there was absolutely nothing to be vexed about. What was there strange or wonderful, for instance, in the fish or in the wind's breaking loose from its chain? Suppose the fish were as big as a mountain and its back were as hard as a sturgeon: and in the same way, supposing that away yonder at the end of the world there stood great stone walls and the fierce winds were chained up to the walls . . . if they had not broken loose, why did they tear about all over the sea like maniacs, and struggle to escape like dogs? If they were not chained up, what did become of them when it was calm?

Gusev pondered for a long time about fishes as big as a mountain and stout, rusty chains, then he began to feel dull and thought of his native place to which he was returning after five years' service in the East. He pictured an immense pond covered with snow. . . . On one side of the pond the red-brick building of the potteries with a tall chimney and clouds of black smoke; on the other side—a village. . . . His brother Alexey comes out in a sledge from the fifth yard from the end; behind him sits his little son Vanka in big felt over-boots, and his little girl Akulka, also in big felt boots. Alexey has been drinking, Vanka is laughing, Akulka's face he could not see, she had muffled herself up.

"You never know, he'll get the children frozen . . ." thought Gusev. "Lord send them sense and judgment that they may honour their father and mother and not be wiser than their parents."

"They want re-soleing," a delirious sailor says in a bass voice. "Yes, yes!"

Gusev's thoughts break off, and instead of a pond there suddenly appears apropos of nothing a huge bull's head without eyes, and the horse and sledge are not driving along, but are whirling round and round in a cloud of smoke. But still he was glad he had seen his own folks. He held his breath from delight, shudders ran all over him, and his fingers twitched.

"The Lord let us meet again," he muttered feverishly, but he at once opened his eyes and sought in the darkness for water.

He drank and lay back, and again the sledge was moving, then again the bull's head without eyes, smoke, clouds. . . . And so on till daybreak.

II

The first outline visible in the darkness was a blue circle—the little round window; then little by little Gusev could distinguish his neighbour in the next hammock, Pavel Ivanitch. The man slept sitting up, as he could not breathe lying down. His face was grey, his nose was long and sharp, his eyes looked huge from the terrible thinness of his face, his temples were sunken, his beard was skimpy, his hair was long. . . . Looking at him you could not make out of what class he was, whether he were a gentleman, a merchant, or a peasant. Judging from his expression and his long hair he might have been a hermit or a lay brother in a monastery—but if one listened to what he said it seemed that he could not be a monk. He was worn out by his cough and his illness and by the stifling heat, and breathed with difficulty, moving his parched lips. Noticing that Gusev was looking at him he turned his face towards him and said:

"I begin to guess. . . . Yes. . . . I understand it all perfectly now."

"What do you understand, Pavel Ivanitch?"

"I'll tell you. . . . It has always seemed to me strange that terribly ill as you are you should be here in a steamer where it is so hot and stifling and we are always being tossed up and down, where, in fact, everything threatens you with death; now it is all clear to me. . . . Yes. . . . Your doctors put you on the steamer to get rid of you. They get sick of looking after poor brutes like you. . . . You don't pay them anything, they have a bother with you, and you damage their records with your deaths—so, of course, you are brutes! It's not difficult to get rid of you. . . . All that is necessary is, in the first place, to have no conscience or humanity, and, secondly, to deceive the steamer authorities. The first condition need hardly be considered, in that respect we are artists; and one can always succeed in the second with a little practice. In a crowd of four hundred healthy soldiers and sailors half a dozen sick ones are not conspicuous; well, they drove you all on to the steamer, mixed you with the healthy ones, hurriedly counted you over, and in the confusion nothing amiss was noticed, and when the steamer had started they saw that there were paralytics and consumptives in the last stage lying about on the deck. . . ."

Gusev did not understand Pavel Ivanitch; but supposing he was being blamed, he said in self-defense:

"I lay on the deck because I had not the strength to stand; when we were unloaded from the barge on to the ship I caught a fearful chill."

"It's revolting," Pavel Ivanitch went on. "The worst of it is they know perfectly well that you can't last out the long journey, and yet they put you here. Supposing you get as far as the Indian Ocean, what then? It's horrible to think of it. . . . And that's their gratitude for your faithful, irreproachable service!"

Pavel Ivanitch's eyes looked angry; he frowned contemptuously and said, gasping:

"Those are the people who ought to be plucked in the newspapers till the feathers fly in all directions."

The two sick soldiers and the sailor were awake and already playing cards. The sailor was half reclining in his hammock, the soldiers were sitting near him on the floor in the most uncomfortable attitudes. One of the soldiers had his right arm in a sling, and the hand was swathed up in a regular bundle so that he held his cards under his right arm or in the crook of his elbow while he played with the left. The ship was rolling heavily. They could not stand up, nor drink tea, nor take their medicines.

"Were you an officer's servant?" Pavel Ivanitch asked Gusev.

"Yes, an officer's servant."

"My God, my God!" said Pavel Ivanitch, and he shook his head mournfully. "To tear a man out of his home, drag him twelve thousand miles away, then to drive him into consumption and . . . and what is it all for, one wonders? To turn him into a servant for some Captain Kopeikin or Midshipman Dirka! How logical!"

"It's not hard work, Pavel Ivanitch. You get up in the morning and clean the boots, get the samovar, sweep the rooms, and then you have nothing more to do. The lieutenant is all the day drawing plans, and if you like you can say your prayers, if you like you can read a book or go out into the street. God grant everyone such a life."

"Yes, very nice, the lieutenant draws plans all the day and you sit in the kitchen and pine for home. . . . Plans indeed! . . . It is not plans that matter, but a human life. Life is not given twice, it must be treated mercifully."

"Of course, Pavel Ivanitch, a bad man gets no mercy anywhere, neither at home nor in the army, but if you live as you ought and obey orders, who has any need to insult you? The officers are educated gentlemen, they understand. . . . In five years I was never once in prison, and I was never struck a blow, so help me God, but once."

"What for?"

"For fighting. I have a heavy hand, Pavel Ivanitch. Four Chinamen came into our yard; they were bringing firewood or something, I don't remember. Well, I was bored and I knocked them about a bit, one's nose began bleeding, damn the fellow. . . . The lieutenant saw it through the little window, he was angry and gave me a box on the ear."

"Foolish, pitiful man . . ." whispered Pavel Ivanitch. "You don't understand anything."

He was utterly exhausted by the tossing of the ship and closed his eyes; his head alternately fell back and dropped forward on his breast. Several times he tried to lie down but nothing came of it; his difficulty in breathing prevented it.

"And what did you hit the four Chinamen for?" he asked a little while afterwards.

"Oh, nothing. They came into the yard and I hit them."

And a stillness followed. . . . The card-players had been playing for two hours with enthusiasm and loud abuse of one another, but the motion of the ship overcame them, too; they threw aside the cards and lay down. Again Gusev saw the big pond, the brick building, the village. . . . Again the sledge was coming along, again Vanka was laughing and Akulka, silly little thing, threw open her fur coat and stuck her feet out, as much as to say: "Look, good people, my snowboots are not like Vanka's, they are new ones."

"Five years old, and she has no sense yet," Gusev muttered in delirium. "Instead of kicking your legs you had better come and get your soldier uncle a drink. I will give you something nice."

Then Andron with a flintlock gun on his shoulder was carrying a hare he had killed, and he was followed by the decrepit old Jew Isaitchik, who offers to barter the hare for a piece of soap; then the black calf in the shed, then Domna sewing at a shirt and crying about something, and then again the bull's head without eyes, black smoke. . . .

Overhead someone gave a loud shout, several sailors ran by, they seemed to be dragging something bulky over the deck, something fell with a crash. Again they ran by. . . . Had something gone wrong? Gusev raised his head, listened, and saw that the two soldiers and the sailor were playing cards again; Pavel Ivanitch was sitting up moving his lips. It was stifling, one hadn't strength to breathe, one was thirsty, the water was warm, disgusting. The ship heaved as much as ever.

Suddenly something strange happened to one of the soldiers playing cards. . . . He called hearts diamonds, got muddled in his score, and dropped his cards, then with a frightened, foolish smile looked round at all of them.

"I shan't be a minute, mates, I'll . . ." he said, and lay down on the floor.

Everybody was amazed. They called to him, he did not answer.

"Stepan, maybe you are feeling bad, eh?" the soldier with his arm in a sling asked him. "Perhaps we had better bring the priest, eh?"

"Have a drink of water, Stepan . . ." said the sailor. "Here, lad, drink."

"Why are you knocking the jug against his teeth?" said Gusev angrily. "Don't you see, turnip head?"

"What?"

"What?" Gusev repeated, mimicking him. "There is no breath in him, he is dead! That's what! What nonsensical people, Lord have mercy on us . . . !"

III

The ship was not rocking and Pavel Ivanitch was more cheerful. He was no longer ill-humoured. His face had a boastful, defiant, mocking expression. He looked as though he wanted to say: "Yes, in a minute I will tell you something that will make you split your sides with laughing." The little round window was open and a soft breeze was blowing on Pavel Ivanitch. There was a sound of voices, of the plash of oars in the water. . . . Just under the little window someone began droning in a high, unpleasant voice: no doubt it was a Chinaman singing.

"Here we are in the harbour," said Pavel Ivanitch, smiling ironically. "Only another month and we shall be in Russia. Well, worthy gentlemen and warriors! I shall arrive at Odessa and from there go straight to Harkov. In Harkov I have a friend, a literary man. I shall go to him and say, 'Come, old man, put aside your horrid subjects, ladies' amours and the beauties of nature, and show up human depravity.' "

For a minute he pondered, then said:

"Gusev, do you know how I took them in?"

"Took in whom, Pavel Ivanitch?"

"Why, these fellows. . . . You know that on this steamer there is only a first-class and a third-class, and they only allow peasants—that is the riff-raff—to go in the third. If you have got on a reefer jacket and have the faintest resemblance to a gentleman or a bourgeois you must go first-class, if you please. You must fork out five hundred roubles if you die for it. Why, I ask, have you made such a rule? Do you want to raise the prestige of educated Russians thereby? Not a bit of it. We don't let you go third-class simply because a decent person can't go third-class; it is very horrible and disgusting. Yes, indeed. I am very grateful for such solicitude for decent people's welfare. But in any case, whether it is nasty there or nice, five hundred roubles I haven't got. I haven't pilfered government money. I haven't exploited the natives, I haven't trafficked in contraband, I have flogged no one to death, so judge whether I have the right to travel first-class and even less to reckon myself of the educated class? But you won't catch them with logic. . . . One has to resort to deception. I put on a workman's coat and high boots, I assumed a drunken, servile mug and went to the agents: 'Give us a little ticket, your honour,' said I. . . ."

"Why, what class do you belong to?" asked a sailor.

"Clerical. My father was an honest priest, he always told the great ones of the world the truth to their faces; and he had a great deal to put up with in consequence."

Pavel Ivanitch was exhausted with talking and gasped for breath, but still went on:

"Yes, I always tell people the truth to their faces. I am not afraid of anyone or anything. There is a vast difference between me and all of you in that respect. You are in darkness, you are blind, crushed; you see nothing and what you do see you don't understand. . . . You are told the wind breaks loose from its chain, that you are beasts, Petchenyegs, and you believe it; they punch you in the neck, you kiss their hands; some animal in a sable-lined coat robs you and then tips you fifteen kopecks and you: 'Let me kiss your hand, sir.' You are pariahs, pitiful people. . . . I am a different sort. My eyes are open, I see it all as clearly as a hawk or an eagle when it floats over the earth, and I understand it all. I am a living protest. I see irresponsible tyranny—I protest. I see cant and hypocrisy—I protest. I see swine triumphant—I protest. And I cannot be suppressed, no Spanish Inquisition can make me hold my tongue. No. . . . Cut out my tongue and I would protest in dumb show; shut me up in a cellar—I will shout from it to be heard half a mile away, or I will starve myself to death that they may have another weight on their black consciences. Kill me and I will haunt them with my ghost. All my acquaintances say to me: 'You are a most insufferable person, Pavel Ivanitch.' I am proud of such a reputation. I have served three years in the far East, and I shall be remembered there for a hundred years: I had rows with everyone. My friends write to me from Russia, 'Don't come back,' but here I am going back to spite them . . . yes. . . . That is life as I understand it. That is what one can call life."

Gusev was looking at the little window and was not listening. A boat was swaying on the transparent, soft, turquoise water all bathed in hot, dazzling sunshine. In it there were naked Chinamen holding up cages with canaries and calling out:

"It sings, it sings!"

Another boat knocked against the first; the steam cutter darted by. And then there came another boat with a fat Chinaman sitting in it, eating rice with little sticks.

Languidly the water heaved, languidly the white seagulls floated over it.

"I should like to give that fat fellow one in the neck," thought Gusev, gazing at the stout Chinaman, with a yawn.

He dozed off, and it seemed to him that all nature was dozing, too. Time flew swiftly by; imperceptibly the day passed, imperceptibly the darkness came on. . . . The steamer was no longer standing still, but moving on further.

IV

Two days passed, Pavel Ivanitch lay down instead of sitting up; his eyes were closed, his nose seemed to have grown sharper.

"Pavel Ivanitch," Gusev called to him. "Hey, Pavel Ivanitch."

Pavel Ivanitch opened his eyes and moved his lips.

"Are you feeling bad?"

"No . . . it's nothing . . ." answered Pavel Ivanitch, gasping. "Nothing; on the contrary . . . I am rather better. . . . You see I can lie down. . . . I am a little easier. . . ."

"Well, thank God for that, Pavel Ivanitch."

"When I compare myself with you I am sorry for you . . . poor fellow. My lungs are all right, it is only a stomach cough. . . . I can stand hell, let alone the Red Sea. Besides I take a critical attitude to my illness and to the medicines they give me for it. While you . . . you are in darkness. . . . It's hard for you, very, very hard!"

The ship was not rolling, it was calm, but as hot and stifling as a bath-house; it was not only hard to speak but even hard to listen. Gusev hugged his knees, laid his head on them and thought of his home. Good heavens, what a relief it was to think of snow and cold in that stifling heat! You drive in a sledge, all at once the horses take fright at something and bolt. . . . Regardless of the road, the ditches, the ravines, they dash like mad things, right through the village, over the pond by the pottery works, out across the open fields. "Hold on," the pottery hands and the peasants shout, meeting them. "Hold on." But why? Let the keen, cold wind beat in one's face and bite one's hands; let the lumps of snow, kicked up by the horses' hoofs, fall on one's cap, on one's back, down one's collar, on one's chest; let the runners ring on the snow, and the traces and the sledge be smashed, deuce take them one and all! And how delightful when the sledge upsets and you go flying full tilt into a drift, face downwards in the snow, and then you get up white all over with icicles on your moustaches; no cap, no gloves, your belt undone. . . . People laugh, the dogs bark. . . .

Pavel Ivanitch half opened one eye, looked at Gusev with it, and asked softly:

"Gusev, did your commanding officer steal?"

"Who can tell, Pavel Ivanitch! We can't say, it didn't reach us."

And after that a long time passed in silence. Gusev brooded, muttered something in delirium, and kept drinking water; it was hard for him to talk and hard to listen, and he was afraid of being talked to. An hour passed, a second, a third; evening came on, then night, but he did not notice it. He still sat dreaming of the frost.

There was a sound as though someone came into the hospital, and voices were audible, but a few minutes passed and all was still again.

"The Kingdom of Heaven and eternal peace," said the soldier with his arm in a sling. "He was an uncomfortable man."

"What?" asked Gusev. "Who?"

"He is dead, they have just carried him up."

"Oh, well," muttered Gusev, yawning, "the Kingdom of Heaven be his."

"What do you think?" the soldier with his arm in a sling asked Gusev. "Will he be in the Kingdom of Heaven or not?"

"Who is it you are talking about?"

"Pavel Ivanitch."

"He will be . . . he suffered so long. And there is another thing, he belonged to the clergy, and the priests always have a lot of relations. Their prayers will save him."

The soldier with the sling sat down on a hammock near Gusev and said in an undertone:

"And you, Gusev, are not long for this world. You will never get to Russia."

"Did the doctor or his assistant say so?" asked Gusev.

"It isn't that they said so, but one can see it. . . . One can see directly when a man's going to die. You don't eat, you don't drink; it's dreadful to see how thin you've got. It's consumption, in fact. I say it, not to upset you, but because maybe you would like to have the sacrament and extreme unction. And if you have any money you had better give it to the senior officer."

"I haven't written home . . ." Gusev sighed. "I shall die and they won't know."

"They'll hear of it," the sick sailor brought out in a bass voice. "When you die they will put it down in the *Gazette,* at Odessa they will send in a report to the commanding officer there and he will send it to the parish or somewhere. . . ."

Gusev began to be uneasy after such a conversation and to feel a vague yearning. He drank water—it was not that; he dragged himself to the window and breathed the hot, moist air—it was not that; he tried to think of home, of the frost—it was not that. . . . At last it seemed to him one minute longer in the ward and he would certainly expire.

"It's stifling, mates . . ." he said. "I'll go on deck. Help me up, for Christ's sake."

"All right," assented the soldier with the sling. "I'll carry you, you can't walk, hold on to my neck."

Gusev put his arm round the soldier's neck, the latter put his unhurt arm round him and carried him up. On the deck sailors and time-expired soldiers were lying asleep side by side; there were so many of them it was difficult to pass.

"Stand down," the soldier with the sling said softly. "Follow me quietly, hold on to my shirt. . . ."

It was dark. There was no light on deck, nor on the masts, nor anywhere on the sea around. At the furthest end of the ship the man on watch was standing perfectly still like a statue, and it looked as though he were asleep. It seemed as though the steamer were abandoned to itself and were going at its own will.

"Now they will throw Pavel Ivanitch into the sea," said the soldier with the sling. "In a sack and then into the water."

"Yes, that's the rule."

"But it's better to lie at home in the earth. Anyway, your mother comes to the grave and weeps."

"Of course."

There was a smell of hay and of dung. There were oxen standing with drooping heads by the ship's rail. One, two, three; eight of them! And there was a little horse. Gusev put out his hand to stroke it, but it shook its head, showed its teeth, and tried to bite his sleeve.

"Damned brute . . ." said Gusev angrily.

The two of them, he and the soldier, threaded their way to the head of the ship, then stood at the rail and looked up and down. Overhead deep sky, bright stars, peace and stillness, exactly as at home in the village, below darkness and disorder. The tall waves were resounding, no one could tell why. Whichever wave you looked at each one was trying to rise higher than all the rest and to chase and crush the next one; after it a third as fierce and hideous flew noisily, with a glint of light on its white crest.

The sea has no sense and no pity. If the steamer had been smaller and not made of thick iron, the waves would have crushed it to pieces without the slightest compunction, and would have devoured all the people in it with no distinction of saints or sinners. The steamer had the same cruel and meaningless expression. This monster with its huge beak was dashing onwards, cutting millions of waves in its path; it had no fear of the darkness nor the wind, nor of space, nor of solitude, caring for nothing, and if the ocean had its people, this monster would have crushed them, too, without distinction of saints or sinners.

"Where are we now?" asked Gusev.

"I don't know. We must be in the ocean."

"There is no sight of land. . . ."

"No indeed! They say we shan't see it for seven days."

The two soldiers watched the white foam with the phosphorus light on it and were silent, thinking. Gusev was the first to break the silence.

"There is nothing to be afraid of," he said, "only one is full of dread as though one were sitting in a dark forest; but if, for instance, they let a boat down on to the water this minute and an officer ordered me to go a hundred miles over the sea to catch fish, I'd go. Or, let's say, if a Christian were to fall into the water this minute, I'd go in after him. A German or a Chinaman I wouldn't save, but I'd go in after a Christian."

"And are you afraid to die?"

"Yes. I am sorry for the folks at home. My brother at home, you know, isn't steady; he drinks, he beats his wife for nothing, he does not honour his parents. Everything will go to ruin without me, and father and my old mother will be begging their bread, I shouldn't wonder. But my legs won't bear me, brother, and it's hot here. Let's go to sleep."

V

Gusev went back to the ward and got into his hammock. He was again tormented by a vague craving, and he could not make out what he wanted. There was an oppression on his chest, a throbbing in his head, his mouth was so dry that it was difficult for him to move his tongue. He dozed, and murmured in his sleep, and, worn out with nightmares, his cough, and the stifling heat, towards morning he fell into a sound sleep. He dreamed that they were just taking the bread out of the oven in the barracks and he climbed into the stove and had a steam bath in it, lashing himself with a bunch of birch twigs. He slept for two days, and at midday on the third two sailors came down and carried him out.

He was sewn up in sailcloth and to make him heavier they put with him two iron weights. Sewn up in the sailcloth he looked like a carrot or a radish: broad at the head and narrow at the feet. . . . Before sunset they brought him up to the deck and put him on a plank; one end of the plank lay on the side of the ship, the other on a box, placed on a stool. Round him stood the soldiers and the officers with their caps off.

"Blessed be the Name of the Lord . . ." the priest began. "As it was in the beginning, is now, and ever shall be."

"Amen," chanted three sailors.

The soldiers and the officers crossed themselves and looked away at the waves. It was strange that a man should be sewn up in sailcloth and should soon be flying into the sea. Was it possible that such a thing might happen to anyone?

The priest strewed earth upon Gusev and bowed down. They sang "Eternal Memory."

The man on watch duty tilted up the end of the plank, Gusev slid off and flew head foremost, turned a somersault in the air and splashed into the sea. He was covered with foam and for a moment looked as though he were wrapped in lace, but the minute passed and he disappeared in the waves.

He went rapidly towards the bottom. Did he reach it? It was said to be three miles to the bottom. After sinking sixty or seventy feet, he began moving more and more slowly, swaying rhythmically, as though he were hesitating and, carried along by the current, moved more rapidly sideways than downwards.

Then he was met by a shoal of the fish called harbour pilots. Seeing the dark body the fish stopped as though petrified, and suddenly turned round and disappeared. In less than a minute they flew back swift as an arrow to Gusev, and began zig-zagging round him in the water.

After that another dark body appeared. It was a shark. It swam under Gusev with dignity and no show of interest, as though it did not notice him, and sank down upon its back, then it turned belly upwards, basking in the warm, transparent water and languidly opened its jaws with two rows of teeth. The harbour pilots are delighted, they stop to see what will come next. After playing a little with the body the shark nonchalantly puts its jaws under it, cautiously touches it with its teeth, and the sail-cloth is rent its full length from head to foot; one of the weights falls out and frightens the harbour pilots, and striking the shark on the ribs goes rapidly to the bottom.

Overhead at this time the clouds are massed together on the side where the sun is setting; one cloud like a triumphal arch, another like a lion, a third like a pair of scissors. . . . From behind the clouds a broad, green shaft of light pierces through and stretches to the middle of the sky; a little later another, violet-coloured, lies beside it; next that, one of gold, then one rose-coloured. . . . The sky turns a soft lilac. Looking at this gorgeous, enchanted sky, at first the ocean scowls, but soon it, too, takes tender, joyous, passionate colours for which it is hard to find a name in human speech.

Stephen Crane

Stephen Crane (1871–1900) was born in Newark, New Jersey, the fourteenth child of a Methodist minister. A rebel from childhood, Crane enjoyed the activities against which his father inveighed: baseball, theatergoing, and free association with women. He attended several colleges for short periods. His first novel, Maggie: A Girl of the Streets *(1893) exposed slum conditions and Bowery life, about which he knew very little at first hand. Subsequently, he worked as a reporter and war correspondent and after reporting the Greco-Turkish War, he and Cora Taylor, the former proprietress of a Jacksonville, Fla. nightclub-brothel, lived as man and wife in England for the last three years of his life. To stave off bankruptcy, Crane turned out many tales and sketches. He died of tuberculosis and his body was returned by Cora to New Jersey for burial. His most famous work is* The Red Badge of Courage *(1895). His fiction often traces the conflict between the limited individual and the massive forces of nature and society ranged against him.* *(See page 69 of Introduction.)*

THE BLUE HOTEL

The Palace Hotel at Fort Romper was painted a light blue, a shade that is on the legs of a kind of heron, causing the bird to declare its position against any background. The Palace Hotel, then, was always screaming and howling in a way that made the dazzling winter landscape of Nebraska seem only a gray swampish hush. It stood alone on the prairie, and when the snow was falling the town two hundred yards away was not visible. But when the traveller alighted at the railway station he was obliged to pass the Palace Hotel before he could come upon the company of low clapboard houses which composed Fort Romper, and it was not to be thought that any traveller could pass the Palace Hotel without looking at it. Pat Scully, the proprietor, had proved himself a master of strategy when he chose his paints. It is true that on clear days, when the great transcontinental expresses, long lines of swaying Pullmans, swept through Fort Romper, passengers were overcome at the sight, and the cult that knows the brown-reds and the subdivisions of the dark greens of the East expressed shame, pity, horror, in a laugh. But to the citizens of this prairie town and to the people who would naturally stop there, Pat Scully had performed a feat. With this opulence and splendor, these creeds, classes, egotisms, that streamed through Romper on the rails day after day, they had no color in common.

As if the displayed delights of such a blue hotel were not sufficiently enticing, it was Scully's habit to go every morning and every evening to meet the leisurely trains that stopped at Romper and work his seductions upon any man that he might see wavering, gripsack in hand.

One morning, when a snow-crusted engine dragged its long string of freight cars and its one passenger coach to the station, Scully performed the marvel of catching three men. One was a shaky and quick-eyed Swede, with a great shining cheap valise; one was a tall bronzed cowboy, who was on his way to a ranch near the Dakota line; one was a little silent man from the East, who didn't look it, and didn't announce it. Scully practically made them prisoners. He was so nimble and merry and kindly that each probably felt it would be the height of brutality to try to escape. They trudged off over the creaking board sidewalks in the wake of the eager little Irishman. He wore a heavy fur cap sqeezed tightly down on his head. It caused his two red ears to stick out stiffly, as if they were made of tin.

At last, Scully, elaborately, with boisterous hospitality, conducted them through the portals of the blue hotel. The room which they entered was small. It seemed to be merely a proper temple for the enormous stove, which, in the center, was humming with godlike violence. At various points on its surface the iron had become luminous and glowed yellow from the heat. Beside the stove Scully's son Johnnie was playing High-Five with an old farmer who had whiskers both gray and sandy. They were quarreling. Frequently the old farmer turned his face towards a box of sawdust—colored brown from tobacco juice—that was behind the stove, and spat with an air of great impatience and irritation. With a loud flourish of words Scully destroyed the game of cards, and bustled his son upstairs with part of the baggage of the new guests. He himself conducted them to three basins of the coldest water in the world. The cowboy and the Easterner burnished themselves fiery red with his water, until it seemed to be some kind of metal polish. The Swede, however, merely dipped his fingers gingerly and with trepidation. It was notable that throughout this series of small ceremonies the three travellers were made to feel that Scully was very benevolent. He was conferring great favors upon them. He handed the towel from one to another with an air of philanthropic impulse.

Afterward they went to the first room, and, sitting about the stove, listened to Scully's officious clamor at his daughters, who were preparing the midday meal. They reflected in the silence of experienced men who tread carefully amid new people. Nevertheless, the old farmer, stationary, invincible in his chair near the warmest part of the stove, turned his face from the sawdust box frequently and addressed a glowing commonplace to the strangers. Usually he was answered in short but adequate sentences by either the cowboy or the Easterner. The Swede said nothing. He seemed to be occupied in making furtive estimates of each man in the room. One might have thought that he had the sense of silly suspicion which comes to guilt. He resembled a badly frightened man.

Later, at dinner, he spoke a little, addressing his conversation entirely to Scully. He volunteered that he had come from New York, where for ten years he had worked as a tailor. These facts seemed to strike Scully as fascinating, and afterward he volunteered that he had lived at Romper for fourteen years. The Swede asked about the crops and the price of labor. He seemed barely to listen to Scully's extended replies. His eyes continued to rove from man to man.

Finally, with a laugh and a wink, he said that some of these Western communities were very dangerous; and after his statement he straightened his legs under the table, tilted his head, and laughed again, loudly. It was plain that the demonstration had no meaning to the others. They looked at him wondering and in silence.

II

As the men trooped heavily back into the front room, the two little windows presented views of a turmoiling sea of snow. The huge arms of the wind were making attempts—mighty, circular, futile—to embrace the flakes as they sped. A gate-post like a still man with a blanched face stood aghast amid his profligate fury. In a hearty voice Scully announced the presence of a blizzard. The guests of the blue hotel, lighting their pipes, assented with grunts of lazy masculine contentment. No island of the sea could be exempt in the degree of this little room with its humming stove. Johnnie, son of Scully, in a tone which defined his opinion of his ability as a card player, challenged the old farmer of both gray and sandy whiskers to a game of High-Five. The farmer agreed with a contemptuous and bitter scoff. They sat close to the stove, and squared their knees under a wide board. The cowboy and the Easterner watched the game with interest. The Swede remained near the window, aloof, but with a countenance that showed signs of an inexplicable excitement.

The play of Johnnie and the gray-beard was suddenly ended by another quarrel. The old man arose while casting a look of heated scorn at his adversary. He slowly buttoned his coat, and then stalked with fabulous dignity from the room. In the discreet silence of all the other men the Swede laughed. His laughter rang somehow childish. Men by this time had begun to look at him askance, as if they wished to inquire what ailed him.

A new game was formed jocosely. The cowboy volunteered to become the partner of Johnnie, and they all then turned to ask the Swede to throw in his lot with the little Easterner. He asked some questions about the game, and, learning that it wore many names, and that he had played it when it was under an alias, he accepted the invitation. He strode towards the men nervously, as if he expected to be assaulted. Finally, seated, he gazed from face to face and laughed shrilly. This laugh was so strange that the Easterner looked up quickly, the cowboy sat intent and with his mouth open, and Johnnie paused, holding the cards with still fingers.

Afterward there was a short silence. Then Johnnie said, "Well, let's get at it. Come on now!" They pulled their chairs forward until their knees were bunched under the board. They began to play, and their interest in the game caused the others to forget the manner of the Swede.

The cowboy was a board-whacker. Each time that he held superior cards he whanged them, one by one, with exceeding force, down upon the improvised table, and took the tricks with a glowing air of prowess and pride that sent thrills of indignation into the hearts of his opponents. A game with a board-whacker in it is sure to become intense. The countenances of the Easterner and the Swede were miserable whenever the cowboy thundered down his aces and kings, while Johnnie, his eyes gleaming with joy, chuckled and chuckled.

Because of the absorbing play none considered the strange ways of the Swede. They paid strict heed to the game. Finally, during a lull caused by a new deal, the Swede suddenly addressed Johnnie: "I suppose there have been a good many men killed in this room." The jaws of the others dropped and they looked at him.

"What the hell are you talking about?" said Johnnie.

The Swede laughed again his blatant laugh, full of a kind of false courage and defiance. "Oh, you know what I mean all right," he answered.

"I'm a liar if I do!" Johnnie protested. The card game was halted, and the men stared at the Swede. Johnnie evidently felt that as the son of the proprietor he should make a direct inquiry. "Now, what might you be drivin' at, mister?" he asked. The Swede winked at him. It was a wink full of cunning. His fingers shook on the edge of the board. "Oh, maybe you think I have been to nowhere. Maybe you think I'm a tenderfoot?"

"I don't know nothin' about you," answered Johnnie, "and I don't give a damn where you've been. All I got to say is that I don't know what you're driving at. There hain't never been nobody killed in this room."

The cowboy, who had been steadily gazing at the Swede, then spoke: "What's wrong with you, mister?"

Apparently it seemed to the Swede that he was formidably menaced. He shivered and turned white near the corners of his mouth. He sent an appealing glance in the direction of the little Easterner. During these moments he did not forget to wear his air of advanced pot-valor. "They say they don't know what I mean," he remarked mockingly to the Easterner.

The latter answered after prolonged and cautious reflection. "I don't understand you," he said, impassively.

The Swede made a movement then which announced that he thought he had encountered treachery from the only quarter where he had expected sympathy, if not help. "Oh, I see you are all against me. I see—"

The cowboy was in a state of deep stupefaction. "Say," he cried, as he tumbled the deck violently down upon the board "—say, what are you gettin' at, hey?"

The Swede sprang up with the celerity of a man escaping from a snake on the floor. "I don't want to fight!" he shouted. "I don't want to fight!"

The cowboy stretched his long legs indolently and deliberately. His hands were in his pockets. He spat into the sawdust box. "Well, who the hell thought you did?" he inquired.

The Swede backed rapidly toward a corner of the room. His hands were out protectingly in front of his chest, but he was making an obvious struggle to control his fright. "Gentlemen," he quavered, "I suppose I am going to be killed before I can leave this house! I suppose I am going to be killed before I leave this house!" In his eyes was the dying-swan look. Through the windows could be seen the snow turning blue in the shadow of dusk. The wind tore at the house and some loose thing beat regularly against the clapboards like a spirit tapping.

A door opened, and Scully himself entered. He paused in surprise as he noted the tragic attitude of the Swede. Then he said, "What's the matter here?"

The Swede answered him swiftly and eagerly: "These men are going to kill me."

"Kill you!" ejaculated Scully. "Kill you! What are you talkin'?"

The Swede made the gesture of a martyr.

Scully wheeled sternly upon his son. "What is this, Johnnie?"

The lad had grown sullen. "Dammed if I know," he answered. "I can't make no sense to it." He began to shuffle the cards, fluttering them together with an angry snap. "He says a good many men have been killed in this room, or something like that. And he says he's goin' to be killed here too. I don't know what ails him. He's crazy, I shouldn't wonder."

Scully then looked for explanation to the cowboy, but the cowboy simply shrugged his shoulders.

"Kill you?" said Scully again to the Swede. "Kill you? Man, you're off your nut."

"Oh, I know," burst out the Swede. "I know what will happen. Yes, I'm crazy—yes. Yes, of course, I'm crazy—yes. But I know one thing—"

There was a sort of sweat of misery and terror upon his face. "I know I won't get out of here alive."

The cowboy drew a deep breath, as if his mind was passing into the last stages of dissolution. "Well, I'm doggoned," he whispered to himself.

Scully wheeled suddenly and faced his son. "You've been troublin' this man!"

Johnnie's voice was loud with its burden of grievance. "Why, good Gawd, I ain't done nothin' to 'im."

The Swede broke in. "Gentlemen, do not disturb yourselves. I will leave this house. I will go away, because"—he accused them dramatically with his glance—"because I do not want to be killed."

Scully was furious with his son. "Will you tell me what is the matter, you young divil? What's the matter, anyhow? Speak out!"

"Blame it!" cried Johnnie in despair, "don't I tell you I don't know? He—he says we want to kill him, and that's all I know. I can't tell what ails him."

The Swede continued to repeat: "Never mind, Mr. Scully; never mind. I will leave this house. I will go away, because I do not wish to be killed. Yes, of course, I am crazy—yes. But I know one thing! I will go away. I will leave this house. Never mind, Mr. Scully; never mind. I will go away."

"You will not go 'way," said Scully. "You will not go 'way until I hear the reason of this business. If anybody has troubled you I will take care of him. This is my house. You are under my roof, and I will not allow any peaceable man to be troubled here." He cast a terrible eye upon Johnnie, the cowboy, and the Easterner.

"Never mind, Mr. Scully; never mind. I will go away. I do not wish to be killed." The Swede moved towards the door which opened upon the stairs. It was evidently his intention to go at once for his baggage.

"No, no," shouted Scully peremptorily; but the white-faced man slid by him and disappeared. "Now," said Scully severely, "what does this mane?"

Johnnie and the cowboy cried together: "Why, we didn't do nothin' to 'im!"

Scully's eyes were cold. "No," he said, "you didn't?"

Johnnie swore a deep oath. "Why, this is the wildest loon I ever see. We didn't do nothin' at all. We were jest sittin' here playin' cards, and he—"

The father suddenly spoke to the Easterner. "Mr. Blanc," he asked, "what has these boys been doin'?"

The Easterner reflected again. "I didn't see anything wrong at all," he said at last, slowly.

Scully began to howl. "But what does it mane?" He stared ferociously at his son. "I have a mind to lather you for this, me boy."

Johnnie was frantic. "Well, what have I done?" he bawled at his father.

III

"I think you are tongue-tied," said Scully finally to his son, the cowboy, and the Easterner; and at the end of this scornful sentence he left the room.

Upstairs the Swede was swiftly fastening the straps of his great valise. Once his back happened to be half turned towards the door, and, hearing a noise there, he wheeled and sprang up, uttering a loud cry. Scully's wrinkled visage showed grimly in the light of the small lamp he carried. This yellow effulgence, streaming upward, colored only his prominent features, and left his eyes, for instance, in mysterous shadow. He resembled a murderer.

"Man! man!" he exclaimed, "have you gone daffy?"

"Oh, no! Oh, no!" rejoined the other. "There are people in this world who know pretty nearly as much as you do—understand?"

For a moment they stood gazing at each other. Upon the Swede's deathly pale cheeks were two spots brightly crimson and sharply edged, as if they had been carefully painted. Scully placed the light on the table and sat himself on the edge of the bed. He spoke ruminatively. "By cracky, I never heard of such a thing in my life. It's a complete muddle. I can't, for the soul of me, think how you ever got this idea into your head." Presently he lifted his eyes and asked: "And did you sure think they were going to kill you?"

The Swede scanned the old man as if he wished to see into his mind. "I did," he said at last. He obviously suspected that this answer might precipitate an outbreak. As he pulled on a strap his whole arm shook, the elbow wavering like a bit of paper.

Scully banged his hand impressively on the footboard of the bed. "Why, man, we're goin' to have a line of ilictric street cars in this town next spring."

" 'A line of electric street cars,' " repeated the Swede, stupidly.

"And," said Scully, "there's a new railroad goin' to be built down from Broken Arm to here. Not to mintion the four churches and the smashin' big brick schoolhouse. Then there's the big factory, too. Why, in two years Romper'll be a met-tro-*pol*-is."

Having finished the preparation of his baggage, the Swede straightened himself. "Mr. Scully," he said, with sudden hardihood, "how much do I owe you?"

"You don't owe me anythin'," said the old man angrily.

"Yes, I do," retorted the Swede. He took seventy-five cents from his pocket and tendered it to Scully; but the latter snapped his fingers in disdainful refusal. However, it happened that they both stood gazing in a strange fashion at three silver pieces on the Swede's open palm.

"I'll not take your money," said Scully at last. "Not after what's been goin' on here." Then a plan seemed to strike him. "Here," he cried, picking up his lamp and moving towards the door. "Here! Come with me a minute."

"No," said the Swede, in overwhelming alarm.

"Yes," urged the old man. "Come on! I want you to come and see a picter—just across the hall—in my room."

The Swede must have concluded that his hour was come. His jaw dropped and his teeth showed like a dead man's. He ultimately followed Scully across the corridor, but he had the step of one hung in chains.

Scully flashed the light high on the wall of his own chamber. There was revealed a ridiculous photograph of a little girl. She was leaning against a balustrade of gorgeous decoration, and the formidable bang to her hair was prominent. The figure was as graceful as an upright sled-stake, and, withal, it was the hue of lead. "There," said Scully, tenderly, "that's the picter of my little girl that died. Her name was Carrie. She had the purtiest hair you ever saw! I was that fond of her, she—"

Turning then, he saw that the Swede was not contemplating the picture at all, but instead, was keeping keen watch on the gloom in the rear.

"Look, man!" cried Scully, heartily. "That's the picter of my little gal that died. Her name was Carrie. And then here's the picter of my oldest boy, Michael. He's a lawyer in Lincoln, an' doin' well. I gave that boy a grand eddication, and I'm glad for it now. He's a fine boy. Look at 'im now. Ain't he bold as blazes, him there in Lincoln, an honored an' respicted gintleman! An honored and respicted gintleman," concluded Scully with a flourish. And, so saying, he smote the Swede jovially on the back.

"Now," said the old man, "there's only one more thing." He dropped suddenly to the floor and thrust his head beneath the bed. The Swede could hear his muffled voice. "I'd keep it under me piller if it wasn't for that boy Johnnie. Then there's the old woman—Where is it now? I never put it twice in the same place. Ah, now come out with you!"

Presently he backed clumsily from under the bed, dragging with him an old coat rolled into a bundle. "I've fetched him," he muttered. Kneeling on the floor, he unrolled the coat and extracted from its heart a large yellow-brown whiskey bottle.

His first manoeuver was to hold the bottle up to the light. Reassured, apparently, that nobody had been tampering with it, he thrust it with a generous movement towards the Swede.

The weak-kneed Swede was about to eagerly clutch this element of strength, but he suddenly jerked his hand away and cast a look of horror upon Scully.

"Drink," said the old man affectionately. He had risen to his feet, and now stood facing the Swede.

There was a silence. Then again Scully said: "Drink!"

The Swede laughed wildly. He grabbed the bottle, put it to his mouth; and as his lips curled absurdly around the opening and his throat worked, he kept his glance, burning with hatred, upon the old man's face.

IV

After the departure of Scully the three men, with the card board still upon their knees, preserved for a long time an astounded silence. Then Johnnie said: "That's the doddangedest Swede I ever see."

"He ain't no Swede," said the cowboy, scornfully.

"Well, what is he then?" cried Johnnie. "What is he then?"

"It's my opinion," replied the cowboy deliberately, "he's some kind of a Dutchman." It was a venerable custom of the country to entitle as

Swedes all light-haired men who spoke with a heavy tongue. In consequence the idea of the cowboy was not without its daring. "Yes, sir," he repeated. "It's my opinion this feller is some kind of a Dutchman."

"Well, he says he's a Swede, anyhow," muttered Johnnie, sulkily. He turned to the Easterner: "What do you think, Mr. Blanc?"

"Oh, I don't know," replied the Easterner.

"Well, what do you think makes him act that way?" asked the cowboy.

"Why, he's frightened." The Easterner knocked his pipe against a rim of the stove. "He's clear frightened out of his boots."

"What at?" cried Johnnie and the cowboy together.

The Easterner reflected over his answer.

"What at?" cried the others again.

"Oh, I don't know, but it seems to me this man has been reading dime novels, and he thinks he's right out in the middle of it—the shootin' and stabbin' and all."

"But," said the cowboy, deeply scandalized, "this ain't Wyoming, ner none of them places. This is Nebrasker."

"Yes," added Johnnie, "an' why don't he wait till he gets *out West*?"

The travelled Easterner laughed. "It isn't different there even—not in these days. But he thinks he's right in the middle of hell."

Johnnie and the cowboy mused long.

"It's awful funny," remarked Johnnie at last.

"Yes," said the cowboy. "This is a queer game. I hope we don't git snowed in, because then we'd have to stand this here man bein' around with us all the time. That wouldn't be no good."

"I wish pop would throw him out," said Johnnie.

Presently they heard a loud stamping on the stairs, accompanied by ringing jokes in the voice of old Scully, and laughter, evidently from the Swede. The men around the stove stared vacantly at each other. "Gosh!" said the cowboy. The door flew open and old Scully, flushed and anecdotal, came into the room. He was jabbering at the Swede, who followed him, laughing bravely. It was the entry of two roisterers from a banquet hall.

"Come now," said Scully sharply to the three seated men, "move up and give us a chance at the stove." The cowboy and the Easterner obediently sidled their chairs to make room for the newcomers. Johnnie, however, simply arranged himself in a more indolent attitude, and then remained motionless.

"Come! Git over, there," said Scully.

"Plenty of room on the other side of the stove," said Johnnie.

"Do you think we want to sit in the draught?" roared the father.

But the Swede here interposed with a grandeur of confidence. "No, no. Let the boy sit where he likes," he cried in a bullying voice to the father.

"All right! All right!" said Scully, deferentially. The cowboy and the Easterner exchanged glances of wonder.

The five chairs were formed in a crescent about one side of the stove. The Swede began to talk; he talked arrogantly, profanely, angrily. Johnnie, the cowboy, and the Easterner maintained a morose silence, while old Scully appeared to be receptive and eager, breaking in constantly with sympathetic ejaculations.

Finally the Swede announced that he was thirsty. He moved in his chair, and said that he would go for a drink of water.

"I'll git it for you," cried Scully at once.

"No," said the Swede, contemptuously. "I'll get it for myself." He arose and stalked with the air of an owner off into the executive parts of the hotel.

As soon as the Swede was out of hearing Scully sprang to his feet and whispered intensely to the others: "Upstairs he thought I was tryin' to poison 'im."

"Say," said Johnnie, "this makes me sick. Why don't you throw 'im out in the snow?"

"Why, he's all right now," declared Scully. "It was only that he was from the East, and he thought this was a tough place. That's all. He's all right now."

The cowboy looked with admiration upon the Easterner. "You were straight," he said. "You were on to that there Dutchman."

"Well," said Johnnie to his father, "he may be all right now, but I don't see it. Other time he was scared, but now he's too fresh."

Scully's speech was always a combination of Irish brogue and idiom, Western twang and idiom, and scraps of curiously formal diction taken from the story-books and newspapers. He now hurled a strange mass of language at the head of his son. "What do I keep? What do I keep? What do I keep?" he demanded, in a voice of thunder. He slapped his knee impressively, to indicate that he himself was going to make reply, and that all should heed. "I keep a hotel," he shouted. "A hotel, do you mind? A guest under my roof has sacred privileges. He is to be intimidated by none. Not one word shall he hear that would prijudice him in favor of goin' away. I'll not have it. There's no place in this here town where they can say they iver took in a guest of mine because he was afraid to stay here." He wheeled suddenly upon the cowboy and the Easterner. "Am I right?"

"Yes, Mr. Scully," said the cowboy, "I think you're right."

"Yes, Mr. Scully," said the Easterner, "I think you're right."

V

At six-o'clock supper, the Swede fizzed like a fire-wheel. He sometimes seemed on the point of bursting into riotous song, and in all his madness he was encouraged by old Scully. The Easterner was encased in reserve; the cowboy sat in wide-mouthed amazement, forgetting to eat, while Johnnie wrathily demolished great plates of food. The daughters of the house, when they were obliged to replenish the biscuits, approached as warily as Indians, and, having succeeded in their purpose, fled with ill-concealed trepidation. The Swede domineered the whole feast, and he gave it the appearance of a cruel bacchanal. He seemed to have grown suddenly taller; he gazed, brutally disdainful, into every face. His voice rang through the room. Once when he jabbed out harpoon-fashion with his fork to pinion a biscuit, the weapon nearly impaled the hand of the Easterner, which had been stretched quietly out for the same biscuit.

After supper, as the men filed towards the other room, the Swede smote Scully ruthlessly on the shoulder. "Well, old boy, that was a good, square meal." Johnnie looked hopefully at his father; he knew that shoulder was tender from an old fall; and, indeed, it appeared for a moment as if Scully was going to flame out over the matter, but in the end he smiled a sickly smile and remained silent. The others understood from his manner that he was admitting his responsibility for the Swede's new viewpoint.

Johnnie, however, addressed his parent in an aside. "Why don't you license somebody to kick you downstairs?" Scully scowled darkly by way of reply.

When they were gathered about the stove, the Swede insisted on another game of High-Five. Scully gently deprecated the plan at first, but the Swede turned a wolfish glare upon him. The old man subsided, and the Swede canvassed the others. In his tone there was always a great threat. The cowboy and the Easterner both remarked indifferently that they would play. Scully said that he would presently have to go to meet the 6:58 train, and so the Swede turned menacingly upon Johnnie. For a moment their glances crossed like blades, and then Johnnie smiled and said, "Yes, I'll play."

They formed a square, with the little board on their knees. The Easterner and the Swede were again partners. As the play went on, it was noticeable that the cowboy was not board-whacking as usual. Meanwhile, Scully, near the lamp, had put on his spectacles and, with an appearance curiously like an old priest, was reading a newspaper. In time he went out to meet the 6:58 train, and, despite his precautions, a gust of polar wind whirled into the room as he opened the door. Besides scattering the cards, it chilled the players to the marrow. The Swede cursed frightfully. When Scully returned, his entrance disturbed a cosy and friendly scene. The Swede again cursed. But presently they were once more intent, their heads bent forward and their hands moving swiftly. The Swede had adopted the fashion of board-whacking.

Scully took up his paper and for a long time remained immersed in matters which were extraordinarily remote from him. The lamp burned badly, and once he stopped to adjust the wick. The newspaper, as he turned from page to page, rustled with a slow and comfortable sound. Then suddenly he heard three terrible words: "You are cheatin'!"

Such scenes often prove that there can be little of dramatic import in environment. Any room can present a tragic front; any room can be comic. This little den was now hideous as a torture-chamber. The new faces of the men themselves had changed it upon the instant. The Swede held a huge fist in front of Johnnie's face, while the latter looked steadily over it into the blazing orbs of his accuser. The Easterner had grown pallid; the cowboy's jaw had dropped in that expression of bovine amazement which was one of his important mannerisms. After the three words, the first sound in the room was made by Scully's paper as it floated forgotten to his feet. His spectacles had also fallen from his nose, but by a clutch he had saved them in air. His hand, grasping the spectacles, now remained poised awkwardly and near his shoulder. He stared at the card-players.

Probably the silence was while a second elapsed. Then, if the floor had been suddenly twitched out from under the men they could not have moved quicker. The five had projected themselves headlong towards a common point. It happened that Johnnie, in rising to hurl himself upon the Swede, had stumbled slightly because of his curiously instinctive care for the cards and the board. The loss of the moment allowed time for the arrival of Scully, and also allowed the cowboy time to give the Swede a great push which sent him staggering back. The men found tongue together, and hoarse shouts of rage, appeal, or fear burst from every throat. The cowboy pushed and jostled feverishly at the Swede, and the Easterner and Scully clung wildly to Johnnie; but through the smoky air, above the swaying bodies of the peace-controllers, the eyes of the two warriors ever sought each other in glances of challenge that were at once hot and steely.

Of course the board had been overturned, and now the whole company of cards was scattered over the floor, where the boots of the men trampled the fat and painted kings and queens as they gazed with their silly eyes at the war that was waging above them.

Scully's voice was dominating the yells. "Stop now! Stop, I say! Stop, now—"

Johnnie, as he struggled to burst through the rank formed by Scully and the Easterner, was crying, "Well, he says I cheated! He says I cheated! I won't allow no man to say I cheated! If he says I cheated, he's a —— ——!"

The cowboy was telling the Swede, "Quit, now! Quit, d'ye hear—"

The screams of the Swede never ceased: "He did cheat! I saw him! I saw him—"

As for the Easterner, he was importuning in a voice that was not heeded: "Wait a moment, can't you? Oh, wait a moment. What's the good of a fight over a game of cards? Wait a moment—"

In this tumult no complete sentences were clear. "Cheat"—"Quit"—"He says"—these fragments pierced the uproar and rang out sharply. It was remarkable that, whereas Scully undoubtedly made the most noise, he was the least heard of any of the riotous band.

Then suddenly there was a great cessation. It was as if each man had paused for breath; and although the room was still lighted with the anger of men, it could be seen that there was no danger of immediate conflict, and at once Johnnie, shouldering his way forward, almost succeeded in confronting the Swede, "What did you say I cheated for? What did you say I cheated for? I don't cheat, and I won't let no man say I do!"

The Swede said, "I saw you! I saw you!"

"Well," cried Johnnie, "I'll fight any man what says I cheat!"

"No, you won't," said the cowboy. "Not here."

"Ah, be still, can't you?" said Scully, coming between them.

The quiet was sufficient to allow the Easterner's voice to be heard. He was repeating, "Oh, wait a moment, can't you? What's the good of a fight over a game of cards? Wait a moment!"

Johnnie, his red face appearing above his father's shoulder, hailed the Swede again. "Did you say I cheated?"

The Swede showed his teeth. "Yes."

"Then," said Johnnie, "we must fight."

"Yes, fight," roared the Swede. He was like a demoniac. "Yes, fight! I'll show you what kind of a man I am! I'll show you who you want to fight! Maybe you think I can't fight! Maybe you think I can't! I'll show you, you skin, you card-sharp! Yes, you cheated! You cheated!"

"Well, let's go at it, then, mister," said Johnnie, coolly.

The cowboy's brow was beaded with sweat from his efforts in intercepting all sorts of raids. He turned in despair to Scully. "What are you goin' to do now?"

A change had come over the Celtic visage of the old man. He now seemed all eagerness; his eyes glowed.

"We'll let them fight," he answered, stalwartly. "I can't put up with it any longer. I've stood this damned Swede till I'm sick. We'll let them fight."

VI

The men prepared to go out-of-doors. The Easterner was so nervous that he had great difficulty in getting his arms into the sleeves of his new leather coat. As the cowboy drew his fur cap down over his ears his hands trembled. In fact, Johnnie and old Scully were the only ones who displayed no agitation. These preliminaries were conducted without words.

Scully threw open the door. "Well, come on," he said. Instantly a terrific wind caused the flame of the lamp to struggle at its wick, while a puff of black smoke sprang from the chimney-top. The stove was in mid-current of the blast, and its voice swelled to equal the roar of the storm. Some of the scarred and bedabbled cards were caught up from the floor and dashed helplessly against the farther wall. The men lowered their heads and plunged into the tempest as into a sea.

No snow was falling, but great whirls and clouds of flakes, swept up from the ground by the frantic winds, were streaming southward with the speed of bullets. The covered land was blue and the sheen of an unearthly satin, and there was no other hue save where, at the low, black railway station—which seemed incredibly distant—one light gleamed like a tiny jewel. As the men floundered into thigh-deep drift, it was known that the Swede was bawling out something. Scully went to him, put a hand on his shoulder, and projected an ear. "What's that you say?" he shouted.

"I say," bawled the Swede again, "I won't stand much show against this gang. I know you'll all pitch on me."

Scully smote him reproachfully on the arm. "Tut, man!" The wind tore the words from Scully's lips and scattered them far alee.

"You are all a gang of—" boomed the Swede, but the storm also seized the remainder of this sentence.

Immediately turning their backs upon the wind, the men had swung around a corner to the sheltered side of the hotel. It was the function of the little house to preserve here, amid this great devastation of snow, an irregular V-shape of heavily encrusted grass, which crackled beneath the feet. One could imagine the great drifts piled against the windward side. When the party reached the comparative peace of this spot it was found that the Swede was still bellowing.

"Oh, I know what kind of a thing this is! I know you'll all pitch on me. I can't lick you all!"

Scully turned upon him panther fashion. "You'll not have to whip all of us. You'll have to whip my son Johnnie. An' the man what troubles you durin' that time will have me to deal with."

The arrangements were swiftly made. The two men faced each other, obedient to the harsh commands of Scully, whose face, in the subtly luminous gloom, could be seen in the austere impersonal lines that are pictured on the countenances of the Roman veterans. The Easterner's teeth were chattering, and he was hopping up and down like a mechanical toy. The cowboy stood rock-like.

The contestants had not stripped off any clothing. Each was in his ordinary attire. Their fists were up, and they eyed each other in a calm that had the elements of leonine cruelty in it.

During this pause, the Easterner's mind, like a film, took lasting impressions of three men—the iron-nerved master of the ceremony; the Swede, pale, motionless, terrible; and Johnnie, serene yet ferocious, brutish yet heroic. The entire prelude had in it a tragedy greater than the tragedy of action, and this aspect was accentuated by the long, mellow cry of the blizzard, as it sped the tumbling and wailing flakes into the black abyss of the south.

"Now!" said Scully.

The two combatants leaped forward and crashed together like bullocks. There was heard the cushioned sound of blows, and of a curse squeezing out from between the tight teeth of one.

As for the spectators, the Easterner's pent-up breath exploded from him with a pop of relief, absolute relief from the tension of the preliminaries. The cowboy bounded into the air with a yowl. Scully was immovable as from supreme amazement and fear at the fury of the fight which he himself had permitted and arranged.

For a time the encounter in the darkness was such a perplexity of flying arms that it presented no more detail than would a swiftly revolving wheel. Occasionally a face, as if illumined by a flash of light, would shine out, ghastly and marked with pink spots. A moment later, the men might have been known as shadows, if it were not for the involuntary utterance of oaths that came from them in whispers.

Suddenly a holocaust of warlike desire caught the cowboy, and he bolted forward with the speed of a broncho. "Go it, Johnnie! go it! Kill him! Kill him!"

Scully confronted him. "Kape back," he said; and by his glance the cowboy could tell that this man was Johnnie's father.

To the Easterner there was a monotony of unchangeable fighting that was an abomination. This confused mingling was eternal to his sense, which was concentrated in a longing for the end, the priceless end. Once the fighters lurched near him, and as he scrambled hastily backward he heard them breathe like men on the rack.

"Kill him, Johnnie! Kill him! Kill him! Kill him!" The cowboy's face was contorted like one of those agony masks in museums.

"Keep still," said Scully, icily.

Then there was a sudden loud grunt, incomplete, cut short, and Johnnie's body swung away from the Swede and fell with sickening heaviness to the grass. The cowboy was barely in time to prevent the mad Swede from flinging himself upon his prone adversary. "No, you don't," said the cowboy, interposing an arm. "Wait a second."

Scully was at his son's side. "Johnnie! Johnnie, me boy!" His voice had a quality of melancholy tenderness. "Johnnie! Can you go on with it?" He looked anxiously down into the bloody, pulpy face of his son.

There was a moment of silence, and then Johnnie answered in his ordinary voice, "Yes, I—it—yes."

Assisted by his father he struggled to his feet. "Wait a bit now till you get your wind," said the old man.

A few paces away the cowboy was lecturing the Swede. "No, you don't! Wait a second!"

The Easterner was plucking at Scully's sleeve. "Oh, this is enough," he pleaded. "This is enough! Let it go as it stands. This is enough!"

"Bill," said Scully, "git out of the road." The cowboy stepped aside. "Now." The combatants were actuated by a new caution as they advanced towards collision. They glared at each other, and then the Swede aimed a lightning blow that carried with it his entire weight. Johnnie was evidently half stupid from weakness, but he miraculously dodged, and his fist sent the over-balanced Swede sprawling.

The cowboy, Scully, and the Easterner burst into a cheer that was like a chorus of triumphant soldiery, but before its conclusion the Swede had scuffled agilely to his feet and come in berserk abandon at his foe. There was another perplexity of flying arms, and Johnnie's body again swung away and fell, even as a bundle might fall from a roof. The Swede instantly staggered to a little wind-waved tree and leaned against it, breathing like an engine, while his savage and flame-lit eyes roamed from face to face as the men bent over Johnnie. There was a splendor of isolation in his situation at this time which the Easterner felt once when, lifting his eyes from the man on the ground, he beheld that mysterious and lonely figure waiting.

"Are you any good yet, Johnnie?" asked Scully in a broken voice.

The son gasped and opened his eyes languidly. After a moment he answered, "No—I ain't any good—any—more." Then, from shame and bodily ill, he began to weep, the tears furrowing down through the bloodstains on his face. "He was too—too—too heavy for me."

Scully straightened and addressed the waiting figure. "Stranger," he said, evenly, "it's all up with our side." Then his voice changed into that vibrant huskiness which is commonly the tone of the most simple and deadly announcements. "Johnnie is whipped."

Without replying, the victor moved off on the route to the front door of the hotel.

The cowboy was formulating new and unspellable blasphemies. The Easterner was startled to find that they were out in a wind that seemed to come direct from the shadowed arctic floes. He heard again the wail of the snow as it was flung to its grave in the south. He knew now that all this time the cold had been sinking into him deeper and deeper, and he wondered that he had not perished. He felt indifferent to the condition of the vanquished man.

"Johnnie, can you walk?" asked Scully.

"Did I hurt—hurt him any?" asked the son.

"Can you walk, boy? Can you walk?"

Johnnie's voice was suddenly strong. There was a robust impatience in it. "I asked you whether I hurt him any?"

"Yes, yes, Johnnie," answered the cowboy, consolingly; "he's hurt a good deal."

They raised him from the ground, and as soon as he was on his feet he went tottering off, rebuffing all attempts at assistance. When the party rounded the corner they were fairly blinded by the pelting of the snow. It burned their faces like fire. The cowboy carried Johnnie through the drift to the door. As they entered, some cards again rose from the floor and beat against the wall.

The Easterner rushed to the stove. He was so profoundly chilled that he almost dared to embrace the glowing iron. The Swede was not in the room. Johnnie sank into a chair and, folding his arms on his knees, buried his face in them. Scully, warming one foot and then the other at a rim of the stove, muttered to himself with Celtic mournfulness. The cowboy had removed his fur cap, and with a dazed and rueful air he was running one hand through his tousled locks. From overhead they could hear the creaking of boards, as the Swede tramped here and there in his room.

The sad quiet was broken by the sudden flinging open of a door that led toward the kitchen. It was instantly followed by an inrush of women. They precipitated themselves upon Johnnie amid a chorus of lamentation. Before they carried their prey off to the kitchen, there to be bathed and harangued with that mixture of sympathy and abuse which is a feat of their sex, the mother straightened herself and fixed old Scully with an eye of stern reproach. "Shame be upon you, Patrick Scully!" she cried. "Your own son, too. Shame be upon you!"

"There, now! Be quiet, now!" said the old man, weakly.

"Shame be upon you, Patrick Scully!" The girls, rallying to this slogan, sniffed disdainfully in the direction of those trembling accomplices, the cowboy and the Easterner. Presently they bore Johnnie away, and left the three men to dismal reflection.

VII

"I'd like to fight this here Dutchman myself," said the cowboy, breaking a long silence.

Scully wagged his head sadly. "No, that wouldn't do. It wouldn't be right. It wouldn't be right."

"Well, why wouldn't it?" argued the cowboy. "I don't see no harm in it."

"No," answered Scully, with mournful heroism. "It wouldn't be right. It was Johnnie's fight, and now we mustn't whip the man just because he whipped Johnnie."

"Yes, that's true enough," said the cowboy; "but—he better not get fresh with me, because I couldn't stand no more of it."

"You'll not say a word to him," commanded Scully, and even then they heard the tread of the Swede on the stairs. His entrance was made theatric. He swept the door back with a bang and swaggered to the middle of the room. No one looked at him. "Well," he cried, insolently, at Scully, "I s'pose you'll tell me now how much I owe you?"

The old man remained stolid. "You don't owe me nothin'."

"Huh!" said the Swede, "huh! Don't owe 'im nothin'."

The cowboy addressed the Swede. "Stranger, I don't see how you come to be so gay around here."

Old Scully was instantly alert. "Stop!" he shouted, holding his hand forth, fingers upward. "Bill, you shut up!"

The cowboy spat carelessly into the sawdust box. "I didn't say a word, did I?" he asked.

"Mr. Scully," called the Swede, "how much do I owe you?" It was seen that he was attired for departure, and that he had his valise in his hand.

"You don't owe me nothin'," repeated Scully in the same imperturbable way.

"Huh!" said the Swede. "I guess you're right. I guess if it was any way at all, you'd owe me somethin'. That's what I guess." He turned to the cowboy. " 'Kill him! Kill him! Kill him!' " he mimicked, and then guffawed victoriously. " 'Kill him!' " He was convulsed with ironical humor.

But he might have been jeering the dead. The three men were immovable and silent, staring with glassy eyes at the stove.

The Swede opened the door and passed into the storm, giving one derisive glance backward at the still group.

As soon as the door was closed, Scully and the cowboy leaped to their feet and began to curse. They tramped to and fro, waving their arms and smashing into the air their fists. "Oh, but that was a hard minute!" wailed Scully. "That was a hard minute! Him there leerin' and scoffin'! One bang at his nose was worth forty dollars to me that minute! How did you stand it, Bill?"

"How did I stand it?" cried the cowboy in a quivering voice. "How did I stand it? Oh!"

The old man burst into sudden brogue. "I'd loike to take that Swade," he wailed, "and hould 'im down on a shtone flure and bate 'im to a jelly wid a shtick!"

The cowboy groaned in sympathy. "I'd like to git him by the neck and ha-ammer him"—he brought his hand down on a chair with a noise like a pistol-shot—"hammer that there Dutchman until he couldn't tell himself from a dead coyote!"

"I'd bate 'im until he—"

"I'd show *him* some things—"

And then together they raised a yearning, fanatic cry—"Oh-o-oh! if we only could—"

"Yes!"

"Yes!"

"And then I'd—"

"O-o-oh!"

VIII

The Swede, tightly gripping his valise, tacked across the face of the storm as if he carried sails. He was following a line of little naked, gasping trees which, he knew, must mark the way of the road. His face, fresh from the pounding of Johnnie's fist, felt more pleasure than pain in the wind and the driving snow. A number of square shapes loomed upon him finally, and he knew them as the houses of the main body of the town. He found a street and made travel along it, leaning heavily upon the wind whenever, at a corner, a terrific blast caught him.

He might have been in a deserted village. We picture the world as thick with conquering and elate humanity, but here, with the bugles of the tempest pealing, it was hard to imagine a peopled earth. One viewed the existence of man then as a marvel, and conceded a glamor of wonder to these lice which were caused to cling to a whirling, fire-smote, ice-locked, disease-stricken, space-lost bulb. The conceit of man was explained by this storm to be the very engine of life. One was a coxcomb not to die in it. However, the Swede found a saloon.

In front of it an indomitable red light was burning, and the snowflakes were made blood-color as they flew through the circumscribed territory of the lamp's shining. The Swede pushed open the door of the saloon and entered. A sanded expanse was before him, and at the end of it four men sat about a table drinking. Down one side of the room extended a radiant bar, and its guardian was leaning upon his elbows listening to the talk of the men at the table. The Swede dropped his valise upon the floor and, smiling fraternally upon the barkeeper, said, "Gimme some whiskey, will you?" The man placed a bottle, a whiskey-glass, and a glass of ice-thick water upon the bar. The Swede poured himself an abnormal portion of whiskey and drank it in three gulps. "Pretty bad night," remarked the bartender, indifferently. He was making the pretension of blindness which is usually a distinction of his class; but it could have been seen that he was furtively studying the half-erased blood stains on the face of the Swede. "Bad night," he said again.

"Oh, it's good enough for me," replied the Swede, hardily, as he poured himself some more whiskey. The barkeeper took his coin and manœuvered it through its reception by the highly nickelled cash-machine. A bell rang; a card labelled "20 cts." had appeared.

"No," continued the Swede, "this isn't too bad weather. It's good enough for me."

"So?" murmured the barkeeper, languidly.

The copious drams made the Swede's eyes swim, and he breathed a trifle heavier. "Yes, I like this weather. It suits me." It was apparently his design to impart a deep significance to these words.

"So?" murmured the bartender again. He turned to gaze dreamily at the scroll-like birds and bird-like scrolls which had been drawn with soap upon the mirrors in back of the bar.

"Well, I guess I'll take another drink," said the Swede, presently. "Have something?"

"No, thanks; I'm not drinkin'," answered the bartender. Afterward he asked, "How did you hurt your face?"

The Swede immediately began to boast loudly. "Why, in a fight. I thumped the soul out of a man down here at Scully's hotel."

The interest of the four men at the table was at last aroused.

"Who was it?" said one.

"Johnnie Scully," blustered the Swede. "Son of the man what runs it. He will be pretty near dead for some weeks, I can tell you. I made a nice thing of him. I did. He couldn't get up. They carried him in the house. Have a drink?"

Instantly the men in some subtle way encased themselves in reserve. "No, thanks," said one. The group was of curious formation. Two were prominent local businessmen; one was the district attorney; and one was a professional gambler of the kind known as "square." But a scrutiny of the group would not have enabled an observer to pick the gambler from the men of more reputable pursuits. He was, in fact, a man so delicate in manner, when among people of fair class, and so judicious in his choice of victims, that in the strictly masculine part of the town's life he had come to be explicitly trusted and admired. People called him a thoroughbred. The fear and contempt with which his craft was regarded were undoubtedly the reason why his quiet dignity shone conspicuously above the quiet dignity of men who might be merely hatters, billiard-markers, or grocery-clerks. Beyond an occasional unwary traveller who came by rail, this gambler was supposed to prey solely upon reckless and senile farmers, who, when flush with good crops, drove into town in all the pride and confidence of an absolutely invulnerable stupidity. Hearing at times in circuitous fashion of the despoilment of such a farmer, the important men of Romper invariably laughed in contempt of the victim, and if they thought of the wolf at all, it was with a kind of pride at the knowledge that he would never dare think of attacking their wisdom and courage. Besides, it was popular that this gambler had a real wife and two real children in a neat cottage in a suburb, where he led an exemplary home life; and when any one even suggested a discrepancy in his character, the crowd immediately vociferated descriptions of this virtuous family circle.

Then men who led exemplary home lives, and men who did not lead exemplary home lives, all subsided in a bunch, remarking that there was nothing more to be said.

However, when a restriction was placed upon him—as, for instance, when a strong clique of members of the new Pollywog Club refused to permit him, even as a spectator, to appear in the rooms of the organization—the candor and gentleness with which he accepted the judgment disarmed many of his foes and made his friends more desperately partisan. He invariably distinguished between himself and a respectable Romper man so quickly and frankly that his manner actually appeared to be a continual broadcast compliment.

And one must not forget to declare the fundamental fact of his entire position in Romper. It is irrefutable that in all affairs outside his business, in all matters that occur eternally and commonly between man and man, this thieving card-player was so generous, so just, so moral, that, in a contest, he could have put to flight the consciences of nine-tenths of the citizens of Romper.

And so it happened that he was seated in this saloon with the two prominent local merchants and the district attorney.

The Swede continued to drink raw whiskey, meanwhile babbling at the barkeeper and trying to induce him to indulge in potations. "Come on. Have a drink. Come on. What—no? Well, have a little one, then. By gawd, I've whipped a man tonight, and I want to celebrate. I whipped him good, too. Gentlemen," the Swede cried to the men at the table, "have a drink?"

"Ssh!" said the barkeeper.

The group at the table, although furtively attentive, had been pretending to be deep in talk, but now a man lifted his eyes towards the Swede and said, shortly, "Thanks. We don't want any more."

At this reply the Swede ruffled out his chest like a rooster. "Well," he exploded, "it seems I can't get anybody to drink with me in this town. Seems so, don't it? Well!"

"Ssh!" said the barkeeper.

"Say," snarled the Swede, "don't you try to shut me up. I won't have it. I'm a gentleman, and I want people to drink with me. And I want 'em to drink with me now. *Now*—do you understand?" He rapped the bar with his knuckles.

Years of experience had calloused the bartender. He merely grew sulky. "I hear you," he answered.

"Well," cried the Swede, "listen hard then. See those men over there? Well, they're going to drink with me, and don't you forget it. Now you watch."

"Hi!" yelled the barkeeper, "this won't do!"

"Why won't it?" demanded the Swede. He stalked over to the table, and by chance laid his hand upon the shoulder of the gambler. "How about this?" he asked wrathfully. "I asked you to drink with me."

The gambler simply twisted his head and spoke over his shoulder. "My friend, I don't know you."

"Oh, hell!" answered the Swede, "come and have a drink."

"Now, my boy," advised the gambler, kindly, "take your hand off my shoulder and go 'way and mind your own business." He was a little, slim man, and it seemed strange to hear him use this tone of heroic patronage to the burly Swede. The other men at the table said nothing.

"What! You won't drink with me, you little dude? I'll make you, then! I'll make you!" The Swede had grasped the gambler frenziedly at the throat, and was dragging him from his chair. The other men sprang up. The barkeeper dashed around the corner of his bar. There was a great tumult, and then was seen a long blade in the hand of the gambler. It shot forward, and a human body, this citadel of virtue, wisdom, power, was pierced as easily as if it had been a melon. The Swede fell with a cry of supreme astonishment.

The prominent merchants and the district attorney must have at once tumbled out of the place backward. The bartender found himself hanging limply to the arm of a chair and gazing into the eyes of a murderer.

"Henry," said the latter, as he wiped his knife on one of the towels that hung beneath the bar rail, "you tell 'em where to find me. I'll be home, waiting for 'em." Then he vanished. A moment afterward the barkeeper was in the street dinning through the storm for help and, moreover, companionship.

The corpse of the Swede, alone in the saloon, had its eyes fixed upon a dreadful legend that dwelt atop of the cash-machine: "This registers the amount of your purchase."

Months later, the cowboy was frying pork over the stove of a little ranch near the Dakota line, when there was a quick thud of hoofs outside, and presently the Easterner entered with the letters and the papers.

"Well," said the Easterner at once, "the chap that killed the Swede has got three years. Wasn't much, was it?"

"He has? Three years?" The cowboy poised his pan of pork, while he ruminated upon the news. "Three years. That ain't much."

"No. It was a light sentence," replied the Easterner as he unbuckled his spurs. "Seems there was a good deal of sympathy for him in Romper."

"If the bartender had been any good," observed the cowboy, thoughtfully, "he would have gone in and cracked that there Dutchman on the head with a bottle in the beginnin' of it and stopped all this here murderin'."

"Yes, a thousand things might have happened," said the Easterner, tartly.

The cowboy returned his pan of pork to the fire, but his philosophy continued. "It's funny, ain't it? If he hadn't said Johnnie was cheatin' he'd be alive this minute. He was an awful fool. Game played for fun, too. Not for money. I believe he was crazy."

"I feel sorry for that gambler," said the Easterner.

"Oh, so do I," said the cowboy. "He don't deserve none of it for killin' who he did."

"The Swede might not have been killed if everything had been square."

"Might not have been killed?" exclaimed the cowboy. "Everythin' square? Why, when he said that Johnnie was cheatin' and acted like such a jackass? And then in the saloon he fairly walked up to git hurt?" With these arguments the cowboy browbeat the Easterner and reduced him to rage.

"You're a fool!" cried the Easterner, viciously. "You're a bigger jackass than the Swede by a million majority. Now let me tell you one thing. Let me tell you something. Listen! Johnnie *was* cheating!"

" 'Johnnie,' " said the cowboy, blankly. There was a minute of silence, and then he said, robustly, "Why, no. The game was only for fun."

"Fun or not," said the Easterner, "Johnnie was cheating. I saw him. I know it. I saw him. And I refused to stand up and be a man. I let the Swede fight it out alone. And you—you were simply puffing around the place and wanting to fight. And then old Scully himself! We are all in it! This poor gambler isn't even a noun. He is kind of an adverb. Every sin is the result of collaboration. We, five of us, have collaborated in the murder of this Swede. Usually there are from a dozen to forty women really involved in every murder, but in this case it seems to be only five men—you, I, Johnnie, old Scully; and that fool of an unfortunate gambler came merely as a culmination, the apex of a human movement, and gets all the punishment."

The cowboy, injured and rebellious, cried out blindly into this fog of mysterious theory: "Well, I didn't do anythin', did I?"

Joseph Conrad

Joseph Conrad (1857–1924) was born in the Polish Ukraine, of a well-to-do family with revolutionary interests. At seventeen he began a sea career that lasted twenty years. He knew little English when he became a naturalized British citizen in 1886, but soon acquired great command of the language, retiring in 1894 to take up writing. His stories deal with permutations of character in the face of moral decay, disclosing, in his words, "the stress and passion within the core of each convincing moment" of life. His best-known works are Lord Jim *(1900) and* Heart of Darkness *(1902).* *(See page 70 of Introduction.)*

IL CONDE

"Vedi Napoli e poi mori"

The first time we got into conversation was in the National Museum in Naples, in the rooms on the ground floor containing the famous collection of bronzes from Herculaneum and Pompeii—that marvellous legacy of antique art whose delicate perfection has been preserved for us by the catastrophic fury of a volcano.

He addressed me first, over the celebrated Resting Hermes which we had been looking at side by side. He said the right things about that wholly admirable piece. Nothing profound. His taste was natural rather than cultivated. He had obviously seen many fine things in his life and appreciated them: but he had no jargon of a dilettante or the connoisseur. A hateful tribe. He spoke like a fairly intelligent man of the world, a perfectly unaffected gentleman.

We had known each other by sight for some few days past. Staying in the same hotel—good, but not extravagantly up-to-date—I had noticed him in the vestibule going in and out. I judged he was an old and valued client. The bow of the hotel-keeper was cordial in its deference, and he acknowledged it with familiar courtesy. For the servants he was *Il Conde*. There was some squabble over a man's parasol—yellow-silk-with-white-lining sort of thing—the waiters had discovered abandoned outside the dining-room door. Our gold-laced door-keeper recognised it, and I heard him directing one of the lift-boys to run after *Il Conde* with it. Perhaps he was the only count staying in the hotel, or perhaps he had the distinction of being *the* Count *par excellence*, conferred upon him because of his tried fidelity to the house.

Having conversed at the Museo—(and, by-the-bye, he had expressed his dislike of the busts and statues of Roman emperors in the gallery of marbles; their faces were too vigorous, too pronounced for him)—having conversed already in the morning, I did not think I was intruding when in the evening, finding the dining-room very full, I proposed to share his little table. Judging by the quiet urbanity of his consent he did not think so either. His smile was very attractive.

He dined in an evening waistcoat and a "smoking" (he called it so) with a black tie. All this of very good cut, not new—just as these things should be. He was, morning or evening, very correct in his dress. I have no doubt that his whole existence had been correct, well ordered, and conventional, undisturbed by startling events. His white hair brushed upwards off a lofty forehead gave him the air of an idealist, of an imaginative man. His white moustache, heavy but carefully trimmed and arranged, was not unpleasantly tinted a golden yellow in the middle. The faint scent of some very good perfume and of good cigars (that last an odour quite remarkable to come upon in Italy) reached me across the table. It was in his eyes that his age showed most. They were a little weary with creased eyelids. He must have been sixty or a couple of years more. And he was communicative. I would not go so far as to call it garrulous—but distinctly communicative.

He had tried various climates, of Abbazia, of the Riviera, of other places too, he told me, but the only one which suited him was the climate of the Gulf of Naples. The ancient Romans, who, he pointed out to me, were men expert in the art of living, knew very well what they were doing when they built their villas on these shores, in Baiæ, in Vico, in Capri. They came down to this seaside in search of health, bringing with them their trains of mimes and flute-players to amuse their leisure. He thought it extremely probable that the Romans of the higher classes were specially predisposed to painful rheumatic affections.

This was the only personal opinion I heard him express. It was based on no special erudition. He knew no more of the Romans than an average informed man of the world is expected to know. He argued from personal experience. He had suffered himself from a painful and dangerous rheumatic affection till he found relief in this particular spot of Southern Europe.

This was three years ago, and ever since he had taken up his quarters on the shores of the gulf, either in one of the hotels in Sorrento or hiring a small villa in Capri. He had a piano, a few books: picked up transient acquaintances of a day, week, or month in the stream of travellers from all Europe. One can imagine him going out for his walks in the streets and lanes, becoming known to beggars, shopkeepers, children, country people; talking amiably over the walls to the *contadini*—and coming back to his rooms or his villa to sit before the piano, with his white hair brushed up and his thick, orderly moustache, "to make a little music for myself." And, of course, for a change there was Naples near by—life, movement, animation, opera. A little amusement, as he said, is necessary for health. Mimes and flute-players, in fact. Only, unlike the magnates of ancient Rome, he had no affairs of the city to call him away from these moderate delights. He had no affairs at all. Probably he had never had any grave affairs to attend to in his life. It was a kindly existence, with its joys and sorrows regulated by the course of Nature—marriages, births, deaths—ruled by the prescribed usages of good society and protected by the State.

He was a widower; but in the months of July and August he ventured to cross the Alps for six weeks on a visit to his married daughter. He told me her name. It was that of a very aristocratic family. She had a castle—in Bohemia, I think. This is as near as I ever came to ascertaining his nationality. His own name, strangely enough, he never mentioned. Perhaps he thought I had seen it on the published list. Truth to say, I never looked. At any rate, he was a good European—he spoke four languages to my certain knowledge—and a man of fortune. Not of a great fortune evidently and appropriately. I imagine that to be extremely rich would have appeared to him improper, *outré*—too blatant altogether. And obviously, too, the fortune was not of his making. The making of a fortune cannot be achieved without some roughness. It is a matter of temperament. His nature was too kindly for strife. In the course of conversation he mentioned his estate quite by the way, in reference to that painful and alarming rheumatic affection. One year, staying incautiously beyond the Alps as late as the middle of September, he had been laid up for three months in that lonely country house with no one but his valet and the caretaking couple to attend to him. Because, as he expressed it, he "kept no establishment there." He had only gone for a couple of days to confer with his land agent. He promised himself never to be so imprudent in the future. The first weeks of September would find him on the shores of his beloved gulf.

Sometimes in travelling one comes upon such lonely men, whose only business is to wait for the unavoidable. Deaths and marriages have made a solitude round them, and one really cannot blame their endeavours to make the waiting as easy as possible. As he remarked to me, "At my time of life freedom from physical pain is a very important matter."

It must not be imagined that he was a wearisome hypochondriac. He was really much too well-bred to be a nuisance. He had an eye for the small weaknesses of humanity. But it was a good-natured eye. He made a restful, easy, pleasant companion for the hours between dinner and bedtime. We spent three evenings together, and then I had to leave Naples in a hurry to look after a friend who had fallen seriously ill in Taormina. Having nothing to do, *Il Conde* came to see me off at the station. I was somewhat upset, and his idleness was always ready to take a kindly form. He was by no means an indolent man.

He went along the train peering into the carriages for a good seat for me, and then remained talking cheerily from below. He declared he would miss me that evening very much, and announced his intention of going after dinner to listen to the band in the public garden, the Villa Nazionale. He would amuse himself by hearing excellent music and looking at the best society. There would be a lot of people, as usual.

I seem to see him yet—his raised face with a friendly smile under the thick moustaches, and his kind, fatigued eyes. As the train began to move, he addressed me in two languages: first in French, saying, "*Bon voyage*"; then, in his very good, somewhat emphatic English, encouragingly, because he could see my concern, "All—will—be—well—yet!"

My friend's illness having taken a decidedly favourable turn, I returned to Naples on the tenth day. I cannot say I had given much thought to *Il Conde* during my absence, but, entering the dining-room, I looked for him in his habitual place. I had an idea he might have gone back to Sorrento to his piano and his books and his fishing. He was great friends with all the boatmen, and fished a good deal with lines from a boat. But I made out his white head in the crowd of heads, and even from a distance noticed something unusual in his attitude. Instead of sitting erect, gazing all round with alert urbanity, he drooped over his plate. I stood opposite him for some time before he looked up, a little wildly, if such a strong word can be used in connection with his correct appearance.

"Ah, my dear sir! Is it you?" he greeted me. "I hope all is well."

He was very nice about my friend. Indeed, he was always nice, with the niceness of people whose hearts are genuinely humane. But this time it cost him an effort. His attempts at general conversation broke down into dullness. It occurred to me he might have been indisposed. But before I could frame the inquiry he muttered:

"You find me here very sad."

"I am sorry for that," I said. "You haven't had bad news, I hope?"

It was very kind of me to take an interest. No. It was not that. No bad news, thank God. And he became very still as if holding his breath. Then, leaning forward a little, and in an odd tone of awed embarrassment, he took me into his confidence.

"The truth is that I have had a very—a very—how shall I say?—abominable adventure happen to me."

The energy of the epithet was sufficiently startling in that man of moderate feelings and toned-down vocabulary. The word unpleasant I should have thought would have fitted amply the worst experience likely to befall a man of his stamp. And an adventure, too! Incredible! But it is in human nature to believe the worst; and I confess I eyed him stealthily, wondering what he had been up to. In a moment, however, my unworthy suspicions vanished. There was a fundamental refinement of nature about the man which made me dismiss all idea of some more or less disreputable scrape.

"It is very serious. Very serious." He went on nervously, "I will tell you after dinner, if you will allow me."

I expressed my perfect acquiescence by a little bow, nothing more. I wished him to understand that I was not likely to hold him to that offer, if he thought better of it later on. We talked of indifferent things, but with a sense of difficulty quite unlike our former easy, gossipy intercourse. The hand raising a piece of bread to his lips, I noticed, trembled slightly. This symptom, in regard to my reading of the man, was no less than startling.

In the smoking-room he did not hang back at all. Directly we had taken our usual seats he leaned sideways over the arm of his chair and looked straight into my eyes earnestly.

"You remember," he began, "that day you went away? I told you then I would go to the Villa Nazionale to hear some music in the evening."

I remembered. His handsome old face, so fresh for his age, unmarked by any trying experience, appeared haggard for an instant. It was like the passing of a shadow. Returning his steadfast gaze, I took a sip of my black coffee. He was systematically minute in his narrative, simply in order, I think, not to let his excitement get the better of him.

After leaving the railway station, he had an ice, and read the paper in a café. Then he went back to the hotel, dressed for dinner, and dined with a good appetite. After dinner he lingered in the hall (there were chairs and tables there) smoking his cigar, talked to the little girl of the Primo Tenore of the San Carlo Theatre, and exchanged a few words with that "amiable lady" the wife of the Primo Tenore. There was no performance that evening, and these people were going to the Villa also. They went out of the hotel. Very well.

At the moment of following their example—it was half-past nine already—he remembered he had a rather large sum of money in his pocket-book. He entered, therefore, the office and deposited the greater part of it with the book-keeper of the hotel. This done, he took a carozella and drove to the seashore. He got out of the cab and entered the Villa on foot from the Largo di Vittoria end.

He stared at me very hard. And I understood then how really impressionable he was. Every small fact and event of that evening stood out in his memory as if endowed with mystic significance. If he did not mention to me the colour of the pony which drew the carozella, and the aspect of the man who drove, it was a mere oversight arising from his agitation, which he repressed manfully.

He had then entered the Villa Nazionale from the Largo di Vittoria end. The Villa Nazionale is a public pleasure-ground laid out in grass plots, bushes, and flower-beds between the houses of the Riviera di Chiaja and the waters of the bay. Alleys of trees, more or less parallel, stretch its whole length—which is considerable. On the Riviera di Chiaja side the electric tramcars run close to the railings. Between the garden and the sea is the fashionable drive, a broad road bordered by a low wall, beyond which the Mediterranean splashes with gentle murmurs when the weather is fine.

As life goes on late at night in Naples, the broad drive was all astir with a brilliant swarm of carriage lamps moving in pairs—some creeping slowly, others running rapidly under the thin, motionless line of electric lamps defining the shore. And a brillant swarm of stars hung above the land humming with voices, piled up with houses, glittering with lights—and over the silent, flat shadows of the sea.

The gardens themselves are not very well lit. Our friend went forward in the warm gloom, his eyes fixed upon a distant luminous region extending nearly across the whole width of the Villa, as if the air had glowed there with its own cold, bluish, and dazzling light. This magic spot, behind the black trunks of trees and masses of inky foliage, breathed out sweet sounds mingled with bursts of brassy roar, sudden clashes of metal, and grave, vibrating thuds.

As he walked on, all these noises combined together into a piece of elaborate music whose harmonious phrases came persuasively through a great disorderly murmur of voices and shuffling of feet on the gravel of that open space. An enormous crowd immersed in the electric light, as if in a bath of some radiant and tenuous fluid shed upon their heads by luminous globes, drifted in its hundreds round the band. Hundreds more sat on chairs in more or less concentric circles, receiving unflinching the great waves of sonority that ebbed out into the darkness. The Count penetrated the throng, drifted with it in tranquil enjoyment, listening, and looking at the faces. All people of good society: mothers with their daughters, parents and children, young men and young women all talking, smiling, nodding to each other. Very many pretty faces, and very many pretty toilettes. There was, of course, a quantity of diverse types: showy old fellows with white moustaches, fat men, thin men, officers in uniform; but what predominated, he told me, was the South Italian type of young man, with a colourless, clear complexion, red lips, jet-black little moustache, and liquid black eyes so wonderfully effective in leering or scowling.

Withdrawing from the throng, the Count shared a little table in front of the café with a young man of just such a type. Our friend had some lemonade. The young man was sitting moodily before an empty glass.

He looked up once, and then looked down again. He also tilted his hat forward. Like this—

The Count made the gesture of a man pulling his hat down over his brow, and went on:

"I think to myself: he is sad; something is wrong with him; young men have their troubles. I take no notice of him, of course. I pay for my lemonade, and go away."

Strolling about in the neighbourhood of the band, the Count thinks he saw twice that young man wandering alone in the crowd. Once their eyes met. It must have been the same young man, but there were so many there of that type that he could not be certain. Moreover, he was not very much concerned, except in so far that he had been struck by the marked, peevish discontent of that face.

Presently, tired of the feeling of confinement one experiences in a crowd, the Count edged away from the band. An alley, very sombre by contrast, presented itself invitingly with its promise of solitude and coolness. He entered it, walking slowly on till the sound of the orchestra became distinctly deadened. Then he walked back and turned about once more. He did this several times before he noticed that there was somebody occupying one of the benches.

The spot being midway between two lamp-posts, the light was faint.

The man lolled back in the corner of the seat, his legs stretched out, his arms folded, and his head drooping on his breast. He never stirred, as though he had fallen asleep there, but when the Count passed by next time he had changed his attitude. He sat leaning forward. His elbows were propped on his knees, and his hands were rolling a cigarette. He never looked up from that occupation.

The Count continued his stroll away from the band. He returned slowly, he said. I can imagine him enjoying to the full, but with his usual tranquillity, the balminess of this Southern night and the sounds of music softened delightfully by the distance.

Presently, he approached for the third time the man on the garden seat, still leaning forward with his elbows on his knees. It was a dejected pose. In the semi-obscurity of the alley his high shirt collar and his cuffs made small patches of vivid whiteness. The Count said that he had noticed him getting up brusquely as if to walk away, but almost before he was aware of it the man stood before him asking in a low, gentle tone whether the signore would have the kindness to oblige him with a light.

The Count answered this request by a polite "Certainly," and dropped his hands with the intention of exploring both pockets of his trousers for the matches.

"I dropped my hands," he said, "but I never put them in my pockets. I felt a pressure there—"

He put the tip of his finger on a spot close under his breast-bone, the very spot of the human body where a Japanese gentleman begins the operations of the *hara-kiri,* which is a form of suicide following upon dishonour, upon an intolerable outrage to the delicacy of one's feelings.

"I glance down," the Count continued in an awestruck voice, "and what do I see? A knife! A long knife—"

"You don't mean to say," I exclaimed, amazed, "that you have been held up like this in the Villa at half-past ten o'clock, within a stone's-throw of a thousand people?"

He nodded several times, staring at me with all his might.

"The clarionet," he declared solemnly, "was finishing his solo, and I assure you I could hear every note. Then the band crashed *fortissimo*, and that creature rolled its eyes and gnashed its teeth, hissing at me with the greatest ferocity, 'Be silent! No noise, or—' "

I could not get over my astonishment.

"What sort of knife was it?" I asked stupidly.

"A long blade. A stiletto—perhaps a kitchen knife. A long, narrow blade. It gleamed. And his eyes gleamed. His white teeth too. I could see them. He was very ferocious. I thought to myself, 'If I hit him he will kill me.' How could I fight with him? He had the knife and I had nothing. I am nearly seventy, you know, and that was a young man. I seemed even to recognise him. The moody young man of the café. The young man I met in the crowd. But I could not tell. There are so many like him in this country."

The distress of that moment was reflected in his face. I should think that physically he must have been paralysed by surprise. His thoughts, however, remained extremely active. They ranged over every alarming possibility. The idea of setting up a vigorous shouting for help occurred to him too. But he did nothing of the kind, and the reason why he refrained gave me a good opinion of his mental self-possession. He saw in a flash that nothing prevented the other from shouting too.

"That young man might in an instant have thrown away his knife and pretended I was the aggressor. Why not? He might have said I attacked him. Why not? It was one incredible story against another! He might have said anything—bring some dishonouring charge against me—what do I know? By his dress he was no common robber. He seemed to belong to the better classes. What could I say? He was an Italian—I am a foreigner. Of course, I have my passport, and there is our consul—but to be arrested, dragged at night to the police office like a criminal!"

He shuddered. It was in his character to shrink from scandal much more than from mere death. And certainly for many people this would have always remained—considering certain peculiarities of Neapolitan manners—a deucedly queer story. The Count was no fool. His belief in the respectable placidity of life having received this rude shock, he thought that now anything might happen. But also a notion came into his head that this young man was perhaps merely an infuriated lunatic.

This was for me the first hint of his attitude towards this adventure. In his exaggerated delicacy of sentiment he felt that nobody's self-esteem need be affected by what a madman may choose to do to one. It became apparent, however, that the Count was to be denied that consolation. He enlarged upon the abominably savage way in which that young man rolled his glistening eyes and gnashed his white teeth. The band was going now through a slow movement of solemn braying by all the trombones, with deliberately repeated bangs of the big drum.

"But what did you do?" I asked, greatly excited.

"Nothing," answered the Count. "I let my hands hang down very still. I told him quietly I did not intend making a noise. He snarled like a dog, then said in an ordinary voice:

" '*Vostro portofolio.*'

"So I naturally," continued the Count—and from this point acted the whole thing in pantomime. Holding me with his eyes, he went through all the motions of reaching into his inside breast-pocket, taking out a pocket-book, and handing it over. But that young man, still bearing steadily on the knife, refused to touch it.

He directed the Count to take the money out himself, received it into his left hand, motioned the pocket-book to be returned to the pocket, all this being done to the sweet trilling of flutes and clarionets sustained by the emotional drone of the hautboys. And the "young man," as the Count called him, said, "This seems very little."

"It was, indeed, only 340 or 360 lire," the Count pursued. "I had left my money in the hotel, as you know. I told him this was all I had on me. He shook his head impatiently and said:

" '*Vostro orologio.*' "

The Count gave me the dumb show of pulling out his watch, detaching it. But, as it happened, the valuable gold half-chronometer he possessed had been left at a watchmaker's for cleaning. He wore that evening (on a leather guard) the Waterbury fifty-franc thing he used to take with him on his fishing expeditions. Perceiving the nature of this booty, the well-dressed robber made a contemptuous clicking sound with his tongue like this, "Tse-ah!" and waved it away hastily. Then, as the Count was returning the disdained object to his pocket, he demanded with a threateningly increased pressure of the knife on the epigastrium, by way of reminder:

"*Vostri anelli.*"

"One of the rings," went on the Count, "was given me many years ago by my wife; the other is the signet ring of my father. I said, 'No. *That* you shall not have!' "

Here the Count reproduced the gesture corresponding to that declaration by clapping one hand upon the other, and pressing both thus against his chest. It was touching in its resignation. "That you shall not have," he repeated firmly, and closed his eyes, fully expecting—I don't know whether I am right in recording that such an unpleasant word had passed his lips—fully expecting to feel himself being—I really hesitate to say—being disembowelled by the push of the long, sharp blade resting murderously against the pit of his stomach—the very seat, in all human beings, of anguishing sensations.

Great waves of harmony went on flowing from the band.

Suddenly the Count felt the nightmarish pressure removed from the sensitive spot. He opened his eyes. He was alone. He had heard nothing.

It is probable that the young man had departed, with light steps, some time before, but the sense of the horrid pressure had lingered even after the knife had gone. A feeling of weakness came over him. He had just time to stagger to the garden seat. He felt as though he had held his breath for a long time. He sat all in a heap, panting with the shock of the reaction.

The band was executing, with immense bravura, the complicated finale. It ended with a tremendous crash. He heard it unreal and remote, as if his ears had been stopped, and then the hard clapping of a thousand, more or less, pairs of hands, like a sudden hail-shower passing away. The profound silence which succeeded recalled him to himself.

A tramcar resembling a long glass box wherein people sat with their heads strongly lighted, ran along swiftly within sixty yards of the spot where he had been robbed. Then another rustled by, and yet another going the other way. The audience about the band had broken up, and were entering the alley in small conversing groups. The Count sat up straight and tried to think calmly of what had happened to him. The vileness of it took his breath away again. As far as I can make out he was disgusted with himself. I do not mean to say with his behaviour. Indeed, if his pantomimic rendering of it for my information was to be trusted, it was simply perfect. No, it was not that. He was not ashamed. He was shocked at being the selected victim, not of robbery so much as of contempt. His tranquillity had been wantonly desecrated. His lifelong, kindly nicety of outlook had been defaced.

Nevertheless, at that stage, before the iron had time to sink deep, he was able to argue himself into comparative equanimity. As his agitation calmed down somewhat, he became aware that he was frightfully hungry. Yes, hungry. The sheer emotion had made him simply ravenous. He left the seat and, after walking for some time, found himself outside the gardens and before an arrested tramcar, without knowing very well how he came there. He got in as if in a dream, by a sort of instinct. Fortunately, he found in his trousers pocket a copper to satisfy the conductor. Then the car stopped, and as everybody was getting out, he got out too. He recognised the Piazza San Ferdinando, but apparently it did not occur to him to take a cab and drive to the hotel. He remained in distress on the Piazza like a lost dog, thinking vaguely of the best way of getting something to eat at once.

Suddenly he remembered his twenty-franc piece. He explained to me that he had had that piece of French gold for something like three years. He used to carry it about with him as a sort of reserve in case of accident. Anybody is liable to have his pocket picked—a quite different thing from a brazen and insulting robbery.

The monumental arch of the Galleria Umberto faced him at the top of a noble flight of stairs. He climbed these without loss of time, and directed his steps towards the Café Umberto. All the tables outside were occupied by a lot of people who were drinking. But as he wanted something to eat, he went inside the café, which is divided into aisles by square pillars set all round with long looking-glasses. The Count sat down on a red plush bench against one of these pillars, waiting for his risotto. And his mind reverted to his abominable adventure.

He thought of the moody, well-dressed young man, with whom he had exchanged glances in the crowd around the bandstand, and who, he felt confident, was the robber. Would he recognise him again? Doubtless. But he did not want ever to see him again. The best thing was to forget this humiliating episode.

The Count looked round anxiously for the coming of his risotto, and, behold! to the left against the wall—there sat the young man. He was alone at a table, with a bottle of some sort of wine or syrup and a carafe of iced water before him. The smooth olive cheeks, the red lips, the little jet-black moustache turned up gallantly, the fine black eyes a little heavy and shaded by long eyelashes, that peculiar expression of cruel discontent to be seen only in the busts of some Roman emperors—it was he, no doubt at all. But that was a type. The Count looked away hastily. The young officer over there reading a paper was like that too. Same type. Two young men farther away playing draughts also resembled—

The Count lowered his head, with the fear in his heart of being everlastingly haunted by the vision of that young man. He began to eat his risotto. Presently he heard the young man on his left call the waiter in a bad-tempered tone.

At the call, not only his own waiter, but two other idle waiters belonging to a quite different row of tables, rushed towards him with obsequious alacrity, which is not the general characteristic of the waiters in the Café Umberto. The young man muttered something, and one of the waiters walking rapidly to the nearest door called out into the galleria, "Pasquale! O Pasquale!"

Everybody knows Pasquale, the shabby old fellow who, shuffling between the tables, offers for sale cigars, cigarettes, picture postcards, and matches to the clients of the café. He is in many respects an engaging scoundrel. The Count saw the grey-haired, unshaven ruffian enter the café, the glass case hanging from his neck by a leather strap, and, at a word from the waiter, make his shuffling way with a sudden spurt to the young man's table. The young man was in need of a cigar, with which Pasquale served him fawningly. The old pedlar was going out, when the Count, on a sudden impulse, beckoned to him.

Pasquale approached, the smile of deferential recognition combining oddly with the cynical, searching expression of his eyes. Leaning his case on the table, he lifted the glass lid without a word. The Count took a box of cigarettes, and, urged by a fearful curiosity, asked as casually as he could:

"Tell me, Pasquale, who is that young signore sitting over there?"

The other bent over his box confidentially.

"That, Signor Conde," he said, beginning to rearrange his wares busily and without looking up, "that is a young Cavaliere of a very good family from Bari. He studies in the University here, and is the chief, *capo*, of an association of young men—of very nice young men."

He paused, and then, with mingled discretion and pride of knowledge, murmured the explanatory word "Camorra" and shut down the lid. "A very powerful Camorra," he breathed out. "The professors themselves respect it greatly . . . *una lira e cinquanti centesimi,* Signor Conde."

Our friend paid with the gold piece. While Pasquale was making up the change, he observed that the young man, of whom he had heard so much in a few words, was watching the transaction covertly. After the old vagabond had withdrawn with a bow, the Count settled with the waiter and sat still. A numbness, he told me, had come over him.

The young man paid too, got up, and crossed over, apparently for the purpose of looking at himself in the mirror set in the pillar nearest to the Count's seat. He was dressed all in black, with a dark green bow tie. The Count looked round, and was startled by meeting a vicious glance out of the corners of the other's eyes. The young Cavaliere from Bari (according to Pasquale; but Pasquale is, of course, an accomplished liar) went on arranging his tie, settling his hat before the glass, and meantime he spoke just loud enough to be heard by the Count. He spoke through his teeth with the most insulting venom of contempt and gazing straight into the mirror:

"Ah! So you had some gold on you—you old liar—you old *birba*—you *furfante!* But you are not done with me yet."

The fiendishness of his expression vanished like lightning, and he lounged out of the café with a moody, impassive face.

The poor Count, after telling me this last episode, fell back trembling in his chair. His forehead broke into perspiration. There was a wanton insolence in the spirit of this outrage which appalled even me. What it was to the Count's delicacy I won't attempt to guess. I am sure that if he had been not too refined to do such a blatantly vulgar thing as dying from apoplexy in a café, he would have had a fatal stroke there and then. All irony apart, my difficulty was to keep him from seeing the full extent of my commiseration. He shrank from every excessive sentiment, and my commiseration was practically unbounded. It did not surprise me to hear that he had been in bed a week. He had got up to make his arrangements for leaving Southern Italy for good and all.

And the man was convinced that he could not live through a whole year in any other climate!

No argument of mine had any effect. It was not timidity, though he did say to me once: "You do not know what a Camorra is, my dear sir. I am a marked man." He was not afraid of what could be done to him. His delicate conception of his dignity was defiled by a degrading experience. He couldn't stand that. No Japanese gentleman, outraged in his exaggerated sense of honour, could have gone about his preparations for *hara-kiri* with greater resolution. To go home really amounted to suicide for the poor Count.

There is a saying of Neapolitan patriotism, intended for the information of foreigners, I presume: "See Naples and then die." *Vedi Napoli e poi mori.* It is a saying of excessive vanity, and everything excessive was abhorrent to the nice moderation of the poor Count. Yet, as I was seeing him off at the railway station, I thought he was behaving with singular fidelity to its conceited spirit. *Vedi Napoli!* . . . He had seen it! He had seen it with startling thoroughness—and now he was going to his grave. He was going to it by the *train de luxe* of the International Sleeping-Car Company, via Trieste and Vienna. As the four long, sombre coaches pulled out of the station, I raised my hat with the solemn feeling of paying the last tribute of respect to a funeral cortège. *Il Conde's* profile, much aged already, glided away from me in stony immobility, behind the lighted pane of glass—*Vedi Napoli e poi mori!*

Thomas Mann

Thomas Mann (1875–1955), German novelist, was born at Lübeck of a wealthy middle-class family. After a brief period of office work, he took up writing early in life. During World War I he defended German authoritarianism, but later he became highly critical of it. In the 1930's he called boldly on Germans to unite against Hitlerism, and soon found it necessary to move to the United States. He was awarded the Nobel Prize for Literature in 1929. His writings reveal his deep humanistic passion and his preoccupation with the spiritual crisis in Europe. His skillful use of the device of the leitmotiv is the result, in his words, "of an extraordinarily keen conscientiousness in the choice of every word, the coining of every phrase," because each may serve as "motif, link, symbol, citation or association." Among his more popular works are Buddenbrooks *(1900),* Death in Venice *(1912), and* The Magic Mountain *(1924), a brilliant comic-philosophical novel.* *(See p. 65 of Introduction.)*

LITTLE HERR FRIEDEMANN

1

It was the nurse's fault. In vain Frau Consul Friedemann, when the matter was first suspected, had solemnly urged her to relinquish so heinous a vice; in vain she had dispensed to her daily a glass of red wine in addition to her nourishing stout. It suddenly came to light that the girl had actually sunk so low as to drink the methylated spirits intended for the coffee machine; and before a replacement for her had arrived, before she could be sent away, the accident had happened. One day, when little Johannes was about a month old, his mother and three adolescent sisters returned from a walk to find that he had fallen from the swaddling table and was lying on the floor making a horribly faint whimpering noise, with the nurse standing by looking stupidly down at him.

The doctor's face, as he carefully but firmly probed the limbs of the crooked, twitching little creature, wore an exceedingly serious expression; the three girls stood in a corner sobbing, and Frau Friedemann prayed aloud in her mortal anguish.

Even before the baby was born it had been the poor woman's lot to see her husband, the consul for the Netherlands, reft from her by an illness both sudden and acute, and she was still too broken in spirit to be even capable of hoping that the life of her little Johannes might be spared. Two days later, however, the doctor squeezed her hand encouragingly and pronounced that there was now absolutely no question of any immediate danger; above all, the slight concussion of the brain had completely cleared up. This, he explained, was obvious if one looked at the child's eyes: there had been a vacant stare in them at first which had now quite disappeared. . . . "Of course," he added, "we must wait and see how things go on—and we must hope for the best, you know, hope for the best. . . ."

2

The gray gabled house in which Johannes Friedemann grew up was near the north gate of the old, scarcely medium-sized merchant city. Its front door opened onto a spacious stone-paved hall, from which a stair with white wooden banisters led to the upper floors. On the first was the living room with its walls papered in a faded landscape pattern, and its heavy mahogany table draped in crimson plush, with high-backed chairs and settees standing stiffly round it.

Here, as a child, he would sit perhaps on a little stool by his mother's feet, listening to her as she told him some tale full of wonders, and as he listened he would gaze at her smooth gray hair and her kind gentle face, and breathe in the slight fragrance of scent that always hung about her. Or perhaps he would get her to show him the portrait of his father, an amiable gentleman with gray side-whiskers. He was (said Johannes's mother) now living in heaven, waiting for them all to join him there.

Behind the house was a little garden, and during the summer they would spend a good deal of their time in it, notwithstanding the almost perpetual sickly sweet exhalations from a nearby sugar refinery. In the garden stood an old gnarled walnut tree, and in its shade little Johannes would often sit on a low wooden stool cracking nuts, while Frau Friedemann and her three daughters, now grown up, together occupied a gray canvas tent. But Frau Friedemann would often raise her eyes from her needlework and glance tenderly and sadly across at her son.

Little Johannes was no beauty, with his pigeon chest, his steeply humped back and his disproportionately long skinny arms, and as he squatted there on his stool, nimbly and eagerly cracking his nuts, he was certainly a strange sight. But his hands and feet were small and neatly shaped, and he had great liquid brown eyes, a sensitive mouth and soft light brown hair. In fact, although his face sat so pitifully low down between his shoulders, it might almost have been described as beautiful after all.

3

When he was seven he was sent to school, and now the years passed uniformly and rapidly. Every day, walking past the gabled houses and shops with the quaintly solemn gait that deformed people often have, he made his way to the old schoolhouse with its Gothic vaulting; and at home, when he had done his homework, he would perhaps read some of his beautiful books with their brightly colored illustrations, or potter about in the garden, while his sisters kept house for their ailing mother. The girls also went to parties, for the Friedemanns moved in the best local society; but unfortunately none of the three had yet married, for their family fortune was by no means large and they were distinctly plain.

Johannes too occasionally got an invitation from one or other of his contemporaries, but it was no great pleasure for him to associate with them. He was unable to join in their games, and since they always treated him with embarrassed reserve, it was impossible for any real companionship to develop.

Later there came a time when he would often hear them discuss certain matters in the school yard; wide-eyed and attentive, he would listen in silence as they talked of their passions for this little girl or that. Such experiences, he decided, obviously engrossing though they were for the others, belonged like gymnastics and ball games to the category of things for which he was not suited. This was at times a rather saddening thought; but after all, he had long been accustomed to going his own way and not sharing the interests of other people.

It nevertheless came to pass—he was sixteen years old at the time—that he found himself suddenly enamored of a girl of his own age. She was the sister of one of his classmates, a blond, exuberant creature whom he had met at her brother's house. He felt a strange uneasiness in her company, and the studied self-conscious cordiality with which she too treated him saddened him profoundly.

One summer afternoon when he was taking a solitary walk along the promenade outside the old city wall, he heard whispered words being exchanged behind a jasmine bush. He cautiously peeped through the branches, and there on a seat sat this girl and a tall red-haired boy whom he knew very well by sight; the boy's arm was round her and he was pressing a kiss on her lips, which with much giggling she reciprocated. When Johannes had seen this he turned on his heel and walked softly away.

His head had sunk lower than ever between his shoulders, his hands were trembling and a sharp, biting pain rose from his chest and seemed to choke him. But he swallowed it down, and resolutely drew himself up as straight as he could. "Very well," he said to himself, "that is over. I will never again concern myself with such things. To the others they mean joy and happiness, but to me they can only bring grief and suffering. I am done with it all. It is finished for me. Never again."

The decision was a relief to him. He had made a renunciation, a renunciation forever. He went home and took up a book or played the violin, which he had learnt to do despite his deformity.

4

At seventeen he left school to go into business, like everyone else of his social standing, and he became an apprentice in Herr Schlievogt's big timber firm down by the river. They treated him with special consideration, he for his part was amiable and cooperative, and the years passed by in a peaceful and well-ordered manner. But in his twenty-first year his mother died after a long illness.

This was a great sorrow for Johannes Friedemann, and one that he long cherished. He savored this sorrow, he surrendered himself to it as one surrenders oneself to a great happiness, he nourished it with innumerable memories from his childhood and made the most of it, as his first major experience.

Is not life in itself a thing of goodness, irrespective of whether the course it takes for us can be called a "happy" one? Johannes Friedemann felt that this was so, and he loved life. He had renounced the greatest happiness it has to offer, but who shall say with what passionate care he cultivated those pleasures that were accessible to him? A walk in springtime through the parks outside the town, the scent of a flower, the song of a bird—surely these were things to be thankful for?

He also well understood that a capacity for the enjoyment of life presupposes education, indeed that it increases automatically as one's education increases: and he took pains to educate himself. He loved music and attended any concerts that were given in the town. And although it was uncommonly odd to watch him play, he did himself become not a bad violinist and took pleasure in every beautiful and tender note he was able to draw from his instrument. And by dint of much reading he had in the course of time acquired a degree of literary taste which in that town was probably unique. He was versed in all the latest publications both in Germany and abroad, he knew how to savor the exquisite rhythms of a poem, he could appreciate the subtle atmosphere of a finely written short story. . . . One might indeed almost say that he was an epicurean.

He came to see that there is nothing that cannot be enjoyed and that it is almost absurd to distinguish between happy and unhappy experiences. He accepted all his sensations and moods as they came to him, he welcomed and cultivated them, whether they were sad or glad. Even his unfulfilled wishes and ardent longings were precious to him for their own sake: he would tell himself that if any of them ever came to fulfillment the best part of the pleasure would be over. Is not the sweet pain of vague desires and hopes on a still spring evening richer in delight than any fulfillment the summer could bring? Ah yes, little Herr Friedemann was an epicurean and no mistake.

This was something of which the people who passed him in the street, greeting him with that mixture of cordiality and pity to which he had so long been accustomed, were doubtless unaware. They did not know that this unfortunate cripple, strutting so quaintly and solemnly along in his light gray overcoat and his shiny top hat (for oddly enough he was a little vain of his appearance) was a man to whom life was very sweet, this life of his that flowed so gently by, unmarked by any strong emotions but filled with a quiet and delicate happiness of which he had taught himself the secret.

5

But Herr Friedemann's chief and most absorbing passion was for the theater. He had an uncommonly strong sense of drama and at moments of high theatrical effect or tragic catastrophe the whole of his little body would quiver with emotion. At the principal theater of the town he had a seat permanently reserved for him in the front row, and he would go there regularly, sometimes accompanied by his three sisters. Since their mother's death they had lived on in the big house which they and their brother jointly owned, and did all the housekeeping for themselves and him.

They were, alas, still unmarried; but they had long reached an age at which one sets aside all such expectations, for the eldest of them Friederike, was seventeen years older than Herr Friedemann. She and her sister Henriette were rather too tall and thin, whereas Pfiffi, the youngest, looked regrettably short and plump. This youngest girl moreover had an odd habit of wriggling and wetting the corners of her mouth whenever she spoke.

Little Herr Friedemann did not pay much attention to the three girls, but they stuck loyally together and were always of the same opinion. In particular, whenever any engagement between persons of their acquaintance was announced, they would unanimously declare that this was *very* gratifying news.

Their brother went on living with them even after he had left Herr Schlievogt's timber firm and set up on his own by taking over some small business, some sort of agency which did not demand much exertion. He lived in a couple of rooms on the ground floor of the house, in order not to have to climb the stairs except at mealtimes, for he occasionally suffered from asthma.

On his thirtieth birthday, a fine warm June day, he was sitting after lunch in the gray tent in the garden, leaning against a new soft neck rest which Henriette had made for him, with a good cigar in his mouth and a good book in his hand. Now and then he would put the book aside, listen to the contented twittering of the sparrows in the old walnut tree and look at the neat gravel drive that led up to the house and at the lawn with its bright flower beds.

Little Herr Friedemann was clean-shaven, and his face had scarcely changed at all except for a slight sharpening of his features. He wore his soft light brown hair smoothly parted on one side.

Once, he lowered the book right onto his lap, gazed up at the clear blue sky and said to himself: "Well, that's thirty years gone. And now I suppose there will be another ten or perhaps another twenty, God knows. They will come upon me silently and pass by without any commotion, as the others have done, and I look forward to them without a qualm."

6

It was in July of that year that the new military commandant for the district was appointed, a change of office that caused a considerable stir. The stout and jovial gentleman who had held the post for many years had been a great favorite with local society, and his departure was regretted. And now, for God knows what reason, it must needs be Herr von Rinnlingen who was sent from the capital to replace him.

It seemed, in fact, to be not a bad exchange, for the new lieutenant colonel, who was married but had no children, rented a very spacious villa in the southern suburbs, from which it was concluded that he intended to keep house in some style. At all events the rumor that he was quite exceptionally rich found further confirmation in the fact that he brought with him four servants, five riding and carriage horses, a landau and a light hunting brake.

Shortly after their arrival he and his wife had been to pay calls on all the best families, and everyone was talking about them; the chief object of interest however was definitely not Herr von Rinnlingen himself, but his wife. The men were dumbfounded by her and did not at first know what to think; but the ladies most decidedly did not approve of Gerda von Rinnlingen's character and ways.

"Of course, one can tell at once that she comes from the capital," observed Frau Hagenström, the lawyer's wife, in the course of conversation with Henriette Friedemann. "One doesn't mind that, one doesn't mind her smoking and riding—naturally not! But her behavior isn't merely free and easy, it's unrefined, and even that isn't quite the right word. . . . She's by no means ugly, you know, some might even think her pretty—and yet she totally lacks feminine charm, her eyes and her laugh and her movements are simply not at all calculated to appeal to men. She is no flirt, and far be it from me to find fault with her for that, goodness knows—but can it be right for so young a woman, a woman of twenty-four, to show absolutely no sign of . . . a certain natural grace and attractiveness? My dear, I am not very good at expressing myself, but I know what I mean. The men still seem to be quite stunned, poor dears: mark my words, they will all be sick to death of her in a few weeks' time."

"Well," said Fräulein Friedemann, "she has made a very good marriage, anyway."

"Oh, as to her husband!" exclaimed Frau Hagenström. "You should see how she treats him! You will see it soon enough! I am the last person to deny that up to a point a married woman should act toward the opposite sex with a certain reserve. But how does she behave to her own husband? She has a way of freezing him with her eyes and calling him '*mon cher ami*' in pitying tones, which I find quite outrageous! You have only to look at *him*—a fine upstanding first-class officer and gentleman of forty, well behaved and well mannered and very well preserved! They've been married for four years . . . My dear. . . ."

7

The scene of little Herr Friedemann's first encounter with Frau von Rinnlingen was the main street of the town, a street lined almost entirely with shops and offices. He was vouchsafed this first sight of her at midday, just after leaving the stock exchange, where he had been making his modest contribution to the morning's business.

He was trudging along, a tiny and solemn figure, beside Herr Stephens, the wholesale merchant, who was an unusually large and solid man with round-trimmed side-whiskers and formidably bushy eyebrows. They were both wearing top hats, and had opened their overcoats as it was a very hot day. They were discussing politics, and their walking sticks tapped the pavement in regular rhythm. But when they were about halfway down the street Herr Stephens suddenly remarked: "Bless me, here comes that Rinnlingen woman driving toward us."

"Well, that's a lucky coincidence," replied Herr Friedemann in his high-pitched, rather strident voice, and peered expectantly ahead. "I've never yet set eyes on her, you know. Ah, so that is the yellow brake."

And so indeed it was: Frau von Rinnlingen was using the light yellow hunting brake today, and she herself was driving the pair of thoroughbreds; the groom sat behind her with his arms folded. She wore a loose-fitting, very light-colored coat, and her skirt was of a light color as well. From under her little round straw hat with its brown leather band came her luxuriant auburn hair, well curled at the sides and thickly tressed at the back where it fell almost to her shoulders. The complexion of her oval face was pale, and there were blue shadows in the corners of her unusually close-set eyes. Across her short but finely shaped nose ran a very becoming little ridge of freckles; the beauty or otherwise of her mouth, however, was hard to judge, for she kept protruding and withdrawing her lower lip, chafing it continually against the other.

Herr Stephens greeted Frau von Rinnlingen with an exceedingly respectful salutation as her carriage drew abreast of them, and little Herr Friedemann also raised his hat and stared at her very attentively. She lowered her whip, inclined her head slightly and drove slowly past, glancing at the houses and shopwindows on either side.

A few paces further on Herr Stephens remarked: "She's been out for a drive and now she's on her way home."

Little Herr Friedemann made no reply but gazed down at the pavement in front of him. Then he suddenly looked up at Stephens and asked: "What did you say?"

And Herr Stephens, the wholesale trader, repeated his perspicacious observation.

8

Three days later, at noon, Johannes Friedemann returned home from his regular morning walk. Luncheon was served at half-past twelve, so there would be time for him to spend another half hour in his "office" which was just to the right of the front door. But as he was about to enter it the maid came up to him in the hall and said:

"There are visitors, Herr Friedemann."

"In my room?" he asked.

"No, upstairs with the ladies, sir."

"But who are they?"

"Lieutenant Colonel and Frau von Rinnlingen."

"Oh," said Herr Friedemann, "then of course I'll . . ."

And he climbed the stairs to the first floor and walked across the lobby toward the room with the landscape wallpaper. But with the handle of the tall white door already in his hand, he suddenly stopped, drew back a pace, turned and went slowly down again the way he had come. And although he was completely alone he said out loud to himself:

"No. Better not."

He went into his "office," sat down at his desk and took up a newspaper. But presently he let it drop again, and sat with his head turned to one side, looking out of the window. Thus he remained till the maid came and announced that luncheon was served; then he went upstairs to the dining room where his sisters were already waiting for him, and seated himself on his chair on top of three volumes of music.

Henriette, ladling out the soup, said:

"Who do you think has been here, Johannes?"

"Well?" he asked.

"The new lieutenant colonel with his wife."

"Indeed? That is very kind of them."

"Yes," said Pfiffi, dribbling at the corners of her mouth, "I think they are both very agreeable people."

"Anyway," said Friederike, "we must return the call without delay. I suggest we go on Sunday, the day after tomorrow."

"On Sunday," said Henriette and Pfiffi.

"You'll come with us of course, Johannes?" asked Friederike.

"Naturally!" said Pfiffi, wriggling. Herr Friedemann had completely ignored the question and was swallowing his soup, silently and apprehensively. He seemed somehow to be listening, listening to some uncanny noise from nowhere.

9

The following evening there was a performance of *Lohengrin* at the city theater, and all well-educated people were present. The small auditorium was packed from top to bottom and filled with the hum of voices, the smell of gas and a medley of scent. But every eyeglass, in the stalls and in the circles, was trained on box number thirteen, just to the right of the stage; for there, this evening, Herr and Frau von Rinnlingen had appeared for the first time, and now was the chance to give them a thorough inspection.

When little Herr Friedemann, in faultless evening dress with a glistening white pigeon-breasted shirtfront, entered his box—box thirteen—he stopped dead on the threshold: his hand rose to his brow and for a moment his nostrils dilated convulsively. But then he took his seat, the seat immediately to the left of Frau von Rinnlingen.

As he sat down she contemplated him attentively, protruding her lower lip; she then turned and exchanged a few words with her husband, who was standing behind her. He was a tall well-built man with upturned moustaches and a tanned, good-humored face.

When the prelude began and Frau von Rinnlingen leaned forward over the balustrade, Herr Friedemann gave her a quick, furtive, sideways look. She was wearing a light-colored evening gown and was even slightly décolletée, unlike any other woman present. Her sleeves were wide and ample and her white evening gloves came up to her elbows. Tonight there was something voluptuous about her figure which had not been noticeable the other day under her loose coat; her bosom rose and fell slowly and firmly, and her heavy auburn tresses hung low down behind her head.

Herr Friedemann was pale, much paler than usual, and below his smoothly parted brown hair little drops of sweat stood out on his forehead. Frau von Rinnlingen had removed her left glove and was resting her bare arm on the red plush balustrade: a round, pale arm, with pale blue veins running through it and through her hand, on which she wore no rings. This arm lay constantly just where he could see it; there was no help for that.

The violins sang, the trombones blared, Telramund was struck down, the orchestra sounded a general triumph and little Herr Friedemann sat motionless, pale and silent, with his head drooping right down between his shoulders, one forefinger propped against his mouth and the other hand thrust under his lapel.

As the curtain fell, Frau von Rinnlingen rose to leave the box with her husband. Herr Friedemann, without looking at them, saw them go; he drew his handkerchief across his brow, stood up suddenly, got as far as the door that led into the corridor, then turned back again, resumed his seat, and sat on without stirring in the same posture as before.

When the bell rang and his neighbors came back into the box, he sensed that Frau von Rinnlingen was looking at him, and involuntarily he raised his head and returned her gaze. When their eyes met, so far from turning hers away, she went on scrutinizing him without a trace of embarrassment until he himself felt humiliated and compelled to look down. His pallor increased, and a strange, bittersweet rage welled up inside him. . . . The music began.

Toward the end of that act Frau von Rinnlingen happened to drop her fan and it fell to the ground beside Herr Friedemann. Both of them stooped simultaneously, but she reached it first and said with a mocking smile:

"Thank you."

His head had been close to hers, and for a moment, unavoidably, he had caught the warm fragrance of her breast. His face was contorted, his whole body was convulsed and his heart throbbed with such appalling violence that he could not breathe. He sat for half a minute longer, then pushed back his chair, got up quietly and quietly left the box.

10

The clamor of the orchestra followed him as he crossed the corridor, reclaimed his top hat and light gray overcoat and stick from the cloakroom and went downstairs and out into the street.

It was a warm, still evening. In the gaslight the gray gabled houses stood silent against the sky, and the stars gleamed and glistened softly. Only a few people passed Herr Friedemann in the street, their steps re-echoing along the pavement. Someone greeted him but he did not notice; his head was bowed low and his misshapen chest shuddered as he gasped for breath. Now and then, scarcely audibly, he exclaimed to himself:

"Oh my God! my God!"

He examined his feelings with horrified apprehension, realizing that his so carefully cherished, prudently cultivated sensibility had now been torn up by the roots and stirred into wild upheaval. And suddenly, quite overcome by emotion, drunk with vertiginous desire, he leaned against a lamppost and whispered in trembling anguish:

"Gerda!"

There was complete silence. Far and wide there was not a soul to be seen. Little Herr Friedemann pulled himself together and trudged on. He had reached the top of the street in which the theater stood and which ran quite steeply down to the river, and now he was walking northward along the main street toward his house. . . .

How she had looked at him! Was it possible? She had forced him to look away! She had humbled him with her gaze! Was she not a woman and he a man? And had not her strange brown eyes positively quivered with pleasure as she had done so?

Again he felt that impotent, voluptuous hatred welling up inside him, but then he thought of the moment when her head had touched his, when he had breathed her fragrance—and once more he stopped, half straightened his deformed back, and again murmured helplessly, desperately, distractedly:

"Oh my God! my God!"

Then mechanically he resumed his slow advance along the empty, echoing streets, through the sultry evening air, and walked on till he reached his house. He paused for a moment in the hall to sniff its cool, dank atmosphere, then went into his "office."

He sat down at his desk beside the open window and stared straight in front of him at a big yellow rose which someone had put for him there in a glass of water. He took it and inhaled its fragrance with closed eyes; but then, with a sad, weary gesture, he put it aside. No, no! All that was over. What was that sweet smell to him now? What were any of them now, these things that had hitherto constituted his "happiness"? . . .

He turned and looked out into the silent street. Now and then the sound of passing footsteps approached and faded. The stars glittered in the sky. How dead tired he was growing, how weak he felt! The thoughts seemed to drain from his head, and his despair began to dissolve into a great soft sadness. A few lines of poetry floated through his mind, he seemed to hear the music of *Lohengrin* again, to see again Frau von Rinnlingen sitting beside him, her white arm resting on the red plush. Then he fell into a heavy, feverish sleep.

11

Often he was on the point of waking up, yet dreaded to do so and sank back every time into unconsciousness. But when it was broad daylight he opened his eyes and gazed sorrowfully round. All that had happened was still vividly present to him; it was as if sleep had not interrupted his suffering at all.

His head was heavy and his eyes hot, but when he had washed and dabbed his forehead with eau de cologne he felt better, and quietly resumed his seat by the window, which was still open. It was still very early, about five o'clock in the morning. Occasionally a baker's boy passed, but there was no one else to be seen. In the house opposite all the blinds were still down. But the birds were twittering, and the sky was blue and radiant. It was an absolutely beautiful Sunday morning.

A feeling of well-being and confidence came over little Herr Friedemann. What was there to be afraid of? Had anything changed? Last night, admittedly, he had suffered a bad attack; very well, but that must be the last of it! It was still not too late, it was still possible to avert disaster! He would have to avoid everything that might occasion a renewal of the attack; he felt strong enough to do so. He felt strong enough to overcome this thing, to nip it completely in the bud. . . .

When half-past seven struck Friederike brought in his coffee and set it down on the round table in front of the leather sofa by the far wall.

"Good morning, Johannes," she said, "here is your breakfast."

"Thank you," said Herr Friedemann. Then he added: "Friederike dear, I am sorry, but I am afraid you will have to pay that call without me. I don't feel well enough to come with you. I haven't slept well, I have a headache—in short, I must ask you to excuse me. . . ."

Friederike replied:

"What a pity. I think you should certainly call on them another time. But it's true that you're not looking well. Shall I lend you my headache pencil?"[1]

"No, thank you," said Herr Friedemann. "It will pass." And Friederike left the room.

Standing at the table, he slowly drank his coffee and ate a crescent-shaped roll. He was pleased with himself and proud of his strong-mindedness. When he had finished he took a cigar and sat down again at the window. Breakfast had done him good and he felt happy and hopeful. He took up a book, read, smoked and looked out from time to time into the dazzling sunlight.

The street had grown lively now; through his window he could hear the clatter of carriages, the sound of voices and the bells from the horse tramway. But the birds twittered through it all, and a soft warm breeze stirred in the shining blue sky.

At ten o'clock he heard his sisters crossing the hall and the front door

[1] Translated also as a "menthol pencil," the menthol stick was used for inhalation and for cooling the forehead with a gentle stroking motion.—Ed.

creaking open, and presently he saw the three ladies walk past his window, but thought nothing much of it. An hour passed; he felt happier and happier.

A kind of elation began to fill him. How balmy the air was, and how the birds sang! Why should he not go for a short walk? And then suddenly, spontaneously, the sweet and terrifying thought simply surged up inside him: Why not call on her? Warning apprehensions followed the impulse, but with an almost muscular effort he suppressed them and added with exultant resolve: I will call on her!

And he put on his black Sunday suit, took his hat and stick and hurried, breathing rapidly, right across the town to the southern suburb. His head rose and fell busily with every step, but he saw no one, and remained absorbed in his exalted mood until he had reached the chestnut-lined avenue and the red villa that bore at its entrance the name "Lieutenant Colonel von Rinnlingen."

12

At this point he began to tremble and his heart pounded convulsively against his ribs. But he crossed the outer hall and rang the doorbell. The die was cast now and there was no going back. Let it take its course, he thought. In him there was a sudden deathly stillness.

The door was thrown open, the manservant came across the hall toward him, received his card and carried it smartly up the red-carpeted stairs. Herr Friedemann stared motionless at the red carpet till the servant came back and declared that his mistress would be glad if Herr Friedemann would kindly come up.

On the first floor he placed his walking stick outside the door of the drawing room, and glanced at himself in the mirror. He was very pale, his eyes were red and above them the hair clung to his forehead; the hand in which he held his top hat was trembling uncontrollably.

The manservant opened the door and he went in. It was a fairly large, half-darkened room; the curtains were drawn. On the right stood a grand piano, and armchairs upholstered in brown silk were grouped about the round table in the center. A landscape in a massive gilt frame hung on the wall on the left above the sofa. The wallpaper was also dark. Palm trees stood in the bay window at the far end.

A minute passed before Frau von Rinnlingen emerged from the curtained doorway on the right and advanced noiselessly toward him across the deep-piled brown carpet. She was wearing a quite simply cut dress with a red and black check pattern. From the bay window a shaft of light, full of dancing motes of dust, fell straight onto her heavy red hair, so that for a moment it flashed like gold. She was looking straight at him, studying him with her strange eyes, and protruding her lower lip as usual.

"Frau Commandant," began Herr Friedemann, looking up at her, for his head reached only to her chest, "my sisters have already paid you their respects and I should like to do so myself as well. When you honored them with a call I was unfortunately not at home . . . to my great regret. . . ."

He could think of absolutely no more to say, but she stood gazing implacably at him as if she meant to force him to continue speaking. The blood suddenly rushed to his head. "She wants to torment me and mock me!" he thought, "and she has guessed my feelings! Her eyes are simply quivering . . . !" Finally she said in a quite high clear voice:

"It is very kind of you to have come. I was sorry, too, to miss you the other day. Won't you please take a seat?"

She sat down quite close to him and leaned back in her chair, laying her arms on the armrests. He sat leaning forward, holding his hat between his knees. She said:

"Do you know that your sisters were here only a quarter of an hour ago? They told me you were ill."

"That is true," replied Herr Friedemann, "I did not feel well this morning. I thought I should not be able to go out. I must ask you to excuse my late arrival."

"You still do not look quite well," she remarked calmly, with her eyes fixed steadily on him. "You are pale, and your eyes are inflamed. Perhaps your health is usually not very good?"

"Oh . . ." stammered Herr Friedemann, "in general I cannot complain. . . ."

"I am often ill too," she went on, still not averting her gaze, "but no one ever notices it. My nerves are bad and I have very odd moods sometimes."

She paused, lowered her chin to her breast and looked up at him expectantly. But he made no answer. He sat on in silence looking at her, wide-eyed and thoughtful. How strangely she talked, and what an extraordinary effect her clear, cynical voice had on him! His heart was beating more quietly now; he felt as if he were dreaming. Frau von Rinnlingen spoke again:

"If I am not mistaken, you left the theater last night before the end of the opera?"

"Yes, Frau Commandant."

"I was sorry you did. You were a very appreciative neighbor, although it was not a good performance, or only a relatively good one. I suppose you are fond of music? Do you play the piano?"

"I play the violin a little," said Herr Friedemann. "That is to say—really hardly at all. . . ."

"You play the violin?" she asked. Then she gazed past him for a moment and seemed to reflect.

"But then we could play together now and then," she said suddenly. "I can accompany a little. I should be glad to have found someone here who . . . Will you come?"

"I shall be delighted to place myself at your disposal," he replied. He still had the feeling that he was in a dream. There was a pause. Then suddenly her face changed. He saw it twist into a scarcely perceptible expression of cruel mockery, and saw again, for the third time, that uncanny tremor in her eyes as they unswervingly scrutinized him. He blushed scarlet, and not knowing where to look, helpless, distraught, he let his head droop right down between his shoulders and stared in utter dismay at the carpet. But again, for a moment, that impotent, sweet, agonizing fury shuddered and trickled through him. . . .

When with a desperate effort he raised his eyes again she was no longer looking at him, but gazing calmly over his head toward the door. He forced himself to utter a few words:

"And are you tolerably satisfied so far with your stay in our town, Frau Commandant?"

"Oh, yes," said Frau von Rinnlingen indifferently, "yes indeed. Why should I not be satisfied? Of course, I do feel somewhat constrained and conspicuous, but. . . . By the way," she added at once, "before I forget: we are thinking of inviting some people round in a few days' time. Just a small informal party. We might play a little music and talk about this and that. . . . Also we have rather a pretty garden behind the house; it goes right down to the river. In short, you and your ladies will of course be sent an invitation, but I should like to ask you here and now if we may have the pleasure of your company: shall we?"

Herr Friedemann had scarcely expressed his thanks and signified his acceptance when the door handle was pressed smartly down and the lieutenant colonel entered. They both rose, and as Frau von Rinnlingen introduced the men to each other her husband bowed to her and to Herr Friedemann with equal courtesy. His tanned face was glistening in the heat.

As he removed his gloves he said something or other in his loud energetic voice to Herr Friedemann, who stared up at him with wide, vacant eyes, fully expecting to be slapped benevolently on the shoulder. Meanwhile the commandant turned to his wife. Standing with heels together and slightly bowing to her from the waist, he said in a noticeably softer voice:

"I hope you have asked Herr Friedemann if he will come to our little gathering, my dear? If you agree, I think we should arrange for it to take place in a week's time. I hope this weather will last and that we shall be able to use the garden as well."

"As you please," replied Frau von Rinnlingen, gazing past him.

Two minutes later Herr Friedemann took his leave. As he bowed again at the door his eyes met hers, which were expressionlessly fixed on him.

13

He went on his way, not returning into town but involuntarily taking a side road that led off the avenue toward the old fortified wall by the river, where there was a well-kept park with shady paths and seats.

He walked hurriedly, aimlessly, without raising his eyes. He was flushed with an unbearable heat, he could feel it licking up in him and subsiding like flames, and his weary head throbbed relentlessly. . . .

Were those not her eyes still gazing into his? Not empty of expression as they had been when he left her, but with that earlier gaze, that quivering cruelty which had filled them the very moment after she had spoken to him so strangely and softly. Did she take delight in his helplessness, in driving him to distraction? And oh, if she did read his feelings, could she not at least feel some pity? . . .

Down by the river he had walked along the bank, beside the old city wall overgrown with green, and he sat down on a seat half encircled by jasmine bushes. The sweetish fragrance hung heavily in the air all around him. In front of him the sun brooded over the tremulous water.

How weary and worn-out he felt, and yet what an agonizing turmoil filled him! Surely the best thing to do would be to take one more look round him and then walk straight down into the silent water, where he would suffer for a few moments and then be free and rescued from existence and at peace! Oh, all he wanted was peace, peace! Yet not peace in an empty, unheeding nothingness, but a quiet place in gentle sunlight, where he might sit and think good, quiet thoughts.

At that instant all his deep love for life came back to him, piercing his heart with poignant nostalgia for his lost happiness. But then he looked about him, he looked at the mute, infinite tranquillity and indifference of nature, he saw the river wending its way in the sun, saw the grass waving and the flowers standing each in its place, just where it had bloomed, waiting to wither and be blown away: he saw all these things, all bowing in dumb submission to their existence—and suddenly he was overcome by that feeling of goodwill, of acceptance of necessity, which can in a certain sense lift us above all the adversities of fate.

He remembered that afternoon of his thirtieth birthday, when he had been happy in the possession of a quiet mind and had told himself that he could look forward, without fear or hope, to the remainder of his life. He had seen ahead of him neither brightness nor shadow, but a future bathed in gentle twilight, stretching away to a point where it merged almost imperceptibly into the dark; and with a calm and confident smile he had surveyed the years that were yet to come. How long ago had that day been?

Then this woman had come, she had had to come, it was his fate, she herself was his fate, she alone! Had he not sensed this from the very first moment? She had come, and he had tried to defend his peace of mind—but for her there had to be this rebellion within him of everything he had suppressed since his youth, because he had known instinctively that for him it meant misery and destruction. It had seized him with terrible, irresistible violence and it was destroying him!

It was destroying him, that he knew. But why go on with the vain agonizing struggle? Let it all take its course! Let him continue on his way, with his eyes closed to the gaping abyss beyond, obedient to fate, obedient to the invincible, sweetly tormenting power from which there is no escape.

The water gleamed, the jasmine breathed out its heavy pungent scent, the birds twittered in the branches all round him, and between the trees shone a dense velvet blue sky. But little hunchbacked Herr Friedemann did not stir from his seat. He sat on and on, leaning forward with his head bowed down into his hands.

14

Everyone agreed that the Rinnlingen party was a vast success. About thirty people sat round the long, tastefully decorated table which ran the length of the large dining room; the butler and two hired waiters were already hurrying round serving ices, the room was filled with the clink and clatter of glasses and tableware and the warm aroma of food mingled with scent. The guests included a genial assemblage of men of business with their wives and daughters, almost the entire corps of officers from the garrison, an elderly doctor whom everyone liked, a few lawyers and other representatives of the best local society. Also present was a student of mathematics, a nephew of the commandant's who was here visiting his relatives; he was engaged in profound conversation with Fräulein Hagenström, who sat opposite Herr Friedemann.

The latter had been placed at the far end of the table, on a fine velvet cushion, next to the rather plain wife of the headmaster of the classical grammar school. He was not far from Frau von Rinnlingen, who had been escorted in to table by Consul Stephens. It was astonishing what a change had come over little Herr Friedemann in the last week. Perhaps it was partly the white gaslight in the dining room that made his face look so alarmingly pale; but his cheeks were sunken, his eyes reddened, dark rings surrounded them, they shone with an unspeakable sadness; and he seemed more stunted and crippled than ever. He drank a lot of wine, and occasionally addressed a remark to his neighbor.

Frau von Rinnlingen had so far spoken not a word to Herr Friedemann at table; now she leaned forward a little and called across to him:

"I've been waiting in vain these last few days for you to pay me a visit with your fiddle."

He gazed at her vacantly for a moment before answering. She was wearing a light, gay evening gown that left her white neck showing, and in her gleaming hair she had fastened a Maréchal Niel rose in full bloom. Her cheeks were slightly flushed this evening, but there were blue shadows, as always, in the corners of her eyes.

Herr Friedemann looked down at his place and stammered out some kind of reply; whereupon he also had to answer the headmaster's wife, who inquired whether he was fond of Beethoven. At this point however Lieutenant Colonel von Rinnlingen, at the head of the table, exchanged glances with his wife, tapped his glass and said:

"Ladies and gentlemen, I suggest we take our coffee in the other rooms. And it must be rather pleasant in the garden too, on an evening like this: if anyone cares to take a spot of air out there, I'll be very glad to do the same."

Lieutenant von Deidesheim tactfully cracked a joke to break the silence which followed, and everyone rose from table amid peals of laughter. Herr Friedemann was one of the last to leave the dining room with his partner; he escorted her, through the room decorated in medieval style in which the guests were already beginning to smoke, into the dimly lit luxurious drawing room, and there took leave of her.

He was most carefully attired, in faultless evening dress with a dazzlingly white shirt and with patent leather shoes on his slender, neatly shaped feet. From time to time it could be observed that he was wearing red silk socks.

He looked out into the corridor and saw that quite large numbers of people were already going downstairs into the garden. But he sat down with his cigar and his coffee near the door of the medieval smoking room, in which a few of the gentlemen were standing around talking, and from here he looked into the drawing room.

At a table immediately to the right of the door a small circle had formed around the student, who was discoursing volubly. He had asserted that more than one parallel to a given straight line could be drawn through one and the same point; Dr. Hagenström's wife had exclaimed: "But that's impossible!" and he was now proving his proposition so cogently that everyone was pretending to have understood it.

But at the back of the room, on the divan, by the low lamp with the red shade, sat Gerda von Rinnlingen, in conversation with young Fräulein Stephens. She sat half reclined against the yellow silk cushion, with her legs crossed, and was smoking a cigarette in a leisurely manner, blowing the smoke out through her nose and protruding her lower lip, Fräulein Stephens sat facing her bolt upright like a statue, answering her with a nervous smile.

No one noticed little Herr Friedemann, and no one noticed that his large eyes were fixed incessantly on Frau von Rinnlingen. He sat limply and gazed at her. There was no passion in his gaze, scarcely even any pain; only a dull, dead expression of senseless, powerless, will-less surrender.

About ten minutes passed in this manner; then Frau von Rinnlingen suddenly got up, and without looking at him, as if she had been secretly observing him all this time, she walked over and stopped in front of him. He rose to his feet, looked up at her and heard her say:

"Would you like to come into the garden with me, Herr Friedemann?"

He answered:

"With pleasure, Frau Commandant."

15

"So you haven't yet seen our garden?" she asked him as they went downstairs. "It's quite big. I hope there won't be too many people there already; I should like to get away from them all for a little. I got a headache during dinner; perhaps that red wine was too strong for me. . . . This is our way out, through this door." It was a glass door leading from the hall into a small cool passage, from which they went down a few steps into the open air.

It was a wonderfully warm clear starlit night, and all the flower beds were pouring out their fragrance. The full moon was shining down on the garden, and along the gleaming white gravel paths the guests were strolling about, talking and smoking. One group had gathered round the fountain, where the elderly doctor whom everyone liked was causing general merriment by sailing paper boats.

Frau von Rinnlingen walked past them with a slight inclination of the head, and pointed into the distance where the elegant flower garden darkened into a park.

"Let's go down the center avenue," she said. At the head of it stood two short thick obelisks.

At the far end of the dead-straight chestnut-lined avenue they could see the greenish glint of the moonlit river. All round them it was dark and cool. Here and there a side path branched off; these probably all curved down to the river as well. For a long time not a sound could be heard.

"There's a pretty place beside the water," she said, "where I've often been. We could sit there and talk for a few minutes. Look, now and then one can see a star glittering between the leaves."

He made no answer, and stared at the green glimmering surface of the water as they approached it. The far bank was visible, where the public gardens were and the old city wall. At the end of the avenue, as they emerged onto the open grass that sloped down to the river, Frau von Rinnlingen said:

"Here is our spot, a little to the right; look, there's no one else there."

The seat they sat down on had its back to the park, a few yards to one side of the avenue. It was warmer here than among the great trees. The crickets chirped in the grass, which at the very edge of the water ended in a thin line of reeds. The river gleamed palely in the moonlight.

They both sat in silence for a while, looking at the water. Then he listened with a sudden shock of emotion, for she was speaking again in that soft, gentle, pensive voice he had heard a week ago.

"How long have you had your disability, Herr Friedemann?" she asked. "Were you born with it?"

He swallowed, for his throat felt constricted as if he were choking. Then he answered gently and politely:

"No, Frau Commandant. When I was a baby I was dropped on the floor, and that caused it."

"And how old are you now?" she went on.

"Thirty, Frau Commandant."

"Thirty," she repeated. "So you have not been happy during these thirty years?"

Herr Friedemann shook his head, and his lips trembled. "No," he said. "It was a lie and an illusion."

"So you believed you were happy?" she asked.

"I tried to," he said, and she replied:

"That was brave of you."

A minute passed. Only the crickets chirped, and the trees behind them rustled softly.

Then she said: "I have had some experience of unhappiness. These summer nights by the water are the best remedy for it."

He made no reply to this, but gestured weakly, pointing across to the opposite bank, where all was peaceful and dark.

"I sat there the other day," he said.

"Just after you had been to see me?" she asked.

He merely nodded.

Then suddenly, shuddering all over, he started to his feet, uttering a sobbing noise, a moan of sorrow which was somehow at the same time a cry of relief, and slowly sank to the ground in front of her. He had put his hand on hers, which had lain beside him on the seat; he clutched it now and seized the other as well; and as this little, totally deformed creature knelt there before her, quivering convulsively and burying his face in her lap, he stammered out in a hardly human, strangled voice:

"You know! I know that you know . . . Let me . . . I can't go on . . . Oh my God . . . my God. . . ."

She did not push him away, nor did she lower her head toward him. She sat erect, leaning back slightly, and her small close-set eyes, which seemed to mirror the liquid glint of the water, stared intently straight ahead, beyond him, into the distance.

And then, with a sudden violent movement, with a short, proud, scornful laugh, she had snatched her hands from his burning fingers, seized him by the arm, flung him sideways right onto the ground, leaped to her feet and vanished into the avenue.

He lay there with his face in the grass, stunned and desperate, with his body shuddering and twitching. He picked himself up, took two steps and collapsed again onto the grass. He was lying by the water's edge.

What was really his state of mind, his motive in what followed? Perhaps it was that same voluptuous hatred he had felt when she humbled him with her eyes; and now that he was lying here on the ground like a dog she had kicked, did this hatred perhaps degenerate into an insane fury which had to be translated into action, even if it was only action against himself —did it become an access of self-disgust, a craving to annihilate himself, to tear himself to pieces, to blot himself out . . . ?

He dragged himself on his stomach further down the slope, lifted the upper part of his body and let it drop into the water. He did not raise his head again; even his legs on the bank lay still.

The splash had silenced the crickets for a moment. Now they began their chirping as before, the park rustled softly and down the long avenue came the muted sound of laughter.

James Joyce

James Joyce (1882–1941) was born in Dublin, the eldest of ten children, and graduated from University College, Dublin, with a degree in modern languages. He left Dublin to study medicine in Paris but soon returned because his mother had fallen ill. In Ireland he taught at a private school, met Nora Barnacle, a chambermaid, and left Ireland with her to settle finally in Trieste, where he taught at a Berlitz school. Joyce had been writing poetry and sketches for years, always encountering difficulty in securing publication. He gained a small but devoted following after the appearance of Dubliners *(1914) and* Portrait of the Artist As a Young Man *(1916). In 1922,* Ulysses *was published amid the furor over its alleged immorality. His last major work,* Finnegan's Wake, *appeared in 1939. Joyce, an acknowledged master of modern literature, claimed that in* Dubliners, *his collection of short stories, his "intention was to write a chapter of the moral history of my country. . . ."* *(See page 79 of Introduction.)*

COUNTERPARTS

The bell rang furiously and, when Miss Parker went to the tube, a furious voice called out in a piercing North of Ireland accent:

—Send Farrington here!

Miss Parker returned to her machine, saying to a man who was writing at a desk:

—Mr Alleyne wants you upstairs.

The man muttered *Blast him!* under his breath and pushed back his chair to stand up. When he stood up he was tall and of great bulk. He had a hanging face, dark wine-coloured, with fair eyebrows and moustache; his eyes bulged forward slightly and the whites of them were dirty. He lifted up the counter and, passing by the clients, went out of the office with a heavy step.

He went heavily upstairs until he came to the second landing, where a door bore a brass plate with the inscription *Mr Alleyne*. Here he halted, puffing with labour and vexation, and knocked. The shrill voice cried:

—Come in!

The man entered Mr Alleyne's room. Simultaneously Mr Alleyne, a little man wearing gold-rimmed glasses on a clean-shaven face, shot his head up over a pile of documents. The head itself was so pink and hairless that it seemed like a large egg reposing on the papers. Mr Alleyne did not lose a moment:

—Farrington? What is the meaning of this? Why have I always to complain of you? May I ask you why you haven't made a copy of that contract between Bodley and Kirwan? I told you it must be ready by four o'clock.

—But Mr Shelley said, sir—

—*Mr Shelley said, sir. . . .* Kindly attend to what I say and not to what *Mr Shelley says, sir.* You have always some excuse or another for shirking work. Let me tell you that if the contract is not copied before this evening I'll lay the matter before Mr Crosbie. . . . Do you hear me now?

—Yes, sir.

—Do you hear me now? . . . Ay and another little matter! I might as well be talking to the wall as talking to you. Understand once for all that you get a half an hour for your lunch and not an hour and a half. How many courses do you want, I'd like to know. . . . Do you mind me, now?

—Yes, sir.

Mr Alleyne bent his head again upon his pile of papers. The man stared fixedly at the polished skull which directed the affairs of Crosbie & Alleyne, gauging its fragility. A spasm of rage gripped his throat for a few moments and then passed, leaving after it a sharp sensation of thirst. The man recognized the sensation and felt that he must have a good night's drinking. The middle of the month was passed and, if he could get the copy done in time, Mr Alleyne might give him an order on the cashier. He stood still, gazing fixedly at the head upon the pile of papers. Suddenly Mr Alleyne began to upset all the papers, searching for something. Then, as if he had been unaware of the man's presence till that moment, he shot up his head again, saying:

—Eh? Are you going to stand there all day? Upon my word, Farrington, you take things easy!

—I was waiting to see . . .

—Very good, you needn't wait to see. Go downstairs and do your work.

The man walked heavily towards the door and, as he went out of the room, he heard Mr Alleyne cry after him that if the contract was not copied by evening Mr Crosbie would hear of the matter.

He returned to his desk in the lower office and counted the sheets which remained to be copied. He took up his pen and dipped it in the ink but he continued to stare stupidly at the last words he had written: *In no case shall the said Bernard Bodley be* . . . The evening was falling and in a few minutes they would be lighting the gas: then he could write. He felt that he must slake the thirst in his throat. He stood up from his desk and, lifting the counter as before, passed out of the office. As he was passing out the chief clerk looked at him inquiringly.

—It's all right, Mr Shelley, said the man, pointing with his finger to indicate the objective of his journey.

The chief clerk glanced at the hat-rack but, seeing the row complete, offered no remark. As soon as he was on the landing the man pulled a shepherd's plaid cap out of his pocket, put it on his head and ran quickly down the rickety stairs. From the street door he walked on furtively on the inner side of the path towards the corner and all at once dived into a doorway. He was now safe in the dark snug of O'Neill's shop, and, filling up the little window that looked into the bar with his inflamed face, the colour of dark wine or dark meat, he called out:

—Here, Pat, give us a g.p., like a good fellow.

The curate brought him a glass of plain porter. The man drank it at a gulp and asked for a caraway seed. He put his penny on the counter and, leaving the curate to grope for it in the gloom, retreated out of the snug as furtively as he had entered it.

Darkness, accompanied by a thick fog, was gaining upon the dusk of February and the lamps in Eustace Street had been lit. The man went up by the houses until he reached the door of the office, wondering whether he could finish his copy in time. On the stairs a moist pungent odour of perfumes saluted his nose: evidently Miss Delacour had come while he was out in O'Neill's. He crammed his cap back again into his pocket and re-entered the office, assuming an air of absent-mindedness.

—Mr Alleyne has been calling for you, said the chief clerk severely. Where were you?

The man glanced at the two clients who were standing at the counter as if to intimate that their presence prevented him from answering. As the clients were both male the chief clerk allowed himself a laugh.

—I know that game, he said. Five times in one day is a little bit. . . . Well, you better look sharp and get a copy of our correspondence in the Delacour case for Mr Alleyne.

This address in the presence of the public, his run upstairs and the porter he had gulped down so hastily confused the man and, as he sat down at his desk to get what was required, he realized how hopeless was the task of finishing his copy of the contract before half past five. The dark damp night was coming and he longed to spend it in the bars, drinking with his friends amid the glare of gas and the clatter of glasses. He got out the Delacour correspondence and passed out of the office. He hoped Mr Alleyne would not discover that the last two letters were missing.

The moist pungent perfume lay all the way up to Mr Alleyne's room. Miss Delacour was a middle-aged woman of Jewish appearance. Mr Alleyne was said to be sweet on her or on her money. She came to the office often and stayed a long time when she came. She was sitting beside his desk now in an aroma of perfumes, smoothing the handle of her umbrella and nodding the great black feather in her hat. Mr Alleyne had swivelled his chair round to face her and thrown his right foot jauntily upon his left knee. The man put the correspondence on the desk and bowed respectfully but neither Mr Alleyne nor Miss Delacour took any notice of his bow. Mr Alleyne tapped a finger on the correspondence and then flicked it towards him as if to say: *That's all right: you can go.*

The man returned to the lower office and sat down again at his desk. He stared intently at the incomplete phrase: *In no case shall the said Bernard Bodley be* . . . and thought how strange it was that the last three words began with the same letter. The chief clerk began to hurry Miss Parker, saying she would never have the letters typed in time for post. The man listened to the clicking of the machine for a few minutes and then set to work to finish his copy. But his head was not clear and his mind wandered away to the glare and rattle of the public-house. It was a night for hot punches. He struggled on with his copy, but when the clock struck five he had still fourteen pages to write. Blast it! He couldn't finish it in time. He longed to execrate aloud, to bring his fist down on something violently. He was so enraged that he wrote *Bernard Bernard* instead of *Bernard Bodley* and had to begin again on a clean sheet.

He felt strong enough to clear out the whole office single-handed. His body ached to do something, to rush out and revel in violence. All the indignities of his life enraged him. . . . Could he ask the cashier privately for an advance? No, the cashier was no good, no damn good: he wouldn't give an advance. . . . He knew where he would meet the boys: Leonard and O'Halloran and Nosey Flynn. The barometer of his emotional nature was set for a spell of riot.

His imagination had so abstracted him that his name was called twice before he answered. Mr Alleyne and Miss Delacour were standing outside the counter and all the clerks had turned round in anticipation of something. The man got up from his desk. Mr Alleyne began a tirade of abuse, saying that two letters were missing. The man answered that he knew nothing about them, that he had made a faithful copy. The tirade continued: it was so bitter and violent that the man could hardly restrain his fist from descending upon the head of the manikin before him.

—I know nothing about any other two letters, he said stupidly.

—*You—know—nothing*. Of course you know nothing, said Mr Alleyne. Tell me, he added, glancing first for approval to the lady beside him, do you take me for a fool? Do you think me an utter fool?

The man glanced from the lady's face to the little egg-shaped head and back again; and, almost before he was aware of it, his tongue had found a felicitous moment:

—I don't think, sir, he said, that that's a fair question to put to me.

There was a pause in the very breathing of the clerks. Everyone was astounded (the author of the witticism no less than his neighbours) and Miss Delacour, who was a stout amiable person, began to smile broadly. Mr Alleyne flushed to the hue of a wild rose and his mouth twitched with a dwarf's passion. He shook his fist in the man's face till it seemed to vibrate like the knob of some electric machine:

—You impertinent ruffian! You impertinent ruffian! I'll make short work of you! Wait till you see! You'll apologize to me for your impertinence or you'll quit the office instanter! You'll quit this, I'm telling you, or you'll apologize to me!

. . . . . .

He stood in a doorway opposite the office watching to see if the cashier would come out alone. All the clerks passed out and finally the cashier came out with the chief clerk. It was no use trying to say a word to him when he was with the chief clerk. The man felt that his position was bad enough. He had been obliged to offer an abject apology to Mr Alleyne for his impertinence but he knew what a hornet's nest the office would be for him. He could remember the way in which Mr Alleyne had hounded little Peake out of the office in order to make room for his own nephew. He felt savage and thirsty and revengeful, annoyed with himself and with everyone else. Mr Alleyne would never give him an hour's rest; his life would be a hell to him. He had made a proper fool of himself this time. Could he not keep his tongue in his cheek? But they had never pulled together from the first, he and Mr Alleyne, ever since the day Mr Alleyne had overheard him mimicking his North of Ireland accent to amuse Higgins and Miss Parker: that had been the beginning of it. He might have tried Higgins for the money, but sure Higgins never had anything for himself. A man with two establishments to keep up, of course he couldn't. . . .

He felt his great body again aching for the comfort of the public-house. The fog had begun to chill him and he wondered could he touch Pat in

O'Neill's. He could not touch him for more than a bob—and a bob was no use. Yet he must get money somewhere or other: he had spent his last penny for the g.p. and soon it would be too late for getting money anywhere. Suddenly, as he was fingering his watch-chain, he thought of Terry Kelly's pawn-office in Fleet Street. That was the dart! Why didn't he think of it sooner?

He went through the narrow alley of Temple Bar quickly, muttering to himself that they could all go to hell because he was going to have a good night of it. The clerk in Terry Kelly's said *A crown!* but the consignor held out for six shillings; and in the end the six shillings was allowed him literally. He came out of the pawn-office joyfully, making a little cylinder of the coins between his thumb and fingers. In Westmoreland Street the footpaths were crowded with young men and women returning from business and ragged urchins ran here and there yelling out the names of the evening editions. The man passed through the crowd, looking on the spectacle generally with proud satisfaction and staring masterfully at the office-girls. His head was full of the noises of tram-gongs and swishing trolleys and his nose already sniffed the curling fumes of punch. As he walked on he preconsidered the terms in which he would narrate the incident to the boys:

—So, I just looked at him—coolly, you know, and looked at her. Then I looked back at him again—taking my time, you know. *I don't think that that's a fair question to put to me,* says I.

Nosey Flynn was sitting up in his usual corner of Davy Bryne's and, when he heard the story, he stood Farrington a half-one, saying it was as smart a thing as ever he heard. Farrington stood a drink in his turn. After a while O'Halloran and Paddy Leonard came in and the story was repeated to them. O'Halloran stood tailors of malt, hot, all round and told the story of the retort he had made to the chief clerk when he was in Callan's of Fownes's Street; but, as the retort was after the manner of the liberal shepherds in the eclogues, he had to admit that it was not so clever as Farrington's retort. At this Farrington told the boys to polish off that and have another.

Just as they were naming their poisons who should come in but Higgins! Of course he had to join in with the others. The men asked him to give his version of it, and he did so with great vivacity for the sight of five small hot whiskies was very exhilarating. Everyone roared laughing when he showed the way in which Mr Alleyne shook his fist in Farrington's face. Then he imitated Farrington, saying, *And here was my nabs, as cool as you please,* while Farrington looked at the company out of his heavy dirty eyes, smiling and at times drawing forth stray drops of liquor from his moustache with the aid of his lower lip.

When that round was over there was a pause. O'Halloran had money but neither of the other two seemed to have any; so the whole party left the shop somewhat regretfully. At the corner of Duke Street Higgins and Nosey Flynn bevelled off to the left while the other three turned back towards the city. Rain was drizzling down on the cold streets and, when they reached the Ballast Office, Farrington suggested the Scotch House.

The bar was full of men and loud with the noise of tongues and glasses. The three men pushed past the whining match-sellers at the door and formed a little party at the corner of the counter. They began to exchange stories. Leonard introduced them to a young fellow named Weathers who was performing at the Tivoli as an acrobat and knock-about *artiste*. Farrington stood a drink all round. Weathers said he would take a small Irish and Apollinaris. Farrington, who had definite notions of what was what, asked the boys would they have an Apollinaris too; but the boys told Tim to make theirs hot. The talk became theatrical. O'Halloran stood a round and then Farrington stood another round, Weathers protesting that the hospitality was too Irish. He promised to get them in behind the scenes and introduce them to some nice girls. O'Halloran said that he and Leonard would go but that Farrington wouldn't go because he was a married man; and Farrington's heavy dirty eyes leered at the company in token that he understood he was being chaffed. Weathers made them all have just one little tincture at his expense and promised to meet them later on at Mulligan's in Poolbeg Street.

When the Scotch House closed they went round to Mulligan's. They went into the parlour at the back and O'Halloran ordered small hot specials all round. They were all beginning to feel mellow. Farrington was just standing another round when Weathers came back. Much to Farrington's relief he drank a glass of bitter this time. Funds were running low but they had enough to keep them going. Presently two young women with big hats and a young man in a check suit came in and sat at a table close by. Weathers saluted them and told the company that they were out of the Tivoli. Farrington's eyes wandered at every moment in the direction of one of the young women. There was something striking in her appearance. An immense scarf of peacock-blue muslin was wound round her hat and knotted in a great bow under her chin; and she wore bright yellow gloves, reaching to the elbow. Farrington gazed admiringly at the plump arm which she moved very often and with much grace; and when, after a little time, she answered his gaze he admired still more her large dark brown eyes. The oblique staring expression in them fascinated him. She glanced at him once or twice and, when the party was leaving the room, she brushed against his chair and said *O, pardon!* in a London accent. He watched her leave the room in the hope that she would look back at him, but he was disappointed. He cursed his want of money and cursed all the rounds he had stood, particularly all the whiskies and Apollinaris which he had stood to Weathers. If there was one thing that he hated it was a sponge. He was so angry that he lost count of the conversation of his friends.

When Paddy Leonard called him he found that they were talking about feats of strength. Weathers was showing his biceps muscle to the company and boasting so much that the other two had called on Farrington to uphold the national honour. Farrington pulled up his sleeve accordingly and showed his biceps muscle to the company. The two arms were examined and compared and finally it was agreed to have a trial of strength. The table was cleared and the two men rested their elbows on it, clasping hands. When Paddy Leonard said *Go!* each was to try to bring down the other's hand on to the table. Farrington looked very serious and determined.

The trial began. After about thirty seconds Weathers brought his opponent's hand slowly down on to the table. Farrington's dark wine-coloured face flushed darker still with anger and humiliation at having been defeated by such a stripling.

—You're not to put the weight of your body behind it. Play fair, he said.

—Who's not playing fair? said the other.

—Come on again. The two best out of three.

The trial began again. The veins stood out on Farrington's forehead, and the pallor of Weathers' complexion changed to peony. Their hands and arms trembled under the stress. After a long struggle Weathers again brought his opponent's hand slowly on to the table. There was a murmur of applause from the spectators. The curate, who was standing beside the table, nodded his red head toward the victor and said with loutish familiarity:

—Ah! that's the knack!

—What the hell do you know about it? said Farrington fiercely, turning on the man. What do you put in your gab for?

—Sh, sh! said O'Halloran, observing the violent expression of Farrington's face. Pony up, boys. We'll have just one little smahan more and then we'll be off.

A very sullen-faced man stood at the corner of O'Connell Bridge waiting for the little Sandymount tram to take him home. He was full of smouldering anger and revengefulness. He felt humiliated and discontented; he did not even feel drunk; and he had only twopence in his pocket. He cursed everything. He had done for himself in the office, pawned his watch, spent all his money; and he had not even got drunk. He began to feel thirsty again and he longed to be back again in the hot reeking public-house. He had lost his reputation as a strong man, having been defeated twice by a mere boy. His heart swelled with fury and, when he thought of the woman in the big hat who had brushed against him and said *Pardon!* his fury nearly choked him.

His tram let him down at Shelbourne Road and he steered his great body along in the shadow of the wall of the barracks. He loathed returning to his home. When he went in by the side-door he found the kitchen empty and the kitchen fire nearly out. He bawled upstairs:

—Ada! Ada!

His wife was a little sharp-faced woman who bullied her husband when he was sober and was bullied by him when he was drunk. They had five children. A little boy came running down the stairs.

—Who is that? said the man, peering through the darkness.

—Me, pa.

—Who are you? Charlie?

—No, pa. Tom.

—Where's your mother?

—She's out at the chapel.

—That's right. . . . Did she think of leaving any dinner for me?

—Yes, pa. I—

—Light the lamp. What do you mean by having the place in darkness? Are the other children in bed?

The man sat down heavily on one of the chairs while the little boy lit the lamp. He began to mimic his son's flat accent, saying half to himself: *At the chapel. At the chapel, if you please!* When the lamp was lit he banged his fist on the table and shouted:

—What's for my dinner?

—I'm going . . . to cook it, pa, said the little boy.

The man jumped up furiously and pointed to the fire.

—On that fire! You let the fire out! By God, I'll teach you to do that again!

He took a step to the door and seized the walking-stick which was standing behind it.

—I'll teach you to let the fire out! he said, rolling up his sleeve in order to give his arm free play.

The little boy cried *O, pa!* and ran whimpering round the table, but the man followed him and caught him by the coat. The little boy looked about him wildly but, seeing no way of escape, fell upon his knees.

—Now, you'll let the fire out the next time! said the man, striking at him viciously with the stick. Take that, you little whelp!

The boy uttered a squeal of pain as the stick cut his thigh. He clasped his hands together in the air and his voice shook with fright.

—O, pa! he cried. Don't beat me, pa! And I'll . . . I'll say a *Hail Mary* for you. . . . I'll say a *Hail Mary* for you, pa, if you don't beat me. . . . I'll say a *Hail Mary*. . . .

Katherine Mansfield

Katherine Mansfield (1888–1923) was born in Wellington, New Zealand. She left New Zealand permanently in 1909, and thereafter lived either in England or on the Continent. In 1918 she married John Middleton Murry, the English critic and essayist. She died of tuberculosis in 1923. Her stories are greatly influenced by Chekhov, whom she admired ardently. She experimented with stream-of-consciousness techniques, particularly with shifts in time and point of view, all of which had significant influence later on Virginia Woolf's style. "It is not the business of the artist," she writes, "to impose his vision of life upon the existing world [but] to create his own world in *this world. . . . We single out, we bring into the light—we put up higher." Her best-known collections of short stories are* Bliss and Other Stories *(1920) and* The Garden Party *(1922).* *(See page 82 of Introduction.)*

A DILL PICKLE

And then, after six years, she saw him again. He was seated at one of those little bamboo tables decorated with a Japanese vase of paper daffodils. There was a tall plate of fruit in front of him, and very carefully, in a way she recognized immediately as his "special" way, he was peeling an orange.

He must have felt that shock of recognition in her for he looked up and met her eyes. Incredible! He didn't know her! She smiled; he frowned. She came towards him. He closed his eyes an instant, but opening them his face lit up as though he had struck a match in a dark room. He laid down the orange and pushed back his chair, and she took her little warm hand out of her muff and gave it to him.

"Vera!" he exclaimed. "How strange. Really, for a moment I didn't know you. Won't you sit down? You've had lunch? Won't you have some coffee?"

She hesitated, but of course she meant to.

"Yes, I'd like some coffee." And she sat down opposite him.

"You've changed. You've changed very much," he said, staring at her with that eager, lighted look. "You look so well. I've never seen you look so well before."

"Really?" She raised her veil and unbuttoned her high fur collar. "I don't feel very well. I can't bear this weather, you know."

"Ah, no. You hate the cold. . . ."

"Loathe it." She shuddered. "And the worst of it is that the older one grows . . ."

He interrupted her. "Excuse me," and tapped on the table for the waitress. "Please bring some coffee and cream." To her: "You are sure you won't eat anything? Some fruit, perhaps. The fruit here is very good."

"No, thanks. Nothing."

"Then that's settled." And smiling just a hint too broadly he took up the orange again. "You were saying—the older one grows—"

"The colder," she laughed. But she was thinking how well she remembered that trick of his—the trick of interrupting her—and of how it used to exasperate her six years ago. She used to feel then as though he, quite suddenly, in the middle of what she was saying, put his hand over her lips, turned from her, attended to something different, and then took his hand away, and with just the same slightly too broad smile, gave her his attention again. . . . Now we are ready. That is settled.

"The colder!" He echoed her words, laughing too. "Ah, ah. You still say the same things. And there is another thing about you that is not changed at all—your beautiful voice—your beautiful way of speaking." Now he was very grave; he leaned towards her, and she smelled the warm, stinging scent of the orange peel. "You have only to say one word and I would know your voice among all other voices. I don't know what it is—I've often wondered—that makes your voice such a—haunting memory. . . . Do you remember that first afternoon we spent together at Kew Gardens? You were so surprised because I did not know the names of any flowers. I am still just as ignorant for all your telling me. But whenever it is very fine and warm, and I see some bright colours—it's awfully strange—I hear your voice saying: 'Geranium, marigold and verbena.' And I feel those three words are all I recall of some forgotten, heavenly language. . . . You remember that afternoon?"

"Oh, yes, very well." She drew a long, soft breath, as though the paper daffodils between them were almost too sweet to bear. Yet, what had remained in her mind of that particular afternoon was an absurd scene over the tea table. A great many people taking tea in a Chinese pagoda, and he behaving like a maniac about the wasps—waving them away, flapping at them with his straw hat, serious and infuriated out of all proportion to the occasion. How delighted the sniggering tea drinkers had been. And how she had suffered.

But now, as he spoke, that memory faded. His was the truer. Yes, it had been a wonderful afternoon, full of geranium and marigold and verbena, and—warm sunshine. Her thoughts lingered over the last two words as though she sang them.

In the warmth, as it were, another memory unfolded. She saw herself sitting on a lawn. He lay beside her, and suddenly, after a long silence, he rolled over and put his head in her lap.

"I wish," he said, in a low, troubled voice, "I wish that I had taken poison and were about to die—here now!"

At that moment a little girl in a white dress, holding a long, dripping water lily, dodged from behind a bush, stared at them, and dodged back again. But he did not see. She leaned over him.

"Ah, why do you say that? I could not say that."

But he gave a kind of soft moan, and taking her hand he held it to his cheek.

"Because I know I am going to love you too much—far too much. And I shall suffer so terribly, Vera, because you never, never will love me."

He was certainly far better looking now than he had been then. He had lost all that dreamy vagueness and indecision. Now he had the air of a man who has found his place in life, and fills it with a confidence and an assurance which was, to say the least, impressive. He must have made money, too. His clothes were admirable, and at that moment he pulled a Russian cigarette case out of his pocket.

"Won't you smoke?"

"Yes, I will." She hovered over them. "They look very good."

"I think they are. I get them made for me by a little man in St. James's Street. I don't smoke very much. I'm not like you—but when I do, they must be delicious, very fresh cigarettes. Smoking isn't a habit with me; it's a luxury—like perfume. Are you still so fond of perfumes? Ah, when I was in Russia . . ."

She broke in: "You've really been to Russia?"

"Oh, yes. I was there for over a year. Have you forgotten how we used to talk of going there?"

"No, I've not forgotten."

He gave a strange half laugh and leaned back in his chair. "Isn't it curious. I have really carried out all those journeys that we planned. Yes, I have been to all those places that we talked of, and stayed in them long enough to—as you used to say, 'air oneself' in them. In fact, I have spent the last three years of my life travelling all the time. Spain, Corsica, Siberia, Russia, Egypt. The only country left is China, and I mean to go there, too, when the war is over."

As he spoke, so lightly, tapping the end of his cigarette against the ash-tray, she felt the strange beast that had slumbered so long within her bosom stir, stretch itself, yawn, prick up its ears, and suddenly bound to its feet, and fix its longing, hungry stare upon those faraway places. But all she said was, smiling gently: "How I envy you."

He accepted that. "It has been," he said, "very wonderful—especially Russia. Russia was all that we had imagined, and far, far more. I even spent some days on a river boat on the Volga. Do you remember that boatman's song that you used to play?"

"Yes." It began to play in her mind as she spoke.

"Do you ever play it now?"

"No, I've no piano."

He was amazed at that. "But what has become of your beautiful piano?"

She made a little grimace. "Sold. Ages ago."

"But you were so fond of music," he wondered.

"I've no time for it now," said she.

He let it go at that. "That river life," he went on, "is something quite special. After a day or two you cannot realize that you have ever known another. And it is not necessary to know the language—the life of the boat creates a bond between you and the people that's more than sufficient. You eat with them, pass the day with them, and in the evening there is that endless singing."

She shivered, hearing the boatman's song break out again loud and tragic, and seeing the boat floating on the darkening river with melancholy trees on either side. . . . "Yes, I should like that," said she, stroking her muff.

"You'd like almost everything about Russian life," he said warmly. "It's so informal, so impulsive, so free without question. And then the peasants are so splendid. They are such human beings—yes, that is it. Even the man who drives your carriage has—has some real part in what is happening. I remember the evening a party of us, two friends of mine and the wife of one of them, went for a picnic by the Black Sea. We took supper and champagne and ate and drank on the grass. And while we were eating the coachman came up. 'Have a dill pickle,' he said. He wanted to share with us. That seemed to me so right, so—you know what I mean?"

And she seemed at that moment to be sitting on the grass beside the mysteriously Black Sea, black as velvet, and rippling against the banks in silent, velvet waves. She saw the carriage drawn up to one side of the road, and the little group on the grass, their faces and hands white in the moonlight. She saw the pale dress of the woman outspread and her folded parasol, lying on the grass like a huge pearl crochet hook. Apart from them, with his supper in a cloth on his knees, sat the coachman. "Have a dill pickle," said he, and although she was not certain what a dill pickle was, she saw the greenish glass jar with a red chili like a parrot's beak glimmering through. She sucked in her cheeks; the dill pickle was terribly sour. . . .

"Yes, I know perfectly what you mean," she said.

In the pause that followed they looked at each other. In the past when they had looked at each other like that they had felt such a boundless understanding between them that their souls had, as it were, put their arms round each other and dropped into the same sea, content to be drowned, like mournful lovers. But now, the surprising thing was that it was he who held back. He who said:

"What a marvellous listener you are. When you look at me with those wild eyes I feel that I could tell you things that I would never breathe to another human being."

Was there just a hint of mockery in his voice or was it her fancy? She could not be sure.

"Before I met you," he said, "I had never spoken of myself to anybody. How well I remember one night, the night that I brought you the little Christmas tree, telling you all about my childhood. And of how I was so miserable that I ran away and lived under a cart in our yard for two days without being discovered. And you listened, and your eyes shone, and I felt that you had even made the little Christmas tree listen too, as in a fairy story."

But of that evening she had remembered a little pot of caviare. It had cost seven and sixpence. He could not get over it. Think of it—a tiny jar like that costing seven and sixpence. While she ate it he watched her, delighted and shocked.

"No, really, that is eating money. You could not get seven shillings into a little pot that size. Only think of the profit they must make. . . ." And he had begun some immensely complicated calculations. . . . But now good-bye to the caviare. The Christmas tree was on the table, and the little boy lay under the cart with his head pillowed on the yard dog.

"The dog was called Bosun," she cried delightedly.

But he did not follow. "Which dog? Had you a dog? I don't remember a dog at all."

"No, no. I mean the yard dog when you were a little boy." He laughed and snapped the cigarette case to.

"Was he? Do you know I had forgotten that. It seems such ages ago. I cannot believe that it is only six years. After I had recognized you to-day —I had to take such a leap—I had to take a leap over my whole life to get back to that time. I was such a kid then." He drummed on the table. "I've often thought how I must have bored you. And now I understand so perfectly why you wrote to me as you did—although at the time that letter nearly finished my life. I found it again the other day, and I couldn't help laughing as I read it. It was so clever—such a true picture of me." He glanced up. "You're not going?"

She had buttoned her collar again and drawn down her veil.

"Yes, I am afraid I must," she said, and managed a smile. Now she knew that he had been mocking.

"Ah, no, please," he pleaded. "Don't go just for a moment," and he caught up one of her gloves from the table and clutched at it as if that would hold her. "I see so few people to talk to nowadays, that I have turned into a sort of barbarian," he said. "Have I said something to hurt you?"

"Not a bit," she lied. But as she watched him draw her glove through his fingers, gently, gently, her anger really did die down, and besides, at the moment he looked more like himself of six years ago. . . .

"What I really wanted then," he said softly, "was to be a sort of carpet—to make myself into a sort of carpet for you to walk on so that you need not be hurt by the sharp stones and the mud that you hated so. It was nothing more positive than that—nothing more selfish. Only I did desire, eventually, to turn into a magic carpet and carry you away to all those lands you longed to see."

As he spoke she lifted her head as though she drank something; the strange beast in her bosom began to purr. . . .

"I felt that you were more lonely than anybody else in the world," he went on, "and yet, perhaps, that you were the only person in the world who was really, truly alive. Born out of your time," he murmured, stroking the glove, "fated."

Ah, God! What had she done! How had she dared to throw away her happiness like this. This was the only man who had ever understood her. Was it too late? Could it be too late? *She* was that glove that he held in his fingers. . . .

"And then the fact that you had no friends and never had made friends with people. How I understood that, for neither had I. Is it just the same now?"

"Yes," she breathed. "Just the same. I am as alone as ever."

"So am I," he laughed gently, "just the same."

Suddenly with a quick gesture he handed her back the glove and scraped his chair on the floor. "But what seemed to me so mysterious then is perfectly plain to me now. And to you, too, of course. . . . It simply was that we were such egoists, so self-engrossed, so wrapped up in ourselves that we hadn't a corner in our hearts for anybody else. Do you know," he cried, naive and hearty, and dreadfully like another side of that old self again, "I began studying a Mind System when I was in Russia, and I found that we were not peculiar at all. It's quite a well known form of . . ."

She had gone. He sat there, thunder-struck, astounded beyond words. . . . And then he asked the waitress for his bill.

"But the cream has not been touched," he said. "Please do not charge me for it."

Sherwood Anderson

Sherwood Anderson (1876–1941), born in Camden and reared in Clyde, Ohio, left for Chicago in 1896 to work as a laborer. After brief service in the army, he returned to Chicago and worked as an advertising copywriter. He wrote two novels before the publication of Winesburg, Ohio *(1919) brought him immediate fame. His novel* Dark Laughter *(1925) was a best-seller. After brief trips to Paris and parts of the United States, Anderson settled on a Virginia farm and continued to write. His stories and novels stressed the importance of love and communication between people. They often depicted the dehumanizing effects of the new American industrialization. Other well-known short stories by Anderson are "Death in the Woods" and "I Want to Know Why."* *(See page 68 of Introduction.)*

THE EGG

My father was, I am sure, intended by nature to be a cheerful, kindly man. Until he was thirty-four years old he worked as a farmhand for a man named Thomas Butterworth whose place lay near the town of Bidwell, Ohio. He had then a horse of his own, and on Saturday evenings drove into town to spend a few hours in social intercourse with other farmhands. In town he drank several glasses of beer and stood about in Ben Head's saloon—crowded on Saturday evenings with visiting farmhands. Songs were sung and glasses thumped on the bar. At ten o'clock father drove home along a lonely country road, made his horse comfortable for the night, and himself went to bed, quite happy in his position in life. He had at that time no notion of trying to rise in the world.

It was in the spring of his thirty-fifth year that father married my mother, then a country school-teacher, and in the following spring I came wriggling and crying into the world. Something happened to the two people. They became ambitious. The American passion for getting up in the world took possession of them.

It may have been that mother was responsible. Being a school-teacher she had no doubt read books and magazines. She had, I presume, read of how Garfield, Lincoln, and other Americans rose from poverty to fame and greatness, and as I lay beside her—in the days of her lying-in—she may have dreamed that I would some day rule men and cities. At any rate she induced father to give up his place as a farmhand, sell his horse, and embark on an independent enterprise of his own. She was a tall silent woman with a long nose and troubled gray eyes. For herself she wanted nothing. For father and myself she was incurably ambitious.

The first venture into which the two people went turned out badly. They rented ten acres of poor stony land on Grigg's Road, eight miles from Bidwell, and launched into chicken-raising. I grew into boyhood on the place and got my first impressions of life there. From the beginning they were impressions of disaster, and if, in my turn, I am a gloomy man inclined to see the darker side of life, I attribute it to the fact that what should have been for me the happy joyous days of childhood were spent on a chicken farm.

One unversed in such matters can have no notion of the many and tragic things that can happen to a chicken. It is born out of an egg, lives for a few weeks as a tiny fluffy thing such as you will see pictured on Easter cards, then becomes hideously naked, eats quantities of corn and meal bought by the sweat of your father's brow, gets diseases called pip, cholera, and other names, stands looking with stupid eyes at the sun, becomes sick and dies. A few hens and now and then a rooster, intended to serve God's mysterious ends, struggle through to maturity. The hens lay eggs out of which come other chickens and the dreadful cycle is thus made complete. It is all unbelievably complex. Most philosophers must have been raised on chicken farms. One hopes for so much from a chicken and is so dreadfully disillusioned. Small chickens, just setting out on the journey of life, look so bright and alert and they are in fact so dreadfully stupid. They are so much like people they mix one up in one's judgments of life. If disease does not kill them, they wait until your expectations are thoroughly aroused and then walk under the wheels of a wagon—to go squashed and dead back to their maker. Vermin infest their youth, and fortunes must be spent for curative powders. In later life I have seen how a literature has been built up on the subject of fortunes to be made out of the raising of chickens. It is intended to be read by the gods who have just eaten of the tree of the knowledge of good and evil. It is a hopeful literature and declares that much may be done by simple ambitious people who own a few hens. Do not be led astray by it. It was not written for you. Go hunt for gold on the frozen hills of Alaska, put your faith in the honesty of a politician, believe if you will that the world is daily growing better and that good will triumph over evil, but do not read and believe the literature that is written concerning the hen. It was not written for you.

I, however, digress. My tale does not primarily concern itself with the hen. If correctly told it will center on the egg. For ten years my father and mother struggled to make our chicken farm pay and then they gave up their struggle and began another. They moved into the town of Bidwell, Ohio, and embarked in the restaurant business. After ten years of worry with incubators that did not hatch, and with tiny—and in their own way lovely—balls of fluff that passed on into semi-naked pullethood and from that into dead henhood, we threw all aside and, packing our belongings on a wagon, drove down Grigg's Road toward Bidwell, a tiny caravan of hope looking for a new place from which to start on our upward journey through life.

We must have been a sad-looking lot, not, I fancy, unlike refugees fleeing from a battlefield. Mother and I walked in the road. The wagon that contained our goods had been borrowed for the day from Mr. Albert Griggs, a neighbor. Out of its sides stuck the legs of cheap chairs, and at the back of the pile of beds, tables, and boxes filled with kitchen utensils was a crate of live chickens, and on top of that the baby carriage in which I had been wheeled about in my infancy. Why we stuck to the baby carriage I don't know. It was unlikely other children would be born and the wheels were broken. People who have few possessions cling tightly to those they have. That is one of the facts that make life so discouraging.

Father rode on top of the wagon. He was then a bald-headed man of forty-five, a little fat, and from long association with mother and the chickens he had become habitually silent and discouraged. All during our ten years on the chicken farm he had worked as a laborer on neighboring farms and most of the money he had earned had been spent for remedies to cure chicken diseases, on Wilmer's White Wonder Cholera Cure or Professor Bidlow's Egg Producer or some other preparations that mother found advertised in the poultry papers. There were two little patches of hair on father's head just above his ears. I remember that as a child I used to sit looking at him when he had gone to sleep in a chair before the stove on Sunday afternoons in the winter. I had at that time already begun to read books and have notions of my own, and the bald path that led over the top of his head was, I fancied, something like a broad road, such a road as Caesar might have made on which to lead his legions out of Rome and into the wonders of an unknown world. The tufts of hair that grew above father's ears were, I thought, like forests. I fell into a half-sleeping, half-waking state and dreamed I was a tiny thing going along the road into a far beautiful place where there were no chicken farms and where life was a happy eggless affair.

One might write a book concerning our flight from the chicken farm into town. Mother and I walked the entire eight miles—she to be sure that nothing fell from the wagon and I to see the wonders of the world. On the seat of the wagon beside father was his greatest treasure. I will tell you of that.

On a chicken farm, where hundreds and even thousands of chickens come out of eggs, surprising things sometimes happen. Grotesques are born out of eggs as out of people. The accident does not often occur—perhaps once in a thousand births. A chicken is, you see, born that has four legs, two pairs of wings, two heads, or what not. The things do not live. They go quickly back to the hand of their maker that has for a moment trembled. The fact that the poor little things could not live was one of the tragedies of life to father. He had some sort of notion that if he could but bring into henhood or roosterhood a five-legged hen or a two-headed rooster his fortune would be made. He dreamed of taking the wonder about the county fairs and of growing rich by exhibiting it to other farmhands.

At any rate, he saved all the little monstrous things that had been born on our chicken farm. They were preserved in alcohol and put each in its own glass bottle. These he had carefully put into a box, and on our journey into town it was carried on the wagon seat beside him. He drove the horses with one hand and with the other clung to the box. When we got to our destination, the box was taken down at once and the bottles removed. All during our days as keepers of a restaurant in the town of Bidwell, Ohio, the grotesques in their little glass bottles sat on a shelf back of the counter. Mother sometimes protested, but father was a rock on the subject of his treasure. The grotesques were, he declared, valuable. People, he said, liked to look at strange and wonderful things.

Did I say that we embarked in the restaurant business in the town of Bidwell, Ohio? I exaggerated a little. The town itself lay at the foot of a low hill and on the shore of a small river. The railroad did not run through the town and the station was a mile away to the north at a place called Pickleville. There had been a cider mill and pickle factory at the station, but before the time of our coming they had both gone out of business. In the morning and in the evening busses came down to the station along a road called Turner's Pike from the hotel on the main street of Bidwell. Our going to the out-of-the-way place to embark in the restaurant business was mother's idea. She talked of it for a year and then one day went off and rented an empty store building opposite the railroad station. It was her idea that the restaurant would be profitable. Traveling men, she said, would be always waiting around to take trains out of town and town people would come to the station to await incoming trains. They would come to the restaurant to buy pieces of pie and drink coffee. Now that I am older I know that she had another motive in going. She was ambitious for me. She wanted me to rise in the world, to get into a town school and become a man of the towns.

At Pickleville father and mother worked hard, as they always had done. At first there was the necessity of putting our place into shape to be a restaurant. That took a month. Father built a shelf on which he put tins of vegetables. He painted a sign on which he put his name in large red letters. Below his name was the sharp command—"EAT HERE"—that was so seldom obeyed. A showcase was bought and filled with cigars and tobacco. Mother scrubbed the floors and the walls of the room. I went to school in the town and was glad to be away from the farm from the presence of the discouraged, sad-looking chickens. Still I was not very joyous. In the evening I walked home from school along Turner's Pike and remembered the children I had seen playing in the town school yard. A troop of little girls had gone hopping about and singing. I tried that. Down along the frozen road I went hopping solemnly on one leg. "Hippity Hop To The Barber Shop," I sang shrilly. Then I stopped and looked doubtfully about. I was afraid of being seen in my gay mood. It must have seemed to me that I was doing a thing that should not be done by one who, like myself, had been raised on a chicken farm where death was a daily visitor.

Mother decided that our restaurant should remain open at night. At ten in the evening a passenger train went north past our door followed by a local freight. The freight crew had switching to do in Pickelville, and when the work was done they came to our restaurant for hot coffee and food. Sometimes one of them ordered a fried egg. In the morning at four they returned north-bound and again visited us. A little trade began to grow up. Mother slept at night and during the day tended the restaurant and fed our boarders while father slept. He slept in the same bed mother had occupied during the night and I went off to the town of Bidwell and to school. During the long nights, while mother and I slept, father cooked meats that were to go into sandwiches for the lunch baskets of our boarders. Then an idea in regard to getting up in the world came into his head. The American spirit took hold of him. He also became ambitious.

In the long nights when there was little to do, father had time to think. That was his undoing. He decided that he had in the past been an unsuccessful man because he had not been cheerful enough and that in the future he would adopt a cheerful outlook on life. In the early morning he came upstairs and got into bed with mother. She woke and the two talked. From my bed in the corner I listened.

It was father's idea that both he and mother should try to entertain the people who came to eat at our restaurant. I cannot now remember his words, but he gave the impression of one about to become in some obscure way a kind of public entertainer. When people, particularly young people from the town of Bidwell, came into our place, as on very rare occasions they did, bright entertaining conversation was to be made. From father's words I gathered that something of the jolly innkeeper effect was to be sought. Mother must have been doubtful from the first, but she said nothing discouraging. It was father's notion that a passion for the company of himself and mother would spring up in the breasts of the younger people of the town of Bidwell. In the evening bright happy groups would come singing down Turner's Pike. They would troop shouting with joy and laughter into our place. There would be song and festivity. I do not mean to give the impression that father spoke so elaborately of the matter. He was, as I have said, an uncommunicative man. "They want some place to go. I tell you they want some place to go," he said over and over. That was as far as he got. My own imagination has filled in the blanks.

For two or three weeks this notion of father's invaded our house. We did not talk much, but in our daily lives tried earnestly to make smiles take the place of glum looks. Mother smiled at the boarders and I, catching the infection, smiled at our cat. Father became a little feverish in his anxiety to please. There was, no doubt, lurking somewhere in him, a touch of the spirit of the showman. He did not waste much of his ammunition on the railroad men he served at night, but seemed to be waiting for a young man or woman from Bidwell to come in to show what he could do. On the counter in the restaurant there was a wire basket kept always filled with eggs, and it must have been before his eyes when the idea of being entertaining was born in his brain. There was something pre-natal about the way eggs kept themselves connected with the development of his idea. At any rate, an egg ruined his new impulse in life. Late one night I was awakened by a roar of anger coming from father's throat. Both mother and I sat upright in our beds. With trembling hands she lighted a lamp that stood on a table by her head. Downstairs the front door of our restaurant went shut with a bang and in a few minutes father tramped up the stairs. He held an egg in his hand and his hand trembled as though he were having a chill. There was a half-insane light in his eyes. As he stood glaring at us I was sure he intended throwing the egg at either mother or me. Then he laid it gently on the table beside the lamp and dropped on his knees beside mother's bed. He began to cry like a boy, and I, carried away by his grief, cried with him. The two of us filled the little upstairs room with our wailing voices. It is ridiculous, but of the picture we made I can remember only the fact that mother's hand continually stroked the bald path that ran across the top of his head. I have forgotten what mother said to him and how she induced him to tell her of what had happened downstairs. His explanation also has gone out of my mind. I remember only my own grief and fright and the shiny path over father's head glowing in the lamplight as he knelt by the bed.

As to what happened downstairs. For some unexplainable reason I know the story as well as though I had been a witness to my father's discomfiture. One in time gets to know many unexplainable things. On that evening young Joe Kane, son of a merchant of Bidwell, came to Pickleville to meet his father, who was expected on the ten-o'clock evening train from the South. The train was three hours late and Joe came into our place to loaf about and to wait for its arrival. The local freight train came in and the freight crew were fed. Joe was left alone in the restaurant with father.

From the moment he came into our place the Bidwell young man must have been puzzled by my father's actions. It was his notion that father was angry at him for hanging around. He noticed that the restaurant-keeper was apparently disturbed by his presence and he thought of going out. However, it began to rain and he did not fancy the long walk to town and back. He bought a five-cent cigar and ordered a cup of coffee. He had a newspaper in his pocket and took it out and began to read. "I'm waiting for the evening train. It's late," he said apologetically.

For a long time father, whom Joe Kane had never seen before, remained silently gazing at his visitor. He was no doubt suffering from an attack of stage fright. As so often happens in life he had thought so much and so often of the situation that now confronted him that he was somewhat nervous in its presence.

For one thing, he did not know what to do with his hands. He thrust one of them nervously over the counter and shook hands with Joe Kane. "How-de-do," he said. Joe Kane put his newspaper down and stared at him. Father's eyes lighted on the basket of eggs that sat on the counter and he began to talk. "Well," he began hesitatingly, "well, you have heard of Christopher Columbus, eh?" He seemed to be angry. "That Christopher Columbus was a cheat," he declared emphatically. "He talked of making an egg stand on its end. He talked, he did, and then he went and broke the end of the egg."

My father seemed to his visitor to be beside himself at the duplicity of Christopher Columbus. He muttered and swore. He declared it was wrong to teach children that Christopher Columbus was a great man when, after all, he cheated at the critical moment. He had declared he would make an egg stand on end and then, when his bluff had been called, he had done a trick. Still grumbling at Columbus, father took an egg from the basket on the counter and began to walk up and down. He rolled the egg between the palms of his hands. He smiled genially. He began to mumble words regarding the effect to be produced on an egg by the electricity that comes out of the human body. He declared that, without breaking its shell and by virtue of rolling it back and forth in his hands, he could stand the egg on its end. He explained that the warmth of his hands and the gentle rolling movement he gave the egg created a new center of gravity, and Joe Kane was mildly interested. "I have handled thousands of eggs," father said. "No one knows more about eggs than I do."

He stood the egg on the counter and it fell on its side. He tried the trick again and again, each time rolling the egg between the palms of his hands and saying the words regarding the wonders of electricity and the laws of gravity. When after a half-hour's effort he did succeed in making the egg stand for a moment, he looked up to find that his visitor was no longer watching. By the time he had succeeded in calling Joe Kane's attention to the success of his effort, the egg had again rolled over and lay on its side.

Afire with the showman's passion and at the same time a good deal disconcerted by the failure of his first effort, father now took the bottles containing the poultry monstrosities down from their place on the shelf and began to show them to his visitor. "How would you like to have seven legs and two heads like this fellow?" he asked, exhibiting the most remarkable of his treasures. A cheerful smile played over his face. He reached over the counter and tried to slap Joe Kane on the shoulder as he had seen men do in Ben Head's saloon when he was a young farmhand and drove to town on Saturday evenings. His visitor was made a little ill by the sight of the body of the terribly deformed bird floating in the alcohol in the bottle and got up to go. Coming from behind the counter, father took hold of the young man's arm and led him back to his seat. He grew a little angry and for a moment had to turn his face away and force himself to smile. Then he put the bottles back on the shelf. In an outburst of generosity he fairly compelled Joe Kane to have a fresh cup of coffee and another cigar at his expense. Then he took a pan and filling it with vinegar, taken from a jug that sat beneath the counter, he declared himself about to do a new trick. "I will heat this egg in this pan of vinegar," he said. "Then I will put it through the neck of a bottle without breaking the shell. When the egg is inside the bottle it will resume its normal shape and the shell will become hard again. Then I will give the bottle with the egg in it to you. You can take it about with you wherever you go. People will want to know how you got the egg in the bottle. Don't tell them. Keep them guessing. That is the way to have fun with this trick."

Father grinned and winked at his visitor. Joe Kane decided that the man who confronted him was mildly insane but harmless. He drank the cup of coffee that had been given him and began to read his paper again. When the egg had been heated in vinegar, father carried it on a spoon to the counter and going into a back room got an empty bottle. He was angry because his visitor did not watch him as he began to do his trick, but nevertheless went cheerfully to work. For a long time he struggled, trying to get the egg to go through the neck of the bottle. He put the pan of vinegar back on the stove, intending to reheat the egg, then picked it up and burned his fingers. After a second bath in the hot vinegar, the shell of the egg had been softened a little, but not enough for his purpose. He worked and worked and a spirit of desperate determination took possession of him. When he thought that at last the trick was about to be consummated, the delayed train came in at the station and Joe Kane started to go nonchalantly out at the door. Father made a last desperate effort to conquer the egg and make it do the thing that would establish his reputation as one who knew how to entertain guests who came into his restaurant. He worried the egg. He attempted to be somewhat rough with it. He swore and the sweat stood out on his forehead. The egg broke under his hand. When the contents spurted over his clothes, Joe Kane, who had stopped at the door, turned and laughed.

A roar of anger rose from my father's throat. He danced and shouted a string of inarticulate words. Grabbing another egg from the basket on the counter, he threw it, just missing the head of the young man as he dodged through the door and escaped.

Father came upstairs to mother and me with an egg in his hand. I do not know what he intended to do. I imagine he had some idea of destroying it, of destroying all eggs, and that he intended to let mother and me see him begin. When, however, he got into the presence of mother, something happened to him. He laid the egg gently on the table and dropped on his knees by the bed as I have already explained. He later decided to close the restaurant for the night and to come upstairs and get into bed. When he did so, he blew out the light and after much muttered conversation both he and mother went to sleep. I suppose I went to sleep also, but my sleep was troubled. I awoke at dawn and for a long time looked at the egg that lay on the table. I wondered why eggs had to be and why from the egg came the hen who again laid the egg. The question got into my blood. It has stayed there, I imagine, because I am the son of my father. At any rate, the problem remains unsolved in my mind. And that, I conclude, is but another evidence of the complete and final triumph of the egg—at least as far as my family is concerned.

Italo Svevo

Italo Svevo, the pseudonym of Ettore Schmitz (1861–1928), was born in Trieste of a wealthy middle-class German-Italian family. He was tutored in English by James Joyce, who became a friend, and who helped to bring his neglected work to the attention of critics. Svevo's first two novels, declared by critics as "wanting in refinement," were read by Joyce, who was so moved by them as to memorize parts of the work. Joyce's recommendation of Svevo carried weight in the twenties, and in 1926 Svevo was "discovered" in his own country. His heroes have sometimes been called

"Triestian brothers of Charlie Chaplin." His works include The Nice Old Man and the Pretty Girl *(1930) and* As a Man Grows Older *(1932) both of which were published posthumously.* *(See page 82 of Introduction.)*

TRAITOROUSLY

Signor Maier set out for Reveni's home still not completely decided whether to ask for help and solace. The two men had been good friends all their life; they had both started from the bottom, and, by working every day from morning till evening, had both succeeded in making a great deal of money. Dealing in two entirely different lines, there had never existed the slightest competition between them, and despite their never having worked as partners, their friendship, which dated back to early youth, had remained firm and unchanged until their declining years. Unchanged but lifeless: their wives never called on each other, and they themselves met daily only for a quarter of an hour in the Stock Exchange. Both had now passed their sixtieth year.

After a sleepless night, Maier had decided to write to his old friend for an appointment. And now, as he was on his way to it, he turned over a vague plan by which his old friend should be asked to help him, but in such a way (as he would try to present it to him) that Reveni would be running no personal risk. Of course, in his own eyes help was due to him. So many years of honest, successful work swept away by a moment of thoughtlessness! It was intolerable. Seeking to branch out, the old merchant had let himself be talked into a contract putting him in the hands of a third party; and they, having squeezed every last bit of credit from Maier's signature, had pulled up stake and quit Trieste, leaving behind nothing but a few pieces of worthless furniture. At first Signor Maier had determined, as honesty required, to meet all his obligations. But it had now come to seem unjust that he should have to assume responsibilities not his own. If Reveni, who was a notoriously decent man, would relieve him at least for the time being of part of the burden, Maier's prospects for the future would be rosier. Maier could not recall having ever turned down a similar request himself. He remembered (and very clearly) having signed that contract—another gesture of confidence in human nature, as it seemed to him now, forgetting that the original motive for drawing up the contract had merely been to make money.

If Fate meant to favour him, it would certainly act through Reveni, who, without even being asked, would offer to help him. He expected this of Fate. And then—but not until then—he could lay his plan before his old friend who, if he was in a mood to take such risks, would accept it. Maier himself felt no risk was involved. He was only asking for the long-term credit he knew he deserved. Despite his old age, he was still an enterprising man, and against that one time when he had let himself be swindled he could cite hundreds of instances in which he had escaped from similar traps. So there was really no question of risk.

Reveni's home was in the centre of the town. Maier mounted the staircase, and from the moment the butler opened the door he felt nothing but envy. At present he also had a large heavily furnished anteroom hung with tapestries, and a small thickly carpeted chamber within, like the one in which Signor Reveni and his wife were waiting to offer him coffee. Ah, but he wouldn't have them for long! His poor wife was already out looking for a smaller, more modest flat. Here everything had the solid, confident look of a home that had existed for a long time and would long so continue. At his own home, on the other hand, everything was about to fly out of the window. Except for his wife's jewelry everything was still there, but it looked as if the rest were all ready to take flight.

Though the two men were the same age, Signor Reveni was much heavier and sallower than Maier. And seated as he was in a large armchair opposite Maier, who was himself sitting in an equally large chair, but timidly, perched on the edge of it, he—this man who had accumulated and accumulated without ever letting himself be tricked into signing an instrument like the one that had ruined Maier—seemed awe-inspiring.

Signora Reveni served the coffee. She was a woman who dressed with a certain ostentatiousness, all frills and lace, even at home. She was wearing a morning dress that would have looked ravishing on a younger, more beautiful woman.

Maier began to sip his coffee, thinking, "Is she going to leave us to ourselves?"

It soon appeared that the Signora felt she had to let him know that she did not intend to leave them alone together: she told him that her Giovanni had not been well for some days and that he spent the afternoons at home, being looked after by her.

Maier thought it strange that a man who looked healthy enough, and had just got up from lunch, not only had to stay at home but to be continually watched over by his wife. From this, he felt, he must deduce that Reveni and his wife had already decided not to help him. He recalled that the wife was notoriously the more close-fisted of the two and that Reveni himself had once told him how she had managed to rid him of a poor relative who had been pestering him for money. And now, no sooner had Reveni received Maier's request for an appointment, than here she was hurrying to help him.

He felt humiliated—downright offended. Maier could not imagine being classed with a poor and insistent beggar. Quite the contrary, considering he had come with a business proposition that would benefit Reveni if he agreed to have a hand in it. In an effort to pull himself together, to cleanse himself of every trace of inferiority, Maier settled back into his own armchair too, in direct imitation of Reveni's posture. With a slight nod, he thanked the Signora as she handed him another cup of coffee. And the effort he made was such that feelings of inferiority actually seemed to have been purged from his system. He would propose nothing to Reveni. He would pretend instead that he had asked for the appointment for an altogether different reason. But what reason? It was hard to find one, because these two old friends had very rarely met to talk about business. Business was no good, then. But was there some other field in which he might need Reveni's advice? Then he remembered that a few weeks before a friend had vaguely asked whether he would accept a post as a town councillor. Perhaps he could ask Reveni for advice about this.

But Reveni immediately brought up the very topic that had brought Maier to him.

"Why, that Barabich!" he exclaimed. "To think that Barabich, the scion of a fine old Triestine family, has stooped to such a thing! And where is he now? They say he's already had time to reach Corfu."

To Maier that didn't sound at all like the prelude to the offer of help he was expecting from Fate—something else entirely! Reveni, in fact, sounded as though he sympathized more with the swindler than with the victim.

Maier once again settled himself somewhat more comfortably in the armchair, taking care, with his hands trembling as they were, not to drop his cup. He forced himself to wear an attitude of resolute indifference.

"You understand of course," he said, "I *had* to denounce him. Now it hardly matters to me if he gets off scot-free."

The Signora had poured her husband another cup and was passing it to him; with her eyes on the cup, she took a step or two in order to reach him and then immediately turned to Maier.

"Think of the mother in the case!" she said, pained. As in her dress, in the sound of her voice, and every movement of hers, the Signora was determined to inject great sweetness into her words. So, in this affair that meant ruin for Maier, her first thought was for the culprit's mother. And to think that she, for all her airs of a *gran signora,* had been a cabaret singer in her youth, undressing in public as long as anyone would pay her to do so. Had she nurtured this ill will for him because, years ago, Maier had tried to stop Reveni from marrying her?

It was no longer possible to feign indifference. Flushed with anger, and with a bitter smile, Maier exclaimed: "You will understand that I don't give a damn about that mother, considering that her son is about to make another mother—I mean, my wife—suffer terribly."

"I see, I see," the Signora murmured, still as sweetly as ever. And she sat down beside the table and filled her own cup from the steaming coffee-machine.

It was as if she were only now beginning to see; and she obviously still didn't see everything, for then it would have been up to her to say either that she or her husband were prepared to help him or that they didn't want to hear any more about it.

Reveni broke in. He seemed to feel that the affair could be considered from only one angle—that of his poor friend. A little uneasily, he stretched himself out in his armchair, looked up and grunted, "An ugly business, a very ugly business!" He sighed and, finally looking Maier in the face, added, "You've had a stroke of really bad luck."

In other words, this meant that the matter was so serious that any intervention on his part to ease the situation was entirely out of the question. So, no help; and Maier could spare himself the humiliation of asking. He rose, set down the demitasse, which he had emptied without even tasting the coffee, and, settling back in his chair again, said with an offhand gesture, "To be sure, there's money involved—and quite a good deal —but not all the money I had. It's unpleasant to think that I'll have less to leave my son, but at least he'll get more from me at my death than I got when my father died."

Reveni's aloof attitude, of a man who did not wish to hear any more than suited him, changed, and he exclaimed, evidently genuinely delighted: "Then I was right! Your difficulties have not set you back as much as they're saying about town. My good friend, let me shake your hand! I'm happier to hear this than if I'd just made I don't know how much!"

Reveni was wide awake now. He had even got out of his chair to go and shake Maier's hand. Maier found himself unable to show much gratitude for such a demonstration of joy, and he let his hand lie limply in his friend's, so that the other returned to his chair. Maier thought: "They're ready to share my joy, but they weren't ready to share my pain." His mind flashed back over his day's activities: his fortune had been completely wiped out by that speculation—completely!—and he was still not sure that in the drawer of some unknown party there might not be more engagements than he could meet. His son stood to inherit absolutely nothing if, in the few years left to him, Maier couldn't continue in active business. On his own he had been able to take stock and make some exact calculations. But now, in his friend's presence, everything seemed more confused. Wouldn't it perhaps be wise to conceal his true position even from Reveni so as to regain the credit he needed to stay in business? This tactical scheme, though not properly thought out yet, restored his courage a little. The Signora, as if to show her own joy at such good news, offered him another cup of coffee, which he accepted with a grateful smile—a smile that cost him some effort. Meanwhile, in token of his gratitude, he swallowed the whole cupful of coffee, though it was more than he usually took.

Now that it was clear that Maier's situation was not too grave, Reveni seemed to find himself able to speak his mind:

"I confess I would never have trusted Barabich myself. I heard about your partnership only after it had all been settled. But everybody in Trieste knew that all Barabich's previous deals had ended badly."

"Yes, but never to this extent!" Maier protested. "It always looked as if he managed things perfectly well, but that everything he undertook was dogged by bad luck."

Reveni gestured dubiously:

"I don't trust a man who's been set afloat so often and has always sunk. It's pretty clear he doesn't know how to swim. Barabich's career began ten years ago, with that business everybody talked so much about at the time, all those loads of Chinese rice. Remember how much money went overboard then! Then, all of a sudden, he was an industrial promoter. Now, it's true that some of the concerns he promoted actually prospered; but they prospered without him, because at a given stage people would feel it was time to cut free from him. Nothing bad was said about him—quite the contrary. In fact, there was a great deal of talk about his honesty; but still nobody was able to explain how it was that he wasn't connected with the businesses any more. And then how did he live? Until he snared you, all he did was talk, talk, talk. He talked about developing the Argentine, and the Klondike—both of them schemes that couldn't have brought in much, seeing that he never actually went in for them. And then he discovered another distant land—motor-car manufacture. It strikes me as incredible that a man of your experience would want to follow him there."

For Maier it was terrible, the fact that Reveni was right. He remembered how he had been lured by visions of enormous quick profits. But now, in order to defend himself, he remembered also how much he had liked Barabich, who was younger than himself and so self-confident and bubbling over with ideas—they gave him the air of an expert. He wanted to remember only his fondness for him.

"I was led into it out of a desire to help Barabich, too. I felt sorry that a talented man like him should have to remain such a mediocrity."

For a moment, seemingly hesitant to reply, Reveni said nothing. Then he gave Maier a searching look, as if trying to determine if he was really serious. Presently he remembered something that made up his mind for him, and he spoke, laughing and trying unsuccessfully to make Maier laugh too.

"Remember old Almeni? It was because of him that we had our first and last business conference—remember? After lots of insisting on his part he managed to get us—you, me and two friends of ours—all together to decide whether to lend him the money to open a bar, in the middle of the town, to be run by him and his son. It had to be luxurious, and so he needed considerable funds, for only by making it a de-luxe place would he have been certain of a return. Neither you nor I fully understood businesses of that nature, but another of our prospective partners did and explained it to us, seriously doubting whether such a venture would be successful in this town. And the upshot was we decided that the main thing about the deal was the enormous help it would be to Almeni, who was a fine old chap, with a family to support, and who had never, despite his many excellent qualities, managed to raise himself out of the rut. Then we two broke in—you and I—and agreed with one voice that in this world of ours there have to be business dealings and there have to be good deeds, but that a good deed in the guise of business was bad business—all the more because it would no longer be a good deed. We finished by all agreeing to give the old fellow a little immediate help, simply because he deserved it, but nothing more. I remember our arguments perfectly, and I'm surprised you've forgotten them."

Maier felt he must defend himself vigorously. It was too much for Reveni not only to refuse help but to make out that he was justified in doing so.

"There's a great difference between Almeni and Barabich; Almeni was simply an old fool, whereas Barabich was a shrewd and cultivated young man, with the single defect of being a thief."

Maier had spoken so heatedly, and his face had flushed so red with anger, that Signora Reveni felt she ought to intervene. The day before she had seen Signora Maier with her daughter:

"What a little darling your daughter is, with those innocent gazelle-eyes of hers! (The gazelle being a sweet animal, Signora Reveni included it in her vocabulary.)

Maier would not have been placated, even if she had called him himself by the name of some charming animal! A thought struck him. Not only did he recall the Almeni episode, but he was also pretty certain that he had been the one who had thought of the arguments which Reveni was expounding as if they were his. What insight he had had in those days! He was reminded of his one-time intelligence only to be hit all the more by the shame of his recent mistake.

And moved by self-pity, with actual tears in his eyes, he said to Reveni: "Life is long, too long; it is made up of so many days, in every one of which there's time to make the error that will cancel out the wisdom and effort of all the other days. Only one day . . . compared with all the others."

Reveni gazed into space, perhaps to search his own long life for the day when he had made a mistake that might have jeopardized the work of all the other days. He agreed with Maier, but perhaps only to calm him. He did not seem particularly concerned by either the dangers he had faced or those he was likely to face. "Yes," he said, "life is long, very long, and full of dangers."

Maier felt Reveni was incapable of putting himself in his shoes and he couldn't blame him, because everyone knows how hard it is to think of the cold which others suffer when one is warm and cozy oneself; but he noticed that while Reveni was speaking, his wife looked at him with a smile of perfect confidence, of abandon, a look that seemed to say, "Why, what a strange fancy! No, no, *you* couldn't make mistakes!"

And because of that, his dislike for the woman mounted to the point where he felt he could no longer stand her presence. He got to his feet and forced himself to make a courteous gesture towards her: he extended his hand, saying that he had to leave because of pressing business. He had decided to visit Reveni at his office the next day, not to ask for help, just to convince him that life really was long and that he should not condemn a man for one day's rashness—one day out of so many. Having shaken the Signora's hand, he turned back to Reveni. Reveni suddenly let out a peculiar sound. In a voice pitched somewhat lower than usual, he softly mumbled some incomprehensible word; Maier tried to catch it but failed, as it is hard to retain a series of meaningless syllables. Curious, he turned round. The Signora had already rushed terrified to her husband's side, crying: "What's the matter?"

Reveni lay sprawling in his armchair. But after a moment he was still able to say to his wife, quite clearly and as though he had recovered: "I've got a pain here." And he moved his hand which, incapable of making the desired gesture, simply rose from the arm of the chair. Then, for a while, nothing more: he lay motionless, his head lolling upon his chest. He let out another sigh, like a lament, and no more. The Signora propped him up, screaming into his ear: "Giovanni, Giovanni! What is it?"

Maier dabbed away the tears prompted by his own distresses and turned to his friend. He instantly guessed what was happening, but was still so wrapped up in his own affairs that his first thought was: "He's going! He couldn't help me now even if he wanted to."

He had to make a violent effort to throw off this abject self-centredness and act like a man. He went over to the woman, saying gently: "Don't be frightened, Signora. It's only a fainting-spell. But would you like me to call the doctor?"

She was down on her knees in front of her husband. A tear-stained face looked up at Maier, obviously relaxing in the hope his words had inspired. "Yes, Yes! Call the doctor!" And she gave him a telephone number.

Maier rushed off in the direction from which he had entered, but the Signora, still on her knees, called out: "No—the other way!"—an outcry softened by a sob. Then, opening the opposite door, Maier found himself in a dining-room in which two maids were clearing the table. He ordered them into the next room to help their mistress and, quickly locating the telephone, dialled the number she had given him.

He did not get connected at once, and, trembling with impatience, he anxiously asked himself: "Is he dying—or already dead?" Then, as he waited, he felt himself filling with compassion. "So this is how one dies!" And then: "He can't agree to help any more, but he can't refuse either!"

The doctor promised to come at once. Maier put the receiver back and paused a little before returning to Signora Reveni. He glanced round the room. What luxury! His relations with Reveni had been very tenuous after Reveni's marriage, and their wives had never had anything to do with each other. He was seeing their dining-room now for the first time: light flooded in from the great windows and gleamed from the marble skirting along the walls, from the gilt mouldings of the doors, from the crystalware still on the table. Everything was solidly in place, irremovable, because the poor devil in the next room had never done a foolish thing. Nor would he.

"Which of us two is the better off?" Maier thought.

With the maids' help, Signora Reveni had laid her husband's body out on the sofa. She was still busying herself over him. She had soaked his face with vinegar and was holding a little bottle of smelling-salts under his nose. He was now—there was no doubt about it—a corpse. His eyes had shut of their own accord, but the left eyeball protruded visibly.

Feeling himself such a stranger to the woman, Maier did not dare say anything to her. He remembered the address of Reveni's daughter and considered going back to the telephone; on second thoughts, however, he decided to go and see her in person, as she lived not very far away.

"I think," he said hesitantly to Signora Reveni, "I think I'll go over to Signora Alice's and tell her that her father is not feeling well."

"Yes, do!" sobbed the Signora.

Maier flew out of the door not so much because he was in a hurry, for no one could help Reveni now, as to escape the presence of that corpse.

And once down in the street he questioned himself again: "Which of us two is the better off?" How peaceful he looked, laid out on the sofa. Strange!—it was all over, his gloating over his own successes, which were magnified by Maier's errors. He had rejoined the great majority, whence, unmoving, he was staring now with that one protruding eye of his, free of joy and free of pain. The world ran on, but what had happened proved its utter pointlessness. The fate that had befallen Reveni made his own fate of perfect unimportance.

Italo Svevo

THE MOTHER

In a valley shut in by wooded hills, and smiling in its spring colours, stood side by side two large, bare houses, all stone and cement. They might have been built by the same hands. The gardens, too, shut in by hedges and facing each other, were of the same size and form. But the lot of the inmates was very different.

In one of the gardens, while the dog was asleep on its chain and the farmer was busy with his fruit trees, some chickens shut off in a corner were exchanging views on their exciting experiences. There were others older in the garden, but the tiny ones, whose bodies had not yet lost the shape of the egg from which they had come, liked to discuss among themselves the life in to which they had been plunged, because they were not yet so used to it that they did not see it. They had already suffered and enjoyed, for a life of a few days is longer than it can possibly seem to anyone who has endured it for years, and they knew much, seeing that they had brought a part of their great experience with them from the egg. In fact, they had hardly come into the light before they had learnt that they must look well into things, first with one eye, then with the other, to see whether they were to eat them or be on their guard against them.

And they talked of the world and its vastness, with the trees and the hedges that shut it in, and the house, so enormous and tall. These were all things they could already see, but they saw them better when they talked about them.

One of them, covered with yellow down, gorged full and therefore idle, was not satisfied with talking about the things visible, but drew from the warmth of the sun a memory, which he suddenly expressed: "Undoubtedly we are well off, because there is the sun, but I have heard that in this world you can be still better off, and I am very sorry about it, and I will tell you, so that you may be sorry too. The farmer's daughter said that we are poor specimens because we have not got a mother. She spoke so feelingly that she made me cry."

Another one, whiter and some hours younger than the first, so that he still remembered with gratitude the pleasant warmth that he was born from protested: "We have had a mother. It is that little box, which is always warm, no matter how cold it is, and which the chickens come out of full blown."

The yellow one, who had long had the peasant girl's words vividly impressed on his brain, and had therefore had time to magnify them by dwelling on them, dreaming of the mother till he had imagined her as large as the whole garden and as good as bird-food, exclaimed with a contempt that was meant as much for his interlocutor as for the mother of which he was talking: "If it were a question of a dead mother, everyone would have one. But this mother is alive and runs much faster than we can. Perhaps she has wheels like the peasant's cart. So she can come to you without you having to call for her, to warm you when you are likely to be frozen by the cold of this world. It must be nice to have a mother like that near you at night."

A third chicken broke in, brother of the others because he had come out of the same incubator, though it had fashioned him a little differently, with a broader beak and shorter little legs. They called him the bad-mannered chicken, because, when he ate, you could hear his beak clapping together, whereas he was really a duckling who, in his own country, would have passed for a model of manners. In his presence also the girl had talked of a mother. That had happened at the time when a chicken had died of cold and exposure in the grass, with the other chicks round him, not trying to help him, because they do not feel other people's cold. And the duckling, with the air of simplicity which the huge end of his beak gave his tiny face, declared emphatically that, when there is a mother, chickens cannot die.

The desire for a mother soon invaded the whole brood and it was keener, more disturbing, in the minds of the older chicks. Childish illnesses often attack grown-ups and are more dangerous to them. So also do ideas, sometimes. The picture of the mother, as it had taken shape in those little heads heated by the spring, developed in an extraordinary degree, and everything that was good was called mother, fine weather and plenty of food; and when the chickens, ducklings or little turkeys were ill, they became real brothers because they were sighing for the same mother.

One day one of the eldest swore that he would find his mother. He was determined not to live without one any longer. He was the only one of them who had been christened and he was called "Come-Come" because, when the girl with the corn in her apron called, "Come, come," he was always the first to do so. He was already vigorous, a cockerel in whose generous soul the spirit of combat was budding. Tall and lithe as a rapier, he wanted a mother first and foremost to admire him: the mother who was said to be able to give every blessing and therefore also to satisfy ambition and vanity.

One day Come-Come boldly leaped through the thick hedge that surrounded his native garden. In the open he stood suddenly still in amazement. Where could he find his mother in that enormous valley over which was a blue sky even more vast? It was hopeless for one as small as himself to search that immensity. So he did not go too far from his native garden, the world he knew, and thoughtfully made the round of it. Thus he found himself in front of the hedge of the other garden.

"If my mother were in there," he thought, "I should find her in a moment." After escaping from the difficulties of infinite space he had no more hesitation. With a bound he went through that hedge also and found himself in a garden very like the one he had left.

Here also there was a flock of tiny chickens fluttering in the long grass. But here was also an animal not to be found in the other garden. A huge chicken, perhaps ten times the size of Come-Come, was lording it in the midst of little creatures covered only with down, and they, as was clear in a moment, regarded this great, bulky animal as their master and protector. And it looked after them all. It gave warning to those straying too far away with a noise not very unlike that which the girl in the other garden made with her own chickens. But this was not all. Every now and then it bent down over the weakest, covering them with all its body, clearly to give them its own heat.

"This is the mother," thought Come-Come with joy. "I have found her and I shan't leave her. How she will love me! I am stronger and better looking than any of those. And it will be easy for me to be obedient, because I love her already. How beautiful and majestic she is! I will help her to look after all these other stupid creatures too."

Without looking at him the mother called. Come-Come drew nearer, believing that she was calling him. He saw that she was busy scratching the earth with rapid blows of her huge claws, and stood still, watching curiously what she was doing, for it was the first time he had seen the operation. When she stopped, a tiny worm was wriggling on the ground in front of her from which she had scratched the grass. Then she clucked while the chickens round her looked at her ecstatically without understanding.

"Idiots," thought Come-Come. "They don't even understand that she wants them to eat that worm." And fired by his enthusiasm to obey her, he pounced quickly upon his prey and swallowed it.

And then—poor Come-Come—the mother darted furiously upon him. He did not understand at once, because he still suspected that, having only just found him, she had a violent desire to caress him. He would thankfully have welcomed all her caresses, of which he knew nothing, and which he therefore admitted might hurt. But the blows that rained upon him from that hard beak were certainly not kisses. They left no room for doubt. He tried to run away, but the great bird pushed him down, rolled him over and jumped upon him, driving her claws into his stomach.

With a superhuman effort Come-Come got upon his legs and ran to the hedge. In his mad race he knocked over some of the chicks, leaving them there cheeping desperately with their legs in the air. He was thus able to escape, because his enemy stopped for a moment by the fallen. Reaching the hedge, Come-Come, with a leap, and despite all the trunks and branches, managed to hurl his agile little body into safety.

The mother, however, was held up by a thick tangle of foliage. And there she remained, majestically looking out as from a window on the intruder, who had also stopped, exhausted. She looked at him with her terrible round eyes red with anger. "Who are you that dared to steal the food I dug out of the ground with so much trouble?"

"I am Come-Come," said the chicken humbly. "But who are you and why have you hurt me so?"

She made but one answer to both his questions. "I am mother," and turned her back contemptuously upon him.

Some time later Come-Come, now a splendid cock, was in quite a different farmyard. And one day he heard all his new comrades talking affectionately and regretfully of their mother.

Marvelling at his own cruel fate, he said sadly: "My mother, on the contrary, was a horrible monster, and it would have been better for me if I had never known her."

Franz Kafka

Franz Kafka (1883–1924) was born in Prague to a middle-class German-Jewish family. After receiving a law degree he worked briefly as a lawyer, writing on the side. Except for a few short tales, his major works were published posthumously by his friend Max Brod, who disregarded Kafka's instructions to destroy them. Haunted by doubt and guilt, prompted in part by a domineering father, Kafka's stories involve the perplexities of the human mind and psyche in a world that is irrational, yet subject to a remote elusive power. His best-known works are The Trial *(1925)* The Castle *(1926), and* Amerika *(1927).* *(See page 75 of Introduction.)*

A COUNTRY DOCTOR

I was in great perplexity; I had to start on an urgent journey; a seriously ill patient was waiting for me in a village ten miles off; a thick blizzard of snow filled all the wide spaces between him and me; I had a gig, a light gig with big wheels, exactly right for our country roads; muffled in furs, my bag of instruments in my hand, I was in the courtyard all ready for the journey; but there was no horse to be had, no horse. My own horse had died in the night, worn out by the fatigues of this icy winter; my servant girl was now running round the village trying to borrow a horse; but it was hopeless, I knew it, and I stood there forlornly, with the snow gathering more and more thickly upon me, more and more unable to move. In the gateway the girl appeared, alone, and waved the lantern; of course, who would lend a horse at this time for such a journey? I strode through the courtyard once more; I could see no way out; in my confused distress I kicked at the dilapidated door of the yearlong uninhabited pigsty. It flew open and flapped to and fro on its hinges. A steam and smell as of horses came out from it. A dim stable lantern was swinging inside from a rope. A man, crouching on his hams in that low space, showed an open blue-eyed face. "Shall I yoke up?" he asked, crawling out on all fours. I did not know what to say and merely stooped down to see what else was in the sty. The servant girl was standing beside me. "You never know what you're going to find in your own house," she said, and we both laughed. "Hey there, Brother, hey there, Sister!" called the groom, and two horses, enormous creatures with powerful flanks, one after the other, their legs tucked close to their bodies, each well-shaped head lowered like a camel's, by sheer strength of buttocking squeezed out through the door hole which they filled entirely. But at once they were standing up, their legs long and their bodies steaming thickly. "Give him a hand," I said, and the willing girl hurried to help the groom with the harnessing. Yet hardly was she beside him when the groom clipped hold of her and pushed his face against hers. She screamed and fled back to me; on her cheek stood out in red the marks of two rows of teeth. "You brute," I yelled in fury, "do you want a whipping?" but in the same moment reflected that the man was a stranger; that I did not know where he came from, and that of his own free will he was helping me out when everyone else had failed me. As if he knew my thoughts he took no offense at my threat but, still busied with the horses, only turned round once towards me. "Get in," he said then, and indeed: everything was ready. A magnificent pair of horses, I observed, such as I had never sat behind, and I climbed in happily. "But I'll drive, you don't know the way," I said. "Of course," said he, "I'm not coming with you anyway, I'm staying with Rose." "No," shrieked Rose, fleeing into the house with a justified presentiment that her fate was inescapable; I heard the door chain rattle as she put it up; I heard the key turn in the lock; I could see, moreover, how she put out the lights in the entrance hall and in further flight all through the rooms to keep herself from being discovered. "You're coming with me," I said to the groom, "or I won't go, urgent as my journey is. I'm not thinking of paying for it by handing the girl over to you." "Gee up!" he said; clapped his hands; the gig whirled off like a log in a freshet; I could just hear the door of my house splitting and bursting as the groom charged at it and then I was deafened and blinded by a storming rush that steadily buffeted all my senses. But this only for a moment, since, as if my patient's farmyard had opened out just before my courtyard gate, I was already there; the horses had come quietly to a standstill; the blizzard had stopped; moonlight all around; my patient's parents hurried out of the house, his sister behind them; I was almost lifted out of the gig; from their confused ejaculations I gathered not a word; in the sickroom the air was almost unbreathable; the neglected stove was smoking; I wanted to push open a window; but first I had to look at my patient. Gaunt, without any fever, not cold, not warm, with vacant eyes, without a shirt, the youngster heaved himself up from under the feather bedding, threw his arms round my neck, and whispered in my ear: "Doctor, let me die." I glanced round the room; no one had heard it; the parents were leaning forward in silence waiting for my verdict; the sister had set a chair for my handbag; I opened the bag and hunted among my instruments; the boy kept clutching at me from his bed to remind me of his entreaty; I picked up a pair of tweezers, examined them in the candlelight and laid them down again. "Yes," I thought blasphemously, "in cases like this the gods are helpful, send the missing horse, add to it a second because of the urgency, and to crown everything bestow even a groom—" And only now did I remember Rose again; what was I to do, how could I rescue her, how could I pull her away from under that groom at ten miles' distance, with a team of horses I couldn't control. These horses, now, they had somehow slipped the reins loose, pushed the windows open from outside, I did not know how; each of them had stuck a head in at a window and, quite unmoved by the startled cries of the family, stood eyeing the patient. "Better go back at once," I thought, as if the horses were summoning me to the return journey, yet I permitted the patient's sister, who fancied that I was dazed by the heat, to take my fur coat from me. A glass of rum was poured out for me, the old man clapped me on the shoulder, a familiarity justified by this offer of his treasure. I shook my head; in the narrow confines of the old man's thoughts I felt ill; that was my only reason for refusing the drink. The mother stood by the bedside and cajoled me towards it; I yielded, and, while one of the horses whinnied loudly to the ceiling, laid my head to the boy's breast, which shivered under my wet beard. I confirmed what I already knew; the boy was quite sound, something a little wrong with his circulation, saturated with coffee by his solicitous mother, but sound and best turned out of bed with one shove. I am no world reformer and so I let him lie. I was the district doctor and did my duty to the uttermost, to the point where it became almost too much. I was badly paid and yet generous and helpful to the poor. I had still to see that Rose was all right, and then the boy might have his way and I wanted to die too. What was I doing there in that endless winter! My horse was dead, and not a single person in the village would lend me another. I had to get my team out of the pigsty; if they hadn't chanced to be horses I should have had to travel with swine. That was how it was. And I nodded to the family. They knew nothing about it, and, had they known, would not have believed it. To write prescriptions is easy, but to come to an understanding with people is hard. Well, this should be the end of my visit, I had once more been called out needlessly, I was used to that, the whole district made my life a torment with my night bell, but that I should have to sacrifice Rose this time as well, the pretty girl who had lived in my house for years almost without my noticing her—that sacrifice was too much to ask, and I had somehow to get it reasoned out in my head with the help of what craft I could muster, in order not to let fly at this family, which with the best will in the world could not restore Rose to me. But as I shut my bag and put an arm out for my fur coat, the family meanwhile standing together, the father sniffing at the glass of rum in his hand, the mother, apparently disappointed in me—why, what do people expect?—biting her lips with tears in her eyes, the sister fluttering a blood-soaked towel, I was somehow ready to admit conditionally that the boy might be ill after all. I went towards him, he welcomed me smiling as if I were bringing him the most nourishing invalid broth—ah, now both horses were whinnying together; the noise, I suppose, was ordained by heaven to assist my examination of the patient—and this time I discovered that the boy was indeed ill. In his right side, near the hip, was an open wound as big as the palm of my hand. Rose-red, in many variations of shade, dark in the hollows, lighter at the edges, softly granulated, with irregular clots of blood, open as a surface mine to the daylight. That was how it looked from a distance. But on a closer inspection there was another complication. I could not help a low whistle of surprise. Worms, as thick and as long as my little finger, themselves rose-red and blood-spotted as well, were wriggling from their fastness in the interior of the wound towards the light, with small white heads and many little legs. Poor boy, you were past helping. I had discovered your great wound; this blossom in your side was destroying you. The family was pleased; they saw me busying myself; the sister told the mother, the mother the father, the father told several guests who were coming in, through the moonlight at the open door, walking on tiptoe, keeping their balance with outstretched arms. "Will you save me?" whispered the boy with a sob, quite blinded by the life within his wound. That is what people are like in my district. Always expecting the impossible from the doctor. They have lost their ancient beliefs; the parson sits at home and unravels his vestments, one after another; but the doctor is supposed to be omnipotent with his merciful surgeon's hand. Well, as it pleases them; I have not thrust my services on them; if they misuse me for sacred ends, I let that happen to me too; what better do I want, old country doctor that I am, bereft of my servant girl! And so they came, the family and the village elders, and stripped my clothes off me; a school choir with the teacher at the head of it stood before the house and sang these words to an utterly simple tune:

> Strip his clothes off, then he'll heal us,
> If he doesn't, kill him dead!
> Only a doctor, only a doctor.

Then my clothes were off and I looked at the people quietly, my fingers in my beard and my head cocked to one side. I was altogether composed and equal to the situation and remained so, although it was no help to me, since they now took me by the head and feet and carried me to the bed. They laid me down in it next to the wall, on the side of the wound. Then they all left the room; the door was shut; the singing stopped; clouds covered the moon; the bedding was warm around me; the horses' heads in the open windows wavered like shadows. "Do you know," said a voice in my ear, "I have very little confidence in you. Why, you were only blown in here, you didn't come on your own feet. Instead of helping me, you're cramping me on my deathbed. What I'd like best is to scratch your eyes out." "Right," I said, "it is a shame. And yet I am a doctor. What am I to do? Believe me, it is not too easy for me either." "Am I supposed to be content with this apology? Oh, I must be, I can't help it. I always have to put up with things. A fine wound is all I brought into the world; that was my sole endowment." "My young friend," said I, "your mistake is: you have not a wide enough view. I have been in all the sickrooms, far and wide, and I tell you: your wound is not so bad. Done in a tight corner with two strokes of the ax. Many a one proffers his side and can hardly hear the ax in the forest, far less that is coming nearer to him." "Is that really so, or are you deluding me in my fever?" "It is really so, take the word of honor of an official doctor." And he took it and lay still. But now it was time for me to think of escaping. The horses were still standing faithfully in their places. My clothes, my fur coat, my bag were quickly collected; I didn't want to waste time dressing; if the horses raced home as they had come, I should only be springing, as it were, out of this bed into my own. Obediently a horse backed away from the window; I threw my bundle into the gig; the fur coat missed its mark and was caught on a hook only by the sleeve. Good enough. I swung myself on to the horse. With the reins loosely trailing, one horse barely fastened to the other, the gig swaying behind, my fur coat last of all in the snow. "Gee up!" I said, but there was no galloping; slowly, like old men, we crawled through the snowy wastes; a long time echoed behind us the new but faulty song of the children:

> O be joyful, all you patients,
> The doctor's laid in bed beside you!

Never shall I reach home at this rate; my flourishing practice is done for; my successor is robbing me, but in vain, for he cannot take my place; in my house the disgusting groom is raging; Rose is his victim; I do not want to think about it any more. Naked, exposed to the frost of this most unhappy of ages, with an earthly vehicle, unearthly horses, old man that I am, I wander astray. My fur coat is hanging from the back of the gig, but I cannot reach it, and none of my limber pack of patients lifts a finger. Betrayed! Betrayed! A false alarm on the night bell once answered—it cannot be made good, not ever.

Franz Kafka

A LITTLE FABLE

"Alas," said the mouse, "the world is growing smaller every day. At the beginning it was so big that I was afraid, I kept running and running, and I was glad when at last I saw walls far away to the right and left, but these long walls have narrowed so quickly that I am in the last chamber already, and there in the corner stands the trap that I must run into." "You only need to change your direction," said the cat, and ate it up.

Rudyard Kipling

Rudyard Kipling (1865–1936) was born in Bombay, India. After an education in England, he worked for seven years as a journalist in India, during which time he published several volumes of prose sketches and light verse. By 1889 he was established as a prominent writer. He was awarded the Nobel Prize for Literature in 1907, but in the following decades his reputation suffered a decline. The popular view of him as a "jingoistic imperialist" has hindered proper appreciation of the development of his art and his perception. His works include such popular tales as Captains Courageous *(1897) and* Kim *(1901), as well as the short-story collections* Plain Tales from the Hills *(1887) and* Debits and Credits *(1926).* *(See page 64 of Introduction.)*

THE GARDENER

Every one in the village knew that Helen Turrell did her duty by all her world, and by none more honourably than by her only brother's unfortunate child. The village knew, too, that George Turrell had tried his family severely since early youth, and were not surprised to be told that, after many fresh starts given and thrown away, he, an Inspector of Indian Police, had entangled himself with the daughter of a retired noncommissioned officer, and had died of a fall from a horse a few weeks before his child was born. Mercifully, George's father and mother were both dead, and though Helen, thirty-five and independent, might well have washed her hands of the whole disgraceful affair, she most nobly took charge, though she was, at the time, under threat of lung trouble which had driven her to the South of France. She arranged for the passage of the child and a nurse from Bombay, met them at Marseilles, nursed the baby through an attack of infantile dysentery due to the carelessness of the nurse, whom she had had to dismiss, and at last, thin and worn but triumphant, brought the boy late in the autumn, wholly restored, to her Hampshire home.

All these details were public property, for Helen was as open as the day, and held that scandals are only increased by hushing them up. She admitted that George had always been rather a black sheep, but things might have been much worse if the mother had insisted on her right to keep the boy. Luckily, it seemed that people of that class would do almost anything for money, and, as George had always turned to her in his scrapes, she felt herself justified—her friends agreed with her—in cutting the whole noncommissioned officer connection, and giving the child every advantage. A christening, by the Rector, under the name of Michael, was the first step. So far as she knew herself, she was not, she said, a child-lover, but, for all his faults, she had been very fond of George, and she pointed out that little Michael had his father's mouth to a line; which made something to build upon.

As a matter of fact, it was the Turrell forehead, broad, low, and well-shaped, with the widely-spaced eyes beneath it, that Michael had most faithfully reproduced. His mouth was somewhat better cut than the family type. But Helen, who would concede nothing good to his mother's side, vowed he was a Turrell all over, and, there being no one to contradict, the likeness was established.

In a few years Michael took his place, as accepted as Helen had always been—fearless, philosophical, and fairly good-looking. At six, he wished to know why he could not call her "Mummy," as other boys called their mothers. She explained that she was only his auntie, and that aunties were not quite the same as mummies, but that, if it gave him pleasure, he might call her "Mummy" at bedtime, for a pet-name between themselves.

Michael kept his secret most loyally, but Helen, as usual, explained the fact to her friends; which when Michael heard, he raged.

"Why did you tell? *Why* did you tell?" came at the end of the storm.

"Because it's always best to tell the truth," Helen answered, her arm around him as he shook in his cot.

"All right, but when the troof's ugly I don't think it's nice."

"Don't you, dear?"

"No, I don't, and"—she felt the small body stiffen—"now you've told, I won't call you 'Mummy' any more—not even at bedtimes."

"But isn't that rather unkind?" said Helen, softly.

"I don't care! I don't care! You've hurted me in my insides and I'll hurt you back. I'll hurt you as long as I live!"

"Don't, oh, don't talk like that, dear! You don't know what—"

"I will! And when I'm dead I'll hurt you worse!"

"Thank goodness, I shall be dead long before you, darling."

"Huh! Emma says, 'Never know your luck.' " (Michael had been talking to Helen's elderly, flat-faced maid.) "Lots of little boys die quite soon. So'll I. *Then* you'll see!"

Helen caught her breath and moved towards the door, but the wail of "Mummy! Mummy!" drew her back again, and the two wept together.

At ten years old, after two terms at a prep school, something or somebody gave him the idea that his civil status was not quite regular. He attacked Helen on the subject, breaking down her stammered defences with the family directness.

"Don't believe a word of it," he said, cheerily, at the end. "People wouldn't have talked like they did if my people had been married. But don't you bother, Auntie. I've found out all about my sort in English Hist'ry and the Shakespeare bits. There was William the Conqueror to begin with, and—oh, heaps more, and they all got on first-rate. 'Twon't make any difference to you, my being *that*—will it?"

"As if anything could—" she began.

"All right. We won't talk about it any more if it makes you cry." He never mentioned the thing again of his own will, but when, two years later, he skilfully managed to have measles in the holidays, as his temperature went up to the appointed one hundred and four he muttered of nothing else, till Helen's voice, piercing at last his delirium, reached him with assurance that nothing on earth or beyond could make any difference between them.

The terms at his public school and the wonderful Christmas, Easter, and summer holidays followed each other, variegated and glorious as jewels on a string; and as jewels Helen treasured them. In due time Michael developed his own interests, which ran their courses and gave way to others; but his interest in Helen was constant and increasing throughout. She repaid it with all that she had of affection or could command of counsel and money; and since Michael was no fool, the war took him just before what was like to have been a most promising career.

He was to have gone up to Oxford, with a scholarship, in October. At the end of August he was on the edge of joining the first holocaust of public-school boys who threw themselves into the Line; but the captain of his O.T.C., where he had been sergeant for nearly a year, headed him off and steered him directly to a commission in a battalion so new that half of it still wore the old Army red, and the other half was breeding meningitis through living overcrowdedly in damp tents. Helen had been shocked at the idea of direct enlistment.

"But it's in the family," Michael laughed.

"You don't mean to tell me that you believed that old story all this time?" said Helen. (Emma, her maid, had been dead now several years.) "I gave you my word of honour—and I give it again—that—that it's all right. It is indeed."

"Oh, *that* doesn't worry me. It never did," he replied valiantly. "What I meant was, I should have got into the show earlier if I'd enlisted—like my grandfather."

"Don't talk like that! Are you afraid of its ending so soon, then?"

"No such luck. You know what K. says."

"Yes. But my banker told me last Monday it couldn't *possibly* last beyond Christmas—for financial reasons."

" 'Hope he's right, but our Colonel—and he's a Regular—says it's going to be a long job."

Michael's battalion was fortunate in that, by some chance which meant several "leaves," it was used for coast-defence among shallow trenches on the Norfolk coast; thence sent north to watch the mouth of a Scotch estuary, and, lastly, held for weeks on a baseless rumour of distant service. But, the very day that Michael was to have met Helen for four whole hours at a railway-junction up the line, it was hurled out, to help make good the wastage of Loos, and he had only just time to send her a wire of farewell.

In France luck again helped the battalion. It was put down near the Salient, where it led a meritorious and unexacting life, while the Somme was being manufactured; and enjoyed the peace of the Armentières and

Laventie sectors when that battle began. Finding that it had sound views on protecting its own flanks and could dig, a prudent Commander stole it out of its own Division, under pretence of helping to lay telegraphs, and use it round Ypres at large.

A month later, and just after Michael had written Helen that there was nothing special doing and therefore no need to worry, a shell-splinter dropping out of a wet dawn killed him at once. The next shell uprooted and laid down over the body what had been the foundation of a barn wall, so neatly that none but an expert would have guessed that anything unpleasant had happened.

By this time the village was old in experience of war, and, English fashion, had evolved a ritual to meet it. When the postmistress handed her seven-year-old daughter the official telegram to take to Miss Turrell, she observed to the Rector's gardener: "It's Miss Helen's turn now." He replied, thinking of his own son: "Well, he's lasted longer than some." The child herself came to the front-door weeping aloud, because Master Michael had often given her sweets. Helen, presently, found herself pulling down the house-blinds one after one with great care, and saying earnestly to each: "Missing *always* means dead." Then she took her place in the dreary procession that was impelled to go through an inevitable series of unprofitable emotions. The Rector, of course, preached hope and prophesied word, very soon, from a prison camp. Several friends, too, told her perfectly truthful tales, but always about other women, to whom, after months and months of silence, their missing had been miraculously restored. Other people urged her to communicate with infallible Secretaries of organisations who could communicate with benevolent neutrals, who could extract accurate information from the most secretive of Hun prison commandants. Helen did and wrote and signed everything that was suggested or put before her.

Once, on one of Michael's leaves, he had taken her over a munition factory, where she saw the progress of a shell from blank-iron to the all but finished article. It struck her at the time that the wretched thing was never left alone for a single second; and "I'm being manufactured into a bereaved next-of-kin," she told herself, as she prepared her documents.

In due course, when all the organisations had deeply or sincerely regretted their inability to trace, etc., something gave way within her and all sensation—save of thankfulness for the release—came to an end in blessed passivity. Michael had died and her world had stood still and she had been one with the full shock of that arrest. Now she was standing still and the world was going forward, but it did not concern her—in no way or relation did it touch her. She knew this by the ease with which she could slip Michael's name into talk and incline her head to the proper angle, at the proper murmur of sympathy.

In the blessed realisation of that relief, the Armistice with all its bells broke over her and passed unheeded. At the end of another year she had overcome her physical loathing of the living and returned young, so that she could take them by the hand and almost sincerely wish them well. She had no interest in any aftermath, national or personal, of the War, but, moving at an immense distance, she sat on various relief committees and held strong views—she heard herself delivering them—about the site of the proposed village War Memorial.

Then there came to her, as next of kin, an official intimation, backed by a page of a letter to her in indelible pencil, a silver identity-disc, and a watch, to the effect that the body of Lieutenant Michael Turrell had been found, identified, and re-interred in Hagenzeele Third Military Cemetery—the letter of the row and the grave's number in that row duly given.

So Helen found herself moved on to another process of the manufacture—to a world full of exultant or broken relatives, now strong in the certainty that there was an altar upon earth where they might lay their love. These soon told her, and by means of time-tables made clear, how easy it was and how little it interfered with life's affairs to go and see one's grave.

"*So* different," as the Rector's wife said, "if he'd been killed in Mesopotamia, or even Gallipoli."

The agony of being waked up to some sort of second life drove Helen across the Channel, where, in a new world of abbreviated titles, she learnt that Hagenzeele Third could be comfortably reached by an afternoon train which fitted in with the morning boat, and that there was a comfortable little hotel not three kilometers from Hagenzeele itself, where one could spend quite a comfortable night and see one's grave next morning. All this she had from a Central Authority who lived in a board and tarpaper shed on the skirts of a razed city full of whirling lime-dust and blown papers.

"By the way," said he, "you know your grave, of course?"

"Yes, thank you," said Helen, and showed its row and number typed on Michael's own little typewriter. The officer would have checked it, out of one of his many books; but a large Lancashire woman thrust between them and bade him tell her where she might find her son, who had been corporal in the A.S.C. His proper name, she sobbed, was Anderson, but, coming of respectable folk, he had of course enlisted under the name of Smith; and had been killed at Dickiebush, in early 'Fifteen. She had not his number nor did she know which of his two Christian names he might have used with his alias; but her Cook's tourist ticket expired at the end of Easter week, and if by then she could not find her child she should go mad. Whereupon she fell forward on Helen's breast; but the officer's wife came out quickly from a little bedroom behind the office, and the three of them lifted the woman on to the cot.

"They are often like this," said the officer's wife, loosening the right bonnet-strings. "Yesterday she said he'd been killed at Hooge. Are you sure you know your grave? It makes such a difference."

"Yes, thank you," said Helen, and hurried out before the woman on the bed should begin to lament again.

Tea in a crowded mauve and blue striped wooden structure, with a false front, carried her still further into the nightmare. She paid her bill beside a stolid, plain-featured Englishwoman, who, hearing her inquire about the train to Hagenzeele, volunteered to come with her.

"I'm going to Hagenzeele myself," she explained. "Not to Hagenzeele Third; mine is Sugar Factory, but they call it La Rosière now. It's just south of Hagenzeele Three. Have you got your room at the hotel there?"

"Oh yes, thank you. I've wired."

"That's better. Sometimes the place is quite full, and at others there's hardly a soul. But they've put bathrooms into the old Lion d'Or—that's the hotel on the west side of Sugar Factory—and it draws off a lot of people, luckily."

"It's all new to me. This is the first time I've been over."

"Indeed! This is my ninth time since the Armistice. Not on my own account. *I* haven't lost any one, thank God—but, like every one else, I've a lot of friends at home who have. Coming over as often as I do, I find it helps them to have some one just look at the—the place and tell them about it afterwards. And one can take photos for them, too. I get quite a list of commissions to execute." She laughed nervously and tapped her slung Kodak. "There are two or three to see at Sugar Factory this time, and plenty of others in the cemeteries all about. My system is to save them up, and arrange them, you know. And when I've got enough commissions for one area to make it worth while, I pop over and execute them. It *does* comfort people."

"I suppose so," Helen answered, shivering as they entered the little train.

"Of course it does. (Isn't it lucky we've got window-seats?) It must do or they wouldn't ask one to do it, would they? I've a list of quite twelve or fifteen commissions here"—she tapped the Kodak again—"I must sort them out to-night. Oh, I forgot to ask you. What's yours?"

"My nephew," said Helen. "But I was very fond of him."

"Ah yes! I sometimes wonder whether *they* know after death? What do you think?"

"Oh, I don't—I haven't dared to think much about that sort of thing," said Helen, almost lifting her hands to keep her off.

"Perhaps that's better," the woman answered. "The sense of loss must be enough, I expect. Well, I won't worry you any more."

Helen was grateful, but when they reached the hotel Mrs. Scarsworth (they had exchanged names) insisted on dining at the same table with her, and after the meal, in the little, hideous salon full of low-voiced relatives, took Helen through her "commissions" with biographies of the dead, where she happened to know them, and sketches of their next of kin. Helen endured till nearly half-past nine, ere she fled to her room.

Almost at once there was a knock at her door and Mrs. Scarsworth entered; her hands, holding the dreadful list, clasped before her.

"Yes—yes—*I* know," she began. "You're sick of me, but I want to tell you something. You—you aren't married are you? Then perhaps you won't. . . . But it doesn't matter. I've *got* to tell some one. I can't go on any longer like this."

"But please—" Mrs. Scarsworth had backed against the shut door, and her mouth worked dryly.

"In a minute," she said. "You—you know about these graves of mine I was telling you about downstairs, just now? They really *are* commissions. At least several of them are." Her eyes wandered round the room. "What extraordinary wall-papers they have in Belgium, don't you think? . . . Yes. I swear they are commissions. But there's *one,* d'you see, and—and he was more to me than anything else in the world. Do you understand?"

Helen nodded.

"More than any one else. And, of course, he oughtn't to have been. He ought to have been nothing to me. But he *was.* He *is.* That's why I do the commissions, you see. That's all."

"But why do you tell me?" Helen asked desperately.

"Because I'm *so* tired of lying. Tired of lying—always lying—year in and year out. When I don't tell lies I've got to act 'em and I've got to think 'em always. *You* don't know what that means. He was everything to me that he oughtn't to have been—the one real thing—the only thing that ever happened to me in all my life; and I've had to pretend he wasn't. I've had to watch every word I said, and think out what lie I'd tell next, for years and years!"

"How many years?" Helen asked.

"Six years and four months before, and two and three-quarters after. I've gone to him eight times, since. To-morrow'll make the ninth, and—and I can't—I *can't* go to him again with nobody in the world knowing. I want to be honest with some one before I go. Do you understand? It doesn't matter about *me.* I was never truthful, even as a girl. But it isn't worthy of *him.* So—so I—I had to tell you. I can't keep it up any longer. Oh, I can't!"

She lifted her joined hands almost to the level of her mouth, and brought them down sharply, still joined, to full arms' length below her waist. Helen reached forward, caught them, bowed her head over them, and murmured: "Oh, my dear! My dear!" Mrs. Scarsworth stepped back, her face all mottled.

"My God!" said she. "Is *that* how you take it?"

Helen could not speak, the woman went out; but it was a long while before Helen was able to sleep.

Next morning, Mrs. Scarsworth left early on her round of commissions, and Helen walked alone to Hagenzeele Third. The place was still in the making, and stood some five or six feet above the metalled road, which it flanked for hundreds of yards. Culverts across a deep ditch served for entrances through the unfinished boundary wall. She climbed a few wooden-faced earthen steps and then met the entire crowded level of the thing in one held breath. She did not know that Hagenzeele Third counted twenty-one thousand dead already. All she saw was a merciless sea of black crosses, bearing little strips of stamped tin at all angles across their faces. She could distinguish no order or arrangement in their mass; nothing but a waist-high wilderness as of weeds stricken dead, rushing at her. She went forward, moved to the left and the right hopelessly, wondering by what guidance she should ever come to her own. A great distance away there was a line of whiteness. It proved to be a block of some two or three hundred graves whose headstones had already been set, whose flowers were planted out, and whose new-sown grass showed green. Here she could see clear-cut letters at the ends of the rows, and, referring to her slip, realised that it was not here she must look.

A man knelt behind a line of headstones—evidently a gardener, for he was firming a young plant in the soft earth. She went towards him, her paper in her hand. He rose at her approach and without prelude or salutation asked: "Who are you looking for?"

"Lieutenant Michael Turrell—my nephew," said Helen slowly and word for word, as she had many thousands of times in her life.

The man lifted his eyes and looked at her with infinite compassion before he turned from the fresh-sown grass towards the naked black crosses.

"Come with me," he said, "and I will show you where your son lies."

When Helen left the Cemetery she turned for a last look. In the distance she saw the man bending over his young plants; and she went away, supposing him to be the gardener.

F. Scott Fitzgerald

F. Scott Fitzgerald (1896–1940) was born in St. Paul, Minnesota, and attended Newman, a Catholic preparatory school, and Princeton University, where he wrote several "Triangle" shows. He served in the army briefly, saw no actual combat, but while stationed near Montgomery, Alabama, met Zelda Sayre, with whom he immediately fell in love. They married when his first novel, This Side of Paradise, *was accepted for publication in 1920. His meteoric success, his struggle to maintain the level and intensity of life associated with the "Jazz Age" boom, his commuting between lavish European and American resorts, led to a physical and emotional crisis which he movingly chronicled in his book of essays,* The Crack-Up *(1936). His wife's mental illness and the pressure for money to support her and his daughter drew him to Hollywood, where he spent his last years writing for the movies. His most famous novel is* The Great Gatsby *(1925); during a twenty-five year period, he wrote more than one hundred and fifty short stories and sketches. His work often describes the manners and morals of upper-class Americans.* *(See page 63 of Introduction.)*

DALYRIMPLE GOES WRONG

I

In the millenium an educational genius will write a book to be given to every young man on the date of his disillusion. This work will have the flavor of Montaigne's essays and Samuel Butler's notebooks—and a little of Tolstoi and Marcus Aurelius. It will be neither cheerful nor pleasant but will contain numerous passages of striking humor. Since first-class minds never believe anything very strongly until they've experienced it, its value will be purely relative . . . all people over thirty will refer to it as "depressing."

This prelude belongs to the story of a young man who lived, as you and I do, before the book.

II

The generation which numbered Bryan Dalyrimple drifted out of adolescence to a mighty fanfare of trumpets. Bryan played the star in an affair which included a Lewis gun and a nine-day romp behind the retreating German lines, so luck triumphant or sentiment rampant awarded him a row of medals and on his arrival in the States he was told that he was second in importance only to General Pershing and Sergeant York. This was a lot of fun. The governor of his State, a stray congressman, and a citizens' committee gave him enormous smiles and "By God, Sirs," on the dock at Hoboken; there were newspaper reporters and photographers who said "would you mind" and "if you could just"; and back in his home town there were old ladies, the rims of whose eyes grew red as they talked to him, and girls who hadn't remembered him so well since his father's business went blah! in nineteen-twelve.

But when the shouting died he realized that for a month he had been the house guest of the mayor, that he had only fourteen dollars in the world, and that "the name that will live forever in the annals and legends of this State" was already living there very quietly and obscurely.

One morning he lay late in bed and just outside his door he heard the up-stairs maid talking to the cook. The up-stairs maid said that Mrs. Hawkins, the mayor's wife, had been trying for a week to hint Dalyrimple out of the house. He left at eleven o'clock in intolerable confusion, asking that his trunk be sent to Mrs. Beebe's boarding-house.

Dalyrimple was twenty-three and he had never worked. His father had given him two years at the State University and passed away about the time of his son's nine-day romp, leaving behind him some mid-Victorian furniture and a thin packet of folded papers that turned out to be grocery bills. Young Dalyrimple had very keen gray eyes, a mind that delighted the army psychological examiners, a trick of having read it—whatever it was—some time before, and a cool hand in a hot situation. But these things did not save him a final unresigned sigh when he realized that he had to go to work—right away.

It was early afternoon when he walked into the office of Theron G. Macy, who owned the largest wholesale grocery house in town. Plump, prosperous, wearing a pleasant but quite unhumorous smile, Theron G. Macy greeted him warmly.

"Well—how do, Bryan? What's on your mind?"

To Dalyrimple, straining with his admission, his own words, when they came, sounded like an Arab beggar's whine for alms.

"Why—this question of a job." ("This question of a job" seemed somehow more clothed than just "a job.")

"A job?" An almost imperceptible breeze blew across Mr. Macy's expression.

"You see, Mr. Macy," continued Dalyrimple, "I feel I'm wasting time. I want to get started at something. I had several chances about a month ago but they all seem to have—gone—"

"Let's see," interrupted Mr. Macy. "What were they?"

"Well, just at the first the governor said something about a vacancy on his staff. I was sort of counting on that for a while, but I hear he's given it to Allen Gregg, you know, son of G. P. Gregg. He sort of forgot what he said to me—just talking, I guess."

"You ought to push those things."

"Then there was that engineering expedition, but they decided they'd have to have a man who knew hydraulics, so they couldn't use me unless I paid my own way."

"You had just a year at the university?"

"Two. But I didn't take any science or mathematics. Well, the day the battalion paraded, Mr. Peter Jordan said something about a vacancy in his store. I went around there to-day and I found he meant a sort of floorwalker—and then you said something one day"—he paused and waited for the older man to take him up, but noting only a minute wince continued—"about a position, so I thought I'd come and see you."

"There was a position," confessed Mr. Macy reluctantly, "but since then we've filled it." He cleared his throat again. "You've waited quite a while."

"Yes, I suppose I did. Everybody told me there was no hurry—and I'd had these various offers."

Mr. Macy delivered a paragraph on present-day opportunities which Dalyrimple's mind completely skipped.

"Have you had any business experience?"

"I worked on a ranch two summers as a rider."

"Oh, well," Mr. Macy disparaged this neatly, and then continued: "What do you think you're worth?"

"I don't know."

"Well, Bryan, I tell you, I'm willing to strain a point and give you a chance."

Dalyrimple nodded.

"Your salary won't be much. You'll start by learning the stock. Then you'll come in the office for a while. Then you'll go on the road. When could you begin?"

"How about to-morrow?"

"All right. Report to Mr. Hanson in the stock-room. He'll start you off."

He continued to regard Dalyrimple steadily until the latter, realizing that the interview was over, rose awkwardly.

"Well, Mr. Macy, I'm certainly much obliged."

"That's all right. Glad to help you, Bryan."

After an irresolute moment, Dalyrimple found himself in the hall. His forehead was covered with perspiration, and the room had not been hot.

"Why the devil did I thank the son of a gun?" he muttered.

III

Next morning Mr. Hanson informed him coldly of the necessity of punching the time-clock at seven every morning, and delivered him for instruction into the hands of a fellow worker, one Charley Moore.

Charley was twenty-six, with that faint musk of weakness hanging about him that is often mistaken for the scent of evil. It took no psychological examiner to decide that he had drifted into indulgence and laziness as casually as he had drifted into life, and was to drift out. He was pale and his clothes stank of smoke; he enjoyed burlesque shows, billiards, and Robert Service, and was always looking back upon his last intrigue or forward to his next one. In his youth his taste had run to loud ties, but now it seemed to have faded, like his vitality, and was expressed in pale-lilac four-in-hands and indeterminate gray collars. Charley was listlessly struggling that losing struggle against mental, moral, and physical anaemia that takes place ceaselessly on the lower fringe of the middle classes.

The first morning he stretched himself on a row of cereal cartons and carefully went over the limitations of the Theron G. Macy Company.

"It's a piker organization. My Gosh! Lookit what they give me. I'm quittin' in a coupla months. Hell! Me stay with this bunch!"

The Charley Moores are always going to change jobs next month. They do, once or twice in their careers, after which they sit around comparing their last job with the present one, to the infinite disparagement of the latter.

"What do you get?" asked Dalyrimple curiously.

"Me. I get sixty." This rather defiantly.

"Did you start at sixty?"

"Me? No, I started at thirty-five. He told me he'd put me on the road after I learned the stock. That's what he tells 'em all!"

"How long've you been here?" asked Dalyrimple with a sinking sensation.

"Me? Four years. My last year, too, you bet your boots."

Dalyrimple rather resented the presence of the store detective as he resented the time-clock, and he came into contact with him almost immediately through the rule against smoking. This rule was a thorn in his side. He was accustomed to his three or four cigarettes in a morning, and after three days without it he followed Charley Moore by a circuitous route up a flight of back stairs to a little balcony where they indulged in peace. But this was not for long. One day in his second week the detective met him in a nook of the stairs, on his descent, and told him sternly that next time he'd be reported to Mr. Macy. Dalyrimple felt like an errant schoolboy.

Unpleasant facts came to his knowledge. There were "cavedwellers" in the basement who had worked there for ten or fifteen years at sixty dollars a month, rolling barrels and carrying boxes through damp, cement-walled corridors, lost in that echoing half-darkness between seven and five-thirty and, like himself, compelled several times a month to work until nine at night.

At the end of a month he stood in line and received forty dollars. He pawned a cigarette-case and a pair of field-glasses and managed to live—to eat, sleep, and smoke. It was, however, a narrow scrape; as the ways and means of economy were a closed book to him and the second month brought no increase, he voiced his alarm.

"If you've got a drag with old Macy, maybe he'll raise you," was Charley's disheartening reply. "But he didn't raise *me* till I'd been here nearly two years."

"I've got to live," said Dalyrimple simply. "I could get more pay as a laborer on the railroad but, Golly, I want to feel I'm where there's a chance to get ahead."

Charles shook his head sceptically and Mr. Macy's answer next day was equally unsatisfactory.

Dalyrimple had gone to the office just before closing time.

"Mr. Macy, I'd like to speak to you."

"Why—yes." The unhumorous smile appeared. The voice was faintly resentful.

"I want to speak to you in regard to more salary."

Mr. Macy nodded.

"Well," he said doubtfully, "I don't know exactly what you're doing. I'll speak to Mr. Hanson."

He knew exactly what Dalyrimple was doing, and Dalyrimple knew he knew.

"I'm in the stock-room—and, sir, while I'm here I'd like to ask you how much longer I'll have to stay there."

"Why—I'm not sure exactly. Of course it takes some time to learn the stock."

"You told me two months when I started."

"Yes. Well, I'll speak to Mr. Hanson."

Dalyrimple paused, irresolute.

"Thank you, sir."

Two days later he again appeared in the office with the result of a count that had been asked for by Mr. Hesse, the bookkeeper. Mr. Hesse was engaged and Dalyrimple, waiting, began idly fingering a ledger on the stenographer's desk.

Half unconsciously he turned a page—he caught sight of his name—it was a salary list:

Dalyrimple
Demming
Donahoe
Everett

His eyes stopped——

Everett $60

So Tom Everett, Macy's weak-chinned nephew, had started at sixty—and in three weeks he had been out of the packing-room and into the office.

So that was it! He was to sit and see man after man pushed over him: sons, cousins, sons of friends, irrespective of their capabilities, while *he* was cast for a pawn, with "going on the road" dangled before his eyes—put off with the stock remark: "I'll see; I'll look into it." At forty, perhaps, he would be a bookkeeper like old Hesse, tired, listless Hesse with dull routine for his stint and a dull background of boarding-house conversation.

This was a moment when a genie should have pressed into his hand the book for disillusioned young men. But the book has not been written.

A great protest swelling into revolt surged up in him. Ideas half forgotten, chaotically perceived and assimilated, filled his mind. Get on—that was the rule of life—and that was all. How he did it, didn't matter—but to be Hesse or Charley Moore.

"I won't!" he cried aloud.

The bookkeeper and the stenographers looked up in surprise.

"What?"

For a second Dalyrimple stared—then walked up to the desk.

"Here's that data," he said brusquely. "I can't wait any longer."

Mr. Hesse's face expressed surprise.

It didn't matter what he did—just so he got out of this rut. In a dream he stepped from the elevator into the stock-room, and walking to an unused aisle, sat down on a box, covering his face with his hands.

His brain was whirring with the frightful jar of discovering a platitude for himself.

"I've got to get out of this," he said aloud and then repeated, "I've got to get out"—and he didn't mean only out of Macy's wholesale house.

When he left at five-thirty it was pouring rain, but he struck off in the opposite direction from his boarding-house, feeling, in the first cool moisture that oozed soggily through his old suit, an odd exultation and freshness. He wanted a world that was like walking through rain, even though he could not see far ahead of him, but fate had put him in the world of Mr. Macy's fetid storerooms and corridors. At first merely the overwhelming need of change took him, then half-plans began to formulate in his imagination.

"I'll go East—to a big city—meet people—bigger people—people who'll help me. Interesting work somewhere. My God, there *must* be."

With sickening truth it occurred to him that his facility for meeting people was limited. Of all places it was here in his own town that he should be known, was known—famous—before the waters of oblivion had rolled over him.

You had to cut corners, that was all. Pull—relationship—wealthy marriages—

For several miles the continued reiteration of this preoccupied him and then he perceived that the rain had become thicker and more opaque in the heavy gray of twilight and that the houses were falling away. The district of full blocks, then of big houses, then of scattering little ones, passed and great sweeps of misty country opened out on both sides. It was hard walking here. The sidewalk had given place to a dirt road, streaked with furious brown rivulets that splashed and squashed around his shoes.

Cutting corners—the words began to fall apart, forming curious phrasings—little illuminated pieces of themselves. They resolved into sentences, each of which had a strangely familiar ring.

Cutting corners meant rejecting the old childhood principles that success came from faithfulness to duty, that evil was necessarily punished or virtue necessarily rewarded—that honest poverty was happier than corrupt riches.

It meant being hard.

This phrase appealed to him and he repeated it over and over. It had to do somehow with Mr. Macy and Charley Moore—the attitudes, the methods of each of them.

He stopped and felt his clothes. He was drenched to the skin. He looked about him and, selecting a place in the fence where a tree sheltered it, perched himself there.

In my credulous years—he thought—they told me that evil was a sort of dirty hue, just as definite as a soiled collar, but it seems to me that evil is only a manner of hard luck, or heredity-and-environment, or "being found out." It hides in the vacillations of dubs like Charley Moore as certainly as it does in the intolerance of Macy, and if it ever gets much more tangible it becomes merely an arbitrary label to paste on the unpleasant things in other people's lives.

In fact—he concluded—it isn't worth worrying over what's evil and what isn't. Good and evil aren't any standard to me—and they can be a devil of a bad hindrance when I want something. When I want something bad enough, common sense tells me to go and take it—and not get caught.

And then suddenly Dalyrimple knew what he wanted first. He wanted fifteen dollars to pay his overdue board bill.

With a furious energy he jumped from the fence, whipped off his coat, and from its black lining cut with his knife a piece about five inches square. He made two holes near its edge and then fixed it on his face, pulling his hat down to hold it in place. It flapped grotesquely and then dampened and clung to his forehead and cheeks.

Now. . . . The twilight had merged to dripping dusk . . . black as pitch. He began to walk quickly back toward town, not waiting to remove the mask but watching the road with difficulty through the jagged eye-holes. He was not conscious of any nervousness . . . the only tension was caused by a desire to do the thing as soon as possible.

He reached the first sidewalk, continued on until he saw a hedge far from any lamp-post, and turned in behind it. Within a minute he heard several series of footsteps—he waited—it was a woman and he held his breath until she passed . . . and then a man, a laborer. The next passer, he felt, would be what he wanted . . . the laborer's footfalls died far up the drenched street . . . other steps grew near, grew suddenly louder.

Dalyrimple braced himself:

"Put up your hands!"

The man stopped, uttered an absurd little grunt, and thrust pudgy arms skyward.

Dalyrimple went through the waistcoat.

"Now, you shrimp," he said, setting his hand suggestively to his own hip pocket, "you run, and stamp—loud! If I hear your feet stop I'll put a shot after you!"

Then he stood there in sudden uncontrollable laughter as audibly frightened footsteps scurried away into the night.

After a moment he thrust the roll of bills into his pocket, snatched off his mask, and running quickly across the street, darted down an alley.

IV

Yet, however Dalyrimple justified himself intellectually, he had many bad moments in the weeks immediately following his decision. The tremendous pressure of sentiment and inherited tradition kept raising riot with his attitude. He felt morally lonely.

The noon after his first venture he ate in a little lunch-room with Charley Moore and, watching him unspread the paper, waited for a remark about the hold-up of the day before. But either the hold-up was not mentioned or Charley wasn't interested. He turned listlessly to the sporting sheet, read Doctor Crane's crop of seasoned bromides, took in an editorial on ambition with his mouth slightly ajar, and then skipped to Mutt and Jeff.

Poor Charley—with his faint aura of evil and his mind that refused to focus, playing a lifeless solitaire with cast-off mischief.

Yet Charley belonged on the other side of the fence. In him could be stirred up all the flamings and denunciations of righteousness; he would weep at a stage heroine's lost virtue, he could become lofty and contemptuous at the idea of dishonor.

On my side, thought Dalyrimple, there aren't any resting-places; a man who's a strong criminal is after the weak criminals as well, so it's all guerilla warfare over here.

What will it all do to me? he thought, with a persistent weariness. Will it take the color out of life with the honor? Will it scatter my courage and dull my mind?—despiritualize me completely—does it mean eventual barrenness, eventual remorse, failure?

With a great surge of anger, he would fling his mind upon the barrier—and stand there with the flashing bayonet of his pride. Other men who broke the laws of justice and charity lied to all the world. He at any rate would not lie to himself. He was more than Byronic now: not the spiritual rebel, Don Juan; not the philosophical rebel, Faust; but a new psychological rebel of his own century—defying the sentimental a priori forms of his own mind—

Happiness was what he wanted—a slowly rising scale of gratifications of the normal appetites—and he had a strong conviction that the materials, if not the inspiration of happiness, could be bought with money.

V

The night came that drew him out upon his second venture, and as he walked the dark street he felt in himself a great resemblance to a cat—a certain supple, swinging litheness. His muscles were rippling smoothly and sleekly under his spare, healthy flesh—he had an absurd desire to bound along the street, to run dodging among trees, to turn "cart-wheels" over soft grass.

It was not crisp, but in the air lay a faint suggestion of acerbity, inspirational rather than chilling.

"The moon is down—I have not heard the clock!"

He laughed in delight at the line which an early memory had endowed with a hushed, awesome beauty.

He passed a man, and then another a quarter of a mile afterward.

He was on Philmore Street now and it was very dark. He blessed the city council for not having put in new lamp-posts as a recent budget had recommended. Here was the red-brick Sterner residence which marked the beginning of the avenue; here was the Jordon house, the Eisenhaurs', the Dents', the Markhams', the Frasers'; the Hawkins', where he had been a guest; the Willoughbys', the Everetts', colonial and ornate; the little cottage where lived the Watts old maids between the imposing fronts of the Macys' and the Krupstadts'; the Craigs'—

Ah . . . *there!* He paused, wavered violently—far up the street was a blot, a man walking, possibly a policeman. After an eternal second he found himself following the vague, ragged shadow of a lamp-post across a lawn, running bent very low. Then he was standing tense, without breath or need of it, in the shadow of his limestone prey.

Interminably he listened—a mile off a cat howled, a hundred yards away another took up the hymn in a demoniacal snarl, and he felt his heart dip and swoop, acting as shock-absorber for his mind. There were other sounds; the faintest fragment of song far away; strident, gossiping laughter from a back porch diagonally across the alley; and crickets, crickets singing in the patched, patterned, moonlit grass of the yard. Within the house there seemed to lie an ominous silence. He was glad he did not know who lived here.

His slight shiver hardened to steel; the steel softened and his nerves became pliable as leather; gripping his hands he gratefully found them supple, and taking out knife and pliers he went to work on the screen.

So sure was he that he was unobserved that, from the dining-room where in a minute he found himself, he leaned out and carefully pulled the screen up into position, balancing it so it would neither fall by chance nor be a serious obstacle to a sudden exit.

Then he put the open knife in his coat pocket, took out his pocket-flash, and tiptoed around the room.

There was nothing here he could use—the dining-room had never been included in his plans, for the town was too small to permit disposing of silver.

As a matter of fact his plans were of the vaguest. He had found that with a mind like his, lucrative in intelligence, intuition, and lightning decision, it was best to have but the skeleton of a campaign. The machine-gun episode had taught him that. And he was afraid that a method preconceived would give him two points of view in a crisis—and two points of view meant wavering.

He stumbled slightly on a chair, held his breath, listened, went on, found the hall, found the stairs, started up; the seventh stair creaked at his step, the ninth, the fourteenth. He was counting them automatically. At the third creak he paused again for over a minute—and in that minute he felt more alone than he had ever felt before. Between the lines on patrol, even when alone, he had had behind him the moral support of half a billion people; now he was alone, pitted against that same moral pressure—a bandit. He had never felt this fear, yet he had never felt this exultation.

The stairs came to an end, a doorway approached; he went in and listened to regular breathing. His feet were economical of steps and his body swayed sometimes at stretching as he felt over the bureau, pocketing all articles which held promise—he could not have enumerated them ten seconds afterward. He felt on a chair for possible trousers, found soft garments, women's lingerie. The corners of his mouth smiled mechanically.

Another room . . . the same breathing, enlivened by one ghastly snort that sent his heart again on its tour of his breast. Round object—watch; chain; roll of bills; stick-pins; two rings—he remembered that he had got rings from the other bureau. He started out, winced as a faint glow flashed in front of him, facing him. God!—it was the glow of his own wrist-watch on his outstretched arm.

Down the stairs. He skipped two creaking steps but found another. He was all right now, practically safe; as he neared the bottom he felt a slight boredom. He reached the dining-room—considered the silver—again decided against it.

Back in his room at the boarding-house he examined the additions to his personal property:

Sixty-five dollars in bills.

A platinum ring with three medium diamonds, worth, probably, about seven hundred dollars. Diamonds were going up.

A cheap gold-plated ring with the initials O. S. and the date inside—'03—probably a class-ring from school. Worth a few dollars. Unsalable.

A red-cloth case containing a set of false teeth.

A silver watch.

A gold chain worth more than the watch.

An empty ring-box.

A little ivory Chinese god—probably a desk ornament.

A dollar and sixty-two cents in small change.

He put the money under his pillow and the other things in the toe of an infantry boot, stuffing a stocking in on top of them. Then for two hours his mind raced like a high-power engine here and there through his life, past and future, through fear and laughter. With a vague, inopportune wish that he were married, he fell into a deep sleep about half past five.

VI

Though the newspaper account of the burglary failed to mention the false teeth, they worried him considerably. The picture of a human waking in the cool dawn and groping for them in vain, of a soft, toothless breakfast, of a strange, hollow, lisping voice calling the police station, of weary, dispirited visits to the dentist, roused a great fatherly pity in him.

Trying to ascertain whether they belonged to a man or a woman, he took them carefully out of the case and held them up near his mouth. He moved his own jaws experimentally; he measured with his fingers; but he failed to decide: they might belong either to a large-mouthed woman or a small-mouthed man.

On a warm impulse he wrapped them in brown paper from the bottom of his army trunk, and printed FALSE TEETH on the package in clumsy pencil letters. Then, the next night, he walked down Philmore Street, and shied the package onto the lawn so that it would be near the door. Next day the paper announced that the police had a clew—they knew that the burglar was in town. However, they didn't mention what the clew was.

VII

At the end of a month "Burglar Bill of the Silver District" was the nurse-girl's standby for frightening children. Five burglaries were attributed to him, but though Dalyrimple had only committed three, he considered that majority had it and appropriated the title to himself. He had once been seen—"a large bloated creature with the meanest face you ever laid eyes on." Mrs. Henry Coleman, awaking at two o'clock at the beam of an electric torch flashed in her eye, could not have been expected to recognize Bryan Dalyrimple at whom she had waved flags last Fourth of July, and whom she had described as "not at all the daredevil type, do you think?"

When Dalyrimple kept his imagination at white heat he managed to glorify his own attitude, his emancipation from petty scruples and remorses—but let him once allow his thought to rove unarmored, great unexpected horrors and depressions would overtake him. Then for reassurance he had to go back to think out the whole thing over again. He found that it was on the whole better to give up considering himself as a rebel. It was more consoling to think of every one else as a fool.

His attitude toward Mr. Macy underwent a change. He no longer felt a dim animosity and inferiority in his presence. As his fourth month in the store ended he found himself regarding his employer in a manner that was almost fraternal. He had a vague but very assured conviction that Mr. Macy's innermost soul would have abetted and approved. He no longer worried about his future. He had the intention of accumulating several thousand dollars and then clearing out—going east, back to France, down to South America. Half a dozen times in the last two months he had been about to stop work, but a fear of attracting attention to his being in funds prevented him. So he worked on, no longer in listlessness, but with contemptuous amusement.

VIII

Then with astounding suddenness something happened that changed his plans and put an end to his burglaries.

Mr. Macy sent for him one afternoon and with a great show of jovial mystery asked him if he had an engagement that night. If he hadn't, would he please call on Mr. Alfred J. Fraser at eight o'clock. Dalyrimple's wonder was mingled with uncertainty. He debated with himself whether it were not his cue to take the first train out of town. But an hour's consideration decided him that his fears were unfounded and at eight o'clock he arrived at the big Fraser house in Philmore Avenue.

Mr. Fraser was commonly supposed to be the biggest political influence in the city. His brother was Senator Fraser, his son-in-law was Congressman Demming, and his influence, though not wielded in such a way as to make him an objectionable boss, was strong nevertheless.

He had a great, huge face, deep-set eyes, and a barn-door of an upper lip, the mélange approaching a worthy climax in a long professional jaw.

During his conversation with Dalyrimple his expression kept starting toward a smile, reached a cheerful optimism, and then receded back to imperturbability.

"How do you do, sir?" he said, holding out his hand. "Sit down. I suppose you're wondering why I wanted you. Sit down."

Dalyrimple sat down.

"Mr. Dalyrimple, how old are you?"

"I'm twenty-three."

"You're young. But that doesn't mean you're foolish. Mr. Dalyrimple, what I've got to say won't take long. I'm going to make you a proposition. To begin at the beginning, I've been watching you ever since last Fourth of July when you made that speech in response to the loving-cup."

Dalyrimple murmured disparagingly, but Fraser waved him to silence.

"It was a speech I've remembered. It was a brainy speech, straight from the shoulder, and it got to everybody in that crowd. I know. I've watched crowds for years." He cleared his throat, as if tempted to digress on his knowledge of crowds—then continued. "But, Mr. Dalyrimple, I've seen too many young men who promised brilliantly go to pieces, fail through want of steadiness, too many high-power ideas, and not enough willingness to work. So I waited. I wanted to see what you'd do. I wanted to see if you'd go to work, and if you'd stick to what you started."

Dalyrimple felt a glow settle over him.

"So," continued Fraser, "when Theron Macy told me you'd started down at his place, I kept watching you, and I followed your record through him. The first month I was afraid for a while. He told me you were getting restless, too good for your job, hinting around for a raise—"

Dalyrimple started.

"—But he said after that you evidently made up your mind to shut up and stick to it. That's the stuff I like in a young man! That's the stuff that wins out. And don't think I don't understand. I know how much harder it was for you, after all that silly flattery a lot of old women had been giving you. I know what a fight it must have been—"

Dalyrimple's face was burning brightly. He felt young and strangely ingenuous.

"Dalyrimple, you've got brains and you've got the stuff in you—and that's what I want. I'm going to put you into the State Senate."

"The *what?*"

"The State Senate. We want a young man who has got brains, but is solid and not a loafer. And when I say State Senate I don't stop there. We're up against it here, Dalyrimple. We've got to get some young men into politics—you know the old blood that's been running on the party ticket year in and year out."

Dalyrimple licked his lips.

"You'll run me for the State Senate?"

"I'll *put* you in the State Senate."

Mr. Fraser's expression had now reached the point nearest a smile and Dalyrimple in a happy frivolity felt himself urging it mentally on—but it stopped, locked, and slid from him. The barn-door and the jaw were separated by a line straight as a nail. Dalyrimple remembered with an effort that it was a mouth, and talked to it.

"But I'm through," he said. "My notoriety's dead. People are fed up with me."

"Those things," answered Mr. Fraser, "are mechanical. Linotype is a resuscitator of reputations. Wait till you see the *Herald*, beginning next week—that is if you're with us—that is," and his voice hardened slightly, "if you haven't got too many ideas yourself about how things ought to be run."

"No," said Dalyrimple, looking him frankly in the eyes. "You'll have to give me a lot of advice at first."

"Very well. I'll take care of your reputation then. Just keep yourself on the right side of the fence."

Dalyrimple started at this repetition of a phrase he had thought of so much lately. There was a sudden ring of the door-bell.

"That's Macy now," observed Fraser, rising. "I'll go let him in. The servants have gone to bed."

He left Dalyrimple there in a dream. The world was opening up suddenly—The State Senate, the United States Senate—so life was this after all—cutting corners—cutting corners—common sense, that was the rule. No more foolish risks now unless necessity called—but it was being hard that counted—Never to let remorse or self-reproach lose him a night's sleep—let his life be a sword of courage—there was no payment—all that was drivel—drivel. He sprang to his feet with clenched hands in a sort of triumph.

"Well, Bryan," said Mr. Macy stepping through the portières.

The two older men smiled their half-smiles at him.

"Well, Bryan," said Mr. Macy again.

Dalyrimple smiled also.

"How do, Mr. Macy?"

He wondered if some telepathy between them had made this new appreciation possible—some invisible realization. . . .

Mr. Macy held out his hand.

"I'm glad we're to be associated in this scheme—I've been for you all along—especially lately. I'm glad we're to be on the same side of the fence."

"I want to thank you, sir," said Dalyrimple simply. He felt a whimsical moisture gathering back of his eyes.

Ernest Hemingway

Ernest Hemingway (1899–1961), born in Oak Park, Illinois, was the son of a doctor whose hobbies were hunting and fishing. After graduating from high school, he obtained the first of a series of newspaper-reporting jobs on the Kansas City Star, *where the training helped to develop his unique style. Rejected by the army, he managed to serve in the First World War as an ambulance driver for the Italian army. His wartime experiences and his own injury served as bases for his early fiction. He achieved fame with* The Sun Also Rises *(1926), and from then to the end of his life, he made no move that failed to attract public attention. After hospitalization for depression in the Mayo Clinic, he committed suicide in Ketchum, Idaho, where he is buried. Of his writing, he said, "I always try to write on the principle of the iceberg. There is seven-eighths of it under water for every part that shows." Hemingway received the Nobel Prize for literature in 1954.* *(See page 64 of Introduction.)*

SOLDIER'S HOME

Krebs went to the war from a Methodist college in Kansas. There is a picture which shows him among his fraternity brothers, all of them wearing exactly the same height and style collar. He enlisted in the Marines in 1917 and did not return to the United States until the second division returned from the Rhine in the summer of 1919.

There is a picture which shows him on the Rhine with two German girls and another corporal. Krebs and the corporal look too big for their uniforms. The German girls are not beautiful. The Rhine does not show in the picture.

By the time Krebs returned to his home town in Oklahoma the greeting of heroes was over. He came back much too late. The men from the town who had been drafted had all been welcomed elaborately on their return. There had been a great deal of hysteria. Now the reaction had set in. People seemed to think it was rather ridiculous for Krebs to be getting back so late, years after the war was over.

At first Krebs, who had been at Belleau Wood, Soissons, the Champagne, St. Mihiel and in the Argonne, did not want to talk about the war at all. Later he felt the need to talk but no one wanted to hear about it. His town had heard too many atrocity stories to be thrilled by actualities. Krebs found that to be listened to at all he had to lie, and after he had done this twice he, too, had a reaction against the war and against talking about it. A distaste for everything that had happened to him in the war set in because of the lies he had told. All of the times that had been able to make him feel cool and clear inside himself when he thought of them; the times so long back when he had done the one thing, the only thing for a man to do, easily and naturally, when he might have done something else, now lost their cool, valuable quality and then were lost themselves.

His lies were quite unimportant lies and consisted in attributing to himself things other men had seen, done or heard of, and stating as facts certain apocryphal incidents familiar to all soldiers. Even his lies were not sensational at the pool room. His acquaintances, who had heard detailed accounts of German women found chained to machine guns in the Argonne forest and who could not comprehend, or were barred by their patriotism from interest in, any German machine gunners who were not chained, were not thrilled by his stories.

Krebs acquired the nausea in regard to experience that is the result of untruth or exaggeration, and when he occasionally met another man who had really been a soldier and they talked a few minutes in the dressing room at a dance he fell into the easy pose of the old soldier among other soldiers: that he had been badly, sickeningly frightened all the time. In this way he lost everything.

During this time, it was late summer, he was sleeping late in bed, getting up to walk down town to the library to get a book, eating lunch at home, reading on the front porch until he became bored and then walking down through the town to spend the hottest hours of the day in the cool dark of the pool room. He loved to play pool.

In the evening he practiced on his clarinet, strolled down town, read and went to bed. He was still a hero to his two young sisters. His mother would have given him breakfast in bed if he had wanted it. She often came in when he was in bed and asked him to tell her about the war, but her attention always wandered. His father was non-committal.

Before Krebs went away to the war he had never been allowed to drive the family motor car. His father was in the real estate business and always wanted the car to be at his command when he required it to take clients out into the country to show them a piece of farm property. The car always stood outside the First National Bank building where his father had an office on the second floor. Now, after the war, it was still the same car.

Nothing was changed in the town except that the young girls had grown up. But they lived in such a complicated world of already defined alliances and shifting feuds that Krebs did not feel the energy or the courage to break into it. He liked to look at them, though. There were so many good-looking young girls. Most of them had their hair cut short. When he went away only little girls wore their hair like that or girls that were fast. They all wore sweaters and shirt waists with round Dutch collars. It was a pattern. He liked to look at them from the front porch as they walked on the other side of the street. He liked to watch them walking under the shade of the trees. He liked the round Dutch collars above their sweaters. He liked their silk stockings and flat shoes. He like their bobbed hair and the way they walked.

When he was in town their appeal to him was not very strong. He did not like them when he saw them in the Greek's ice cream parlor. He did not want them themselves really. They were too complicated. There was something else. Vaguely he wanted a girl but he did not want to have to work to get her. He would have liked to have a girl but he did not want to have to spend a long time getting her. He did not want to get into the intrigue and the politics. He did not want to have to do any courting. He did not want to tell any more lies. It wasn't worth it.

He did not want any consequences. He did not want any consequences ever again. He wanted to live along without consequences. Besides he did not really need a girl. The army had taught him that. It was all right to pose as though you had to have a girl. Nearly everybody did that. But it wasn't true. You did not need a girl. That was the funny thing. First a fellow boasted how girls mean nothing to him, that he never thought of them, that they could not touch him. Then a fellow boasted that he could not get along without girls, that he had to have them all the time, that he could not go to sleep without them.

That was all a lie. It was all a lie both ways. You did not need a girl unless you thought about them. He learned that in the army. Then sooner or later you always got one. When you were really ripe for a girl you always got one. You did not have to think about it. Sooner or later it would come. He had learned that in the army.

Now he would have liked a girl if she had come to him and not wanted to talk. But here at home it was all too complicated. He knew he could never get through it all again. It was not worth the trouble. That was the thing about French girls and German girls. There was not all this talking. You couldn't talk much and you did not need to talk. It was simple and you were friends. He thought about France and then he began to think about Germany. On the whole he had liked Germany better. He did not want to leave Germany. He did not want to come home. Still, he had come home. He sat on the front porch.

He liked the girls that were walking along the other side of the street. He liked the look of them much better than the French girls or the German girls. But the world they were in was not the world he was in. He would like to have one of them. But it was not worth it. They were such a nice pattern. He liked the pattern. It was exciting. But he would not go through all the talking. He did not want one badly enough. He liked to look at them all, though. It was not worth it. Not now when things were getting good again.

He sat there on the porch reading a book on the war. It was a history and he was reading about all the engagements he had been in. It was the most interesting reading he had ever done. He wished there were more maps. He looked forward with a good feeling to reading all the really good histories when they would come out with good detail maps. Now he was really learning about the war. He had been a good soldier. That made a difference.

One morning after he had been home about a month his mother came into his bedroom and sat on the bed. She smoothed her apron.

"I had a talk with your father last night, Harold," she said, "and he is willing for you to take the car out in the evenings."

"Yeah?" said Krebs, who was not fully awake. "Take the car out? Yeah?"

"Yes. Your father has felt for some time that you should be able to take the car out in the evenings whenever you wished but we only talked it over last night."

"I'll bet you made him," Krebs said.

"No. It was your father's suggestion that we talk the matter over."

"Yeah. I'll bet you made him," Krebs sat up in bed.

"Will you come down to breakfast, Harold?" his mother said.

"As soon as I get my clothes on," Krebs said.

His mother went out of the room and he could hear her frying something downstairs while he washed, shaved and dressed to go down into the dining-room for breakfast. While he was eating breakfast his sister brought in the mail.

"Well, Hare," she said. "You old sleepyhead. What do you ever get up for?"

Krebs looked at her. He liked her. She was his best sister.

"Have you got the paper?" he asked.

She handed him the Kansas City *Star* and he shucked off its brown wrapper and opened it to the sporting page. He folded the *Star* open and propped it against the water pitcher with his cereal dish to steady it, so he could read while he ate.

"Harold," his mother stood in the kitchen doorway, "Harold, please don't muss up the paper. Your father can't read his *Star* if it's been mussed."

"I won't muss it," Krebs said.

His sister sat down at the table and watched him while he read.

"We're playing indoor over at school this afternoon," she said. "I'm going to pitch."

"Good," said Krebs. "How's the old wing?"

"I can pitch better than lots of the boys. I tell them all you taught me. The other girls aren't much good."

"Yeah?" said Krebs.

"I tell them all you're my beau. Aren't you my beau, Hare?"

"You bet."

"Couldn't your brother really be your beau just because he's your brother?"

"I don't know."

"Sure you know. Couldn't you be my beau, Hare, if I was old enough and if you wanted to?"

"Sure. You're my girl now."

"Am I really your girl?"

"Sure."

"Do you love me?"

"Uh, huh."

"Will you love me always?"

"Sure."

"Will you come over and watch me play indoor?"

"Maybe."

"Aw, Hare, you don't love me. If you loved me, you'd want to come over and watch me play indoor."

Krebs' mother came into the dining-room from the kitchen. She carried a plate with two fried eggs and some crisp bacon on it and a plate of buckwheat cakes.

"You run along, Helen," she said. "I want to talk to Harold."

She put the eggs and bacon down in front of him and brought in a jug of maple syrup for the buckwheat cakes. Then she sat down across the table from Krebs.

"I wish you'd put down the paper a minute, Harold," she said.

Krebs took down the paper and folded it.

"Have you decided what you are going to do yet, Harold?" his mother said, taking off her glasses.

"No," said Krebs.

"Don't you think it's about time?" His mother did not say this in a mean way. She seemed worried.

"I hadn't thought about it," Krebs said.

"God has some work for everyone to do," his mother said. "There can be no idle hands in His Kingdom."

"I'm not in His Kingdom," Krebs said.

"We are all of us in His Kingdom."

Krebs felt embarrassed and resentful as always.

"I've worried about you so much, Harold," his mother went on. "I know the temptations you must have been exposed to. I know how weak men are. I know what your own dear grandfather, my own father, told us about the Civil War and I have prayed for you. I pray for you all day long, Harold."

Krebs looked at the bacon fat hardening on his plate.

"Your father is worried, too," his mother went on. "He thinks you have lost your ambition, that you haven't got a definite aim in life. Charley Simmons, who is just your age, has a good job and is going to be married. The boys are all settling down; they're all determined to get somewhere; you can see that boys like Charley Simmons are on their way to being really a credit to the community."

Krebs said nothing.

"Don't look that way, Harold," his mother said. "You know we love you and I want to tell you for your own good how matters stand. Your father does not want to hamper your freedom. He thinks you should be allowed to drive the car. If you want to take some of the nice girls out riding with you, we are only too pleased. We want you to enjoy yourself. But you are going to have to settle down to work, Harold. Your father doesn't care what you start in at. All work is honorable as he says. But you've got to make a start at something. He asked me to speak to you this morning and then you can stop in and see him at his office."

"Is that all?" Krebs said.

"Yes. Don't you love your mother, dear boy?"

"No," Krebs said.

His mother looked at him across the table. Her eyes were shiny. She started crying.

"I don't love anybody," Krebs said.

It wasn't any good. He couldn't tell her, he couldn't make her see it. It was silly to have said it. He had only hurt her. He went over and took hold of her arm. She was crying with her head in her hands.

"I didn't mean it," he said. "I was just angry at something. I didn't mean I didn't love you."

His mother went on crying. Krebs put his arm on her shoulder.

"Can't you believe me, mother?"

His mother shook her head.

"Please, please, mother. Please believe me."

"All right," his mother said chokily. She looked up at him. "I believe you, Harold."

Krebs kissed her hair. She put her face up to him.

"I'm your mother," she said. "I held you next to my heart when you were a tiny baby."

Krebs felt sick and vaguely nauseated.

"I know, Mummy," he said. "I'll try and be a good boy for you."

"Would you kneel and pray with me, Harold?" his mother asked.

They knelt down beside the dining-room table and Krebs's mother prayed.

"Now, you pray, Harold," she said.

"I can't," Krebs said.

"Try, Harold."

"I can't."

"Do you want me to pray for you?"

"Yes."

So his mother prayed for him and then they stood up and Krebs kissed his mother and went out of the house. He had tried so to keep his life from being complicated. Still, none of it had touched him. He had felt sorry for his mother and she had made him lie. He would go to Kansas City and get a job and she would feel all right about it. There would be one more scene maybe before he got away. He would not go down to his father's office. He would miss that one. He wanted his life to go smoothly. It had just gotten going that way. Well, that was all over now, anyway. He would go over to the schoolyard and watch Helen play indoor baseball.

D. H. Lawrence

D. H. Lawrence (1885–1930), English novelist, was born in a village in Nottinghamshire, where his father worked as a coal miner and his mother was a school teacher. Through the influence of his ambitious mother, he developed an early interest in literature. When his first novel, The White Peacock *(1911), was published, he gave up teaching at an elementary school in order to devote himself to writing. He married divorcee Frieda von Richthofen in 1914, and began a series of travels in Europe, Asia, Australia, and America, where he lived for some years before his death. Lawrence's work deals with the relationship between an individual's inner emotional life and its mystical connection with the physical world. Many of his novels and short stories are concerned with the necessity for readjustment in sexual relationships. Among his major works are the autobiographical novel* Sons and Lovers *(1913),* The Rainbow *(1915),* Women in Love *(1920), and* Lady Chatterley's Lover *(1928).* *(See page 76 of Introduction.)*

THE MAN WHO LOVED ISLANDS

I

There was a man who loved islands. He was born on one, but it didn't suit him, as there were too many other people on it, besides himself. He wanted an island all of his own: not necessarily to be alone on it, but to make it a world of his own.

An island, if it is big enough, is no better than a continent. It has to be really quite small, before it *feels* like an island; and this story will show how tiny it has to be, before you can presume to fill it with your own personality.

Now circumstances so worked out that this lover of islands, by the time he was thirty-five, actually acquired an island of his own. He didn't own it as freehold property, but he had a ninety-nine years' lease of it, which, as far as a man and an island are concerned, is as good as everlasting. Since, if you are like Abraham, and want your offspring to be numberless as the sands of the sea-shore, you don't choose an island to start breeding on. Too soon there would be overpopulation, overcrowding, and slum conditions. Which is a horrid thought, for one who loves an island for its insulation. No, an island is a nest which holds one egg, and one only. This egg is the islander himself.

The island acquired by our potential islander was not in the remote oceans. It was quite near at home, no palm trees nor boom of surf on the reef, nor any of that kind of thing; but a good solid dwelling-house, rather gloomy, above the landing-place, and beyond, a small farmhouse with sheds, and a few outlying fields. Down on the little landing-bay were three cottages in a row, like coastguards' cottages, all neat and whitewashed.

What could be more cosy and home-like? It was four miles if you walked all around your island, through the gorse and the blackthorn bushes, above the steep rocks of the sea and down in the little glades where the primroses grew. If you walked straight over the two humps of hills, the length of it, through the rocky fields where the cows lay chewing, and through the rather sparse oats, on into the gorse again, and so to the low cliffs' edge, it took you only twenty minutes. And when you came to the edge, you could see another, bigger island lying beyond. But the sea was between you and it. And as you returned over the turf where the short, downland cowslips nodded, you saw to the east still another island, a tiny one this time, like the calf of the cow. This tiny island also belonged to the islander.

Thus it seems that even islands like to keep each other company.

Our islander loved his island very much. In early spring, the little ways and glades were a snow of blackthorn, a vivid white among the Celtic stillness of close green and grey rock, blackbirds calling out in the whiteness their first long, triumphant calls. After the blackthorn and the nestling primroses came the blue apparition of hyacinths, like elfin lakes and slipping sheets of blue, among the bushes and under the glade of trees. And many birds with nests you could peep into, on the island all your own. Wonderful what a great world it was!

Followed summer, and the cowslips gone, the wild roses faintly fragrant through the haze. There was a field of hay, the foxgloves stood looking down. In a little cove, the sun was on the pale granite where you bathed, and the shadow was in the rocks. Before the mist came stealing, you went home through the ripening oats, the glare of the sea fading from the high air as the fog-horn started to moo on the other island. And then the sea-fog went, it was autumn, the oat-sheaves lying prone, the great moon, another island, rose golden out of the sea, and rising higher, the world of the sea was white.

So autumn ended with rain, and winter came, dark skies and dampness and rain, but rarely frost. The island, your island, cowered dark, holding away from you. You could feel, down in the wet, sombre hollows, the resentful spirit coiled upon itself, like a wet dog coiled in gloom, or a snake that is neither asleep nor awake. Then in the night, when the wind left off blowing in great gusts and volleys, as at sea, you felt that your island was a universe, infinite and old as the darkness; not an island at all, but an infinite dark world where all the souls from all the other bygone nights lived on, and the infinite distance was near.

Strangely, from your little island in space, you were gone forth into the dark, great realms of time, where all the souls that never die veer and swoop on their vast, strange errands. The little earthly island has dwindled, like a jumping-off place, into nothingness, for you have jumped off, you know not how, into the dark wide mystery of time, where the past is vastly alive, and the future is not separated off.

This is the danger of becoming an islander. When, in the city, you wear your white spats and dodge the traffic with the fear of death down your spine, then you are quite safe from the terrors of infinite time. The moment is your little islet in time, it is the spatial universe that careers round you.

But once isolate yourself on a little island in the sea of space, and the moment begins to heave and expand in great circles, the solid earth is gone, and your slippery, naked dark soul finds herself out in the timeless world, where the chariots of the so-called dead dash down the old streets of centuries, and souls crowd on the footways that we, in the moment, call bygone years. The souls of all the dead are alive again, and pulsating actively around you. You are out in the other infinity.

Something of this happened to our islander. Mysterious "feelings" came upon him that he wasn't used to; strange awareness of old, far-gone men, and other influences; men of Gaul, with big moustaches, who had been on his island, and had vanished from the face of it, but not out of the air of night. They were there still, hurtling their big, violent, unseen bodies through the night. And there were priests, with golden knives and mistletoe; then other priests with a crucifix; then pirates with murder on the sea.

Our islander was uneasy. He didn't believe, in the day-time, in any of this nonsense. But at night it just was so. He had reduced himself to a single point in space, and, a point being that which has neither length nor breath, he had to step off it into somewhere else. Just as you must step into the sea, if the waters wash your foothold away, so he had, at night, to step off into the other worlds of undying time.

He was uncannily aware, as he lay in the dark, that the blackthorn grove that seemed a bit uncanny even in the realm of space and day, at night was crying with old men of an invisible race, around the altar stone. What was a ruin under the hornbeam trees by day, was a moaning of blood-stained priests with crucifixes, on the ineffable night. What was a cave and a hidden beach between coarse rocks, became in the invisible dark the purple-lipped imprecation of pirates.

To escape any more of this sort of awareness, our islander daily concentrated upon his material island. Why should it not be the Happy Isle at last? Why not the last small isle of the Hesperides, the perfect place, all filled with his own gracious, blossom-like spirit? A minute world of pure perfection, made by man himself.

He began, as we begin all our attempts to regain Paradise, by spending money. The old, semi-feudal dwelling-house he restored, let in more light, put clear lovely carpets on the floor, clear, flower-petal curtains at the sullen windows, and wines in the cellars of rock. He brought over a buxom housekeeper from the world, and a soft-spoken, much-experienced butler. These two were to be islanders.

In the farmhouse he put a bailiff, with two farm-hands. There were Jersey cows, tinkling a slow bell, among the gorse. There was a call to meals at midday, and the peaceful smoking of chimneys at evening, when rest descended.

A jaunty sailing-boat with a motor accessory rode in the shelter in the bay, just below the row of three white cottages. There was also a little yawl, and two row-boats drawn up on the sand. A fishing-net was drying on its supports, a boatload of new white planks stood criss-cross, a woman was going to the well with a bucket.

In the end cottage lived the skipper of the yacht, and his wife and son. He was a man from the other, large island, at home on this sea. Every fine day he went out fishing, with his son, every fair day there was fresh fish in the island.

In the middle cottage lived an old man and wife, a very faithful couple. The old man was a carpenter, and man of many jobs. He was always working, always the sound of his plane or his saw; lost in his work, he was another kind of islander.

In the third cottage was a mason, a widower with a son and two daughters. With the help of his boy, this man dug ditches and built fences, raised buttresses and erected a new out-building, and hewed stone from the little quarry. One daughter worked at the big house.

It was a quiet, busy little world. When the islander brought you over as his guest, you met first the dark-bearded, thin, smiling skipper, Arnold, then his boy Charles. At the house, the smooth-lipped butler who had lived all over the world valeted you, and created that curious creamy-smooth, disarming sense of luxury around you which only a perfect and rather untrustworthy servant can create. He disarmed you and had you at his mercy. The buxom housekeeper smiled and treated you with the subtly respectful familiarity that is only dealt out to the true gentry. And the rosy maid threw a glance at you, as if you were very wonderful, coming from the great outer world. Then you met the smiling but watchful bailiff, who came from Cornwall, and the shy farm-hand from Berkshire, with his clean wife and two little children: then the rather sulky farm-hand from Suffolk. The mason, a Kent man, would talk to you by the yard if you let him. Only the old carpenter was gruff and elsewhere absorbed.

Well then, it was a little world to itself, and everybody feeling very safe, and being very nice to you, as if you were really something special. But it was the islander's world, not yours. He was the Master. The special smile, the special attention was to the Master. They all knew how well off they were. So the islander was no longer Mr. So-and-so. To everyone on the island, even to you yourself, he was "the Master."

Well, it was ideal. The Master was no tyrant. Ah, no! He was a delicate, sensitive, handsome Master, who wanted everything perfect and everybody happy. Himself, of course, to be the fount of this happiness and perfection.

But in his way, he was a poet. He treated his guests royally, his servants liberally. Yet he was shrewd, and very wise. He never came the boss over his people. Yet he kept his eye on everything, like a shrewd, blue-eyed young Hermes. And it was amazing what a lot of knowledge he had at hand. Amazing what he knew about Jersey cows, and cheese-making, ditching and fencing, flowers and gardening, ships and the sailing of ships. He was a fount of knowledge about everything, and this knowledge he imparted to his people in an odd, half-ironical, half-portentous fashion, as if he really belonged to the quaint, half-real world of the gods.

They listened to him with their hats in their hands. He loved white clothes; or creamy white; and cloaks, and broad hats. So, in fine weather, the bailiff would see the elegant tall figure in creamy-white serge coming like some bird over the fallow, to look at the weeding of the turnips. Then there would be a doffing of hats, and a few minutes of whimsical, shrewd, wise talk, to which the bailiff answered admiringly, and the farm-hands listened in silent wonder, leaning on their hoes. The bailiff was almost tender, to the Master.

Or, on a windy morning, he would stand with his cloak blowing in the sticky sea-wind, on the edge of the ditch that was being dug to drain a little swamp, talking in the teeth of the wind to the man below, who looked up at him with steady and inscrutable eyes.

Or at evening in the rain he would be seen hurrying across the yard, the broad hat turned against the rain. And the farm-wife would hurriedly exclaim: "The Master! Get up, John, and clear him a place on the sofa." And then the door opened, and it was a cry of: "Why, of all things, if it isn't the Master! Why, have ye turned out then, of a night like this, to come across to the like of we?" And the bailiff took his cloak, and the farm-wife his hat, the two farm-hands drew their chairs to the back, he sat on the sofa and took a child up near him. He was wonderful with children, talked to them simply wonderful, made you think of Our Saviour Himself, said the woman.

He was always greeted with smiles, and the same peculiar deference, as if he were a higher, but also frailer being. They handled him almost tenderly, and almost with adulation. But when he left, or when they spoke of him, they had often a subtle, mocking smile on their faces. There was no need to be afraid of "the Master." Just let him have his own way. Only the old carpenter was sometimes sincerely rude to him; so he didn't care for the old man.

It is doubtful whether any of them really liked him, man to man, or even woman to man. But then it is doubtful if he really liked any of them, as man to man, or man to woman. He wanted them to be happy, and the little world to be perfect. But anyone who wants the world to be perfect must be careful not to have real likes or dislikes. A general goodwill is all you can afford.

The sad fact is, alas, that general goodwill is always felt as something of an insult, by the mere object of it; and so it breeds a quite special brand of malice. Surely general goodwill is a form of egoism, that it should have such a result!

Our islander, however, had his own resources. He spent long hours in his library, for he was compiling a book of references to all the flowers mentioned in the Greek and Latin authors. He was not a great classical scholar; the usual public-school equipment. But there are such excellent translations nowadays. And it was so lovely, tracing flower after flower as it blossomed in the ancient world.

So the first year on the island passed by. A great deal had been done. Now the bills flooded in, and the Master, conscientious in all things, began to study them. The study left him pale and breathless. He was not a rich man. He knew he had been making a hole in his capital to get the island into running order. When he came to look, however, there was hardly anything left but hole. Thousands and thousands of pounds had the island swallowed into nothingness.

But surely the bulk of the spending was over! Surely the island would now begin to be self-supporting, even if it made no profit! Surely he was safe. He paid a good many of the bills, and took a little heart. But he had had a shock, and the next year, the coming year, there must be economy, frugality. He told his people so in simple and touching language. And they said: "Why, surely! Surely!"

So, while the wind blew and the rain lashed outside, he would sit in his library with the bailiff over a pipe and pot of beer, discussing farm projects. He lifted his narrow, handsome face, and his blue eyes became dreamy. "*What* a wind!" It blew like cannon-shots. He thought of his island, lashed with foam, and inaccessible, and he exulted. . . . No, he must not lose it. He turned back to the farm projects with the zest of genius, and his hands flicked white emphasis, while the bailiff intoned: "Yes, sir! Yes, sir! You're right, Master!"

But the man was hardly listening. He was looking at the Master's blue lawn shirt and curious pink tie with the fiery red stone, at the enamel sleeve-links, and at the ring with the peculiar scarab. The brown, searching eyes of the man of the soil glanced repeatedly over the fine, immaculate figure of the Master, with a sort of slow, calculating wonder. But if he happened to catch the Master's bright, exalted glance, his own eye lit up with a careful cordiality and deference, as he bowed his head slightly.

Thus between them they decided what crops should be sown, what fertilizers should be used in different places, which breed of pigs should be imported, and which line of turkeys. That is to say, the bailiff, by continually cautiously agreeing with the Master, kept out of it, and let the young man have his own way.

The Master knew what he was talking about. He was brilliant at grasping the gist of a book, and knowing how to apply his knowledge. On the whole, his ideas were sound. The bailiff even knew it. But in the man of the soil there was no answering enthusiasm. The brown eyes smiled their cordial deference, but the thin lips never changed. The Master pursed his own flexible mouth in a boyish versatility, as he cleverly sketched in his ideas to the other man, and the bailiff made eyes of admiration, but in his heart he was not attending, he was only watching the Master as he would have watched a queer, caged animal, quite without sympathy, not implicated.

So, it was settled, and the Master rang for Elvery, the butler, to bring a sandwich. He, the Master, was pleased. The butler saw it, and came back with anchovy and ham sandwiches, and a newly opened bottle of vermouth. There was always a newly opened bottle of something.

It was the same with the mason. The Master and he discussed the drainage of a bit of land, and more pipes were ordered, more special bricks, more this, more that.

Fine weather came at last; there was a little lull in the hard work on the island. The Master went for a short cruise in his yacht. It was not really a yacht, just a little bit of a thing. They sailed along the coast of the mainland, and put in at the ports. At every port some friend turned up, the butler made elegant little meals in the cabin. Then the Master was invited to villas and hotels, his people disembarked him as if he were a prince.

And oh, how expensive it turned out! He had to telegraph to the bank for money. And he went home again to economise.

The marsh-marigolds were blazing in the little swamp where the ditches were being dug for drainage. He almost regretted, now, the work in hand. The yellow beauties would not blaze again.

Harvest came, and a bumper crop. There must be a harvest-home supper. The long barn was now completely restored and added to. The carpenter had made long tables. Lanterns hung from the beams of the high-pitched roof. All the people of the island were assembled. The bailiff presided. It was a gay scene.

Towards the end of the supper the Master, in a velvet jacket, appeared with his guests. Then the bailiff rose and proposed "The Master! Long life and health to the Master!" All the people drank the health with great enthusiasm and cheering. The Master replied with a little speech: They were on an island in a little world of their own. It depended on them all to make this world a world of true happiness and content. Each must do his part. He hoped he himself did what he could, for his heart was in his island, and with the people of his island.

The butler responded: As long as the island had such a Master, it could not help but be a little heaven for all the people on it. This was seconded with virile warmth by the bailiff and the mason, the skipper was beside himself. Then there was dancing, the old carpenter was fiddler.

But under all this, things were not well. The very next morning came the farm-boy to say that a cow had fallen over the cliff. The Master went to look. He peered over the not very high declivity, and saw her lying dead on a green ledge under a bit of late-flowering broom. A beautiful, expensive creature, already looking swollen. But what a fool, to fall so unnecessarily!

It was a question of getting several men to haul her up the bank, and then of skinning and burying her. No one would eat the meat. How repulsive it all was!

This was symbolic of the island. As sure as the spirits rose in the human breast, with a movement of joy, an invisible hand struck malevolently out of the silence. There must not be any joy, nor even any quiet peace. A man broke a leg, another was crippled with rheumatic fever. The pigs had some strange disease. A storm drove the yacht on a rock. The mason hated the butler, and refused to let his daughter serve at the house.

Out of the very air came a stony, heavy malevolence. The island itself seemed malicious. It would go on being hurtful and evil for weeks at a time. Then suddenly again one morning it would be fair, lovely as a morning in Paradise, everything beautiful and flowing. And everybody would begin to feel a great relief, and a hope for happiness.

Then as soon as the Master was opened out in spirit like an open flower, some ugly blow would fall. Somebody would send him an anonymous note, accusing some other person on the island. Somebody else would come hinting things against one of his servants.

"Some folks think they've got an easy job out here, with all the pickings they make!" the mason's daughter screamed at the suave butler, in the Master's hearing. He pretended not to hear.

"My man says this island is surely one of the lean kine of Egypt, it would swallow a sight of money, and you'd never get anything back out of it," confided the farm-hand's wife to one of the Master's visitors.

The people were not contented. They were not islanders. "We feel we're not doing right by the children," said those who had children. "We feel we're not doing right by ourselves," said those who had no children. And the various families fairly came to hate one another.

Yet the island was so lovely. When there was a scent of honeysuckle and the moon brightly flickering down on the sea, then even the grumblers felt a strange nostalgia for it. It set you yearning, with a wild yearning; perhaps for the past, to be far back in the mysterious past of the island, when the blood had a different throb. Strange floods of passion came over you, strange violent lusts and imaginations of cruelty. The blood and the passion and the lust which the island had known. Uncanny dreams, half-dreams, half-evocated yearnings.

The Master himself began to be a little afraid of his island. He felt here strange, violent feelings he had never felt before, and lustful desires that he had been quite free from. He knew quite well now that his people didn't love him at all. He knew that their spirits were secretly against him, malicious, jeering, envious, and lurking to down him. He became just as wary and secretive with regard to them.

But it was too much. At the end of the second year, several departures took place. The housekeeper went. The Master always blamed self-important women most. The mason said he wasn't going to be monkeyed about any more, so he took his departure, with his family. The rheumatic farm-hand left.

And then the year's bills came in, the Master made up his accounts. In spite of good crops, the assets were ridiculous, against the spending. The island had again lost, not hundreds but thousands of pounds. It was incredible. But you simply couldn't believe it! Where had it all gone?

The Master spent gloomy nights and days going through accounts in the library. He was thorough. It became evident, now the housekeeper had gone, that she had swindled him. Probably everybody was swindling him. But he hated to think it, so he put the thought away.

He emerged, however, pale and hollow-eyed from his balancing of unbalanceable accounts, looking as if something had kicked him in the stomach. It was pitiable. But the money had gone, and there was an end of it. Another great hole in his capital. How could people be so heartless?

It couldn't go on, that was evident. He would soon be bankrupt. He had to give regretful notice to his butler. He was afraid to find out how much his butler had swindled him. Because the man was such a wonderful butler, after all. And the farm bailiff had to go. The Master had no regrets in that quarter. The losses on the farm had almost embittered him.

The third year was spent in rigid cutting down of expenses. The island was still mysterious and fascinating. But it was also treacherous and cruel, secretly, fathomlessly malevolent. In spite of all its fair show of white blossom and bluebells, and the lovely dignity of foxgloves bending their rose-red bells, it was your implacable enemy.

With reduced staff, reduced wages, reduced splendour, the third year went by. But it was fighting against hope. The farm still lost a good deal. And once more there was a hole in that remnant of capital. Another hole in that which was already a mere remnant round the old holes. The island was mysterious in this also: it seemed to pick the very money out of your pocket, as if it were an octopus with invisible arms stealing from you in every direction.

Yet the Master still loved it. But with a touch of rancour now.

He spent, however, the second half of the fourth year intensely working on the mainland, to be rid of it. And it was amazing how difficult he found it, to dispose of an island. He had thought that everybody was pining for such an island as his; but not at all. Nobody would pay any price for it. And he wanted now to get rid of it, as a man who wants a divorce at any cost.

It was not till the middle of the fifth year that he transferred it, at a considerable loss to himself, to an hotel company who were willing to speculate in it. They were to turn it into a handy honeymoon-and-golf island.

There, take that, island which didn't know when it was well off. Now be a honeymoon-and-golf island!

II

THE SECOND ISLAND

The islander had to move. But he was not going to the mainland. Oh, no! He moved to the smaller island, which still belonged to him. And he took with him the faithful old carpenter and wife, the couple he never really cared for; also a widow and daughter, who had kept house for him the last year; also an orphan lad, to help the old man.

The small island was very small; but being a hump of rock in the sea, it was bigger than it looked. There was a little track among the rocks and bushes, winding and scrambling up and down around the islet, so that it took you twenty minutes to do the circuit. It was more than you would have expected.

Still, it was an island. The islander moved himself, with all his books, into the commonplace six-roomed house up to which you had to scramble from the rocky landing-place. There were also two joined-together cottages. The old carpenter lived in one, with his wife and the lad, the widow and daughter lived in the other.

At last all was in order. The Master's books filled two rooms. It was already autumn, Orion lifting out of the sea. And in the dark nights, the Master could see the lights on his late island, where the hotel company were entertaining guests who would advertise the new resort for honeymoon-golfers.

On his lump of rock, however, the Master was still master. He explored the crannies, the odd hand-breadths of grassy level, the steep little cliffs where the last harebells hung and the seeds of summer were brown above the sea, lonely and untouched. He peered down the old well. He examined the stone pen where the pig had been kept. Himself, he had a goat.

Yes, it was an island. Always, always underneath among the rocks the Celtic sea sucked and washed and smote its feathery greyness. How many different noises of the sea! Deep explosions, rumblings, strange long sighs and whistling noises; then voices, real voices of people clamouring as if they were in a market, under the waters: and again, the far-off ringing of a bell, surely an actual bell! Then a tremendous trilling noise, very long and alarming, and an undertone of hoarse gasping.

On this island there were no human ghosts, no ghosts of any ancient race. The sea, and the spume and the weather, had washed them all out, washed them out so there was only the sound of the sea itself, its own ghost, myriad-voiced, communing and plotting and shouting all winter long. And only the smell of the sea, with a few bristly bushes of gorse and coarse tufts of heather, among the grey, pellucid rocks, in the grey, more-pellucid air. The coldness, the greyness, even the soft, creeping fog of the sea, and the islet of rock humped up in it all, like the last point in space.

Green star Sirius stood over the sea's rim. The island was a shadow. Out at sea a ship showed small lights. Below, in the rocky cove, the row-boat and the motor-boat were safe. A light shone in the carpenter's kitchen. That was all.

Save, of course, that the lamp was lit in the house, where the widow was preparing supper, her daughter helping. The islander went in to his meal. Here he was no longer the Master, he was an islander again and he had peace. The old carpenter, the widow and daughter were all faithfulness itself. The old man worked while ever there was light to see, because he had a passion for work. The widow and her quiet, rather delicate daughter of thirty-three worked for the Master, because they loved looking after him, and they were infinitely grateful for the haven he provided them. But they didn't call him "the Master." They gave him his name: "Mr. Cathcart, sir!" softly and reverently. And he spoke back to them also softly, gently, like people far from the world, afraid to make a noise.

The island was no longer a "world." It was a sort of refuge. The islander no longer struggled for anything. He had no need. It was as if he and his few dependants were a small flock of sea-birds alighted on this rock, as they travelled through space, and keeping together without a word. The silent mystery of travelling birds.

He spent most of his day in his study. His book was coming along. The widow's daughter could type out his manuscript for him, she was not uneducated. It was the one strange sound on the island, the typewriter. But soon even its spattering fitted in with the sea's noises, and the wind's.

The months went by. The islander worked away in his study, the people of the island went quietly about their concerns. The goat had a little black kid with yellow eyes. There were mackerel in the sea. The old man went fishing in the row-boat with the lad, when the weather was calm enough; they went off in the motor-boat to the biggest island for the post. And they brought supplies, never a penny wasted. And the days went by, and the nights, without desire, without ennui.

The strange stillness from all desire was a kind of wonder to the islander. He didn't want anything. His soul at last was still in him, his spirit was like a dim-lit cave under water, where strange sea-foliage expands upon the watery atmosphere, and scarcely sways, and a mute fish shadowily slips in and slips away again. All still and soft and uncrying, yet alive as rooted seaweed is alive.

The islander said to himself: "Is this happiness?" He said to himself: "I am turned into a dream. I feel nothing, or I don't know what I feel. Yet it seems to me I am happy."

Only he had to have something upon which his mental activity could work. So he spent long, silent hours in his study, working not very fast, nor very importantly, letting the writing spin softly from him as if it were drowsy gossamer. He no longer fretted whether it were good or not, what he produced. He slowly, softly spun it like gossamer, and if it were to melt away as gossamer in autumn melts, he would not mind. It was only the soft evanescence of gossamy things which now seemed to him permanent. The very mist of eternity was in them. Whereas stone buildings, cathedrals for example, seemed to him to howl with temporary resistance, knowing they must fall at last; the tension of their long endurance seemed to howl forth from them all the time.

Sometimes he went to the mainland and to the city. Then he went elegantly, dressed in the latest style, to his club. He sat in a stall at the theatre, he shopped in Bond Street. He discussed terms for publishing his book. But over his face was that gossamy look of having dropped out of the race of progress, which made the vulgar city people feel they had won it over him, and made him glad to go back to his island.

He didn't mind if he never published his book. The years were blending into a soft mist, from which nothing obtruded. Spring came. There was never a primrose on his island, but he found a winter-aconite. There were two little sprayed bushes of blackthorn, and some wind-flowers. He began to make a list of the flowers of his islet, and that was absorbing. He noted a wild currant bush and watched for the elder flowers on a stunted little tree, then for the first yellow rags of the broom, and wild roses. Bladder campion, orchids, stitchwort, celandine, he was prouder of them than if they had been people on his island. When he came across the golden saxifrage, so inconspicuous in a damp corner, he crouched over it in a trance, he knew not for how long, looking at it. Yet it was nothing to look at. As the widow's daughter found, when he showed it her.

He had said to her in real triumph:

"I found the golden saxifrage this morning."

The name sounded splendid. She looked at him with fascinated brown eyes, in which was a hollow ache that frightened him a little.

"Did you, sir? Is it a nice flower?"

He pursed his lips and tilted his brows.

"Well—not showy exactly. I'll show it you if you like."

"I should like to see it."

She was so quiet, so wistful. But he sensed in her a persistency which made him uneasy. She said she was so happy: really happy. She followed him quietly, like a shadow, on the rocky track where there was never room for two people to walk side by side. He went first, and could feel her there, immediately behind him, following so submissively, gloating on him from behind.

It was a kind of pity for her which made him become her lover: though he never realised the extent of the power she had gained over him, and how *she* willed it. But the moment he had fallen, a jangling feeling came upon him, that it was all wrong. He felt a nervous dislike of her. He had not wanted it. And it seemed to him, as far as her physical self went, she had not wanted it either. It was just her will. He went away, and climbed at the risk of his neck down to a ledge near the sea. There he sat for hours, gazing all jangled at the sea, and saying miserably to himself: "We didn't want it. We didn't really want it."

It was the automatism of sex that had caught him again. Not that he hated sex. He deemed it, as the Chinese do, one of the great life-mysteries. But it had become mechanical, automatic, and he wanted to escape that. Automatic sex shattered him, and filled him with a sort of death. He thought he had come through, to a new stillness of desirelessness. Perhaps beyond that there was a new fresh delicacy of desire, an unentered frail communion of two people meeting on untrodden ground.

Be that as it might, this was not it. This was nothing new or fresh. It was automatic, and driven from the will. Even she, in her true self, hadn't wanted it. It was automatic in her.

When he came home, very late, and saw her face white with fear and apprehension of his feeling against her, he pitied her, and spoke to her delicately, reassuringly. But he kept himself remote from her.

She gave no sign. She served him with the same silence, the same hidden hunger to serve him, to be near where he was. He felt her love following him, to be near where he was. He felt her love following him with strange, awful persistency. She claimed nothing. Yet now, when he met her bright, brown, curiously vacant eyes, he saw in them the mute question. The question came direct at him, with a force and a power of will he never realised.

So he succumbed, and asked her again.

"Not," she said, "if it will make you hate me."

"Why should it?" he replied, nettled. "Of course not."

"You know I would do anything on earth for you."

It was only afterwards, in his exasperation, he remembered what she said, and was more exasperated. Why should she pretend to do this *for him?* Why not herself? But in his exasperation, he drove himself deeper in. In order to achieve some sort of satisfaction, which he never did achieve, he abandoned himself to her. Everybody on the island knew. But he did not care.

Then even what desire he had left him, and he felt only shattered. He felt that only with her will had she wanted him. Now he was shattered and full of self-contempt. His island was smirched and spoiled. He had lost his place in the rare, desireless levels of Time to which he had at last arrived, and he had fallen right back. If only it had been true, delicate desire between them, and a delicate meeting on the third rare place where a man might meet a woman, when they were both true to the frail, sensitive, crocus-flame of desire in them. But it had been no such thing: automatic, an act of will, not of true desire, it left him feeling humiliated.

He went away from the islet, in spite of her mute reproach. And he wandered about the continent, vainly seeking a place where he could stay. He was out of key; he did not fit in the world any more.

There came a letter from Flora—her name was Flora—to say she was afraid she was going to have a child. He sat down as if he were shot, and he remained sitting. But he replied to her: "Why be afraid? If it is so, it is so, and we should rather be pleased than afraid."

At this very moment, it happened there was an auction of islands. He got the maps, and studied them. And at the auction he bought, for very little money, another island. It was just a few acres of rock away in the north, on the outer fringe of the isles. It was low, it rose low out of the great ocean. There was not a building, not even a tree on it. Only northern sea-turf, a pool of rain-water, a bit of sedge, rock, and sea-birds. Nothing else. Under the weeping wet western sky.

He made a trip to visit his new possession. For several days, owing to the seas, he could not approach it. Then, in a light sea-mist, he landed, and saw it hazy, low, stretching apparently a long way. But it was illusion. He walked over the wet, springy turf, and dark-grey sheep tossed away from him, spectral, bleating hoarsely. And he came to the dark pool, with the sedge. Then on in the dampness, to the grey sea sucking angrily among the rocks.

This was indeed an island.

So he went home to Flora. She looked at him with guilty fear, but also with a triumphant brightness in her uncanny eyes. And again he was gentle, he reassured her, even he wanted her again, with that curious desire that was almost like toothache. So he took her to the mainland, and they were married, since she was going to have his child.

They returned to the island. She still brought in his meals, her own along with them. She sat and ate with him. He would have it so. The widowed mother preferred to stay in the kitchen. And Flora slept in the guest-room of his house, mistress of his house.

His desire, whatever it was, died in him with nauseous finality. The child would still be months coming. His island was hateful to him, vulgar, a suburb. He himself had lost all his finer distinction. The weeks passed in a sort of prison, in humiliation. Yet he stuck it out, till the child was born. But he was meditating escape. Flora did not even know.

A nurse appeared, and ate at table with them. The doctor came sometimes, and, if the sea were rough, he too had to stay. He was cheery over his whisky.

They might have been a young couple in Golders Green.

The daughter was born at last. The father looked at the baby, and felt depressed, almost more than he could bear. The millstone was tied round his neck. But he tried not to show what he felt. And Flora did not know. She still smiled with a kind of half-witted triumph in her joy, as she got well again. Then she began again to look at him with those aching, suggestive, somehow impudent eyes. She adored him so.

This he could not stand. He told her that he had to go away for a time. She wept, but she thought she had got him. He told her he had settled the best part of his property on her, and wrote down for her what income it would produce. She hardly listened, only looked at him with those heavy, adoring, impudent eyes. He gave her a cheque-book, with the amount of her credit duly entered. This did arouse her interest. And he told her, if she got tired of the island, she could choose her home wherever she wished.

She followed him with those aching, persistent brown eyes, when he left, and he never even saw her weep.

He went straight north, to prepare his third island.

III

THE THIRD ISLAND

The third island was soon made habitable. With cement and the big pebbles from the shingle beach, two men built him a hut, and roofed it with corrugated iron. A boat brought over a bed and table, and three chairs, with a good cupboard, and a few books. He laid in a supply of coal and paraffin and food—he wanted so little.

The house stood near the flat shingle bay where he landed, and where he pulled up his light boat. On a sunny day in August the men sailed away and left him. The sea was still and pale blue. On the horizon he saw the small mail-steamer slowly passing northwards, as if she were walking. She served the outer isles twice a week. He could row out to her if need be, in calm weather, and he could signal her from a flagstaff behind his cottage.

Half a dozen sheep still remained on the island, as company; and he had a cat to rub against his legs. While the sweet, sunny days of the northern autumn lasted, he would walk among the rocks, and over the springy turf of his small domain, always coming to the ceaseless, restless sea. He looked at every leaf, that might be different from another, and he watched the endless expansion and contraction of the water-tossed seaweed. He had never a tree, not even a bit of heather to guard. Only the turf, and tiny turf-plants, and the sedge by the pool, the seaweed in the ocean. He was glad. He didn't want trees or bushes. They stood up like people, too assertive. His bare, low-pitched island in the pale blue sea was all he wanted.

He no longer worked at his book. The interest had gone. He liked to sit on the low elevation of his island, and see the sea: nothing but the pale, quiet sea. And to feel his mind turn soft and hazy, like the hazy ocean. Sometimes, like a mirage, he would see the shadow of land rise hovering to northwards. It was a big island beyond. But quite without substance.

He was soon almost startled when he perceived the steamer on the near horizon, and his heart contracted with fear, lest it were going to pause and molest him. Anxiously he watched it go, and not till it was out of sight did he feel truly relieved, himself again. The tension of waiting for human approach was cruel. He did not want to be approached. He did not want to hear voices. He was shocked by the sound of his own voice, if he inadvertently spoke to his cat. He rebuked himself for having broken the great silence. And he was irritated when his cat would look up at him and mew faintly, plaintively. He frowned at her. And she knew. She was becoming wild, lurking in the rocks, perhaps fishing.

But what he disliked most was when one of the lumps of sheep opened its mouth and baa-ed its hoarse, raucous baa. He watched it, and it looked to him hideous and gross. He came to dislike the sheep very much.

He wanted only to hear the whispering sound of the sea, and the sharp cries of the gulls, cries that came out of another world to him. And best of all, the great silence.

He decided to get rid of the sheep when the boat came. They were accustomed to him now, and stood and stared at him with yellow or colourless eyes, in an insolence that was almost cold ridicule. There was a suggestion of cold indecency about them. He disliked them very much. And when they jumped with staccato jumps off the rocks, and their hoofs made the dry, sharp hit, and the fleece flopped on their square backs, he found them repulsive, degrading.

The fine weather passed, and it rained all day. He lay a great deal on his bed, listening to the water trickling from his roof into the zinc water-butt, looking through the open door at the rain, the dark rocks, the hidden sea. Many gulls were on the island now: many sea-birds of all sorts. It was another world of life. Many of the birds he had never seen before. His old impulse came over him, to send for a book, to know their names. In a flicker of the old passion, to know the name of everything he saw, he even decided to row out to the steamer. The names of these birds! He must know their names, otherwise he had not got them, they were not quite alive to him.

But the desire left him, and he merely watched the birds as they wheeled or walked around him, watched them vaguely, without discrimination. All interest had left him. Only there was one gull, a big, handsome fellow, who would walk back and forth, back and forth in front of the open door of the cabin, as if he had some mission there. He was big, and pearl-grey, and his roundnesses were as smooth and lovely as a pearl. Only the folded wings had shut black pinions, and on the closed black feathers were three very distinct white dots, making a pattern. The islander wondered very much, why this bit of trimming on the bird out of the far, cold seas. And as the gull walked back and forth, back and forth in front of the cabin, strutting on pale-dusky gold feet, holding up his pale yellow beak, that was curved at the tip, with curious alien importance, the man wondered over him. He was portentous, he had a meaning.

Then the bird came no more. The island, which had been full of sea-birds, the flash of wings, the sound and cut of wings and sharp eerie cries in the air, began to be deserted again. No longer they sat like living eggs on the rocks and turf, moving their heads, but scarcely rising into flight round his feet. No longer they ran across the turf among the sheep, and lifted themselves upon low wings. The host had gone. But some remained, always.

The days shortened, and the world grew eerie. One day the boat came: as if suddenly, swooping down. The islander found it a violation. It was torture to talk to those two men, in their homely clumsy clothes. The air of familiarity around them was very repugnant to him. Himself, he was neatly dressed, his cabin was neat and tidy. He resented any intrusion, the clumsy homeliness, the heavy-footedness of the two fishermen was really repulsive to him.

The letters they had brought he left lying unopened in a little box. In one of them was his money. But he could not bear to open even that one. Any kind of contact was repulsive to him. Even to read his name on an envelope. He hid the letters away.

And the hustle and horror of getting the sheep caught and tied and put in the ship made him loathe with profound repulsion the whole of the animal creation. What repulsive god invented animals and evil-smelling men? To his nostrils, the fishermen and the sheep alike smelled foul; an uncleanness on the fresh earth.

He was still nerve-racked and tortured when the ship at last lifted sail and was drawing away, over the still sea. And sometimes, days after, he would start with repulsion, thinking he heard the munching of sheep.

The dark days of winter drew on. Sometimes there was no real day at all. He felt ill, as if he were dissolving, as if dissolution had already set in inside him. Everything was twilight, outside, and in his mind and soul. Once, when he went to the door, he saw black heads of men swimming in his bay. For some moments he swooned unconscious. It was the shock, the horror of unexpected human approach. The horror in the twilight! And not till the shock had undermined him and left him disembodied, did he realise that the black heads were the heads of seals swimming in. A sick relief came over him. But he was barely conscious, after the shock. Later on, he sat and wept with gratitude, because they were not men. But he never realised that he wept. He was too dim. Like some strange, ethereal animal, he no longer realised what he was doing.

Only he still derived his single satisfaction from being alone, absolutely alone, with the space soaking into him. The grey sea alone, and the footing of his sea-washed island. No other contact. Nothing human to bring its horror into contact with him. Only space, damp, twilit, sea-washed space! This was the bread of his soul.

For this reason, he was most glad when there was a storm, or when the sea was high. Then nothing could get at him. Nothing could come through to him from the outer world. True, the terrific violence of the wind made him suffer badly. At the same time, it swept the world utterly out of existence for him. He always liked the sea to be heavily rolling and tearing. Then no boat could get at him. It was like eternal ramparts round his island.

He kept no track of time, and no longer thought of opening a book. The print, the printed letters, so like the depravity of speech, looked obscene. He tore the brass label from his paraffin stove. He obliterated any bit of lettering in his cabin.

His cat had disappeared. He was rather glad. He shivered at her thin, obtrusive call. She had lived in the coal-shed. And each morning he had put her a dish of porridge, the same as he ate. He washed her saucer with repulsion. He did not like her writhing about. But he fed her scrupulously. Then one day she did not come for her porridge; she always mewed for it. She did not come again.

He prowled about his island in the rain, in a big oilskin coat, not knowing what he was looking at, nor what he went out to see. Time had ceased to pass. He stood for long spaces, gazing from a white, sharp face, with those keen, far-off blue eyes of his, gazing fiercely and almost cruelly at the dark sea under the dark sky. And if he saw the labouring sail of a fishing-boat away on the cold waters, a strange malevolent anger passed over his features.

Sometimes he was ill. He knew he was ill, because he staggered as he walked, and easily fell down. Then he paused to think what it was. And he went to his stores and took out dried milk and malt, and ate that. Then he forgot again. He ceased to register his own feelings.

The days were beginning to lengthen. All winter the weather had been comparatively mild, but with much rain, much rain. He had forgotten the sun. Suddenly, however, the air was very cold, and he began to shiver. A fear came over him. The sky was level and grey, and never a star appeared at night. It was very cold. More birds began to arrive. The island was freezing. With trembling hands he made a fire in his grate. The cold frightened him.

And now it continued, day after day, a dull, deathly cold. Occasional crumblings of snow were in the air. The days were greyly longer, but no change in the cold. Frozen grey daylight. The birds passed away, flying away. Some he saw lying frozen. It was as if all life were drawing away, contracting away from the north, contracting southwards. "Soon," he said to himself, "it will all be gone, and in all these regions nothing will be alive." He felt a cruel satisfaction in the thought.

Then one night there seemed to be a relief; he slept better, did not tremble half-awake, and writhe so much, half-conscious. He had become so used to the quaking and writhing of his body, he hardly noticed it. But when for once it slept deep, he noticed that.

He woke in the morning to a curious whiteness. His window was muffled. It had snowed. He got up and opened his door, and shuddered. Ugh! How cold! All white, with a dark leaden sea, and black rocks curiously speckled with white. The foam was no longer pure. It seemed dirty. And the sea ate at the whiteness of the corpse-like land. Crumbles of snow were silting down the dead air.

On the ground the snow was a foot deep, white and smooth and soft, windless. He took a shovel to clear round his house and shed. The pallor of morning darkened. There was a strange rumbling of far-off thunder in the frozen air, and through the newly-falling snow, a dim flash of lightning. Snow now fell steadily down in the motionless obscurity.

He went out for a few minutes. But it was difficult. He stumbled and fell in the snow, which burned his face. Weak, faint, he toiled home. And when he recovered, took the trouble to make hot milk.

It snowed all the time. In the afternoon again there was a muffled rumbling of thunder, and flashes of lightning blinking reddish through the falling snow. Uneasy, he went to bed and lay staring fixedly at nothingness.

Morning seemed never to come. An eternity long he lay and waited for one alleviating pallor on the night. And at last it seemed the air was paler. His house was a cell faintly illuminated with white light. He realised the snow was walled outside his window. He got up, in the dead cold. When he opened his door, the motionless snow stopped him in a wall as high as his breast. Looking over the top of it, he felt the dead wind slowly driving, saw the snow-powder lift and travel like a funeral train. The blackish sea churned and champed, seeming to bite at the snow, impotent. The sky was grey, but luminous.

He began to work in a frenzy, to get at his boat. If he was to be shut in, it must be by his own choice, not by the mechanical power of the elements. He must get to the sea. He must be able to get at his boat.

But he was weak, and at times the snow overcame him. It fell on him, and he lay buried and lifeless. Yet every time he struggled alive before it was too late, and fell upon the snow with the energy of fever. Exhausted, he would not give in. He crept indoors and made coffee and bacon. Long since he had cooked so much. Then he went at the snow once more. He must conquer the snow, this new, white brute force which had accumulated against him.

He worked in the awful, dead wind, pushing the snow aside, pressing it with his shovel. It was cold, freezing hard in the wind, even when the sun came out for a while, and showed him his white, lifeless surroundings, the black sea rolling sullen, flecked with dull spume, away to the horizons. Yet the sun had power on his face. It was March.

He reached the boat. He pushed the snow away, then sat down under the lee of the boat, looking at the sea, which swirled nearly to his feet, in the high tide. Curiously natural the pebbles looked, in a world gone all uncanny. The sun shone no more. Snow was falling in hard crumbs, that vanished as if by a miracle as they touched the hard blackness of the sea. Hoarse waves rang in the shingle, rushing up at the snow. The wet rocks were brutally black. And all the time the myriad swooping crumbs of snow, demonish, touched the dark sea and disappeared.

During the night there was a great storm. It seemed to him he could hear the vast mass of snow striking all the world with a ceaseless thud; and over it all, the wind roared in strange hollow volleys, in between which came a jump of blindfold lightning, then the low roll of thunder heavier than the wind. When at last the dawn faintly discoloured the dark, the storm had more or less subsided, but a steady wind drove on. The snow was up to the top of his door.

Sullenly, he worked to dig himself out. And he managed through sheer persistency to get out. He was in the tail of a great drift, many feet high. When he got through, the frozen snow was not more than two feet deep. But his island was gone. Its shape was all changed, great heaping white hills rose where no hills had been, inaccessible, and they fumed like volcanoes, but with snow powder. He was sickened and overcome.

His boat was in another, smaller drift. But he had not the strength to clear it. He looked at it helplessly. The shovel slipped from his hands, and he sank in the snow, to forget. In the snow itself, the sea resounded.

Something brought him to. He crept to his house. He was almost without feeling. Yet he managed to warm himself, just that part of him which leaned in snow-sleep over the coal fire. Then again he made hot milk. After which, carefully, he built up the fire.

The wind dropped. Was it night again? In the silence, it seemed he could hear the panther-like dropping of infinite snow. Thunder rumbled nearer, crackled quick after the bleared reddened lightning. He lay in bed in a kind of stupor. The elements! The elements! His mind repeated the word dumbly. You can't win against the elements.

How long it went on, he never knew. Once, like a wraith, he got out and climbed to the top of a white hill on his unrecognisable island. The sun was hot. "It is summer," he said to himself, "and the time of leaves." He looked stupidly over the whiteness, of his foreign island, over the waste of the lifeless sea. He pretended to imagine he saw the wink of a sail. Because he knew too well there would never again be a sail on that stark sea.

As he looked, the sky mysteriously darkened and chilled. From far off came the mutter of the unsatisfied thunder, and he knew it was the signal of the snow rolling over the sea. He turned, and felt its breath on him.

Sigrid Undset

Sigrid Undset (1882–1949), Norwegian novelist, was born in Denmark. She attended the first Norwegian coeducational school, run by a leading feminist, who prophesied that Sigrid would one day "prove the intellectual equality of the sexes." She married a painter, A. C. Starsvad, in 1911, and was divorced in 1922. Her interest in the early history of the Church led to her conversion to Catholicism in 1924. In 1928, she won the Nobel Prize for Literature, and in 1947, the Grand Cross of St. Olaf. Through her father, a historian and archeologist, and also because of what she called her growing disbelief in the "isms" of progress, she turned to medieval history, and the medieval period forms the setting of her best-known stories. These are Kristin Lavransdatter, *in three parts (1920–22) and* Olav Audunssøn *(1925–27), written at the time she joined the Catholic Church, and later translated under the title* The Master of Hestviken *(1928–30).* *(See page 83 of Introduction.)*

SIMONSEN

Simonsen paused a moment at the gate entrance, and dug out his old grease-worn wallet, in order to put away a testimonial he held in his hand. But before he did so, he smoothed the soiled paper out and read it through, although he knew it by heart already.

"Anton Simonsen has been a warehouse clerk in our employ for three years. During that time he has proved himself a willing, sober, and industrious worker.

"The Hercules Machine Shops,
By N. NIELSEN."

No, that testimonal wouldn't help him very far. It was pretty damn cheap of the manager—confound him! He was surely not so averse ordinarily to cramming his customers full of lies about one thing and another—shipping dates and the like, but when it came to giving a poor devil a reference which might help him get a job, that was another matter. "Yes, but I can't very well write that your work has been entirely satisfactory," the old devil had said. But the word "sober," at any rate, he had forced him to put in. That wasn't in the first draft. He—Simonsen—had insisted that he put it in. "It seems to me, Simonsen," the manager had said, "that you've smelled of liquor at all hours of the day almost." But at that he had opened up on him. "I've taken a drink now and again, it is true, Mr. Manager," he had said, "but that I venture you'd have done too if you had to dig around all day in that clammy warehouse. But there's no one can say that Anton Simonsen has ever been drunk on the job. Not even a bit on edge once." Well, at that the old wind-bag had had to give in, and the girl copyist had had to rewrite the testimonial with the word "sober" in it. So there it was—such as it was! It didn't amount to very much, it is true, and, what was worse, he had none better to show.

"Look out there, you damn fool!"

Simonsen jumped to one side, in towards the wall. A wagon loaded with iron beams swung rattling through the gate. The big horses steamed and sweat as they dug in with all their might to get the load over the stone bridge at the gateway entrance. The driver yelled something after him, but Simonsen could not hear what it was he said, for it was drowned in the rattle and rumble of the iron beams.

He put the testimonial away and stuck the wallet in his breast pocket. He glowered with hostile eyes after the wagon. It had come to a stop up against the warehouse, just opposite a huge crane, which with its pulleys and chains projected out from a dark hole, between barred windows, in the smoky red-brick wall. The flanks of the horses were steaming white, and the hairs on their sides were plastered together in little wet tufts. The driver had not blanketed them; he stood talking with another fellow.

Simonsen buttoned his winter coat, comparatively new and in fair condition, straightened up, and threw his stomach out. There rose within him a feeling of bourgeois dignity; he still considered himself a better member of society than this ruffian driver, even though the fellow did berate him. And with this self-consciousness there was vaguely merged another feeling, which had stirred within him at the sight of the two work-horses, as they tugged away and flexed the muscles of their perspiring flanks. He stepped in through the gate.

"It seems to me you ought to cover your horses. There's certainly no sense in letting the poor creatures stand unprotected this way in the cold—sweaty as they are."

The driver—a tall, lanky brute—faced about and looked down at him.

"Any of your business, fatty?"

"What do you suppose would happen to you if I were to go up to the office and report how you're treating their horses?"

"Beat it, and quickly. What's it to you any way? No call for you to butt in." And the driver moved threateningly towards him.

Simonsen drew back a bit, but, he reflected, the fellow would hardly dare touch him here, and he thrust his paunch out still more.

"Well, I merely wanted to call to your attention that they can see you from the office window—how you are treating the company's horses."

With that he faced about, and all at once his self-assurance left him. For just as he passed through the gate a man rushed down the stairs and swept by him—red-faced and blond and light-haired—dressed in fur cap and coat and swinging a silver-headed cane—the same man he had interviewed at the time he had applied for the position.

It was beginning to grow dark outside. It was going towards four o'clock already. Olga, no doubt, would scold a bit when he came home so late for dinner. Oh well, he'd simply have to tell her he'd had to stay the extra hour at the warehouse.

Simonsen trudged rapidly down Torvgaten. He seemed to mince and drag his steps at the same time, and what with his large round paunch and his bowed arms he suggested a rubber ball rolling and bouncing along. He was slight of build and short-necked, and his face was fat and flabby, with bleary eyes that lay deeply hid beneath his eyebrows, bloodshot cheeks, and a blueish something of a nose above a drooping grayish-yellow mustache.

It was a wretched Saturday afternoon in early December, and the air was thick with a cold, gray fog, which both smelled and tasted of gas and soot. Out in the street the sleighs skidded over the hard-frozen, rut-worn snow, and on the walks the stream of humanity swept, dark and heavy, past the lighted, frosty shop windows. Every moment, as he trudged along, immersed in his own thoughts, there was some one who ran into him and glowered angrily back at him.

Not that there was much in the way of thoughts stirring in his mind. For he kept pushing them aside. Surely he would find something. So that he'd not have to let Olga know that he had been laid off, finally, beginning with the first of the year. Life certainly was a struggle!

There was no hurry; he still had the better part of a month left before the beginning of the year. But if worse came to worst, he would have to write to Sigurd. Sigurd could easily get him another job. That wasn't too much to ask of a son who was as well established as Sigurd was. It would not be any fun, to be sure; this would be the fourth time. But then it was only four times in eight years. It was eight years ago exactly this coming New Year that Sigurd had got him that place in the office—all because that elegant daughter-in-law—the vixen—had felt he was not swell enough to have around her home in Fredrikstad. It was unfortunate, to be sure, that he had messed up things in all three places, but that wasn't his fault. In the office it had been the women—the shrews—who had got it in for him, as though it was any of their business what sort of man he was as long as he minded his work—and that he had done. And he had never tried to become too familiar with any of them. On that score he was clear. They needn't worry—upstart, washed-out hussies they were. Yes, and then there was the lumber warehouse. There certainly he had been proper and orderly in every way, for it was just at the time that he had taken up with Olga. True, he had not been accustomed to work of that kind, but if it had not been for malice on the part of the foreman he would never have lost that job. And after that he had got into the machine shop. Ah, it was no easy matter for a man already well up towards sixty to learn to master all the mysterious intricacies—all new to him—in connection with the selling and the shipping and the storing and what not. The warehouse foreman was a lazy scamp, and always he—Simonsen—had to shoulder the blame. And right from the start they had been disagreeable to him—from the manager and the chief clerk, who were forever reminding him that he was there only temporarily, and kept asking him whether he didn't have something else in view, down to the warehouse foreman and the other foremen and the teamsters—and the lady cashier, always so crabby and sour and cross and irritable every time he came up and asked for part of his pay in advance.

A gray feeling of restlessness and despondency settled over him like a clammy fog. He shuddered when he thought how Olga would fret and stew when he came home, and how extremely disagreeable Sigurd and his wife would be when they learned that he had been laid off, and how he would be starting in again at some new place, where, dazed and fearful and at his wits' end, he would be rushing around at new tasks, which he did not understand and probably never would come to know—in another warehouse or perhaps another office, full of strangers, unfamiliar and hostile—always cowering beneath constant reprimands and complaints, passively awaiting, half expecting another dismissal, just as he had rushed about and humbled himself, sluggish and old and stupid, through all his other jobs.

Simonsen was, in spite of all, however, somewhat adept at keeping unpleasant thoughts at arm's length. In reality he had gone through life that way, had humbled himself, and had come to look upon dismissals and reprimands and cross words and unpleasantnesses as inevitable. So it had been at sea, and so it had been at the docks when he was with Isachsen, and so it had been at home with his wife, as long as she lived. Cross and dour and severe and disagreeable—his daughter-in-law was not altogether unlike her for that matter. Well, Sigurd had been only too well repaid for aspiring to marry Captain Myhre's climbing daughter. Ah, how cozy their home had been those years immediately after Laura died! The boy had got a good start, and kind he had always been to his old father, had paid royally for his keep and everything. Not that he had been altogether unhappy here either at first, as a bachelor again and a man about town—he had been into things, had had a good time and lots of fun and all that—and later when he took up with Olga he had in reality—he couldn't deny it—been very comfortable—most of the time, at any rate. A little disagreeable, to be sure, it had been at the time Olga became with child, but Olga was not altogther to blame for that, and she had reconciled herself to it immediately when he had promised her marriage. Even yet, of course, she raised a fuss about it at times and insisted he go through with it and marry her. Not that he didn't some time intend to do it—he'd have done it long ago, had it not been for the disagreeable complications he foresaw with Sigurd and his wife. But some day surely an easy, respectable job must fall to his lot, which would be his permanently—and when Olga was able to enlarge her dressmaking establishment, and Henry, her boy, got into the office, where he was now running errands—for that he had been promised; the fellow was rounding out quite satisfactorily—well, they might then at last get a cozy little place and be happy together. He could sit in the sofa with his glass of toddy and his pipe, while Olga went about her work in a leisurely way, and Svanhild sat near him and studied her lessons. For Olga was a real genuine soul, and no one should have occasion to say about Svanhild that she was an illegitimate child—when the time came for her to start school.

Simonsen had by now reached Ruselökveien. The fog lay thick and clammy in the narrow street, streaked here and there by yellow-green light from frozen shop windows, and in all of them, wherever the heat from the gas light or the lamp had cleared a space on the frosted windows, could be seen displays of Christmas tree baskets, whether it was a general merchandise shop or a delicatessen or a tobacco shop. The reddish glare from the huge exhibition windows of the two-story bazaar on the other side of the street oozed unctuously out into the fog. The gas lamps up on the Terrace were just barely discernible. But the private dwellings beyond were entirely lost. Not a single ray of light penetrated to the street from them, although they could be sensed vaguely as towering walls in the fog—which, as it were, dwarfed the street below into a mere gutter.

Simonsen trudged along mincingly. The walks in many places, where the ice had not been cut away, were slippery. Children swarmed about on all sides. Out in the street, between vans and sleighs, they attempted to slide, if it were only along an icy rut in the rough, irregular, brown layer of hard frozen snow.

"Svanhild!"

Simonsen called sharply to a little girl in a dirty white cap. She had crawled up on the bank of snow, piled high along the walk, and let herself slide down into the street on her wee tiny skis, which were quite black from the soot and the dirty snow, and had almost no bend left in them.

The child stood stock still in the middle of the street and looked up at Simonsen as he straddled the snow bank and went out to her. Her blue eyes testified to a guilty conscience, as she brushed her light hair up under her cap, and wiped her little nose with her red-mittened hand.

"And how many times have you been told, Svanhild, that you are not to run out into the street! Why can't you be a good girl and play in the court?"

Svanhild glanced up timidly.

"But I can't very well ski in the court—for there's no hill there, and—"

"Suppose a wagon came along and ran over you, or a drunken man came up and ran away with you—what do you think papa and mamma would say then?"

Svanhild was ashamed and said nothing. Simonsen helped her onto the walk again, and they tripped away hand in hand, her tiny, strip-like skis clattering down the bare walk.

"Do you think papa will take you out walking to-night, if you're a bad girl, and won't do as you're told to?—I suppose they've already had dinner?"

"Oh, yes, mamma and Henry and I have eaten long ago—"

Hm! Simonsen trudged in through the gate. A white metal sign read: "Mrs. Olga Martinsen. Dressmaking Establishment. Children's and Boys' Clothes. Third Floor Rear." Simonsen crossed the court diagonally, and glanced up towards a lighted window, against which some fashion journals leaned. Then he picked up Svanhild's skis under his arm and led the child up the narrow back stairway.

Outside Olga's hall door a couple of youngsters stood reading a paper-bound book in the glare of a kitchen lamp which had been hung out. Simonsen grumbled something and let himself in.

The hall was dark. At the farther end a streak of light issued through the door from the living room. Simonsen went into his own room. It was dark there too—and cold. He shivered as he lit the lamp. She had let the fire go out.

"Run in, Svanhild, and tell mamma I am here."

He opened the door to the room adjoining. At the table, overflowing with cut and half-sewed garments and scraps of lining, sat Miss Abrahamsen bent over her sewing. She had fastened a newspaper to one side of the lamp, and all the light fell on her little yellow spinster face and diminutive brown hands. There was a little reflection of light from the two steel sewing machines, and in towards the wall could be seen the white beds of Olga and Svanhild.

"And you're at it harder than ever, Miss Abrahamsen."

"Ah yes—one has to, you know."

"Yes, isn't this Christmas business the funniest thing—it's almost as if the world was coming to an end."

Svanhild slipped in from the living room.

"Mamma says to say your dinner is in the warming oven."

"Well, I guess I'll stay right here and make myself comfortable, Miss Abrahamsen; it's so cold in my room—and then, too, I'll have pleasant company."

Miss Abrahamsen had quietly cleared a corner of the table, while Simonsen brought out the dinner—cabbage soup and sausages.

"Hm! Not so bad. Now if one only had—," Simonsen got up and tapped on the door to the living room.

"Oh, Olga—"

"Why good evening, Simonsen! And how are you?"

He opened the door and peered in.

"Well, if it isn't Miss Hellum! And you're having another new dress again?"

Olga, her mouth full of pins, was busy fitting Miss Hellum, arranging the folds over her bust before the console mirror.

"About so, I guess."

Olga removed the lamp from the nickel holder on the wall and held it up.

"It seems all right. You're sure it's not crooked in the back, Mrs. Martinsen?"

Two girls who sat waiting over on the plush sofa in the twilight laid aside their fashion journal, looked at each other and smiled, looked at Miss Hellum and smiled again to each other. "Heavens!" one of them whispered audibly. They were dressed exactly alike, with rather short jackets, little neck pieces of fur, and nice-looking felt hats with feathers on. Simonsen was still at the door—they embarrassed him a bit.

"Well, what do you think, Simonsen? Is it going to be pretty?"

"Ah, it is remarkable how that color suits you, Miss Hellum—but then anything looks well on the beautiful, as the saying goes."

"Oh, you—!" Miss Hellum exclaimed and chuckled.

Lovely girl—this Miss Hellum! Olga cut around the neck, and Miss

Hellum bent her head and shuddered a little as the cold scissors touched her skin. A lovely full neck, with yellow curly hair all the way down, and arms that were soft and round.

"Costly stuff too, I imagine," Simonsen remarked, as he touched the silk—and her arm—while Olga worked on the sleeve.

"For shame, Simonsen," Miss Hellum laughed. Olga looked daggers. She pushed him aside, as she tugged at the sleeve.

"Oh yes, that reminds me—Olga, couldn't Henry run down and get a bottle or two of beer?"

"Henry's had to go down to the office again, poor fellow—some estimate or other that had to be copied, he said."

"Poor fellow—he had to go down again, did he?—It seems to me it's getting to be almost every Saturday afternoon. Ah yes, life is a struggle! It was almost four o'clock before I got away from the warehouse. Oh, if one were only young and beautiful, Miss Hellum!"

Svanhild peeped in.

"Come in here, Svanhild! Do you remember my name to-day?"

"Miss Hellum," Svanhild smiled modestly.

"I suppose you'd like some candy to-day too, wouldn't you?" Miss Hellum opened her purse and brought out a little bag.

"Oh ho. What do you say now, Svanhild? Your hand, Svanhild! and a pretty curtsy."

Svanhild whispered her thanks, offered her hand, and curtsied. And she took to breaking apart the pieces of camphorated candy which had stuck together.

Miss Hellum talked and laughed while she put on her wraps.

"Well, I'll expect it ready for a final fitting Tuesday next then, about this time. And you won't disappoint me, Mrs. Martinsen, will you? Well, good-bye! Good-bye, Simonsen! And good-bye, Svanhild!"

Simonsen gallantly opened the door, and Miss Hellum swept out, the feathers on her hat swaying as she went, her muskrat neck piece flung loosely down over her shoulders.

"Whew!" one of the girls on the sofa giggled. "Not so bad, either."

"Say, she is a regular one all right."

Simonsen withdrew again to Miss Abrahamsen and his dinner, which had got cold. Olga came in after a while with the coffee and poured it.

"Really, it's beyond me, Anton—it's perfectly ridiculous the way you carry on! What can you be thinking of—when there are others around, too, listening!"

"Who were those silly gigglers anyway?"

"The minister's hired girl on the Terrace and a friend of hers. It seems to me you have made it difficult enough as it is for me—without carrying on in this way with that Hellum woman. Well, they'll have something to talk about now—as if they didn't have enough already."

"Come on, I don't imagine it was as bad as all that."

The door bell rang. Miss Abrahamsen went out to answer it.

"It is Miss Larsen."

Olga set aside her cup and picked up a basted dress and threw it over her arm.

"Never a moment's peace!"

Miss Abrahamsen bent forward over her sewing again.

Mrs. Martinsen and Miss Abrahamsen sat and sewed all day Sunday. They put off their dinner till it was too dark to work, and when it was over, Olga lit the lamp, and they took up their sewing again.

"That vestee of Miss Olsen's, weren't you working on it, Miss Abrahamsen, a while ago?"

Miss Abrahamsen set her machine whirring.

"I laid it on the table."

Olga searched the table—and then the floor—for it.

"Svanhild, you haven't seen a little white bib, have you—of lace?"

"No, mamma, I haven't," Svanhild answered from the corner by the window. And she jumped up and began hunting too, but first she settled her doll in the up-turned footstool, which served as a cradle, and covered it carefully.

"Astrid is sleeping. She has diphtheria and scarlet fever," she protested, as her mother rummaged around among the doll clothes. But Olga took the patient out of her cradle. The doll was wrapped in a white pleated bit of lace, carefully fastened about with safety pins.

"Heavens, child, are you crazy! And if she hasn't torn a hole in it with the pins! You naughty girl!" and she cuffed Svanhild on the ear. "Oh, what shall I do now—this costly lace of Miss Olsen's too!"

Svanhild howled.

"But I thought it was only a rag, mamma!"

"Haven't I told you you're not to touch anything, not even what's on the floor? What a naughty girl you are!"

Miss Abrahamsen inspected the vestee.

"I think I can take up the pleats, and then press it and repleat it, so as to bring the tear inside one of the folds—I don't think it will show any—."

Svanhild kept right on howling.

"Well, what's the matter now, Svanhild—crying like this when you know papa is taking a nap?"

Olga was furious as she explained the trouble.

"What a naughty little girl you are, Svanhild—to play such tricks on mamma! For shame,—this isn't my little Svanhild!"

"It seems to me you might take her out, Anton. It's not particularly good for you either to be lying around and sleeping all day."

Simonsen scolded the child industriously as he went off with her. But he comforted her when they had reached the hall and he put on her wraps.

"Come, don't cry any more now! Shame on you for crying so! We'll go over in the park and slide. You know it wasn't nice of you. So wipe your nose now. Papa'll take you sliding—come along, sweetheart.

Olga was perhaps a bit too severe at times with Svanhild. Not, of course, that children were not to be punished—when they had done something wrong. But Svanhild took everything so to heart—she was still hiccoughing on the sled behind him—poor little thing!

The evening sky rose darkly purple high over the towers and spires on the Terrace. The weather had cleared up. There was left only a thin sooty streak of fog in the street, around the lights, as Simonsen trudged along, pulling his daughter on the sled.

The palace park was such a pretty place. The heavy hoar-frost on the trees and the bushes everywhere sparkled in the reflection from the lamps. And such a mass of children everywhere! On every least little incline they were coasting and skiing. The main slide simply swarmed with them. Big naughty boys—sometimes five or six to a sled—hooted and yelled as they sped down over the icy crust, swinging a thin narrow pole, like the tail of a rat, behind them. But Simonsen knew of a quiet little hill, farther in, where he and Svanhild had been in the habit of coasting before in the evenings. And really Svanhild had a grand time. Papa stood at the top and gave her a good start, and Svanhild yelled "Look out!" so loud that her thin little voice almost cracked, and Simonsen too roared "Look out there!" from way down inside, although apart from themselves there were only two small boys in sport shoes and knitted caps on the whole hill. Simonsen took the initiative and made their acquaintance. They were Alf and Johannes Hauge, and their father was an office manager, and lived in Parkveien. Simonsen started all three of them down; they were to see whose sled was the fastest, but he gave Svanhild the most vigorous push, and she won. And he ran down after them and helped Svanhild up the hill again, for otherwise she would have stuck fast in the snow every time she went through the crust.

But after a while Svanhild began to whimper.

"Papa, my feet are so cold."

"Well, then you must run—let's go up on the road and run around a bit."

Svanhild ran and cried—her toes hurt her so.

"Oh ho! You must run much faster, Svanhild—let's see if you can catch papa!"

He bounced along with wee tiny steps like a rubber ball. And Svanhild ran after him as fast as she could, and caught him, till she grew warm again and cheerful and happy.

But by that time they had lost track of their sled. Simonsen looked for it above the hill and below the hill and in between the bushes—it was nowhere to be found. Alf and Johannes had seen it stand over by a large tree in the road some time back, but that was all they knew. And—oh yes—some big rough boys had gone by—that Simonsen too remembered. It was most likely they who had taken it.

Svanhild was heartbroken and cried—it really hurt one to see her. Simonsen thought of Olga. She wouldn't grow any sweeter, touchy as she was nowadays. What scamps those boys were! To steal a poor little girl's sled! To think that children could be so mean!

"Don't cry, Svanhild sweetheart—we'll find your sled again all right."

Simonsen went about from hill to hill and inquired after a little blue painted sled. Svanhild trudged along with him and cried, and Alf and Johannes followed them, both holding fast to the rope of their sled, while they told, as their eyes bulged, of all they had heard about big rough boys, who went about stealing sleds, and ran down children, and threw chunks of ice on the slides.

There was no trace of the sled to be found, but up on the main road they met a smartly dressed angry lady, who turned out to be Alf's and Johannes' nurse, and who scolded them for not coming home long ago and promised them they would catch it from papa and mamma. She wasn't at all concerned to learn that the little girl was named Svanhild and that she had lost her sled—as she scolded and shuffled away, holding each of the boys in an iron grip. Then Simonsen was almost hit in the eye by a steering pole and in the shins by a sharp sled runner.

"Well, Svanhild, they've apparently made away with your sled—I don't imagine we'll ever see it again," Simonsen sighed, dejected. "But don't cry so now, little sweetheart. Papa'll get you a new sled for Christmas. Come, let's go down Carl Johan and look at the shop windows—they're so beautiful to-night—perhaps we'll see a nice new sled for you too—" and he brightened up.

Svanhild and her papa went down and looked at the shops. And when they came up to a window in front of which the stream of people had stopped and formed one dark stationary milling mass of humanity, Simonsen raised her on his arms, and struggled and edged his way through, till they were right in front of the brilliantly lighted window, where they continued to stand as long as there was one single item left to talk about and guess the price of. In some places there were Christmas trees, colorfully arrayed, and lighted with electric bulbs. Svanhild was also to have a Christmas tree on Christmas Eve. In one window there was a regular Christmas party of lady dolls, smartly dressed—as Svanhild would be when she grew up. And in another shop, which dealt in trunks and bags, there was a wee tiny crocodile in a wee tiny water basin. There they had to stand a long time speculating as to whether it was alive. At last it moved one eye just the least bit—just think, it was alive! And this little crocodile, when it grew up, would be so large that it could swallow a whole Svanhild in a single bite.

"But now it can't bite any, can it?"

"No, now it can't hurt you."

Up near Eketorvet there was a movie camera in a window among moving picture advertisements. Svanhild, who had been to the movies with papa—three times already—had to remember all they had seen—the two little girls who had been kidnapped by robbers in an automobile, and all the rest. Forgotten was the sled they had lost, and mamma, who sat pursing her lips over her sewing, till she grew tired and cross. Forgotten was everything now—except that Svanhild was papa's little girl, and that Christmas Eve was only seventeen days off.

Then they passed by a sporting goods shop, with many sleds, large and small, on display in the window, and the grandest of them all—the one with the fiery red and the roses painted on it and the bronze gilt iron braces—Svanhild was to get from her papa for Christmas.

After that they had to have something to warm them up a bit. Simonsen knew of a cozy little temperance café, since it was Sunday, and the wine shop was closed. There were no other people present, and the waitress behind the counter was not insusceptible to Simonsen's flirtatious banter while he had his coffee and sandwich and Svanhild had a piece of cake and a sip now and then of papa's coffee.

"You needn't tell mamma," Simonsen saw fit to caution her, as he winked one eye. But Svanhild knew better than to tell mamma anything, whenever she and papa on their evening walks dropped into one place or other, and she had a stick of candy, from which—mamma thought—little girls got a toothache, and papa had something to drink, from which—mamma thought—he got a bad stomach. But mamma always was so busy, and it made her cross. Papa too was busy when he was at the warehouse, and Henry when he was at the office. When one was grown up one had to work terribly hard, Svanhild had learned.

After Sunday came Monday and five other gray week-days. Svanhild sat on the floor in the sewing room and played by herself, for papa now came home so late in the evening that he could not take her out walking. Papa, too, was cross now, Svanhild noticed—whether it was because he had so much to do at the office, or because mamma had so much to do that she scarce had time to prepare dinner or get his supper until late in the evening. And Henry, too, was irritable, for lady customers used the room in which he ordinarily slept, for fitting and trying on till late at night, and kept him from getting to bed as he should. But Svanhild comforted herself with the thought of the new sled she was to get for Christmas.

On the fifteenth Anton Simonsen wrote to his son. He was tired of running around looking for jobs—which he didn't get anyway. And having done so he faced the future blithely again. He had time once more to take Svanhild out walking evenings, and to help her ski in the park, and they talked of the new sled she was to get.

On the eighteenth, just as he was nailing up a case of machinery, the warehouse foreman came over and told him he was wanted at the telephone. It was Sigurd, who was in town, and invited him to drop in and have coffee with him at the Café Augustin—couldn't he beg off a couple of hours after dinner—that they might talk things over a bit?

"And how is Mossa—and the children?"

The children were all right, thanks. And Mossa had come in with him—intended to make some purchases for Christmas.

"Come to think of it, son, it's well-nigh hopeless to expect even an hour off now, busy as we are just before Christmas," Simonsen explained.

Sigurd himself undertook to see the manager about it.

"Well, in that case, all right—you're very kind! 'Hello' to Mossa."

It was just like her! Of course she wouldn't ask him to have dinner with them—oh no! But—by George!—he'd have beer and even something stronger before he turned up for that bout!

"Do you think that's necessary?" Mrs. Mossa Carling asked her husband, who was in the act of uncorking a bottle of punch.

"It seems to me we ought to have a glass of punch for father anyway."

"Well, all right—as you please, dear!" Mrs. Carling thrust out her double chin as far as she could. She was not pretty. Her eyelids grew thicker out towards the temples, so that her small gray eyes seemed to creep in towards the bridge of the nose; her face was full and fresh in color, but her mouth was narrow and small and her lips thin, and her chest, finally, was hollow and undersized, while below she was full and broad.

She was sitting in the center of the plush sofa, directly underneath the electric chandelier, whose three globes lit up the hotel room—the two iron bedsteads, the two mahogany washstands, the two small tables and the wardrobe with the mirror, the two easy chairs in front of the larger table, on which stood an ash tray on a doily in the center of a chenille runner.

There was a hesitant knock on the door, and Simonsen entered cautiously. He shook hands with both of them.

"Good afternoon, Sigurd—glad to see you again, son—good afternoon, good afternoon Mossa—it's nice to see you once again too—and just as young and pretty as ever—"

Mossa rang for the coffee, and poured it, while Sigurd filled the glasses.

Simonsen kept eyeing his daughter-in-law, who sat silent, her mouth tightly drawn, as he talked with Sigurd. Leisurely and with many flourishes the conversation drifted over to the main business.

"You don't mind if we smoke, do you Mossa? Here, father—a cigar—?

"And now this matter you wrote about. I was up at the office to-day and had a talk with your manager. He seems to be of the same opinion as I. The city's not quite the place for you. The work here is too strenuous for a man of your age—he seemed to think so too. And I can't get you anything else either for that matter—"

Simonsen said nothing. But Mossa took up the thread.

"Sigurd is himself in a subordinate position, you will have to remember—to some extent at least. The board is not likely to relish having Sigurd forever asking the firm's connections to take his father into their business. He has already done so three times—and you've messed up everything. I may as well tell you outright that Sigurd had some very serious difficulties after he had got you this last place, which you have just been let out of, as I understand—"

"That I had, I assure you. As I say, you don't quite fit in here. You're too old, too, to be constantly trying new things. And there is therefore only one way in which I can help you. I can get you a position up at the Menstad plant in Öimark—nice, easy work. To be sure, the wages aren't much—sixty kroner to begin with, if I'm not mistaken. But, as I say, that place I can get for you."

Simonsen said nothing.

"Well—that is the only way I can help you," Sigurd Carling repeated.

"Well—what do you say—shall I get it for you, father?" he asked after a brief pause.

The father cleared his throat a few times before he spoke.

"Well, it's like this, Sigurd—I don't know whether you've heard about it or not—but the fact is I'm engaged—to the woman I've been lodging with these last six years. So I suppose I'll have to talk it over some with Olga first—see what she thinks. Olga—that's her name," he explained, "Mrs. Olga Martinsen; she is a widow."

There was an uncomfortably long pause. Simonsen played with the tassels on the armchair.

"She is a genuine, thorough, good woman in every way, Olga is—and she has a large thriving sewing establishment here in town. So it's a question whether she'd care to move up into that Godforsaken country up there. And her son has an office job in the city too."

"Is this the woman—" Sigurd spoke very deliberately, "that you are said—from what I have heard—to have had a child with—?"

"We have a little girl, yes—Svanhild by name. She will be five years next April."

"So!" It was Mossa speaking. "So you have a daughter with the woman you are lodging with—who is such a good, proper woman in every way!"

"Well, so Olga is! Orderly and proper—and industrious and hard working, too. And furthermore kind."

"It is really strange, father," Mrs. Mossa made herself very sweet as she spoke, "that you haven't married this excellent Mrs. Martinsen before. It seems to me you had ample reason to do so long ago."

"Let me tell you, Mossa dear," Simonsen beamed with delight, proud of what he was inventing, "I did not want to see my wife work and struggle so hard, and so I waited in hopes of finding something better. But marry Olga I have promised on my word of honor I would, and that promise I'll stand by, as long as my name's Anton Simonsen!"

"Ah," Mossa became sweeter and sweeter, "but sixty kroner a month is not a great deal to get married on—and support a wife and child. And any great amount of sewing of course Olga can't figure on up in Öimark."

"The worst of course, father, is that you have this child. But I suppose Mrs. Martinsen could somehow be made to understand the situation—we might perhaps come to some sort of agreement with her."

"One thing you'll have to remember, Sigurd—there's your little sister, Svanhild. I shouldn't want her to suffer because she is an illegitimate child. It seems to me, Sigurd, you're incurring a grave responsibility by interfering in this matter."

Mossa broke in on him almost before he had finished, and now there was not the slightest suggestion of sweetness in her voice.

"When you speak of responsibility, father—for *your* illegitimate child—you really strike me as very funny. Sigurd offers to get you a position—for the fourth time—in Öimark. Here he is unable to get anything. Why, if you don't think you can leave the city because of your private affairs, you are quite at liberty to remain. If you can find a position here and get married on it—why, that's your affair and not ours. But Sigurd can obviously not help you in any other way. Surely he must think first and foremost of his own wife and children."

Mrs. Mossa had arrayed herself in her silk petticoat and draped herself in her new set of furs, when she mounted the stairs the next morning to Mrs. Martinsen's establishment in the rear apartment in Ruselökveien. She pressed the button underneath Simonsen's soiled card with a determined finger.

The woman who let her in was little, plump and dark. She had pretty blue eyes, set in a faded, sun-starved face.

"Is this Mrs. Martinsen? I am Mrs. Carling. I should like to speak with you."

Olga opened a bit hesitantly the door to the nearest room.

"Won't you come in here? I'm sorry there's no fire in here. But we're sewing in the other rooms."

Mrs. Mossa sailed in and seated herself in the only easy chair in the room. It was a room furnished as rooms for rent usually are. On the white dresser scarf stood, conscientiously arranged, photographs of the former Mrs. Simonsen, of Sigurd and herself—their engagement photographs—and two group pictures of the grandchildren.

"Now, my dear Mrs. Martinsen,"—Olga stood over by the dresser observing her—"there are one or two things I'd like very much to talk over with you. Won't you sit down?"

"Thanks—but I am very busy. What was it Madam wished?"

"Well, I won't keep you very long. Simonsen—my husband's father—is apparently, from what we gathered from him yesterday, under certain obligations to you. Now I don't know whether he has fully informed you as to his position?"

"You mean the position in Öimark?—Indeed, he has."

"Well now, you understand, of course, it's quite a small place. If he should take it, he would temporarily not be in a position to fulfill his obligations to you."

"Thank you!" Olga spoke rapidly and to the point. "But it's not necessary to trouble Madam with these affairs. We have just agreed—Simonsen and I—have decided to get married right away."

"Well, in that case, Mrs. Martinsen, I must call your attention to one thing: Simonsen can expect no support of any kind from my husband—absolutely none. He has a large family himself. And for four people to live on sixty kroner a month. Besides the little girl, which is said to be my father-in-law's, you have another child too?"

"My son will remain here—I have a sister in Trondhjemsveien whom he can stay with. And our plan was to sort of make our home in Fredrikstad. Simonsen would come down Saturdays—and I would run a dressmaking shop in the city."

"I see. Well, that might not seem unreasonable either. But there is this to remember, you see—there are more than enough seamstresses in Fredrikstad already. It is questionable, *Miss* Martinsen, whether it would pay you to give up your business here and try to establish a new one there."

Olga started.

"*Mrs.* Martinsen, I beg your pardon. For that, I see, is how you style yourself. My husband and I, to be sure, have done a bit of investigating. It need not surprise you surely, that we should want to know what sort of person it was he had taken up with."

Olga sniffed scornfully.

"Well, that's all the same to me, Mrs. Simonsen—Mrs. Carling, I mean —pardon me. But the fact is that Simonsen doesn't seem to hold it against me that the man I was to marry deserted me for America and left me to provide for myself and my little baby as best I could. And Simonsen has promised me—time and time again he has said to me, 'Don't worry, I shall never go back on you, Olga!' And then I don't see why it should concern you at all, Mrs. Carling. We shan't ever trouble you, or run in on you—and seeing your husband hasn't cared to keep his father's name—"

"My dear Mrs. Martinsen," Mossa waved her hand and thrust out her chin. "Not so hysterical—please! I've surely never dreamed of interfering in your affairs. On the contrary, I came here with the best of intentions. I merely wanted to enlighten you—in case you ever imagined Simonsen would be a good provider. I must confess, I don't think you'll attain anything, if you marry him, except the privilege of supporting him as well as the child. If you recall, my dear father-in-law has really never been what you might call an up-and-coming man. We have no guarantee that he will not be as shiftless in the future as he has been in the past. So there you are! Do you think it will be easy for a man of his age—with a family— always to be getting new positions?

"I am here in all friendliness to make you an offer on behalf of my husband. So far you have managed to get along without being married. Now, my husband would offer you something—we had thought of five hundred kroner—to cover any loss you might suffer by reason of your lodger leaving you thus suddenly. It's without any conditions, you understand. If my father-in-law should subsequently attain a position that would enable him to marry, we'd have no desire or occasion to interfere. As you quite rightly said, that is none of our business. And as regards your little girl, my husband and I have talked the matter over and would offer her a home with us."

"Never—as long as I live!" Olga flashed. "Part with Svanhild! That you may rest assured I'll never, never consent to."

"All right—as you please, of course. And you and my father-in-law will, of course, suit yourselves, if you want to marry on sixty kroner a month— give up your livelihood here, and undertake to start anew in Fredrikstad, which I can promise you will be very difficult. It is so perfectly incomprehensible to me what you want with Simonsen anyway. Heavens, to marry —you already call yourself 'Mrs.' In your circle people aren't so particular about some little affair you may have had with one of your lodgers. That you ever took up with Simonsen—really you must excuse me for saying it—in my opinion it doesn't speak very well for you. In plain language he's really nothing but an old swine!"

Olga interrupted here.

"You might just as well stop right here, Mrs. Carling. But I'll tell you, in plain language, what it was I wanted with Anton Simonsen. One thing and another there may be about him that one might object to. But I noticed one thing very soon, whatever else one might say, he had a kind heart. And there are not too many kind people around, let me tell you! And no sooner did he realize that I took pains and wanted to make him comfortable than he began to feel at home, and straightened up and became regular in his habits, as he might have done sooner, in my opinion, had he been made comfortable before. No, you can't deny—Anton's kind-hearted and grateful. And then his fondness for Svanhild—really he goes too far in his love for the child—he is downright spoiling her. I am fond of Simonsen, let me tell you, Mrs. Carling."

Mossa rose and thrust her gloved finger tips in between the lace frills of her muff.

"Of course—if you're in *love* with Simonsen—that's another matter."

She sailed out.

That Mr. Sigurd Carling had a high opinion of his wife's sagacity is true enough. He had so often heard others say—that he had come to believe it himself—that it was Miss Mossa Myhre who had put life into Sigurd Carl Simonsen when he was a mere clerk and had made him the man he was. But he had nevertheless had his doubts as to whether she was the proper person to come to an understanding with Mrs. Martinsen. For there was no denying that she looked at things quite rigorously, and this Olga, it appeared, had had two children a bit irregularly. Mossa could on occasion be rather sharp and disagreeable. He was sorry therefore afterwards—he had been foolish to let her go. For some kind of understanding had to be arrived at. Should the father come down to Fredrikstad and live, with a wife and child whom he could not provide for—it was as clear as day what the end would be. Never would he feel secure against unexpected, unforeseen demands for assistance—and then all the other aggravations which always trailed his father. And everlasting difficulties with Mossa.

The affair had to be settled—and that immediately, before the old fellow had time to slip one over on them first. He had been up at the Hercules Machine Shops and had ordered the two new turbines, and had at the same time said a few words *en passant* relative to his father. Simonsen—it was now arranged—was to leave Christmas Eve, in order that he might go home with them and spend Christmas with his family.

Later he started off himself to see Mrs. Martinsen.

Olga's eyes were red from much weeping when Simonsen came home to dinner. Carling had been there. He had been very nice for that matter, she said. He had asked to see Svanhild, and he had set her on his knee, and had promised her something for Christmas. Later he had talked with

Olga. It was this miserable debt of hers—she was behind in her rent, and had bills at various shops here and there—so she had accepted the money. He had promised her fifteen kroner a month for Svanhild—that was something sure anyway—and she had to consider Henry too—he wouldn't be able to take care of himself entirely for some time yet. Fifteen kroner a month, he had said, for the time being—"until my father becomes self-supporting and can marry you." Olga was sitting on Simonsen's knee, in his cold room, in the easy chair in front of the dresser with the family portraits, and she wept, and he caressed and comforted her.

"Really, Anton, I don't know—! What else was there I could do? If he won't help you—why, there's no other way out. And I understood from the way he talked—he won't help in any other way. If they are so set against us, I don't suppose we could make a go of it in Fredrikstad either, you see—"

She blew her nose and dried away her tears, and then started to cry again.

"One must take what comes—must stand a lot when one is poor."

But persuade Simonsen to go down and spend Christmas with them—that Sigurd and Mossa were unable to do. They held out the prospect of a Christmas tree and the grandchildren and goose and ale and wine and head-cheese all through the Christmas holidays. But the old man was firm—he wanted to spend Christmas with Olga and the children. All they could get him to promise was that he would run down the day after Christmas. For Sigurd had given him twenty-five kroner by way of a Christmas gift. It was best therefore to get him away from the city, lest he go gadding about during the holidays with money in his pockets and nothing to do. It was preferable after all that the old fellow did his Christmas drinking with them—under supervision.

The day before Christmas Eve, when Simonsen came home, he had the sled under one arm. And he hummed in a deep bass as he lit the lamp in his room and undid his packages.

There was something in the way of drinks for the holidays—aquavit and punch and port for Olga. With a little ale now he'd be all set. A pipe for Henry. It didn't cost a great deal—it was mostly to show the lad he hadn't forgotten him—and a manly thing to get too it was for that matter. Otherwise he had been almost niggardly. The waist material for Olga cost only one forty-five, but he had bought her a brooch too for three seventy-five—and really it looked like something worth at least ten kroner. Simonsen took it out of the box—ah, wouldn't she be delighted! And for Miss Abrahamsen, too, he would get something—by way of remembrance. Some trifling thing—he could easily afford it.

And then the sled! Simonsen, after removing the table cloth from the table, unwrapped it and placed it on exhibition.

"Oh, Olga dear, can you come here for a second?" he called out into the sewing room.

"Well, what is it? I'm very busy—"

Simonsen moved the lamp over to the table.

"And what do you suppose Svanhild'll say to that, Olga?"

"But the veneer, Anton!" And Olga placed newspapers underneath the sled and lamp. "Yes—a beautiful—lovely—sled—"

"And see here," and Simonsen unbuckled the cushion and showed her the painted roses. "The cushion was extra, of course, you understand."

"Hm! It cost quite a bit, I imagine?"

"Five kroner and twenty-five öre—with the cushion," Simonsen proclaimed proudly.

"That seems a lot of money to put into a thing like that, Anton. She's still so young—she might have been satisfied, even if it had not been quite so grand." And Olga sighed.

"Oh, well, seeing we have a few pennies to spend, we might as well do it. It's only fun, it seems to me, to give a little liberally. And now that you'll be rid of your debt— I've not forgotten my sweetheart either, you'll see," and he nudged her playfully. "Can you get me a couple of glasses, Olga? I've bought some port—we'll see how you like it—it was mostly for your sake, you see, that I bought it."

Olga glanced at the row of bottles on the dresser. She sighed again. Then she brought in the glasses.

It was late Christmas Eve before Mrs. Martinsen had finished her work. But finally everything was in order. Henry had delivered the last of the dresses as soon as they were done, and Olga and Miss Abrahamsen had straightened up and gathered everything in bundles on the chairs and the table in the sewing room. Miss Abrahamsen had had her coffee and cake, and had received a bottle of eau de cologne from Simonsen before she left.

After that Olga went into the living room. She cleared the table of the fashion journals and the chairs of dress goods and materials for lining, and gathered up the buttons and pins on the console in glass trays. Then she lit the Christmas tree, which she had trimmed the evening before.

Svanhild and Henry and Simonsen came in. The elders sat down in the plush chairs. But Svanhild danced about and was happy, greatly captivated by all the lights,—caught sight of the sled—and shouted for joy,—ran back to the tree and scarcely knew what to do with herself.

Simonsen beamed, and Olga smiled, although her eyes were red. Simonsen had noticed them several times during the afternoon. It would be just his luck to have her start crying to-night—when he so wanted them all to be happy.

He brought in his gifts, and he smiled mischievously; no doubt she thought the waist material a meager gift. Then he brought out a bottle of eau de cologne—he had given in to his desire to be extravagant when he was in the fifty öre shop getting something for Miss Abrahamsen. And there was even a sewing basket for Olga, and a little match box, which looked like silver, for Henry. The boy thanked him as a matter of course, and laid the pipe and the box in the window, where he sprawled lazily in a chair.

Then finally the brooch!

"These other things, you see, are kind of practical—I wanted you to have something else too, Olga—."

Olga opened the box, and tears came into her eyes.

"But so many things, Anton!"

Simonsen gave a grand flourish of the hand.

"I hope you'll keep me in mind when you wear it, Olga, dear."

"I certainly shall, Anton!"

"And, say,—what about the box that came this evening for Svanhild?"

Olga brought it in.

It was addressed "Little Miss Svanhild, care of Mrs. Martinsen's Dressmaking Establishment." Olga opened it. On a card inside was written "A Merry Christmas." It was from Sigurd Carling, and it was a doll—but oh, what a doll!

It had yellow curly hair and eyes that opened and closed, and it was dressed in a white coat with a white fur cap and muff, and there was a tiny pair of skates hung over one arm—that was the grandest of all. Svanhild was struck speechless—but Simonsen prated. He and Svanhild were equally delighted with the doll.

"Well, I suppose mamma had better put this away for you—it wouldn't do, you see, to play with it except on Sundays."

"After all, Sigurd is kind," he said to Olga, who came in with the glasses and a pitcher of hot water. "That's what I've always said—Sigurd is really kind at heart—it's that confounded wife of his that winds him round her finger, for he is really kind."

Simonsen brewed himself a hot toddy, and Olga had some port. Svanhild, too, was given a little port in a glass by herself as she sat on papa's knee.

"Won't you come over here too, Henry, and brew yourself a toddy—you're almost a grown man now, you know."

Henry rose somewhat reluctantly. He avoided looking at Simonsen. He had a pale freckled face and hard light-colored eyes. He looked thin and slight in the man-sized clothes he wore.

"Well, skaal then, all three!—This is what I call having a cozy time! Aren't we having a cozy time, Olga?"

"Yes, indeed!" She sat biting her lips, for the tears came into her eyes. "If only one could know where we'd be next Christmas—!"

Simonsen lit his cigar. He seemed a bit annoyed.

"Don't you want to try your pipe, Henry? There's some tobacco on my dresser—if you don't happen to have any yourself."

"No thanks!" was Henry's only reply.

"Ah yes—next Christmas—" Olga sighed and struggled to keep from crying.

"It's not easy to know what one doesn't know," Simonsen remarked, and leaned back in the sofa. "This certainly was a good cigar! Well, skaal, Olga! Who knows—perhaps we'll all be celebrating next Christmas with the peasants in the country! They celebrate Christmas royally up in Öimark, I am told. I really think you'd like living in the country, Olga—I really do. It wouldn't be so bad—all you'd have to do would be to step outside and chop down your own Christmas tree. How would you like that, Svanhild—go with papa into the woods and get a Christmas tree, and haul it home on your sled?"

Svanhild beamed ecstatically.

"And Henry'd have to beg off a few days at the office and come and celebrate Christmas with us."

Henry smiled—a bit scornfully.

"Wouldn't that be fun, Svanhild—go down to the station and meet Henry at the train? How would you like living with papa and mamma on a big farm in the country—with cows and horses and pigs and chickens and everything? And nice Sigurd, who gave you your doll—he has a little girl about your age too, and a boy a bit larger, and a wee tiny baby—you could go down and play with them in the city."

"And I'd go down and drink tea with that swell daughter-in-law of yours—if that's what you mean, Anton!"

"I don't see why *that* should follow."

"How can you sit and talk such nonsense!" Olga laughed, and then began to cry.

"But, Olga, what are you crying for now, my dear. Why must you always take it that way—?"

"Well, how do you want me to take it? I ought to be grateful, too, I suppose—that this swell daughter-in-law of yours flung in my face that Henry's father once deserted me, and that now you're leaving me. And we'll be left here with our shame—my children and I—my unfathered children! You think, as they do, I suppose, I am only fit to slave away forever, sewing for these fancy females you carry on with so scandalously. But I guess it's natural that all you people think you can treat me just as you please! Well, that's what I get—I should have known what sort you men were—when you've had what you want from a poor woman—why off you go and leave her sitting with the bag."

"But Olga!"

"Ah, it's easy enough for you. I should say so! All you need do is to move up into the country—and then take to drink and women again and all the rest, and run around wallowing in mire, as you were when I first took hold of you. Oh God, how simple and foolish I was to believe you and let you do with me as you pleased!"

"But Olga, for heaven's sake, think of the children!"

"Oh, don't worry—they hear it, you may rest assured—in the yard and on the stairs. They might just as well hear it from me too."

"But—it's Christmas Eve to-night—surely you ought to remember that," Simonsen protested paternally.

Olga wept quietly, her head on the table. Simonsen placed his hand over on her shoulder.

"But, Olga—surely you know—you know very well that I am fond of you. And Svanhild? Do you think perhaps I shall ever forget my little innocent child? On that score you may rest assured, Olga. I shan't ever betray you or leave you—what I've promised I'll keep!"

"The poor thing!" Olga sat up and blew her nose. "It won't be you, I'm afraid, who'll decide about that, Anton."

"One thing there is, Olga, you must remember," he put one arm about her neck and held Svanhild with the other, and he straightened up and thrust his stomach out, "there's one greater than either Sigurd or Mossa who presides over all of us."

"But isn't it time to sing some Christmas songs?" he asked after a bit. He took a sip of his toddy and cleared his throat. " 'Oh, blessed ever is Christmas Eve'—shall we sing that? Svanhild knows that, I'm sure. All right, Svanhild, sweetheart."

Svanhild sang whole-heartedly, and Simonsen hobbled along, falling by the wayside at the high notes, but always starting afresh at the beginning of each verse. After a little Olga too joined them with her tear-broken voice. Only Henry did not sing.

And after Olga had gone out to tend to the cream pudding and the spare ribs, Simonsen and Svanhild still went on singing.

And then finally the last morning came. The alarm clock in Olga's room sounded, but Simonsen merely rolled over, half-dozing in the dark—it was so cold to get up. Everything was gray and gloomy. Especially the prospect of having to get up and go out in the cold—away from everything.

Such a bed—with feather ticks on top and underneath—he had never experienced in any of the many places he had lived in before.

Olga opened the door, and in the light from her own room she set down the tray she was carrying, lit the lamp, and moved the tray over on the bed. There was coffee and cake.

"You'll have to hurry, I guess, Anton."

"I suppose so."

Simonsen sighed. He drew her over to him and patted her, in the intervals of dipping his cakes and drinking his coffee.

"Ah, what excellent coffee you have to-day, Olga dear—can't you sit down and have some with me?"

"I'm afraid I must get busy and start breakfast—"

Simonsen crawled out of bed and got his clothes on. He thrust the last few items into his hand-bag and locked both bags. Then he went into Olga's room.

He crossed over to the bed where Svanhild lay sleeping. He stood there for some time, his hands in his pockets, looking at her. Dear little Svanhild!

He peered into the living room too. It was pitch dark and icy cold. Henry had gone off to Nordmarken early Christmas morning with some friends of his. He fussed about in there awhile—came up against Svanhild's Christmas tree in the dark and set the tinsel trimmings tinkling. Ah—he sighed, when—if ever—would he see the place again!

And he returned to Olga's room. It was warm and comfortable. The lower end of the table had been cleared, where Olga and Miss Abrahamsen sat all day sewing; a white table cloth had been laid, and breakfast all ready—head-cheese and ale and dram and everything—and the lamp glowed peacefully and hummed softly as it burned. A bit of light fell upon Svanhild, asleep in her little bed, her pretty hair down over her forehead. His poor little girl!

There was a warmth and coziness in the room. Ah, how comfortable he had been here—with her—Olga—and Svanhild. His eyes filled with tears—he let the tears run—did not wipe them away—in order that Olga might see them. His flabby blue-red cheeks were quite wet when Olga came in with the coffee.

"Well, we'd better eat," she said.

"Yes, we may as well. And Svanhild—? Don't you think she might have liked to go to the train with us—have a ride in the sleigh?"

"I thought of it, Anton, but it's so dark and cold outside. Perhaps I'd better wake her anyway—she can have a drop of coffee with us."

She went over to the bed—shook the child gently.

"Svanhild, don't you want to get up and have coffee with papa and mamma?"

Svanhild blinked her eyes as she sat in her night-dress on Simonsen's knee. The coffee wakened her a bit, but she was quite still and spiritless—since the grown ups were so quiet.

"Where are you going, papa?"

"To Fredrikstad, of course."

"But when are you coming back?"

"Oh, I imagine you'll be coming down to me first."

"In the country—you told about?"

"Why, yes—"

"You can go sliding with me again there papa—can't you?"

"There we can go sliding—I should say so!"

The door bell rang. Olga looked out. The sleigh had arrived. The carrier's boy came and took Simonsen's bags down.

Simonsen kissed Svanhild and got up, and stood a moment with her in his arms.

"And now, Svanhild, you must be a nice good little girl—while papa is away."

"I'll be good," Svanhild answered.

Olga went out into the kitchen and turned off the gas—since Svanhild was to be home alone—and came in again, and stood ready, her finger on the wick of the lamp.

"Well, Anton—"

He gave Svanhild a resounding kiss, put her in her bed, and covered her up.

"Well, good-by, Svanhild dear!"

Olga put out the light, and they went out. In the hall he put his arms about her and pressed her close to him, and they kissed each other.

They sat silent in the sleigh as they shuffled down the streets in the dark morning. Nor had they anything to say to each other as they strolled about in the cold uninviting station hall. But she was ever at his heels—when he bought his ticket, when he checked his baggage—stood right behind him, small and dressed in black and looking short and square in her wraps.

They made their way leisurely into the waiting room and sat looking up at the station clock.

"We got here early enough surely," Olga remarked.

"We did that—and that's always best when one is travelling. It was a shame, Olga, that you had to get up so early—now in the holidays."

"Oh well," she said. "But perhaps we'd better go out and make sure of a seat on the train."

Simonsen got himself and his belongings stowed away in a smoking car. And he stood at the window and Olga below on the station platform.

"Well, take care of yourself,Olga—and write often—how you're getting on—"

"And you do the same, Anton."

They began to close the doors down the line. Olga stepped up on the runboard, and they kissed each other again.

"Well, Olga, you've been mighty good to me."

"No more than you to me, Anton. And have a good trip!"

The locomotive whistled—a jerk ran down the length of the train—and it began to move forward. Olga and Simonsen got out their handkerchiefs, and waved to each other, as long as they could see anything.

The train thundered away at the first gray sign of dawn—past the homes at Bækkelaget—at Norstrand—at Ljan. Some of the windows were already lit up. The icy gray of the fjord was just visible, on the lower side of the track, with islands scattered about.

How uncomfortable! Simonsen, alone in the car, puffed at his cigar, and looked out the window. Farms and forests swept by—swam by—grayish brown fields with strips of snow in the furrows—black woods—

Well—Olga was probably home by now. He wondered what she might be doing. Dressing Svanhild perhaps. She intended to sew to-day—she had said. So Svanhild would have to sit on the floor over by the window and play with her doll rags. There was no papa now to take her out coasting in the park.

Ah, that cozy room with the two warm beds in—and the lamp, and the sewing all spread out, and the bits of rag on the floor, which one was forever wading around in—and Svanhild over by the window—his dear little child!

He could see her sitting quiet all by herself. Now and then a Miss Hellum or some other came over and offered her some candy. Svanhild would surely miss her papa a lot!

It was all wrong, all wrong.

For a moment he was about to explode within—because it was not as it should be. His heart—what life had left him of it—fairly burned within him.

"Svanilla—Svanilla dear," he muttered to himself.

But he pushed the thoughts aside.

The little innocent child, who was so good, so very good. Surely she would be all right!

He wiped his eyes. There was, after all, some one mightier than they who ruled such things. Yes—one had to console oneself with the thought that there was after all a higher destiny that ruled everything.

William Faulkner

William Faulkner (1897–1962) was born in New Albany, Mississippi, the great-grandson of plantation owner, Civil War colonel, and minor novelist William C. Falkner, details of whose life figure prominently in several Faulkner novels. He attended the University of Mississippi briefly and enlisted in the Royal Canadian Air Force in 1918, but the war ended before he was commissioned. He held a series of minor jobs in the following years, and settled in Oxford, Mississippi, which was to serve as basis for his fictional town, Jefferson, in the mythical Yoknapatawpha County of his novels. In later years, Faulkner was writer-in-residence at the University of Virginia. He won the Nobel Prize for literature in 1949. His novels are often tragic accounts of the destructive power of the mythic past as it impinges on the lives of contemporary Southerners. His best-known novels include The Sound and the Fury *(1929) and* Absalom, Absalom! *(1936).* *(See page 81 of Introduction.)*

DEATH DRAG

I

The airplane appeared over town with almost the abruptness of an apparition. It was travelling fast; almost before we knew it was there it was already at the top of a loop; still over the square, in violation of both city and government ordinance. It was not a good loop either, performed viciously and slovenly and at top speed, as though the pilot were either a very nervous man or in a hurry, or (and this queerly: there is in our town an ex-army aviator. He was coming out of the post office when the airplane appeared going south; he watched the hurried and ungraceful loop and he made the comment) as though the pilot were trying to make the minimum of some specified manœuvre in order to save gasoline. The airplane came over the loop with one wing down, as though about to make an Immelmann turn. Then it did a half roll, the loop three-quarters complete, and without any break in the whine of the full-throttled engine and still at top speed and with that apparition-like suddenness, it disappeared eastward toward our airport. When the first small boys reached the field, the airplane was on the ground, drawn up into a fence corner at the end of the field. It was motionless and empty. There was no one in sight at all. Resting there, empty and dead, patched and shabby and painted awkwardly with a single thin coat of dead black, it gave again that illusion of ghostliness, as though it might have flown there and made that loop and landed by itself.

Our field is still in an embryonic state. Our town is built upon hills, and the field, once a cotton field, is composed of forty acres of ridge and gully, upon which, by means of grading and filling, we managed to build an X-shaped runway into the prevailing winds. The runways are long enough in themselves, but the field, like our town, is controlled by men who were of middle age when younger men first began to fly, and so the clearance is not always good. On one side is a grove of trees which the owner will not permit to be felled; on another is the barnyard of a farm: sheds and houses, a long barn with a roof of rotting shingles, a big haycock. The airplane had come to rest in the fence corner near the barn. The small boys and a Negro or two and a white man, descended from a halted wagon in the road, were standing quietly about it when two men in helmets and lifted goggles emerged suddenly around the corner of the barn. One was tall, in a dirty coverall. The other was quite short, in breeches and puttees and a soiled, brightly patterned overcoat which looked as if he had got wet in it and it had shrunk on him. He walked with a decided limp.

They had stopped at the corner of the barn. Without appearing to actually turn their heads, they seemed to take in at one glance the entire scene, quickly. The tall man spoke. "What town is this?"

One of the small boys told him the name of the town.

"Who lives here?" the tall man said.

"Who lives here?" the boy repeated.

"Who runs this field? Is it a private field?"

"Oh. It belongs to the town. They run it."

"Do they all live here? The ones that run it?"

The white man, the Negroes, the small boys, all watched the tall man.

"What I mean, is there anybody in this town that flies, that owns a ship? Any strangers here that fly?"

"Yes," the boy said. "There's a man lives here that flew in the war, the English army."

"Captain Warren was in the Royal Flying Corps," a second boy said.

"That's what I said," the first boy said.

"You said the English army," the second boy said.

The second man, the short one with the limp, spoke. He spoke to the tall man, quietly, in a dead voice, in the diction of Weber and Fields in vaudeville, making his *wh's* into *v's* and his *th's* into *d's*. "What does that mean?" he said.

"It's all right," the tall man said. He moved forward. "I think I know him." The short man followed, limping, terrific, crablike. The tall man had a gaunt face beneath a two-days' stubble. His eyeballs looked dirty, too, with a strained, glaring expression. He wore a dirty helmet of cheap, thin cloth, though it was January. His goggles were worn, but even we could tell that they were good ones. But then everybody quit looking at him to look at the short man; later, when we older people saw him, we said among ourselves that he had the most tragic face we had ever seen; an expression of outraged and convinced and indomitable despair, like that of a man carrying through choice a bomb which, at a certain hour each day, may or may not explode. He had a nose which would have been out of proportion to a man six feet tall. As shaped by his close helmet, the entire upper half of his head down to the end of his nose would have fitted a six-foot body. But below that, below a lateral line bisecting his head from the end of his nose to the back of his skull, his jaw, the rest of his face, was not two inches deep. His jaw was a long, flat line clapping-to beneath his nose like the jaw of a shark, so that the tip of his nose and the tip of his jaw almost touched. His goggles were merely flat pieces of window-glass held in felt frames. His helmet was leather. Down the back of it, from the top to the hem, was a long savage tear, held together top and bottom by strips of adhesive tape almost black with dirt and grease.

From around the corner of the barn there now appeared a third man, again with that abrupt immobility, as though he had materialized there out of thin air; though when they saw him he was already moving toward the group. He wore an overcoat above a neat civilian suit; he wore a cap. He was a little taller than the limping man, and broad, heavily built. He was handsome in a dull, quiet way; from his face, a man of infrequent speech. When he came up the spectators saw that he, like the limping man, was also a Jew. That is, they knew at once that two of the strangers were of a different race from themselves, without being able to say what the difference was. The boy who had first spoken probably revealed by his next speech what they thought the difference was. He, as well as the other boys, was watching the man who limped.

"Were you in the war?" the boy said. "In the air war?"

The limping man did not answer. Both he and the tall man were watching the gate. The spectators looked also and saw a car enter the gate and come down the edge of the field toward them. Three men got out of the car and approached. Again the limping man spoke quietly to the tall man: "Is that one?"

"No," the tall man said, without looking at the other. He watched the newcomers, looking from face to face. He spoke to the oldest of the three. "Morning," he said. "You run this field?"

"No," the newcomer said. "You want the secretary of the Fair Association. He's in town."

"Any charge to use it?"

"I don't know. I reckon they'll be glad to have you use it."

"Go on and pay them," the limping man said.

The three newcomers looked at the airplane with that blank, knowing, respectful air of groundlings. It reared on its muddy wheels, the propeller motionless, rigid, with a quality immobile and poised and dynamic. The nose was big with engine, the wings taut, the fuselage streaked with oil behind the rusting exhaust pipes. "Going to do some business here?" the oldest one said.

"Put you on a show," the tall man said.

"What kind of show?"

"Anything you want. Wing-walking; death-drag."

"What's that? Death-drag?"

"Drop a man onto the top of a car and drag him off again. Bigger the crowd, the more you'll get."

"You will get your money's worth," the limping man said.

The boys still watched him. "Were you in the war?" the first boy said.

The third stranger had not spoken up to this time. He now said: "Let's get on to town."

"Right," the tall man said. He said generally, in his flat, dead voice, the same voice which the three strangers all seemed to use, as though it were their common language: "Where can we get a taxi? Got one in town?"

"We'll take you to town," the men who had come up in the car said.

"We'll pay," the limping man said.

"Glad to do it," the driver of the car said. "I won't charge you anything. You want to go now?"

"Sure," the tall man said. The three strangers got into the back seat, the other three in front. Three of the boys followed them to the car.

"Lemme hang on to town, Mr. Black?" one of the boys said.

"Hang on," the driver said. The boys got onto the running boards. The car returned to town. The three in front could hear the three strangers talking in the back. They talked quietly, in low, dead voices, somehow quiet and urgent, discussing something among themselves, the tall man and the handsome one doing most of the talking. The three in front heard only one speech from the limping man: "I won't take less. . . ."

"Sure," the tall man said. He leaned forward and raised his voice a little: "Where'll I find this Jones, this secretary?"

The driver told him.

"Is the newspaper or the printing shop near there? I want some handbills?"

"I'll show you," the driver said. "I'll help you get fixed up."

"Fine," the tall man said. "Come out this afternoon and I'll give you a ride, if I have time."

The car stopped at the newspaper office. "You can get your handbills here," the driver said.

"Good," the tall man said. "Is Jones's office on this street?"

"I'll take you there, too," the driver said.

"You see about the editor," the tall man said. "I can find Jones, I guess." They got out of the car. "I'll come back here," the tall man said. He went on down the street, swiftly, in his dirty coverall and helmet. Two other men had joined the group before the newspaper office. They all entered, the limping man leading, followed by the three boys.

"I want some handbills," the limping man said. "Like this one." He took from his pocket a folded sheet of pink paper. He opened it; the editor, the boys, the five men, leaned to see it. The lettering was black and bold:

DEMON DUNCAN
DAREDEVIL OF THE AIR
DEATH DEFYING SHOW WILL BE GIVEN
UNDER THE AUSPICES OF . . . .
THIS P.M. AT TWO P.M.
COME ONE COME ALL AND SEE DEMON DUNCAN
DEFY DEATH IN DEATH DROP & DRAG OF DEATH

"I want them in one hour," the limping man said.

"What you want in this blank space?" the editor said.

"What you got in this town?"

"What we got?"

"What auspices? American Legion? Rotary Club? Chamber of Commerce?"

"We got all of them."

"I'll tell you which one in a minute, then," the limping man said. "When my partner gets back."

"You have to have a guarantee before you put on the show, do you?" the editor said.

"Why, sure. Do you think I should put on a daredevil without auspices? Do you think I should for a nickel maybe jump off the airplane?"

"Who's going to jump?" one of the later comers said; he was a taxi-driver.

The limping man looked at him. "Don't you worry about that," he said. "Your business is just to pay the money. We will do all the jumping you want, if you pay enough."

"I just asked which one of you all was the jumper."

"Do I ask you whether you pay me in silver or in greenbacks?" the limping man said. "Do I ask you?"

"No," the taxi-driver said.

"About these bills," the editor said. "You said you wanted them in an hour."

"Can't you begin on them, and leave that part out until my partner comes back?"

"Suppose he don't come before they are finished?"

"Well, that won't be my fault, will it?"

"All right," the editor said. "Just so you pay for them."

"You mean, I should pay without a auspices on the handbill?"

"I ain't in this business for fun," the editor said.

"We'll wait," the limping man said.

They waited.

"Were you a flyer in the war, Mister?" the boy said.

The limping man turned upon the boy his long, misshapen, tragic face. "The war? Why should I fly in a war?"

"I thought maybe because of your leg. Captain Warren limps, and he flew in the war. I reckon you just do it for fun?"

"For fun? What for fun? Fly? Gruss Gott. I hate it, I wish the man what invented them was here; I would put him into that machine yonder and I would print on his back, Do not do it, one thousand times."

"Why do you do it, then?" the man who had entered with the taxi-driver said.

"Because of that Republican Coolidge. I was in business, and that Coolidge ruined business; ruined it. That's why. For fun? Gruss Gott."

They looked at the limping man. "I suppose you have a license?" the second late-comer said.

The limping man looked at him. "A license?"

"Don't you have to have a license to fly?"

"Oh; a license. For the airplane to fly; sure, I understand. Sure. We got one. You want to see it?"

"You're supposed to show it to anybody that wants to see it, aren't you?"

"Why, sure. You want to see it?"

"Where is it?"

"Where should it be? It's nailed to the airplane, where the government put it. Did you thought maybe it was nailed to me? Did you thought maybe I had a engine on me and maybe wings? It's on the airplane. Call a taxi and go to the airplane and look at it."

"I run a taxi," the driver said.

"Well, run it. Take this gentleman out to the field where he can look at the license on the airplane."

"It'll be a quarter," the driver said. But the limping man was not looking at the driver. He was leaning against the counter. They watched him take a stick of gum from his pocket and peel it. They watched him put the gum into his mouth. "I said it'll be a quarter, Mister," the driver said.

"Was you talking to me?" the limping man said.

"I thought you wanted a taxi out to the airport."

"Me? What for? What do I want to go out to the airport for? I just come from there. I ain't the one that wants to see that license. I have already seen it. I was there when the government nailed it onto the airplane."

II

Captain Warren, the ex-army flyer, was coming out of the store, where he met the tall man in the dirty coverall. Captain Warren told about it in the barber shop that night, when the airplane was gone.

"I hadn't seen him in fourteen years, not since I left England for the front in '17. 'So it was you that rolled out of that loop with two passengers and a twenty model Hisso smokepot?' I said.

" 'Who else saw me?' he said. So he told me about it, standing there, looking over his shoulder every now and then. He was sick; a man stopped behind him to let a couple of ladies pass, and Jock whirled like he might have shot the man if he'd had a gun, and while we were in the café some one slammed a door at the back and I thought he would come out of his monkey suit. 'It's a little nervous trouble I've got,' he told me. 'I'm all right.' I had tried to get him to come out home with me for dinner, but he wouldn't. He said that he had to kind of jump himself and eat before he knew it, sort of. We had started down the street and we were passing the restaurant when he said: 'I'm going to eat,' and he turned and ducked in like a rabbit and sat down with his back to the wall and told Vernon to bring him the quickest thing he had. He drank three glasses of water and then Vernon brought him a milk bottle full and he drank most of that before the dinner came up from the kitchen. When he took off his helmet, I saw that his hair was pretty near white, and he is younger than I am. Or he was, up there when we were in Canada training. Then he told me what the name of his nervous trouble was. It was named Ginsfarb. The little one; the one that jumped off the ladder."

"What was the trouble?" we asked. "What were they afraid of?"

"They were afraid of inspectors," Warren said. "They had no licenses at all."

"There was one on the airplane."

"Yes. But it did not belong to that airplane. That one had been grounded by an inspector when Ginsfarb bought it. The license was for another airplane that had been wrecked, and some one had helped Ginsfarb compound another felony by selling the license to him. Jock had lost his license about two years ago when he crashed a big plane full of Fourth-of-July holidayers. Two of the engines quit, and he had to land. The airplane smashed up some and broke a gas line, but even then they would have been all right if a passenger hadn't got scared (it was about dusk) and struck a match. Jock was not so much to blame, but the passengers all burned to death, and the government is strict. So he couldn't get a license, and he couldn't make Ginsfarb even pay to take out a parachute rigger's license. So they had no license at all; if they were ever caught, they'd all go to the penitentiary."

"No wonder his hair was white," some one said.

"That wasn't what turned it white," Warren said. "I'll tell you about that. So they'd go to little towns like this one, fast, find out if there was anybody that might catch them, and if there wasn't, they'd put on the show and then clear out and go to another town, staying away from the cities. They'd come in and get handbills printed while Jock and the other one would try to get underwritten by some local organization. They wouldn't let Ginsfarb do this part, because he'd stick out for his price too long and they'd be afraid to risk it. So the other two would do this, get what they could, and if they could not get what Ginsfarb told them to, they'd take what they could and then try to keep Ginsfarb fooled until it was too late. Well, this time Ginsfarb kicked up. I guess they had done it too much on him.

"So I met Jock on the street. He looked bad, I offered him a drink, but he said he couldn't even smoke any more. All he could do was drink water; he said he usually drank about a gallon during the night, getting up for it.

" 'You look like you might have to jump yourself to sleep, too,' I said.

" 'No, I sleep fine. The trouble is, the nights aren't long enough. I'd like to live at the North Pole from September to April, and at the South Pole from April to September. That would just suit me.'

" 'You aren't going to last long enough to get there,' I said.

" 'I guess so. It's a good engine. I see to that.'

" 'I mean, you'll be in jail.'

"Then he said: 'Do you think so? Do you guess I could?'

"We went on to the café. He told me about the racket, and showed me one of those Demon Duncan handbills. 'Demon Duncan?' I said.

" 'Why not? Who would pay to see a man named Ginsfarb jump from a ship?'

" 'I'd pay to see that before I'd pay to see a man named Duncan do it,' I said.

"He hadn't thought of that. Then he began to drink water, and he told me that Ginsfarb had wanted a hundred dollars for the stunt, but that he and the other fellow only got sixty.

" 'What are you going to do about it?' I said.

" 'Try to keep him fooled and get this thing over and get to hell away from here,' he said.

" 'Which one is Ginsfarb?' I said. The little one that looks like a shark?'

"Then he began to drink water. He emptied my glass too at one shot and tapped it on the table. Vernon brought him another glass. 'You must be thirsty,' Vernon said.

" 'Have you got a pitcher of it?' Jock said.

" 'I could fill you a milk bottle.'

" 'Let's have it,' Jock said. 'And give me another glass while I'm waiting.' Then he told me about Ginsfarb, why his hair had turned gray.

" 'How long have you been doing this?' I said.

" 'Ever since the 26th of August.'

" 'This is just January,' I said.

" 'What about it?'

" 'The 26th of August is not six months past.' "

"He looked at me. Vernon brought the bottle of water. Jock poured a glass and drank it. He began to shake, sitting there, shaking and sweating, trying to fill the glass again. Then he told me about it, talking fast, filling the glass and drinking.

"Jake (the other one's name is Jake something; the good-looking one) drives the car, the rented car. Ginsfarb swaps onto the car from the ladder. Jock said he would have to fly the ship into position over a Ford or a Chevrolet running on three cylinders, trying to keep Ginsfarb from jumping from twenty or thirty feet away in order to save gasoline in the ship and in the rented car. Ginsfarb goes out on the bottom wing with his ladder, fastens the ladder onto a strut, hooks himself into the other end of the ladder, and drops off; everybody on the ground thinks that he has done what they all came to see: fallen off and killed himself. That's what he calls his death-drop. Then he swaps from the ladder onto the top of the car, and the ship comes back and he catches the ladder and is dragged off again. That's his death-drag.

"Well, up till the day when Jock's hair began to turn white, Ginsfarb, as a matter of economy, would do it all at once; he would get into position above the car and drop off on his ladder and then make contact with the car, and sometimes Jock said the ship would not be in the air three minutes. Well, on this day the rented car was a bum or something; anyway, Jock had to circle the field four or five times while the car was getting into position, and Ginsfarb, seeing his money being blown out the exhaust pipes, finally refused to wait for Jock's signal and dropped off anyway. It was all right, only the distance between the ship and the car was not as long as the rope ladder. So Ginsfarb hit on the car, and Jock had just enough soup to zoom and drag Ginsfarb, still on the ladder, over a high-power electric line, and he held the ship in that climb for twenty minutes while Ginsfarb climbed back up the ladder with his leg broken. He held the ship in a climb with his knees, with the throttle wide open and the engine revving about eleven hundred, while he reached back and opened that cupboard behind the cockpit and dragged out a suitcase and propped the stick so he could get out on the wing and drag Ginsfarb back into the ship. He got Ginsfarb in the ship and on the ground again and Ginsfarb says: 'How far did we go?' and Jock told him they had flown with full throttle for thirty minutes and Ginsfarb says: 'Will you ruin me yet?' "

III

The rest of this is composite. It is what we (groundlings, dwellers in and backbone of a small town interchangeable with the duplicate of ten thousand little dead clottings of human life about the land) saw, refined and clarified by the expert, the man who had himself seen his own lonely and scudding shadow upon the face of the puny and remote earth.

The three strangers arrived at the field, in the rented car. When they got out of the car, they were arguing in tense, dead voices, the pilot and the handsome man against the man who limped. Captain Warren said they were arguing about the money.

"I want to see it," Ginsfarb said. They stood close; the handsome man took something from his pocket.

"There. There it is. See?" he said.

"Let me count it myself," Ginsfarb said.

"Come on, come on," the pilot hissed, in his dead, tense voice. "We tell you we got the money! Do you want an inspector to walk in and take the money and the ship too and put us in jail? Look at all these people waiting."

"You fooled me before," Ginsfarb said.

"All right," the pilot said. "Give it to him. Give him his ship too. And he can pay for the car when he gets back to town. We can get a ride in; there's a train out of here in fifteen minutes."

"You fooled me once before," Ginsfarb said.

"But we're not fooling you now. Come on. Look at all these people."

They moved toward the airplane, Ginsfarb limping terrifically, his back stubborn, his face tragic, outraged, cold. There was a good crowd: country people in overalls; the men a general dark clump against which the bright dresses of the women, the young girls, showed. The small boys and several men were already surrounding the airplane. We watched the limping man begin to take objects from the body of it: a parachute, a rope ladder. The handsome man went to the propeller. The pilot got into the back seat.

"Off!" he said, sudden and sharp. "Stand back, folks. We're going to wring the old bird's neck."

They tried three times to crank the engine.

"I got a mule, Mister," a countryman said. "How much'll you pay for a tow?"

The three strangers did not laugh. The limping man was busy attaching the rope ladder to one wing.

"You can't tell me," a countrywoman said. "Even he ain't that big a fool."

The engine started then. It seemed to lift bodily from the ground a small boy who stood behind it and blow him aside like a leaf. We watched it turn and trundle down the field.

"You can't tell me that thing's flying," the countrywoman said. "I reckon the Lord give me eyes. I can see it ain't flying. You folks have been fooled."

"Wait," another voice said. "He's got to turn into the wind."

"Ain't there as much wind right there or right here as there is down yonder?" the woman said. But it did fly. It turned back toward us; the noise became deafening. When it came broadside on to us, it did not seem to be going fast, yet we could see daylight beneath the wheels and the earth. But it was not going fast; it appeared rather to hang gently just above the earth until we saw that, beyond and beneath it, trees and earth in panorama were fleeing backward at dizzy speed, and then it tilted and shot skyward with a noise like a circular saw going into a white oak log. "There ain't nobody in it!" the countrywoman said. "You can't tell me!"

The third man, the handsome one in the cap, had got into the rented car. We all knew it: a battered thing which the owner would rent to any one who would make a deposit of ten dollars. He drove to the end of the field, faced down the runway, and stopped. We looked back at the airplane. It was high, coming back toward us; some one cried suddenly, his voice puny and thin: "There! Out on the wing! See?"

"It ain't!" the countrywoman said. "I don't believe it!"

"You saw them get in it," some one said.

"I don't believe it!" the woman said.

Then we sighed; we said, "Aaahhhhhhh"; beneath the wing of the airplane there was a falling dot. We knew it was a man. Some way we knew that that lonely, puny, falling shape was that of a living man like ourselves. It fell. It seemed to fall for years, yet when it checked suddenly up without visible rope or cord, it was less far from the airplane than was the end of the delicate pen-slash of the profiled wing.

"It ain't a man!" the woman shrieked.

"You know better," the man said. "You saw him get in it."

"I don't care!" the woman cried. "It ain't a man! You take me right home this minute!"

The rest is hard to tell. Not because we saw so little; we saw everything that happened, but because we had so little in experience to postulate it with. We saw that battered rented car moving down the field, going faster, jouncing in the broken January mud, then the sound of the airplane blotted it, reduced it to immobility; we saw the dangling ladder and the shark-faced man swinging on it beneath the death-colored airplane. The end of the ladder raked right across the top of the car, from end to end, with the limping man on the ladder and the capped head of the handsome man leaning out of the car. And the end of the field was coming nearer, and the airplane was travelling faster than the car, passing it. And nothing happened. "Listen!" some one cried. "They are talking to one another!"

Captain Warren told us what they were talking about, the two Jews yelling back and forth at one another: the shark-faced man on the dangling ladder that looked like a cobweb, the other one in the car; the fence, the end of the field, coming closer.

"Come on!" the man in the car shouted.

"What did they pay?"

"Jump!"

"If they didn't pay that hundred, I won't do it."

Then the airplane zoomed, roaring, the dangling figure on the gossamer ladder swinging beneath it. It circled the field twice while the man got the car into position again. Again the car started down the field; again the airplane came down with its wild, circular-saw drone which died into a splutter as the ladder and the clinging man swung up to the car from behind; again we heard the two puny voices shrieking at one another with a quality at once ludicrous and horrible: the one coming out of the very air itself, shrieking about something sweated out of the earth and without value anywhere else:

"How much did you say?"

"Jump!"

"What? How much did they pay?"

"Nothing! Jump!"

"Nothing?" the man on the ladder wailed in a fading, outraged shriek. "Nothing?" Again the airplane was dragging the ladder irrevocably past the car, approaching the end of the field, the fences, the long barn with its rotting roof. Suddenly we saw Captain Warren beside us; he was using words we had never heard him use.

"He's got the stick between his knees," Captain Warren said. "Exalted suzerain of mankind; saccharine and sacred symbol of eternal rest." We had forgot about the pilot, the man still in the airplane. We saw the airplane, tilted upward, the pilot standing upright in the back seat, leaning over the side and shaking both hands at the man on the ladder. We could hear him yelling now as again the man on the ladder was dragged over the car and past it, shrieking:

"I won't do it! I won't do it!" He was still shrieking when the airplane zoomed; we saw him, a diminishing and shrieking spot against the sky above the long roof of the barn: "I won't do it! I won't do it!" Before, when the speck left the airplane, falling, to be snubbed up by the ladder, we knew that it was a living man; again, when the speck left the ladder, falling, we knew that it was a living man, and we knew that there was no ladder to snub him up now. We saw him falling against the cold, empty January sky until the silhouette of the barn absorbed him; even from here, his attitude froglike, outraged, implacable. From somewhere in the crowd a woman screamed, though the sound was blotted out by the sound of the airplane. It reared skyward with its wild, tearing noise, the empty ladder swept backward beneath it. The sound of the engine was like a groan, a groan of relief and despair.

IV

Captain Warren told us in the barber shop on that Saturday night.

"Did he really jump off, onto that barn?" we asked him.

"Yes. He jumped. He wasn't thinking about being killed, or even hurt. That's why he wasn't hurt. He was too mad, too in a hurry to receive justice. He couldn't wait to fly back down. Providence knew that he was too busy and that he deserved justice, so Providence put that barn there with the rotting roof. He wasn't even thinking about hitting the barn; if he'd tried to, let go of his belief in a cosmic balance to bother about landing, he would have missed the barn and killed himself."

It didn't hurt him at all, save for a long scratch on his face that bled a lot, and his overcoat was torn completely down the back, as though the tear down the back of the helmet had run on down the overcoat. He came out of the barn running before we got to it. He hobbled right among us, with his bloody face, his arms waving, his coat dangling from either shoulder.

"Where is that secretary?" he said.

"What secretary?"

"That American Legion secretary." He went on, limping fast, toward where a crowd stood about three women who had fainted. "You said you would pay a hundred dollars to see me swap to that car. We pay rent on the car and all, and now you would—"

"You got sixty dollars," some one said.

The man looked at him. "Sixty? I said one hundred. Then you would let me believe it was one hundred and it was just sixty; you would see me risk my life for sixty dollars. . . ." The airplane was down; none of us were aware of it until the pilot sprang suddenly upon the man who limped. He jerked the man around and knocked him down before we could grasp the pilot. We held the pilot, struggling, crying, the tears streaking his dirty, unshaven face. Captain Warren was suddenly there, holding the pilot.

"Stop it!" he said. "Stop it!"

The pilot ceased. He stared at Captain Warren, then he slumped and sat on the ground in his thin, dirty garment, with his unshaven face, dirty, gaunt, with his sick eyes, crying. "Go away," Captain Warren said. "Let him alone for a minute."

We went away, back to the other man, the one who limped. They had lifted him and he drew the two halves of his overcoat forward and looked at them. Then he said: "I want some chewing gum."

Some one gave him a stick. Another offered him a cigarette. "Thanks," he said. "I don't burn up no money. I ain't got enough of it yet." He put the gum into his mouth. "You would take advantage of me. If you thought I would risk my life for sixty dollars, you fool yourself."

"Give him the rest of it," some one said. "Here's my share."

The limping man did not look around. "Make it up to a hundred, and I will swap to the car like on the handbill," he said.

Somewhere a woman screamed behind him. She began to laugh and to cry at the same time. "Don't . . ." she said, laughing and crying at the same time. "Don't let . . ." until they led her away. Still the limping man had not moved. He wiped his face on his cuff and he was looking at his bloody sleeve when Captain Warren came up.

"How much is he short?" Warren said. They told Warren. He took out some money and gave it to the limping man.

"You want I should swap to the car?" he said.

"No," Warren said. "You get that crate out of here quick as you can."

"Well, that's your business," the limping man said. "I got witnesses I offered to swap." He moved; we made way and watched him, in his severed and dangling overcoat, approach the airplane. It was on the runway, the engine running. The third man was already in the front seat. We watched the limping man crawl terrifically in beside him. They sat there, looking forward.

The pilot began to get up. Warren was standing beside him. "Ground it," Warren said. "You are coming home with me."

"I guess we'd better get on," the pilot said. He did not look at Warren. Then he put out his hand. "Well . . ." he said.

Warren did not take his hand. "You come on home with me," he said.

"Who'd take care of that bastard?"

"Who wants to?"

"I'll get him right, some day. Where I can beat hell out of him."

"Jock," Warren said.

"No," the other said.

"Have you got an overcoat?"

"Sure I have."

"You're a liar." Warren began to pull off his overcoat.

"No," the other said; "I don't need it." He went on toward the machine. "See you some time," he said over his shoulder. We watched him get in, heard an airplane come to life, come alive. It passed us, already off the ground. The pilot jerked his hand once, stiffly; the two heads in the front seat did not turn nor move. Then it was gone, the sound was gone.

Warren turned. "What about that car they rented?" he said.

"He give me a quarter to take it back to town," a boy said.

"Can you drive it?"

"Yes, sir. I drove it out here. I showed him where to rent it."

"The one that jumped?"

"Yes, sir." The boy looked a little aside. "Only I'm a little scared to take it back. I don't reckon you could come with me."

"Why, scared?" Warren said.

"That fellow never paid nothing down on it, like Mr. Harris wanted. He told Mr. Harris he might not use it, but if he did use it in his show, he would pay Mr. Harris twenty dollars for it instead of ten like Mr. Harris wanted. He told me to take it back and tell Mr. Harris he never used the car. And I don't know if Mr. Harris will like it. He might get mad."

Richard Wright

Richard Wright (1908–1960) was born on a farm near Natchez, Mississippi. His father's desertion of the family and his mother's partial paralysis contributed to a barren and impoverished childhood. Wright lived in orphanages and with various relatives; his early experiences are movingly detailed in Black Boy *(1945) and several other autobiographical works. He fled the South in 1927, but found life in Chicago equally difficult for a black man. Wright read widely, particularly H. L. Mencken, Sinclair Lewis, and Theodore Dreiser, who validated his own experiences with social injustice. He joined the Communist Party (which he soon left) and began to publish stories, poetry, and essays in radical journals. For most of the Depression, he worked in the WPA Federal Writers Project and the Federal Negro Theater. His first major work was a collection of short stories,* Uncle Tom's Children *(1938). His novel* Native Son *(1940) was a great success. Wright later turned to existentialism. He spent the last thirteen years of his life in Europe, mostly France. He was the first major twentieth-century black writer to treat with sophistication and complexity the loneliness and alienation of black life in the ghetto.* *(See p. 67 of Introduction.)*

BRIGHT AND MORNING STAR

I

She stood with her black face some six inches from the moist windowpane and wondered when on earth would it ever stop raining. It might keep up like this all week, she thought. She heard rain droning upon the roof, and high up in the wet sky her eyes followed the silent rush of a bright shaft of yellow that swung from the airplane beacon in far-off Memphis. Momently she could see it cutting through the rainy dark; it would hover a second like a gleaming sword above her head, then vanish. She sighed, troubling, Johnny-Boys been trampin in this slop all day wid no decent shoes on his feet. . . . Through the window she could see the rich black earth sprawling outside in the night. There was more rain than the clay could soak up; pools stood everywhere. She yawned and mumbled: "Rains good n bad. It kin make seeds bus up thu the groun, er it kin bog things down lika watah-soaked coffin." Her hands were folded loosely over her stomach and the hot air of the kitchen traced a filmy veil of sweat on her forehead. From the cook stove came the soft singing of burning wood, and now and then a throaty bubble rose from a pot of simmering greens.

"Shucks, Johnny-Boy coulda let somebody else do all tha runnin in the rain. Theres others bettah fixed fer it than he is. But, naw! Johnny-Boy ain the one t trust nobody t do nothin. Hes gotta do it *all* hissef. . . ."

She glanced at a pile of damp clothes in a zinc tub. Waal, Ah bettah git t work. She turned, lifted a smoothing iron with a thick pad of cloth, touched a spit-wet finger to it with a quick, jerking motion: *smiiitz!* Yeah; its hot! Stooping, she took a blue work-shirt from the tub and shook it out. With a deft twist of her shoulder she caught the iron in her right hand; the fingers of her left hand took a piece of wax from a tin box and a frying sizzle came as she smeared the bottom. She was thinking of nothing now; her hands followed a life-long ritual of toil. Spreading a sleeve, she ran the hot iron to and fro until the wet cloth became stiff. She was deep in the midst of her work when a song rose up out of the far-off days of her childhood and broke through half-parted lips:

Hes the Lily of the Valley, the Bright n Mawnin Star
Hes the Fariest of Ten Thousan t mah soul . . .

A gust of wind dashed rain against the window. Johnny-Boy oughta c mon home n eat his suppah. Aw, Lawd! Itd be fine ef Sug could eat wid us tonight! Itd be like ol times! Mabbe aftah all it won't be long fo he comes back. Tha lettah Ah got from im las week said *Don give up hope. . . .* Yeah; we gotta live in hope. Then both of her sons, Sug and Johnny-Boy, would be back with her.

With an involuntary nervous gesture, she stopped and stood still, listening. But the only sound was the lulling fall of rain. Shucks, ain no usa me ackin this way, she thought. Ever time they gits ready to hol them meetings Ah gits jumpity. Ah been a lil scared ever since Sug went t jail. She heard the clock ticking and looked. Johnny-Boys a *hour* late! He sho mus be havin a time doin all tha trampin, trampin thu the mud. . . . But her fear was a quiet one; it was more like an intense brooding than a fear; it was a sort of hugging of hated facts so closely that she could feel their grain, like letting cold water run over her hand from a faucet on a winter morning.

She ironed again, faster now, as if she felt the more she engaged her body in work the less she would think. But how could she forget Johnny-Boy out there on those wet fields rounding up white and black Communists for a meeting tomorrow? And that was just what Sug had been doing when the sheriff had caught him, beat him, and tried to make him tell who and where his comrades were. Po Sug! They sho musta beat the boy somethin awful! But, thank Gawd, he didnt talk! He ain no weaklin, Sug ain! Hes been lion-hearted all his life long.

That had happened a year ago. And now each time those meetings came around, the old terror surged back. While shoving the iron, a cluster of toiling days returned; days of washing and ironing to feed Johnny-Boy and Sug so they could do party work; days of carrying a hundred pounds of white folks' clothes upon her head across fields sometimes wet and sometimes dry. But in those days a hundred pounds was nothing to carry carefully balanced upon her head while stepping by instinct over the corn and cotton rows. The only time it had seemed heavy was when she had heard of Sug's arrest. She had been coming home one morning with a bundle upon her head, her hands swinging idly by her sides, walking slowly with her eyes in front of her, when Bob, Johnny-Boy's pal, had called from across the fields and had come and told her that the sheriff had got Sug. That morning the bundle had become heavier than she could ever remember.

And with each passing week now, though she spoke of it to no one, things were becoming heavier. The tubs of water and the smoothing iron and the bundle of clothes were becoming harder to lift, with her back aching so; and her work was taking longer, all because Sug was gone and she didn't know just when Johnny-Boy would be taken too. To ease the ache of anxiety that was swelling her heart, she hummed, then sang softly:

He walks wid me, He talks wid me
He tells me Ahm His own. . . .

Guiltily, she stopped and smiled. Looks like Ah jus cant seem t fergit them ol songs, no mattah how hard Ah tries. . . . She had learned them when she was a little girl living and working on a farm. Every Monday morning from the corn- and cotton-fields the slow strains had floated from her mother's lips, lonely and haunting; and later, as the years had filled with gall, she had learned their deep meaning. Long hours of scrubbing floors for a few cents a day had taught her who Jesus was, what a great boon it was to cling to Him, to be like Him and suffer without a mumbling word. She had poured the yearning of her life into the songs, feeling buoyed with a faith beyond this world. The figure of the Man nailed in agony to the Cross, His burial in a cold grave, His transfigured Resurrection, His being breath and clay, God and Man—all had focused her feelings upon an imagery which had swept her life into a wondrous vision.

But as she had grown older, a cold white mountain, the white folks and their laws, had swum into her vision and shattered her songs and their spell of peace. To her that white mountain was temptation, something to lure her from her Lord, a part of the world God had made in order that she might endure it and come through all the stronger, just as Christ had risen with greater glory from the tomb. The days crowded with trouble had enhanced her faith and she had grown to love hardship with a bitter pride; she had obeyed the laws of the white folks with a soft smile of secret knowing.

After her mother had been snatched up to heaven in a chariot of fire, the years had brought her a rough workingman and two black babies, Sug and Johnny-Boy, all three of whom she had wrapped in the charm and magic of her vision. Then she was tested by no less than God; her man died, a trial which she bore with the strength shed by the grace of her vision; finally even the memory of her man faded into the vision itself, leaving her with two black boys growing tall, slowly into manhood.

Then one day grief had come to her heart when Johnny-Boy and Sug had walked forth, demanding their lives. She had sought to fill their eyes with her vision, but they would have none of it. And she had wept when they began to boast of the strength shed by a new and terrible vision.

But she had loved them, even as she loved them now; bleeding, her heart had followed them. She could have done no less, being an old woman in a strange world. And day by day her sons had ripped from her startled eyes her old vision, and image by image had given her a new one, different, but great and strong enough to fling her into the light of another grace. The wrongs and sufferings of black men had taken the place of Him nailed to the Cross; the meager beginnings of the party had become another Resurrection; and the hate of those who would destroy her new faith had quickened in her a hunger to feel how deeply her new strength went.

"Lawd, Johnny-Boy," she would sometimes say, "Ah jus wan them white folks t try t make me tell *who* is *in* the party n who *ain!* Ah jus wan em t try, n Ahll show em somethin they never thought a black woman could have!"

But sometimes, like tonight, while lost in the forgetfulness of work, the past and the present would become mixed in her; while toiling under a strange star for a new freedom, the old songs would slip from her lips with their beguiling sweetness.

The iron was getting cold. She put more wood into the fire, stood again at the window, and watched the yellow blade of light cut through the wet darkness. Johnny-Boy ain here yit. . . . Then, before she was aware of it, she was still, listening for sounds. Under the drone of rain she heard the slosh of feet in mud. Tha ain Johnny-Boy. She knew his long, heavy footsteps in a million. She heard feet come on the porch. Some woman. . . . She heard bare knuckles knock three times, then once. Thas some of them comrades! She unbarred the door, cracked it a few inches, and flinched from the cold rush of damp wind.

"Whos tha?"

"Its me!"

"Who?"

"Me, Reva!"

She flung the door open.

"Lawd, chile c mon in!"

She stepped to one side and a thin, blond-haired white girl ran through the door; as she slid the bolt she heard the girl gasping and shaking her wet clothes. Somethings wrong! Reva wouldna walked a mile t mah house in all this slop fer nothin! tha gals stuck onto Johnny-Boy. Ah wondah ef anythin happened t im?

"Git on inter the kitchen, Reva, where its warm."

"Lawd, Ah sho is wet!"

"How yuh reckon yuhd be, in all tha rain?"

"Johnny-Boy ain here *yit?*" asked Reva.

"Naw! N ain no usa yuh worryin bout im. Jus yuh git them shoes off! Yuh wanna ketch yo deatha col?" She stood looking absently. Yeah; its somethin about the party er Johnny-Boy thas gone wrong. Lawd, Ah wondah ef her pa knows how she feels bout Johnny-Boy? "Honey, yuh hadnt oughta come out in sloppy weather like this."

"Ah had t come, An Sue."

She led Reva to the kitchen.

"Git them shoes off n git close t the stove so yuhll git dry!"

"An Sue, Ah got somethin t tell yuh . . ."

The words made her hold her breath. Ah bet its somethin bout Johnny-Boy!

"Whut, honey?"

"The sheriff wuz by our house tonight. He come t see pa."

"Yeah?"

"He done got word from somewheres bout tha meetin tomorrow."

"Is it Johnny-Boy, Reva?"

"Aw, naw, An Sue! Ah ain hearda word bout im. Ain yuh seen im tonight?"

"He ain come home t eat yit."

"Where kin he be?"

"Lawd knows, chile."

"Somebodys gotta tell them comrades tha meetings off," said Reva. "The sheriffs got men watchin our house. Ah had t slip out t git here widout em followin me."

"Reva?"

"Hunh?"

"Ahma ol woman n Ah wans yuh t tell me the truth."

"Whut, An Sue?"

"Yuh ain tryin t fool me, is yuh?"

"*Fool* yuh?"

"Bout Johnny-Boy?"

"Lawd, naw, An Sue!"

"Ef theres anythin wrong jus tell me, chile. Ah kin stan it."

She stood by the ironing board, her hands as usual folded loosely over her stomach, watching Reva pull off her water-clogged shoes. She was feeling that Johnny-Boy was already lost to her; she was feeling the pain that would come when she knew it for certain; and she was feeling that she would have to be brave and bear it. She was like a person caught in a swift current of water and knew where the water was sweeping her and did not want to go on but had to go on to the end.

"It ain nothin bout Johnny-Boy, An Sue," said Reva. "But we gotta do somethin er we'll all git inter trouble."

"How the sheriff know about the meetin?"

"Thas whut pa wans t know."

"Somebody done turned Judas."

"Sho looks like it."

"Ah bet it wuz some of them new ones," she said.

"Its hard t tell," said Reva.

"Lissen, Reva, yuh oughta stay here n git dry, but yuh bettah git back n tell yo pa Johnny-Boy ain here n Ah don know when hes gonna show up. *Some*bodys gotta tell them comrades t stay erway from you pas house."

She stood with her back to the window, looking at Reva's wide blue eyes. Po critter! Gotta go back thu all tha slop! Though she felt sorry for Reva, not once did she think that it would not have to be done. Being a woman, Reva was not suspect; she would *have* to go. It was just as natural for Reva to go back through the cold rain as it was for her to iron night and day, or for Sug to be in jail. Right now, Johnny-Boy was out there on those dark fields trying to get home. Lawd, don let em git im tonight! In spite of herself her feelings became torn. She loved her son, and loving him, she loved what he was trying to do. Johnny-Boy was happiest when he was working for the party, and her love for him was for his happiness. She frowned, trying hard to fit something together in her feelings: for her to try to stop Johnny-Boy was to admit that all the toil of years meant nothing; and to let him go meant that sometime or other he would be caught, like Sug. In facing it this way she felt a little stunned, as though she had come suddenly upon a blank wall in the dark. But outside in the rain were people, white and black, whom she had known all her life. Those people depended upon Johnny-Boy, loved him, and looked to him as a man and leader. Yeah; hes gotta keep on; he cant stop now. . . . She looked at Reva; she was crying and pulling her shoes back on with reluctant fingers.

"Whut yuh carryin on that way fer, chile?"

"Yuh done los Sug, now yuh sending Johnny-Boy . . ."

"Ah got t, honey."

She was glad she could say that. Reva believed in black folks and not for anything in the world would she falter before her. In Reva's trust and acceptance of her she had found her first feelings of humanity; Reva's love was her refuge from shame and degradation. If in the early days of her life the white mountain had driven her back from the earth, then in her last days Reva's love was drawing her toward it, like the beacon that swung through the night outside. She heard Reva sobbing.

"Hush, honey!"

"Mah brothers in jail too! Ma cries ever day . . ."

"Ah know, honey."

She helped Reva with her coat; her fingers felt the scant flesh of the girl's shoulders. She don git ernuff t eat, she thought. She slipped her arms around Reva's waist and held her close for a moment.

"Now, yuh stop that cryin."

"A-a-ah c-c-cant hep it. . . ."

"Everythingll be awright; Johnny-Boyll be back."

"Yuh think so?"

"Sho, chile. Cos he will."

Neither of them spoke again until they stood in the doorway. Outside they could hear water washing through the ruts of the street.

"Be sho n send Johnny-Boy t tell the folks t stay erway from pas house," said Reva.

"Ahll tell im. Don yuh worry."

"Good-by!"

"Good-by!"

Leaning against the door jamb, she shook her head slowly and watched Reva vanish through the falling rain.

II

She was back at her board, ironing, when she heard feet sucking in the mud of the back yard; feet she knew from long years of listening were Johnny-Boy's. But tonight, with all the rain and fear, his coming was like a leaving, was almost more than she could bear. Tears welled to her eyes and she blinked them away. She felt that he was coming so that she could give him up; to see him now was to say good-by. But it was a good-by she knew she could never say; they were not that way toward each other. All day long they could sit in the same room and not speak; she was his mother and he was her son. Most of the time a nod or a grunt would carry all the meaning that she wanted to convey to him, or he to her. She did not even turn her head when she heard him come stomping into the kitchen. She heard him pull up a chair, sit, sigh, and draw off his muddy shoes; they fell to the floor with heavy thuds. Soon the kitchen was full of the scent of his drying socks and his burning pipe. Tha boys hongry! She paused and looked at him over her shoulder; he was puffing at his pipe with his head tilted back and his feet propped up on the edge of the stove; his eyelids drooped and his wet clothes steamed from the heat of the fire. Lawd, tha boy gits mo like his pa ever day he lives, she mused, her lips breaking in a slow faint smile. Hols tha pipe in his mouth just like his pa usta hol his. Wondah how they woulda got erlong ef his pa hada lived? They oughta liked each other, they so mucha like. She wished there could have been other children besides Sug, so Johnny-Boy would not have to be so much alone. A man needs a woman by his side. . . . She thought of Reva; she liked Reva; the brightest glow her heart had ever known was when she had learned that Reva loved Johnny-Boy. But beyond Reva were cold white faces. Ef theys caught it means *death*. . . . She jerked around when she heard Johnny-Boy's pipe clatter to the floor. She saw him pick it up, smile sheepishly at her, and wag his head.

"Gawd, Ahm sleepy," he mumbled.

She got a pillow from her room and gave it to him.

"Here," she said.

"Hunh," he said, putting the pillow between his head and the back of the chair.

They were silent again. Yes, she would have to tell him to go back out into the cold rain and slop; maybe to get caught; maybe for the last time; she didn't know. But she would let him eat and get dry before telling him that the sheriff knew of the meeting to be held at Lem's tomorrow. And she would make him take a big dose of soda before he went out; soda always helped to stave off a cold. She looked at the clock. It was eleven. Theres time yit. Spreading a newspaper on the apron of the stove, she placed a heaping plate of greens upon it, a knife, a fork, a cup of coffee, a slab of cornbread, and a dish of peach cobbler.

"Yo suppahs ready," she said.

"Yeah," he said.

He did not move. She ironed again. Presently, she heard him eating. When she could no longer hear his knife tinkling against the edge of the plate, she knew he was through. It was almost twelve now. She would let him rest a little while longer before she told him. Till one er'clock, mabbe. Hes so tired. . . . She finished her ironing, put away the board, and stacked the clothes in her dresser drawer. She poured herself a cup of black coffee, drew up a chair, sat down, and drank.

"Yuh almos dry," she said, not looking around.

"Yeah," he said, turning sharply to her.

The tone of voice in which she had spoken had let him know that more was coming. She drained her cup and waited a moment longer.

"Reva wuz here."

"Yeah?"

"She lef bout a hour ergo."

"Whut she say?"

"She said ol man Lem hada visit from the sheriff today."

"Bout the meetin?"

"Yeah."

She saw him stare at the coals glowing red through the crevices of the stove and run his fingers nervously through his hair. She knew he was wondering how the sheriff had found out. In the silence he would ask a wordless question and in the silence she would answer wordlessly. Johnny-Boys too trustin, she thought. Hes trying t make the party big n hes takin in folks fastern he kin git t know em. You cant trust ever white man yuh meet. . . .

"Yuh know, Johnny-Boy, yuh been takin in a lotta them white folks lately . . ."

"Aw, ma!"

"But, Johnny-Boy . . ."

"Please, don talk t me bout tha now, ma."

"Yuh ain t ol t lissen n learn, son," she said.

"Ah know whut yuh gonna say, ma. N yuh wrong. Yuh cant judge folks jus by how yuh feel bout em n by how long yuh done knowed em. Ef we start tha we wouldn't have *no*body in the party. When folks pledge they word t be with us, then we gotta take em in. Wes too weak t be choosy."

He rose abruptly, rammed his hands into his pockets, and stood facing the window; she looked at his back in a long silence. She knew his faith; it was deep. He had always said that black men could not fight the rich bosses alone; a man could not fight with every hand against him. But he believes so hard hes blind, she thought. At odd times they had had these arguments before; always she would be pitting her feelings against the hard necessity of his thinking, and always she would lose. She shook her head. Po Johnny-Boy; he don know. . . .

"But ain nona our folks tol, Johnny-Boy," she said.

"How yuh know?" he asked. His voice came low and with a tinge of anger. He still faced the window, and now and then the yellow blade of light flicked across the sharp outline of his black face.

"Cause Ah know em," she said.

"*Any*body mighta tol," he said.

"It wuznt nona *our* folks," she said again.

She saw his hand sweep in a swift arc of disgust.

"*Our* folks! Ma, who in Gawds name is *our* folks?"

"The folks we wuz born n raised wid, son. The folks we *know!*"

"We cant make the party grow tha way, ma."

"It mighta been Booker," she said.

"Yuh don know."

". . . er Blattberg . . ."

"Fer Chrissakes!"

". . . er any of the fo-five others whut joined las week."

"Ma, yuh jus don wan me t go out tonight," he said.

"Yo ol ma wans yuh t be careful, son."

"Ma, when yuh start doubtin folks in the party, then there ain no end."

"Son, Ah knows ever black man n woman in this parta the county," she said, standing too. "Ah watched em grow up; Ah even heped birth n nurse some of em; Ah knows em *all* from way back. There ain none of em that *coulda* tol! The folks Ah know jus don open they dos n ast death t walk in! Son, it wuz some of them *white* folks! Yuh jus mark mah word n wait n see!"

"Why is it gotta be *white* folks?" he asked. "Ef they tol, then theys jus Judases, thas all."

"Son, look at whuts befo yuh."

He shook his head and sighed.

"Ma, Ah done tol yuh a hundred times. Ah cant see white n Ah cant see black," he said. "Ah sees rich men n Ah sees po men."

She picked up his dirty dishes and piled them in a pan. Out of the corners of her eyes she saw him sit and pull on his wet shoes. Hes goin! When she put the last dish away he was standing, fully dressed, warming his hands over the stove. Jus a few mo minutes now n he'll be gone, like Sug, mabbe. Her throat tightened. This black mans fight takes *ever*thin! Looks like Gawd put us in this world jus t beat us down!

"Keep this, ma," he said.

She saw a crumpled wad of money in his outstretched fingers.

"Naw; yuh keep it. Yuh might need it."

"It ain mine, ma. It berlongs t the party."

"But, Johnny-Boy, yuh might hafta go erway!"

"Ah kin make out."

"Don fergit yosef too much, son."

"Ef Ah don come back theyll need it."

He was looking at her face and she was looking at the money.

"Yuh keep tha," she said slowly. "Ahll give em the money."

"From where?"

"Ah got some."

"Where yuh git it from?"

She sighed.

"Ah been savin a dollah a week fer Sug ever since hes been in jail."

"Lawd, ma!"

She saw the look of puzzled love and wonder in his eyes. Clumsily, he put the money back into his pocket.

"Ahm gone," he said.

"Here; drink this glass of soda watah."

She watched him drink, then put the glass away.

"Waal," he said.

"Take the stuff outta yo pockets!"

She lifted the lid of the stove and he dumped all the papers from his pocket into the fire. She followed him to the door and made him turn round.

"Lawd, yuh tryin to maka revolution n yuh cant even keep yo coat buttoned." Her nimble fingers fastened his collar high around his throat. "There!"

He pulled the brim of his hat low over his eyes. She opened the door, and with the suddenness of the cold gust of wind that struck her face, he was gone. She watched the black fields and the rain take him, her eyes burning. When the last faint footstep could no longer be heard, she closed the door, went to her bed, lay down, and pulled the cover over her while fully dressed. Her feelings coursed with the rhythm of the rain: Hes gone! Lawd, Ah *know* hes gone! Her blood felt cold.

III

She was floating in a grey void somewhere between sleeping and dreaming and then suddenly she was wide awake, hearing and feeling in the same instant the thunder of the door crashing in and a cold wind filling the room. It was pitch black and she stared, resting on her elbows, her mouth open, not breathing, her ears full of the sound of tramping feet and booming voices. She knew at once: They lookin fer im! Then, filled with her will, she was on her feet, rigid, waiting, listening.

"The lamps burnin!"

"Yuh see her?"

"Naw!"

"Look in the kitchen!"

"Gee, this place smells like niggers!"

"Say, somebodys here er been here!"

"Yeah; theres fire in the stove!"

"Mabbe hes been here n gone?"

"Boy, look at these jars of jam!"

"Niggers make good jam!"

"Git some bread!"

"Heres some cornbread!"

"Say, lemme git some!"

"Take it easy! Theres plenty here!"

"Ahma take some of this stuff home!"

"Look, heres a pota greens!"

"N some hot cawffee!"

"Say, yuh guys! C mon! Cut it out! We didnt come here fer a feas!"

She walked slowly down the hall. They lookin fer im, but they ain got im yit! She stopped in the doorway, her gnarled black hands as always, folded over her stomach, but tight now, so tightly the veins bulged. The kitchen was crowded with white men in glistening raincoats. Though the lamp burned, their flashlights still glowed in red fists. Across her floor she saw the muddy tracks of their boots.

"Yuh white folks git outta mah house!"

There was quick silence; every face turned toward her. She saw a sudden movement, but did not know what it meant until something hot and wet slammed her squarely in the face. She gasped, but did not move. Calmly, she wiped the warm, greasy liquor of greens from her eyes with her left hand. One of the white men had thrown a handful of greens out of the pot at her.

"How they taste, ol bitch?"

"Ah ast yuh t git outta mah house!"

She saw the sheriff detach himself from the crowd and walk toward her.

"Now, Anty . . ."

"White man, don yuh *Anty* me!"

"Yuh ain got the right sperit!"

"Sperit hell! Yuh git these men outta mah house!"

"Yuh ack like yuh don like it!"

"Naw, Ah don like it, n yuh knows dam waal Ah don!"

"Whut yuh gonna do bout it?"

"Ahm tellin yuh t git outta mah house!"

"Gittin sassy?"

"Ef telling yuh t git outta mah house is sass, then Ahm sassy!"

Her words came in a tense whisper; but beyond, back of them, she was watching, thinking, judging the men.

"Listen, Anty," the sheriff's voice came soft and low. "Ahm here t hep yuh. How come yah wanna ack this way?"

"Yuh ain never heped yo *own* sef since yuh been born," she flared. "How kin the likes of yuh hep me?"

One of the white men came forward and stood directly in front of her.

"Lissen, nigger woman, yuh talkin t *white* men!"

"Ah don care who Ahm talkin t!"

"Yuhll wish some day yuh did!"

"Not t the likes of yuh!"

"Yuh need somebody t teach yuh how t be a good nigger!"

"*Yuh* cant teach it t me!"

"Yuh gonna change yo tune."

"Not longs mah bloods warm!"

"Don git smart now!"

"Yuh git outta mah house!"

"Spose we don go?" the sheriff asked.

They were crowded around her. She had not moved since she had taken her place in the doorway. She was thinking only of Johnny-Boy as she stood there, giving and taking words; and she knew that they, too, were thinking of Johnny-Boy. She knew they wanted him, and her heart was daring them to take him from her.

"Spose we don go?" the sheriff asked again.

"Twenty of yuh runnin over one ol woman! Now, ain yuh white men glad yuh so brave?"

The sheriff grabbed her arm.

"C mon, now! Yuh done did ernuff sass fer one night. Wheres tha nigger son of yos?"

"Don yuh wished yuh knowed?"

"Yuh wanna git slapped?"

"Ah ain never seen one of yo kind tha wuznt too low fer . . ."

The sheriff slapped her straight across her face with his open palm. She fell back against a wall and sank to her knees.

"Is tha whut white men do t nigger women?"

She rose slowly and stood again, not even touching the place that ached from his blow, her hands folded over her stomach.

"Ah ain never seen one of yo kind tha wuznt too low fer . . ."

He slapped her again; she reeled backward several feet and fell on her side.

"Is tha whut we too low t do?"

She stood before him again, dry-eyed, as though she had not been struck. Her lips were numb and her chin was wet with blood.

"Aw, let her go! Its the nigger we wan!" said one.

"Wheres that nigger son of yos?" the sheriff asked.

"Find im," she said.

"By Gawd, ef we hafta find im we'll kill im!"

"He wont be the only nigger yuh ever killed," she said.

She was consumed with a bitter pride. There was nothing on this earth, she felt then, that they could not do to her but that she could take. She stood on a narrow plot of ground from which she would die before she was pushed. And then it was, while standing there, feeling warm blood seeping down her throat, that she gave up Johnny-Boy, gave him up to the white folks. She gave him up because they had come tramping into her heart, demanding him, thinking they could get him by beating her, thinking they could scare her into making her tell where he was. She gave him up because she wanted them to know that they could not get what they wanted by bluffing and killing.

"Wheres this meetin gonna be?" the sheriff asked.

"Don yuh wish yuh knowed?"

"Ain there gonna be a meetin?"

"How come yuh astin me?"

"There *is* gonna be a meetin," said the sheriff.

"Is it?"

"Ah gotta great mind t choke it outta yuh!"

"Yuh so smart," she said.

"We ain playin wid yuh!"

"Did Ah say yuh wuz?"

"Tha nigger son of yos is erroun here somewheres n we aim t find im," said the sheriff. "Ef yuh tell us where he is n ef he talks, mabbe he'll git off easy. But ef we hafta find im, we'll kill im! Ef we hafta find im, then yuh git a sheet t put over im in the mawnin, see? Gut yuh a sheet, cause hes gonna be dead!"

"He wont be the only nigger yuh ever killed," she said again.

The sheriff walked past her. The others followed. Yuh didnt git whut yuh wanted! she thought exultingly. N yuh ain gonna *never* git it! Hotly, something ached in her to make them feel the intensity of her pride and freedom; her heart groped to turn the bitter hours of her life into words of a kind that would make them feel that she had taken all they had done to her in her stride and could still take more. Her faith surged so strongly in her she was all but blinded. She walked behind them to the door, knotting and twisting her fingers. She saw them step to the muddy ground. Each whirl of the yellow beacon revealed glimpses of slanting rain. Her lips moved, then she shouted:

"Yuh didnt git whut yuh wanted! N yuh ain gonna nevah git it!"

The sheriff stopped and turned; his voice came low and hard.

"Now, by Gawd, thas ernuff outta yuh!"

"Ah know when Ah done said ernuff!"

"Aw, naw, yuh don!" he said. "Yuh don know when yuh done said ernuff, but Ahma teach yuh ternight!"

He was up the steps and across the porch with one bound. She backed into the hall, her eyes full on his face.

"Tell me when yuh gonna stop talkin!" he said, swinging his fist.

The blow caught her high on the cheek; her eyes went blank; she fell on her face. She felt the hard heel of his wet shoes coming into her temple and stomach.

"Lemme hear yuh talk some mo!"

She wanted to, but could not; pain numbed and choked her. She lay still, and somewhere out of the grey void of unconsciousness she heard someone say: *aw fer chrissakes leave her erlone its the nigger we wan. . . .*

IV

She never knew how long she had lain huddled in the dark hallway. Her first returning feeling was of a nameless fear crowding the inside of her, then a deep pain spreading from her temple downward over her body. Her ears were filled with the drone of rain and she shuddered from the cold wind blowing through the door. She opened her eyes and at first saw nothing. As if she were imagining it, she knew she was half-lying and half-sitting in a corner against a wall. With difficulty she twisted her neck, and what she saw made her hold her breath—a vast white blur was suspended directly above her. For a moment she could not tell if her fear was from the blur or if the blur was from her fear. Gradually the blur resolved itself into a huge white face that slowly filled her vision. She was stone still, conscious really of the effort to breathe, feeling somehow that she existed only by the mercy of that white face. She had seen it before; its fear had gripped her many times; it had for her the fear of all the white faces she had ever seen in her life. *Sue* . . . As from a great distance, she heard her name being called. She was regaining consciousness now, but the fear was coming with her. She looked into the face of a white man, wanting to scream out for him to go, yet accepting his presence because she felt she had to. Though some remote part of her mind was active, her limbs were powerless. It was as if an invisible knife had split her in two, leaving one half of her lying there helpless, while the other half shrank in dread from a forgotten but familiar enemy. *Sue its me Sue its me* . . . Then all at once the voice came clearly.

"Sue, its me! Its Booker!"

And she heard an answering voice speaking inside of her, Yeah, its Booker . . . The one whut jus joined . . . She roused herself, struggling for full consciousness; and as she did so she transferred to the person of Booker the nameless fear she felt. It seemed that Booker towered above her as a challenge to her right to exist upon the earth.

"Yuh awright?"

She did not answer; she started violently to her feet and fell.

"Sue, yuh hurt!"

"Yeah," she breathed.

"Where they hit yuh?"

"Its mah head," she whispered.

She was speaking even though she did not want to; the fear that had hold of her compelled her.

"They beat yuh?"

"Yeah."

"Them bastards! Them Gawddam bastards!"

She heard him saying it over and over; then she felt herself being lifted.

"Naw!" she gasped.

"Ahma take yuh t the kitchen!"

"Put me down!"

"But yuh cant stay here like this!"

She shrank in his arms and pushed her hands against his body; when she was in the kitchen she freed herself, sank into a chair, and held tightly to its back. She looked wonderingly at Booker. There was nothing about him that should frighten her so, but even that did not ease her tension. She saw him go to the water bucket, wet his handkerchief, wring it, and offer it to her. Distrustfully, she stared at the damp cloth.

"Here; put this on yo fohead . . ."

"Naw!"

"C mon; itll make yuh feel bettah!"

She hesitated in confusion. What right had she to be afraid when someone was acting as kindly as this toward her? Reluctantly, she leaned forward and pressed the damp cloth to her head. It helped. With each passing minute she was catching hold of herself, yet wondering why she felt as she did.

"Whut happened?"

"Ah don know."

"Yuh feel bettah?"

"Yeah."

"Who all wuz here?"

"Ah don know," she said again.

"Yo head still hurt?"

"Yeah."

"Gee, Ahm sorry."

"Ahm awright," she sighed and buried her face in her hands.

She felt him touch her shoulder.

"Sue, Ah got some bad news fer yuh . . ."

She knew; she stiffened and grew cold. It had happened; she stared dry-eyed, with compressed lips.

"Its mah Johnny-Boy," she said.

"Yeah; Ahm awful sorry t hafta tell yuh this way. But Ah thought yuh oughta know . . ."

Her tension eased and a vacant place opened up inside of her. A voice whispered, Jesus, hep me!

"W-w-where is he?"

"They got im out t Foleys Woods tryin t make im tell who the others is."

"He ain gonna tell," she said. "They just as waal kill im, cause he ain gonna nevah tell."

"Ah hope he don," said Booker. "But he didnt hava chance t tell the others. They grabbed im jus as he got t the woods."

Then all the horror of it flashed upon her; she saw flung out over the rainy countryside an array of shacks where white and black comrades were sleeping; in the morning they would be rising and going to Lem's; then they would be caught. And that meant terror, prison, and death. The comrades would have to be told; she would have to tell them; she could not entrust Johnny-Boy's work to another, and especially not to Booker as long as she felt toward him as she did. Gripping the bottom of the chair with both hands, she tried to rise; the room blurred and she swayed. She found herself resting in Booker's arms.

"Lemme go!"

"Sue, yuh too weak t walk!"

"Ah gotta tell em!" she said.

"Set down, Sue! Yuh hurt! Yuh sick!"

When seated, she looked at him helplessly.

"Sue, lissen! Johnny-Boys caught. Ahm here. Yuh tell me who they is n Ahll tell em."

She stared at the floor and did not answer. Yes; she was too weak to go. There was no way for her to tramp all those miles through the rain tonight. But should she tell Booker? If only she had somebody like Reva to talk to! She did not want to decide alone; she must make no mistake about this. She felt Booker's fingers pressing on her arm and it was as though the white mountain was pushing her to the edge of a sheer height; she again exclaimed inwardly, Jesus, hep me! Booker's white face was at her side, waiting. Would she be doing right to tell him? Suppose she did not tell and then the comrades were caught? She could not ever forgive herself for doing a thing like that. But maybe she was wrong; maybe her fear was what Johnny-Boy had always called "jus foolishness." She remembered his saying, Ma we cant make the party grow ef we start doubtin everybody . . .

"Tell me who they is, Sue, n Ahll tell em. Ah jus joined n Ah don know who they is."

"Ah don know who they is," she said.

"Yuh *gotta* tell me who they is, Sue!"

"Ah tol yuh Ah don know!"

"Yuh *do* know! C mon! Set up n talk!"

"Naw!"

"Yuh wan em all t git *killed*?"

She shook her head and swallowed. Lawd, Ah don blieve in this man!

"Lissen, Ahll call the names n yuh tell me which ones is in the party n which ones ain, see?"

"Naw!"

"Please, Sue!"

"Ah don know," she said.

"Sue, yuh ain doin right by em. Johnny-Boy wouldnt wan yuh t be this way. Hes out there holdin up his end. Les hol up ours . . ."

"Lawd, Ah don know . . ."

"Is yuh scareda me cause Ahm *white*? Johnny-Boy ain like tha. Don let all the work we done go fer nothin."

She gave up and bowed her head in her hands.

"Is it Johnson? Tell me, Sue?"

"Yeah," she whispered in horror; a mounting horror of feeling herself being undone.

"Is it Green?"

"Yeah."

"Murphy?"

"Lawd, Ah don know!"

"Yuh gotta tell me, Sue!"

"Mistah Booker, please leave me erlone . . ."

"Is it Murphy?"

She answered yes to the names of Johnny-Boy's comrades; she answered until he asked her no more. Then she thought, How he know the sheriffs men is watchin Lems house? She stood up and held onto her chair, feeling something sure and firm within her.

"How yuh know bout Lem?"

"Why . . . How Ah know?"

"Whut yuh doin here this tima night? How yuh know the sheriff got Johnny-Boy?"

"Sue, don yuh blieve in me?"

She did not, but she could not answer. She stared at him until her lips hung open; she was searching deep within herself for certainty.

"You meet Reva?" she asked.

"Reva?"

"Yeah; Lems gal?"

"Oh, yeah. Sho, Ah met Reva."

"She tell yuh?"

She asked the question more of herself than of him; she longed to believe.

"Yeah," he said softly. "Ah reckon Ah oughta be goin t tell em now."

"Who?" she asked. "Tell *who*?"

The muscles of her body were stiff as she waited for his answer; she felt as though life depended upon it.

"The comrades," he said.

"Yeah," she sighed.

She did not know when he left; she was not looking or listening. She just suddenly saw the room empty and from her the thing that had made her fearful was gone.

V

For a space of time that seemed to her as long as she had been upon the earth, she sat huddled over the cold stove. One minute she would say to herself, They both gone now; Johnny-Boy n Sug . . . Mabbe Ahll never see em ergin. Then a surge of guilt would blot out her longing. "Lawd, Ah shouldna tol!" she mumbled. "But no man kin be so lowdown as t do a think like tha . . ." Several times she had an impulse to try to tell the comrades herself; she was feeling a little better now. But what good would that do? She had told Booker the names. He jus couldnt be a Judas t po folks like us . . . *He couldnt!*

"An Sue!"

That Reva! Her heart leaped with an anxious gladness. She rose without answering and limped down the dark hallway. Through the open door, against the background of rain, she saw Reva's face, lit now and then to whiteness by the whirling beams of the beacon. She was about to call, but a thought checked her. Jesus, hep me! Ah gotta tell her bout Johnny-Boy . . . Lawd, Ah cant!

"An Sue, yuh there?"

"C mon in, chile!"

She caught Reva and held her close for a moment without speaking.

"Lawd, Ahm sho glad yuh here," she said at last.

"Ah thought somethin had happened t yuh," said Reva, pulling away. "Ah saw the do open . . . Pa tol me to come back n stay wid yuh tonight . . ." Reva paused and started, "W-w-whuts the mattah?"

She was so full of having Reva with her that she did not understand what the question meant.

"Hunh?"

"Yo neck . . ."

"Aw, it ain nothin, chile. C mon in the kitchen."

"But theres blood on yo neck!"

"The sheriff wuz here . . ."

"Them fools! Whut they wanna bother yuh fer? Ah could kill em! So hep me Gawd, Ah could!"

"It ain nothin," she said.

She was wondering how to tell Reva about Johnny-Boy and Booker.

Ahll wait a lil while longer, she thought. Now that Reva was here, her fear did not seem as awful as before.

"C mon, lemme fix yo head, An Sue. Yuh hurt."

They went to the kitchen. She sat silent while Reva dressed her scalp. She was feeling better now; in just a little while she would tell Reva. She felt the girl's finger pressing gently upon her head.

"Tha hurt?"

"A lil, chile."

"Yuh po thing."

"It ain nothin."

"Did Johnny-Boy come?"

She hesitated.

"Yeah."

"He done gone t tell the others?"

Reva's voice sounded so clear and confident that it mocked her. Lawd, Ah cant tell this chile . . .

"Yuh tol im, didn't yuh, An Sue?"

"Y-y-yeah . . ."

"Gee! Thas good! Ah tol pa he didnt hafta worry ef Johnny-Boy got the news. Mabbe thingsll come out awright."

"Ah hope . . ."

She could not go on; she had gone as far as she could. For the first time that night she began to cry.

"Hush, An Sue! Yuh awways been brave. Itll be awright!"

"Aain nothin awright, chile. The worls jus too much fer us, Ah reckon."

"Ef yuh cry that way itll make me cry."

She forced herself to stop. Naw; Ah cant carry on way in fronta Reva . . . Right now she had a deep need for Reva to believe in her. She watched the girl get pine-knots from behind the stove, rekindle the fire, and put on the coffee pot.

"Yuh wan some cawffee?" Reva asked.

"Naw, honey."

"Aw, c mon, An Sue."

"Jusa lil, honey."

"Thas the way to be. Oh, say, Ah fergot," said Reva, measuring out spoonsful of coffee. "Pa tol me t tell yuh t watch out fer tha Booker man. Hes a stool."

She showed not one sign of outward movement or expression, but as the words fell from Reva's lips she went limp inside.

"Pa tol me soon as Ah got back home. He got word from town . . ."

She stopped listening. She felt as though she had been slapped to the extreme outer edge of life, into a cold darkness. She knew now what she had felt when she had looked up out of her fog of pain and had seen Booker. It was the image of all the white folks, and the fear that went with them, that she had seen and felt during her lifetime. And again, for the second time that night, something she had felt had come true. All she could say to herself was, Ah didnt like im! Gawd knows, Ah didnt! Ah tol Johnny-Boy it wuz some of them white folks . . .

"Here; drink yo cawffee . . ."

She took the cup; her fingers trembled, and the steaming liquid spilt onto her dress and leg.

"Ahm sorry, An Sue!"

Her leg was scalded, but the pain did not bother her.

"Its awright," she said.

"Wait; lemme put some lard on tha burn!"

"It don hurt."

"Yuh worried bout somethin."

"Naw, honey."

"Lemme fix yuh so mo cawffee."

"Ah don wan nothin now, Reva."

"Waal, buck up. Don be tha way . . ."

They were silent. She heard Reva drinking. No; she would not tell Reva; Reva was all she had left. But she had to do something, some way, somehow. She was undone too much as it was; and to tell Reva about Booker or Johnny-Boy was more than she was equal to; it would be too coldly shameful. She wanted to be alone and fight this thing out with herself.

"Go t bed, honey. Yuh tired."

"Naw; Ahm awright, An Sue."

She heard the bottom of Reva's empty cup clank against the top of the stove. Ah *got* t make her go t bed! Yes; Booker would tell the names of the comrades to the sheriff. If she could only stop him some way! That was the answer, the point, the star that grew bright in the morning of new hope. Soon, maybe half an hour from now, Booker would reach Foley's Woods. Hes boun t go the long way, cause he don know no short cut, she thought. Ah could wade the creek n beat im there. . . . But what would she do after that?

"Reva, honey, go t bed. Ahm awright. Yuh need res."

"Ah ain sleepy, An Sue."

"Ah knows whuts bes fer yuh, chile. Yuh tired n wet."

"Ah wanna stay up wid yuh."

She forced a smile and said:

"Ah don think they gonna hurt Johnny-Boy . . ."

"Fer *real,* An Sue?"

"Sho, honey."

"But Ah wanna wait up wid yuh."

"Thas mah job, honey. Thas whut a mas fer, t wait up fer her chullun."

"Good night, An Sue."

"Good night, honey."

She watched Reva pull up and leave the kitchen; presently she heard the shucks in the mattress whispering, and she knew that Reva had gone to bed. She was alone. Through the cracks of the stove she saw the fire dying to grey ashes; the room was growing cold again. The yellow beacon continued to flit past the window and the rain still drummed. Yes; she was alone; she had done this awful thing alone; she must find some way out, alone. Like touching a festering sore, she put her finger upon that moment when she had shouted her defiance to the sheriff, when she had shouted to feel her strength. She had lost Sug to save others; she had let Johnny-Boy go to save others; and then in a moment of weakness that came from too much strength she had lost all. If she had not shouted to the sheriff, she would have been strong enough to have resisted Booker; she would have been able to tell the comrades herself. Something tightened in her as she remembered and understood the fit of fear she had felt on coming to herself in the dark hallway. A part of her life she thought she had done away with forever had had hold of her then. She had thought the soft, warm past was over; she had thought that it did not mean much when now she sang: *"Hes the Lily of the Valley, the Bright n Mawnin Star"* . . . The days when she had sung that song were the days when she had not hoped for anything on this earth, the days when the cold mountain had driven her into the arms of Jesus. She had thought that Sug and Johnny-Boy had taught her to forget Him, to fix her hope upon the fight of black men for freedom. Through the gradual years she had believed and worked with them, had felt strength shed from the grace of their terrible vision. That grace had been upon her when she had let the sheriff slap her down; it had been upon her when she had risen time and again from the floor and faced him. But she had trapped herself with her own hunger; to water the long, dry thirst of her faith her pride had made a bargain which her flesh could not keep. Her having told the names of Johnny-Boy's comrades was but an incident in a deeper horror. She stood up and looked at the floor while call and counter-call, loyalty and counter-loyalty struggled in her soul. Mired she was between two abandoned worlds, living, but dying without the strength of the grace that either gave. The clearer she felt it the fuller did something well up from the depths of her for release; the more urgent did she feel the need to fling into her black sky another star, another hope, one more terrible vision to give her the strength to live and act. Softly and restlessly she walked about the kitchen, feeling herself naked against the night, the rain, the world; and shamed whenever the thought of Reva's love crossed her mind. She lifted her empty hands and looked at her writhing fingers. Lawd, whut kin Ah do now? She could still wade the creek and get to Foley's Woods before Booker. And then what? How could she manage to see Johnny-Boy or Booker? Again she heard the sheriff's threatening voice: Git yuh a sheet, cause hes gonna be dead! The sheet! Thas it, the *sheet!* Her whole being leaped with will; the long years of her life bent toward a moment of focus, a point. Ah kin go wid mah sheet! Ahll be doin whut he said! Lawd Gawd in Heaven, Ahma go lika nigger woman wid mah windin sheet t git mah dead son! But then what? She stood straight and smiled grimly; she had in her heart the whole meaning of her life; her entire personality was poised on the brink of a total act. Ah know! Ah *know!* She thought of Johnny-Boy's gun in the dresser drawer. Ahll hide the gun in the sheet n go aftah Johnny-Boy's body. . . . She tiptoed to her room, eased out the dresser drawer, and got a sheet. Reva was sleeping; the darkness was filled with her quiet breathing. She groped in the drawer and found the gun. She wound the gun in the sheet and held them both under her apron. Then she stole to the bedside and watched Reva. Lawd, hep her! But mabbe shes bettah off. This had t happen sometime . . . She n Johnny-Boy couldna been together in this here South . . . N Ah couldnt tell her bout Booker. Itll come out awright n she wont nevah know. Reva's trust would never be shaken. She caught her breath as the shucks in the mattress rustled dryly; then all was quiet and she breathed easily again. She tiptoed to the door, down the hall, and stood on the porch. Above her the yellow beacon whirled through the rain. She went over muddy ground, mounted a slope, stopped, and looked back at her house. The lamp glowed in her window, and the yellow beacon that swung every few seconds seemed to feed it with light. She turned and started across the fields, holding the gun and sheet tightly, thinking, Po Reva . . . Po critter . . . Shes fas ersleep . . .

VI

For the most part she walked with her eyes half shut, her lips tightly compressed, leaning her body against the wind and the driving rain, feeling the pistol in the sheet sagging cold and heavy in her fingers. Already she was getting wet; it seemed that her feet found every puddle of water that stood between the corn rows.

She came to the edge of the creek and paused, wondering at what point was it low. Taking the sheet from under her apron, she wrapped the gun in it so that her finger could be upon the trigger. Ahll cross here, she thought. At first she did not feel the water; her feet were already wet. But the water grew cold as it came up to her knees; she gasped when it reached her waist. Lawd, this creeks high! When she had passed the middle, she knew that she was out of danger. She came out of the water, climbed a grassy hill, walked on, turned a bend, and saw the lights of autos gleaming ahead. Yeah; theys still there! She hurried with her head down. Wondah did Ah beat im here? Lawd, A *hope* so! A vivid image of Booker's white face hovered a moment before her eyes, and a surging will rose up in her so hard and strong that it vanished. She was among the autos now. From nearby came the hoarse voices of the men.

"Hey, yuh!"

She stopped, nervously clutching the sheet. Two white men with shotguns came toward her.

"Whut in hell yuh doin out here?"

She did not answer.

"Didnt yuh hear somebody speak t yuh?"

"Ahm comin aftah mah son," she said humbly.

"Yo *son*?"

"Yessuh."

"Whut yo son doin out here?"

"The sheriffs got im."

"Holy Scott! Jim, its the niggers ma!"

"Whut yuh got there?" asked one.

"A sheet."

"A *sheet*?"

"Yessuh."

"Fer whut?"

"The sheriff tol me t bring a sheet t git his body."

"Waal, waal . . ."

"Now, ain tha somethin?"

The white men looked at each other.

"These niggers sho love one ernother," said one.

"N tha ain no lie," said the other.

"Take me t the sheriff," she begged.

"Yuh ain givin us *orders*, is yuh?"

"Nawsuh."

"We'll take yuh when wes good n ready."

"Yessuh."

"So yuh wan his body?"

"Yessuh."

"Waal, he ain dead yit."

"They gonna kill im," she said.

"Ef he talks they wont."

"He ain gonna talk," she said.

"How yuh know?"

"Cause he ain."

"We got ways of makin niggers talk."

"Yuh ain got no way fer im."

"Yuh thinka lot of that black Red, don yuh?"

"Hes mah son."

"Why don yuh teach im some sense?"

"Hes mah son," she said again.

"Lissen, ol nigger woman, yuh stand there wid yo hair white. Yuh got bettah sense than t blieve tha niggers kin make a revolution . . ."

"A black republic," said the other one, laughing.

"Take me t the sheriff," she begged.

"Yuh his ma," said one. "Yuh kin make im talk n tell whos in this thing wid im."

"He ain gonna talk," she said.

"Don yuh wan im t live?"

She did not answer.

"C mon, les take her t Bradley."

They grabbed her arms, and she clutched hard at the sheet and gun; they led her toward the crowd in the woods. Her feelings were simple; Booker would not tell; she was there with the gun to see to that. The louder became the voices of the men the deeper became her feeling of wanting to right the mistake she had made; of wanting to fight her way back to solid ground. She would stall for time until Booker showed up. Oh, ef theyll only lemme git close t Johnny-Boy! As they led her near the crowd she saw white faces turning and looking at her and heard a rising clamor of voices.

"Whos tha?"

"A nigger woman!"

"Whut she doin out here?"

"This is his ma!" called one of the men.

"Whut she wans?"

"She brought a sheet t cover his body!"

"He ain dead yit!"

"They tryin t make im talk!"

"But he will be dead soon ef he don open up!"

"Say, look! The niggers ma brought a sheet t cover up his body!"

"Now, ain that sweet?"

"Mabbe she wans t hol a prayer meetin!"

"Did she git a preacher?"

"Say, go git Bradley!"

"O.K.!"

The crowd grew quiet. They looked at her curiously; she felt their cold eyes trying to detect some weakness in her. Humbly, she stood with the sheet covering the gun. She had already accepted all that they could do to her.

The sheriff came.

"So yuh brought yo sheet, hunh?"

"Yessuh," she whispered.

"Looks like them slaps we gave yuh learned yuh some sense, didnt they?"

She did not answer.

"Yuh don need tha sheet. Yo son ain dead yit," he said, reaching toward her.

She backed away, her eyes wide.

"Naw!"

"Now, lissen, Anty!" he said. "There ain no use in yuh ackin a fool! Go in there n tell tha nigger son of yos t tell us whos in this wid im, see? Ah promise we won't kill im ef he talks. We'll let him git outta town."

"There ain nothin Ah kin tell im," she said.

"Yuh wan us t kill im?"

She did not answer. She saw someone lean toward the sheriff and whisper.

"Bring her erlong," the sheriff said.

They led her to a muddy clearing. The rain streamed down through the ghostly glare of the flashlights. As the men formed a semi-circle she saw Johnny-Boy lying in a trough of mud. He was tied with rope; he lay hunched, and one side of his face rested in a pool of black water. His eyes were staring questioningly at her.

"Speak t im," said the sheriff.

If she could only tell him why she was here! But that was impossible; she was close to what she wanted and she stared straight before her with compressed lips.

"Say, nigger!" called the sheriff, kicking Johnny-Boy. "Heres yo ma!"

Johnny-Boy did not move or speak. The sheriff faced her again.

"Lissen, Anty," he said. "Yuh got mo say wid im than anybody. Tell im t talk n hava chance. Whut he wanna pertect the other niggers n white folks fer?"

She slid her finger about the trigger of the gun and looked stonily at the mud.

"Go t him," said the sheriff.

She did not move. Her heart was crying out to answer the amazed question in Johnny-Boy's eyes. But there was no way now.

"Waal, yuhre astin fer it. By Gawd, we gotta way to *make* yuh talk t im," he said, turning away. "Say, Tim, git one of them logs n turn that nigger upside-down n put his legs on it!"

A murmur of assent ran through the crowd. She bit her lips; she knew what that meant.

"Yuh wan yo nigger son crippled?" she heard the sheriff ask.

She did not answer. She saw them roll the log up; they lifted Johnny-Boy and laid him on his face and stomach, then they pulled his legs over the log. His kneecaps rested on the sheer top of the log's back and the toes of his shoes pointed groundward. So absorbed was she in watching that she felt that it was she who was being lifted and made ready for torture.

"Git a crowbar!" said the sheriff.

A tall, lank man got a crowbar from a nearby auto and stood over the log. His jaws worked slowly on a wad of tobacco.

"Now, its up t yuh, Anty," the sheriff said. "Tell the man wuht t do!"

She looked into the rain. The sheriff turned.

"Mabbe she think wes playin. Ef she don say nothin, then break em at the kneecaps!"

"O.K., Sheriff!"

She stood waiting for Booker. Her legs felt weak; she wondered if she would be able to wait much longer. Over and over she said to herself, Ef he came now Ahd kill em both!

"She ain sayin nothin, Sheriff."

"Waal, Gawddammit, let im have it!"

The crowbar came down and Johnny-Boy's body lunged in the mud and water. There was a scream. She swayed, holding tight to the gun and sheet.

"Hol im! Git the other leg!"

The crowbar fell again. There was another scream.

"Yuh break em?" asked the sheriff.

The tall man lifted Johnny-Boy's legs and let them drop limply again, dropping rearward from the kneecaps. Johnny-Boy's body lay still. His head rolled to one side and she could not see his face.

"Jus lika broke sparrow wing," said the man, laughing softly.

Then Johnny-Boy's face turned to her; he screamed.

"Go way, ma! Go way!"

It was the first time she had heard his voice since she had come out to the woods; she all but lost control of herself. She started violently forward, but the sheriff's arm checked her.

"Aw, naw! Yuh had yo chance!" He turned to Johnny-Boy. "She kin go ef yuh talk."

"Mistah, he ain gonna talk," she said.

"Go way, ma!" said Johnny-Boy.

"Shoot im! Don make im suffah so," she begged.

"He'll either talk or he'll never hear yuh ergin," the sheriff said. "Theres other things we kin do t im."

She said nothing.

"What yuh come here fer, ma?" Johnny-Boy sobbed.

"Ahm gonna split his eardrums," the sheriff said. "Ef yuh got anythin t say t im yuh bettah say it *now!*"

She closed her eyes. She heard the sheriff's feet sucking in mud. Ah could save im! She opened her eyes; there were shouts of eagerness from the crowd as it pushed in closer.

"Bus em, Sheriff!"

"Fix im so he cant hear!"

"He knows how t do it, too!"

"He busted a Jew boy tha way once!"

She saw the sheriff stoop over Johnny-Boy, place his flat palm over one ear, and strike his fist against it with all his might. He placed his palm over the other ear and struck again. Johnny-Boy moaned, his head rolling from side to side, his eyes showing white amazement in a world without sound.

"Yuh wouldnt talk t im when yuh had the chance," said the sheriff. "Try n talk now."

She felt warm tears on her cheeks. She longed to shoot Johnny-Boy and let him go. But if she did that they would take the gun from her, and Booker would tell who the others were. Lawd, hep me! The men were talking loudly now, as though the main business was over. It seemed ages that she stood there watching Johnny-Boy roll and whimper in his world of silence.

"Say, Sheriff, heres somebody lookin fer yuh!"

"Who is it?"

"Ah don know!"

"Bring em in!"

She stiffened and looked around wildly, holding the gun tight. Is tha Booker? Then she held still, feeling that her excitement might betray her. Mabbe Ah kin shoot em both! Mabbe Ah kin shoot *twice!* The sheriff stood in front of her, waiting. The crowd parted and she saw Booker hurrying forward.

"Ah know em all, Sheriff!" he called.

He came full into the muddy clearing where Johnny-Boy lay.

"Yuh mean yuh got the names?"

"Sho! The ol nigger . . ."

She saw his lips hang open and silent when he saw her. She stepped forward and raised the sheet.

"Whut . . ."

She fired, once; then, without pausing, she turned, hearing them yell.

She aimed at Johnny-Boy, but they had their arms around her, bearing her to the ground, clawing at the sheet in her hand. She glimpsed Booker lying sprawled in the mud, on his face, his hands stretched out before him; then a cluster of yelling men blotted him out. She lay without struggling, looking upward through the rain at the white faces above her. And she was suddenly at peace; they were not a white mountain now; they were not pushing her any longer to the edge of life. Its awright . . .

"She shot Booker!"

"She hada gun in the sheet!"

"She shot im right thu the head!"

"Whut she shoot im fer?"

"Kill the bitch!"

"Ah *thought* something wuz wrong bout her!"

"Ah wuz fer givin it t her from the firs!"

"Thas whut yuh git for treatin a nigger nice!"

"Say, Bookers dead!"

She stopped looking into the white faces, stopped listening. She waited, giving up her life before they took it from her; she had done what she wanted. Ef only Johnny-Boy . . . She looked at im; he lay looking at her with tired eyes. Ef she could only tell im! But he lay already buried in a grave of silence.

"Whut yuh kill im fer, hunh?"

It was the sheriff's voice; she did not answer.

"Mabbe she wuz shootin at yuh, Sheriff?"

"Whut yuh kill im fer?"

She felt the sheriff's foot come into her side; she closed her eyes.

"Yuh black bitch!"

"Let her have it!"

"Yuh reckon she foun out bout Booker?"

"She mighta."

"Jesus Chris, whut yuh dummies *waitin* on!"

"Yeah; kill her!"

"Kill em *both!*"

"Let her know her nigger sons dead firs!"

She turned her head toward Johnny-Boy; he lay looking puzzled in a world beyond the reach of voices. At leas he cant hear, she thought.

"C mon, let im have it!"

She listened to hear what Johnny-Boy could not. They came, two of them, one right behind the other, so close together that they sounded like one shot. She did not look at Johnny-Boy now; she looked at the white faces of the men, hard and wet in the glare of the flashlights.

"Yuh hear tha, nigger woman?"

"Did tha surprise im? Hes in hell now, wonderin whut hit im!"

"C mon! Give it t her, Sheriff!"

"Lemme shoot her, Sheriff! It wuz mah pal she shot!"

"Awright, Pete! Thas fair ernuff!"

She gave up as much of her life as she could before they took it from her. But the sound of the shot and the streak of fire that tore its way through her chest forced her to live again, intensely. She had not moved, save for the slight jarring impact of the bullet. She felt the heat of her own blood warming her cold, wet back. She yearned suddenly to talk. "Yuh didnt git whut yuh wanted! N yuh ain gonna nevah git it! Yuh didnt kill me; Ah come here by mahsef . . ." She felt rain falling into her wide-open, dimming eyes and heard faint voices. Her lips moved soundlessly. *Yuh didnt git yuh didnt yuh didnt* . . . Focused and pointed she was, buried in the depths of her star, swallowed in its peace and strength, and not feeling her flesh growing cold, cold as the rain that fell from the invisible sky upon the doomed living and the dead that never dies.

Katherine Anne Porter

Katherine Anne Porter (1894–   ) was born in Indian Creek, Texas, of pioneer stock, distantly related to Daniel Boone. Reared a Catholic, she attended convent schools and worked as a journalist for many years before the first volume of stories, Flowering Judas, *appeared in 1930. A near-fatal attack of influenza during the World War I epidemic was the basis of her short novel,* Pale Horse, Pale Rider, *and her recuperation in Mexico in the 1920s brought her into contact with the colorful artists and revolutionaries who people her fiction. Noted for its careful craftsmanship, Miss Porter's literary output was small, confined to stories and short novels until the publication in 1962 of her massive novel,* Ship of Fools. *Her stories often treat the conflict between generations as revealed through the sensitive perception of a young woman or child, as in this story.* *(See page 78 of Introduction.)*

THE DOWNWARD PATH TO WISDOM

In the square bedroom with the big window Mama and Papa were lolling back on their pillows handing each other things from the wide black tray on the small table with crossed legs. They were smiling and they smiled even more when the little boy, with the feeling of sleep still in his skin and hair, came in and walked up to the bed. Leaning against it, his bare toes wriggling in the white fur rug, he went on eating peanuts which he took from his pajama pocket. He was four years old.

"Here's my baby," said Mama. "Lift him up, will you?"

He went limp as a rag for Papa to take him under the arms and swing him up over a broad, tough chest. He sank between his parents like a bear cub in a warm litter, and lay there comfortably. He took another peanut between his teeth, cracked the shell, picked out the nut whole and ate it.

"Running around without his slippers again," said Mama. "His feet are like icicles."

"He crunches like a horse," said Papa. "Eating peanuts before breakfast will ruin his stomach. Where did he get them?"

"You brought them yesterday," said Mama, with exact memory, "in a grisly little cellophane sack. I have asked you dozens of times not to bring him things to eat. Put him out, will you? He's spilling shells all over me."

Almost at once the little boy found himself on the floor again. He moved around to Mama's side of the bed and leaned confidingly near her and began another peanut. As he chewed he gazed solemnly in her eyes.

"Bright-looking specimen, isn't he?" asked Papa, stretching his long legs and reaching for his bathrobe. "I suppose you'll say it's my fault he's dumb as an ox."

"He's my little baby, my only baby," said Mama richly, hugging him, "and he's a dear lamb." His neck and shoulders were quite boneless in her firm embrace. He stopped chewing long enough to receive a kiss on his crumby chin. "He's sweet as clover," said Mama. The baby went on chewing.

"Look at him staring like an owl," said Papa.

Mama said, "He's an angel and I'll never get used to having him."

"We'd be better off if we never *had* had him," said Papa. He was walking about the room and his back was turned when he said that. There was silence for a moment. The little boy stopped eating, and stared deeply at his Mama. She was looking at the back of Papa's head, and her eyes were almost black. "You're going to say that just once too often," she told him in a low voice. "I hate you when you say that."

Papa said, "You spoil him to death. You never correct him for anything. And you don't take care of him. You let him run around eating peanuts before breakfast."

"You gave him the peanuts, remember that," said Mama. She sat up and hugged her only baby once more. He nuzzled softly in the pit of her arm. "Run along, my darling," she told him in her gentlest voice, smiling at him straight in the eyes. "Run along," she said, her arms falling away from him. "Get your breakfast."

The little boy had to pass his father on the way to the door. He shrank into himself when he saw the big hand raised above him. "Yes, get out of here and stay out," said Papa, giving him a little shove toward the door. It was not a hard shove, but it hurt the little boy. He slunk out, and trotted down the hall trying not to look back. He was afraid something was coming after him, he could not imagine what. Something hurt him all over, he did not know why.

He did not want his breakfast; he would not have it. He sat and stirred it round in the yellow bowl, letting it stream off the spoon and spill on the table, on his front, on the chair. He liked seeing it spill. It was hateful stuff, but it looked funny running in white rivulets down his pajamas.

"Now look what you're doing, dirty boy," said Marjory. "You dirty little old boy."

The little boy opened his mouth to speak for the first time. "You're dirty yourself," he told her.

"That's right," said Marjory, leaning over him and speaking so her voice would not carry. "That's right, just like your papa. Mean," she whispered, "mean."

The little boy took up his yellow bowl full of cream and oatmeal and sugar with both hands and brought it down with a crash on the table. It burst and some of the wreck lay in chunks and some of it ran all over everything. He felt better.

"You see?" said Marjory, dragging him out of the chair and scrubbing him with a napkin. She scrubbed him as roughly as she dared until he cried out. "That's just what I said. That's exactly it." Through his tears he saw her face terribly near, red and frowning under a stiff white band, looking like the face of somebody who came at night and stood over him and scolded him when he could not move or get away. "Just like your papa, *mean.*"

The little boy went out into the garden and sat on a green bench dangling his legs. He was clean. His hair was wet and his blue woolly pull-over made his nose itch. His face felt stiff from the soap. He saw Marjory going past a window with the black tray. The curtains were still closed at the window he knew opened into Mama's room. Papa's room. Mommanpoppasroom, the word was pleasant, it made a mumbling snapping noise between his lips; it ran in his mind while his eyes wandered about looking for something to do, something to play with.

Mommanpoppas' voices kept attracting his attention. Mama was being cross with Papa again. He could tell by the sound. That was what Marjory always said when their voices rose and fell and shot up to a point and crashed and rolled like the two tomcats who fought at night. Papa was being cross, too, much crosser than Mama this time. He grew cold and disturbed and sat very still, wanting to go to the bathroom, but it was just next to Mommanpoppasroom; he didn't dare think of it. As the voices grew louder he could hardly hear them any more, he wanted so badly to go to the bathroom. The kitchen door opened suddenly and Marjory ran out, making the motion with her hand that meant he was to come to her. He didn't move. She came to him, her face still red and frowning, but she was not angry; she was scared just as he was. She said, "Come on, honey, we've got to go to your gran'ma's again." She took his hand and pulled him. "Come on quick, your gran'ma is waiting for you." He slid off the bench. His mother's voice rose in a terrible scream, screaming something he could not understand, but she was furious; he had seen her clenching her fists and stamping in one spot, screaming with her eyes shut; he knew how she looked. She was screaming in a tantrum, just as he remembered having heard himself. He stood still, doubled over, and all his body seemed to dissolve, sickly, from the pit of his stomach.

"Oh, my God," said Marjory. "Oh, my God. Now look at you. Oh, my God. I can't stop to clean you up."

He did not know how he got to his grandma's house, but he was there at last, wet and soiled, being handled with disgust in the big bathtub. His grandma was there in long black skirts saying, "Maybe he's sick; maybe we should send for the doctor."

"I don't think so, m'am," said Marjory. "He hasn't et anything; he's just scared."

The little boy couldn't raise his eyes, he was so heavy with shame. "Take this note to his mother," said Grandma.

She sat in a wide chair and ran her hands over his head, combing his hair with her fingers; she lifted his chin and kissed him. "Poor little fellow," she said. "Never you mind. You always have a good time at your grandma's, don't you? You're going to have a nice little visit, just like the last time."

The little boy leaned against the stiff, dry-smelling clothes and felt horribly grieved about something. He began to whimper and said, "I'm hungry. I want something to eat." This reminded him. He began to bellow at the top of his voice; he threw himself upon the carpet and rubbed his nose in a dusty woolly bouquet of roses. "I want my peanuts," he howled. "Somebody took my peanuts."

His grandma knelt beside him and gathered him up so tightly he could hardly move. She called in a calm voice above his howls to Old Janet in the doorway, "Bring me some bread and butter with strawberry jam."

"I want peanuts," yelled the little boy desperately.

"No, you don't, darling," said his grandma. "You don't want horrid old peanuts to make you sick. You're going to have some of grandma's nice fresh bread with good strawberries on it. That's what you're going to have." He sat afterward very quietly and ate and ate. His grandma sat near him and Old Janet stood by, near a tray with a loaf and a glass bowl of jam upon the table at the window. Outside there was a trellis with tube-shaped red flowers clinging all over it, and brown bees singing.

"I hardly know what to do," said Grandma, "it's very . . ."

"Yes, m'am," said Old Janet, "it certainly is . . ."

Grandma said, "I can't possibly see the end of it. It's a terrible . . ."

"It certainly is bad," said Old Janet, "all this upset all the time and him such a baby."

Their voices ran on soothingly. The little boy ate and forgot to listen. He did not know these women, except by name. He could not understand what they were talking about; their hands and their clothes and their voices were dry and far away; they examined him with crinkled eyes without any expression that he could see. He sat there waiting for whatever they would do next with him. He hoped they would let him go out and play in the yard. The room was full of flowers and dark red curtains and big soft chairs, and the windows were open, but it was still dark in there somehow; dark, and a place he did not know, or trust.

"Now drink your milk," said Old Janet, holding out a silver cup.

"I don't want any milk," he said, turning his head away.

"Very well, Janet, he doesn't have to drink it," said Grandma quickly. "Now run out in the garden and play, darling. Janet, get his hoop."

A big strange man came home in the evenings who treated the little boy very confusingly. "Say 'please,' and 'thank you,' young man," he would roar, terrifyingly, when he gave any smallest object to the little boy. "Well, fellow, are you ready for a fight?" he would say, again, doubling up huge, hairy fists and making passes at him. "Come on now, you must learn to box." After the first few times this was fun.

"Don't teach him to be rough," said Grandma. "Time enough for all that."

"Now, Mother, we don't want him to be a sissy," said the big man. "He's got to toughen up early. Come on now, fellow, put up your mitts." The little boy liked this new word for hands. He learned to throw himself upon the strange big man, whose name was Uncle David, and hit him on the chest as hard as he could; the big man would laugh and hit him back with his huge, loose fists. Sometimes, but not often, Uncle David came home in the middle of the day. The little boy missed him on the other days, and would hang on the gate looking down the street for him. One evening he brought a large square package under his arm.

"Come over here, fellow, and see what I've got," he said, pulling off quantities of green paper and string from the box which was full of flat, folded colors. He put something in the little boy's hand. It was limp and silky and bright green with a tube on the end. "Thank you," said the little boy nicely, but not knowing what to do with it.

"Balloons," said Uncle David in triumph. "Now just put your mouth here and blow hard." The little boy blew hard and the green thing began to grow round and thin and slivery.

"Good for your chest," said Uncle David. "Blow some more." The little boy went on blowing and the balloon swelled steadily.

"Stop," said Uncle David, "that's enough." He twisted the tube to keep the air in. "That's the way," he said. "Now I'll blow one, and you blow one, and let's see who can blow up a big balloon the fastest."

They blew and blew, especially Uncle David. He puffed and panted and blew with all his might, but the little boy won. His balloon was perfectly round before Uncle David could even get started. The little boy was so proud he began to dance and shout, "I beat, I beat," and blew in his balloon again. It burst in his face and frightened him so he felt sick. "Ha ha, ho ho ho," whooped Uncle David. "That's the boy. I bet I can't do that. Now let's see." He blew until the beautiful bubble grew and wavered and burst into thin air, and there was only a small colored rag in his hand. This was a fine game. They went on with it until Grandma came in and said, "Time for supper now. No, you can't blow balloons at the table. Tomorrow maybe." And it was all over.

The next day, instead of being given balloons, he was hustled out of bed early, bathed in warm soapy water and given a big breakfast of soft-boiled eggs with toast and jam and milk. His grandma came in to kiss him good morning. "And I hope you'll be a good boy and obey your teacher," she told him.

"What's teacher?" asked the little boy.

"Teacher is at school," said Grandma. "She'll tell you all sorts of things and you must do as she says."

Mama and Papa had talked a great deal about School, and how they must send him there. They had told him it was a fine place with all kinds of toys and other children to play with. He felt he knew about School. "I didn't know it was time, Grandma," he said. "Is it today?"

"It's this very minute," said Grandma. "I told you a week ago."

Old Janet came in with her bonnet on. It was a prickly looking bundle held with a black rubber band under her back hair. "Come on," she said. "This is my busy day." She wore a dead cat slung around her neck, its sharp ears bent over under her baggy chin.

The little boy was excited and wanted to run ahead. "Hold to my hand like I told you," said Old Janet. "Don't go running off like that and get yourself killed."

"I'm going to get killed, I'm going to get killed," sang the little boy, making a tune of his own.

"Don't say that, you give me the creeps," said Old Janet. "Hold to my hand now." She bent over and looked at him, not at his face but at something on his clothes. His eyes followed hers.

"I declare," said Old Janet, "I did forget. I was going to sew it up. I might have known. I *told* your grandma it would be that way from now on."

"What?" asked the little boy.

"Just look at yourself," said Old Janet crossly. He looked at himself. There was a little end of him showing through the slit in his short blue flannel trousers. The trousers came halfway to his knees above, and his socks came halfway to his knees below, and all winter long his knees were cold. He remembered now how cold his knees were in cold weather. And how sometimes he would have to put the part of him that came through the slit back again, because he was cold there too. He saw at once what was wrong, and tried to arrange himself, but his mittens got in the way. Janet said, "Stop that, you bad boy," and with a firm thumb she set him in order, at the same time reaching under his belt to pull down and fold his knit undershirt over his front.

"There now," she said, "try not to disgrace yourself today." He felt guilty and red all over, because he had something that showed when he was dressed that was not supposed to show then. The different women who bathed him always wrapped him quickly in towels and hurried him into his clothes, because they saw something about him he could not see for himself. They hurried him so he never had a chance to see whatever it was they saw, and though he looked at himself when his clothes were off, he could not find out what was wrong with him. Outside, in his clothes, he knew he looked like everybody else, but inside his clothes there was something bad the matter with him. It worried him and confused him and he wondered about it. The only people who never seemed to notice there was something wrong with him were Mommanpoppa. They never called him a bad boy, and all summer long they had taken all his clothes off and let him run in the sand beside a big ocean.

"Look at him, isn't he a love?" Mama would say and Papa would look, and say, "He's got a back like a prize fighter." Uncle David was a prize fighter when he doubled up his mitts and said, "Come on, fellow."

Old Janet held him firmly and took long steps under her big rustling skirts. He did not like Old Janet's smell. It made him a little quivery in the stomach; it was just like wet chicken feathers.

School was easy. Teacher was a square-shaped woman with square short hair and short skirts. She got in the way sometimes, but not often. The people around him were his size; he didn't have always to be stretching his neck up to faces bent over him, and he could sit on the chairs without having to climb. All the children had names, like Frances and Evelyn and Agatha and Edward and Martin, and his own name was Stephen. He was not Mama's "Baby," nor Papa's "Old Man"; he was not Uncle David's "Fellow" or Grandma's "Darling," or even Old Janet's "Bad Boy." He was Stephen. He was learning to read, and to sing a tune to some strange-looking letters or marks written in chalk on a blackboard. You talked one kind of lettering, and you sang another. All the children talked and sang in turn, and then all together. Stephen thought it a fine game. He felt awake and happy. They had soft clay and paper and wires and squares of colors in tin boxes to play with, colored blocks to build houses with. Afterward they all danced in a big ring, and then they danced in pairs, boys with girls. Stephen danced with Frances, and Frances kept saying, "Now you just follow me." She was a little taller than he was, and her hair stood up in short, shiny curls, the color of an ash tray on Papa's desk. She would say, "You can't dance." "I can dance too," said Stephen, jumping around holding her hands, "I can, too, dance." He was certain of it. "*You* can't dance," he told Frances, "you can't dance at all."

Then they had to change partners, and when they came round again, Frances said, "I don't *like* the way you dance." This was different. He felt uneasy about it. He didn't jump quite so high when the phonograph record started going dumdiddy dumdiddy again. "Go ahead, Stephen, you're doing fine," said Teacher, waving her hands together very fast. The dance ended, and they all played "relaxing" for five minutes. They relaxed by swinging their arms back and forth, then rolling their heads round and round. When Old Janet came for him he didn't want to go home. At lunch his grandma told him twice to keep his face out of his plate. "Is that what they teach you at school?" she asked. Uncle David was at home. "Here you are, fellow," he said and gave Stephen two balloons. "Thank you," said Stephen. He put the balloons in his pocket and forgot about them. "I told you that boy could learn something," said Uncle David to Grandma. "Hear him say 'thank you'?"

In the afternoon at school Teacher handed out big wads of clay and told the children to make something out of it. Anything they liked. Stephen decided to make a cat, like Mama's Meeow at home. He did not like Meeow, but he thought it would be easy to make a cat. He could not get the clay to work at all. It simply fell into one lump after another. So he stopped, wiped his hands on his pull-over, remembered his balloons and began blowing one.

"Look at Stephen's horse," said Frances. "Just look at it."

"It's not a horse, it's a cat," said Stephen. The other children gathered around. "It looks like a horse, a little," said Martin.

"It is a cat," said Stephen, stamping his foot, feeling his face turning hot. The other children all laughed and exclaimed over Stephen's cat that looked like a horse. Teacher came down among them. She sat usually at the top of the room before a big table covered with papers and playthings. She picked up Stephen's lump of clay and turned it round and examined it with her kind eyes. "Now, children," she said, "everybody has the right to make anything the way he pleases. If Stephen says this is a cat, it *is* a cat. Maybe you were thinking about a horse, Stephen?"

"It's a *cat,*" said Stephen. He was aching all over. He knew then he should have said at first. "Yes, it's a horse." Then they would have let him alone. They would never have known he was trying to make a cat. "It's Meeow," he said in a trembling voice, "but I forgot how she looks."

His balloon was perfectly flat. He started blowing it up again, trying not to cry. Then it was time to go home, and Old Janet came looking for him. While Teacher was talking to other grown-up people who came to take other children home, Frances said, "Give me your balloon; I haven't got a balloon." Stephen handed it to her. He was happy to give it. He reached in his pocket and took out the other. Happily, he gave her that one too. Frances took it, then handed it back. "Now you blow up one and I'll blow up the other, and let's have a race," she said. When their balloons were only half filled Old Janet took Stephen by the arm and said, "Come on here, this is my busy day."

Frances ran after them, calling, "Stephen, you give me back my balloon," and snatched it away. Stephen did not know whether he was surprised to find himself going away with Frances' balloon, or whether he was surprised to see her snatching it as if it really belonged to her. He was badly mixed up in his mind, and Old Janet was hauling him along. One thing he knew, he liked Frances, he was going to see her again tomorrow, and he was going to bring her more balloons.

That evening Stephen boxed awhile with his Uncle David, and Uncle David gave him a beautiful orange. "Eat that," he said, "it's good for your health."

"Uncle David, may I have some more balloons?" asked Stephen.

"Well, what do you say first?" asked Uncle David, reaching for the box on the top bookshelf.

"Please," said Stephen.

"That's the word," said Uncle David. He brought out two balloons, a red and a yellow one. Stephen noticed for the first time they had letters on them, very small letters that grew taller and wider as the balloon grew rounder. "Now that's all, fellow," said Uncle David. "Don't ask for any more because that's all." He put the box back on the bookshelf, but not before Stephen had seen that the box was almost full of balloons. He didn't say a word, but went on blowing, and Uncle David blew also. Stephen thought it was the nicest game he had ever known.

He had only one left, the next day, but he took it to school and gave it to Frances. "There are a lot," he said, feeling very proud and warm; "I'll bring you a lot of them."

Frances blew it up until it made a beautiful bubble, and said, "Look, I want to show you something." She took a sharp-pointed stick they used in working the clay; she poked the balloon, and it exploded. "Look at that," she said.

"That's nothing," said Stephen, "I'll bring you some more."

After school, before Uncle David came home, while Grandma was resting, when Old Janet had given him his milk and told him to run away and not bother her, Stephen dragged a chair to the bookshelf, stood upon it and reached into the box. He did not take three or four as he believed he intended; once his hands were upon them he seized what they could hold and jumped off the chair, hugging them to him. He stuffed them into his reefer pocket where they folded down and hardly made a lump.

He gave them all to Frances. There were so many, Frances gave most of them away to the other children. Shephen, flushed with his new joy, the lavish pleasure of giving presents, found almost at once still another happiness. Suddenly he was popular among the children; they invited him specially to join whatever games were up; they fell in at once with his own notions for play, and asked him what he would like to do next. They had festivals of blowing up the beautiful globes, fuller and rounder and thinner, changing as they went from deep color to lighter, paler tones, growing glassy thin, bubbly thin, then bursting with a thrilling loud noise like a toy pistol.

For the first time in his life Stephen had almost too much of something he wanted, and his head was so turned he forgot how this fullness came about, and no longer thought of it as a secret. The next day was Saturday, and Frances came to visit him with her nurse. The nurse and Old Janet sat in Old Janet's room drinking coffee and gossiping, and the children sat on the side porch blowing balloons. Stephen chose an apple-colored one and Frances a pale green one. Between them on the bench lay a tumbled heap of delights still to come.

"I once had a silver balloon," said Frances, "a beyootiful silver one, not round like these; it was a long one. But these are even nicer, I think," she added quickly, for she did want to be polite.

"When you get through with that one," said Stephen, gazing at her with the pure bliss of giving added to loving, "you can blow up a blue one and then a pink one and a yellow one and a purple one." He pushed the heap of limp objects toward her. Her clear-looking eyes, with fine little rays of brown in them like the spokes of a wheel, were full of approval for Stephen. "I wouldn't want to be greedy, though, and blow up all your balloons."

"There'll be plenty more left," said Stephen, and his heart rose under his thin ribs. He felt his ribs with his fingers and discovered with some surprise that they stopped somewhere in front, while Frances sat blowing balloons rather halfheartedly. The truth was, she was tired of balloons. After you blow six or seven your chest gets hollow and your lips feel puckery. She had been blowing balloons steadily for three days now. She had begun to hope they were giving out. "There's boxes and boxes more of them, Frances," said Stephen happily. "Millions more. I guess they'd last and last if we didn't blow too many every day."

Frances said somewhat timidly, "I tell you what. Let's rest awhile and fix some liquish water. Do you like liquish?"

"Yes, I do," said Stephen, "but I haven't got any."

"Couldn't we buy some?" asked Frances. "It's only a cent a stick, the nice rubbery, twisty kind. We can put it in a bottle with some water, and shake it and shake it, and it makes foam on top like soda pop and we can drink it. I'm kind of thirsty," she said in a small, weak voice. "Blowing balloons all the time makes you thirsty, I think."

Stephen, in silence, realized a dreadful truth and a numb feeling crept over him. He did not have a cent to buy licorice for Frances and she was tired of his balloons. This was the first real dismay of his whole life, and he aged at least a year in the next minute, huddled, with his deep, serious blue eyes focused down his nose in intense speculation. What could he do to please Frances that would not cost money? Only yesterday Uncle David had given him a nickel, and he had thrown it away on gumdrops. He regretted that nickel so bitterly his neck and forehead were damp. He was thirsty too.

"I tell you what," he said, brightening with a splendid idea, lamely trailing off on second thought, "I know something we can do, I'll—I . . ."

"I *am* thirsty," said Frances with gentle persistence. "I think I'm so thirsty maybe I'll have to go home." She did not leave the bench, though, but sat, turning her grieved mouth toward Stephen.

Stephen quivered with the terrors of the adventure before him, but he said boldly, "I'll make some lemonade. I'll get sugar and lemon and some ice and we'll have lemonade."

"Oh, I love lemonade," cried Frances. "I'd rather have lemonade than liquish."

"You stay right here," said Stephen, "and I'll get everything."

He ran around the house, and under Old Janet's window he heard the dry, chattering voices of the two old women whom he must outwit. He sneaked on tiptoe to the pantry, took a lemon lying there by itself, a handful of lump sugar and a china teapot, smooth, round, with flowers and leaves all over it. These he left on the kitchen table while he broke a piece of ice with a sharp metal pick he had been forbidden to touch. He put the ice in the pot, cut the lemon and squeezed it as well as he could—a lemon was tougher and more slippery than he had thought—and mixed sugar and water. He decided there was not enough sugar so he sneaked back and took another handful. He was back on the porch in an astonishingly short time, his face tight, his knees trembling, carrying iced lemonade to thirsty Frances with both his devoted hands.

A pace distant from her he stopped, literally stabbed through with a thought. Here he stood in broad daylight carrying a teapot with lemonade in it, and his grandma or Old Janet might walk through the door at any moment.

"Come on, Frances," he whispered loudly. "Let's go round to the back behind the rose bushes where it's shady." Frances leaped up and ran like a deer beside him, her face wise with knowledge of why they ran; Stephen ran stiffly, cherishing his teapot with clenched hands.

It was shady behind the rose bushes, and much safer. They sat side by side on the dampish ground, legs doubled under, drinking in turn from the slender spout. Stephen took his just share in large, cool, delicious swallows. When Frances drank she set her round pink mouth daintily to the spout and her throat beat steadily as a heart. Stephen was thinking he had really done something pretty nice for Frances. He did not know where his own happiness was; it was mixed with the sweet-sour taste in his mouth and a cool feeling in his bosom because Frances was there drinking his lemonade which he had got for her with great danger.

Frances said, "My, what big swallows you take," when his turn came next.

"No bigger than yours," he told her downrightly. "You take awfully big swallows."

"Well," said Frances, turning this criticism into an argument for her rightness about things, "that's the way to drink lemonade anyway." She peered into the teapot. There was quite a lot of lemonade left and she was beginning to feel she had enough. "Let's make up a game and see who can take the biggest swallows."

This was such a wonderful notion they grew reckless, tipping the spout into their opened mouths above their heads until lemonade welled up and ran over their chins in rills down their fronts. When they tired of this there was still lemonade left in the pot. They played first at giving the rosebush a drink and ended by baptizing it. "Name father son holygoat," shouted Stephen, pouring. At this sound Old Janet's face appeared over the low hedge, with the tan, disgusted-looking face of Frances' nurse hanging over her shoulder.

"Well, just as I thought," said Old Janet. "Just as I expected." The bag under her chin waggled.

"We were thirsty," he said; "we were awfully thirsty." Frances said nothing, but she gazed steadily at the toes of her shoes.

"Give me that teapot," said Old Janet, taking it with a rude snatch. "Just because you're thirsty is no reason," said Old Janet. "You can ask for things. You don't have to steal."

"We didn't steal," cried Frances suddenly. "We didn't. We didn't!"

"That's enough from you, missy," said her nurse. "Come straight out of there. You have nothing to do with this."

"Oh, I don't know," said Old Janet with a hard stare at Frances' nurse. "*He* never did such a thing before, by himself."

"Come on," said the nurse to Frances, "this is no place for you." She held Frances by the wrist and started walking away so fast Frances had to run to keep up. "Nobody can call *us* thieves and get away with it."

"You don't have to steal, even if others do," said Old Janet to Stephen, in a high carrying voice. "If you so much as pick up a lemon in somebody else's house you're a little thief." She lowered her voice then and said, "Now I'm going to tell your grandma and you'll see what you get."

"He went in the icebox and left it open," Janet told Grandma, "and he got into the lump sugar and spilt it all over the floor. Lumps everywhere underfoot. He dribbled water all over the clean kitchen floor, and he baptized the rose bush, blaspheming. And he took your Spode teapot."

"I didn't either," said Stephen loudly, trying to free his hand from Old Janet's big hard fist.

"Don't tell fibs," said Old Janet; "that's the last straw."

"Oh, dear," said Grandma. "He's not a baby any more." She shut the book she was reading and pulled the wet front of his pull-over toward her. "What's this sticky stuff on him?" she asked and straightened her glasses.

"Lemonade," said Old Janet. "He took the last lemon."

They were in the big dark room with the red curtains. Uncle David walked in from the room with the bookcases, holding a box in his uplifted hand. "Look here," he said to Stephen. "What's become of all my balloons?"

Stephen knew well that Uncle David was not really asking a question.

Stephen, sitting on a footstool at his grandma's knee, felt sleepy. He leaned heavily and wished he could put his head on her lap, but he might go to sleep, and it would be wrong to go to sleep while Uncle David was still talking. Uncle David walked about the room with his hands in his pockets, talking to Grandma. Now and then he would walk over to a lamp and, leaning, peer into the top of the shade, winking in the light, as if he expected to find something there.

"It's simply in the blood, I told her," said Uncle David. "I told her she would simply have to come and get him, and keep him. She asked me if I meant to call him a thief and I said if she could think of a more exact word I'd be glad to hear it."

"You shouldn't have said that," commented Grandma calmly.

"Why not? She might as well know the facts. . . . I suppose he can't help it," said Uncle David, stopping now in front of Stephen and dropping his chin into his collar, "I shouldn't expect too much of him, but you can't begin too early—"

"The trouble is," said Grandma, and while she spoke she took Stephen by the chin and held it up so that he had to meet her eye; she talked steadily in a mournful tone, but Stephen could not understand. She ended, "It's not just about the balloons, of course."

"It *is* about the balloons," said Uncle David angrily, "because balloons now mean something worse later. But what can you expect? His father—well, it's in the blood. He—"

"That's your sister's husband you're talking about," said Grandma, "and there is no use making things worse. Besides, you don't really *know*."

"I *do* know," said Uncle David. And he talked again very fast, walking up and down. Stephen tried to understand, but the sounds were strange and floating just over his head. They were talking about his father, and they did not like him. Uncle David came over and stood above Stephen and Grandma. He hunched over them with a frowning face, a long, crooked shadow from him falling across them to the wall. To Stephen he looked like his father, and he shrank against his grandma's skirts.

"The question is, what to do with him now?" asked Uncle David. "If we keep him here, he'd just be a—I won't be bothered with him. Why can't they take care of their own child? That house is crazy. Too far gone already, I'm afraid. No training. No example."

"You're right, they must take him and keep him," said Grandma. She ran her hands over Stephen's head; tenderly she pinched the nape of his neck between thumb and forefinger. "You're your Grandma's darling," she told him, "and you've had a nice long visit, and now you're going home. Mama is coming for you in a few minutes. Won't that be nice?"

"I want my mama," said Stephen, whimpering, for his grandma's face frightened him. There was something wrong with her smile.

Uncle David sat down. "Come over here, fellow," he said, wagging a forefinger at Stephen. Stephen went over slowly, and Uncle David drew him between his wide knees in their loose, rough clothes. "You ought to be ashamed of yourself," he said, "stealing Uncle David's balloons when he had already given you so many."

"It wasn't that," said Grandma quickly. "Don't say that. It will make an impression—"

"I hope it does," said Uncle David in a louder voice; "I hope he remembers it all his life. If he belonged to me I'd give him a good thrashing."

Stephen felt his mouth, his chin, his whole face jerking. He opened his mouth to take a breath, and tears and noise burst from him. "Stop that, fellow, stop that," said Uncle David, shaking him gently by the shoulders, but Stephen could not stop. He drew his breath again and it came back in a howl. Old Janet came to the door.

"Bring me some cold water," called Grandma. There was a flurry, a commotion, a breath of cool air from the hall, the door slammed, and Stephen heard his mother's voice. His howl died away, his breath sobbed and fluttered, he turned his dimmed eyes and saw her standing there. His heart turned over within him and he bleated like a lamb, "Maaaaama," running toward her. Uncle David stood back as Mama swooped in and fell on her knees beside Stephen. She gathered him to her and stood up with him in her arms.

"What are you doing to my baby?" she asked Uncle David in a thickened voice. "I should never have let him come here. I should have known better—"

"You always should know better," said Uncle David, "and you never do. And you never will. You haven't got it here," he told her, tapping his forehead.

"David," said Grandma, "that's your—"

"Yes, I know, she's my sister," said Uncle David. "I know it. But if she must run away and marry a—"

"Shut up," said Mama.

"And bring more like him into the world, let her keep them at home. I say let her keep—"

Mama set Stephen on the floor and, holding him by the hand, she said to Grandma all in a rush as if she were reading something, "Good-by, Mother. This is the last time, really the last. I can't bear it any longer. Say good-by to Stephen; you'll never see him again. You let this happen. It's your fault. You know David was a coward and a bully and a self-righteous little beast all his life and you never crossed him in anything. You let him bully me all my life and you let him slander my husband and call my baby a thief, and now this is the end. . . . He calls my baby a thief over a few horrible little balloons because he doesn't like my husband. . . ."

She was panting and staring about from one to the other. They were all standing. Now Grandma said, "Go home, daughter. Go away, David. I'm sick of your quarreling. I've never had a day's peace or comfort from either of you. I'm sick of you both. Now let me alone and stop this noise. Go away," said Grandma in a wavering voice. She took out her handkerchief and wiped first one eye and then the other and said, "All this hate, hate—what is it for? . . . So this is the way it turns out. Well, let me alone."

"You and your little advertising balloons," said Mama to Uncle David. "The big honest businessman advertises with balloons and if he loses one he'll be ruined. And your beastly little moral notions . . ."

Grandma went to the door to meet Old Janet, who handed her a glass of water. Grandma drank it all, standing there.

"Is your husband coming for you, or are you going home by yourself?" she asked Mama.

"I'm driving myself," said Mama in a far-away voice as if her mind had wandered. "You know he wouldn't set foot in this house."

"I should think not," said Uncle David.

"Come on, Stephen darling," said Mama. "It's far past his bedtime," she said, to no one in particular. "Imagine keeping a baby up to torture him about a few miserable little bits of colored rubber." She smiled at Uncle David with both rows of teeth as she passed him on the way to the door, keeping between him and Stephen. "Ah, where would we be without high moral standards," she said, and then to Grandma, "Good night, Mother," in quite her usual voice. "I'll see you in a day or so."

"Yes, indeed," said Grandma cheerfully, coming out into the hall with Stephen and Mama. "Let me hear from you. Ring me up tomorrow. I hope you'll be feeling better."

"I feel very well now," said Mama brightly, laughing. She bent down and kissed Stephen. "Sleepy, darling? Papa's waiting to see you. Don't go to sleep until you've kissed your papa good night."

Stephen woke with a sharp jerk. He raised his head and put out his chin a little. "I don't want to go home," he said; "I want to go to school. I don't want to see Papa, I don't like him."

Mama laid her palm over his mouth softly. "Darling, don't."

Uncle David put his head out with a kind of snort. "There you are," he said. "There you've got a statement from headquarters."

Mama opened the door and ran, almost carrying Stephen. She ran across the sidewalk, jerking open the car door and dragging Stephen in after her. She spun the car around and dashed forward so sharply Stephen was almost flung out of the seat. He sat braced then with all his might, hands digging into the cushions. The car speeded up and the trees and houses whizzed by all flattened out. Stephen began suddenly to sing to himself, a quiet, inside song so Mama would not hear. He sang his new secret; it was a comfortable, sleepy song: "I hate Papa, I hate Mama, I hate Grandma, I hate Uncle David, I hate Old Janet, I hate Marjory, I hate Papa, I hate Mama . . ."

His head bobbed, leaned, came to rest on Mama's knee, eyes closed. Mama drew him closer and slowed down, driving with one hand.

Eudora Welty

Eudora Welty (1909–   ) was born in Jackson, Mississippi, attended Mississippi State College for Women and graduated from the University of Wisconsin. She held a number of writing jobs before publishing her first stories, collected in A Curtain of Green *(1941). Among her awards have been two Guggenheim fellowships and several O. Henry prizes. Miss Welty's stories deal with her native Mississippi and the often peculiar events in the lives of her small-town characters. She achieves brilliant comic effects through her use of colloquial speech. Although rooted to a particular locality, her stories seem to transcend their place and time. Among her other works are the novels* Delta Wedding *(1946) and* The Ponder Heart *(1954), and a short story collection,* The Wide Net *(1943). Her most recent work is* The Optimist's Daughter *(1972). "Death of a Traveling Salesman" was her first published story (1936).* *(See page 68 of Introduction.)*

DEATH OF A TRAVELING SALESMAN

R. J. Bowman, who for fourteen years had traveled for a shoe company through Mississippi, drove his Ford along a rutted dirt path. It was a long day! The time did not seem to clear the noon hurdle and settle into soft afternoon. The sun, keeping its strength here even in winter, stayed at the top of the sky, and every time Bowman stuck his head out of the dusty car to stare up the road, it seemed to reach a long arm down and push against the top of his head, right through his hat—like the practical joke of an old drummer, long on the road. It made him feel all the more angry and helpless. He was feverish, and he was not quite sure of the way.

This was his first day back on the road after a long siege of influenza. He had had very high fever, and dreams, and had become weakened and pale, enough to tell the difference in the mirror, and he could not think clearly. . . . All afternoon, in the midst of his anger, and for no reason, he had thought of his dead grandmother. She had been a comfortable soul. Once more Bowman wished he could fall into the big feather bed that had been in her room. . . . Then he forgot her again.

This desolate hill country! And he seemed to be going the wrong way—it was as if he were going back, far back. There was not a house in sight. . . . There was no use wishing he were back in bed, though. By paying the hotel doctor his bill he had proved his recovery. He had not even been sorry when the pretty trained nurse said good-by. He did not like illness, he distrusted it, as he distrusted the road without signposts. It angered him. He had given the nurse a really expensive bracelet, just because she was packing up her bag and leaving.

But now—what if in fourteen years on the road he had never been ill before and never had an accident? His record was broken, and he had even begun almost to question it. . . . He had gradually put up at better hotels, in the bigger towns, but weren't they all, eternally, stuffy in summer and drafty in winter? Women? He could only remember little rooms within little rooms, like a nest of Chinese paper boxes, and if he thought of one woman he saw the worn loneliness that the furniture of that room seemed built of. And he himself—he was a man who always wore rather wide-brimmed black hats, and in the wavy hotel mirrors had looked something like a bull-fighter, as he paused for that inevitable instant on the landing, walking downstairs to supper. . . . He leaned out of the car again, and once more the sun pushed at his head.

Bowman had wanted to reach Beulah by dark, to go to bed and sleep off his fatigue. As he remembered, Beulah was fifty miles away from the last town, on a graveled road. This was only a cow trail. How had he ever come to such a place? One hand wiped the sweat from his face, and he drove on.

He had made the Beulah trip before. But he had never seen this hill or this petering-out path before—or that cloud, he thought shyly, looking up and then down quickly—any more than he had seen this day before. Why did he not admit he was simply lost and had been for miles? . . . He was not in the habit of asking the way of strangers, and these people never knew where the very roads they lived on went to; but then he had not even been close enough to anyone to call out. People standing in the fields now and then, or on top of the haystacks, had been too far away, looking like leaning sticks or weeds, turning a little at the solitary rattle of his car across their countryside, watching the pale sobered winter dust where it chunked out behind like big squashes down the road. The stares of these distant people had followed him solidly like a wall, impenetrable, behind which they turned back after he had passed.

The cloud floated there to one side like the bolster on his grandmother's bed. It went over a cabin on the edge of a hill, where two bare chinaberry trees clutched at the sky. He drove through a heap of dead oak leaves, his wheels stirring their weightless sides to make a silvery melancholy whistle as the car passed through their bed. No car had been along this way ahead of him. Then he saw that he was on the edge of a ravine that fell away, a red erosion, and that this was indeed the road's end.

He pulled the brake. But it did not hold, though he put all his strength into it. The car, tipped toward the edge, rolled a little. Without doubt, it was going over the bank.

He got out quietly, as though some mischief had been done him and he had his dignity to remember. He lifted his bag and sample case out, set them down, and stood back and watched the car roll over the edge. He heard something—not the crash he was listening for, but a slow, unuproarious crackle. Rather distastefully he went to look over, and he saw that his car had fallen into a tangle of immense grapevines as thick as his arm, which caught it and held it, rocked it like a grotesque child in a dark cradle, and then, as he watched, concerned somehow that he was not still inside it, released it gently to the ground.

He sighed.

Where am I? he wondered with a shock. Why didn't I do something? All his anger seemed to have drifted away from him. There was the house, back on the hill. He took a bag in each hand and with almost childlike willingness went toward it. But his breathing came with difficulty, and he had to stop to rest.

It was a shotgun house, two rooms and an open passage between, perched on the hill. The whole cabin slanted a little under the heavy heaped-up vine that covered the roof, light and green, as though forgotten from summer. A woman stood in the passage.

He stopped still. Then all of a sudden his heart began to behave strangely. Like a rocket set off, it began to leap and expand into uneven patterns of beats which showered into his brain, and he could not think. But in scattering and falling it made no noise. It shot up with great power, almost elation, and fell gently, like acrobats into nets. It began to pound profoundly, then waited irresponsibly, hitting in some sort of inward mockery first at his ribs, then against his eyes, then under his shoulder blades, and against the roof of his mouth when he tried to say, "Good afternoon, madam." But he could not hear his heart—it was as quiet as ashes falling. This was rather comforting; still, it was shocking to Bowman to feel his heart beating at all.

Stock-still in his confusion, he dropped his bags, which seemed to drift in slow bulks gracefully through the air and to cushion themselves on the gray prostrate grass near the doorstep.

As for the woman standing there, he saw at once that she was old. Since she could not possibly hear his heart, he ignored the pounding and now looked at her carefully, and yet in his distraction dreamily, with his mouth open.

She had been cleaning the lamp, and held it, half blackened, half clear, in front of her. He saw her with the dark passage behind her. She was a big woman with a weather-beaten but unwrinkled face; her lips were held tightly together, and her eyes looked with a curious dulled brightness into his. He looked at her shoes, which were like bundles. If it were summer she would be barefoot. . . . Bowman, who automatically judged a woman's age on sight, set her age at fifty. She wore a formless garment of some gray coarse material, rough-dried from a washing, from which her arms appeared pink and unexpectedly round. When she never said a word, and sustained her quiet pose of holding the lamp, he was convinced of the strength in her body.

"Good afternoon, madam," he said.

She stared on, whether at him or at the air around him he could not tell, but after a moment she lowered her eyes to show that she would listen to whatever he had to say.

"I wonder if you would be interested—" He tried once more. "An accident—my car . . ."

Her voice emerged low and remote, like a sound across a lake. "Sonny he ain't here."

"Sonny?"

"Sonny ain't here now."

Her son—a fellow able to bring my car up, he decided in blurred relief. He pointed down the hill. "My car's in the bottom of the ditch. I'll need help."

"Sonny ain't here, but he'll be here."

She was becoming clearer to him and her voice stronger, and Bowman saw that she was stupid.

He was hardly surprised at the deepening postponement and tedium of his journey. He took a breath, and heard his voice speaking over the silent blows of his heart. "I was sick. I am not strong yet. . . . May I come in?"

He stooped and laid his big black hat over the handle on his bag. It was a humble motion, almost a bow, that instantly struck him as absurd and betraying of all his weakness. He looked up at the woman, the wind blowing his hair. He might have continued for a long time in this unfamiliar attitude; he had never been a patient man, but when he was sick he had learned to sink submissively into the pillows, to wait for his medicine. He waited on the woman.

Then she, looking at him with blue eyes, turned and held open the door, and after a moment Bowman, as if convinced in his action, stood erect and followed her in.

Inside, the darkness of the house touched him like a professional hand, the doctor's. The woman set the half-cleaned lamp on a table in the center of the room and pointed, also like a professional person, a guide, to a chair with a yellow cowhide seat. She herself crouched on the hearth, drawing her knees up under the shapeless dress.

At first he felt hopefully secure. His heart was quieter. The room was enclosed in the gloom of yellow pine boards. He could see the other room, with the foot of an iron bed showing, across the passage. The bed had been made up with a red-and-yellow pieced quilt that looked like a map or a picture, a little like his grandmother's girlhood painting of Rome burning.

He had ached for coolness, but in this room it was cold. He stared at the hearth with dead coals lying on it and iron pots in the corners. The hearth and smoked chimney were of the stone he had seen ribbing the hills, mostly slate. Why is there no fire? he wondered.

And it was so still. The silence of the fields seemed to enter and move familiarly through the house. The wind used the open hall. He felt that he was in a mysterious, quiet, cool danger. It was necessary to do what? . . . To talk.

"I have a nice line of women's low-priced shoes . . ." he said.

But the woman answered, "Sonny'll be here. He's strong. Sonny'll move your car."

"Where is he now?"

"Farms for Mr Redmond."

Mr Redmond. Mr Redmond. That was someone he would never have to encounter, and he was glad. Somehow the name did not appeal to him. . . . In a flare of touchiness and anxiety, Bowman wished to avoid even mention of unknown men and their unknown farms.

"Do you two live here alone?" He was surprised to hear his old voice, chatty, confidential, inflected for selling shoes, asking a question like that—a thing he did not even want to know.

"Yes. We are alone."

He was surprised at the way she answered. She had taken a long time to say that. She had nodded her head in a deep way too. Had she wished to affect him with some sort of premonition? he wondered unhappily. Or was it only that she would not help him, after all, by talking with him? For he was not strong enough to receive the impact of unfamiliar things without a little talk to break their fall. He had lived a month in which nothing had happened except in his head and his body—an almost inaudible life of heartbeats and dreams that came back, a life of fever and privacy, a delicate life which had left him weak to the point of—what? Of begging. The pulse in his palm leapt like a trout in a brook.

He wondered over and over why the woman did not go ahead with cleaning the lamp. What prompted her to stay there across the room, silently bestowing her presence upon him? He saw that with her it was not a time for doing little tasks. Her face was grave; she was feeling how right she was. Perhaps it was only politeness. In docility he held his eyes stiffly wide; they fixed themselves on the woman's clasped hands as though she held the cord they were strung on.

Then, "Sonny's coming," she said.

He himself had not heard anything, but there came a man passing the window and then plunging in at the door, with two hounds beside him. Sonny was a big enough man, with his belt slung low about his hips. He looked at least thirty. He had a hot, red face that was yet full of silence. He wore muddy blue pants and an old military coat stained and patched. World War? Bowman wondered. Great God, it was a Confederate coat. On the back of his light hair he had a wide filthy black hat which seemed to insult Bowman's own. He pushed down the dogs from his chest. He was strong, with dignity and heaviness in his way of moving. . . . There was the resemblance to his mother.

They stood side by side. . . . He must account again for his presence here.

"Sonny, this man, he had his car to run off over the prec'pice an' wants to know if you will git it out for him," the woman said after a few minutes.

Bowman could not even state his case.

Sonny's eyes lay upon him.

He knew he should offer explanations and show money—at least appear either penitent or authoritative. But all he could do was to shrug slightly.

Sonny brushed by him going to the window, followed by the eager dogs, and looked out. There was effort even in the way he was looking, as if he could throw his sight out like a rope. Without turning Bowman felt that his own eyes could have seen nothing: it was too far.

"Got me a mule out there an' got me a block an' tackle," said Sonny meaningfully. "I *could* catch me my mule an' git me my ropes, an' before long I'd git your car out the ravine."

He looked completely around the room, as if in meditation, his eyes roving in their own distance. Then he pressed his lips firmly and yet shyly together, and with the dogs ahead of him this time, he lowered his head and strode out. The hard earth sounded, cupping to his powerful way of walking—almost a stagger.

Mischievously, at the suggestion of those sounds, Bowman's heart leapt again. It seemed to walk about inside him.

"Sonny's goin' to do it," the woman said. She said it again, singing it almost, like a song. She was sitting in her place by the hearth.

Without looking out, he heard some shouts and the dogs barking and the pounding of hoofs in short runs on the hill. In a few minutes Sonny passed under the window with a rope, and there was a brown mule with quivering, shining, purple-looking ears. The mule actually looked in the window. Under its eyelashes it turned target-like eyes into his. Bowman averted his head and saw the woman looking serenely back at the mule, with only satisfaction in her face.

She sang a little more, under her breath. It occurred to him, and it seemed quite marvelous, that she was not really talking to him, but rather following the thing that came about with words that were unconscious and part of her looking.

So he said nothing, and this time when he did not reply he felt a curious and strong emotion, not fear, rise up in him.

This time, when his heart leapt, something—his soul—seemed to leap too, like a little colt invited out of a pen. He stared at the woman while the frantic nimbleness of his feeling made his head sway. He could not move; there was nothing he could do, unless perhaps he might embrace this woman who sat there growing old and shapeless before him.

But he wanted to leap up, to say to her, I have been sick and I found out then, only then, how lonely I am. Is it too late? My heart puts up a struggle inside me, and you may have heard it, protesting against emptiness. . . . It should be full, he would rush on to tell her, thinking of his heart now as a deep lake, it should be holding love like other hearts. It should be flooded with love. There would be a warm spring day . . .

Come and stand in my heart, whoever you are, and a whole river would cover your feet and rise higher and take your knees in whirlpools, and draw you down to itself, your whole body, your heart too.

But he moved a trembling hand across his eyes, and looked at the placid crouching woman across the room. She was still as a statue. He felt ashamed and exhausted by the thought that he might, in one more moment, have tried by simple words and embraces to communicate some strange thing—something which seemed always to have just escaped him . . .

Sunlight touched the furthest pot on the hearth. It was late afternoon. This time tomorrow he would be somewhere on a good graveled road, driving his car past things that happened to people, quicker than their happening. Seeing ahead to the next day, he was glad, and knew that this was no time to embrace an old woman. He could feel in his pounding temples the readying of his blood for motion and for hurrying away.

"Sonny's hitched up your car by now," said the woman. "He'll git it out the ravine right shortly."

"Fine!" he cried with his customary enthusiasm.

Yet it seemed a long time that they waited. It began to get dark. Bowman was cramped in his chair. Any man should know enough to get up and walk around while he waited. There was something like guilt in such stillness and silence.

But instead of getting up, he listened. . . . His breathing restrained, his eyes powerless in the growing dark, he listened uneasily for a warning sound, forgetting in wariness what it would be. Before long he heard something—soft, continuous, insinuating.

"What's that noise?" he asked, his voice jumping into the dark. Then wildly he was afraid it would be his heart beating so plainly in the quiet room, and she would tell him so.

"You might hear the stream," she said grudgingly.

Her voice was closer. She was standing by the table. He wondered why she did not light the lamp. She stood there in the dark and did not light it.

Bowman would never speak to her now, for the time was past. I'll sleep in the dark, he thought, in his bewilderment pitying himself.

Heavily she moved on to the window. Her arm, vaguely white, rose straight from her full side and she pointed out into the darkness.

"That white speck's Sonny," she said, talking to herself.

He turned unwillingly and peered over her shoulder; he hesitated to rise and stand beside her. His eyes searched the dusky air. The white speck floated smoothly toward her finger, like a leaf on a river, growing whiter in the dark. It was as if she had shown him something secret, part of her life, but had offered no explanation. He looked away. He was moved almost to tears, feeling for no reason that she had made a silent declaration equivalent to his own. His hand waited upon his chest.

Then a step shook the house, and Sonny was in the room. Bowman felt how the woman left him there and went to the other man's side.

"I done got your car out, mister," said Sonny's voice in the dark. "She's settin' a-waitin' in the road, turned to go back where she come from."

"Fine!" said Bowman, projecting his own voice to loudness. "I'm surely much obliged—I could never have done it myself—I was sick. . . ."

"I could do it easy," said Sonny.

Bowman could feel them both waiting in the dark, and he could hear the dogs panting out in the yard, waiting to bark when he should go. He felt strangely helpless and resentful. Now that he could go, he longed to stay. From what was he being deprived? His chest was rudely shaken by the violence of his heart. These people cherished something here that he could not see, they withheld some ancient promise of food and warmth and light. Between them they had a conspiracy. He thought of the way she had moved away from him and gone to Sonny, she had flowed toward him. He was shaking with cold, he was tired, and it was not fair. Humbly and yet angrily he stuck his hand into his pocket.

"Of course I'm going to pay you for everything—"

"We don't take money for such," said Sonny's voice belligerently.

"I want to pay. But do something more . . . Let me stay—to-night. . . . " He took another step toward them. If only they could see him, they would know his sincerity, his real need! His voice went on, "I'm not very strong yet, I'm not able to walk far, even back to my car, maybe, I don't know—I don't know exactly where I am—"

He stopped. He felt as if he might burst into tears. What would they think of him!

Sonny came over and put his hands on him. Bowman felt them pass (they were professional too) across his chest, over his hips. He could feel Sonny's eyes upon him in the dark.

"You ain't no revenuer come sneakin' here, mister, ain't got no gun?"

To this end of nowhere! And yet *he* had come. He made a grave answer. "No."

"You can stay."

"Sonny," said the woman, "you'll have to borry some fire."

"I'll go git it from Redmond's," said Sonny.

"What?" Bowman strained to hear their words to each other.

"Our fire, it's out, and Sonny's got to borry some, because it's dark an' cold," she said.

"But matches—I have matches—"

"We don't have no need for 'em," she said proudly. "Sonny's goin' after his own fire."

"I'm goin' to Redmond's," said Sonny with an air of importance, and he went out.

After they had waited a while, Bowman looked out the window and saw a light moving over the hill. It spread itself out like a little fan. It zigzagged along the field, darting and swift, not like Sonny at all. . . . Soon enough, Sonny staggered in, holding a burning stick behind him in tongs, fire flowing in his wake, blazing light into the corners of the room.

"We'll make a fire now," the woman said, taking the brand.

When that was done she lit the lamp. It showed its dark and light. The whole room turned golden-yellow like some sort of flower, and the walls smelled of it and seemed to tremble with the quiet rushing of the fire and the waving of the burning lampwick in its funnel of light.

The woman moved among the iron pots. With the tongs she dropped hot coals on top of the iron lids. They made a set of soft vibrations, like the sound of a bell far away.

She looked up and over at Bowman, but he could not answer. He was trembling. . . .

"Have a drink, mister?" Sonny asked. He had brought in a chair from the other room and sat astride it with his folded arms across the back. Now we are all visible to one another, Bowman thought, and cried, "Yes sir, you bet, thanks!"

"Come after me and do just what I do," said Sonny.

It was another excursion into the dark. They went through the hall, out to the back of the house, past a shed and a hooded well. They came to a wilderness of thicket.

"Down on your knees," said Sonny.

"What?" Sweat broke out on his forehead.

He understood when Sonny began to crawl through a sort of tunnel that the bushes made over the ground. He followed, startled in spite of himself when a twig or a thorn touched him gently without making a sound, clinging to him and finally letting him go.

Sonny stopped crawling and, crouched on his knees, began to dig with both his hands into the dirt. Bowman shyly struck matches and made a light. In a few minutes Sonny pulled up a jug. He poured out some of the whisky into a bottle from his coat pocket, and buried the jug again. "You never know who's liable to knock at your door," he said, and laughed. "Start back," he said, almost formally. "Ain't no need for us to drink outdoors, like hogs."

At the table by the fire, sitting opposite each other in their chairs, Sonny and Bowman took drinks out of the bottle, passing it across. The dogs slept; one of them was having a dream.

"This is good," said Bowman. "This is what I needed." It was just as though he were drinking the fire off the hearth.

"He makes it," said the woman with quiet pride.

She was pushing the coals off the pots, and the smells of corn bread and coffee circled the room. She set everything on the table before the men, with a bone-handled knife stuck into one of the potatoes, splitting out its golden fiber. Then she stood for a minute looking at them, tall and full above them where they sat. She leaned a little toward them.

"You all can eat now," she said, and suddenly smiled.

Bowman had just happened to be looking at her. He set his cup back on the table in unbelieving protest. A pain pressed at his eyes. He saw that she was not an old woman. She was young, still young. He could think of no number of years for her. She was the same age as Sonny, and she belonged to him. She stood with the deep dark corner of the room behind her, the shifting yellow light scattering over her head and her gray formless dress, trembling over her tall body when it bent over them in its sudden communication. She was young. Her teeth were shining and her eyes glowed. She turned and walked slowly and heavily out of the room, and he heard her sit down on the cot and then lie down. The pattern on the quilt moved.

"She's goin' to have a baby," said Sonny, popping a bite into his mouth.

Bowman could not speak. He was shocked with knowing what was really in this house. A marriage, a fruitful marriage. That simple thing. Anyone could have had that.

Somehow he felt unable to be indignant or protest, although some sort of joke had certainly been played upon him. There was nothing remote or mysterious here—only something private. The only secret was the ancient communication between two people. But the memory of the woman's waiting silently by the cold hearth, of the man's stubborn journey a mile away to get fire, and how they finally brought out their food and drink and filled the room proudly with all they had to show, was suddenly too clear and too enormous within him for response. . . .

"You ain't as hungry as you look," said Sonny.

The woman came out of the bedroom as soon as the men had finished, and ate her supper while her husband stared peacefully into the fire.

Then they put the dogs out, with the food that was left.

"I think I'd better sleep here by the fire, on the floor," said Bowman.

He felt that he had been cheated, and that he could afford now to be generous. Ill though he was, he was not going to ask them for their bed. He was through with asking favors in this house, now that he understood what was there.

"Sure, mister."

But he had not known yet how slowly he understood. They had not meant to give him their bed. After a little interval they both rose and looking at him gravely went into the other room.

He lay stretched by the fire until it grew low and dying. He watched every tongue of blaze lick out and vanish. "There will be special reduced prices on all footwear during the month of January," he found himself repeating quietly, and then he lay with his lips tight shut.

How many noises the night had! He heard the stream running, the fire dying, and he was sure now that he heard his heart beating, too, the sound it made under his ribs. He heard breathing, round and deep, of the man and his wife in the room across the passage. And that was all. But emotion swelled patiently within him, and he wished that the child were his.

He must get back to where he had been before. He stood weakly before the red coals and put on his overcoat. It felt too heavy on his shoulders. As he started out he looked and saw that the woman had never got through with cleaning the lamp. On some impulse he put all the money from his billfold under its fluted glass base, almost ostentatiously.

Ashamed, shrugging a little, and then shivering, he took his bags and went out. The cold of the air seemed to lift him bodily. The moon was in the sky.

On the slope he began to run, he could not help it. Just as he reached the road, where his car seemed to sit in the moonlight like a boat, his heart began to give off tremendous explosions like a rifle, bang bang bang.

He sank in fright onto the road, his bags falling about him. He felt as if all this had happened before. He covered his heart with both hands to keep anyone from hearing the noise it made.

But nobody heard it.

Jean-Paul Sartre

Jean-Paul Sartre (1905–), French writer and leading contemporary existentialist, was born in Paris. His mother was a niece of Albert Schweitzer. Sartre took his degree in philosophy, and later taught the subject at the Lycée Henri IV, a renowned Parisian high school. During World War II he was captured by the Germans, but escaped after a year, and, with Albert Camus, began publishing an underground paper for the French Resistance Movement. He refused the Nobel Prize for Literature in 1964 as a matter of principle. In regard to fiction, he insists on the freedom of characters to move and live, in fictional "duration" independent of an omniscient or absolute plan. "The time has come to say that the novelist is not God," he writes, and "Every one of my characters, after having done anything, may still do anything whatever." His many works include The Age of Reason *(1945) and* No Exit *(1944), a play.* *(See page 74 of Introduction.)*

THE WALL

They pushed us into a big white room and I began to blink because the light hurt my eyes. Then I saw a table and four men behind the table, civilians, looking over the papers. They had bunched another group of prisoners in the back and we had to cross the whole room to join them. There were several I knew and some others who must have been foreigners. The two in front of me were blond with round skulls; they looked alike. I supposed they were French. The smaller one kept hitching up his pants; nerves.

It lasted about three hours; I was dizzy and my head was empty; but the room was well heated and I found that pleasant enough: for the past 24 hours we hadn't stopped shivering. The guards brought the prisoners up to the table, one after the other. The four men asked each one his name and occupation. Most of the time they didn't go any further—or they would simply ask a question here and there: "Did you have anything to do with the sabotage of munitions?" Or "Where were you the morning of the 9th and what were you doing?" They didn't listen to the answers or at least didn't seem to. They were quiet for a moment and then looking straight in front of them began to write. They asked Tom if it were true he was in the International Brigade; Tom couldn't tell them otherwise because of the papers they found in his coat. They didn't ask Juan anything but they wrote for a long time after he told them his name.

"My brother José is the anarchist," Juan said, "you know he isn't here any more. I don't belong to any party, I never had anything to do with politics."

They didn't answer. Juan went on, "I haven't done anything. I don't want to pay for somebody else."

His lips trembled. A guard shut him up and took him away. It was my turn.

"Your name is Pablo Ibbieta?"

"Yes."

The man looked at the papers and asked me, "Where's Ramon Gris?"

"I don't know."

"You hid him in your house from the 6th to the 19th."

"No."

They wrote for a minute and then the guards took me out. In the corridor Tom and Juan were waiting between two guards. We started walking. Tom asked one of the guards, "So?"

"So what?" the guard said.

"Was that the cross-examination or the sentence?"

"Sentence," the guard said.

"What are they going to do with us?"

The guard answered dryly, "Sentence will be read in your cell."

As a matter of fact, our cell was one of the hospital cellars. It was terrifically cold there because of the drafts. We shivered all night and it wasn't much better during the day. I had spent the previous five days in a cell in a monastery, a sort of hole in the wall that must have dated from the middle ages: since there were a lot of prisoners and not much room, they locked us up anywhere. I didn't miss my cell; I hadn't suffered too much from the cold but I was alone; after a long time it gets irritating. In the cellar I had company. Juan hardly ever spoke: he was afraid and he was too young to have anything to say. But Tom was a good talker and he knew Spanish well.

There was a bench in the cellar and four mats. When they took us back we sat and waited in silence. After a long moment, Tom said, "We're screwed."

"I think so too," I said, "but I don't think they'll do anything to the kid."

"They don't have a thing against him," said Tom. "He's the brother of a militiaman and that's all."

I looked at Juan: he didn't seem to hear. Tom went on, "You know what they do in Saragossa? They lay the men down on the road and run over them with trucks. A Moroccan deserter told us that. They said it was to save ammunition."

"It doesn't save gas," I said.

I was annoyed at Tom: he shouldn't have said that.

"Then there's officers walking along the road," he went on, "supervising it all. They stick their hands in their pockets and smoke cigarettes. You think they finish off the guys? Hell no. They let them scream. Sometimes for an hour. The Moroccan said he damned near puked the first time."

"I don't believe they'll do that here," I said. "Unless they're really short on ammunition."

Day was coming in through four airholes and a round opening, they had made in the ceiling on the left, and you could see the sky through it. Through this hole, usually closed by a trap, they unloaded coal into the cellar. Just below the hole there was a big pile of coal dust; it had been used to heat the hospital but since the beginning of the war the patients were evacuated and the coal stayed there, unused; sometimes it even got rained on because they had forgotten to close the trap.

Tom began to shiver. "Good Jesus Christ I'm cold," he said. "Here it goes again."

He got up and began to do exercises. At each movement his shirt opened on his chest, white and hairy. He lay on his back, raised his legs in the air and bicycled. I saw his great rump trembling. Tom was husky but he had too much fat. I thought how rifle bullets or the sharp points of bayonets would soon be sunk into this mass of tender flesh as in a lump of butter. It wouldn't have made me feel like that if he'd been thin.

I wasn't exactly cold, but I couldn't feel my arms and shoulders any more. Sometimes I had the impression I was missing something and began to look around for my coat and then suddenly remembered they hadn't given me a coat. It was rather uncomfortable. They took our clothes and gave them to their soldiers leaving us only our shirts—and those canvas pants that hospital patients wear in the middle of summer. After a while Tom got up and sat next to me, breathing heavily.

"Warmer?"

"Good Christ, no. But I'm out of wind."

Around eight o'clock in the evening a major came in with two *falangistas*. He had a sheet of paper in his hand. He asked the guard, "What are the names of those three?"

"Steinbock, Ibbieta and Mirbal," the guard said.

The major put on his eyeglasses and scanned the list: "Steinbock . . . Steinbock . . . Oh yes . . . You are sentenced to death. You will be shot tomorrow morning." He went on looking. "The other two as well."

"That's not possible," Juan said. "Not me."

The major looked at him amazed. "What's your name?"

"Juan Mirbal," he said.

"Well, your name is there," said the major. "You're sentenced."

"I didn't do anything," Juan said.

The major shrugged his shoulders and turned to Tom and me.

"You're Basque?"

"Nobody is Basque."

He looked annoyed. "They told me there were three Basques. I'm not going to waste my time running after them. Then naturally you don't want a priest?"

We didn't even answer.

He said, "A Belgian doctor is coming shortly. He is authorized to spend the night with you." He made a military salute and left.

"What did I tell you," Tom said. "We get it."

"Yes," I said "it's a rotten deal for the kid."

I said that to be decent but I didn't like the kid. His face was too thin and fear and suffering had disfigured it, twisting all his features. Three days before he was a smart sort of kid, not too bad; but now he looked like an old fairy and I thought how he'd never be young again, even if they were to let him go. It wouldn't have been too hard to have a little pity for him but pity disgusts me, or rather it horrifies me. He hadn't said anything more but he had turned grey; his face and hands were both grey. He sat down again and looked at the ground with round eyes. Tom was good-hearted, he wanted to take his arm, but the kid tore himself away violently and made a face.

"Let him alone," I said in a low voice, "you can see he's going to blubber."

Tom obeyed regretfully; he would have liked to comfort the kid, it would have passed his time and he wouldn't have been tempted to think about himself. But it annoyed me: I'd never thought about death because I never had any reason to, but now the reason was here and there was nothing to do but think about it.

Tom began to talk. "So you think you've knocked guys off, do you?" he asked me. I didn't answer. He began explaining to me that he had knocked off six since the beginning of August; he didn't realize the situation and I could tell he didn't *want* to realize it. I hadn't quite realized it myself, I wondered if it hurt much, I thought of bullets, I imagined their burning hail through my body. All that was beside the real question; but I was calm: we had all night to understand. After a while Tom stopped talking and I watched him out of the corner of my eye; I saw he too had turned grey and he looked rotten; I told myself "Now it starts." It was almost dark, a dim glow filtered through the airholes and the pile of coal and made a big stain beneath the spot of sky; I could already see a star through the hole in the ceiling: the night would be pure and icy.

The door opened and two guards came in, followed by a blonde man in a tan uniform. He saluted us. "I am the doctor," he said. "I have authorization to help you in these trying hours."

He had an agreeable and distinguished voice. I said, "What do you want here?"

"I am at your disposal. I shall do all I can to make your last moments less difficult."

"What did you come here for? There are others, the hospital's full of them."

"I was sent here," he answered with a vague look. "Ah! Would you like to smoke?" he added hurriedly, "I have cigarettes and even cigars."

He offered us English cigarettes and *puros*, but we refused. I looked him in the eyes and he seemed irritated. I said to him, "You aren't here on an errand of mercy. Besides, I know you. I saw you with the fascists in the barracks yard the day I was arrested."

I was going to continue, but something surprising suddenly happened to me; the presence of this doctor no longer interested me. Generally when I'm on somebody I don't let go. But the desire to talk left me completely; I shrugged and turned my eyes away. A little later I raised my head; he was watching me curiously. The guards were sitting on a mat. Pedro, the tall thin one, was twiddling his thumbs, the other shook his head from time to time to keep from falling asleep.

"Do you want a light?" Pedro suddenly asked the doctor. The other nodded "Yes": I think he was about as smart as a log, but he surely wasn't bad. Looking in his cold blue eyes it seemed to me that his only sin was lack of imagination. Pedro went out and came back with an oil lamp which he set on the corner of the bench. It gave a bad light but it was better than nothing: they had left us in the dark the night before. For a long time I watched the circle of light the lamp made on the ceiling. I was fascinated. Then suddenly I woke up, the circle of light disappeared and I felt myself crushed under an enormous weight. It was not the thought of death, or fear; it was nameless. My cheeks burned and my head ached.

I shook myself and looked at my two friends. Tom had hidden his face in his hands. I could only see the fat white nape of his neck. Little Juan was the worst, his mouth was open and his nostrils trembled. The doctor went to him and put his hand on his shoulder to comfort him: but his eyes stayed cold. Then I saw the Belgian's hand drop stealthily along Juan's arm, down to the wrist. Juan paid no attention. The Belgian took his wrist between three fingers, distractedly, the same time drawing back a little and turning his back to me. But I leaned backward and saw him take a watch from his pocket and look at it for a moment, never letting go of the wrist. After a minute he let the hand fall inert and went and leaned his back against the wall, then, as if he suddenly remembered something very important which had to be jotted down on the spot, he took a notebook from his pocket and wrote a few lines. "Bastard," I thought angrily, "let him come and take my pulse. I'll shove my fist in his rotten face."

He didn't come but I felt him watching me. I raised my head and returned his look. Impersonally, he said to me, "Doesn't it seem cold to you here?" He looked cold, he was blue.

"I'm not cold," I told him.

He never took his hard eyes off me. Suddenly I understood and my hands went to my face: I was drenched in sweat. In this cellar, in the midst of winter, in the midst of drafts, I was sweating. I ran my hands through my hair, gummed together with perspiration; at the same time I saw my shirt was damp and sticking to my skin: I had been dripping for an hour and hadn't felt it. But that swine of a Belgian hadn't missed a thing; he had seen the drops rolling down my cheeks and thought: this is the manifestation of an almost pathological state of terror; and he had felt normal and proud of being alive because he was cold. I wanted to stand up and smash his face but no sooner had I made the slightest gesture than my rage and shame were wiped out; I fell back on the bench with indifference.

I satisfied myself by rubbing my neck with my handkerchief because now I felt the sweat dropping from my hair onto my neck and it was unpleasant. I soon gave up rubbing, it was useless; my handkerchief was already soaked and I was still sweating. My buttocks were sweating too and my damp trousers were glued to the bench.

Suddenly Juan spoke. "You're a doctor?"

"Yes," the Belgian said.

"Does it hurt . . . very long?"

"Huh? When . . . ? Oh, no," the Belgian said paternally. "Not at all. It's over quickly." He acted as though he were calming a cash customer.

"But I . . . they told me . . . sometimes they have to fire twice."

"Sometimes," the Belgian said, nodding. "It may happen that the first volley reaches no vital organs."

"Then they have to reload their rifles and aim all over again?" He thought for a moment and then added hoarsely, "That takes time!"

He had a terrible fear of suffering, it was all he thought about: it was his age. I never thought much about it and it wasn't fear of suffering that made me sweat.

I got up and walked to the pile of coal dust. Tom jumped up and threw me a hateful look: I had annoyed him because my shoes squeaked. I wondered if my face looked as frightened as his: I saw he was sweating too. The sky was superb, no light filtered into the dark corner and I had only to raise my head to see the Big Dipper. But it wasn't like it had been: the night before I could see a great piece of sky from my monastery cell and each hour of the day brought me a different memory. Morning, when the sky was a hard, light blue, I thought of beaches on the Atlantic; at noon I saw the sun and I remembered a bar in Seville where I drank *manzanilla* and ate olives and anchovies; afternoons I was in the shade and I thought of the deep shadow which spreads over half a bull-ring leaving the other half shimmering in sunlight; it was really hard to see the whole world reflected in the sky like that. But now I could watch the sky as much as I pleased, it no longer evoked anything in me. I liked that better. I came back and sat near Tom. A long moment passed.

Tom began speaking in a low voice. He had to talk, without that he wouldn't have been able to recognize himself in his own mind. I thought he was talking to me but he wasn't looking at me. He was undoubtedly afraid to see me as I was, grey and sweating: we were alike and worse than mirrors of each other. He watched the Belgian, the living.

"Do you understand?" he said. "I don't understand."

I began to speak in a low voice too. I watched the Belgian. "Why? What's the matter?"

"Something is going to happen to us that I can't understand."

There was a strange smell about Tom. It seemed to me I was more sensitive than usual to odors. I grinned. "You'll understand in a while."

"It isn't clear," he said obstinately. "I want to be brave but first I have to know . . . Listen, they're going to take us into the courtyard. Good. They're going to stand up in front of us. How many?"

"I don't know. Five or eight. Not more."

"All right. There'll be eight. Someone'll holler 'aim!' and I'll see eight rifles looking at me. I'll think how I'd like to get inside the wall, I'll push against it with my back . . . with every ounce of strength I have, but the wall will stay, like in a nightmare. I can imagine all that. If you only knew how well I can imagine it."

"All right, all right!" I said, "I can imagine it too."

"It must hurt like hell. You know, they aim at the eyes and the mouth to disfigure you," he added mechanically. "I can feel the wounds already; I've had pains in my head and in my neck for the past hour. Not real pains. Worse. This is what I'm going to feel tomorrow morning. And then what?"

I well understood what he meant but I didn't want to act as if I did. I had pains too, pains in my body like a crowd of tiny scars. I couldn't get used to it. But I was like him, I attached no importance to it. "After," I said, "you'll be pushing up daisies."

He began to talk to himself: he never stopped watching the Belgian. The Belgian didn't seem to be listening. I knew what he had come to do; he wasn't interested in what we thought; he came to watch our bodies, bodies dying in agony while yet alive.

"It's like a nightmare," Tom was saying. "You want to think something, you always have the impression that it's all right, that you're going to understand and then it slips, it escapes you and fades away. I tell myself there will be nothing afterwards. But I don't understand what it means. Sometimes I almost can . . . and then it fades away and I start thinking about the pains again, bullets, explosions. I'm a materialist, I swear it to you; I'm not going crazy. But something's the matter. I see my corpse; that's not hard but *I'm* the one who sees it, with *my* eyes. I've got to think . . . think that I won't see anything anymore and the world will go on for the others. We aren't made to think that, Pablo. Believe me: I've already stayed up a whole night waiting for something. But this isn't the same: this will creep up behind us, Pablo, and we won't be able to prepare for it."

"Shut up," I said, "Do you want me to call a priest?"

He didn't answer. I had already noticed he had the tendency to act like a prophet and call me Pablo, speaking in a toneless voice. I didn't like that: but it seems all the Irish are that way. I had the vague impression he smelled of urine. Fundamentally, I hadn't much sympathy for Tom and I didn't see why, under the pretext of dying together, I should have any more. It would have been different with some others. With Ramon Gris, for example. But I felt alone between Tom and Juan. I liked that better, anyhow: with Ramon I might have been more deeply moved. But I was terribly hard just then and I wanted to stay hard.

He kept on chewing his words, with something like distraction. He certainly talked to keep himself from thinking. He smelled of urine like an old prostate case. Naturally, I agreed with him, I could have said everything he said: it isn't *natural* to die. And since I was going to die, nothing seemed natural to me, not this pile of coal dust, or the bench, or Pedro's ugly face. Only it didn't please me to think the same things as Tom. And I knew that, all through the night, every five minutes, we would keep on thinking things at the same time. I looked at him sideways and for the first time he seemed strange to me: he wore death on his face. My pride was wounded: for the past 24 hours I had lived next to Tom, I had listened to him, I had spoken to him and I knew we had nothing in common. And now we looked as much alike as twin brothers, simply because we were going to die together. Tom took my hand without looking at me.

"Pablo, I wonder . . . I wonder if it's really true that everything ends."

I took my hand away and said, "Look between your feet, you pig."

There was a big puddle between his feet and drops fell from his pants-leg.

"What is it," he asked, frightened.

"You're pissing in your pants," I told him.

"It isn't true," he said furiously. "I'm not pissing. I don't feel anything."

The Belgian approached us. He asked with false solicitude, "Do you feel ill?"

Tom did not answer. The Belgian looked at the puddle and said nothing.

"I don't know what it is," Tom said ferociously. "But I'm not afraid. I swear I'm not afraid."

The Belgian did not answer. Tom got up and went to piss in a corner. He came back buttoning his fly, and sat down without a word. The Belgian was taking notes.

All three of us watched him because he was alive. He had the motions of a living human being, the cares of a living human being; he shivered in the cellar the way the living are supposed to shiver; he had an obedient, well-fed body. The rest of us hardly felt ours—not in the same way anyhow. I wanted to feel my pants between my legs but I didn't dare; I watched the Belgian, balancing on his legs, master of his muscles, someone who could think about tomorrow. There we were, three bloodless shadows; we watched him and we sucked his life like vampires.

Finally he went over to little Juan. Did he want to feel his neck for some professional motive or was he obeying an impulse of charity? If he was acting by charity it was the only time during the whole night.

He caressed Juan's head and neck. The kid let himself be handled, his eyes never leaving him, then suddenly, he seized the hand and looked at it strangely. He held the Belgian's hand between his own two hands and there was nothing pleasant about them, two grey pincers gripping this fat and reddish hand. I suspected what was going to happen and Tom must have suspected it too: but the Belgian didn't see a thing, he smiled paternally. After a moment the kid brought the fat red hand to his mouth and tried to bite it. The Belgian pulled away quickly and stumbled back against the wall. For a second he looked at us with horror, he must have suddenly understood that we were not men like him. I began to laugh and one of the guards jumped up. The other was asleep, his wide open eyes were blank.

I felt relaxed and over-excited at the same time. I didn't want to think any more about what would happen at dawn, at death. It made no sense. I only found words or emptiness. But as soon as I tried to think of anything else I saw rifle barrels pointing at me. Perhaps I lived through my execution twenty times; once I even thought it was for good: I must have slept a minute. They were dragging me to the wall and I was struggling; I was asking for mercy. I woke up with a start and looked at the Belgian: I was afraid I might have cried out in my sleep. But he was stroking his moustache, he hadn't noticed anything. If I had wanted to, I think I could have slept a while; I had been awake for 48 hours. I was at the end of my rope. But I didn't want to lose two hours of life: they would come to wake me up at dawn, I would follow them, stupefied with sleep and I would have croaked without so much as an "Oof!"; I didn't want that, I didn't want to die like an animal, I wanted to understand. Then I was afraid of having nightmares. I got up, walked back and forth, and, to change my ideas, I began to think about my past life. A crowd of memories came back to me pell-mell. There were good and bad ones—or at least I called them that *before*. There were faces and incidents. I saw the face of a little *novillero* who was gored in Valencia during the *Feria*, the face of one of my uncles, the face of Ramon Gris. I remembered my whole life: how I was out of work for three months in 1926, how I almost starved to death. I remembered a night I spent on a bench in Grenada: I hadn't eaten for three days. I was angry, I didn't want to die. That made me smile. How madly I ran after happiness, after women, after liberty. Why? I wanted to free Spain, I admired Pi y Margall, I joined the anarchist movement, I spoke in public meetings: I took everything as seriously as if I were immortal.

At that moment I felt that I had my whole life in front of me and I thought, "It's a damned lie." It was worth nothing because it was finished. I wondered how I'd been able to walk, to laugh with the girls: I wouldn't have moved so much as my little finger if I had only imagined I would die like this. My life was in front of me, shut, closed, like a bag and yet everything inside of it was unfinished. For an instant I tried to judge it. I wanted to tell myself, this is a beautiful life. But I couldn't pass judgment on it; it was only a sketch; I had spent my time counterfeiting eternity, I had understood nothing. I missed nothing: there were so many things I could have missed, the taste of *manzanilla* or the baths I took in summer in a little creek near Cadiz; but death had disenchanted everything.

The Belgian suddenly had a bright idea. "My friends," he told us, "I will undertake—if the military administration will allow it—to send a message for you, a souvenir to those who love you . . ."

Tom mumbled, "I don't have anybody."

I said nothing. Tom waited an instant then looked at me with curiosity. "You don't have anything to say to Concha?"

"No."

I hated this tender complicity: it was my own fault, I had talked about Concha the night before, I should have controlled myself. I was with her for a year. Last night I would have given an arm to see her again for five minutes. That was why I talked about her, it was stronger than I was. Now I had no more desire to see her, I had nothing more to say to her. I would not even have wanted to hold her in my arms: my body filled me with horror because it was grey and sweating—and I wasn't sure that her body didn't fill me with horror. Concha would cry when she found out

I was dead, she would have no taste for life for months afterward. But I was still the one who was going to die. I thought of her soft, beautiful eyes. When she looked at me something passed from her to me. But I knew it was over: if she looked at me *now* the look would stay in her eyes, it wouldn't reach me. I was alone.

Tom was alone too but not in the same way. Sitting cross-legged, he had begun to stare at the bench with a sort of smile, he looked amazed. He put out his hand and touched the wood cautiously as if he were afraid of breaking something, then drew back his hand quickly and shuddered. If I had been Tom I wouldn't have amused myself by touching the bench; this was some more Irish nonsense, but I too found that objects had a funny look: they were more obliterated, less dense than usual. It was enough for me to look at the bench, the lamp, the pile of coal dust, to feel that I was going to die. Naturally I couldn't think clearly about my death but I saw it everywhere, on things, in the way things fell back and kept their distance, discreetly, as people who speak quietly at the bedside of a dying man. It was *his* death which Tom had just touched on the bench.

In the state I was in, if someone had come and told me I could go home quietly, that they would leave me my life whole, it would have left me cold: several hours or several years of waiting is all the same when you have lost the illusion of being eternal. I clung to nothing, in a way I was calm. But it was a horrible calm—because of my body; my body, I saw with its eyes, I heard with its ears, but it was no longer me; it sweated and trembled by itself and I didn't recognize it any more. I had to touch it and look at it to find out what was happening, as if it were the body of someone else. At times I could still feel it, I felt sinkings, and fallings, as when you're in a plane taking a nosedive, or I felt my heart beating. But that didn't reassure me. Everything that came from my body was all cockeyed. Most of the time it was quiet and I felt no more than a sort of weight, a filthy presence against me; I had the impression of being tied to an enormous vermin. Once I felt my pants and I felt they were damp; I didn't know whether it was sweat or urine, but I went to piss on the coal pile as a precaution.

The Belgian took out his watch, looked at it. He said, "It is three-thirty."

Bastard! He must have done it on purpose. Tom jumped; we hadn't noticed time was running out; night surrounded us like a shapeless, somber mass, I couldn't even remember that it had begun.

Little Juan began to cry. He wrung his hands, pleaded, "I don't want to die. I don't want to die."

He ran across the whole cellar waving his arms in the air then fell sobbing on one of the mats. Tom watched him with mournful eyes, without the slightest desire to console him. Because it wasn't worth the trouble: the kid made more noise than we did, but he was less touched: he was like a sick man who defends himself against his illness by fever. It's much more serious when there isn't any fever.

He wept: I could clearly see he was pitying himself; he wasn't thinking about death. For one second, one single second, I wanted to weep myself, to weep with pity for myself. But the opposite happened: I glanced at the kid, I saw his thin sobbing shoulders and I felt inhuman: I could pity neither the others nor myself. I said to myself, "I want to die cleanly."

Tom had gotten up, he placed himself just under the round opening and began to watch for daylight. I was determined to die cleanly and I only thought of that. But ever since the doctor told us the time, I felt time flying, flowing away drop by drop.

It was still dark when I heard Tom's voice: "Do you hear them?"

Men were marching in the courtyard.

"Yes."

"What the hell are they doing? They can't shoot in the dark."

After a while we heard no more. I said to Tom, "It's day."

Pedro got up, yawning, and came to blow out the lamp. He said to his buddy, "Cold as hell."

The cellar was all grey. We heard shots in the distance.

"It's starting," I told Tom. "They must do it in the court in the rear."

Tom asked the doctor for a cigarette. I didn't want one; I didn't want cigarettes or alcohol. From that moment on they didn't stop firing.

"Do you realize what's happening," Tom said.

He wanted to add something but kept quiet, watching the door. The door opened and a lieutenant came in with four soldiers. Tom dropped his cigarette.

"Steinbock?"

Tom didn't answer. Pedro pointed him out.

"Juan Mirbal?"

"On the mat."

"Get up," the lieutenant said.

Juan did not move. Two soldiers took him under the arms and set him on his feet. But he fell as soon as they released him.

The soldiers hesitated.

"He's not the first sick one," said the lieutenant. "You two carry him; they'll fix it up down there."

He turned to Tom. "Let's go."

Tom went out between two soldiers. Two others followed, carrying the kid by the armpits. He hadn't fainted; his eyes were wide open and tears ran down his cheeks. When I wanted to go out the lieutenant stopped me.

"You Ibbieta?"

"Yes."

"You wait here; they'll come for you later."

They left. The Belgian and the two jailers left too, I was alone. I did not understand what was happening to me but I would have liked it better if they had gotten it over with right away. I heard shots at almost regular intervals; I shook with each one of them. I wanted to scream and tear out my hair. But I gritted my teeth and pushed my hands in my pockets because I wanted to stay clean.

After an hour they came to get me and led me to the first floor, to a small room that smelt of cigars and where the heat was stifling. There were two officers sitting smoking in the armchairs, papers on their knees.

"You're Ibbieta?"

"Yes."

"Where is Ramon Gris?"

"I don't know."

The one questioning me was short and fat. His eyes were hard behind his glasses. He said to me, "Come here."

I went to him. He got up and took my arms, staring at me with a look that should have pushed me into the earth. At the same time he pinched my biceps with all his might. It wasn't to hurt me, it was only a game: he wanted to dominate me. He also thought he had to blow his stinking breath square in my face. We stayed for a moment like that, and I almost felt like laughing. It takes a lot to intimidate a man who is going to die; it didn't work. He pushed me back violently and sat down again. He said, "It's his life against yours. You can have yours if you tell us where he is."

These men dolled up with their riding crops and boots were still going to die. A little later than I, but not too much. They busied themselves looking for names in their crumpled papers, they ran after other men to imprison or suppress them; they had opinions on the future of Spain and on other subjects. Their little activities seemed shocking and burlesqued to me; I couldn't put myself in their place, I thought they were insane. The little man was still looking at me, whipping his boots with the riding crop. All his gestures were calculated to give him the look of a live and ferocious beast.

"So? You understand?"

"I don't know where Gris is," I answered. "I thought he was in Madrid."

The other officer raised his pale hand indolently. This indolence was also calculated. I saw through all their little schemes and I was stupefied to find there were men who amused themselves that way.

"You have a quarter of an hour to think it over," he said slowly. "Take him to the laundry, bring him back in fifteen minutes. If he still refuses he will be executed on the spot."

They knew what they were doing: I had passed the night in waiting; then they had made me wait an hour in the cellar while they shot Tom and Juan and now they were locking me up in the laundry; they must have prepared their game the night before. They told themselves that nerves eventually wear out and they hoped to get me that way.

They were badly mistaken. In the laundry I sat on a stool because I felt very weak and I began to think. But not about their proposition. Of course I knew where Gris was; he was hiding with his cousins, four kilometers from the city. I also knew that I would not reveal his hiding place unless they tortured me (but they didn't seem to be thinking about that). All that was perfectly regulated, definite and in no way interested me. Only I would have liked to understand the reasons for my conduct. I would rather die than give up Gris. Why? I didn't like Ramon Gris any more. My friendship for him had died a little while before dawn at the same time as my love for Concha, at the same time as my desire to live. Undoubtedly I thought highly of him: he was tough. But it was not for this reason that I consented to die in his place; his life had no more value than mine; no life had value. They were going to slap a man up against a wall and shoot at him till he died, whether it was I or Gris or somebody else made no difference. I knew he was more useful than I to the cause of Spain but I thought to hell with Spain and anarchy; nothing was important. Yet I was there, I could save my skin and give up Gris and I refused to do it. I found that somehow comic; it was obstinacy. I thought, "I must be stubborn!" And a droll sort of gaiety spread over me.

They came for me and brought me back to the two officers. A rat ran out from under my feet and that amused me. I turned to one of the *falangistas* and said, "Did you see the rat?"

He didn't answer. He was very sober, he took himself seriously. I wanted to laugh but I held myself back because I was afraid that once I got started I wouldn't be able to stop. The *falangista* had a moustache. I said to him again, "You ought to shave off your moustache, idiot." I thought it funny that he would let the hairs of his living being invade his face. He kicked me without great conviction and I kept quiet.

"Well," said the fat officer, "have you thought about it?"

I looked at them with curiosity, as insects of a very rare species. I told them, "I know where he is. He is hidden in the cemetery. In a vault or in the gravediggers' shack."

It was a farce. I wanted to see them stand up, buckle their belts and give orders busily.

They jumped to their feet. "Let's go. Molés, go get fifteen men from Lieutenant Lopez. You," the fat man said, "I'll let you off if you're telling the truth, but it'll cost you plenty if you're making monkeys out of us."

They left in a great clatter and I waited peacefully under the guard of *falangistas*. From time to time I smiled, thinking about the spectacle they would make. I felt stunned and malicious. I imagined them lifting up tombstones, opening the doors of the vaults one by one. I represented this situation to myself as if I had been someone else: this prisoner obstinately playing the hero, these grim *falangistas* with their moustaches and their men in uniform running among the graves; it was irresistibly funny. After half an hour the little fat man came back alone. I thought he had come to give the orders to execute me. The others must have stayed in the cemetery.

The officer looked at me. He didn't look at all sheepish. "Take him into the big courtyard with the others," he said. "After the military operations a regular court will decide what happens to him."

"Then they're not . . . not going to shoot me? . . ."

"Not now, anyway. What happens afterwards is none of my business."

I still didn't understand. I asked, "But why . . . ?"

He shrugged his shoulders without answering and the soldiers took me away. In the big courtyard there were about a hundred prisoners, women, children and a few old men. I began walking around the central grass-plot, I was stupefied. At noon they let us eat in the mess hall. Two or three people questioned me. I must have known them, but I didn't answer: I didn't even know where I was.

Around evening they pushed about ten new prisoners into the court. I recognized Garcia, the baker. He said, "What damned luck you have! I didn't think I'd see you alive."

"They sentenced me to death," I said, "and then they changed their minds. I don't know why."

"They arrested me at two o'clock," Garcia said.

"Why?" Garcia had nothing to do with politics.

"I don't know," he said. "They arrest everybody who doesn't think the way they do." He lowered his voice. "They got Gris."

I began to tremble. "When?"

"This morning. He messed it up. He left his cousin's on Tuesday because they had an argument. There were plenty of people to hide him but he didn't want to owe anything to anybody. He said, 'I'd go and hide in Ibbieta's place, but they got him, so I'll go hide in the cemetery.' "

"In the cemetery?"

"Yes. What a fool. Of course they went by there this morning, that was sure to happen. They found him in the gravediggers' shack. He shot at them and they got him."

"In the cemetery!"

Everything began to spin and I found myself sitting on the ground: I laughed so hard I cried.

J. F. Powers

James Farl Powers (1917–   ) was born in Chicago and educated in parochial schools. He attended Northwestern University, but the Depression forced him to leave college. He worked in bookshops, and taught at Marquette University. His first book, Prince of Darkness *(1943), a collection of short stories, was widely praised. He won a Guggenheim fellowship in 1948 and received the National Book Award for his 1962 novel,* Morte d'Urban. *Powers' stories frequently deal with the Catholic clergy, whom he treats with humor, irony, and critical detachment.* *(See p. 67 of Introduction.)*

THE FORKS

That summer when Father Eudex got back from saying Mass at the orphanage in the morning, he would park Monsignor's car, which was long and black and new like a politician's, and sit down in the cool of the porch to read his office. If Monsignor was not already standing in the door, he would immediately appear there, seeing that his car had safely returned, and inquire:

"Did you have any trouble with her?"

Father Eudex knew too well the question meant, Did you mistreat my car?

"No trouble, Monsignor."

"Good," Monsignor said, with imperfect faith in his curate, who was not a car owner. For a moment Monsignor stood framed in the screen door, fumbling his watch fob as for a full-length portrait, and then he was suddenly not there.

"Monsignor," Father Eudex said, rising nervously, "I've got a chance to pick up a car."

At the door Monsignor slid into his frame again. His face expressed what was for him intense interest.

"Yes? Go on."

"I don't want to have to use yours every morning."

"It's all right."

"And there are other times." Father Eudex decided not to be maudlin and mention sick calls, nor be entirely honest and admit he was tired of busses and bumming rides from parishioners. "And now I've got a chance to get one—cheap."

Monsignor, smiling, came alert at *cheap.*

"New?"

"No, I wouldn't say it's new."

Monsignor was openly suspicious now. "What kind?"

"It's a Ford."

"And not new?"

"Not new, Monsignor—but in good condition. It was owned by a retired farmer and had good care."

Monsignor sniffed. He *knew* cars. "V-Eight, Father?"

"No," Father Eudex confessed. "It's a Model A."

Monsignor chuckled as though this were indeed the damnedest thing he had ever heard.

"But in very good condition, Monsignor."

"You said that."

"Yes. And I could take it apart if anything went wrong. My uncle had one."

"No doubt." Monsignor uttered a laugh at Father Eudex's rural origins. Then he delivered the final word, long delayed out of amusement. "It wouldn't be prudent, Father. After all, this isn't a country parish. You know the class of people we get here."

Monsignor put on his Panama hat. Then, apparently mistaking the obstinacy in his curate's face for plain ignorance, he shed a little more light. "People watch a priest, Father. *Damnant quod non intelligunt.* It would never do. You'll have to watch your tendencies."

Monsignor's eyes tripped and fell hard on the morning paper lying on the swing where he had finished it.

"Another flattering piece about that crazy fellow. . . . There's a man who might have gone places if it weren't for his mouth! A bishop doesn't have to get mixed up in all that stuff!"

Monsignor, as Father Eudex knew, meant unions, strikes, race riots—all that stuff.

"A parishioner was saying to me only yesterday it's getting so you can't tell the Catholics from the Communists, with the priests as bad as any. Yes, and this fellow is the worst. He reminds me of that bishop a few years back—at least he called himself a bishop, a Protestant—that was advocating companionate marriages. It's not that bad, maybe, but if you listened to some of them you'd think that Catholicity and capitalism were incompatible!"

"The Holy Father—"

"The Holy Father's in Europe, Father. Mr. Memmers lives in this parish. I'm his priest. What can I tell him?"

"Is it Mr. Memmers of the First National, Monsignor?"

"It is, Father. And there's damned little cheer I can give a man like Memmers. Catholics, priests, and laity alike—yes, and princes of the Church, all talking atheistic communism!"

This was the substance of their conversation, always, the deadly routine in which Father Eudex played straight man. Each time it happened he seemed to participate, and though he should have known better he justified his participation by hoping that it would not happen again, or in quite the same way. But it did, it always did, the same way, and Monsignor, for all his alarums, had nothing to say really and meant one thing only, the thing he never said—that he dearly wanted to be, and was not, a bishop.

Father Eudex could imagine just what kind of bishop Monsignor would be. His reign would be a wise one, excessively so. His mind was made up on everything, excessively so. He would know how to avoid the snares set in the path of the just man, avoid them, too, in good taste and good conscience. He would not be trapped as so many good shepherds before him had been trapped, poor souls—caught in fair-seeming dilemmas of justice that were best left alone, like the first apple. It grieved him, he said, to think of those great hearts broken in silence and solitude. It was the worst kind of exile, alas! But just give him the chance and he would know what to do, what to say, and, more important, what not to do, not to say—neither yea nor nay for him. He had not gone to Rome for nothing. For him the dark forest of decisions would not exist; for him, thanks to hours spent in prayer and meditation, the forest would vanish as dry grass before fire, his fire. He knew the mask of evil already—birth control, indecent movies, salacious books—and would call these things by their right names and dare to deal with them for what they were, these new occasions for the old sins of the cities of the plains.

But in the meantime—oh, to have a particle of the faith that God had in humanity! Dear, trusting God forever trying them beyond their feeble powers, ordering terrible tests, fatal trials by nonsense (the crazy bishop). And keeping Monsignor steadily warming up on the side lines, ready to rush in, primed for the day that would perhaps never dawn.

At one time, so the talk went, there had been reason to think that Monsignor was headed for a bishopric. Now it was too late; Monsignor's intercessors were all dead; the cupboard was bare; he knew it at heart, and it galled him to see another man, this *crazy* man, given the opportunity, and making such a mess of it.

Father Eudex searched for and found a little salt for Monsignor's wound. "The word's going around he'll be the next archbishop," he said.

"I won't believe it," Monsignor countered hoarsely. He glanced at the newspaper on the swing and renewed his horror. "If that fellow's right, Father, I'm"—his voice cracked at the idea—"*wrong!*"

Father Eudex waited until Monsignor had started down the steps to the car before he said, "It could be."

"I'll be back for lunch, Father. I'm taking her for a little spin."

Monsignor stopped in admiration a few feet from the car—her. He was as helpless before her beauty as a boy with a birthday bicycle. He could not leave her alone. He had her out every morning and afternoon and evening. He was indiscriminate about picking people up for a ride in her. He kept her on a special diet—only the best of gas and oil and grease, with daily rubdowns. He would run her only on the smoothest roads and at so many miles an hour. That was to have stopped at the first five hundred, but only now, nearing the thousand mark, was he able to bring himself to increase her speed, and it seemed to hurt him more than it did her.

Now he was walking around behind her to inspect the tires. Apparently O.K. He gave the left rear fender an amorous chuck and eased into the front seat. Then they drove off, the car and he, to see the world, to explore each other further on the honeymoon.

Father Eudex watched the car slide into the traffic, and waited, on edge. The corner cop, fulfilling Father Eudex's fears, blew his whistle and waved his arms up in all four directions, bringing traffic to a standstill. Monsignor pulled expertly out of line and drove down Clover Boulevard in a one-car parade; all others stalled respectfully. The cop, as Monsignor passed, tipped his cap, showing a bald head. Monsignor, in the circumstances, could not acknowledge him, though he knew the man well—a parishioner. He was occupied with keeping his countenance kindly, grim, and exalted, that the cop's faith remain whole, for it was evidently inconceivable to him that Monsignor should ever venture abroad unless to bear the Holy Viaticum, always racing with death.

Father Eudex, eyes baleful but following the progress of the big black car, saw a hand dart out of the driver's window in a wave. Monsignor would combine a lot of business with pleasure that morning, creating what he called "good will for the Church"—all morning in the driver's seat toasting passers-by with a wave that was better than a blessing. How he loved waving to people!

Father Eudex overcame his inclination to sit and stew about things by going down the steps to meet the mailman. He got the usual handful for the Monsignor—advertisements and amazing offers, the unfailing crop of chaff from dealers in church goods, organs, collection schemes, insurance, and sacramental wines. There were two envelopes addressed to Father Eudex, one a mimeographed plea from a missionary society which he might or might not acknowledge with a contribution, depending upon what he thought of the cause—if it was really lost enough to justify a levy on his poverty—and the other a cheque for a hundred dollars.

The cheque came in an eggshell envelope with no explanation except a tiny card, "Compliments of the Rival Tractor Company," but even that was needless. All over town clergymen had known for days that the cheques were on the way again. Some, rejoicing, could hardly wait. Father Eudex, however, was one of those who could.

With the passing of hard times and the coming of the fruitful war years, the Rival Company, which was a great one for public relations, had found the best solution to the excess-profits problem to be giving. Ministers and even rabbis shared in the annual jack pot, but Rival employees were largely Catholic and it was the cheques to the priests that paid off. Again, some thought it was a wonderful idea, and others thought that Rival, plagued by strikes and justly so, had put their alms to work.

There was another eggshell envelope, Father Eudex saw, among the letters for Monsignor, and knew his cheque would be for two hundred, the premium for pastors.

Father Eudex left Monsignor's mail on the porch table by his cigars. His own he stuck in his back pocket, wanting to forget it, and went down the steps into the yard. Walking back and forth on the shady side of the rectory where the lilies of the valley grew and reading his office, he gradually drifted into the back yard, lured by a noise. He came upon Whalen, the janitor, pounding pegs into the ground.

Father Eudex closed the breviary on a finger. "What's it all about, Joe?"

Joe Whalen snatched a piece of paper from his shirt and handed it to Father Eudex. "He gave it to me this morning."

He—it was the word for Monsignor among them. A docile pronoun only, and yet when it meant the Monsignor it said, and concealed, nameless things.

The paper was a plan for a garden drawn up by the Monsignor in his fine hand. It called for a huge fleur-de-lis bounded by smaller crosses—and these Maltese—a fountain, a sundial, and a cloister walk running from the rectory to the garage. Later there would be birdhouses and a ten-foot wall of thick grey stones, acting as a moat against the eyes of the world. The whole scheme struck Father Eudex as expensive and, in this country, Presbyterian.

When Monsignor drew the plan, however, he must have been in his medieval mood. A spouting whale jostled with Neptune in the choppy waters of the fountain. North was indicated in the legend by a winged cherub huffing and puffing.

Father Eudex held the plan up against the sun to see the watermark. The stationery was new to him, heavy, simulated parchment, with the Church of the Holy Redeemer and Monsignor's name embossed, three initials, W. F. X., William Francis Xavier. With all those initials the man could pass for a radio station, a chancery wit had observed, or if his last name had not been Sweeney, Father Eudex added now, for high Anglican.

Father Eudex returned the plan to Whalen, feeling sorry for him and to an extent guilty before him—if only because he was a priest like Monsignor (now turned architect) whose dream of a monastery garden included the overworked janitor under the head of "labour."

Father Eudex asked Whalen to bring another shovel. Together, almost without words, they worked all morning spading up crosses, leaving the big fleur-de-lis to the last. Father Eudex removed his coat first, then his collar, and finally was down to his undershirt.

Toward noon Monsignor rolled into the driveway.

He stayed in the car, getting red in the face, recovering from the pleasure of seeing so much accomplished as he slowly recognized his curate in Whalen's helper. In a still, appalled voice he called across the lawn, "Father," and waited as for a beast that might or might not have sense enough to come.

Father Eudex dropped his shovel and went over to the car, shirtless.

Monsignor waited a moment before he spoke, as though annoyed by the everlasting necessity, where this person was concerned, to explain. "Father," he said quietly at last, "I wouldn't do any more of that—if I were you. Rather, in any event, I wouldn't."

"All right, Monsignor."

"To say the least, it's not prudent. If necessary"—he paused as Whalen came over to dig a cross within earshot—"I'll explain later. It's time for lunch now."

The car, black, beautiful, fierce with chromium, was quiet as Monsignor dismounted, knowing her master. Monsignor went around to the rear, felt a tire, and probed a nasty cinder in the tread.

"Look at that," he said, removing the cinder.

Father Eudex thought he saw the car lift a hoof, gaze around, and thank Monsignor with her headlights.

Monsignor proceeded at a precise pace to the back door of the rectory. There he held the screen open momentarily, as if remembering something or reluctant to enter before himself—such was his humility—but then called to Whalen with an intimacy that could never exist between them.

"Better knock off now, Joe?"

Whalen turned in on himself. "*Joe*—is it!"

Father Eudex removed his clothes from the grass. His hands were all blisters, but in them he found a little absolution. He apologized to Joe for having to take the afternoon off. "I can't make it, Joe. Something turned up."

"Sure, Father."

Father Eudex could hear Joe telling his wife about it that night—yeah, the young one got in wrong with the old one again. Yeah, the old one, he don't believe in it, work, for them.

Father Eudex paused in the kitchen to remember he knew not what. It was in his head, asking to be let in, but he did not place it until he heard Monsignor in the next room complaining about the salad to the housekeeper. It was the voice of dear, dead Aunt Hazel, coming from the summer he was ten. He translated the past into the present: I can't come out and play this afternoon, Joe, on account of my monsignor won't let me.

In the dining room Father Eudex sat down at the table and said grace. He helped himself to a chop, creamed new potatoes, pickled beets, jelly, and bread. He liked jelly. Monsignor passed the butter.

"That's supposed to be a tutti-frutti salad," Monsignor said, grimacing at his. "But she used green olives."

Father Eudex said nothing.

"I said she used green olives."

"I like green olives all right."

"*I* like green olives, but *not* in tutti-frutti salad."

Father Eudex replied by eating a green olive, but he knew it could not end there.

"Father," Monsignor said in a new tone. "How would you like to go away and study for a year?"

"Don't think I'd care for it, Monsignor. I'm not the type."

"You're no canonist, you mean?"

"That's one thing."

"Yes. Well, there are other things it might not hurt you to know. To be quite frank with you, Father, I think you need broadening."

"I guess so," Father Eudex said thickly.

"And still, with your tendencies . . . and with the universities honeycombed with Communists. No, that would never do. I think I meant seasoning, not broadening."

"Oh."

"No offence?"

"No offence."

Who would have thought a little thing like an olive could lead to all this, Father Eudex mused—who but himself, that is, for his association with Monsignor had shown him that anything could lead to everything. Monsignor was a master at making points. Nothing had changed since the day Father Eudex walked into the rectory saying he was the new assistant. Monsignor had evaded Father Eudex's hand in greeting, and a few days later, after he began to get the range, he delivered a lecture on the whole subject of handshaking. It was Middle West to shake hands, or South West, or West in any case, and it was not done where he came from, and —why had he ever come from where he came from? Not to be reduced to shaking hands, you could bet! Handshaking was worse than foot washing and unlike that pious practice there was nothing to support it. And from handshaking Monsignor might go into a general discussion of Father Eudex's failings. He used the open forum method, but he was the only speaker and there was never time enough for questions from the audience. Monsignor seized his examples at random from life. He saw Father Eudex coming out of his bedroom in pyjama bottoms only and so told him about the dressing gown, its purpose, something of its history. He advised Father Eudex to barber his armpits, for it was being done all over now. He let Father Eudex see his bottle of cologne, "Steeple," special for clergymen, and said he should not be afraid of it. He suggested that Father Eudex shave his face oftener, too. He loaned him his Rogers Peet catalogue, which had sketches of clerical blades togged out in the latest, and prayed that he would stop going around looking like a rabbinical student.

He found Father Eudex reading *The Catholic Worker* one day and had not trusted him since. Father Eudex's conception of the priesthood was evangelical in the worst sense, barbaric, gross, foreign to the mind of the Church, which was one of two terms he used as sticks to beat him with. The other was taste. The air of the rectory was often heavy with The Mind of the Church and Taste.

Another thing. Father Eudex could not conduct a civil conversation. Monsignor doubted that Father Eudex could even think to himself with anything like agreement. Certainly any discussion with Father Eudex ended inevitably in argument or sighing. Sighing! Why didn't people talk up if they had anything to say? No, they'd rather sigh! Father, don't ever, ever sigh at me again!

Finally, Monsignor did not like Father Eudex's table manners. This came to a head one night when Monsignor, seeing his curate's plate empty and all the silverware at his place unused except for a single knife, fork, and spoon, exploded altogether, saying it had been on his mind for weeks, and then descending into the vernacular he declared that Father Eudex did not know the forks—now perhaps he could understand that! Meals, unless Monsignor had guests or other things to struggle with, were always occasions of instruction for Father Eudex, and sometimes of chastisement.

And now he knew the worst—if Monsignor was thinking of recommending him for a year of study, in a Sulpician seminary probably, to learn the forks. So this was what it meant to be a priest. *Come, follow me. Going forth, teach ye all nations. Heal the sick, raise the dead, cleanse the lepers, cast out devils.* Teach the class of people we get here? Teach Mr. Memmers? Teach Communists? Teach Monsignors? And where were the poor? The lepers of old? The lepers were in their colonies with nuns to nurse them. The poor were in their holes and would not come out. Mr. Memmers was in his bank, without cheer. The Communists were in their universities, awaiting a sign. And he was at table with Monsignor, and it was enough for the disciple to be as his master, but the housekeeper had used green olives.

Monsignor inquired, "Did you get your cheque today?"

Father Eudex looked up, considered. "I got *a* cheque," he said.

"From the Rival people, I mean?"

"Yes."

"Good. Well, I think you might apply it on the car you're wanting. A decent car. That's a worthy cause." Monsignor noticed that he was not taking it well. "Not that I mean to dictate what you shall do with your little windfall, Father. It's just that I don't like to see you mortifying yourself with a Model A—and disgracing the Church."

"Yes," Father Eudex said, suffering.

"Yes. I dare say you don't see the danger, just as you didn't a while ago when I found you making a spectacle of yourself with Whalen. You just don't see the danger because you just don't think. Not to dwell on it, but I seem to remember some overshoes."

The overshoes! Monsignor referred to them as to the Fall. Last winter Father Eudex had given his overshoes to a freezing picket. It had got back to Monsignor and—good Lord, a man could have his sympathies, but he had no right clad in the cloth to endanger the prestige of the Church by siding in these wretched squabbles. Monsignor said he hated to think of all the evil done by people doing good! Had Father Eudex ever heard of the Albigensian heresy, or didn't the seminary teach that any more?

Father Eudex declined dessert. It was strawberry mousse.

"Delicious," Monsignor said. "I think I'll let her stay."

At that moment Father Eudex decided that he had nothing to lose. He placed his knife next to his fork on the plate, adjusted them this way and that until they seemed to work a combination in his mind, to spring a lock which in turn enabled him to speak out.

"Monsignor," he said. "I think I ought to tell you I don't intend to make use of that money. In fact—to show you how my mind works—I have even considered endorsing the cheque to the strikers' relief fund."

"So," Monsignor said calmly—years in the confessional had prepared him for anything.

"I'll admit I don't know whether I can in justice. And even if I could I don't know that I would. I don't know why . . . I guess hush money, no matter what you do with it, is lousy."

Monsignor regarded him with piercing baby blue eyes. "You'd find it pretty hard to prove, Father, that *any* money *in se* is . . . what you say it is. I would quarrel further with the definition 'hush money.' It seems to me nothing if not rash that you would presume to impugn the motive of the Rival Company in sending out those cheques. You would seem to challenge the whole concept of good works—not that I am ignorant of the misuses to which money can be put." Monsignor, changing tack, tucked it all into a sigh. "Perhaps I'm just a simple soul, and it's enough for me to know personally some of the people in the Rival Company and to know them good people. Many of them Catholic . . ." A throb had crept into Monsignor's voice. He shut it off.

"I don't mean anything that subtle, Monsignor," Father Eudex said. "I'm just telling you, as my pastor, what I'm going to do with the cheque. Or what I'm not going to do with it. I don't know what I'm going to do with it. Maybe send it back."

Monsignor rose from the table, slightly smiling. "Very well, Father. But there's always the poor."

Monsignor took leave of Father Eudex with a laugh. Father Eudex felt it was supposed to fool him into thinking that nothing he had said would be used against him. It showed, rather, that Monsignor was not winded, that he had broken wild curates before, plenty of them, and that he would ride again.

Father Eudex sought the shade of the porch. He tried to read his office, but was drowsy. He got up for a glass of water. The saints in Ireland used to stand up to their necks in cold water, but not for drowsiness. When he came back to the porch a woman was ringing the doorbell. She looked like a customer for rosary beads.

"Hello," he said.

"I'm Mrs. Klein, Father, and I was wondering if you could help me out."

Father Eudex straightened a porch chair for her. "Please sit down."

"It's a German name, Father. Klein was German descent," she said, and added with a silly grin, "It ain't what you think, Father."

"I beg your pardon."

"Klein. Some think it's a Jew name. But they stole it from Klein."

Father Eudex decided to come back to that later. "You were wondering if I could help you?"

"Yes, Father. It's personal."

"Is it matter for confession?"

"Oh no, Father." He had made her blush.

"Then go ahead."

Mrs. Klein peered into the honeysuckle vines on either side of the porch for alien ears.

"No one can hear you, Mrs. Klein."

"Father—I'm just a poor widow," she said, and continued as though Father Eudex had just slandered the man. "Klein was awful good to me, Father."

"I'm sure he was."

"So good . . . and he went and left me all he had." She had begun to cry a little.

Father Eudex nodded gently. She was after something, probably not money, always the best bet—either that or a drunk in the family—but this one was not Irish. Perhaps just sympathy.

"I come to get your advice, Father. Klein always said, 'If you got a problem, Freda, see the priest.' "

"Do you need money?"

"I got more than I can use from the bakery."

"You have a bakery?"

Mrs. Klein nodded down the street. "That's my bakery. It was Klein's. The Purity."

"I go by there all the time," Father Eudex said, abandoning himself to her. He must stop trying to shape the conversation and let her work it out.

"Will you give me your advice, Father?" He felt that she sensed his indifference and interpreted it as his way of rejecting her. She either had no idea how little sense she made or else supreme faith in him, as a priest, to see into her heart.

"Just what is it you're after, Mrs. Klein?"

"He left me all he had, Father, but it's just laying in the bank."

"And you want me to tell you what to do with it?"

"Yes, Father."

Father Eudex thought this might be interesting, certainly a change. He went back in his mind to the seminary and the class in which they had considered the problem of inheritances. Do we have any unfulfilled obligations? Are we sure? . . . Are there any impedimenta?

"Do you have any dependents, Mrs. Klein—any children?"

"One boy, Father. I got him running the bakery. I pay him good—too much, Father."

"Is 'too much' a living wage?"

"Yes, Father. He ain't got a family."

"A living wage is not too much," Father Eudex handed down, sailing into the encyclical style without knowing it.

Mrs. Klein was smiling over having done something good without knowing precisely what it was.

"How old is your son?"

"He's thirty-six, Father."

"Not married?"

"No, Father, but he's got him a girl." She giggled, and Father Eudex, embarrassed, retied his shoe.

"But you don't care to make a will and leave this money to your son in the usual way?"

"I guess I'll have to . . . if I die." Mrs. Klein was suddenly crushed and haunted, but whether by death or charity, Father Eudex did not know.

"You don't have to, Mrs. Klein. There are many worthy causes. And the worthiest is the cause of the poor. My advice to you, if I understand your problem, is to give what you have to someone who needs it."

Mrs. Klein just stared at him.

"You could even leave it to the archdiocese," he said, completing the sentence to himself: but I don't recommend it in your case . . . with your tendencies. You look like an Indian giver to me.

But Mrs. Klein had got enough. "Huh!" she said, rising. "Well! You *are* a funny one!"

And then Father Eudex realized that she had come to him for a broker's tip. It was in the eyes. The hat. The dress. The shoes. "If you'd like to speak to the pastor," he said, "come back in the evening."

"You're a nice young man," Mrs. Klein said, rather bitter now and bent on getting away from him. "But I got to say this—you ain't much of a priest. And Klein said if I got a problem, see the priest—huh! You ain't much of a priest! What time's your boss come in?"

"In the evening," Father Eudex said. "Come any time in the evening."

Mrs. Klein was already down the steps and making for the street.

"You might try Mr. Memmers at the First National," Father Eudex called, actually trying to help her, but she must have thought it was just some more of his nonsense and did not reply.

After Mrs. Klein had disappeared Father Eudex went to his room. In the hallway upstairs Monsignor's voice, coming from the depths of the clerical nap, halted him.

"Who was it?"

"A woman," Father Eudex said. "A woman seeking good counsel."

He waited a moment to be questioned, but Monsignor was not awake enough to see anything wrong with that, and there came only a sigh and a shifting of weight that told Father Eudex he was simply turning over in bed.

Father Eudex walked into the bathroom. He took the Rival cheque from his pocket. He tore it into little squares. He let them flutter into the toilet. He pulled the chain—hard.

He went to his room and stood looking out the window at nothing. He could hear the others already giving an account of their stewardship, but could not judge them. I bought baseball uniforms for the school. I bought the nuns a new washing machine. I purchased a Mass kit for a Chinese missionary. I bought a set of matched irons. Mine helped pay for keeping my mother in a rest home upstate. I gave mine to the poor.

And you, Father?

Saul Bellow

Saul Bellow (1915–   ), born in Quebec, was reared in Chicago, where he has lived since the age of nine. His seven novels and two volumes of stories published since 1944 have earned him two National Book Awards and wide critical and public acclaim. Among his major works are The Adventures of Augie March *(1953) and* Herzog *(1961). Bellow's fiction characteristically asks the "big" question: "What is the meaning of human existence?" And his answer is generally an affirmation of the human need to go on asking. By seeking ultimate meanings, his heroes learn enough about themselves to persevere in the face of an apparently chaotic universe.* *(See page 73 of Introduction.)*

LOOKING FOR MR. GREEN

Whatsoever thy hand findeth to do, do it with thy might. . . .

Hard work? No, it wasn't really so hard. He wasn't used to walking and stair-climbing, but the physical difficulty of his new job was not what George Grebe felt most. He was delivering relief checks in the Negro district, and although he was a native Chicagoan this was not a part of the city he knew much about—it needed a depression to introduce him to it. No, it wasn't literally hard work, not as reckoned in foot-pounds, but yet he was beginning to feel the strain of it, to grow aware of its peculiar difficulty. He could find the streets and numbers, but the clients were not where they were supposed to be, and he felt like a hunter inexperienced in the camouflage of his game. It was an unfavorable day, too—fall, and cold, dark weather, windy. But, anyway, instead of shells in his deep trenchcoat pocket he had the cardboard of checks, punctured for the spindles of the file, the holes reminding him of the holes in player-piano paper. And he didn't look much like a hunter, either; his was a city figure entirely, belted up in his Irish conspirator's coat. He was slender without being tall, stiff in the back, his legs looking shabby in a pair of old tweed pants gone through and fringy at the cuffs. With this stiffness, he kept his head forward, so that his face was red from the sharpness of the weather; and it was an indoors sort of face with gray eyes that persisted in some kind of thought and yet seemed to avoid definiteness of conclusion. He wore sideburns that surprised you somewhat by the tough curl of the blond hair and the effect of assertion in their length. He was not so mild as he looked, nor so youthful; and nevertheless there was no effort on his part to seem what he was not. He was an educated man; he was a bachelor; he was in some ways simple; without lushing, he liked a drink; his luck had not been good. Nothing was deliberately hidden.

He felt that his luck was better than usual today. When he had reported for work that morning he had expected to be shut up in the relief office at a clerk's job, for he had been hired downtown as a clerk, and he was glad to have, instead, the freedom of the streets and welcomed, at least at first, the vigor of the cold and even the blowing of the hard wind. But on the other hand he was not getting on with the distribution of the checks. It was true that it was a city job; nobody expected you to push too hard at a city job. His supervisor, that young Mr. Raynor, had practically told him that. Still, he wanted to do well at it. For one thing, when he knew how quickly he could deliver a batch of checks, he would know also how much time he could expect to clip for himself. And then, too, the clients would be waiting for their money. That was not the most important consideration, though it certainly mattered to him. No, but he wanted to do well, simply for doing-well's sake, to acquit himself decently of a job because he so rarely had a job to do that required just this sort of energy. Of this peculiar energy he now had a superabundance; once it had started to flow, it flowed all too heavily. And, for the time being anyway, he was balked. He could not find Mr. Green.

So he stood in his big-skirted trenchcoat with a large envelope in his hand and papers showing from his pocket, wondering why people should be so hard to locate who were too feeble or sick to come to the station to collect their own checks. But Raynor had told him that tracking them down was not easy at first and had offered him some advice on how to proceed. "If you can see the postman, he's your first man to ask, and your best bet. If you can't connect with him, try the stores and tradespeople around. Then the janitor and the neighbors. But you'll find the closer you come to your man the less people will tell you. They don't want to tell you anything."

"Because I'm a stranger."

"Because you're white. We ought to have a Negro doing this, but we don't at the moment, and of course you've got to eat, too, and this is public employment. Jobs have to be made. Oh, that holds for me too. Mind you, I'm not letting myself out. I've got three years of seniority on you, that's all. And a law degree. Otherwise, you might be back of the desk and I might be going out into the field this cold day. The same dough pays us both and for the same, exact, identical reason. What's my law degree got to do with it? But you have to pass out these checks, Mr. Grebe, and it'll help if you're stubborn, so I hope you are."

"Yes, I'm fairly stubborn."

Raynor sketched hard with an eraser in the old dirt of his desk, left-handed, and said, "Sure, what else can you answer to such a question. Anyhow, the trouble you're going to have is that they don't like to give information about anybody. They think you're a plain-clothes dick or an installment collector, or summons-server or something like that. Till you've been seen around the neighborhood for a few months and people know you're only from the relief."

It was dark, ground-freezing, pre-Thanksgiving weather; the wind played hob with the smoke, rushing it down, and Grebe missed his gloves, which he had left in Raynor's office. And no one would admit knowing Green. It was past three o'clock and the postman had made his last delivery. The nearest grocer, himself a Negro, had never heard the name Tulliver Green, or said he hadn't. Grebe was inclined to think that it was true, that he had in the end convinced the man that he wanted only to deliver a check. But he wasn't sure. He needed experience in interpreting looks and signs and, even more, the will not to be put off or denied and even the force to bully if need be. If the grocer did know, he had got rid of him easily. But since most of his trade was with reliefers, why should he prevent the delivery of a check? Maybe Green, or Mrs. Green, if there was a Mrs. Green, patronized another grocer. And was there a Mrs. Green? It was one of Grebe's great handicaps that he hadn't looked at any of the case records. Raynor should have let him read files for a few hours. But he apparently saw no need for that, probably considering the job unimportant. Why prepare systematically to deliver a few checks?

But now it was time to look for the janitor. Grebe took in the building in the wind and gloom of the late November day—trampled, frost-hardened lots on one side; on the other, an automobile junk yard and then the infinite work of Elevated frames, weak-looking, gaping with rubbish fires; two sets of leaning brick porches three stories high and a flight of cement stairs to the cellar. Descending, he entered the underground passage, where he tried the doors until one opened and he found himself in the furnace room. There someone rose toward him and approached, scraping on the coal grit and bending under the canvas-jacketed pipes.

"Are you the janitor?"

"What do you want?"

"I'm looking for a man who's supposed to be living here. Green."

"What Green?"

"Oh, you maybe have more than one Green?" said Grebe with new, pleasant hope. "This is Tulliver Green."

"I don't think I c'n help you, mister. I don't know any."

"A crippled man."

The janitor stood bent before him. Could it be that he was crippled? Oh, God! what if he was. Grebe's gray eyes sought with excited difficulty to see. But no, he was only very short and stooped. A head awakened from meditation, a strong-haired beard, low, wide shoulders. A staleness of sweat and coal rose from his black shirt and the burlap sack he wore as an apron.

"Crippled how?"

Grebe thought and then answered with the light voice of unmixed candor, "I don't know. I've never seen him." This was damaging, but his only other choice was to make a lying guess, and he was not up to it. "I'm delivering checks for the relief to shut-in cases. If he weren't crippled he'd come to collect himself. That's why I said crippled. Bedridden, chair-ridden—is there anybody like that?"

This sort of frankness was one of Grebe's oldest talents, going back to childhood. But it gained him nothing here.

"No suh. I've got four buildin's same as this that I take care of. I don' know all the tenants, leave alone the tenants' tenants. The rooms turn over so fast, people movin' in and out every day. I can't tell you."

The janitor opened his grimy lips but Grebe did not hear him in the piping of the valves and the consuming pull of air to flame in the body of the furnace. He knew, however, what he had said.

"Well, all the same, thanks. Sorry I bothered you. I'll prowl around up-stairs again and see if I can turn up someone who knows him."

Once more in the cold air and early darkness he made the short circle from the cellarway to the entrance crowded between the brickwork pil-lars and began to climb to the third floor. Pieces of plaster ground under his feet; strips of brass tape from which the carpeting had been torn away marked old boundaries at the sides. In the passage, the cold reached him worse than in the street; it touched him to the bone. The hall toilets ran like springs. He thought grimly as he heard the wind burning around the building with a sound like that of the furnace, that this was a great piece of constructed shelter. Then he struck a match in the gloom and searched for names and numbers among the writings and scribbles on the walls. He saw WHOODY-DOODY GO TO JESUS, and zigzags, caricatures, sexual scrawls, and curses. So the sealed rooms of pyramids were also decorated, and the caves of human dawn.

The information on his card was, TULLIVER GREEN—APT 3D. There were no names, however, and no numbers. His shoulders drawn up, tears of cold in his eyes, breathing vapor, he went the length of the corridor and told himself that if he had been lucky enough to have the temperament for it he would bang on one of the doors and bawl out "Tulliver Green!" until he got results. But it wasn't in him to make an uproar and he continued to burn matches, passing the light over the walls. At the rear, in a corner off the hall, he discovered a door he had not seen before and he thought it best to investigate. It sounded empty when he knocked, but a young Negress answered, hardly more than a girl. She opened only a bit, to guard the warmth of the room.

"Yes suh?"

"I'm from the district relief station on Prairie Avenue. I'm looking for a man named Tulliver Green to give him his check. Do you know him?"

No, she didn't; but he thought she had not understood anything of what he had said. She had a dream-bound, dream-blind face, very soft and black, shut off. She wore a man's jacket and pulled the ends together at her throat. Her hair was parted in three directions, at the sides and trans-versely, standing up at the front in a dull puff.

"Is there somebody around here who might know?"

"I jus' taken this room las' week."

He observed that she shivered, but even her shiver was somnambulistic and there was no sharp consciousness of cold in the big smooth eyes of her handsome face.

"All right, miss, thank you. Thanks," he said, and went to try another place.

Here he was admitted. He was grateful, for the room was warm. It was full of people, and they were silent as he entered—ten people, or a dozen, perhaps more, sitting on benches like a parliament. There was no light, properly speaking, but a tempered darkness that the window gave, and everyone seemed to him enormous, the men padded out in heavy work clothes and winter coats, and the women huge, too, in their sweaters, hats, and old furs. And, besides, bed and bedding, a black cooking range, a piano piled towering to the ceiling with papers, a dining-room table of the old style of prosperous Chicago. Among these people Grebe, with his cold-heightened fresh color and his smaller stature, entered like a schoolboy. Even though he was met with smiles and good will, he knew, before a single word was spoken, that all the currents ran against him and that he would make no headway. Nevertheless he began. "Does anybody here know how I can deliver a check to Mr. Tulliver Green?"

"Green?" It was the man that had let him in who answered. He was in short sleeves, in a checkered shirt, and had a queer, high head, profusely overgrown and long as a shako; the veins entered it strongly from his forehead. "I never heard mention of him. Is this where he live?"

"This is the address they gave me at the station. He's a sick man, and he'll need his check. Can't anybody tell me where to find him?"

He stood his ground and waited for a reply, his crimson wool scarf wound about his neck and drooping outside his trenchcoat, pockets weighted with the block of checks and official forms. They must have realized that he was not a college boy employed afternoons by a bill collector, trying foxily to pass for a relief clerk, recognized that he was an older man who knew himself what need was, who had had more than an average seasoning in hardship. It was evident enough if you looked at the marks under his eyes and at the sides of his mouth.

"Anybody know this sick man?"

"No suh." On all sides he saw heads shaken and smiles of denial. No one knew. And maybe it was true, he considered, standing silent in the earthen, musky human gloom of the place as the rumble continued. But he could never really be sure.

"What's the matter with this man?" said shako-head.

"I've never seen him. All I can tell you is that he can't come in person for his money. It's my first day in this district."

"Maybe they given you the wrong number?"

"I don't believe so. But where else can I ask about him?" He felt that this persistence amused them deeply, and in a way he shared their amusement that he should stand up so tenaciously to them. Though smaller, though slight, he was his own man, he retracted nothing about himself, and he looked back at them, gray-eyed, with amusement and also with a sort of courage. On the bench some man spoke in his throat, the words impossible to catch, and a woman answered with a wild, shrieking laugh, which was quickly cut off.

"Well, so nobody will tell me?"

"Ain't nobody who knows."

"At least, if he lives here, he pays rent to someone. Who manages the building?"

"Greatham Company. That's on Thirty-ninth Street."

Grebe wrote it in his pad. But, in the street again, a sheet of wind-driven paper clinging to his leg while he deliberated what direction to take next, it seemed a feeble lead to follow. Probably this Green didn't rent a flat, but a room. Sometimes there were as many as twenty people in an apartment; the real-estate agent would know only the lessee. And not even the agent could tell you who the renters were. In some places the beds were even used in shifts, watchmen or jitney drivers or short-order cooks in night joints turning out after a day's sleep and surrendering their beds to a sister, a nephew, or perhaps a stranger, just off the bus. There were large numbers of newcomers in this terrific, blight-bitten portion of the city between Cottage Grove and Ashland, wandering from house to house and room to room. When you saw them, how could you know them? They didn't carry bundles on their backs or look picturesque. You only saw a man, a Negro, walking in the street or riding in the car, like everyone else, with his thumb closed on a transfer. And therefore how were you supposed to tell? Grebe thought the Greatham agent would only laugh at his question.

But how much it would have simplified the job to be able to say that Green was old, or blind, or consumptive. An hour in the files, taking a few notes, and he needn't have been at such a disadvantage. When Raynor gave him the block of checks he asked, "How much should I know about these people?" Then Raynor had looked as though he were preparing to accuse him of trying to make the job more important than it was. He smiled, because by then they were on fine terms, but nevertheless he had been getting ready to say something like that when the confusion began in the station over Staika and her children.

Grebe had waited a long time for this job. It came to him through the pull of an old schoolmate in the Corporation Counsel's office, never a close friend, but suddenly sympathetic and interested—pleased to show, moreover, how well he had done, how strongly he was coming on even in these miserable times. Well, he was coming through strongly, along with the Democratic administration itself. Grebe had gone to see him in City Hall, and they had had a counter lunch or beers at least once a month for a year, and finally it had been possible to swing the job. He didn't mind being assigned the lowest clerical grade, nor even being a messenger, though Raynor thought he did.

This Raynor was an original sort of guy and Grebe had taken to him immediately. As was proper on the first day, Grebe had come early, but he waited long, for Raynor was late. At last he darted into his cubicle of an office as though he had just jumped from one of those hurtling huge red

Indian Avenue cars. His thin, rough face was wind-stung and he was grinning and saying something breathlessly to himself. In his hat, a small fedora, and his coat, the velvet collar a neat fit about his neck, and his silk muffler that set off the nervous twist of his chin, he swayed and turned himself in his swivel chair, feet leaving the ground; so that he pranced a little as he sat. Meanwhile he took Grebe's measure out of his eyes, eyes of an unusual vertical length and slightly sardonic. So the two men sat for a while, saying nothing, while the supervisor raised his hat from his miscombed hair and put it in his lap. His cold-darkened hands were not clean. A steel beam passed through the little makeshift room, from which machine belts once had hung. The building was an old factory.

"I'm younger than you; I hope you won't find it hard taking orders from me," said Raynor. "But I don't make them up, either. You're how old, about?"

"Thirty-five."

"And you thought you'd be inside doing paper work. But it so happens I have to send you out."

"I don't mind."

"And it's mostly a Negro load we have in this district."

"So I thought it would be."

"Fine. You'll get along. *C'est un bon boulot.* Do you know French?"

"Some."

"I thought you'd be a university man."

"Have you been in France?" said Grebe.

"No, that's the French of the Berlitz School. I've been at it for more than a year, just as I'm sure people have been, all over the world, office boys in China and braves in Tanganyika. In fact, I damn well know it. Such is the attractive power of civilization. It's overrated, but what do you want? *Que voulez-vous?* I get *Le Rire* and all the spicy papers, just like in Tanganyika. It must be mystifying, out there. But my reason is that I'm aiming at the diplomatic service. I have a cousin who's a courier, and the way he describes it is awfully attractive. He rides in the *wagon-lits* and reads books. While we—What did you do before?"

"I sold."

"Where?"

"Canned meat at Stop and Shop. In the basement."

"And before that?"

"Window shades, at Goldblatt's."

"Steady work?"

"No, Thursdays and Saturdays. I also sold shoes."

"You've been a shoe-dog too. Well. And prior to that? Here it is in your folder." He opened the record. "Saint Olaf's College, instructor in classical languages. Fellow, University of Chicago, 1926–27. I've had Latin, too. Let's trade quotations—*'Dum spiro spero.'* "

" *'Da dextram misero.'* "

" *'Alea jacta est.'* "

" *'Excelsior.'* "

Raynor shouted with laughter, and other workers came to look at him over the partition. Grebe also laughed, feeling pleased and easy. The luxury of fun on a nervous morning.

When they were done and no one was watching or listening, Raynor said rather seriously, "What made you study Latin in the first place? Was it for the priesthood?"

"No."

"Just for the hell of it? For the culture? Oh, the things people think they can pull!" He made his cry hilarious and tragic. "I ran my pants off so I could study for the bar, and I've passed the bar, so I get twelve dollars a week more than you as a bonus for having seen life straight and whole. I'll tell you, as a man of culture, that even though nothing looks to be real, and everything stands for something else, and that thing for another thing, and that thing for a still further one—there ain't any comparison between twenty-five and thirty-seven dollars a week, regardless of the last reality. Don't you think that was clear to your Greeks? They were a thoughtful people, but they didn't part with their slaves."

This was a great deal more than Grebe had looked for in his first interview with his supervisor. He was too shy to show all the astonishment he felt. He laughed a little, aroused, and brushed at the sunbeam that covered his head with its dust. "Do you think my mistake was so terrible?"

"Damn right it was terrible, and you know it now that you've had the whip of hard times laid on your back. You should have been preparing yourself for trouble. Your people must have been well off to send you to the university. Stop me, if I'm stepping on your toes. Did your mother pamper you? Did your father give in to you? Were you brought up tenderly, with permission to go and find out what were the last things that everything else stands for while everybody else labored in the fallen world of appearances?"

"Well, no, it wasn't exactly like that." Grebe smiled. *The fallen world of appearances!* no less. But now it was his turn to deliver a surprise. "We weren't rich. My father was the last genuine English butler in Chicago—"

"Are you kidding?"

"Why should I be?"

"In a livery?"

"In livery. Up on the Gold Coast."

"And he wanted you to be educated like a gentleman?"

"He did not. He sent me to the Armour Institute to study chemical engineering. But when he died I changed schools."

He stopped himself, and considered how quickly Raynor had reached him. In no time he had your valise on the table and all your stuff unpacked. And afterward, in the streets, he was still reviewing how far he might have gone, and how much he might have been led to tell if they had not been interrupted by Mrs. Staika's great noise.

But just then a young woman, one of Raynor's workers, ran into the cubicle exclaiming, "Haven't you heard all the fuss?"

"We haven't heard anything."

"It's Staika, giving out with all her might. The reporters are coming. She said she phoned the papers, and you know she did."

"But what is she up to?" said Raynor.

"She brought her wash and she's ironing it here, with our current, because the relief won't pay her electric bill. She has her ironing board set up by the admitting desk, and her kids are with her, all six. They never are in school more than once a week. She's always dragging them around with her because of her reputation."

"I don't want to miss any of this," said Raynor, jumping up. Grebe, as he followed with the secretary, said, "Who is this Staika?"

"They call her the 'Blood Mother of Federal Street.' She's a professional donor at the hospitals. I think they pay ten dollars a pint. Of course it's no joke, but she makes a very big thing out of it and she and the kids are in the papers all the time."

A small crowd, staff and clients divided by a plywood barrier, stood in the narrow space of the entrance, and Staika was shouting in a gruff, mannish voice, plunging the iron on the board and slamming it on the metal rest.

"My father and mother came in a steerage, and I was born in our house, Robey by Huron. I'm no dirty immigrant. I'm a U.S. citizen. My husband is a gassed veteran from France with lungs weaker'n paper, that hardly can he go to the toilet by himself. These six children of mine, I have to buy the shoes for their feet with my own blood. Even a lousy little white Communion necktie, that's a couple of drops of blood; a little piece of mosquito veil for my Vadja so she won't be ashamed in church for the other girls, they take my blood for it by Goldblatt. That's how I keep goin'. A fine thing if I had to depend on the relief. And there's plenty of people on the rolls—fakes! There's nothin' *they* can't get, that can go and wrap bacon at Swift and Armour any time. They're lookin' for them by the Yards. They never have to be out of work. Only they rather lay in their lousy beds and eat the public's money." She was not afraid, in a predominantly Negro station, to shout this way about Negroes.

Grebe and Raynor worked themselves forward to get a closer view of the woman. She was flaming with anger and with pleasure at herself, broad and huge, a golden-headed woman who wore a cotton cap laced with pink ribbon. She was barelegged and had on black gym shoes, her Hoover apron was open and her great breasts, not much restrained by a man's undershirt, hampered her arms as she worked at the kid's dress on the ironing board. And the children, silent and white, with a kind of locked obstinacy, in sheepskins and lumberjackets, stood behind her. She had captured the station, and the pleasure this gave her was enormous. Yet her grievances were true grievances. She was telling the truth. But she behaved like a liar. The look of her small eyes was hidden, and while she raged she also seemed to be spinning and planning.

"They send me out college case workers in silk pants to talk me out of what I got comin'. Are they better'n me? Who told them? Fire them. Let 'em go and get married, and then you won't have to cut electric from people's budget."

The chief supervisor, Mr. Ewing, couldn't silence her and he stood with folded arms at the head of his staff, bald, bald-headed, saying to his subordinates like the ex-school principal he was, "Pretty soon she'll be tired and go."

"No she won't," said Raynor to Grebe. "She'll get what she wants. She knows more about the relief even than Ewing. She's been on the rolls for years, and she always gets what she wants because she puts on a noisy show. Ewing knows it. He'll give in soon. He's only saving face. If he gets bad publicity, the Commissioner'll have him on the carpet, downtown. She's got him submerged; she'll submerge everybody in time, and that includes nations and governments."

Grebe replied with his characteristic smile, disagreeing completely. Who would take Staika's orders, and what changes could her yelling ever bring about?

No, what Grebe saw in her, the power that made people listen, was that her cry expressed the war of flesh and blood, perhaps turned a little crazy and certainly ugly, on this place and this condition. And at first, when he went out, the spirit of Staika somehow presided over the whole district for him, and it took color from her; he saw her color, in the spotty curb fires, and the fires under the El, the straight alley of flamy gloom. Later, too, when he went into a tavern for a shot of rye, the sweat of beer, association with West Side Polish streets, made him think of her again.

He wiped the corners of his mouth with his muffler, his handkerchief being inconvenient to reach for, and went out again to get on with the delivery of his checks. The air bit cold and hard and a few flakes of snow formed near him. A train struck by and left a quiver in the frames and a bristling icy hiss over the rails.

Crossing the street, he descended a flight of board steps into a basement grocery, setting off a little bell. It was a dark, long store and it caught you with its stinks of smoked meat, soap, dried peaches, and fish. There was a fire wrinkling and flapping in the little stove, and the proprietor was waiting, an Italian with a long, hollow face and stubborn bristles. He kept his hands warm under his apron.

No, he didn't know Green. You knew people but not names. The same man might not have the same name twice. The police didn't know, either, and mostly didn't care. When somebody was shot or knifed they took the body away and didn't look for the murderer. In the first place, nobody would tell them anything. So they made up a name for the coroner and called it quits. And in the second place, they didn't give a goddamn anyhow. But they couldn't get to the bottom of a thing even if they wanted to. Nobody would get to know even a tenth of what went on among these people. They stabbed and stole, they did every crime and abomination you ever heard of, men and men, women and women, parents and children, worse than the animals. They carried on their own way, and the horrors passed off like a smoke. There was never anything like it in the history of the whole world.

It was a long speech, deepening with every word in its fantasy and passion and becoming increasingly senseless and terrible: a swarm amassed by suggestion and invention, a huge, hugging, despairing knot, a human wheel of heads, legs, bellies, arms, rolling through his shop.

Grebe felt that he must interrupt him. He said sharply, "What are you talking about! All I asked was whether you knew this man."

"That isn't even the half of it. I been here six years. You probably don't want to believe this. But suppose it's true?"

"All the same," said Grebe, "there must be a way to find a person."

The Italian's close-spaced eyes had been queerly concentrated, as were his muscles, while he leaned across the counter trying to convince Grebe. Now he gave up the effort and sat down on his stool. "Oh—I suppose. Once in a while. But I been telling you, even the cops don't get anywhere."

"They're always after somebody. It's not the same thing."

"Well, keep trying if you want. I can't help you."

But he didn't keep trying. He had no more time to spend on Green. He slipped Green's check to the back of the block. The next name on the list was FIELD, WINSTON.

He found the back-yard bungalow without the least trouble; it shared a lot with another house, a few feet of yard between. Grebe knew these two-shack arrangements. They had been built in vast numbers in the days before the swamps were filled and the streets raised, and they were all the same—a boardwalk along the fence, well under street level, three or four ball-headed posts for clotheslines, greening wood, dead shingles, and a long, long flight of stairs to the rear door.

A twelve-year-old boy let him into the kitchen, and there the old man was, sitting by the table in a wheelchair.

"Oh, it's d' Government man," he said to the boy when Grebe drew out his checks. "Go bring me my box of papers." He cleared a space on the table.

"Oh, you don't have to go to all that trouble," said Grebe. But Field laid out his papers: Social Security card, relief certification, letters from the state hospital in Manteno, and a naval discharge dated San Diego, 1920.

"That's plenty," Grebe said. "Just sign."

"You got to know who I am," the old man said. "You're from the Government. It's not your check, it's a Government check and you got no business to hand it over till everything is proved."

He loved the ceremony of it, and Grebe made no more objections. Field emptied his box and finished out the circle of cards and letters.

"There's everything I done and been. Just the death certificate and they can close book on me." He said this with a certain happy pride and magnificence. Still he did not sign; he merely held the little pen upright on the golden-green corduroy of his thigh. Grebe did not hurry him. He felt the old man's hunger for conversation.

"I got to get better coal," he said. "I send my little gran'son to the yard with my order and they fill his wagon with screening. The stove ain't made for it. It fall through the grate. The order says Franklin County egg-size coal."

"I'll report it and see what can be done."

"Nothing can be done, I expect. You know and I know. There ain't no little ways to make things better, and the only big thing is money. That's the only sunbeams, money. Nothing is black where it shines, and the only place you see black is where it ain't shining. What we colored have to have is our own rich. There ain't no other way."

Grebe sat, his reddened forehead bridged levelly by his close-cut hair and his cheeks lowered in the wings of his collar—the caked fire shone hard within the isinglass-and-iron frames but the room was not comfortable—sat and listened while the old man unfolded his scheme. This was to create one Negro millionaire a month by subscription. One clever, good-hearted young fellow elected every month would sign a contract to use the money to start a business employing Negroes. This would be advertised by chain letters and word of mouth, and every Negro wage earner would contribute a dollar a month. Within five years there would be sixty millionaires.

"That'll fetch respect," he said with a throat-stopped sound that came out like a foreign syllable. "You got to take and organize all the money that gets thrown away on the policy wheel and horse race. As long as they can take it away from you, they got no respect for you. Money, that's d'sun of human kind!" Field was a Negro of mixed blood, perhaps Cherokee, or Natchez; his skin was reddish. And he sounded, speaking about a golden sun in this dark room, and looked, shaggy and slab-headed, with the mingled blood of his face and broad lips, the little pen still upright in his hand, like one of the underground kings of mythology, old judge Minos himself.

And now he accepted the check and signed. Not to soil the slip, he held it down with his knuckles. The table budged and creaked, the center of the gloomy, heathen midden of the kitchen covered with bread, meat, and cans, and the scramble of papers.

"Don't you think my scheme'd work?"

"It's worth thinking about. Something ought to be done, I agree."

"It'll work if people will do it. That's all. That's the only thing, any time. When they understand it in the same way, all of them."

"That's true," said Grebe, rising. His glance met the old man's.

"I know you got to go," he said. "Well, God bless you, boy, you ain't been sly with me. I can tell it in a minute."

He went back through the buried yard. Someone nursed a candle in a shed, where a man unloaded kindling wood from a sprawl-wheeled baby buggy and two voices carried on a high conversation. As he came up the sheltered passage he heard the hard boost of the wind in the branches and against the house fronts, and then, reaching the sidewalk, he saw the needle-eye red of cable towers in the open icy height hundreds of feet above the river and the factories—those keen points. From here, his view was obstructed all the way to the South Branch and its timber banks, and the cranes beside the water. Rebuilt after the Great Fire, this part of the city was, not fifty years later, in ruins again, factories boarded up, buildings deserted or fallen, gaps of prairie between. But it wasn't desolation that this made you feel, but rather a faltering of organization that set free a huge energy, an escaped, unattached, unregulated power from the giant raw place. Not only must people feel it but, it seemed to Grebe, they were compelled to match it. In their very bodies. He no less than others, he realized. Say that his parents had been servants in their time, whereas he was not supposed to be one. He thought that they had never done any service like this, which no one visible asked for, and probably flesh and blood could not even perform. Nor could anyone show why it should be performed; or see where the performance would lead. That did not mean that he wanted to be released from it, he realized with a grimly pensive face. On the contrary. He had something to do. To be compelled to feel this energy and yet have no task to do—that was horrible; that was suffering; he knew what that was. It was now quitting time. Six o'clock. He could go home if he liked, to his room, that is, to wash in hot water, to pour a drink, lie down on his quilt, read the paper, eat some liver paste on crackers before going out to dinner. But to think of this actually made him feel a little sick, as though he had swallowed hard air. He had six checks left, and he was determined to deliver at least one of these: Mr. Green's check.

So he started again. He had four or five dark blocks to go, past open lots, condemned houses, old foundations, closed schools, black churches, mounds, and he reflected that there must be many people alive who had once seen the neighborhood rebuilt and new. Now there was a second layer of ruins; centuries of history accomplished through human massing. Numbers had given the place forced growth; enormous numbers had also broken it down. Objects once so new, so concrete that it could have occurred to anyone they stood for other things, had crumbled. Therefore, reflected Grebe, the secret of them was out. It was that they stood for themselves by agreement, and were natural and not unnatural by agreement, and when the things themselves collapsed the agreement became visible. What was it, otherwise, that kept cities from looking peculiar? Rome, that was almost permanent, did not give rise to thoughts like these. And was it abidingly real? But in Chicago, where the cycles were so fast and the familiar died out, and again rose changed, and died again in thirty years, you saw the common agreement or covenant, and you were forced to think about appearances and realities. (He remembered Raynor and he smiled. Raynor was a clever boy.) Once you had grasped this, a great many things became intelligible. For instance, why Mr. Field should conceive such a scheme. Of course, if people were to agree to create a millionaire, a real millionaire would come into existence. And if you wanted to know how Mr. Field was inspired to think of this, why, he had within sight of his kitchen window the chart, the very bones of a successful scheme—the El with its blue and green confetti of signals. People consented to pay dimes and ride the crash-box cars, and so it was a success. Yet how absurd it looked; how little reality there was to start with. And yet Yerkes, the great financier who built it, had known that he could get people to agree to do it. Viewed as itself, what a scheme of a scheme it seemed, how close to an appearance. Then why wonder at Mr. Field's idea? He had grasped a principle. And then Grebe remembered, too, that Mr. Yerkes had established the Yerkes Observatory and endowed it with millions. Now how did the notion come to him in his New York museum of a palace or his Aegean-bound yacht to give money to astronomers? Was he awed by the success of his bizarre enterprise and therefore ready to spend money to find out where in the universe being and seeming were identical? Yes, he wanted to know what abides; and whether flesh is Bible grass; and he offered money to be burned in the fire of suns. Okay, then, Grebe thought further, these things exist because people consent to exist with them—we have got so far—and also there is a reality which doesn't depend on consent but within which consent is a game. But what about need, the need that keeps so many vast thousands in position? You tell me that, you *private* little gentleman and *decent* soul—he used these words against himself scornfully. Why is the consent given to misery? And why so painfully ugly? Because there is *something* that is dismal and permanently ugly? Here he sighed and gave it up, and thought it was enough for the present moment that he had a real check in his pocket for a Mr. Green who must be real beyond question. If only his neighbors didn't think they had to conceal him.

This time he stopped at the second floor. He struck a match and found a door. Presently a man answered his knock and Grebe had the check ready and showed it even before he began. "Does Tulliver Green live here? I'm from the relief."

The man narrowed the opening and spoke to someone at his back.

"Does he live here?"

"Uh-uh. No."

"Or anywhere in this building? He's a sick man and he can't come for his dough." He exhibited the check in the light, which was smoky—the air smelled of charred lard—and the man held off the brim of his cap to study it.

"Uh-uh. Never seen the name."

"There's nobody around here that uses crutches?"

He seemed to think, but it was Grebe's impression that he was simply waiting for a decent interval to pass.

"No, suh. Nobody I ever see."

"I've been looking for this man all afternoon"—Grebe spoke out with sudden force—"and I'm going to have to carry this check back to the station. It seems strange not to be able to find a person to *give* him something when you're looking for him for a good reason. I suppose if I had bad news for him I'd find him quick enough."

There was a responsive motion in the other man's face. "That's right, I reckon."

"It almost doesn't do any good to have a name if you can't be found by it. It doesn't stand for anything. He might as well not have any," he went on, smiling. It was as much of a concession as he could make to his desire to laugh.

"Well, now, there's a little old knot-back man I see once in a while. He might be the one you lookin' for. Downstairs."

"Where? Right side or left? Which door?"

"I don't know which. Thin-face little knot-back with a stick."

But no one answered at any of the doors on the first floor. He went to the end of the corridor, searching by matchlight, and found only a stairless exit to the yard, a drop of about six feet. But there was a bungalow near the alley, an old house like Mr. Field's. To jump was unsafe. He ran from the front door, through the underground passage and into the yard. The place was occupied. There was a light through the curtains, upstairs. The name on the ticket under the broken, scoop-shaped mailbox was Green! He exultantly rang the bell and pressed against the locked door. Then the lock clicked faintly and a long staircase opened before him. Someone was slowly coming down—a woman. He had the impression in the weak light that she was shaping her hair as she came, making herself presentable, for he saw her arms raised. But it was for support that they were raised; she was feeling her way downward, down the wall, stumbling. Next he wondered about the pressure of her feet on the treads; she did not seem to be wearing shoes. And it was a freezing stairway. His ring had got her out of bed, perhaps, and she had forgotten to put them on. And then he saw that she was not only shoeless but naked; she was entirely naked, climbing down while she talked to herself, a heavy woman, naked and drunk. She blundered into him. The contact of her breasts, though they touched only his coat, made him go back against the door with a blind shock. See what he had tracked down, in his hunting game!

The woman was saying to herself, furious with insult, "So I cain't ——k, huh? I'll show that sonofabitch kin I, cain't I."

What should he do now? Grebe asked himself. Why, he should go. He should turn away and go. He couldn't talk to this woman. He couldn't keep her standing naked in the cold. But when he tried he found himself unable to turn away.

He said, "Is this where Mr. Green lives?"

But she was still talking to herself and did not hear him.

"Is this Mr. Green's house?"

At last she turned her furious drunken glance on him. "What do you want?"

Again her eyes wandered from him; there was a dot of blood in their enraged brilliance. He wondered why she didn't feel the cold.

"I'm from the relief."

"Awright, what?"

"I've got a check for Tulliver Green."

This time she heard him and put out her hand.

"No, no, for *Mr.* Green. He's got to sign," he said. How was he going to get Green's signature tonight!

"I'll take it. He cain't."

He desperately shook his head, thinking of Mr. Field's precautions about identification. "I can't let you have it. It's for him. Are you Mrs. Green?"

"Maybe I is, and maybe I ain't. Who want to know?"

"Is he upstairs?"

"Awright. Take it up yourself, you goddamn fool."

Sure, he was a goddamn fool. Of course he could not go up because Green would probably be drunk and naked, too. And perhaps he would appear on the landing soon. He looked eagerly upward. Under the light was a high narrow brown wall. Empty! It remained empty!

"Hell with you, then!" he heard her cry. To deliver a check for coal and clothes, he was keeping her in the cold. She did not feel it, but his face was burning with frost and self-ridicule. He backed away from her.

"I'll come tomorrow, tell him."

"Ah, hell with you. Don' never come. What you don' here in the night-time? Don' come back." She yelled so that he saw the breadth of her tongue. She stood astride in the long cold box of the hall and held on to the banister and the wall. The bungalow itself was shaped something like a box, a clumsy, high box pointing into the freezing air with its sharp, wintry lights.

"If you are Mrs. Green, I'll give you the check," he said, changing his mind.

"Give here, then." She took it, took the pen offered with it in her left hand, and tried to sign the receipt on the wall. He looked around, almost as though to see whether his madness was being observed, and came near believing that someone was standing on a mountain of used tires in the auto-junking shop next door.

"But are you Mrs. Green?" he now thought to ask. But she was already climbing the stairs with the check, and it was too late, if he had made an error, if he was now in trouble, to undo the thing. But he wasn't going to worry about it. Though she might not be Mrs. Green, he was convinced that Mr. Green was upstairs. Whoever she was, the woman stood for Green, whom he was not to see this time. Well, you silly bastard, he said to himself, so you think you found him. So what? Maybe you really did find him—what of it? But it was important that there was a real Mr. Green whom they could not keep him from reaching because he seemed to come as an emissary from hostile appearances. And though the self-ridicule was slow to diminish, and his face still blazed with it, he had, nevertheless, a feeling of elation, too. "For after all," he said, "he *could* be found!"

John Cheever

John Cheever (1912–   ) was born in Quincy, Massachusetts, attended Thayer Academy, his only formal education, and published his first short story at the age of sixteen. Since then, his more than one hundred stories and three novels have earned him two Guggenheim fellowships. He has been a major contributor to several magazines, notably The New Yorker, *and his novel* The Wapshot Chronicle *(1957) was a best-seller. His most recent novel is* Bullet Park *(1969). Cheever's short fiction has focused on the lives of sophisticated city-dwellers or suburbanites and their failure, despite worldly success, to find emotional satisfaction in a world that exalts material values.* *(See p. 69 of Introduction.)*

THE ENORMOUS RADIO

Jim and Irene Westcott were the kind of people who seem to strike that satisfactory average of income, endeavor, and respectability that is reached by the statistical reports in college alumni bulletins. They were the parents of two young children, they had been married nine years, they lived on the twelfth floor of an apartment house near Sutton Place, they went to the theatre on an average of 10.3 times a year, and they hoped someday to live in Westchester. Irene Westcott was a pleasant, rather plain girl with soft brown hair and a wide, fine forehead upon which nothing at all had been written, and in the cold weather she wore a coat of fitch skins dyed to resemble mink. You could not say that Jim Westcott looked younger than he was, but you could at least say of him that he seemed to feel younger. He wore his graying hair cut very short, he dressed in the kind of clothes his class had worn at Andover, and his manner was earnest, vehement, and intentionally naïve. The Westcotts differed from their friends, their classmates, and their neighbors only in an interest they shared in serious music. They went to a great many concerts—although they seldom mentioned this to anyone—and they spent a good deal of time listening to music on the radio.

Their radio was an old instrument, sensitive, unpredictable, and beyond repair. Neither of them understood the mechanics of radio—or of any of the other appliances that surrounded them—and when the instrument faltered, Jim would strike the side of the cabinet with his hand. This sometimes helped. One Sunday afternoon, in the middle of a Schubert quartet, the music faded away altogether. Jim struck the cabinet repeatedly, but there was no response; the Schubert was lost to them forever. He promised to buy Irene a new radio, and on Monday when he came home from work he told her that he had got one. He refused to describe it, and said it would be a surprise for her when it came.

The radio was delivered at the kitchen door the following afternoon, and with the assistance of her maid and the handyman Irene uncrated it and brought it into the living room. She was struck at once with the physical ugliness of the large gumwood cabinet. Irene was proud of her living room, she had chosen its furnishings and colors as carefully as she chose her clothes, and now it seemed to her that the new radio stood among her intimate possessions like an aggressive intruder. She was confounded by the number of dials and switches on the instrument panel, and she studied them thoroughly before she put the plug into a wall socket and turned the radio on. The dials flooded with a malevolent green light, and in the distance she heard the music of a piano quintet. The quintet was in the distance for only an instant; it bore down upon her with a speed greater than light and filled the apartment with the noise of music amplified so mightily that it knocked a china ornament from a table to the floor. She rushed to the instrument and reduced the volume. The violent forces that were snared in the ugly gumwood cabinet made her uneasy. Her children came home from school then, and she took them to the Park. It was not until later in the afternoon that she was able to return to the radio.

The maid had given the children their suppers and was supervising their baths when Irene turned on the radio, reduced the volume, and sat down to listen to a Mozart quintet that she knew and enjoyed. The music came through clearly. The new instrument had a much purer tone, she thought, than the old one. She decided that tone was most important and that she could conceal the cabinet behind a sofa. But as soon as she had made her peace with the radio, the interference began. A crackling sound like the noise of a burning powder fuse began to accompany the singing of the strings. Beyond the music, there was a rustling that reminded Irene unpleasantly of the sea, and as the quintet progressed, these noises were joined by many others. She tried all the dials and switches but nothing dimmed the interference, and she sat down, disappointed and bewildered, and tried to trace the flight of the melody. The elevator shaft in her building ran beside the living-room wall, and it was the noise of the elevator that gave her a clue to the character of the static. The rattling of the elevator cables and the opening and closing of the elevator doors were reproduced in her loudspeaker, and, realizing that the radio was sensitive to electrical currents of all sorts, she began to discern through the Mozart the ringing of telephone bells, the dialing of phones, and the lamentation of a vacuum cleaner. By listening more carefully, she was able to distinguish doorbells, elevator bells, electric razors, and Waring mixers, whose sounds had been picked up from the apartments that surrounded hers and transmitted through her loudspeaker. The powerful and ugly instrument, with its mistaken sensitivity to discord, was more than she could hope to master, so she turned the thing off and went into the nursery to see her children.

When Jim Westcott came home that night, he went to the radio confidently and worked the controls. He had the same sort of experience Irene had had. A man was speaking on the station Jim had chosen, and his voice swung instantly from the distance into a force so powerful that it shook the apartment. Jim turned the volume control and reduced the voice. Then, a minute or two later, the interference began. The ringing of telephones and doorbells set in, joined by the rasp of the elevator doors and the whir of cooking appliances. The character of the noise had changed since Irene had tried the radio earlier; the last of the electric razors was being unplugged, the vacuum cleaners had all been returned to their closets, and the static reflected that change in pace that overtakes the city after the sun goes down. He fiddled with the knobs but couldn't get rid of the noises, so he turned the radio off and told Irene that in the morning he'd call the people who had sold it to him and give them hell.

The following afternoon, when Irene returned to the apartment from a luncheon date, the maid told her that a man had come and fixed the radio. Irene went into the living room before she took off her hat or her furs and tried the instrument. From the loudspeaker came a recording of the "Missouri Waltz." It reminded her of the thin, scratchy music from an old-fashioned phonograph that she sometimes heard across the lake where she spent her summers. She waited until the waltz had finished, expecting an explanation of the recording, but there was none. The music was followed by silence, and then the plaintive and scratchy record was repeated. She turned the dial and got a satisfactory burst of Caucasian music—the thump of bare feet in the dust and the rattle of coin jewelry—but in the background she could hear the ringing of bells and a confusion of voices. Her children came home from school then, and she turned off the radio and went to the nursery.

When Jim came home that night, he was tired, and he took a bath and changed his clothes. Then he joined Irene in the living room. He had just turned on the radio when the maid announced dinner, so he left it on, and he and Irene went to the table.

Jim was too tired to make even a pretense of sociability, and there was nothing about the dinner to hold Irene's interest, so her attention wandered from the food to the deposits of silver polish on the candlesticks and from there to the music in the other room. She listened for a few moments to a Chopin prelude and then was surprised to hear a man's voice break in. "For Christ's sake, Kathy," he said, "do you always have to play the piano when I get home?" The music stopped abruptly. "It's the only chance I have," a woman said. "I'm at the office all day." "So am I," the man said. He added something obscene about an upright piano, and slammed a door. The passionate and melancholy music began again.

"Did you hear that?" Irene asked.

"What?" Jim was eating his dessert.

"The radio. A man said something while the music was still going on—something dirty."

"It's probably a play."

"I don't think it *is* a play," Irene said.

They left the table and took their coffee into the living room. Irene asked Jim to try another station. He turned the knob. "Have you seen my garters?" a man asked. "Button me up," a woman said. "Have you seen my garters?" the man said again. "Just button me up and I'll find your garters," the woman said. Jim shifted to another station. "I wish you wouldn't leave apple cores in the ashtrays," a man said. "I hate the smell."

"This is strange," Jim said.

"Isn't it?" Irene said.

Jim turned the knob again. " 'On the coast of Coromandel where the early pumpkins blow,' " a woman with a pronounced English accent said, " 'in the middle of the woods lived the Yonghy-Bonghy-Bò. Two old chairs, and half a candle, one old jug without a handle . . .' "

"My God!" Irene cried. "That's the Sweeneys' nurse."

" 'These were all his worldly goods,' " the British voice continued.

"Turn that thing off," Irene said. "Maybe they can hear *us*." Jim switched the radio off. "That was Miss Armstrong, the Sweeneys' nurse," Irene said. "She must be reading to the little girl. They live in 17-B. I've talked with Miss Armstrong in the Park. I know her voice very well. We must be getting other people's apartments."

"That's impossible," Jim said.

"Well, that was the Sweeneys' nurse," Irene said hotly. "I know her voice. I know it very well. I'm wondering if they can hear us."

Jim turned the switch. First from a distance and then nearer, nearer, as if borne on the wind, came the pure accents of the Sweeneys' nurse again: " '*Lady Jingly! Lady Jingly!*' " she said, " '*Sitting where the pumpkins blow, will you come and be my wife,* said the Yonghy-Bonghy-Bò . . .' "

Jim went over to the radio and said "Hello" loudly into the speaker.

" '*I am tired of living singly,*' " the nurse went on, " '*on this coast so wild and shingly, I'm a-weary of my life; if you'll come and be my wife, quite serene would be my life . . .*' "

"I guess she can't hear us," Irene said. "Try something else."

Jim turned to another station, and the living room was filled with the uproar of a cocktail party that had overshot its mark. Someone was playing the piano and singing the Whiffenpoof Song, and the voices that surrounded the piano were vehement and happy. "Eat some more sandwiches," a woman shrieked. There were screams of laughter and a dish of some sort crashed to the floor.

"Those must be the Fullers, in 11-E," Irene said. "I knew they were giving a party this afternoon. I saw her in the liquor store. Isn't this too divine? Try something else. See if you can get those people in 18-C."

The Westcotts overheard that evening a monologue on salmon fishing in Canada, a bridge game, running comments on home movies of what had apparently been a fortnight at Sea Island, and a bitter family quarrel about an overdraft at the bank. They turned off their radio at midnight and went to bed, weak with laughter. Sometime in the night, their son began to call for a glass of water and Irene got one and took it to his room. It was very early. All the lights in the neighborhood were extinguished, and from the boy's window she could see the empty street. She went into the living room and tried the radio. There was some faint coughing, a moan, and then a man spoke. "Are you all right, darling?" he asked. "Yes," a woman said wearily. "Yes, I'm all right, I guess," and then she added with great feeling, "but, you know, Charlie, I don't feel like myself any more. Sometimes there are about fifteen or twenty minutes in the week when I feel like myself. I don't like to go to another doctor, because the doctor's bills are so awful already, but I just don't feel like myself, Charlie. I just never feel like myself." They were not young, Irene thought. She guessed from the timbre of their voices that they were middle-aged. The restrained melancholy of the dialogue and the draft from the bedroom window made her shiver, and she went back to bed.

The following morning, Irene cooked breakfast for the family—the maid didn't come up from her room in the basement until ten—braided her daughter's hair, and waited at the door until her children and her husband had been carried away in the elevator. Then she went into the living room and tried the radio. "I don't want to go to school," a child screamed. "I hate school. I won't go to school. I hate school." "You will go to school," an enraged woman said. "We paid eight hundred dollars to get you into that school and you'll go if it kills you." The next number on the dial produced the worn record of the "Missouri Waltz." Irene shifted the control and invaded the privacy of several breakfast tables. She overheard demonstrations of indigestion, carnal love, abysmal vanity, faith, and despair. Irene's life was nearly as simple and sheltered as it appeared to be, and the forthright and sometimes brutal language that came from the loudspeaker that morning astonished and troubled her. She continued to listen until her maid came in. Then she turned off the radio quickly, since this insight, she realized, was a furtive one.

Irene had a luncheon date with a friend that day, and she left her apartment at a little after twelve. There were a number of women in the elevator when it stopped at her floor. She stared at their handsome and impassive faces, their furs, and the cloth flowers in their hats. Which one of them had been to Sea Island, she wondered. Which one had overdrawn her bank account? The elevator stopped at the tenth floor and a woman with a pair of Skye terriers joined them. Her hair was rigged high on her head and she wore a mink cape. She was humming the "Missouri Waltz."

Irene had two Martinis at lunch, and she looked searchingly at her friend and wondered what her secrets were. They had intended to go shopping after lunch, but Irene excused herself and went home. She told the maid that she was not to be disturbed; then she went into the living room, closed the doors, and switched on the radio. She heard, in the course of the afternoon, the halting conversation of a woman entertaining her aunt, the hysterical conclusion of a luncheon party, and a hostess briefing her maid about some cocktail guests. "Don't give the best Scotch to anyone who hasn't white hair," the hostess said. "See if you can get rid of that liver paste before you pass those hot things, and could you lend me five dollars? I want to tip the elevator man."

As the afternoon waned, the conversations increased in intensity. From where Irene sat, she could see the open sky above the East River. There were hundreds of clouds in the sky, as though the south wind had broken the winter into pieces and were blowing it north, and on her radio she could hear the arrival of cocktail guests and the return of children and businessmen from their schools and offices. "I found a good-sized diamond on the bathroom floor this morning," a woman said. "It must have fallen out of that bracelet Mrs. Dunston was wearing last night." "We'll sell it," a man said. "Take it down to the jeweller on Madison Avenue and sell it. Mrs. Dunston won't know the difference, and we could use a couple of hundred bucks . . ." " 'Oranges and lemons, say the bells of St. Clement's,' " the Sweeneys' nurse sang. " 'Half-pence and farthings, say the bells of St. Martin's. When will you pay me? say the bells at old Bailey . . .' " "It's not a hat," a woman cried, and at her back roared a cocktail party. "It's not a hat, it's a love affair. That's what Walter Florell said. He said it's not a hat, it's a love affair," and then, in a lower voice, the same woman added, "Talk to somebody, for Christ's sake, honey, talk to somebody. If she catches you standing here not talking to anybody, she'll take us off her invitation list, and I love these parties."

The Westcotts were going out for dinner that night, and when Jim came home, Irene was dressing. She seemed sad and vague, and he brought her a drink. They were dining with friends in the neighborhood, and they walked to where they were going. The sky was broad and filled with light. It was one of those splendid spring evenings that excite memory and desire, and the air that touched their hands and faces felt very soft. A Salvation Army band was on the corner playing "Jesus Is Sweeter." Irene drew on her husband's arm and held him there for a minute, to hear the music. "They're really such nice people, aren't they?" she said. "They have such nice faces. Actually, they're so much nicer than a lot of the people we know." She took a bill from her purse and walked over and dropped it into the tambourine. There was in her face, when she returned to her husband, a look of radiant melancholy that he was not familiar with. And her conduct at the dinner party that night seeemed strange to him, too. She interrupted her hostess rudely and stared at the people across the table from her with an intensity for which she would have punished her children.

It was still mild when they walked home from the party, and Irene looked up at the spring stars. " 'How far that little candle throws its beams,' " she exclaimed. " 'So shines a good deed in a naughty world.' " She waited that night until Jim had fallen asleep, and then went into the living room and turned on the radio.

Jim came home at about six the next night. Emma, the maid, let him in, and he had taken off his hat and was taking off his coat when Irene ran into the hall. Her face was shining with tears and her hair was disordered. "Go up to 16-C, Jim!" she screamed. "Don't take off your coat. Go up to 16-C. Mr. Osborn's beating his wife. They've been quarrelling since four o'clock, and now he's hitting her. Go up there and stop him."

From the radio in the living room, Jim heard screams, obscenities, and thuds. "You know you don't have to listen to this sort of thing," he said. He strode into the living room and turned the switch. "It's indecent," he said. "It's like looking in windows. You know you don't have to listen to this sort of thing. You can turn it off."

"Oh, it's so horrible, it's so dreadful," Irene was sobbing. "I've been listening all day, and it's so depressing."

"Well, if it's so depressing, why do you listen to it? I bought this damned radio to give you some pleasure," he said. "I paid a great deal of money for it. I thought it might make you happy. I wanted to make you happy."

"Don't, don't, don't, don't quarrel with me," she moaned, and laid her head on his shoulder. "All the others have been quarrelling all day. Everybody's been quarrelling. They're all worried about money. Mrs. Hutchinson's mother is dying of cancer in Florida and they don't have enough money to send her to the Mayo Clinic. At least, Mr. Hutchinson says they don't have enough money. And some woman in this building is having an affair with the handyman—with that hideous handyman. It's too disgusting. And Mrs. Melville has heart trouble and Mr. Hendricks is going to lose his job in April and Mrs. Hendricks is horrid about the whole thing and that girl who plays the 'Missouri Waltz' is a whore, a common whore, and the elevator man has tuberculosis and Mr. Osborn has been beating Mrs. Osborn." She wailed, she trembled with grief and checked the stream of tears down her face with the heel of her palm.

"Well, why do you have to listen?" Jim asked again. "Why do you have to listen to this stuff if it makes you so miserable?"

"Oh, don't, don't, don't," she cried. "Life is too terrible, too sordid and awful. But we've never been like that, have we, darling? Have we? I mean we've always been good and decent and loving to one another, haven't we? And we have two children, two beautiful children. Our lives aren't sordid, are they, darling? Are they?" She flung her arms around his neck and drew his face down to hers. "We're happy, aren't we, darling? We are happy, aren't we?"

"Of course we're happy," he said tiredly. He began to surrender his resentment. "Of course we're happy. I'll have that damned radio fixed or taken away tomorrow." He stroked her soft hair. "My poor girl," he said.

"You love me, don't you?" she asked. "And we're not hypercritical or worried about money or dishonest, are we?"

"No, darling," he said.

A man came in the morning and fixed the radio. Irene turned it on cautiously and was happy to hear a California-wine commercial and a recording of Beethoven's Ninth Symphony, including Schiller's "Ode to Joy." She kept the radio on all day and nothing untoward came from the speaker.

A Spanish suite was being played when Jim came home. "Is everything all right?" he asked. His face was pale, she thought. They had some cocktails and went in to dinner to the "Anvil Chorus" from "Il Trovatore." This was followed by Debussy's "La Mer."

"I paid the bill for the radio today," Jim said. "It cost four hundred dollars. I hope you'll get some enjoyment out of it."

"Oh, I'm sure I will," Irene said.

"Four hundred dollars is a good deal more than I can afford," he went on. "I wanted to get something that you'd enjoy. It's the last extravagance we'll be able to indulge in this year. I see that you haven't paid your clothing bills yet. I saw them on your dressing table." He looked directly at her. "Why did you tell me you'd paid them? Why did you lie to me?"

"I just didn't want you to worry, Jim," she said. She drank some water. "I'll be able to pay my bills out of this month's allowance. There were the slipcovers last month, and that party."

"You've got to learn to handle the money I give you a little more intelligently, Irene," he said. "You've got to understand that we won't have as much money this year as we had last. I had a very sobering talk with Mitchell today. No one is buying anything. We're spending all our time promoting new issues, and you know how long that takes. I'm not getting any younger, you know. I'm thirty-seven. My hair will be gray next year. I haven't done as well as I'd hoped to do. And I don't suppose things will get any better."

"Yes, dear," she said.

"We've got to start cutting down," Jim said. "We've got to think of the children. To be perfectly frank with you, I worry about money a great deal. I'm not at all sure of the future. No one is. If anything should happen to me, there's the insurance, but that wouldn't go very far today. I've worked awfully hard to give you and the children a comfortable life," he said bitterly. "I don't like to see all of my energies, all of my youth, wasted in fur coats and radios and slipcovers and—"

"Please, Jim," she said. "Please. They'll hear us."

"*Who'll hear us?* Emma can't hear us."

"The radio."

"Oh, I'm sick!" he shouted. "I'm sick to death of your apprehensiveness. The radio can't hear us. Nobody can hear us. And what if they can hear us? Who cares?"

Irene got up from the table and went into the living room. Jim went to the door and shouted at her from there. "Why are you so Christly all of a sudden? What's turned you overnight into a convent girl? You stole your mother's jewelry before they probated her will. You never gave your sister a cent of that money that was intended for her—not even when she needed it. You made Grace Howland's life miserable, and where was all your piety and your virtue when you went to that abortionist? I'll never forget how cool you were. You packed your bag and went off to have that child murdered as if you were going to Nassau. If you'd had any reasons, if you'd had any good reasons—"

Irene stood for a minute before the hideous cabinet, disgraced and sickened, but she held her hand on the switch before she extinguished the music and the voices, hoping that the instrument might speak to her kindly, that she might hear the Sweeneys' nurse. Jim continued to shout at her from the door. The voice on the radio was suave and noncommittal. "An early-morning railroad disaster in Tokyo," the loudspeaker said, "killed twenty-nine people. A fire in a Catholic hospital near Buffalo for the care of blind children was extinguished early this morning by nuns. The temperature is forty-seven. The humidity is eighty-nine."

Elizabeth Taylor

Elizabeth Taylor (1912–   ) was born in Berkshire, England, and educated at an offspring institution of the Abbey School which Jane Austen briefly attended in the late 18th century. She was over thirty when her novels first began to be published after World War II. Her short stories have appeared mostly in The New Yorker, Harper's Bazaar, *and* Harper's, *and, like her novels, reveal a penetrating, sympathetic understanding of human nature in the best English tradition of the "novels of sensibility." Although her style reflects meticulous craftsmanship, it has sometimes been criticized as "too quiet and unemphatic." Her works include* A Wreath of Roses *(1950),* In a Summer Season *(1961),* The Sleeping Beauty *(1953), and* The Soul of Kindness *(1964).* *(See page 83 of Introduction.)*

SPRY OLD CHARACTER

The Home for the Blind absorbed the surplus of that rural charity so much more pleasant to give than to receive—the cakes left over from the Women's Institute party, and concerts which could no longer tempt appetites more than satisfied by homely monologues and the postmistress's zither. Fruit and vegetables from the Harvest Festival seemed not richer from their blessing but vitiated by being too much arranged, too much stared at. The bread in the shape of a corn sheaf tasted of incense, and, with its mainly visual appeal, was wasted on the blind.

No week went by without some dispiriting jollity being forced upon them. This week it was a choir of schoolgirls singing "Orpheus with His Lute." Which drives me finally up the wall, Harry decided, and clapped his great horny hands together at the end with relief. "Your *nails*, Harry!" Matron had said earlier, as if he were a child; and, like a child, he winced each time the scissors touched him. "You've been biting them again. I shall have to get very cross with you." He imagined her irritating smile: false teeth like china, no doubt; thin lips. He had been on the wrong side of her from the start; had asked her to read out to him the runners at Newmarket. "You old terror! I shall do nothing of the kind. I'm not having that sort of thing here." He was helpless. Reading by touch he regarded as a miracle and beyond him. He had steered clear of books when he could see, and they held even less attraction now that tedious lessons as well as indifference stood in the way; and the *Sporting Life* was not set in Braille, he soon discovered.

His request had scandalized, for, he had soon decided, only the virtuous lose their sight—perhaps as a further test of their saintly patience. None of his friends in London— the Boys—had ever known such a calamity, and rebelliousness, as if at some clerical error, hardened his heart. Set down in this institution after his sister's death, he was a fish out of water. I'm just not the type, he thought, over and over again.

What Harry called the rural setup—the great house in its park, the village, the surrounding countryside—was visually unimaginable to him. His nearest experience of it was Hampstead Heath or the view (ignored) from Goodwood Race Course. Country to him was negative—simply a place where there was not a town. The large rooms of the Home unnerved him. In his sister's parlor he could not go far wrong, edging round the table which took up most of the space; and the heat from the fire, the clock ticking on the dresser, had given him his bearings. After she died he was helpless. The Home had appealed to him as a wonderful alternative to his own picture of himself out in the street with a tray of matches and a card pinned to his breast with some words such as "On My Beam Ends" or, simply, "Blind."

"You'll have the company of others like you," his neighbors had told him. This was not so. He found himself in a society whose existence he had never, in his old egotism, contemplated, and whose ways soon lowered his vitality. He had nothing in common with these faded seamstresses, the prophet-like lay preacher, an old piano tuner who believed he was the reincarnation of Beethoven—with elderly people who had lived more than half a dim lifetime in dark drapers' shops in country towns. They almost might not have been blind, even, for they found their way about the house, its grounds, the village, with pride and confidence. Indoors they bickered about the wireless—for the ladies liked a nice domestic play and thought some of the variety programs "suggestive." The racing results were always switched to something different hastily, before they could contaminate the air.

"I once went to a race meeting," Miss Arbuthnot admitted. She had been a governess in Russia in the czarist days and had taken tea with Rasputin. Now she overrode her companions with her past grandeur. No one knew, perhaps she least of all, what bizarre experience might be related next. "It was at Ascot after the last war. I mean the one before that. I went as chaperon to Lady Allegra Faringdon and one of the Ponsonby cousins."

"Did you see the King and Queen drive down the course?" asked the sycophantic Mrs. Hussey. "What a picture that must be!"

"It is quite a pageant of English life. The cream of the cream, as one might say. But dear, dear me! What a tiring way to spend a day! My poor feet! I wore some pale grey buckskin shoes, and how they *drew!* I daresay they would look very old-fashioned nowadays, but then they were quite *à la.*" She gave her silvery, trilling laugh. "Well, I have been once. I know what it is like, and I know that I give the preference to Henley, even if the crowd there is not so brilliant. Oh, yes, give me Henley any day."

No one would be likely to give her any such thing ever again, but this occurred only to Harry.

"Did you have any luck—with the horses, I mean?" he asked, breaking his sullen silence with his coarse, breathy voice. Exasperation and nostalgia forced him to speak, although to do so invited ridicule. He was driven to broach the subject as lovers are often driven to mention the beloved's name, even in casual conversation with unworthy people.

"Do you mean betting?"

"What else do you go for?" he asked huffily.

"Well, certainly not for that, I hope. For the spectacle, the occasion—a brilliant opening to the London season."

No one thought—their indignation was so centered upon Harry—that she spoke less as a governess than as a duchess. She coloured their lives with her extravagances, whereas Harry only underlined their plight; stumbling, cursing, spilling food, he had brought the word "blindness" into their midst and was a threat to their courage.

Cantankerous old virgin, he thought. Trying to come it over me. A spinster to him was a figure of fun, but now he, not she, sat humble and grumpy and rejected.

The evening of the concert Miss Arbuthnot, with the advantage of her cultured life behind her ("Ah! Chaliapin in *Boris!* After that, one is never quite the same person again"), sat in the front row and led and tempered the applause. A humorous song in country dialect wound up the evening, and her fluting laugh gave the cue for broad-minded appreciation. Then chairs scraped back and talk broke out. Harry tapped his way to a corner and sat there alone.

The girls, told to mingle, to bring their sunshine into these dark lives, began nervously to hand round buns, unsure of how far the blind could help themselves. They were desperately tactful. ("I made the most frightful *faux pas,*" they would chatter in the bus going home. "Dropped the most appalling brick. Wasn't it all depressing? Poor old thing! But it doesn't bear thinking of, of course.")

One girl obediently came towards Harry. "Would you like a cake?"

"That's very kind of you, missie."

She held the plate out awkwardly, but he made no movement towards it.

"Shall I—May I give you one?"

"I should maybe knock them all on the floor if I start feeling about," he said gloomily.

She put a cake into his hand, and as the crumbs began to fall on his waistcoat and knees she looked away, fearing that he might guess the direction of her glance, for she had been told that the blind develop the other senses to an uncanny degree.

Her young voice was a pleasure to him. He was growing used to voices either elderly or condescending. Hoping to detain her a little longer, he said, "You all sang very nice indeed."

"I'm so glad you enjoyed it."

He thought: I'd only have run a mile from it, given half a chance.

"I'm fond of a nice voice," he said. "My mother was a singer."

"Oh, really?" She had not intended to sound so incredulous, but her affectation of brightness had grown out of hand.

"She was a big figure on the halls—in more ways than just the one. A fine great bust and thighs she had, but small feet. Collins' Music Hall and the Met. I daresay you heard of them?"

"I can't really say I have."

"She had her name on the bills—Lottie Throstle. That was her stage name, and a funny, old-fashioned name it must sound nowadays, but you used to have to have something out of the usual run. Louie Breakspear her real name was. I expect you've heard your mum and dad speak of Lottie Throstle."

"I can't remember—"

"She was a good old sort." (She'd have had you taped, he thought. I can hear her now: "Ay can't say, Ay'm sure.") "'Slip Round the Corner, Charlie,' that was her song. Did you ever hear that one?" ("No, Ay can't say Ay hev," he answered for her. No, I thought not. Orpheus and his sodding lute's more your ticket.)

"No, I haven't." She glanced desperately about her.

"What colour dress you got on, miss?"

"White."

"Well, don't be shy! Nothing wrong with a white dress at your age. When you're fat and forty I should advise thinking twice about it. You all got white dresses on?"

"Yes."

Must look like the Virgins' Outing, he thought. What a sight! Never came my way, of course, before now. No one ever served up twenty-five virgins in white to me in those days. Showing common sense on their part, no doubt.

His rough hand groped forward and rasped against her silk frock. "That's nice material! I like nice material. My sister Lily who died was a dressmaker." The girl, rigid, turned her head sharply aside. He smelled the sudden sweat of fear and embarrassment on her skin and drew back his hand.

"Now, young lady, we can't let you monopolize Mr. Breakspear," Matron said, coming swiftly across the room. "Here's Miss Wilcox to have a chat with you, Harry. Miss Wilcox is the choir mistress. She brings the girls here every year to give us this wonderful experience. You know, Miss Wilcox, Harry is quite the naughtiest of all my old darlings. He thinks we treat him so badly. Oh, yes, you do, Harry. You grumble from morning till night. And so lazy! Such a lovely basket he was going to make, but he lost all interest in it in next to no time."

Sullenly he sat beside Miss Wilcox. When coffee was brought to him, he spilled it purposely. He had no pride in overcoming difficulties, as the others had. His waistcoat was evidence of this. He was angry that Matron had mentioned his basketwork, for a very deep shame had overtaken him when they tried to teach him such a craft. He saw a picture of his humiliation, as if through his friends' eyes—the poor old codger, broken, helpless, back to the bottom class at school. "You want to be independent," the teacher had said, seeing him slumped there, idle with misery. He thought they did not understand the meaning of the word.

"You haven't been here long?" Miss Wilcox inquired kindly.

"No, only since my sister Lily died. I went to live along with her when I lost my wife. I've been a widower nineteen years now. She was a good old sort, my wife."

"I'm sure she was."

Why's she so sure, he wondered, when she never as much as clapped eyes on her? She could have been a terrible old tartar for all she knows.

But he liked to talk and none of the others would ever listen to him. He engaged Miss Wilcox, determined to prevent her escaping. "I lost my sight three years ago, on account of a kick I had on the head from a horse. I used to be a horse dealer at one time." Then he remembered that no one spoke about being blind. This apparently trivial matter was never discussed.

"How very interesting!"

"I made a packet of money in those days. At one time I was a driver on the old horse buses. You could see those animals dragging up Highgate

Hill with their noses on the ground nearly. I bought an old mare off of them for a couple of quid, and turned her out on a bit of grass I used to rent. Time I'd fed her up and got her coat nice with dandelion leaves and clover, I sold her for twenty pounds. Everything I touched went right for me in those days. She was the one who kicked me on the head. Francie, we called her. I always wished I could tell the wife what the doctors said. If I'd have said to her, 'You know, Florrie, what they hold Francie did to me all those years ago?' she would never have believed me. But that's what they reckoned. Delayed action they reckoned it was."

"Extraordinary!" Miss Wilcox murmured.

"Now, you old chatterbox!" Matron said. "We're going to sing 'Jerusalem' all together before the girls go home. And none of your nonsense, Harry. He's such an old rascal about hymns, Miss Wilcox."

Once he had refused to join in, believing that hymn-singing was a matter of personal choice, and not *his* choice. Now he knew that the blind are always religious, as they are cheerful, industrious, and independent. He no longer argued but stood up clumsily, feet apart, hands clasped over his paunch, and moved his lips feebly until the music stopped.

In the first weeks of his blindness he had suffered attacks of hysteria as wave upon wave of terror and frustration swept across him. "Your language!" his sister would say, her hand checking the wheel of the sewing machine. "Why don't we go round to the Lion for a beer?" She would button up his overcoat for him, saying, "I can't bear to see you fidgeting with your clothes." He would put on his old bowler hat, and, arm in arm, they would go along the street. "Good evening, Mrs. Simpson. That was Mrs. Simpson went by, Harry." She used no tact or Montessori methods on him. In the pub she would say, "Mind out, you! Let Harry sit down. How would *you* like to be blind?" They were all glad to see him. They read out the winners and prices for him. He knew the scene so well that he had no need to look at it, and the sensation of panic would be eased from him.

Now a deeper despair showed him daily the real tragedy of his blindness. This orderly, aseptic world was not only new to him but beyond his imagining. Food and talk had lost their richness. Central heating provided no warmth; he crouched over radiators with his hands spread over the pipes, his head aching with the dryness of the air. No one buttoned his coat for him. He tapped his way round with his stick, often hitting out viciously and swearing. "There are ladies present," he was told, and, indeed, this was so. They lowered the atmosphere with little jealousies and edged remarks, and irritated with their arguments about birds ("I could not mistake a chaffinch's song, Mrs. Hussey, being country bred and born") or about royalty ("But both Lady Mary *and* Lady May Cambridge were bridesmaids to the Duchess of York"). They always remembered as if it were yesterday, although begging pardon for contradicting. Morale was very high, as it so often is in a community where tragedy is present. Harry was reminded of the blitz, and Cockney resilience and understatement. Although a Cockney himself, he detested understatement. Some Irish strain in him allowed his mind to dwell on the mournful, to spread alarm and despondency, and to envisage with clarity the possibilities of defeat. When he confessed to fear, the Boys had relished the joke. "That'll be the day!" they had said. He had found the burden of their morale very tiring. The war's bad enough in itself, he had thought; as now he thought, Surely it's bad enough being blind, when he was expected to sing hymns and alter all his ways as well.

After the concert, his luck changed; at first, though, it seemed to deteriorate. The still, moist winter weather drew the other inmates out on walks about the village. Only Miss Arbuthnot remained indoors with a slight cold. In the end, the sense of nervousness and irritation she induced in Harry drove him out too. He wandered alone, a little scared, down the drive and out onto the highroad. He followed the brick wall along and turned with it into a narrow lane with a soft surface.

The hedges dripped with moisture, although it was not raining. All about that neighbourhood there was a resinous scent in the air, which was pronounced healthy by Matron, who snuffed it up enthusiastically, as if she were a war horse smelling battle. Harry's tread was now muffled by pine needles, and a fir cone dropped on his shoulder, startling him wretchedly. Every sound in the hedgerow unnerved him; he imagined small bright-eyed animals watching his progress. From not following the curve of the hedge sharply enough, he ran his face against wet hawthorn twigs. He felt giddiness, as if he were wandering in a circle. Bad enough being out by myself in the country, let alone being blind too, he thought as he stumbled in a rut.

He could imagine Matron when he returned—if he returned. "Why, Harry, you naughty old thing, going off like that! Why didn't you go with Mr. Thomas, who knows the neighbourhood so well and could have told you the names of all the birds you heard, and made it nice and interesting!"

The only birds he, Harry, could recognize—and he did not wish to recognize any—were jackdaws (and they were really rooks), who seemed to congregate above him through his walk, wheeling and cawing in an offensive manner; perhaps disputing over him, he thought morbidly, staking their claims before he dropped.

Then suddenly he lost hedge and ditch. He was treading on turf, and the air had widened. He felt a great space about him and the wind blowing, as if he were on a sea cliff, which he knew he could not be in Oxfordshire. With a sense of being confronted by an immense drop—a blind man's vertigo—he dared not take a pace forward but stood swaying a little, near to tears.

He heard rough breathing, and a large dog jumped upon him. In terror, he thrashed about with his stick, the tears now pouring from his eyes, which had no other function.

He heard a woman's voice calling and the squelch of the wet turf as she ran towards him across what he had imagined to be the middle of the air. She beat the dog away and took Harry's arm. "You all right, dear? He's plastered you up properly, but it'll brush off when it's dry."

"I don't know where I am," Harry said, fumbling for his handkerchief.

"It's the common where the bus stops." She pulled his handkerchief from his pocket and gave it to him. "That's our bus over there."

"You a conductress, then?"

"That's right, dear. You're from that Home, are you? It's on the route and we can give you a lift."

"I don't have any coppers on me."

"You needn't worry about that. Just take my arm and we're nearly there. It's a scandal the way they let you wander about."

"The others manage better nor I. I'm not one for the country. It always gives me the wind up."

At the gates of the Home she helped him down, saying, "Any time, dear. Only too pleased. Take care of yourself. Bye-bye!"

No one had noticed his absence, and he concealed his adventure. One of the daily cleaners, with whom he felt more confidence than with the resident staff, brushed his coat for him.

After this the lane that had held such terror was his escape route. The buses came every hour, and he would sometimes be waiting there or the drivers would see him stumbling across the common and would sound the horn in welcome. Sitting in the bus before it drew out, he could enjoy the only normal conversation of his day.

"A shilling each way Flighty Frances! That's not much for a man of your substance, Harry."

"It's just I fancy the name. I had an old mare of the name of Francie. Time was, no doubt, I'd have had a fiver on it. Now I'm left about as free of money as a toad of fleas."

He tried to roll his own cigarettes, but tore the paper and spilled the tobacco until the bus drivers learned to help him. In their company he opened out, became garrulous, waggish, his old manner returning. He came to know one driver from another and to call each by his name. Their camaraderie opened up to him garage gossip, feuds at the depot, a new language, a new life. His relationship with them was not one of equality, for they had too much to give and he nothing. This he sensed, and while taking their badinage and imagining their winks, he played up his part—the lowering role of a proper old character—and extracted what he could from it, even to the extent of hinting and scrounging. His fumblings with his cigarette-making became more piteous than was necessary.

"Oh, for goodness' sake, have a proper cigarette—messing about like that."

"That's all I got the lolly for, mate."

"Whose fault's that—if you've got to drink yourself silly every night?"

"I haven't had a pint since I came down here."

"Well, where's your money gone to? Wild living, I suppose. And women."

"Now, don't you start taking the mike out of me, Fred." He used their names a great deal; the first pride he had felt since his blindness was in distinguishing Fred from Syd or Lil from Marg. The women had more individuality to him, with wider variety of inflection and vocabulary and tone, and the different scents of their powder and their hair.

"Supposing Flighty Frances comes in, what are you going to do with your winnings, Harry? Take us all out for a beer?"

"I'll do that," he said. "I forget the taste of it myself. I could do with a nice brown. It's the price of it, though, and how to find my way back afterwards, and all them old codgers sitting round fanning theirselves each time I free a belch. Very offhand they can be with their ways."

"What do you do all day?"

The driver felt a curiosity about a life so different from his own, imagined a workhouse with old people groping about, arms extended, as if playing blindman's buff.

"We have a nice listen to the wireless set—a lot of music which I never liked the sound of anyway, and plays about sets of people carrying on as if they need their backside kicked. You never met a breed of people like these customers on the wireless; what they get into a rare consternation about is nobody's business. Then we might have some old Army gent give a talk about abroad and the rum ways they get into over there, but personally I've got my own troubles, so I lie back and get in a bit of shut-eye. One night we had a wagonload of virgins up there singing hymns."

He played to the gallery, which repaid him with cigarettes and bonhomie. His repartee became so strained that sometimes he almost waited to hear Florrie, his late wife, say sharply, "That's enough now, Harry. It's about time we heard something from someone else." He had always talked too much; was a bad listener—almost a non-listener, for he simply waited without patience for others to stop talking so that he might cap their story. Well, hurry up, hurry up, he would think. Get a move on with it, man. I got something to say myself on those lines. If you go drivelling on much longer, chances are I'll forget it.

"No, what I'd do—say this horse comes in, bar the fact I'd only make about seven bob all told—but what I'd do is take the bus down to the fair on Saturday. I like a nice lively fair."

"What, and have a go on the coconut shies?"

"I wouldn't mind, Fred," he boasted.

"You can come along with me and Charlie, Saturday evening," Fred said, adding with an ungraciousness he did not intend, "Makes no odds to us."

"Well, I don't know," Harry said. "Have to see what's fixed up for Saturday. I'll let you know tomorrow."

"All right, Harry. We'll get one of the boys to pick you up at the gates Saturday after tea, and we can put you on the last bus along with all those coconuts you're going to knock down."

The bus was stopped at the gates for him. He lifted his white stick in farewell and then walked up the drive, slashing out at the rhododendron hedge and whistling shrilly. Now he was in for a spell of his old difficulty—currying favour. He would not have admitted to Fred that he could not come and go as he pleased, that for the rest of the day he must fawn on Matron and prepare his request.

This he overdid, as a child would, arousing suspicion and lowering himself in his own eyes. He praised the minced meat and went into ecstasies over the prunes and custard. His unctuous voice was a deep abasement to him and an insult to Matron's intelligence.

"My, that's what I call a meal, quite a prewar touch about it. Now say I have another go at that basketwork, ma'am?"

"What are you up to today, Harry?"

"Me?"

"Yes, you."

Later the wind drove gusts of fair music up the hill. Miss Arbuthnot complained, but Harry could not hear the music. Missing so much that the others heard was an added worry to him lately, for to lose hearing as well would finish him as a person. It would leave him at the mercy of his own thoughts, which had always bored him. His tongue did his thinking for him. Other people's talk struck words from him like a light from a match. His phrases were quick and ready-made and soon forgotten, but he feared a silence and they filled it.

Matron found him alone, after the basketmaking class was over. He was involved in a great tangle of withies. His enormous hands, ingrained with dirt, looked so ill-adapted to the task that Matron, stringent as she was about the difficulties of others, found them wretchedly pathetic. So few men of action came her way; the burly, the ham-handed, ended up in other backwaters, she supposed, with gout and dropsy and high blood pressure. She felt, like Harry, that he was not the type. He was certainly ill-matched to his present task of managing the intractable, and even dangerous, tangle of cane.

"When is your birthday, Harry?" she asked, for she was interested in astrology and quite surprised at how many Cancer subjects came her way.

"April the twenty-first. Why?"

"Taurus the Bull," she said.

He began to bristle indignantly, then remembered his purpose and bent his head humbly, a poor, broken bull with a lance in his neck. "You mean," some instinct led him to say, "I'm like a bull in a china shop?"

Her contrition was a miracle. He listened to her hurried explanations with a glow in his heart.

"I only thought you meant I was clumsy about the place," he said. "I don't seem to cotton on to half what the others say, and I keep spilling my dinner."

"But Harry—"

"I've had my sight longer than them, and it takes more getting used to doing without it," he went on, and might have been inspired. "When you've been lucky to have your eyes so long as me, it takes some settling to." *You've still got yours* hung in the air. He managed to insinuate the idea and seem innocent of the thought, but he had lost his innocence and was as cagey as a child. His late wife would have said, "All right, you can come off it now, Harry."

Matron said, "We only want to make you happy, you know. Though sometimes you're such an old reprobate!"

After that he had to endure the impatience of being coaxed to do what he desired, and coquetry was not in his line. He became unsure of himself and the trend of the conversation, and with a Cockney adroitness let the idea of the fair simmer in Matron's mind undisturbed.

Busy again with his basketwork, he let one of the osiers snap back and hit him across the face.

"I'm no spoilsport, Harry," she said.

This daunted him; in all his life he had found that sport was spoiled by those who claimed this to be their last intention. He awaited all the other phrases—"I should hate to be a wet blanket" and "Goodness knows I don't want to criticize."

In his agitation he took up the picking knife to cut an end of cane and cut into the pad of his thumb. At first he felt no pain, but the neatness with which the blade divided his flesh alarmed him. He missed his sight when he needed to feel pain. Blood crawling between his thumb and finger put him into a panic. He imagined the bone laid bare, and his head swam. Pain coming through slowly reassured him more than Matron could.

For the rest of the evening he sat alone in his corner by the radiator, and the steady throbbing of his bandaged thumb kept him company, mixed as it was in his mind—and, no doubt, in Matron's mind too—with the promise of the fair. "I should insist on their bringing you back," she had said. "There's the rough element to contend with on a Saturday night." In other years he had been—proudly—a large part of the rough element himself.

After supper, reminded by the distant sounds of the carrousels, Miss Arbuthnot too began to discuss the rough element—which in her experience was exaggerated beyond anything Harry had ever known. Spinster-like, she described a teeming, Hogarthian scene of pickpockets, drunkards, and what she called, contradictorily, "undesirable women." "Oh, once, I daresay, these fairs were very picturesque—the maypoles and the morris dancing. And so vividly I remember the colourful peasants I saw at the fair at Nijni Novgorod. Such beautiful embroidery. But now what is there left of such a life? So drearily commercial, as all our pleasures are."

She drove their inclinations into the corral; now no one cared to go to the fair except Harry, worldly-wise, crouched over his radiator, nursing his poor hand with his own inner vision still intact.

In the Home there was an aristocracy—never, from decency, mentioned—of those who had once, and even perhaps recently, seen, over those blind from birth. The aristocracy claimed no more than the privilege of kindness and of tact, and the feeling of superiority was tempered by the deftness and efficiency of those who had had longest to adapt themselves to being without sight. Miss Arbuthnot—blinded, Harry imagined, by her own needlework—was the eyes of them all, for she had great inventiveness and authority and could touch up a scene with the skill of an artist. Harry, finding her vision of the fair, the races, the saloon bar unacceptable, had nothing of his own to take its place—only the pig-headed reiteration, "It isn't like that."

"I used to like a roundabout when I was a girl," Mrs. Hussey said timidly.

"Well, there you have it!" said Miss Arbuthnot. "All we have salvaged of the picturesque. The last of a traditional art, in fact. For instance, the carved horses with their bright designs."

"It was going round I liked," Mrs. Hussey said.

With a tug, as of a flag unfurling, an old memory spread out across Harry's mind. He recalled himself as a boy, coming home from school with one of his friends, along the banks of a canal. It was growing dark. His child's eyes had recorded the scene, which his busy life had overlaid and preserved. Now, unexpectedly laid bare, it was more vivid than anything he had witnessed since. Sensually he evoked the magic of that time of day, with the earth about to heel over into darkness; the canal steaming faintly; cranes at a menacing angle across the sky. He and the other boy walked in single file on the muddy path, which was hoof-printed by barge horses. The tufted grass on each side was untidy and hoary with moisture; reeds, at the water's edge, lisped together. Now, in his mind, he followed this path with a painful intensity, fearing an interruption. Almost slyly he tracked down the boy he had been, who, exposed like a lens, had unconsciously taken the imprint of the moment and the place. Now, outside the scene, as if a third person, he walked behind the boys along the path; saw one, then the other, stoop and pick up a stone and skim it across the water. Without speaking, they climbed on the stacks of planks when they came to a timberyard. The air seemed to brace itself against distant thunder. The canal's surface wrinkled in a sudden breeze; then drops of rain spread rings upon it. The boys, trying the door of a long shed, found it unlocked and crept inside to shelter, wiping their wet hands down their trousers. Rain drove against the windows in a flurry, and the thunder came nearer. They stood close to each other just inside the door. The shapes which filled the shed, set out so neatly in rows, became recognizable after a while as carrousel horses, newly carved and as yet unpainted. Harry moved amongst them, ran his hand down their smooth backs, and breathed the smell of the wood. They were drawn up in ranks, pale and strange horses, awaiting their trappings and decorations and flowing tails.

The two boys spoke softly to each other, their voices muted—for the wood shavings and the sawdust, which lay everywhere like snow, had a muffling effect. Nervousness filled them. Harry forced himself to stare at the horses as if to hypnotize them, to check their rearing and bearing down, and became convinced of their hostility. Moving his eyes watchfully, he was always just too late to see a nostril quiver or a head turn, though feeling that this had happened.

The rain fell into the timberyard as if the sky had collapsed—drumming upon the roof of the shed and hissing into the canal. It was dark now, and they thought of their homes. When the horses were swallowed by shadows, the boys were too afraid to speak and strained their ears for the sound of a movement. Lightning broke across the shed, and the creatures seemed to rear up from the darkness, and all their eyes flashed glassily.

The boys, pelting along the footpath, slipping in the squelching mud, their hair in a wet fringe plastered to their foreheads, began after a while to feel their fear recede. The canal was covered with bubbles, sucked at the banks, and swirled into ratholes. Beyond the allotments was the first street lamp, and the boys leaned against it to take deep breaths and to wipe the rain from their faces. "That was only their glass eyes," Harry had said; and there, under the street lamp, the memory ended. He could not pursue himself home but was obliged to take leave of his boyhood there—the child holding his wet jacket across his chest. The evening was lying vaguely before him, with perhaps a box on the ears from Lottie Throstle for getting his boots wet—or had she fetched the tin bath in from the wall in the yard and let him soak his feet in mustard water? She had had her moods, and they defeated his memory.

Miss Arbuthnot was still talking of traditional art and craftsmanship and, rather to her vexation, was upheld in her views by the piano tuner.

Harry leaned sleepily against the radiator, tired from the mental strain of recollection—that patient stalking of his boyhood, tiring to one who had never dwelt on the past or reconsidered a scene. The intensity of the experience was so new to him that he was dazed by it, enriched, and awed by the idea of more treasure lying idle and at his disposal.

That night the pain eased him by giving a different focus to his distress. Nursing his throbbing hand to his chest, he slept his first deep and unbroken sleep since his sister's death.

On Saturday, as it grew dark, he waited for the bus at the top of the drive. His bowler hat was tilted forward, as if to match his feeling of jaunty anticipation; his scarf was tucked into his coat. Muffled up, stooping, with his head thrust from side to side, his reddened, screwed-up eyes turned upward, he looked like a great tortoise balancing on its hind legs—and burdened by the extra carapace of blindness.

At tea he had excited envy in some of the inmates when he at last overcame superstition enough to mention the fair. Miss Arbuthnot had doubled her scorn, but felt herself up against curiosity and surprise and the beginning of a reassessment, in most of their minds, of Harry's character. He had left behind a little stir of conjecture.

He heard the bus coming down the lane and stood ready, his stick raised, to hail it. The unseen headlights spread out, silhouetting him.

"You been hurting your hand?" the conductress asked, helping him into a seat.

"I just cut it. Is that old Fred up in front?"

"No, that's Evan. Fred's been on a different route, but he said to tell you he'd be waiting for you at the depot, along with Jock and Charlie."

Fred's heart sank when he saw Harry climbing down from the bus and smiling like a child. Saddling his friends with the old geezer for an evening was too much of a responsibility, and constraint and false heartiness marked the beginning of the outing. He had explained and apologized over and over again for the impulse which had brought Harry into the party. "Why, that's all right, Fred," they had assured him.

He thought that a beer or two at the Wheatsheaf would make them feel better, but after so much enforced abstinence the drink went to Harry's head with swift effect. He became boastful, swaggering. He invited laughter and threw in a few coarse jests for good measure. Sitting by the fire, his coat trailing about him, he looked a shocking old character, Fred thought. The beer dripped onto his knees; above the straining fly buttons his waistcoat bulged, looped with the tarnished chain of a watch he kept winding and holding to his ear, although he could no longer read it. Every so often he knocked his bowler hat straight with his stick—a slick music-hall gesture. Cocky and garrulous, he attracted attention from those not yet tired of his behaviour or responsible for it, as Fred was. They offered cigarettes and more drink. When at last he was persuaded to go, he lurched into a table, slopping beer from glasses.

Down the wide main street the fair booths were set out. Their lights spread upward through the yellowing leaves of the trees. The tunes of competing carrousels engulfed Harry in a confusion of sound. The four men stopped at a stall for a plateful of whelks and were joined by another bus driver and his wife, whose shrill peacock laughter flew out above all the other sounds.

"How are you keeping, Harry?" she asked. She was eating some pink candy floss on a stick, and her lips and the inside of her mouth were crimson from it. Harry could smell the sickly raspberry smell of her breath.

"Quite nicely, thanks. I had a bit of a cold, but I can't complain."

"Ever such a lot of colds about," she said vaguely.

"And lately I seem to be troubled with my hearing." He could not forgo this chance to talk of himself.

"Well, never mind. Can't have it all ways, I suppose."

He doesn't have it many ways, Fred thought.

"You ought to take me through the Haunted House, you know, Harry. I can't get anyone else to."

"You don't want to go along with an old codger like me."

"I wouldn't trust him in the dark, Vi," Fred said.

"I'll risk it."

She sensed his apprehension as they turned towards the sideshow. From behind the canvas façade, with its painted skeletons, came the sound of wheels running on a track, and spasms of wild laughter. Harry tripped over a cable, and she took his arm. "You're a real old sport," she told him. She paid at the entrance and helped him into a little car like a toast rack. They sat close together. She finished her candy, threw away the stick, and began to lick her fingers. "I've got good care of you," she said. "It's only a bit of kids' fun."

The car started forward, jolting at sharp bends, where sheeted ghosts leaned over them and luminous skulls shone in the darkness. Vi outlaughed everyone, screaming into Harry's ear and gripping his arm with both hands.

"It isn't much for *you*," she kept saying sympathetically. He couldn't see any of the horrific sights that made her gasp, but the jerking, the swift running on, the narrow (he guessed) avoidance of unseen obstacles made him tremble. The close smell was frightening, and when, as part of the macabre adventure, synthetic cobwebs trailed over his face and bony fingers touched his shoulder, he ducked his head fearfully.

"Well, you *are* an old baby," Vi said.

They came out into the light and the crowds again, and as they went towards her husband and the others, she put up her raspberry lips and kissed his cheek.

Her behaviour troubled him. She seemed to rehearse flirtatiousness with him for its own sake—unless it were to excite her audience. She expected no consequence from her coquetry, as if his blindness had made him less than a man. Her husband rarely spoke, and never to her, and Harry could not see his indifferent look.

With ostentatious care Vi guided him through the crowds, her arm in his so closely that he could feel her bosom against his elbow. He was tired now—physically, and with the strain of being at everybody's mercy and of trying to take his colour from other people. His senses, with their extra burden, were fatigued. The braying music cuffed his ears until he longed to clap his hands over them. His uncertain stumblings had made his step drag. Drifting smells—shellfish, petrol, and Vi's raspberry breath—began to nauseate him.

At the coconut shy she was shriller than ever. She stood inside the net, over the ladies' line, and screamed each time she missed, and, when a coconut rocked and did not fall, accused the proprietor, in piteous baby talk, of trickery.

Her husband had walked on, yawning, heedless of her importunities—for she *had* to have a coconut, just as she had *had* to have her fortune told and her turn on the swing boats.

Jock and Charlie followed, and they were lost in the crowd. Fred stayed and watched Vi's anger growing. When he knocked down a coconut she claimed it at once as a trophy. She liked to leave a fair laden with such tributes to her sexual prowess.

"Well, it's just too bad," Fred said, "because I'm taking it home to my wife."

"You're mean. Isn't he mean, Harry?"

Fred, coming closer to her, said softly as he held the coconut to his ear and rattled the milk, "You can have it on one condition."

"What's that?"

"You guess," he said.

She turned her head quickly. "Harry, you'll get a coconut for me, won't you?" She ran her hands up under the lapels of Harry's coat in a film-actressy way and rearranged his scarf.

"That's right, Harry," Fred said. "You told me the other day you were going to have a try. You can't do worse than Vi." Her fury relaxed him. He threw the coconut from one hand to the other and whistled softly, watching her.

Harry was aware that he was being put to some use, but the childish smile he had worn all the evening did not change; it expressed anxiety and the desire to please. Only by pleasing could he live. By complying—as clown, as eunuch—he earned the scraps and shreds they threw to him, the odds and ends left over from their everyday life.

Fred and Vi filled his arms with the wooden balls and led him to the front of the booth. Vi took his stick and stepped back. Someone behind her whispered, "He's blind. How dreadful!" and she turned and said, "Real spry old character, isn't he?" in a proprietary voice. More people pressed up to watch, murmuring sympathetically.

"Aim straight ahead," Fred was saying, and the man in charge was adding his advice. Harry's smile wrinkled up his face and his scarred-looking eyes. "How's that?" he cried, flinging his arm up violently and throwing. The crowd encouraged him, anxious that he should be successful. He threw again.

Fred stepped back, close to Vi, who avoided his glance. Staring ahead, still whistling, he put his hand out and gripped her wrist. She turned her arm furiously, but no one noticed.

"You've been asking for something all the evening, haven't you?" he asked her in a light conversational tone. "One of these days you're going to get it, see? That's right, Harry!" he shouted. "That was a near one! Proper old character. You can't help admiring him."

Vi's hand was still. She looked coolly in front of her, but Fred could sense a change of pulse, an excitement in her, and almost nodded to himself when she began to twist her fingers in his, with a vicious lasciviousness he had foreseen.

A cheer went up as Harry's throw went near to his target. "Next round on the house," the owner said. Harry's smile changed to a desperate grin. His bowler hat was crooked, and all his movements were impeded by his heavy overcoat. Noise shifted and roared round him until he felt giddy and began to sweat.

Insanely the carrousel horses rose and plunged, as if spurred on by the music and the lateness of the hour. Sparks spluttered from the electric cars. Above the trees the sky was bruised with a reddish stain, a polluted light, like a miasma given off by the fair.

The rough good will of the crowd went to Harry's head, and he began to clown and boast, as if he were drunk. Fred and Vi seemed to have vanished. Their voices were lost. He could hear only the carrousel and the thud of the wooden balls as he threw them against the canvas screen, and he feared the moment when his act was over and he must turn, empty-handed, hoping to be claimed.

Flannery O'Connor

Flannery O'Connor (1925–1964) was born in Savannah, Georgia, and reared as an orthodox Catholic. After receiving a Master of Fine Arts degree from the University of Iowa, she spent most of her life on a farm in Milledgeville, Georgia, where her hobby was raising peacocks. Although afflicted with a painful degenerative disease, she continued to write until her death, leaving behind two novels and about two dozen short stories, most of which had originally appeared in small-circulation journals and magazines. Her work is centered on the South—the Georgia Backwoods—and depicts the manifestations of hatred and sinfulness—often expressed through violence—in the twisted psyches of the grotesques who people her fiction. Her works include A Good Man Is Hard To Find *(1955),* Wise Blood *(1952) and* The Violent Bear It Away *(1960).* *(See page 65 of Introduction.)*

GOOD COUNTRY PEOPLE

Besides the neutral expression that she wore when she was alone, Mrs. Freeman had two others, forward and reverse, that she used for all her human dealings. Her forward expression was steady and driving like the advance of a heavy truck. Her eyes never swerved to left or right but turned as the story turned as if they followed a yellow line down the center of it. She seldom used the other expression because it was not often necessary for her to retract a statement, but when she did her face came to a complete stop, there was an almost imperceptible movement of her black eyes, during which they seemed to be receding, and then the observer would see that Mrs. Freeman, though she might stand there as real as several grain sacks thrown on top of each other, was no longer there in spirit. As for getting anything across to her when this was the case, Mrs. Hopewell had given it up. She might talk her head off. Mrs. Freeman could never be brought to admit herself wrong on any point. She would stand there and if she could be brought to say anything, it was something like, "Well, I wouldn't of said it was and I wouldn't of said it wasn't," or letting her gaze range over the top kitchen shelf where there was an assortment of dusty bottles, she might remark, "I see you ain't ate many of them figs you put up last summer."

They carried on their most important business in the kitchen at breakfast. Every morning Mrs. Hopewell got up at seven o'clock and lit her gas heater and Joy's. Joy was her daughter, a large blonde girl who had an artificial leg. Mrs. Hopewell thought of her as a child though she was thirty-two years old and highly educated. Joy would get up while her mother was eating and lumber into the bathroom and slam the door, and before long, Mrs. Freeman would arrive at the back door. Joy would hear her mother call, "Come on in," and then they would talk for a while in low voices that were indistinguishable in the bathroom. By the time Joy came in, they had usually finished the weather report and were on one or the other of Mrs. Freeman's daughters, Glynese or Carramae. Joy called them Glycerin and Caramel, Glynese, a redhead, was eighteen and had many admirers; Carramae, a blonde, was only fifteen but already married and pregnant. She could not keep anything on her stomach. Every morning

Mrs. Freeman told Mrs. Hopewell how many times she had vomited since the last report.

Mrs. Hopewell liked to tell people that Glynese and Carramae were two of the finest girls she knew and that Mrs. Freeman was a *lady* and that she was never ashamed to take her anywhere or introduce her to anybody they might meet. Then she would tell how she had happened to hire the Freemans in the first place and how they were a godsend to her and how she had had them four years. The reason for her keeping them so long was that they were not trash. They were good country people. She had telephoned the man whose name they had given as a reference and he had told her that Mr. Freeman was a good farmer but that his wife was the nosiest woman ever to walk the earth. "She's got to be into everything," the man said. "If she don't get there before the dust settles, you can bet she's dead, that's all. She'll want to know all your business. I can stand him real good," he had said, "but me nor my wife neither could have stood that woman one more minute on this place." That had put Mrs. Hopewell off for a few days.

She had hired them in the end because there were no other applicants but she had made up her mind beforehand exactly how she would handle the woman. Since she was the type who had to be into everything, then, Mrs. Hopewell had decided, she would not only let her be into everything, she would *see to it* that she was into everything—she would give her the responsibility of everything, she would put her in charge. Mrs. Hopewell had no bad qualities of her own but she was able to use other people's in such a constructive way that she never felt the lack. She had hired the Freemans and she had kept them four years.

Nothing is perfect. This was one of Mrs. Hopewell's favorite sayings. Another was: that is life! And still another, the most important, was: well, other people have their opinions too. She would make these statements, usually at the table, in a tone of gentle insistence as if no one held them but her, and the large hulking Joy, whose constant outrage had obliterated every expression from her face, would stare just a little to the side of her, her eyes icy blue, with the look of someone who has achieved blindness by an act of will and means to keep it.

When Mrs. Hopewell said to Mrs. Freeman that life was like that, Mrs. Freeman would say, "I always said so myself." Nothing had been arrived at by anyone that had not first been arrived at by her. She was quicker than Mr. Freeman. When Mrs. Hopewell said to her after they had been on the place a while, "You know, you're the wheel behind the wheel," and winked, Mrs. Freeman had said, "I know it. I've always been quick. It's some that are quicker than others."

"Everybody is different," Mrs. Hopewell said.

"Yes, most people is," Mrs. Freeman said.

"It takes all kinds to make the world."

"I always said it did myself."

The girl was used to this kind of dialogue for breakfast and more of it for dinner; sometimes they had it for supper too. When they had no guest they ate in the kitchen because that was easier. Mrs. Freeman always managed to arrive at some point during the meal and to watch them finish it. She would stand in the doorway if it were summer but in the winter she would stand with one elbow on top of the refrigerator and look down on them, or she would stand by the gas heater, lifting the back of her skirt slightly. Occasionally she would stand against the wall and roll her head from side to side. At no time was she in any hurry to leave. All this was very trying on Mrs. Hopewell but she was a woman of great patience. She realized that nothing is perfect and that in the Freemans she had good country people and that if, in this day and age, you get good country people, you had better hang onto them.

She had had plenty of experience with trash. Before the Freemans she had averaged one tenant family a year. The wives of these farmers were not the kind you would want to be around you for very long. Mrs. Hopewell, who had divorced her husband long ago, needed someone to walk over the fields with her; and when Joy had to be impressed for these services, her remarks were usually so ugly and her face so glum that Mrs. Hopewell would say, "If you can't come pleasantly, I don't want you at all," to which the girl, standing square and rigid-shouldered with her neck thrust slightly forward, would reply, "If you want me, here I am—LIKE I AM."

Mrs. Hopewell excused this attitude because of the leg (which had been shot off in a hunting accident when Joy was ten). It was hard for Mrs. Hopewell to realize that her child was thirty-two now and that for more than twenty years she had had only one leg. She thought of her still as a child because it tore her heart to think instead of the poor stout girl in her thirties who had never danced a step or had any *normal* good times. Her name was really Joy but as soon as she was twenty-one and away from home, she had had it legally changed. Mrs. Hopewell was certain that she had thought and thought until she had hit upon the ugliest name in any language. Then she had gone and had the beautiful name, Joy, changed without telling her mother until after she had done it. Her legal name was Hulga.

When Mrs. Hopewell thought the name, Hulga, she thought of the broad blank hull of a battleship. She would not use it. She continued to call her Joy to which the girl responded but in a purely mechanical way.

Hulga had learned to tolerate Mrs. Freeman, who saved her from taking walks with her mother. Even Glynese and Carramae were useful when they occupied attention that might otherwise have been directed at her. At first she had thought she could not stand Mrs. Freeman for she had found that it was not possible to be rude to her. Mrs. Freeman would take on strange resentments and for days together she would be sullen but the source of her displeasure was always obscure; a direct attack, a positive leer, blatant ugliness to her face—these never touched her. And without warning one day, she began calling her Hulga.

She did not call her that in front of Mrs. Hopewell who would have been incensed but when she and the girl happened to be out of the house together, she would say something and add the name Hulga to the end of it, and the big spectacled Joy-Hulga would scowl and redden as if her privacy had been intruded upon. She considered the name her personal affair. She had arrived at it first purely on the basis of its ugly sound and then the full genius of its fitness had struck her. She had a vision of the name working like the ugly sweating Vulcan who stayed in the furnace and to whom, presumably, the goddess had to come when called. She saw it as the name of her highest creative act. One of her major triumphs was that her mother had not been able to turn her dust into Joy, but the greater one was that she had been able to turn it herself into Hulga. However, Mrs. Freeman's relish for using the name only irritated her. It was as if Mrs. Freeman's beady steel-pointed eyes had penetrated far enough behind her face to reach some secret fact. Something about her seemed to fascinate Mrs. Freeman and then one day Hulga realized that it was the artificial leg. Mrs. Freeman had a special fondness for the details of secret infections, hidden deformities, assaults upon children. Of diseases, she preferred the lingering or incurable. Hulga had heard Mrs. Hopewell give her the details of the hunting accident, how the leg had been literally blasted off, how she had never lost consciousness. Mrs. Freeman could listen to it any time as if it had happened an hour ago.

When Hulga stumped into the kitchen in the morning (she could walk without making the awful noise but she made it—Mrs. Hopewell was certain—because it was ugly-sounding), she glanced at them and did not speak. Mrs. Hopewell would be in her red kimono with her hair tied around her head in rags. She would be sitting at the table, finishing her breakfast and Mrs. Freeman would be hanging by her elbow outward from the refrigerator, looking down at the table. Hulga always put her eggs on the stove to boil and then stood over them with her arms folded, and Mrs. Hopewell would look at her—a kind of indirect gaze divided between her and Mrs. Freeman—and would think that if she would only keep herself up a little, she wouldn't be so bad looking. There was nothing wrong with her face that a pleasant expression wouldn't help. Mrs. Hopewell said that people who looked on the bright side of things would be beautiful even if they were not.

Whenever she looked at Joy this way, she could not help but feel that it would have been better if the child had not taken the Ph.D. It had certainly not brought her out any and now that she had it, there was no more excuse for her to go to school again. Mrs. Hopewell thought it was nice for girls to go to school to have a good time but Joy had "gone through." Anyhow, she would not have been strong enough to go again. The doctors had told Mrs. Hopewell that with the best of care, Joy might see forty-five. She had a weak heart. Joy had made it plain that if it had not been for this condition, she would be far from these red hills and good country people. She would be in a university lecturing to people who knew what she was talking about. And Mrs. Hopewell could very well picture her there, looking like a scarecrow and lecturing to more of the same. Here she went about all day in a six-year-old skirt and a yellow sweat shirt with a faded cowboy on a horse embossed on it. She thought this was funny; Mrs. Hopewell thought it was idiotic and showed simply that she was still a child. She was brilliant but she didn't have a grain of sense. It seemed to

Mrs. Hopewell that every year she grew less like other people and more like herself—bloated, rude, and squint-eyed. And she said such strange things! To her own mother she had said—without warning, without excuse, standing up in the middle of a meal with her face purple and her mouth half full—"Woman! do you ever look inside? Do you ever look inside and see what you are *not?* God!" she had cried sinking down again and staring at her plate, "Malebranche was right: we are not our own light. We are not our own light!" Mrs. Hopewell had no idea to this day what brought that on. She had only made the remark, hoping Joy would take it in, that a smile never hurt anyone.

The girl had taken the Ph.D. in philosophy and this left Mrs. Hopewell at a complete loss. You could say, "My daughter is a nurse," or "My daughter is a school teacher," or even, "My daughter is a chemical engineer." You could not say, "My daughter is a philosopher." That was something that had ended with the Greeks and Romans. All day Joy sat on her neck in a deep chair, reading. Sometimes she went for walks but she didn't like dogs or cats or birds or flowers or nature or nice young men. She looked at nice young men as if she could smell their stupidity.

One day Mrs. Hopewell had picked up one of the books the girl had just put down and opening it at random, she read, "Science, on the other hand, has to assert its soberness and seriousness afresh and declare that it is concerned solely with what-is. Nothing—how can it be for science anything but a horror and a phantasm? If science is right, then one thing stands firm: science wishes to know nothing of nothing. Such is after all the strictly scientific approach to Nothing. We know it by wishing to know nothing of Nothing." These words had been underlined with a blue pencil and they worked on Mrs. Hopewell like some evil incantation in gibberish. She shut the book quickly and went out of the room as if she were having a chill.

This morning when the girl came in, Mrs. Freeman was on Carramae. "She thrown up four times after supper," she said, "and was up twict in the night after three o'clock. Yesterday she didn't do nothing but ramble in the bureau drawer. All she did. Stand up there and see what she could run up on."

"She's got to eat," Mrs. Hopewell muttered, sipping her coffee, while she watched Joy's back at the stove. She was wondering what the child had said to the Bible salesman. She could not imagine what kind of a conversation she could possibly have had with him.

He was a tall gaunt hatless youth who had called yesterday to sell them a Bible. He had appeared at the door, carrying a large black suitcase that weighted him so heavily on one side that he had to brace himself against the door facing. He seemed on the point of collapse but he said in a cheerful voice, "Good morning, Mrs. Cedars!" and set the suitcase down on the mat. He was not a bad-looking young man though he had on a bright blue suit and yellow socks that were not pulled up far enough. He had prominent face bones and a streak of sticky-looking brown hair falling across his forehead.

"I'm Mrs. Hopewell," she said.

"Oh!" he said, pretending to look puzzled but with his eyes sparkling, "I saw it said 'The Cedars,' on the mailbox so I thought you was Mrs. Cedars!" and he burst out in a pleasant laugh. He picked up the satchel and under cover of a pant, he fell forward into her hall. It was rather as if the suitcase had moved first, jerking him after it. "Mrs. Hopewell!" he said and grabbed her hand. "I hope you are well!" and he laughed again and then all at once his face sobered completely. He paused and gave her a straight earnest look and said, "Lady, I've come to speak of serious things."

"Well, come in," she muttered, none too pleased because her dinner was almost ready. He came into the parlor and sat down on the edge of a straight chair and put the suitcase between his feet and glanced around the room as if he were sizing her up by it. Her silver gleamed on the two sideboards; she decided he had never been in a room as elegant as this.

"Mrs. Hopewell," he began, using her name in a way that sounded almost intimate, "I know you believe in Chrustian service."

"Well yes," she murmured.

"I know," he said and paused, looking very wise with his head cocked on one side, "that you're a good woman. Friends have told me."

Mrs. Hopewell never liked to be taken for a fool. "What are you selling?" she asked.

"Bibles," the young man said and his eye raced around the room before he added, "I see you have no family Bible in your parlor, I see that is the one lack you got!"

Mrs. Hopewell could not say, "My daughter is an atheist and won't let me keep the Bible in the parlor." She said, stiffening slightly, "I keep my Bible by my bedside." This was not the truth. It was in the attic somewhere.

"Lady," he said, "the word of God ought to be in the parlor."

"Well, I think that's a matter of taste," she began. "I think . . ."

"Lady," he said, "for a Chrustian, the word of God ought to be in every room in the house besides in his heart. I know you're a Chrustian because I can see it in every line of your face."

She stood up and said, "Well, young man, I don't want to buy a Bible and I smell my dinner burning."

He didn't get up. He began to twist his hands and looking down at them, he said softly, "Well lady, I'll tell you the truth—not many people want to buy one nowadays and besides, I know I'm real simple. I don't know how to say a thing but to say it. I'm just a country boy." He glanced up into her unfriendly face. "People like you don't like to fool with country people like me!"

"Why!" she cried, "good country people are the salt of the earth! Besides, we all have different ways of doing, it takes all kinds to make the world go 'round. That's life!"

"You said a mouthful," he said.

"Why, I think there aren't enough good country people in the world!" she said, stirred. "I think that's what's wrong with it!"

His face had brightened. "I didn't inraduce myself," he said. "I'm

Manley Pointer from out in the country around Willohobie, not even from a place, just from near a place."

"You wait a minute," she said. "I have to see about my dinner." She went out to the kitchen and found Joy standing near the door where she had been listening.

"Get rid of the salt of the earth," she said, "and let's eat."

Mrs. Hopewell gave her a pained look and turned the heat down under the vegetables. "*I* can't be rude to anybody," she murmured and went back into the parlor.

He had opened the suitcase and was sitting with a Bible on each knee.

"You might as well put those up," she told him. "I don't want one."

"I appreciate your honesty," he said. "You don't see any more real honest people unless you go way out in the country."

"I know," she said, "real genuine folks!" Through the crack in the door she heard a groan.

"I guess a lot of boys come telling you they're working their way through college," he said, "but I'm not going to tell you that. Somehow," he said, "I don't want to go to college. I want to devote my life to Chrustian service. See," he said, lowering his voice, "I got this heart condition. I may not live long. When you know it's something wrong with you and you may not live long, well then, lady . . ." He paused, with his mouth open, and stared at her.

He and Joy had the same condition! She knew that her eyes were filling with tears but she collected herself quickly and murmured, "Won't you stay for dinner? We'd love to have you!" and was sorry the instant she heard herself say it.

"Yes mam," he said in an abashed voice, "I would sher love to do that!"

Joy had given him one look on being introduced to him and then throughout the meal had not glanced at him again. He had addressed several remarks to her, which she had pretended not to hear. Mrs. Hopewell could not understand deliberate rudeness, although she lived with it, and she felt she had always to overflow with hospitality to make up for Joy's lack of courtesy. She urged him to talk about himself and he did. He said he was the seventh child of twelve and that his father had been crushed under a tree when he himself was eight years old. He had been crushed very badly, in fact, almost cut in two and was practically not recognizable. His mother had got along the best she could by hard working and she had always seen that her children went to Sunday School and that they read the Bible every evening. He was now nineteen years old and he had been selling Bibles for four months. In that time he had sold seventy-seven Bibles and had the promise of two more sales. He wanted to become a missionary because he thought that was the way you could do most for people. "He who losest his life shall find it," he said simply and he was so sincere, so genuine and earnest that Mrs. Hopewell would not for the world have smiled. He prevented his peas from sliding onto the table by blocking them with a piece of bread which he later cleaned his plate with. She could see Joy observing sidewise how he handled his knife and fork and she saw too that every few minutes, the boy would dart a keen appraising glance at the girl as if he were trying to attract her attention.

After dinner Joy cleared the dishes off the table and disappeared and Mrs. Hopewell was left to talk with him. He told her again about his childhood and his father's accident and about various things that had happened to him. Every five minutes or so she would stifle a yawn. He sat for two hours until finally she told him she must go because she had an appointment in town. He packed his Bibles and thanked her and prepared to leave, but in the doorway he stopped and wrung her hand and said that not on any of his trips had he met a lady as nice as her and he asked if he could come again. She had said she would always be happy to see him.

Joy had been standing in the road, apparently looking at something in the distance, when he came down the steps toward her, bent to the side with his heavy valise. He stopped where she was standing and confronted her directly. Mrs. Hopewell could not hear what he said but she trembled to think what Joy would say to him. She could see that after a minute Joy said something and that then the boy began to speak again, making an excited gesture with his free hand. After a minute Joy said something else at which the boy began to speak once more. Then to her amazement, Mrs. Hopewell saw the two of them walk off together, toward the gate. Joy had walked all the way to the gate with him and Mrs. Hopewell could not imagine what they had said to each other, and she had not yet dared to ask.

Mrs. Freeman was insisting upon her attention. She had moved from the refrigerator to the heater so that Mrs. Hopewell had to turn and face her in order to seem to be listening. "Glynese gone out with Harvey Hill again last night," she said. "She had this sty."

"Hill," Mrs. Hopewell said absently, "is that the one who works in the garage?"

"Nome, he's the one that goes to chiropracter school," Mrs. Freeman said. "She had this sty. Been had it two days. So she says when he brought her in the other night he says, 'Lemme get rid of that sty for you,' and she says, 'How?' and he says, 'You just lay yourself down acrost the seat of that car and I'll show you.' So she done it and he popped her neck. Kept on a-popping it several times until she made him quit. This morning," Mrs. Freeman said, "she ain't got no sty. She ain't got no traces of a sty."

"I never heard of that before," Mrs. Hopewell said.

"He ast her to marry him before the Ordinary," Mrs. Freeman went on, "and she told him she wasn't going to be married in no *office*."

"Well, Glynese is a fine girl," Mrs. Hopewell said. "Glynese and Carramae are both fine girls."

"Carramae said when her and Lyman was married Lyman said it sure felt sacred to him. She said he said he wouldn't take five hundred dollars for being married by a preacher."

"How much would he take?" the girl asked from the stove.

"He said he wouldn't take five hundred dollars," Mrs. Freeman repeated.

"Well we all have work to do," Mrs. Hopewell said.

"Lyman said it just felt more sacred to him," Mrs. Freeman said. "The doctor wants Carramae to eat prunes. Says instead of medicine. Says them cramps is coming from pressure. You know where I think it is?"

"She'll be better in a few weeks," Mrs. Hopewell said.

"In the tube," Mrs. Freeman said. "Else she wouldn't be as sick as she is."

Hulga had cracked her two eggs into a saucer and was bringing them to the table along with a cup of coffee that she had filled too full. She sat down carefully and began to eat, meaning to keep Mrs. Freeman there by questions if for any reason she showed an inclination to leave. She could perceive her mother's eye on her. The first roundabout question would be about the Bible salesman and she did not wish to bring it on. "How did he pop her neck?" she asked.

Mrs. Freeman went into a description of how he had popped her neck. She said he owned a '55 Mercury but that Glynese said she would rather marry a man with only a '36 Plymouth who would be married by a preacher. The girl asked what if he had a '32 Plymouth and Mrs. Freeman said what Glynese had said was a '36 Plymouth.

Mrs. Hopewell said there were not many girls with Glynese's common sense. She said what she admired in those girls was their common sense. She said that reminded her that they had had a nice visitor yesterday, a young man selling Bibles. "Lord," she said, "he bored me to death but he was so sincere and genuine I couldn't be rude to him. He was just good country people, you know," she said, "—just the salt of the earth."

"I seen him walk up," Mrs. Freeman said, "and then later—I seen him walk off," and Hulga could feel the slight shift in her voice, the slight insinuation, that he had not walked off alone, had he? Her face remained expressionless but the color rose into her neck and she seemed to swallow it down with the next spoonful of egg. Mrs. Freeman was looking at her as if they had a secret together.

"Well, it takes all kinds of people to make the world go 'round," Mrs. Hopewell said. "It's very good we aren't all alike."

"Some people are more alike than others," Mrs. Freeman said.

Hulga got up and stumped, with about twice the noise that was necessary, into her room and locked the door. She was to meet the Bible salesman at ten o'clock at the gate. She had thought about it half the night. She had started thinking of it as a great joke and then she had begun to see profound implications in it. She had lain in bed imagining dialogues for them that were insane on the surface but that reached below to depths that no Bible salesman would be aware of. Their conversation yesterday had been of this kind.

He had stopped in front of her and had simply stood there. His face was bony and sweaty and bright, with a little pointed nose in the center of it, and his look was different from what it had been at the dinner table. He was gazing at her with open curiosity, with fascination, like a child watching a new fantastic animal at the zoo, and he was breathing as if he had run a great distance to reach her. His gaze seemed somehow familiar but she could not think where she had been regarded with it before. For almost a minute he didn't say anything. Then on what seemed an insuck of breath, he whispered, "You ever ate a chicken that was two days old?"

The girl looked at him stonily. He might have just put this question up for consideration at the meeting of a philosophical association. "Yes," she presently replied as if she had considered it from all angles.

"It must have been mighty small!" he said triumphantly and shook all over with little nervous giggles, getting very red in the face, and subsiding finally into his gaze of complete admiration, while the girl's expression remained exactly the same.

"How old are you?" he asked softly.

She waited some time before she answered. Then in a flat voice she said, "Seventeen."

His smiles came in succession like waves breaking on the surface of a little lake. "I see you got a wooden leg," he said. "I think you're real brave. I think you're real sweet."

The girl stood blank and solid and silent.

"Walk to the gate with me," he said. "You're a brave sweet little thing and I liked you the minute I seen you walk in the door."

Hulga began to move forward.

"What's your name?" he asked, smiling down on the top of her head.

"Hulga," she said.

"Hulga," he murmured, "Hulga. Hulga. I never heard of anybody name Hulga before. You're shy, aren't you, Hulga?" he asked.

She nodded, watching his large red hand on the handle of the giant valise.

"I like girls that wear glasses," he said. "I think a lot. I'm not like these people that a serious thought don't ever enter their heads. It's because I may die."

"I may die too," she said suddenly and looked up at him. His eyes were very small and brown, glittering feverishly.

"Listen," he said, "don't you think some people was meant to meet on account of what all they got in common and all? Like they both think serious thoughts and all?" He shifted the valise to his other hand so that the hand nearest her was free. He caught hold of her elbow and shook it a little. "I don't work on Saturday," he said. "I like to walk in the woods and see what Mother Nature is wearing. O'er the hills and far away. Pic-nics and things. Couldn't we go on a pic-nic tomorrow? Say yes, Hulga," he said and gave her a dying look as if he felt his insides about to drop out of him. He had even seemed to sway slightly toward her.

During the night she had imagined that she seduced him. She imagined that the two of them walked on the place until they came to the storage barn beyond the two back fields and there, she imagined, that things came to such a pass that she very easily seduced him and that then, of course, she had to reckon with his remorse. True genius can get an idea across even to an inferior mind. She imagined that she took his remorse in hand and changed it into a deeper understanding of life. She took all his shame away and turned it into something useful.

She set off for the gate at exactly ten o'clock, escaping without drawing Mrs. Hopewell's attention. She didn't take anything to eat, forgetting that food is usually taken on a picnic. She wore a pair of slacks and a dirty white shirt, and as an afterthought, she had put some Vapex on the collar of it since she did not own any perfume. When she reached the gate no one was there.

She looked up and down the empty highway and had the furious feeling that she had been tricked, that he had only meant to make her walk to the gate after the idea of him. Then suddenly he stood up, very tall, from behind a bush on the opposite embankment. Smiling, he lifted his hat which was new and wide-brimmed. He had not worn it yesterday and she wondered if he had bought it for the occasion. It was toast-colored with a red and white band around it and was slightly too large for him. He stepped from behind the bush still carrying the black valise. He had on the same suit and the same yellow socks sucked down in his shoes from walking. He crossed the highway and said, "I knew you'd come!"

The girl wondered acidly how he had known this. She pointed to the valise and asked, "Why did you bring your Bibles?"

He took her elbow, smiling down on her as if he could not stop. "You can never tell when you'll need the word of God, Hulga," he said. She had a moment in which she doubted that this was actually happening and then they began to climb the embankment. They went down into the pasture toward the woods. The boy walked lightly by her side, bouncing on his toes. The valise did not seem to be heavy today; he even swung it. They crossed half the pasture without saying anything and then, putting his hand easily on the small of her back, he asked softly, "Where does your wooden leg join on?"

She turned an ugly red and glared at him and for an instant the boy looked abashed. "I didn't mean you no harm," he said. "I only meant you're so brave and all. I guess God takes care of you."

"No," she said, looking forward and walking fast, "I don't even believe in God."

At this he stopped and whistled. "No!" he exclaimed as if he were too astonished to say anything else.

She walked on and in a second he was bouncing at her side, fanning with his hat. "That's very unusual for a girl," he remarked, watching her out of the corner of his eye. When they reached the edge of the wood, he put his hand on her back again and drew her against him without a word and kissed her heavily.

The kiss, which had more pressure than feeling behind it, produced that extra surge of adrenalin in the girl that enables one to carry a packed trunk out of a burning house, but in her, the power went at once to the brain. Even before he released her, her mind, clear and detached and ironic anyway, was regarding him from a great distance, with amusement but with pity. She had never been kissed before and she was pleased to discover that it was an unexceptional experience and all a matter of the mind's control. Some people might enjoy drain water if they were told it was vodka. When the boy, looking expectant but uncertain, pushed her gently away, she turned and walked on, saying nothing as if such business, for her, were common enough.

He came along panting at her side, trying to help her when he saw a root that she might trip over. He caught and held back the long swaying blades of thorn vine until she had passed beyond them. She led the way and he came breathing heavily behind her. Then they came out on a sunlit hillside, sloping softly into another one a little smaller. Beyond, they could see the rusted top of the old barn where the extra hay was stored.

The hill was sprinkled with small pink weeds. "Then you ain't saved?" he asked suddenly, stopping.

The girl smiled. It was the first time she had smiled at him at all. "In my economy," she said, "I'm saved and you are damned but I told you I didn't believe in God."

Nothing seemed to destroy the boy's look of admiration. He gazed at her now as if the fantastic animal at the zoo had put its paw through the bars and given him a loving poke. She thought he looked as if he wanted to kiss her again and she walked on before he had the chance.

"Ain't there somewheres we can sit down sometime?" he murmured, his voice softening toward the end of the sentence.

"In that barn," she said.

They made for it rapidly as if it might slide away like a train. It was a large two-story barn, cool and dark inside. The boy pointed up the ladder that led into the loft and said, "It's too bad we can't go up there."

"Why can't we?" she asked.

"Yer leg," he said reverently.

The girl gave him a contemptuous look and putting both hands on the ladder, she climbed it while he stood below, apparently awestruck. She pulled herself expertly through the opening and then looked down at him and said, "Well, come on if you're coming," and he began to climb the ladder, awkwardly bringing the suitcase with him.

"We won't need the Bible," she observed.

"You never can tell," he said, panting. After he had got into the loft, he was a few seconds catching his breath. She had sat down in a pile of straw. A wide sheath of sunlight, filled with dust particles, slanted over her. She lay back against a bale, her face turned away, looking out the front opening of the barn where hay was thrown from a wagon into the loft. The two pink-speckled hillsides lay back against a dark ridge of woods. The sky was cloudless and cold blue. The boy dropped down by her side and put one arm under her and the other over her and began methodically kissing her face, making little noises like a fish. He did not remove his hat but it was pushed far enough back not to interfere. When her glasses got in his way, he took them off of her and slipped them into his pocket.

The girl at first did not return any of the kisses but presently she began to and after she had put several on his cheek, she reached his lips and remained there, kissing him again and again as if she were trying to draw all the breath out of him. His breath was clear and sweet like a child's and the kisses were sticky like a child's. He mumbled about loving her and about knowing when he first seen her that he loved her, but the mumbling was like the sleepy fretting of a child being put to sleep by his mother. Her mind, throughout this, never stopped or lost itself for a second to her feelings. "You ain't said you loved me none," he whispered finally, pulling back from her. "You got to say that."

She looked away from him off into the hollow sky and then down at a black ridge and then down farther into what appeared to be two green swelling lakes. She didn't realize he had taken her glasses but this landscape could not seem exceptional to her for she seldom paid any close attention to her surroundings.

"You got to say it," he repeated. "You got to say you love me."

She was always careful how she committed herself. "In a sense," she began, "if you use the word loosely, you might say that. But it's not a word I use. I don't have illusions. I'm one of those people who see *through* to nothing."

The boy was frowning. "You got to say it. I said it and you got to say it," he said.

The girl looked at him almost tenderly. "You poor baby," she murmured. "It's just as well you don't understand," and she pulled him by the neck, face-down, against her. "We are all damned," she said, "but some of us have taken off our blindfolds and see that there's nothing to see. It's a kind of salvation."

The boy's astonished eyes looked blankly through the ends of her hair. "Okay," he almost whined, "but do you love me or don'tcher?"

"Yes," she said and added, "in a sense. But I must tell you something. There mustn't be anything dishonest between us." She lifted his head and looked him in the eye. "I am thirty years old," she said. "I have a number of degrees."

The boy's look was irritated but dogged. "I don't care," he said. "I don't care a thing about what all you done. I just want to know if you love me or don'tcher?" and he caught her to him and and wildly planted her face with kisses until she said, "Yes, yes."

"Okay then," he said, letting her go. "Prove it."

She smiled, looking dreamily out on the shifty landscape. She had seduced him without even making up her mind to try. "How?" she asked, feeling that he should be delayed a little.

He leaned over and put his lips to her ear. "Show me where your wooden leg joins on," he whispered.

The girl uttered a sharp little cry and her face instantly drained of color. The obscenity of the suggestion was not what shocked her. As a child she had sometimes been subject to feelings of shame but education had removed the last traces of that as a good surgeon scrapes for cancer; she would no more have felt it over what he was asking than she would have believed in his Bible. But she was as sensitive about the artificial leg as a peacock about his tail. No one ever touched it but her. She took care of it as someone else would his soul, in private and almost with her own eyes turned away. "No," she said.

"I known it," he muttered, sitting up. "You're just playing me for a sucker."

"Oh no no!" she cried. It joins on at the knee. Only at the knee. Why do you want to see it?"

The boy gave her a long penetrating look. "Because," he said, "it's what makes you different. You ain't like anybody else."

She sat staring at him. There was nothing about her face or her round freezing-blue eyes to indicate that this had moved her; but she felt as if her heart had stopped and left her mind to pump her blood. She decided that for the first time in her life she was face to face with real innocence. This boy, with an instinct that came from beyond wisdom, had touched the truth about her. When after a minute, she said in a hoarse high voice, "All right," it was like surrendering to him completely. It was like losing her own life and finding it again, miraculously, in his.

Very gently he began to roll the slack leg up. The artificial limb, in a white sock and brown flat shoe, was bound in a heavy material like canvas and ended in an ugly jointure where it was attached to the stump. The boy's face and his voice were entirely reverent as he uncovered it and said, "Now show me how to take it off and on."

She took it off for him and put it back on again and then he took it off himself, handling it as tenderly as if it were a real one. "See!" he said with a delighted child's face. "Now I can do it myself!"

"Put it back on," she said. She was thinking that she would run away with him and that every night he would take the leg off and every morning put it back on again. "Put it back on," she said.

"Not yet," he murmured, setting it on its foot out of her reach. "Leave it off for a while. You got me instead."

She gave a little cry of alarm but he pushed her down and began to kiss her again. Without the leg she felt entirely dependent on him. Her brain seemed to have stopped thinking altogether and to be about some other function that it was not very good at. Different expressions raced back and forth over her face. Every now and then the boy, his eyes like two steel spikes, would glance behind him where the leg stood. Finally she pushed him off and said, "Put it back on me now."

"Wait," he said. He leaned the other way and pulled the valise toward him and opened it. It had a pale blue spotted lining and there were only two Bibles in it. He took one of these out and opened the cover of it. It was hollow and contained a pocket flask of whiskey, a pack of cards, and a small blue box with printing on it. He laid these out in front of her one at a time in an evenly-spaced row, like one presenting offerings at the shrine of a goddess. He put the blue box in her hand. THIS PRODUCT TO BE USED ONLY FOR THE PREVENTION OF DISEASE, she read, and dropped it. The boy was unscrewing the top of the flask. He stopped and pointed, with a smile, to the deck of cards. It was not an ordinary deck but one with an obscene picture on the back of each card. "Take a swig," he said, offering her the bottle first. He held it in front of her, but like one mesmerized, she did not move.

Her voice when she spoke had an almost pleading sound. "Aren't you," she murmured, "aren't you just good country people?"

The boy cocked his head. He looked as if he were just beginning to understand that she might be trying to insult him. "Yeah," he said, curling his lip slightly, "but it ain't held me back none. I'm as good as you any day in the week."

"Give me my leg," she said.

He pushed it farther away with his foot. "Come on now, let's begin to have us a good time," he said coaxingly. "We ain't got to know one another good yet."

"Give me my leg!" she screamed and tried to lunge for it but he pushed her down easily.

"What's the matter with you all of a sudden?" he asked, frowning as he screwed the top on the flask and put it quickly back inside the Bible. "You just a while ago said you didn't believe in nothing. I thought you was some girl!"

Her face was almost purple. "You're a Christian!" she hissed. "You're a fine Christian! You're just like them all—say one thing and do another. You're a perfect Christian, you're . . ."

The boy's mouth was set angrily. "I hope you don't think," he said in a lofty indignant tone, "that I believe in that crap! I may sell Bibles but I know which end is up and I wasn't born yesterday and I know where I'm going!"

"Give me my leg!" she screeched. He jumped up so quickly that she barely saw him sweep the cards and the blue box back into the Bible and throw the Bible into the valise. She saw him grab the leg and then she saw it for an instant slanted forlornly across the inside of the suitcase with a Bible at either side of its opposite ends. He slammed the lid shut and snatched up the valise and swung it down the hole and then stepped through himself.

When all of him had passed but his head, he turned and regarded her with a look that no longer had any admiration in it. "I've gotten a lot of interesting things," he said. "One time I got a woman's glass eye this way. And you needn't to think you'll catch me because Pointer ain't really my name. I use a different name at every house I call at and don't stay nowhere long. And I'll tell you another thing, Hulga," he said, using the name as if he didn't think much of it, "you ain't so smart. I been believing in nothing ever since I was born!" and then the toast-colored hat disappeared down the hole and the girl was left, sitting on the straw in the dusty sunlight. When she turned her churning face toward the opening, she saw his blue figure struggling successfully over the green speckled lake.

Mrs. Hopewell and Mrs. Freeman, who were in the back pasture, digging up onions, saw him emerge a little later from the woods and head across the meadow toward the highway. "Why, that looks like that nice dull young man that tried to sell me a Bible yesterday," Mrs. Hopewell said, squinting. "He must have been selling them to the Negroes back in there. He was so simple," she said, "but I guess the world would be better off if we were all that simple."

Mrs. Freeman's gaze drove forward and just touched him before he disappeared under the hill. Then she returned her attention to the evil-smelling onion shoot she was lifting from the ground. "Some can't be that simple," she said. "I know I never could."

Bernard Malamud

Bernard Malamud (1914–) was born in Brooklyn, attended City College and Columbia University, and has himself taught at several colleges, including Bennington College in Vermont, where he now lives. In 1959 he won the National Book Award for his volume of short stories, The Magic Barrel. *He is best known for his novels,* The Assistant *(1957),* A New Life *(1961),* The Fixer *(1966), and, most recently,* The Tenants *(1971). Malamud often writes about impoverished American Jewish merchants and small tradesmen and their relationship to one aspect of the Jewish tradition: the conversion of suffering into a celebration of life and spiritual values.* *(See page 66 of Introduction.)*

THE LAST MOHICAN

Fidelman, a self-confessed failure as a painter, came to Italy to prepare a critical study of Giotto, the opening chapter of which he had carried across the ocean in a new pigskin leather brief case, now gripped in his perspiring hand. Also new were his gum-soled oxblood shoes, a tweed suit he had on despite the late-September sun slanting hot in the Roman sky, although there was a lighter one in his bag; and a dacron shirt and set of cotton-dacron underwear, good for quick and easy washing for the traveler. His suitcase, a bulky two-strapped affair which embarrassed him slightly, he had borrowed from his sister Bessie. He planned, if he had any funds left at the end of the year, to buy a new one in Florence. Although he had been in not much of a mood when he had left the U.S.A., Fidelman picked up in Naples, and at the moment, as he stood in front of the Rome railroad station, after twenty minutes still absorbed in his first sight of the Eternal City, he was conscious of a certain exaltation that devolved on him after he had discovered that directly across the many-vehicled piazza stood the remains of the Baths of Diocletian. Fidelman remembered having read that Michelangelo had helped in converting the baths into a church and convent, the latter ultimately changed into the museum that presently was there. "Imagine," he muttered. "Imagine all that history."

In the midst of his imagining. Fidelman experienced the sensation of suddenly seeing himself as he was, to the pinpoint, outside and in, not without bittersweet pleasure; and as the well-known image of his face rose before him he was taken by the depth of pure feeling in his eyes, slightly magnified by glasses, and the sensitivity of his elongated nostrils and often tremulous lips, nose divided from lips by a mustache of recent vintage that looked, Fidelman thought, as if it had been sculptured there, adding to his dignified appearance although he was a little on the short side. Almost at the same moment, this unexpectedly intense sense of his being—it was more than appearance—faded, exaltation having gone where exaltation goes, and Fidelman became aware that there was an exterior source to the strange, almost tri-dimensional reflection of himself he had felt as well as seen. Behind him, a short distance to the right, he had noticed a stranger—give a skeleton a couple of pounds—loitering near a bronze statue on a stone pedestal of the heavy-dugged Etruscan wolf suckling the infant Romulus and Remus, the man contemplating Fidelman already acquisitively so as to suggest to the traveler that he had been mirrored (lock, stock, barrel) in the other's gaze for some time, perhaps since he had stepped off the train. Casually studying him though pretending no, Fidelman beheld a person of about his own height, oddly dressed in brown knickers and black knee-length woolen socks drawn up over slightly bowed, broomstick legs, these grounded in small porous pointed shoes. His yellowed shirt was open at the gaunt throat, both sleeves rolled up over skinny, hairy arms. The stranger's high forehead was bronzed, his black hair thick behind small ears, the dark close-shaven beard tight on the face; his experienced nose was weighted at the tip, and the soft brown eyes, above all, wanted. Though his expression suggested humility he all but licked his lips as he approached the ex-painter.

"Shalom," he greeted Fidelman.

"Shalom," the other hesitantly replied, uttering the word—so far as he recalled—for the first time in his life. My God, he thought, a handout for sure. My first hello in Rome and it has to be a schnorrer.

The stranger extended a smiling hand. "Susskind," he said, "Shimon Susskind."

"Arthur Fidelman." Transferring his brief case to under his left arm while standing astride the big suitcase he shook hands with Susskind. A blue-smocked porter came by, glanced at Fidelman's bag, looked at him, then walked away.

Whether he knew it or not Susskind was rubbing his palms contemplatively together.

"Parla italiano?"

"Not with ease, although I read it fluently. You might say I need the practice."

"Yiddish?"

"I express myself best in English."

"Let it be English then." Susskind spoke with a slight British intonation. "I knew you were Jewish," he said, "the minute my eyes saw you."

Fidelman chose to ignore the remark. "Where did you pick up your knowledge of English?"

"In Israel."

Israel interested Fidelman. "You live there?"

"Once, not now," Susskind answered vaguely. He seemed suddenly bored.

"How so?"

Susskind twitched a shoulder. "Too much heavy labor for a man of my modest health. Also I couldn't stand the suspense."

Fidelman nodded.

"Furthermore, the desert air makes me constipated. In Rome I am lighthearted."

"A Jewish refugee from Israel, no less," Fidelman said with good humor.

"I'm always running," Susskind answered mirthlessly. If he was lighthearted he had yet to show it.

"Where else from, if I may ask?"

"Where else but Germany, Hungary, Poland? Where not?"

"Ah, that's so long ago." Fidelman then noticed the gray in the man's hair. "Well, I'd better be going." He picked up his bag as two porters hovered uncertainly nearby.

But Susskind offered certain services. "You got a hotel?"

"All picked and reserved."

"How long are you staying?"

What business is it of his? However, Fidelman courteously replied, "Two weeks in Rome, the rest of the year in Florence, with a few side trips to Siena, Assisi, Padua and maybe also Venice."

"You wish a guide in Rome?"

"Are you a guide?"

"Why not?"

"No," said Fidelman. "I'll look as I go along to museums, libraries, et cetera."

This caught Susskind's attention. "What are you, a professor?"

Fidelman couldn't help blushing. "Not exactly, really just a student."

"From which institution?"

He coughed a little. "By that I mean professional student, you might say. Call me Trofimov, from Chekhov. If there's something to learn I want to learn it."

"You have some kind of a project?" the other persisted. "A grant?"

"No grant. My money is hard earned. I worked and saved a long time to take a year in Italy. I made certain sacrifices. As for a project, I'm writing on the painter Giotto. He was one of the most important—"

"You don't have to tell me about Giotto," Susskind interrupted with a little smile.

"You've studied his work?"

"Who doesn't know Giotto?"

"That's interesting to me," said Fidelman, secretly irritated. "How do you happen to know him?"

"How do you?"

"I've given a good deal of time and study to his work."

"So I know him too."

I'd better get this over with before it begins to amount up to something, Fidelman thought. He set down his bag and fished with a finger in his leather coin purse. The two porters watched with interest, one taking a sandwich out of his pocket, unwrapping the newspaper and beginning to eat.

"This is for yourself," Fidelman said.

Susskind hardly glanced at the coin as he let it drop into his pants pocket. The porters then left.

The refugee had an odd way of standing motionless, like a cigar store Indian about to burst into flight. "In your luggage," he said vaguely, "would you maybe have a suit you can't use? I could use a suit."

At last he comes to the point. Fidelman, though annoyed, controlled himself. "All I have is a change from the one you now see me wearing. Don't get the wrong idea about me, Mr. Susskind. I'm not rich. In fact I'm poor. Don't let a few new clothes deceive you. I owe my sister money for them."

Susskind glanced down at his shabby baggy knickers. "I haven't had a suit for years. The one I was wearing when I ran away from Germany, fell apart. One day I was walking around naked."

"Isn't there a welfare organization that could help you out—some group in the Jewish community, interested in refugees?"

"The Jewish organizations wish to give me what they wish, not what I wish," Susskind replied bitterly. "The only thing they offer me is a ticket back to Israel."

"Why don't you take it?"

"I told you already, here I feel free."

"Freedom is a relative term."

"Don't tell me about freedom."

He knows all about that too, Fidelman thought. "So you feel free," he said, "but how do you live?"

Susskind coughed, a brutal cough.

Fidelman was about to say something more on the subject of freedom but left it unsaid. Jesus, I'll be saddled with him all day if I don't watch out.

"I'd better be getting off to the hotel." He bent again for his bag.

Susskind touched him on the shoulder and when Fidelman exasperatedly straightened up, the half dollar he had given the man was staring him in the eye.

"On this we both lose money."

"How do you mean?"

"Today the lira sells six twenty-three on the dollar, but for specie they only give you five hundred."

"In that case give it here and I'll let you have a dollar." From his billfold Fidelman quickly extracted a crisp bill and handed it to the refugee.

"Not more?" Susskind sighed.

"Not more," the student answered emphatically.

"Maybe you would like to see Diocletian's bath? There are some enjoyable Roman coffins inside. I will guide you for another dollar."

"No, thanks." Fidelman said goodbye, and lifting the suitcase, lugged it to the curb. A porter appeared and the student, after some hesitation, let him carry it toward the line of small dark-green taxis on the piazza. The porter offered to carry the brief case too but Fidelman wouldn't part with it. He gave the cab driver the address of the hotel, and the taxi took off with a lurch. Fidelman at last relaxed. Susskind, he noticed, had disappeared. Gone with his breeze, he thought. But on the way to the hotel he had an uneasy feeling that the refugee, crouched low, might be clinging to the little tire on the back of the cab; however he didn't look out to see.

Fidelman had reserved a room in an inexpensive hotel not far from the station with its very convenient bus terminal. Then, as was his habit, he got himself quickly and tightly organized. He was always concerned with not wasting time, as if it were his only wealth—not true, of course, though Fidelman admitted he was an ambitious person—and he soon arranged a schedule that made the most of his working hours. Mornings he usually visited the Italian libraries, searching their catalogues and archives, read in poor light, and made profuse notes. He napped for an hour after lunch, then at four, when the churches and museums were re-opening, hurried off to them with lists of frescoes and paintings he must see. He was anxious to get to Florence, at the same time a little unhappy at all he would not have time to take in in Rome. Fidelman promised himself to return if he could afford it, perhaps in the spring, and look at everything he pleased.

After dark he managed to unwind himself and relax. He ate as the Romans did, late, enjoyed a half liter of white wine and smoked a cigarette. Afterward he liked to wander—especially in the old sections near the Tiber. He had read that here, under his feet, were the ruins of Ancient Rome. It was an inspiring business, he, Arthur Fidelman, after all, born a Bronx boy, walking around in all this history. History was mysterious, the remembrance of things unknown, in a way burdensome, in a way a sensuous experience. It uplifted and depressed, why he did not know except that it excited his thoughts more than he thought good for him. This kind of excitement was all right up to a point, perfect maybe for a creative artist, but less so for a critic. A critic ought to live on beans. He walked for miles along the winding Tiber, gazing at the star-strewn skies. Once, after a couple of days in the Vatican Museum, he saw flights of angels—gold, blue, white—intermingled in the sky. "My God, I got to stop using my eyes so much," Fidelman said to himself. But back in his room he sometimes wrote till morning.

Late one night, about a week after his arrival in Rome, as Fidelman was writing a few notes on the Byzantine style mosaics he had seen during the day, there was a knock on the door, and though the student, immersed in his work, was not conscious he had said "Avanti," he must have, for the door opened, and instead of an angel, in came Susskind in his shirt and baggy knickers.

Fidelman, who had all but forgotten the refugee, certainly never thought of him, half rose in astonishment. "Susskind," he exclaimed, "how did you get in here?"

Susskind for a moment stood motionless, then answered with a weary smile, "I'll tell you the truth, I know the clerk."

"But how did you know where I live?"

"I saw you walking in the street so I followed you."

"You mean you saw me accidentally?"

"How else? Did you leave me your address?"

Fidelman resumed his seat. "What can I do for you, Susskind?" He spoke grimly.

The refugee cleared his throat. "Professor, the days are warm but the nights are cold. You see how I go around naked." He held forth bluish arms, goosefleshed. "I came to ask you to reconsider about giving away your old suit."

"And who says it's an old suit?" Fidelman's voice thickened.

"One suit is new, so the other's old."

"Not precisely. I am afraid I have no suit for you, Susskind. The one I presently have hanging in the closet is a little more than a year old and I can't afford to give it away. Besides, it's gabardine, more like a summer suit."

"On me it will be for all seasons."

After a moment's reflection, Fidelman drew out his billfold and counted four single dollars. These he handed to Susskind.

"Buy yourself a warm sweater."

Susskind also counted the money, bill for bill. "If four," he said, "then why not five?"

Fidelman flushed. The man's warped nerve. "Because I happen to have four available," he answered. "That's twenty-five hundred lire. You should be able to buy a warm sweater and have something left over besides."

"I need a suit," Susskind said. "The days are warm but the nights are cold." He rubbed his arms. "What else I need I won't say."

"At least roll down your sleeves if you're so cold."

"That won't help me."

"Listen, Susskind," Fidelman said gently, "I would gladly give you the suit if I could afford to, but I can't. I have barely enough money to squeeze out a year for myself here. I've already told you I am indebted to my sister. Why don't you try to get yourself a job somewhere, no matter how menial? I'm sure that in a short time you'll work yourself up into a decent position."

"A job, he says," Susskind muttered gloomily. "Do you know what it means to get a job in Italy? Who will give me a job?"

"Who gives anybody a job? They have to go out and get it."

"You don't understand, professor. I am an Israeli citizen and this means I can only work for an Israeli company. How many Israeli companies are there here?—maybe two, El Al and Zim, and even if they had a job, they wouldn't give it to me because I have lost my passport. I would be better off now if I were stateless. A stateless person shows his laissez-passer and sometimes he can find a small job."

"But if you lost your passport why didn't you put in for a duplicate?"

"I did but did they give it to me?"

"Why not?"

"Why not? They say I sold it."

"Had they reason to think so?"

"I swear to you somebody stole it."

"Under such circumstances," Fidelman asked, "how do you live?"

"How do I live?" He chomped with his teeth. "I eat air."

"Seriously?"

"Seriously—on air. I also peddle," he confessed, "but to peddle you need a license and that the Italians won't give me. When they caught me peddling I was interned for six months in a work camp."

"Didn't they attempt to deport you?"

"They did but I sold my mother's old wedding ring that I kept in my pocket so many years. The Italians are a humane people. They took the money and let me go but they told me not to peddle more."

"So what do you do now?"

"I peddle. What should I do, beg?—I peddle. But last spring I got sick and gave my little money away to the doctors. I still have a bad cough." He coughed fruitily. "Now I have no capital to buy stock with. Listen, professor, maybe we can go in partnership together? Lend me twenty thousand lire and I will buy ladies' nylon stockings. After I sell them I will return you your money."

"I have no funds to invest, Susskind."

"You will get it back, with interest."

"I honestly am sorry for you," Fidelman said, "but why don't you at least do something practical? Why don't you go to the Joint Distribution Committee, for instance, and ask them to assist you? That's their business."

"I already told you why. They wish me to go back, I wish to stay here."

"I still think going back would be the best thing for you."

"No," cried Susskind angrily.

"If that's your decision, freely made, then why pick on me? Am I responsible for you then, Susskind?"

"Who else?" Susskind loudly replied.

"Lower your voice, please, people are sleeping around here," said Fidelman, beginning to perspire. "Why should I be?"

"You know what responsibility means?"

"I think so."

"Then you are responsible. Because you are a man. Because you are a Jew, aren't you?"

"Yes, goddamn it, but I'm not the only one in the whole wide world. Without prejudice, I refuse the obligation. I am a single individual and can't take on everybody's personal burden. I have the weight of my own to contend with."

He reached for his billfold and plucked out another dollar.

"This makes five. It's more than I can afford but take it and after this please leave me alone. I have made my contribution."

Susskind stood there, oddly motionless, an impassioned statue, and for a moment Fidelman wondered if he would stay all night, but at last the refugee thrust forth a stiff arm, took the fifth dollar and departed.

Early the next morning Fidelman moved out of the hotel into another, less convenient for him, but far away from Shimon Susskind and his endless demands.

This was Tuesday. On Wednesday, after a busy morning in the library, Fidelman entered a nearby trattoria and ordered a plate of spaghetti with tomato sauce. He was reading his *Messaggero,* anticipating the coming of the food, for he was unusually hungry, when he sensed a presence at the table. He looked up, expecting the waiter, but beheld instead Susskind standing there, alas, unchanged.

Is there no escape from him? thought Fidelman, severely vexed. Is this why I came to Rome?

"Shalom, professor," Susskind said, keeping his eyes off the table. "I was passing and saw you sitting here alone, so I came in to say shalom."

"Susskind," Fidelman said in anger, "have you been following me again?"

"How could I follow you?" asked the astonished Susskind. "Do I know where you live now?"

Though Fidelman blushed a little, he told himself he owed nobody an explanation. So he had found out he had moved—good.

"My feet are tired. Can I sit five minutes?"

"Sit."

Susskind drew out a chair. The spaghetti arrived steaming hot. Fidelman sprinkled it with cheese and wound his fork into several tender strands. One of the strings of spaghetti seemed to stretch for miles, so he stopped at a certain point and swallowed the forkful. Having foolishly neglected to cut the long string he was left sucking it, seemingly endlessly. This embarrassed him.

Susskind watched with rapt attention.

Fidelman at last reached the end of the long spaghetti, patted his mouth with a large napkin, and paused in his eating.

"Would you care for a plateful?"

Susskind, eyes hungry, hesitated. "Thanks," he said.

"Thanks yes or thanks no?"

"Thanks no." The eyes looked away.

Fidelman resumed eating, carefully winding his fork; he had had not much practice with this sort of thing and was soon involved in the same dilemma with the spaghetti. Seeing Susskind still watching him, he soon became tense.

"We are not Italians, professor," the refugee said. "Cut it in small pieces with your knife. Then you will swallow it easier."

"I'll handle it as I please," Fidelman responded testily. "This is my business. You attend to yours."

"My business," Susskind sighed, "don't exist. This morning I had to let a wonderful chance get away from me. I had a chance to buy ladies' stockings at three hundred lire if I had money to buy half a gross. I could easily sell them for five hundred a pair. We would have made a nice profit."

"The news doesn't interest me."

"So, if not ladies' stockings, I can also get sweaters, scarves, men's socks, also cheap leather goods, ceramics—whatever would interest you."

"What interests me is what you did with the money I gave you for a sweater."

"It's getting cold, professor," Susskind said worriedly. "Soon comes the November rains, and in winter the tramontana. I thought I ought to save your money to buy a couple of kilos of chestnuts and a bag of charcoal for my burner. If you sit all day on a busy street corner you can sometimes make a thousand lire. Italians like hot chestnuts. But if I do this I will need some warm clothes, maybe a suit."

"A suit," Fidelman remarked sarcastically, "why not an overcoat?"

"I have a coat, poor that it is, but now I need a suit. How can anybody come in company without a suit?"

Fidelman's hand trembled as he laid down his fork. "To my mind you are irresponsible and I won't be saddled with you. I have the right to choose my own problems and the right to my privacy."

"Don't get excited, professor, it's bad for your digestion. Eat in peace." Susskind got up and left the trattoria.

Fidelman hadn't the appetite to finish his spaghetti. He paid the bill, waited ten minutes, then departed, glancing around from time to time to see if he were being followed. He headed down the sloping street to a small piazza where he saw a couple of cabs. Not that he could afford one, but he wanted to make sure Susskind didn't tail him back to his new hotel. He would warn the clerk at the desk never to allow anybody of the refugee's name or description even to make inquiries about him.

Susskind, however, stepped out from behind a plashing fountain at the center of the little piazza. Modestly addressing the speechless Fidelman, he said, "I don't wish to take only, professor. If I had something to give you, I would gladly give it to you."

"Thanks," snapped Fidelman, "just give me some peace of mind."

"That you have to find yourself," Susskind answered.

In the taxi Fidelman decided to leave for Florence the next day, rather than at the end of the week, and once and for all be done with the pest.

That night, after returning to his room from an unpleasurable walk in the Trastevere—he had a headache from too much wine at supper—Fidelman found his door ajar and at once recalled that he had forgotten to lock it, although he had as usual left the key with the desk clerk. He was at first frightened, but when he tried the armadio in which he kept his clothes and suitcase, it was shut tight. Hastily unlocking it, he was relieved to see his blue gabardine suit—a one-button jacket affair, the trousers a little frayed on the cuffs but all in good shape and usable for years to come—hanging amid some shirts the maid had pressed for him; and when he examined the contents of the suitcase he found nothing missing, including, thank God, his passport and traveler's checks. Gazing around the room, Fidelman saw all in place. Satisfied, he picked up a book and read ten pages before he thought of his brief case. He jumped to his feet and began to search everywhere, remembering distinctly that it had been on the night table as he had lain on the bed that afternoon, rereading his chapter. He searched under the bed and behind the night table, then again throughout the room, even on top of and behind the armadio. Fidelman hopelessly opened every drawer, no matter how small, but found neither the brief case, nor, what was far worse, the chapter in it.

With a groan he sank down on the bed, insulting himself for not having made a copy of the manuscript, for he had more than once warned himself that something like this might happen to it. But he hadn't because there were some revisions he had contemplated making, and he had planned to retype the entire chapter before beginning the next. He thought now of complaining to the owner of the hotel, who lived on the floor below, but it was already past midnight and he realized nothing could be done until morning. Who could have taken it? The maid or hall porter? It seemed unlikely they would risk their jobs to steal a piece of leather goods that would bring them only a few thousand lire in a pawn shop. Possibly a sneak thief? He would ask tomorrow if other persons on the floor were missing something. He somehow doubted it. If a thief, he would then and there have ditched the chapter and stuffed the brief case with Fidelman's oxblood shoes, left by the bed, and the fifteen-dollar R. H. Macy sweater that lay in full view on the desk. But if not the maid or porter or a sneak thief, then who? Though Fidelman had not the slightest shred of evidence to support his suspicions he could think of only one person—Susskind. This thought stung him. But if Susskind, why? Out of pique, perhaps, that he had not been given the suit he had coveted, nor was able to pry it out of the armadio? Try as he would, Fidelman could think of no one else and no other reason. Somehow the peddler had followed him home (he had suspected their meeting at the fountain) and had got into his room while he was out to supper.

Fidelman's sleep that night was wretched. He dreamed of pursuing the refugee in the Jewish catacombs under the ancient Appian Way, threatening him a blow on the presumptuous head with a seven-flamed candelabrum he clutched in his hand; while Susskind, clever ghost, who knew the ins and outs of all the crypts and alleys, eluded him at every turn. Then Fidelman's candles all blew out, leaving him sightless and alone in the cemeterial dark; but when the student arose in the morning and wearily drew up the noisy blinds, the yellow Italian, somewhat shrunken, sun winked him cheerfully in both bleary eyes.

Fidelman postponed going to Florence. He reported his loss to the Questura, and though the police were polite and eager to help, they could do nothing for him. On the form on which the inspector noted the complaint, he listed the brief case as worth ten thousand lire, and for "valore del manoscritto" he drew a line. Fidelman, after giving the matter a good deal of thought, did not report Susskind, first, because he had absolutely no proof, for the desk clerk swore he had seen no stranger around in knickers; second, because he was afraid of the consequences for the refugee if he were written down "suspected thief" as well as "unlicensed peddler" and inveterate refugee. He tried instead to rewrite the chapter, which he felt sure he knew by heart, but when he sat down at the desk there were important thoughts, whole paragraphs, even pages that went blank in the mind. He considered sending to America for his notes for the chapter but they were in a barrel in his sister's attic in Levittown, among many notes for other projects. The thought of Bessie, a mother of five, poking around in his things, and the work entailed in sorting the cards, then getting them packaged and mailed to him across the ocean, wearied Fidelman unspeakably; he was certain she would send the wrong ones. He laid down his pen and went into the street, seeking Susskind. He searched for him in neighborhoods where he had seen him before, and though Fidelman spent hours looking, literally days, Susskind never appeared; or if he perhaps did, the sight of Fidelman caused him to vanish. And when the student inquired about him at the Israeli consulate, the clerk, a new man on the job, said he had no record of such a person or his lost passport; on the other hand, the refugee was known at the JDC, but by name and address only, an impossibility, Fidelman thought. They gave him a number to go to but the place had long since been torn down to make way for an apartment house.

Time went without work, without accomplishment. To put an end to this appalling waste Fidelman tried to force himself back into his routine research and picture viewing. He moved out of the hotel, which he now could not stand for the harm it had done him (leaving a telephone number and urging he be called if the slightest clue turned up), and he took a room in a small pensione near the Stazione and here had breakfast and supper rather than go out. He was much concerned with expenditures and carefully recorded them in a notebook he had acquired for the purpose. Nights, instead of wandering in the city, feasting himself on its beauty and mystery, he kept his eyes glued to paper, sitting steadfastly at his desk in an attempt to re-create his initial chapter, because he was lost without a beginning. He had tried writing the second chapter from notes in his possession but it had come to nothing. Always Fidelman needed something solid behind him before he could advance, some worthwhile accomplishment upon which to build another. He worked late but his mood, or inspiration, or whatever it was, had deserted him, leaving him with growing anxiety, almost disorientation; of not knowing—it seemed to him for the first time in months—what he must do next, a feeling that was torture. Therefore he again took up his search for the refugee. He thought now that once he had settled it, knew that the man had or hadn't stolen his chapter—whether he recovered it or not seemed at the moment immaterial—just the knowing of it would ease his mind and again he would feel like working, the crucial element.

Daily he combed the crowded streets, searching for Susskind wherever people peddled. On successive Sunday mornings he took the long ride to the Porta Portese market and hunted for hours among the piles of second-hand goods and junk lining the back streets, hoping his brief case would magically appear, though it never did. He visited the open market at Piazza Fontanella Borghese, and observed the ambulant vendors at Piazza Dante. He looked among fruit and vegetable stalls set up in the streets, whenever he chanced upon them, and dawdled on busy street corners after dark, among beggars and fly-by-night peddlers. After the first cold snap at the end of October, when the chestnut sellers appeared throughout the city, huddled over pails of glowing coals, he sought in their faces the missing Susskind. Where in all of modern and ancient Rome was he? The man lived in the open air—he had to appear somewhere. Sometimes when riding in a bus or tram, Fidelman thought he had glimpsed somebody in a crowd, dressed in the refugee's clothes, and he invariably got off to run after whoever it was—once a man standing in front of the Banco di Santo Spirito, gone when Fidelman breathlessly arrived; and another time he overtook a person in knickers but this one wore a monocle. Sir Ian Susskind?

In November it drearily rained. Fidelman wore a blue beret with his trench coat and a pair of black Italian shoes, smaller, despite their pointed toes, than his burly oxbloods which overheated his feet and whose color he detested. But instead of visiting museums he frequented movie houses, sitting in the cheapest seats and regretting the cost. He was, at odd hours in certain streets, several times solicited by prostitutes, some heartbreakingly pretty, one a slender, unhappy-looking girl with bags under her eyes whom he desired mightily, but Fidelman feared for his health. He had got to know the face of Rome and spoke Italian fairly fluently but his heart was burdened, and in his blood raged a murderous hatred of the bandy-legged refugee—although there were times when he thought he might be wrong—so Fidelman more than once cursed him to perdition.

One Friday night, as the first star glowed over the Tiber, Fidelman, walking aimlessly along the left riverbank, came upon a synagogue and wandered in among a crowd of Sephardim with Italianate faces. One by one they paused before a sink in an antechamber to dip their hands under a flowing faucet, then in the house of worship touched with loose fingers their brows, mouths, and breasts as they bowed to the Ark, Fidelman doing likewise. Where in the world am I? Three rabbis rose from a bench and the service began, a long prayer, sometimes chanted, sometimes accompanied by invisible organ music, but no Susskind anywhere. Fidelman sat at a desk-like pew in the last row where he could inspect the congregants yet keep an eye on the door. The synagogue was unheated and the cold rose like an exudation from the marble floor. The student's freezing nose burned like a lit candle. He got up to go but the beadle, a stout man in a high hat and short caftan, wearing a long thick silver chain around his neck, fixed the student with his powerful left eye.

"From New York?" he inquired, slowly approaching.

Half the congregation turned to see who.

"State, not city," answered Fidelman, nursing an active embarrassment for the attention he was attracting. Taking advantage of a pause, he whispered, "Do you happen to know a man named Susskind? He wears knickers."

"A relative?" The beadle gazed at him sadly.

"Not exactly."

"My own son—killed in the Ardeatine Caves." Tears stood forth in his eyes.

"Ah, for that I'm sorry."

But the beadle had exhausted the subject. He wiped his wet lids with pudgy fingers and the curious Sephardim turned back to their prayer books.

"Which Susskind?" the beadle wanted to know.

"Shimon."

He scratched his ear. "Look in the ghetto."

"I looked."

"Look again."

The beadle walked slowly away and Fidelman sneaked out.

The ghetto lay behind the synagogue for several crooked well-packed blocks, encompassing aristocratic palazzi ruined by age and unbearable numbers, their discolored façades strung with lines of withered wet wash, the fountains in the piazzas, dirt-laden, dry. And dark stone tenements, built partly on centuries-old ghetto walls, inclined towards one another across narrow, cobblestoned streets. In and among the impoverished houses were the wholesale establishments of wealthy Jews, dark holes ending in jeweled interiors, silks and silver of all colors. In the mazed streets wandered the present-day poor, Fidelman among them, oppressed by history although, he joked to himself, it added years to his life.

A white moon shone upon the ghetto, lighting it like dark day. Once he thought he saw a ghost he knew by sight, and hastily followed him through a thick stone passage to a blank wall where shone in white letters under a tiny electric bulb: VIETATO URINARE. Here was a smell but no Susskind.

For thirty lire the student bought a dwarfed blackened banana from a street vendor (not S) on a bicycle and stopped to eat. A crowd of ragazzi gathered to watch.

"Anybody here know Susskind, a refugee wearing knickers?" Fidelman announced, stooping to point with the banana where the pants went beneath the knees. He also made his legs a trifle bowed but nobody noticed.

There was no response until he had finished his fruit, then a thin-faced boy with brown liquescent eyes out of Murillo, piped: "He sometimes works in the Campo Verano, the Jewish section."

There too? thought Fidelman. "Works in the cemetery?" he inquired. "With a shovel?"

"He prays for the dead," the boy answered, "for a small fee."

Fidelman bought him a quick banana and the others dispersed.

In the cemetery, deserted on the Sabbath—he should have come Sunday—Fidelman went among the graves, reading legends on tombstones, many

"Use the reward for that," Fidelman cagily whispered, "buy Holy Mothers."

If he heard, Susskind gave no sign. At the sight of a family of nine emerging from the main portal above, the refugee, calling addio over his shoulder, fairly flew up the steps. But Fidelman uttered no response. I'll get the rat yet. He went off to hide behind a high fountain in the square. But the flying spume raised by the wind wet him, so he retreated behind a massive column and peeked out at short intervals to keep the peddler in sight.

At two o'clock, when St. Peter's closed to visitors, Susskind dumped his goods into his raincoat pockets and locked up shop. Fidelman followed him all the way home, indeed the ghetto, although along a street he had not consciously been on before, which led into an alley where the refugee pulled open a left-handed door, and without transition, was "home." Fidelman, sneaking up close, caught a dim glimpse of an overgrown closet containing bed and table. He found no address on wall or door, nor, to his surprise, any door lock. This for a moment depressed him. It meant Susskind had nothing worth stealing. Of his own, that is. The student promised himself to return tomorrow, when the occupant was elsewhere.

Return he did, in the morning, while the entrepreneur was out selling religious articles, glanced around once and was quickly inside. He shivered—a pitch-black freezing cave. Fidelman scratched up a thick match and confirmed bed and table, also a rickety chair, but no heat or light except a drippy candle stub in a saucer on the table. He lit the yellow candle and searched all over the place. In the table drawer a few eating implements plus safety razor, though where he shaved was a mystery, probably a public toilet. On a shelf above the thin-blanketed bed stood half a flask of red wine, part of a package of spaghetti, and a hard panino. Also an unexpected little fish bowl with a bony goldfish swimming around in Arctic seas. The fish, reflecting the candle flame, gulped repeatedly, threshing its frigid tail as Fidelman watched. He loves pets, thought the student. Under the bed he found a chamber pot, but nowhere a brief case with a fine critical chapter in it. The place was not more than an ice-box someone probably had lent the refugee to come in out of the rain. Alas, Fidelman sighed. Back in the pensione, it took a hot water bottle two hours to thaw him out; but from the visit he never fully recovered.

In this latest dream of Fidelman's he was spending the day in a cemetery all crowded with tombstones, when up out of an empty grave rose this long-nosed brown shade, Virgilio Susskind, beckoning.

Fidelman hurried over.

"Have you read Tolstoy?"

"Sparingly."

"Why is art?" asked the shade, drifting off.

Fidelman, willy-nilly, followed, and the ghost, as it vanished, led him up steps going through the ghetto and into a marble synagogue.

The student, left alone, because he could not resist the impulse, lay down upon the stone floor, his shoulders keeping strangely warm as he stared at the sunlit vault above. The fresco therein revealed this saint in fading blue, the sky flowing from his head, handing an old knight in a thin red robe his gold cloak. Nearby stood a humble horse and two stone hills.

Giotto. San Francesco dona le vesti al cavaliere povero.

Fidelman awoke running. He stuffed his blue gabardine into a paper bag, caught a bus, and knocked early on Susskind's heavy portal.

"Avanti." The refugee, already garbed in beret and raincoat (probably his pajamas), was standing at the table, lighting the candle with a flaming sheet of paper. To Fidelman the paper looked the underside of a typewritten page. Despite himself the student recalled in letters of fire his entire chapter.

"Here, Susskind," he said in a trembling voice, offering the bundle, "I bring you my suit. Wear it in good health."

The refugee glanced at it without expression. "What do you wish for it?"

"Nothing at all." Fidelman laid the bag on the table, called goodbye and left.

He soon heard footsteps clattering after him across the cobblestones.

"Excuse me, I kept this under my mattress for you." Susskind thrust at him the pigskin brief case.

Fidelman savagely opened it, searching frantically in each compartment, but the bag was empty. The refugee was already in flight. With a bellow the student started after him. "You bastard, you burned my chapter!"

"Have mercy," cried Susskind, "I did you a favor."

"I'll do you one and cut your throat."

"The words were there but the spirit was missing."

In a towering rage Fidelman forced a burst of speed, but the refugee, light as the wind in his marvelous knickers, green coattails flying, rapidly gained ground.

The ghetto Jews, framed in amazement in their medieval windows, stared at the wild pursuit. But in the middle of it, Fidelman, stout and short of breath, moved by all he had lately learned, had a triumphant insight.

"Susskind, come back," he shouted, half sobbing. "The suit is yours. All is forgiven."

He came to a dead halt but the refugee ran on. When last seen he was still running.

Heinrich Böll

Heinrich Böll (1917–   ), German novelist, was born in Cologne, and majored in German philosophy. During World War II he fought in the

German army, and was taken prisoner by the advancing Americans in 1945. In the years since the war ended, he has established himself as one of Germany's foremost contemporary writers. He received the Nobel Prize for Literature in 1972. Basically a moralist, akin in spirit to Camus and Kafka, he is mainly concerned with the changing social and moral structure, particularly of a postwar defeated Germany. A strain of powerful, bitter irony runs through many of his stories. His works include The Clown *(1963),* Billiards at Half-Past Nine *(1959) and* End of a Mission *(1968).* *(See page 70 of Introduction.)*

CHRISTMAS EVERY DAY

I

Symptoms of decline have become evident in our family. For a time we were at pains to disregard them, but now we have resolved to face the danger. I dare not, as yet, use the word breakdown, but disturbing facts are piling up at such a rate as to constitute a menace and to compel me to report things that will sound disagreeable to my contemporaries; no one, however, can dispute their reality. The minute fungi of destruction have found lodgement beneath the hard, thick crust of respectability; colonies of deadly parasites that proclaim the end of a whole tribe's irreproachable correctness. Today we must deplore our disregard of Cousin Franz, who began long ago to warn us of the dreadful consequences that would result from an event that was harmless enough in itself. So insignificant indeed was the event that the disproportion of the consequences now terrifies us. Franz warned us betimes. Unfortunately he had too little standing. He had chosen a calling that no member of the family had ever followed before, and none ever should have: he was a boxer. Melancholy even in youth and possessed by a devoutness that was always described as "pious fiddle-faddle," he early adopted ways that worried my Uncle Franz, that good, kind man. He was wont to neglect his schoolwork to a quite abnormal degree. He used to meet disreputable companions in the thickets and deserted parks of the suburbs, and there practice the rough discipline of the prize fight, with no thought for his neglected humanistic heritage. These youngsters early revealed the vices of their generation, which, as has since become abundantly evident, is really worthless. The exciting spiritual combats of earlier centuries simply did not interest them, they were far too concerned with the dubious excitements of their own. At first I thought Franz's piety in contradiction to his systematic exercises in passive and active brutality. But today I begin to suspect a connection. This is a subject I shall have to return to.

And so it was Franz who warned us in good time, who refused above all to have anything to do with certain celebrations, calling the whole thing a folly and a disgrace, and later on declined to participate in those measures that proved necessary for the continuance of what he considered evil. But, as I have said, he had too little standing to get a hearing in the family circle.

Now, to be sure, things have gone so far that we stand helpless, not knowing how to call a halt.

Franz has long since become a famous boxer, but today he rejects the praises that the family lavishes on him with the same indifference he once showed toward their criticism.

His brother, however—my Cousin Johannes, a man for whom I would at any time have walked through fire, the successful lawyer and favorite son of my uncle—Johannes is said to have struck up relations with the Communist Party, a rumor I stubbornly refuse to believe. My Cousin Lucie, hitherto a normal woman, is said to frequent disreputable nightclubs, accompanied by her helpless husband, and to engage in dances that I can only describe as existential. Even Uncle Franz, that good, kind man, is reported to have remarked that he is weary of life, he whom the whole family considered a paragon of vitality and the very model of what we were taught to call a Christian businessman.

Doctor's bills are piling up, psychiatrists and analysts are being called in. Only my Aunt Milla, who must be considered the cause of it all, enjoys the best of health, smiling, well and cheerful, as she has been almost all her life. Her liveliness and cheerfulness are slowly beginning to get on our nerves after our very serious concern about the state of her health. For there was a crisis in her life that threatened to be serious. It is just this that I must explain.

II

In retrospect it is easy enough to determine the source of a disquieting series of events, but only now, when I regard the matter dispassionately, do the things that have been taking place in our family for almost two years appear out of the ordinary.

We might have surmised earlier that something was not quite right. Something in fact was not, and if things ever were quite right—which I doubt—events are now taking place that fill me with consternation.

For a long time Aunt Milla has been famous in our family for her delight in decorating the Christmas tree, a harmless though particularized weakness which is fairly widespread in our country. This weakness of hers was indulgently smiled at by one and all, and the resistance that Franz showed from his earliest days to this "nonsense" was treated with indignation, especially since Franz was in other respects a disturbing young man. He refused to take part in the decoration of the tree. Up to a certain point all this was taken in stride. My aunt had become accustomed to Franz's staying away from the preparations at Advent and also from the celebration itself and only putting in an appearance for the meal. It was not even mentioned.

At the risk of making myself unpopular, I must here mention a fact in defense of which I can only say that it really is a fact. In the years 1939 to 1945 we were at war. In war there is singing, shooting, oratory, fighting, starvation and death—and bombs are dropped. These are thoroughly disagreeable subjects, and I have no desire to bore my contemporaries by dwelling on them. I must only mention them because the war had an influence on the story I am about to tell. For the war registered on my aunt simply as a force that, as early as Christmas 1939, began to threaten her Christmas tree. To be sure, this tree of hers was peculiarly sensitive.

As its principal attraction my Aunt Milla's Christmas tree was furnished with glass gnomes that held cork hammers in their upraised hands. At their feet were bell-shaped anvils, and under their feet candles were fastened. When the heat rose to a certain degree, a hidden mechanism went into operation, imparting a hectic movement to the gnomes' arms; a dozen in number, they beat like mad on the bell-shaped anvils with their cork hammers, thus producing a concerted, high-pitched, elfin tinkling. And at the top of the tree stood a red-cheeked angel, dressed in silver, who at certain intervals opened his lips and whispered "Peace, peace." The mechanical secret of the angel was strictly guarded, and I only learned about it later, when as it happened I had the opportunity of admiring it almost weekly. Naturally in addition to this my aunt's Christmas tree was decorated with sugar rings, cookies, angel hair, marzipan figures and, not to be forgotten, strands of tinsel. I still remember that the proper preparation of these varied decorations cost a good deal of trouble, demanding the help of all, and the whole family on Christmas Eve was too nervous to be hungry. The mood, as people say, was simply terrible, and the one exception was my Cousin Franz, who of course had taken no part in the preparations and was the only one to enjoy the roasts, asparagus, creams and ices. If after that we came for a call on the day after Christmas and ventured the bold conjecture that the secret of the speaking angel resided in the same sort of mechanism that makes certain dolls say "Mama" or "Papa," we were simply greeted by derisive laughter.

Now it is easy to understand that in the neighborhood of falling bombs such a sensitive tree would be in great danger. There were terrible times when the gnomes pitched down from the tree, and once even the angel fell. My aunt was inconsolable. She went to endless pains to restore the tree completely after each air raid so as to preserve it at least through the Christmas holidays. But by 1940 it was out of the question. Once more at the risk of making myself unpopular I must briefly mention here that the number of air raids on our city was considerable, to say nothing of their severity. In any case my aunt's Christmas tree fell victim to the modern art of war (regulations forbid me to say anything about other victims); foreign ballistics experts temporarily extinguished it.

We all sympathized with our aunt, who was an amiable and charming woman, and pretty into the bargain. It pained us that she was compelled, after bitter struggles, endless disputes, scenes and tears, to agree to forego her tree for the duration.

Fortunately—or should I say unfortunately?—this was almost the only aspect of the war that was brought home to my aunt. The bunker my uncle built was really bomb proof; in addition a car was always ready to whisk my Aunt Milla away to places where nothing was to be seen of the immediate effects of war. Everything was done to spare her the sight of the horrible ruins. My two cousins had the good fortune not to see military service in its harshest form. Johannes at once entered my uncle's firm, which played an essential part in the wholesale grocery business of our city. Besides, he suffered from gall bladder trouble. Franz on the other hand became a soldier, but he was only engaged in guarding prisoners, a post which he exploited to the extent of making himself unpopular with his military superiors by treating Russians and Poles like human beings. My Cousin Lucie was not yet married at that time and helped with the business. One afternoon a week she did voluntary war work, embroidering swastikas. But this is not the place to recite the political sins of my relations.

On the whole, then, there was no lack of money or food or reasonable safety, and my aunt's only sorrow was the absence of her tree. My Uncle Franz, that good, kind man, had for almost fifty years rendered invaluable service by purchasing oranges and lemons in tropical and sub-tropical countries and selling them at an appropriate profit. During the war he extended his business to less valuable fruits and to vegetables. After the war, however, the principal objects of his interest became popular once more under the name of citrus fruits and caused sharp competition in business circles. Here Uncle Franz succeeded once more in playing a decisive role by introducing the populace to a taste for vitamins and himself to a sizable fortune. He was almost seventy by that time, however, and wanted to retire and leave the business to his son-in-law. It was then that the event took place which made us smile at the time but which we now recognize as the cause of the whole affair.

My Aunt Milla began again with her Christmas tree. That was harmless in itself; even the tenacity with which she insisted that everything should be "as it used to be" only caused us to smile. At first there was really no reason to take the matter too seriously. To be sure, the war had caused much havoc which it was our duty to put right, but why—so we asked ourselves—deprive a charming old lady of this small joy?

Everyone knows how hard it was at that time to get butter and bacon. And even for my Uncle Franz, who had the best connections, it was impossible in the year 1945 to procure marzipan figures and chocolate rings. It was not until 1946 that everything could be made ready. Fortunately a complete set of gnomes and anvils as well as an angel had been preserved.

I still clearly remember the day on which we were invited. It was in January '47 and it was cold outside. But at my uncle's it was warm and there was no lack of delicacies. When the lights were turned out and the candles lighted, when the gnomes began to hammer and the angel whispered "Peace, peace," I had a vivid feeling of being restored to a time that I had assumed was gone forever.

This experience, however, though surprising was not extraordinary. The extraordinary thing was what happened three months later. My mother—it was now the middle of March—sent me over to find out whether "there was anything doing" with Uncle Franz. She needed fruit. I wandered into the neighboring quarter—the air was mild and it was twilight. Unsuspecting, I walked past the overgrown piles of ruins and the untended parks, turned in at the gate to my uncle's garden and suddenly stopped in amazement. In the evening quiet I could distinctly hear someone singing in my uncle's living room. Singing is a good old German custom, and there are lots of spring songs—but here I clearly heard:

Unto us a child is born!
The King of all creation . . .

I must admit I was confused. Slowly I approached and waited for the end of the song. The curtains were drawn and so I bent down to the keyhole. At that moment the tinkling of the gnomes' bells reached my ear, and I distinctly heard the angel whispering.

I did not have the courage to intrude, and walked slowly home. My report caused general merriment in the family, and it was not until Franz turned up and told us the details that we discovered what had happened.

In our region Christmas trees are dismantled at Candlemas and are then thrown on the rubbish heap where good-for-nothing children pick them up, drag them through ashes and other debris and play all sorts of games with them. This was the time when the dreadful thing happened. On Candlemas Eve after the tree had been lighted for the last time, and Cousin Johannes began to unfasten the gnomes from their clamps, my aunt who had hitherto been so gentle set up a dreadful screaming, so loud and sudden that my cousin was startled, lost control of the swaying tree, and in an instant it was all over; there was a tinkling and ringing; gnomes and bells, anvils and angel, everything pitched down; and my aunt screamed.

She screamed for almost a week. Neurologists were summoned by telegram, psychiatrists came rushing up in taxicabs—but all of them, even the specialists, left with a shrug of the shoulders and a faint expression of dread.

No one could put an end to this shrill and maddening concert. Only the strongest drugs provided a few hours' rest, and the dose of Luminal that one can daily prescribe for a woman in her sixties without endangering her life is, alas, slight. But it is anguish to have a woman in the house screaming with all her might: on the second day the family was completely disorganized. Even the consolation of the priest, who was accustomed to attend the celebration on Holy Eve, remained unavailing: my aunt screamed.

Franz made himself particularly unpopular by advising that a regular exorcism be performed. The minister rebuked him, the family was alarmed by his medieval views, and his reputation for brutality eclipsed for several weeks his reputation as a boxer.

Meanwhile everything was tried to cure my aunt's ailment. She refused nourishment, did not speak, did not sleep; cold water was tried, hot water, foot baths, alternate cold and hot baths; the doctors searched the lexicons for the name of this complex but could not find it. And my aunt screamed. She screamed until my Uncle Franz—that really kind, good man—hit on the idea of putting up a new Christmas tree.

III

The idea was excellent, but to carry it out proved extremely hard. It was now almost the middle of February, and to find a presentable fir tree in the market at that time is naturally difficult. The whole business world has long since turned with happy alacrity to other things. Carnival time is near: masks, pistols, cowboy hats and fanciful gypsy headgear fill the shop windows where angels and angel hair, candles and mangers, were formerly on view. In the candy stores Christmas items have long since gone back to the storeroom, while fireworks now adorn the windows. Nowhere in the regular market is a fir tree to be found.

Finally an expedition of rapacious grandchildren was fitted out with pocket money and a sharp hatchet. They rode to the state forest and came back toward evening, obviously in the best of spirits, with a silver fir. But meanwhile it was discovered that four gnomes, six bell-shaped anvils and the crowning angel had been completely destroyed. The marzipan figures and the cookies had fallen victim to the rapacious grandchildren. This coming generation, too, is worthless, and if any generation was ever of any worth—which I doubt—I am slowly coming to the belief that it was the generation of our fathers.

Although there was no lack of cash or the necessary connections, it took four days more before the decorations were complete. Meanwhile my aunt screamed uninterruptedly. Messages to the German centers of the toy business, which were just then resuming operations, were dispatched by wireless, hurried telephone conversations were carried on, packages were delivered in the night by heated young postal employees, an import license from Czechoslovakia was obtained, by bribery, without delay.

These days will stand out in the chronicle of my uncle's family by reason of the extraordinary consumption of coffee, cigarettes and nervous energy. Meanwhile my aunt fell into a decline: her round face became harsh and angular, her expression of kindliness changed to one of unalterable severity, she did not eat, she did not drink, she screamed constantly, she was attended by two nurses, and the dose of Luminal had to be increased daily.

Franz told us that the whole family was in the grip of a morbid tension when finally, on the twelfth of February, the decoration of the Christmas tree was at last completed. The candles were lighted, the curtains were drawn, my aunt was brought out from her sickroom, and in the family circle there was only the sound of sobs and giggles. My aunt's expression relaxed at the sight of the candles, and when the heat had reached the proper point and the glass gnomes began to pound like mad and finally the angel, too, whispered "Peace, peace," a beautiful smile illuminated her face. Shortly thereafter everyone began to sing "O Tannenbaum." To complete the picture, they had invited the minister, whose custom it was to spend Christmas Eve at my Uncle Franz's; he, too, smiled, he, too, was relieved and joined in the singing.

What no test, no psychological opinion, no expert search for hidden traumas had succeeded in doing, my uncle's sympathetic heart had accomplished. This good, kind man's Christmas-tree therapy had saved the situation.

My aunt was reassured and almost—so they hoped at the time—cured. After more songs had been sung and several plates of cookies had been emptied, everyone was tired and went to bed. And, imagine, my aunt slept without sedatives. The two nurses were dismissed, the doctors shrugged their shoulders, and everything seemed in order. My aunt ate again, drank again, was once more kind and amiable.

But the following evening at twilight, when my uncle was reading his newspaper beside his wife under the tree, she suddenly touched him gently on the arm and said: "Now we will call the children for the celebration. I think it's time." My uncle admitted to us later that he was startled, but he got up and hastily summoned his children and grandchildren and dispatched a messenger for the minister. The latter appeared, somewhat distraught and amazed; the candles were lighted, the gnomes hammered away, the angel whispered, there was singing and eating—and everything seemed in order.

Now all vegetation is subject to certain biological laws, and fir trees torn from the soil have a well-known tendency to wilt and lose their needles, especially if they are kept in a warm room, and in my uncle's house it was warm. The life of the silver fir is somewhat longer than that of the common variety, as the well-known work *Abies Vulgaris and Abies Nobilis* by Doctor Hergenring has shown. But even the life of the silver fir is not unlimited. As Carnival approached it became clear that my aunt would have to be prepared for a new sorrow: the tree was rapidly losing its needles, and at the evening singing a slight frown appeared on her forehead. On the advice of a really outstanding psychologist an attempt was made in light, casual conversation to warn her of the possible end of the Christmas season, especially as the trees outside were now covered with leaves, which is generally taken as a sign of approaching spring whereas in our latitudes the word Christmas connotes wintry scenes. My resourceful uncle proposed one evening that the songs "All the birds are now assembled" and "Come, Lovely May" should be sung, but at the first verse of the former such a scowl appeared on my aunt's face that the singers quickly broke off and intoned "O Tannenbaum." Three days later my Cousin Johannes was instructed to undertake a quiet dismantling operation, but as soon as he stretched out his hand and took the cork hammer from one of the gnomes my aunt broke into such violent screaming that the gnome was immediately given back his implement, the candles were lighted and somewhat hastily but very loudly everyone began to sing "Silent Night."

But the nights were no longer silent; groups of singing, youthful revelers streamed through the city with trumpets and drums, everything was covered with streamers and confetti, masked children crowded the streets, fired guns, screamed, some sang as well, and a private investigation showed that there were as least sixty thousand cowboys and forty thousand gypsy princesses in our city: in short it was Carnival, a holiday that is celebrated in our neighborhood with as much enthusiasm as Christmas or even more. But my aunt seemed blind and deaf: she deplored the Carnival costumes that inevitably appeared at this time in the wardrobes of our household; in a sad voice she lamented the decline of morals that caused people even at Christmas to indulge in such disgraceful practices, and when she discovered a toy balloon in Lucie's bedroom, a balloon that had, to be sure, collapsed but nevertheless clearly showed a white fool's cap painted on it, she broke into tears and besought my uncle to put an end to these unholy activities.

They were forced to realize with horror that my aunt actually believed it was still Christmas Eve. My uncle called a family council, requested consideration for his wife in view of her extraordinary state of mind, and at once got together an expedition to insure that at least the evening celebration would be peacefully maintained.

While my aunt slept the decorations were taken down from the old tree and placed on a new one, and her state of health continued to be satisfactory.

Carnival, too, went by, spring came for fair; instead of "Come Lovely May" one might properly have sung "Lovely May, Thou Art Here." June arrived. Four Christmas trees had already been discarded and none of the newly summoned doctors could hold out hope of improvement. My aunt remained firm. Even that internationally famous authority, Doctor Bless, had returned to his study, shrugging his shoulders, after having pocketed an honorarium in the sum of 1365 marks, thereby demonstrating once more his complete unworldliness. A few tentative attempts to put an end to the celebration or to intermit it were greeted with such outcries from my aunt that these sacrileges had to be abandoned once and for all.

The dreadful thing was that my aunt insisted that all those closest to her must be present. Among these were the minister and the grandchildren. Even the members of the family could only be compelled by extreme severity to appear punctually; with the minister it was even more difficult. For some weeks he kept it up without protest, out of consideration for his aged pensioner, but then he attempted, clearing his throat in embarrassment, to make it clear to my uncle that this could not go on. The actual celebration was short—it lasted only about thirty-eight minutes—but even this brief ceremonial, the minister maintained, could not be kept up indefinitely. He had other obligations, evening conferences with his confratres, duties connected with his cure of souls, not to mention his regular Saturday confessional. He agreed, however, to some weeks' continuance; but toward the end of May, he began energetic attempts to escape. Franz stormed about, seeking accomplices in the family for his plan to have his mother put in an institution. Everyone turned him down.

And yet difficulties continued. One evening the minister was missing and could not be located either telephonically or by messenger, and it became evident that he had simply skipped out. My uncle swore horribly and took the occasion to describe the servants of the Church in words I must decline to repeat. In this extremity one of the chaplains, a man of humble origin, was requested to help out. He did so, but behaved so abominably that it almost resulted in a catastrophe. However, one must bear in mind that it was June and therefore hot; nevertheless the curtains were drawn to give at least an illusion of wintry twilight and in addition the candles had been lighted. Then the celebration began. The chaplain had, to be sure, heard of this extraordinary event but had no proper idea of it. There was general apprehension when he was presented to my aunt as the minister's substitute. Unexpectedly she accepted this change in the program. Well then, the gnomes hammered, the angel whispered, "O Tannenbaum" was sung, then there was the eating of cookies, more singings, and suddenly the chaplain was overcome by a paroxysm of laughter. Later he admitted that it was the line ". . . in winter, too, when snow is falling" that had been too much for him to endure without laughing. He burst out with clerical tactlessness, left the room and was seen no more. All looked at my aunt apprehensively, but she only murmured resignedly something about "proletarians in priest's robes" and put a piece of marzipan in her mouth. We too deplored this event at the time—but today I am inclined to regard it as an outbreak of quite natural hilarity.

Here I must remark, if I am to be true to the facts, that my uncle exploited his connection with the highest Church authorities to lodge a complaint against both the minister and the chaplain. The matter was taken up with utmost correctness, proceedings were instituted on the grounds of neglect of pastoral duty, and in the first instance the two clergymen were exonerated. Further proceedings are in preparation.

Fortunately a pensioned prelate was found in the neighborhood. This charming old gentleman agreed, with amiable matter-of-factness, to hold himself in readiness daily for the evening celebration. But I am anticipating. My Uncle Franz, who was sensible enough to realize that no medical aid would be of avail and who stubbornly refused to try exorcism, was also a good enough businessman to plan economies for the long haul. First of all, by mid-June, the grandchildren's expeditions were stopped because they proved too expensive. My resourceful Cousin Johannes, who was on good terms with all branches of the business world, discovered that Söderbaum and Company were in a position to provide fresh fir trees. For almost two years now this firm has done noble service in sparing my relations' nerves. At the end of six months Söderbaum and Company substantially reduced their charges and agreed to have the period of delivery determined most precisely by their conifer specialist Doctor Alfast, so that three days before the old tree became unpresentable a new one would be delivered and could be decorated at leisure. As an additional precaution two dozen gnomes and three crowning angels were kept constantly in reserve.

To this day the candies remain a sore point. They show a disturbing tendency to melt and drip down from the tree more quickly and completely than wax, at any rate in the summer months. Every effort to preserve them by carefully concealed refrigeration has thus far come to grief, as has a series of attempts to substitute artificial decorations. The family remains, however, gratefully receptive toward any proposal that might result in reducing the costs of this continuing festival.

IV

Meanwhile the daily celebrations in my uncle's house have taken on an almost professional regularity. People assemble under the tree or around the tree. My aunt comes in, the candles are lighted, the gnomes begin to hammer and the angel whispers "Peace, peace," songs are sung, cookies are nibbled, there is a little conversation and then everyone retires, yawning and murmuring "Merry Christmas to you, too." The young people turn to the forms of diversion dictated by the season, while my good, kind Uncle Franz goes to bed when Aunt Milla does. The smoke of the candles lingers in the room, there is the mild aroma of heated fir needles and the smell of spices. The gnomes, slightly phosphorescent, remain motionless in the darkness, their arms raised threateningly, and the angel can be seen in his silvery robes which are obviously phosphorescent too.

Perhaps it is superfluous to state that in our whole family circle the enjoyment of the real Christmas Eve has suffered a considerable diminution: we can, if we like, admire a classical Christmas tree at our uncle's at any time—and it often happens when we are sitting on the veranda in summertime after the toil and trouble of the day, pouring my uncle's mild orange punch down our throats, that the soft tinkling of glass bells comes to us and we can see in the twilight the gnomes hammering away like spry little devils while the angel whispers "Peace, peace." And it is still disconcerting to hear my uncle in mid-summer suddenly whisper to his children: "Please light the tree, Mother will be right out." Then, usually on the dot, the prelate enters, a kindly old gentleman whom we have all taken to our hearts because he plays his role so admirably, if indeed he knows that he is playing one. But no matter: he plays it, white-haired, smiling, with the violet band beneath his collar giving his appearance the final touch of distinction. And it gives one an extraordinary feeling on a mild summer evening to hear the excited cry: "The snuffer, quick, where is the snuffer?" It has even happened during severe thunderstorms that the gnomes have been suddenly impelled to lift their arms without the agency of heat and swing them wildly as though giving a special performance—a phenomenon that people have tried, rather unimaginatively, to explain by the prosaic word "electricity."

A by no means inessential aspect of this arrangement is the financial one. Even though in general our family suffers no lack of cash, such extraordinary expenses upset all calculations. For naturally, despite precautions, the breakage of gnomes, anvils, and hammers is enormous, and the delicate mechanism that causes the angel to speak requires constant care and attention and must now and again be replaced. I have, incidentally, discovered its secret: the angel is connected by a cable with a microphone in the adjoining room, in front of whose metal snout there is a constantly rotating phonograph record which, at proper intervals, whispers "Peace, peace." All these things are the more costly because they are designed for use on only a few occasions during the year, whereas with us they are subjected to daily wear and tear. I was astounded when my uncle told me one day that the gnomes actually had to be replaced every three months, and that a complete set of them cost no less than 128 marks. He said he had requested an engineering friend of his to try strengthening them by a rubber covering without spoiling the beauty of the tone. This experiment was unsuccessful. The consumption of candles, butter-and-almond cookies, marzipan, the regular payments for the trees, doctor's bills and the quarterly honorarium that has to be given to the prelate, altogether, said my uncle, come to an average daily expense of 11 marks, not to mention the nervous wear and tear and other disturbances of health that began to appear in the fall of the first year. These upsets were generally ascribed, at the time, to that autumnal sensibility that is always noticeable.

The real Christmas celebration went off quite normally. Something like a sigh of relief ran through my uncle's family when other families could be seen gathered under Christmas trees, others too had to sing and eat butter-and-almond cookies. But the relief lasted only as long as the Christmas holidays. By the middle of January my Cousin Lucie began to suffer from a strange ailment: at the sight of Christmas trees lying on the streets and on rubbish heaps she broke into hysterical sobs. Then she had a real attack of insanity which the family tried to discount as a nervous breakdown. At a coffee party in a friend's house she struck a dish out of her hostess' hand as the latter was smilingly offering her butter-and-almond cookies. My cousin is, to be sure, what is called a temperamental woman: and so she struck the dish from her friend's hand, went up to the Christmas tree, tore it from its stand and trampled on the glass balls, the artificial mushrooms, the candles and the stars, the while emitting a continuous roar. The assembled ladies fled, including the hostess. They let Lucie rage, and stood waiting for the doctor in the vestibule, forced to give ear to the sound of crashing china within. Painful though it is for me, I must report that Lucie was taken away in a straitjacket.

Sustained hypnotic treatment checked her illness, but the actual cure proceeded very slowly. Above all, release from the evening celebration, which the doctor demanded, seemed to do her visible good; after a few days she began to brighten. At the end of ten days the doctor could risk at least talking to her about butter-and-almond cookies, although she stubbornly persisted in refusing to eat them. The doctor then struck on the inspired idea of feeding her some sour pickles and offering her salads and nourishing meat dishes. That was poor Lucie's real salvation. She laughed once more and began to interject ironic observations into the endless therapeutic interviews she had with her doctor.

To be sure, the vacancy caused by her absence from the evening celebration was painful to my aunt, but it was explained to her by a circumstance that is an adequate excuse in any woman's eyes—pregnancy.

But Lucie had created what is called a precedent: she had proved that although my aunt suffered when someone was absent, she did not immediately begin to scream, and now my Cousin Johannes and his brother-in-law Carl attempted to infringe on the severe regulations, giving sickness as excuse or business appointments or some other quite transparent pretext. But here my uncle remained astonishingly inflexible: with iron severity he decreed that only in exceptional cases upon presentation of acceptable evidence could very short leaves of absence be permitted. For my aunt noticed every further dereliction at once and broke into silent but continuing tears, which gave rise to the most serious apprehensions.

At the end of four weeks Lucie, too, returned and said she was ready to take part once more in the daily ceremony, but her doctor had insisted that a jar of pickles and a platter of nourishing sandwiches should be held in readiness, since her butter-and-almond trauma had proved incurable. Thus for a time, through my uncle's unexpected severity, all breaches of discipline were suppressed.

Shortly after the first anniversary of the daily Christmas celebration, disquieting rumors began to circulate: my Cousin Johannes was said to have consulted a doctor friend of his about my aunt's life expectancy, a truly sinister rumor which throws a disturbing light on a peaceful family's evening gatherings. The doctor's opinion is said to have been crushing for Johannes. All my aunt's vital organs, which had always been sound, were in perfect condition; her father's age at the time of his death had been seventy-eight, and her mother's eighty-six. My aunt herself is sixty-two, and so there is no reason to prophesy an early passing. Still less reason, I consider, to wish for one. After this when my aunt fell ill in midsummer —the poor woman suffered from vomiting and diarrhea—it was hinted that she had been poisoned, but I expressly declare here and now that this rumor was simply the invention of evil-minded relations. The trouble was clearly shown to have been caused by an infection brought into the house by one of the grandchildren. Moreover, analyses that were made of my aunt's stools showed not the slightest traces of poison.

That same summer Johannes gave the first evidences of anti-social inclinations: he resigned from the singing circle and gave notice in writing that he planned to take no further part in the cultivation of the German song. It is only fair for me to add, however, that, despite the academic distinctions he had won, he was always an uncultivated man. For the "Virhymnia" the loss of his bass voice was a serious matter.

My* brother-in-law Carl began secretly to consult travel agencies. The land of his dreams had to have unusual characteristics: no fir trees must grow there and their importation must be forbidden or rendered unfeasible by a high tariff; besides—on his wife's account—the secret of preparing butter-and-almond cookies must be unknown and the singing of German Christmas songs forbidden by law. Carl declared himself ready to undertake hard physical labor.

Since then he has been able to dispense with secrecy because of a complete and very sudden change which has taken place in my uncle. This happened at such a disagreeable level that we have really had cause

* Earlier references to Carl as Johannes' (his) brother-in-law are presumed to be correct. The "my" here, and in subsequent places, is probably an unintentional error.

to be disconcerted. The sober citizen, of whom it could be said that he was as stubborn as he was good and kind, was observed performing actions that are neither more nor less than immoral and will remain so as long as the world endures. Things became known about him, testified to by witnesses, that can only be described by the word adultery. And the most dreadful thing is that he no longer denies them, but claims for himself the right to live in circumstances and in relationships that make special legislation seem justifiable. Awkwardly enough, this sudden change became evident just at the time when the second hearing of the two parish priests was called. My Uncle Franz seems to have made such a deplorable impression as a witness, as disguised plaintiff indeed, that it must be ascribed to him alone that the second hearing turned out favorably for the two priests. But in the meantime all this had become a matter of indifference to Uncle Franz: his downfall is complete, already accomplished.

He too was the first to hit upon the shocking idea of having himself represented by an actor at the evening celebration. He had found an unemployed *bon vivant,* who for two weeks imitated him so admirably that not even his wife noticed the impersonation. Nor did his children notice it either. It was one of the grandchildren who, during a pause in the singing, suddenly shouted: "Grandpapa has on socks with rings," and triumphantly raised the *bon vivant's* trouser leg. This scene must have been terrifying for the poor artist; the family, too, was upset and to avoid disaster struck up a song, as they had done so often before in critical situations. After my aunt had gone to bed, the identity of the artist was quickly established. It was the signal for almost complete collapse.

However one must bear in mind that a year and a half is a long time, and it was mid-summer again, the time when participation in the play is hardest on my relations. Listless in the heat, they nibble at sand tarts and ginger cookies, smile vacantly while they crack dried-out nuts, listen to the indefatigable hammering of the gnomes and wince when the rosy-cheeked angel above their heads whispers "Peace, peace." But they carry on while, despite their summer clothing, sweat streams down their cheeks and necks and soaks their shirts. Or rather: they have carried on so far.

For the moment money plays no part—almost the reverse. People are beginning to whisper that Uncle Franz has adopted business methods, too, which can hardly be described as those of a "Christian businessman." He is determined not to allow any material lessening of the family fortune, a resolution that both calms and alarms us.

The unmasking of the *bon vivant* led to a regular mutiny, as a result of which a compromise was reached: Uncle Franz agreed to pay the expenses of a small theatrical troupe which would replace him, Johannes, my brother-in-law Carl, and Lucie, and it was further understood that one of the four would always take part in person in the evening celebration in order to keep the children in check. Up till now the prelate has not noticed this deception, which can hardly be described as pious. Aside from my aunt and the children, he is the only original figure still in the play.

An exact schedule has been worked out which, in the family circle, is known as the operational program, and thanks to the provision that one of them is always present in person, the actors too are allowed certain vacations. Meanwhile it was observed that the latter were not averse to the celebration and were glad to earn some additional money; thus it was possible to reduce their wages, since fortunately there is no lack of unemployed actors. Carl tells me that there is reason to hope that these "salaries" can be reduced still more, especially as the actors are given a meal and it is well known that art becomes cheaper when food is involved.

I have already briefly mentioned Lucie's unhappy history: now she spends almost all her time in night spots and, on those days when she is compelled to take part in the household celebration, she is beside herself. She wears corduroy britches, colored pullovers, runs around in sandals and she has cut off her splendid hair in order to wear unbecoming bangs and a coiffure that I only recently discovered was once considered modern —it is known as a pony-tail. Although I have so far been unable to observe any overt immorality on her part, but only a kind of exultation, which she herself describes as existentialism, nevertheless I cannot regard this development as desirable; I prefer quiet women, who move decorously to the rhythm of the waltz, know how to recite agreeable verses and whose nourishment is not exclusively sour pickles and goulash seasoned with paprika. My brother-in-law Carl's plans to emigrate seem on the point of becoming a reality: he has found a country, not far from the equator, which seems to answer his requirements, and Lucie is full of enthusiasm; in this country people wear clothes not unlike hers, they love sharp spices and they dance to those rhythms without which she maintains life is no longer possible for her. It is a little shocking that these two do not plan to obey the command "Abide in the land I have given you," but on the other hand I can understand their desire to flee.

Things are worse with Johannes. Unfortunately the evil rumor has proved true: he has become a Communist. He has broken off all relations with the family, pays no attention to anything and takes part in the evening celebration only in the person of his double. His eyes have taken on a fanatical expression, he makes public appearances behaving like a dervish at party meetings, neglects his practice and writes furious articles in the appropriate journals. Strangely enough he now sees more of Franz, who is vainly trying to convert him—and vice versa. Despite all their spiritual estrangement, they seem personally to have grown somewhat closer.

Franz I have not seen in a long time, but I have had news of him. He is said to have fallen into a profound depression, to spend his time in dim churches, and I believe that his piety can be fairly described as exaggerated. After the family misfortunes began he started to neglect his calling, and recently I saw on the wall of a ruined house a faded poster saying: "Last Battle of our Veteran Lenz against Lecoq. Lenz is Hanging up the Gloves." The date on the poster was March, and now we are well into August. Franz is said to have fallen on bad times. I believe he finds himself in a situation which has never before occurred in our family: he is poor. Fortunately he has remained single, and so the social consequences of his irresponsible piety harm only him. He has tried with amazing perseverance to have a guardian appointed for Lucie's children because he considers they are endangered by the daily celebration. But his efforts have remained fruitless; thank God, the children of wealthy people are not exposed to the interference of social institutions.

The one least removed from the rest of the family circle is, for all his deplorable actions, Uncle Franz. To be sure, despite his advanced years, he has a mistress. And his business practices, too, are of a sort that we admire, to be sure, but cannot at all approve. Recently he has appointed an unemployed stage manager to supervise the evening celebration and see that everything runs like clockwork. Everything does in fact run like clockwork.

V

Almost two years have now gone by—a long time. And I could not resist the temptation, during one of my evening strolls, to stop in at my uncle's house, where no true hospitality is any longer possible, since strange actors wander about every evening and the members of the family have devoted themselves to reprehensible pleasures. It was a mild summer evening, and as I turned into the avenue of chestnut trees I heard the verse:

The wintry woods are clad in snow . . .

A passing truck made the rest inaudible. Slowly and softly I approached the house and looked through a crack in the curtains. The similarity of the actors who were present to those of my relations whom they represented was so startling that for an instant I could not recognize which one this evening was the superintendent, as they called him. I could not see the gnomes but I could hear them. Their chirping tinkle has a wave length that can penetrate any wall. The whispering of the angel was inaudible. My aunt seemed to be really happy: she was chatting with the prelate, and it was only later that I recognized my brother-in-law as the one real person present—if that is the right word. I recognized him by the way he rounded and pointed his lips as he blew out a match. Apparently there are unchangeable individual traits. This led me to reflect that the actors, too, were obviously treated to cigars, cigarettes and wine—in addition there was asparagus every evening. If their appetites were shameless—and what artist's is not?—this meant a considerable additional expense for my uncle. The children were playing with dolls and wooden wagons in a corner of the room. They looked pale and tired. Perhaps one really ought to have some consideration for them. I was struck by the idea that they might perhaps be replaced by wax dolls of the kind one sees in the windows of drugstores as advertisements for powdered milk and skin lotions. It seems to me those look quite natural.

As a matter of fact I intend to call the family's attention to the possible effect on the children's temperament of this unnatural daily excitement. Although a certain amount of discipline does no harm, it seems to me that they are being subjected to excessive demands.

I left my observation post when the people inside began to sing: "Silent

Night." I simply could not bear the song. The air was so mild—and for an instant I had the feeling that I was watching an assembly of ghosts. Suddenly I had a craving for sour pickles and this gave me some inkling of how very much Lucie must have suffered.

I have now succeeded in having the children replaced by wax dolls. Their procurement was costly—Uncle Franz hesitated for some time—but one really could not go on irresponsibly feeding the children on marzipan every day and making them sing songs which in the long run might cause them psychic injury. The procurement of the dolls proved to be useful because Carl and Lucie really emigrated and Johannes also withdrew his children from his father's household. I bade farewell to Carl and Lucie and the children as they stood amid large traveling trunks. They seemed happy, if a little worried. Johannes, too, has left our town. Somewhere or other he is engaged in reorganizing a Communist cell.

Uncle Franz is weary of life. Recently he complained to me that people are always forgetting to dust off the dolls. His servants in particular cause him difficulties, and the actors seem inclined to be undisciplined. They drink more than they ought, and some of them have been caught filling their pockets with cigars and cigarettes. I advised my uncle to provide them with colored water and cardboard cigars.

The only reliable ones are my aunt and the prelate. They chat together about the good old times, giggle and seem to enjoy themselves, interrupting their conversation only when a song is struck up.

In any event, the celebration goes on.

My cousin Franz has taken an amazing step. He has been accepted as a lay brother in a nearby monastery. When I saw him for the first time in a cowl I was startled: that large figure, with broken nose, thickened lips and melancholy expression, reminded me more of a prisoner than a monk. He seemed almost to have read my thoughts. "Life is a prison sentence," he said softly. I followed him into the interview room. We conversed haltingly, and he was obviously relieved when the bell summoned him to the chapel for prayers. I remained behind, thoughtful, as he departed: he went in a great hurry, and his haste seemed genuine.

(Translated from the German by Denver Lindley)

Philip Roth

Philip Roth (1933–) was born in Newark, New Jersey, graduated from Bucknell, and received his Master of Arts degree from the University of Chicago. He has taught there and at Harvard University, and at the State University of Iowa's Writers' Workshop. His first book, Goodbye, Columbus *(1959), was a collection of short stories dealing with the lives of contemporary urban middle-class Jewish-Americans. It won him immediate critical acclaim, and he received the National Book Award in 1960.*

His second book was a novel, Letting Go *(1962), about a young man's experiences in college and graduate school, as he falls in love, and is exposed to the intellectual life of New York City and the mid-West. His most recent works are the comic novel* Portnoy's Complaint *(1969) and the political satire* Our Gang *(1971).* *(See page 66 of Introduction.)*

DEFENDER OF THE FAITH

In May of 1945, only a few weeks after the fighting had ended in Europe, I was rotated back to the States, where I spent the remainder of the war with a training company at Camp Crowder, Missouri. Along with the rest of the Ninth Army, I had been racing across Germany so swiftly during the late winter and spring that when I boarded the plane, I couldn't believe its destination lay to the west. My mind might inform me otherwise, but there was an inertia of the spirit that told me we were flying to a new front, where we would disembark and continue our push eastward —eastward until we'd circled the globe, marching through villages along whose twisting, cobbled streets crowds of the enemy would watch us take possession of what, up till then, they'd considered their own. I had changed enough in two years not to mind the trembling of the old people, the crying of the very young, the uncertainty and fear in the eyes of the once arrogant. I had been fortunate enough to develop an infantryman's heart, which, like his feet, at first aches and swells but finally grows horny enough for him to travel the weirdest paths without feeling a thing.

Captain Paul Barrett was my C.O. in Camp Crowder. The day I reported for duty, he came out of his office to shake my hand. He was short, gruff, and fiery, and—indoors or out—he wore his polished helmet liner pulled down to his little eyes. In Europe, he had received a battlefield commission and a serious chest wound, and he'd been returned to the States only a few months before. He spoke easily to me, and at the evening formation he introduced me to the troops. "Gentlemen," he said, "Sergeant Thurston, as you know, is no longer with this company. Your new first sergeant is Sergeant Nathan Marx, here. He is a veteran of the European theater, and consequently will expect to find a company of soldiers here, and not a company of *boys*."

I sat up late in the orderly room that evening, trying half-heartedly to solve the riddle of duty rosters, personnel forms, and morning reports. The Charge of Quarters slept with his mouth open on a mattress on the floor. A trainee stood reading the next day's duty roster, which was posted on the bulletin board just inside the screen door. It was a warm evening, and I could hear radios playing dance music over in the barracks. The trainee, who had been staring at me whenever he thought I wouldn't notice, finally took a step in my direction.

"Hey, Sarge—we having a G.I. party tomorrow night?" he asked. A G.I. party is a barracks cleaning.

"You usually have them on Friday nights?" I asked him.

"Yes," he said, and then he added, mysteriously, "that's the whole thing."

"Then you'll have a G.I. party."

He turned away, and I heard him mumbling. His shoulders were moving, and I wondered if he was crying.

"What's your name, soldier?" I asked.

He turned, not crying at all. Instead, his green-speckled eyes, long and narrow, flashed like fish in the sun. He walked over to me and sat on the edge of my desk. He reached out a hand. "Sheldon," he said.

"Stand on your feet, Sheldon."

Getting off the desk, he said, "Sheldon Grossbart." He smiled at the familiarity into which he'd led me.

"You against cleaning the barracks Friday night, Grossbart?" I said. "Maybe we shouldn't have G.I. parties. Maybe we should get a maid." My tone startled me. I felt I sounded like every top sergeant I had ever known.

"No, Sergeant." He grew serious, but with a seriousness that seemed to be only the stifling of a smile. "It's just—G.I. parties on Friday night, of all nights."

He slipped up onto the corner of the desk again—not quite sitting, but not quite standing, either. He looked at me with those speckled eyes flashing, and then made a gesture with his hand. It was very slight—no more than a movement back and forth of the wrist—and yet it managed to exclude from our affairs everything else in the orderly room, to make the two of us the center of the world. It seemed, in fact, to exclude everything even about the two of us except our hearts.

"Sergeant Thurston was one thing," he whispered, glancing at the sleeping C.Q., "but we thought that with you here things might be a little different."

"We?"

"The Jewish personnel."

"Why?" I asked, harshly. "What's on your mind?" Whether I was still angry at the "Sheldon" business, or now at something else, I hadn't time to tell, but clearly I was angry.

"We thought you—Marx, you know, like Karl Marx. The Marx Brothers. Those guys are all—M-a-r-x. Isn't that how *you* spell it, Sergeant?"

"M-a-r-x."

"Fishbein said—" He stopped. "What I mean to say, Sergeant—" His face and neck were red, and his mouth moved but no words came out. In a moment, he raised himself to attention, gazing down at me. It was as though he had suddenly decided he could expect no more sympathy from me than from Thurston, the reason being that I was of Thurston's faith, and not this. The young man had managed to confuse himself as to what my faith really was, but I felt no desire to straighten him out. Very simply, I didn't like him.

When I did nothing but return his gaze, he spoke, in an altered tone. "You see, Sergeant," he explained to me, "Friday nights, Jews are supposed to go to services."

"Did Sergeant Thurston tell you you couldn't go to them when there was a G.I. party?"

"No."

"Did he say you had to stay and scrub the floors?"

"No, Sergeant."

"Did the Captain say you had to stay and scrub the floors?"

"That isn't it, Sergeant. It's the other guys in the barracks." He leaned toward me. "They think we're goofing off. But we're not. That's when Jews go to services, Friday night. We have to."

"Then go."

"But the other guys make accusations. They have no right."

"That's not the Army's problem, Grossbart. It's a personal problem you'll have to work out yourself."

"But it's un*fair*."

I got up to leave. "There's nothing I can do about it," I said.

Grossbart stiffened and stood in front of me. "But this is a matter of *religion*, sir."

"Sergeant," I said.

"I mean 'Sergeant,' " he said, almost snarling.

"Look, go see the chaplain. You want to see Captain Barrett, I'll arrange an appointment."

"No, no. I don't want to make trouble, Sergeant. That's the first thing they throw up to you. I just want my rights!"

"Damn it, Grossbart, stop whining. You have your rights. You can stay and scrub floors or you can go to shul—"

The smile swam in again. Spittle gleamed at the corners of his mouth. "You mean church, Sergeant."

"I mean shul, Grossbart!"

I walked past him and went outside. Near me, I heard the scrunching of a guard's boots on gravel. Beyond the lighted windows of the barracks, young men in T shirts and fatigue pants were sitting on their bunks, polishing their rifles. Suddenly there was a light rustling behind me. I turned and saw Grossbart's dark frame fleeing back to the barracks, racing to tell his Jewish friends that they were right—that, like Karl and Harpo, I was one of them.

The next morning, while chatting with Captain Barrett, I recounted the incident of the previous evening. Somehow, in the telling, it must have seemed to the Captain that I was not so much explaining Grossbart's position as defending it. "Marx, I'd fight side by side with a nigger if the fella proved to me he was a man. I pride myself," he said, looking out the window, "that I've got an open mind. Consequently, Sergeant, nobody gets special treatment here, for the good *or* the bad. All a man's got to do is prove himself. A man fires well on the range, I give him a weekend pass. He scores high in P.T., he gets a weekend pass. He *earns* it." He turned from the window and pointed a finger at me. "You're a Jewish fella, am I right, Marx?"

"Yes, sir."

"And I admire you. I admire you because of the ribbons on your chest. I judge a man by what he shows me on the field of battle, Sergeant. It's what he's got *here*," he said, and then, though I expected he would point to his heart, he jerked a thumb toward the buttons straining to hold his blouse across his belly. "Guts," he said.

"O.K., sir. I only wanted to pass on to you how the men felt."

"Mr. Marx, you're going to be old before your time if you worry about how the men feel. Leave that stuff to the chaplain—that's his business, not yours. Let's us train these fellas to shoot straight. If the Jewish personnel feels the other men are accusing them of goldbricking—well, I just don't know. Seems awful funny that suddenly the Lord is calling so loud in Private Grossman's ear he's just got to run to church."

"Synogogue," I said.

"Synagogue is right, Sergeant. I'll write that down for handy reference. Thank you for stopping by."

That evening, a few minutes before the company gathered outside the orderly room for the chow formation, I called the C.Q., Corporal Robert LaHill, in to see me. LaHill was a dark, burly fellow whose hair curled out of his clothes wherever it could. He had a glaze in his eyes that made one think of caves and dinosaurs. "LaHill," I said, "when you take the formation, remind the men that they're free to attend church services *whenever* they are held, provided they report to the orderly room before they leave the area."

LaHill scratched his wrist, but gave no indication that he'd heard or understood.

"LaHill," I said, "*church.* You remember? Church, priest, Mass, confession."

He curled one lip into a kind of smile: I took it for a signal that for a second he had flickered back up into the human race.

"Jewish personnel who want to attend services this evening are to fall out in front of the orderly room at 1900," I said. Then, as an afterthought, I added, "By order of Captain Barrett."

A little while later, as the day's last light—softer than any I had seen that year—began to drop over Camp Crowder, I heard LaHill's thick, inflectionless voice outside my window: "Give me your ears, troopers. Toppie says for me to tell you that at 1900 hours all Jewish personnel is to fall out in front, here, if they want to attend the Jewish Mass."

At seven o'clock, I looked out the orderly-room window and saw three soldiers in starched khakis standing on the dusty quadrangle. They looked at their watches and fidgeted while they whispered back and forth. It was getting dimmer, and, alone on the otherwise deserted field, they looked tiny. When I opened the door, I heard the noises of the G.I. party coming from the surrounding barracks—bunks being pushed to the walls, faucets pounding water into buckets, brooms whisking at the wooden floors, cleaning the dirt away for Saturday's inspection. Big puffs of cloth moved round and round on the windowpanes. I walked outside, and the moment my foot hit the ground I thought I heard Grossbart call to the others, "'Ten-*hut!*" Or maybe, when they all three jumped to attention, I imagined I heard the command.

Grossbart stepped forward. "Thank you, sir," he said.

" 'Sergeant,' Grossbart," I reminded him. "You call officers 'sir.' I'm not an officer. You've been in the Army three weeks—you know that."

He turned his palms out at his sides to indicate that, in truth, he and I lived beyond convention. "Thank you, anyway," he said.

"Yes," a tall boy behind him said. "Thanks a lot."

And the third boy whispered, "Thank you," but his mouth barely fluttered, so that he did not alter by more than a lip's movement his posture of attention.

"For what?" I asked.

Grossbart snorted happily. "For the announcement. The Corporal's announcement. It helped. It made it—"

"Fancier." The tall boy finished Grossbart's sentence.

Grossbart smiled. "He means formal, sir. Public," he said to me. "Now it won't seem as though we're just taking off—goldbricking because the work has begun."

"It was by order of Captain Barrett," I said.

"Aaah, but you pull a little weight," Grossbart said. "So we thank you." Then he turned to his companions. "Sergeant Marx, I want you to meet Larry Fishbein."

The tall boy stepped forward and extended his hand. I shook it. "You from New York?" he asked.

"Yes."

"Me, too." He had a cadaverous face that collapsed inward from his cheekbone to his jaw, and when he smiled—as he did at the news of our communal attachment—revealed a mouthful of bad teeth. He was blinking his eyes a good deal, as though he were fighting back tears. "What borough?" he asked.

I turned to Grossbart. "It's five after seven. What time are services?"

"Shul," he said, smiling, "is in ten minutes. I want you to meet Mickey Halpern. This is Nathan Marx, our sergeant."

The third boy hopped forward. "Private Michael Halpern." He saluted.

"Salute officers, Halpern," I said. The boy dropped his hand, and, on its way down, in his nervousness, checked to see if his shirt pockets were buttoned.

"Shall I march them over, sir?" Grossbart asked. "Or are you coming along?"

From behind Grossbart, Fishbein piped up. "Afterward, they're having refreshments. A ladies' auxiliary from St. Louis, the rabbi told us last week."

"The chaplain," Halpern whispered.

"You're welcome to come along," Grossbart said.

To avoid his plea, I looked away, and saw, in the windows of the barracks, a cloud of faces staring out at the four of us. "Hurry along, Grossbart," I said.

"O.K., then," he said. He turned to the others. "Double time, *march!*"

They started off, but ten feet away Grossbart spun around and, running backward, called to me, "Good *shabbus*, sir!" And then the three of them were swallowed into the alien Missouri dusk.

Even after they had disappeared over the parade ground, whose green was now a deep blue, I could hear Grossbart singing the double-time cadence, and as it grew dimmer and dimmer, it suddenly touched a deep memory—as did the slant of the light—and I was remembering the shrill sounds of a Bronx playground where, years ago, beside the Grand Concourse, I had played on long spring evenings such as this. It was a pleasant memory for a young man so far from peace and home, and it brought so many recollections with it that I began to grow exceedingly tender about myself. In fact, I indulged myself in a reverie so strong that I felt as though a hand were reaching down inside me. It had to reach so very far to touch me! It had to reach past those days in the forests of Belgium, and past the dying I'd refused to weep over; past the nights in German farmhouses whose books we'd burned to warm us; past endless stretches when I had shut off all softness I might feel for my fellows, and had managed even to deny myself the posture of a conqueror—the swagger that I, as a Jew, might well have worn as my boots whacked against the rubble of Wesel, Münster, and Braunschweig.

But now one night noise, one rumor of home and time past, and memory plunged down through all I had anesthetized, and came to what I suddenly remembered was myself. So it was not altogether curious that, in search of more of me, I found myself following Grossbart's tracks to Chapel No. 3, where the Jewish services were being held.

I took a seat in the last row, which was empty. Two rows in front of me sat Grossbart, Fishbein, and Halpern, holding little white Dixie cups. Each row of seats was raised higher than the one in front of it, and I could see clearly what was going on. Fishbein was pouring the contents of his cup into Grossbart's, and Grossbart looked mirthful as the liquid made a purple arc between Fishbein's hand and his. In the glaring yellow light, I saw the chaplain standing on the platform at the front; he was chanting the first line of the responsive reading. Grossbart's prayer book remained closed on his lap; he was swishing the cup around. Only Halpern responded to the chant by praying. The fingers of his right hand were spread wide across the cover of his open book. His cap was pulled down low onto his brow, which made it round, like a yarmulke. From time to time, Grossbart wet his lips at the cup's edge; Fishbein, his long yellow face a dying light bulb, looked from here to there, craning forward to catch sight of the faces down the row, then of those in front of him, then behind. He saw me, and his eyelids beat a tattoo. His elbow slid into Grossbart's side, his neck inclined toward his friend, he whispered something, and then, when the congregation next responded to the chant, Grossbart's voice was among the others. Fishbein looked into his book now, too; his lips, however, didn't move.

Finally, it was time to drink the wine. The chaplain smiled down at them as Grossbart swigged his in one long gulp, Halpern sipped, meditating, and Fishbein faked devotion with an empty cup. "As I look down amongst the congregation"—the chaplain grinned at the word—"this night, I see many new faces, and I want to welcome you to Friday-night services here at Camp Crowder. I am Major Leo Ben Ezra, your chaplain."

Though an American, the chaplain spoke deliberately—syllable by syllable, almost—as though to communicate, above all, with the lip readers in his audience. "I have only a few words to say before we adjourn to the refreshment room, where the kind ladies of the Temple Sinai, St. Louis, Missouri, have a nice setting for you."

Applause and whistling broke out. After another momentary grin, the chaplain raised his hands, palms out, his eyes flicking upward a moment, as if to remind the troops where they were and Who Else might be in attendance. In the sudden silence that followed, I thought I heard Grossbart cackle, "Let the goyim clean the floors!" Were those the words? I wasn't sure, but Fishbein, grinning, nudged Halpern. Halpern looked dumbly at him, then went back to his prayer book, which had been occupying him all through the rabbi's talk. One hand tugged at the black kinky hair that stuck out under his cap. His lips moved.

The rabbi continued. "It is about the food that I want to speak to you for a moment. I know, I know, I know," he intoned, wearily, "how in the mouths of most of you the *trafe* food tastes like ashes. I know how you gag, some of you, and how your parents suffer to think of their children eating foods unclean and offensive to the palate. What can I tell you? I can only say, close your eyes and swallow as best you can. Eat what you must to live, and throw away the rest. I wish I could help more. For those of you who find this impossible, may I ask that you try and try, but then come to see me in private. If your revulsion is so great, we will have to seek aid from those higher up."

A round of chatter rose and subsided. Then everyone sang "Ain Kelohainu"; after all those years, I discovered I still knew the words. Then, suddenly, the service over, Grossbart was upon me. "Higher up? He means the General?"

"Hey, Shelly," Fishbein said, "he means God." He smacked his face and looked at Halpern. "How high can you go!"

"Sh-h-h!" Grossbart said. "What do you think, Sergeant?"

"I don't know," I said. "You better ask the chaplain."

"I'm going to. I'm making an appointment to see him in private. So is Mickey."

Halpern shook his head. "No, no, Sheldon—"

"You have rights, Mickey," Grossbart said. "They can't push us around."

"It's O.K.," said Halpern. "It bothers my mother, not me."

Grossbart looked at me. "Yesterday he threw up. From the hash. It was all ham and God knows what else."

"I have a cold—that was why," Halpern said. He pushed his yarmulke back into a cap.

"What about you, Fishbein?" I asked. "You kosher, too?"

He flushed. "A little. But I'll let it ride. I have a very strong stomach, and I don't eat a lot anyway." I continued to look at him, and he held up his wrist to reinforce what he'd just said; his watch strap was tightened to the last hole, and he pointed that out to me.

"But services are important to you?" I asked him.

He looked at Grossbart. "Sure, sir."

" 'Sergeant.' "

"Not so much at home," said Grossbart, stepping between us, "but away from home it gives one a sense of his Jewishness."

"We have to stick together," Fishbein said.

I started to walk toward the door; Halpern stepped back to make way for me.

"That's what happened in Germany," Grossbart was saying, loud enough for me to hear. "They didn't stick together. They let themselves get pushed around."

I turned. "Look, Grossbart. This is the Army, not summer camp."

He smiled. "So?"

Halpern tried to sneak off, but Grossbart held his arm.

"Grossbart, how old are you?" I asked.

"Nineteen."

"And you?" I said to Fishbein.

"The same. The same month, even."

"And what about him?" I pointed to Halpern, who had by now made it safely to the door.

"Eighteen," Grossbart whispered. "But like he can't tie his shoes or brush his teeth himself. I feel sorry for him."

"I feel sorry for all of us, Grossbart," I said, "but just act like a man. Just don't overdo it."

"Overdo what, sir?"

"The 'sir' business, for one thing. Don't overdo that," I said.

I left him standing there. I passed by Halpern, but he did not look at me. Then I was outside, but, behind, I heard Grossbart call, "Hey, Mickey, my *leben*, come on back. Refreshments!"

"*Leben!*" My grandmother's word for me!

One morning a week later, while I was working at my desk, Captain Barrett shouted for me to come into his office. When I entered, he had his helmet liner squashed down so far on his head that I couldn't even see his eyes. He was on the phone, and when he spoke to me, he cupped one hand over the mouthpiece. "Who the hell is Grossbart?"

"Third platoon, Captain," I said. "A trainee."

"What's all this stink about food? His mother called a goddam congressman about the food." He uncovered the mouthpiece and slid his helmet up until I could see his bottom eyelashes. "Yes, sir," he said into the phone. "Yes, sir. I'm still here, sir. I'm asking Marx, here, right now—"

He covered the mouthpiece again and turned his head back toward me. "Lightfoot Harry's on the phone," he said, between his teeth. "This congressman calls General Lyman, who calls Colonel Sousa, who calls the Major, who calls me. They're just dying to stick this thing on me. Whatsa matter?" He shook the phone at me. "I don't feed the troops? What the hell is this?"

"Sir, Grossbart is strange—" Barrett greeted that with a mockingly indulgent smile. I altered my approach. "Captain, he's a very orthodox Jew, and so he's only allowed to eat certain foods."

"He throws up, the congressman said. Every time he eats something, his mother says, he throws up!"

"He's accustomed to observing the dietary laws, Captain."

"So why's his old lady have to call the White House?"

"Jewish parents, sir—they're apt to be more protective than you expect. I mean, Jews have a very close family life. A boy goes away from home, sometimes the mother is liable to get very upset. Probably the boy mentioned something in a letter, and his mother misinterpreted."

"I'd like to punch him one right in the mouth," the Captain said. "There's a goddam war on, and he wants a silver platter!"

"I don't think the boy's to blame, sir. I'm sure we can straighten it out by just asking him. Jewish parents worry—"

"*All* parents worry, for Christ's sake. But they don't get on their high horse and start pulling strings—"

I interrupted, my voice higher, tighter than before. "The home life, Captain, is very important—but you're right, it may sometimes get out of hand. It's a very wonderful thing, Captain, but because it's so close, this kind of thing . . ."

He didn't listen any longer to my attempt to present both myself and Lightfoot Harry with an explanation for the letter. He turned back to the phone. "Sir?" he said. "Sir—Marx, here, tells me Jews have a tendency to be pushy. He says he thinks we can settle it right here in the company. . . . Yes, sir. . . . I *will* call back, sir, soon as I can." He hung up. "Where are the men, Sergeant?"

"On the range."

With a whack on the top of his helmet, he crushed it down over his eyes again, and charged out of his chair. "We're going for a ride," he said.

The Captain drove, and I sat beside him. It was a hot spring day, and under my newly starched fatigues I felt as though my armpits were melting down onto my sides and chest. The roads were dry, and by the time we reached the firing range, my teeth felt gritty with dust, though my mouth had been shut the whole trip. The Captain slammed the brakes on and told me to get the hell out and find Grossbart.

I found him on his belly, firing wildly at the five-hundred-feet target. Waiting their turns behind him were Halpern and Fishbein. Fishbein, wearing a pair of steel-rimmed G.I. glasses I hadn't seen on him before, had the appearance of an old peddler who would gladly have sold you his rifle and the cartridges that were slung all over him. I stood back by the ammo boxes, waiting for Grossbart to finish spraying the distant targets. Fishbein straggled back to stand near me.

"Hello, Sergeant Marx," he said.

"How are you?" I mumbled.

"Fine, thank you. Sheldon's really a good shot."

"I didn't notice."

"I'm not so good, but I think I'm getting the hang of it now. Sergeant, I don't mean to, you know, ask what I shouldn't—" The boy stopped. He was trying to speak intimately, but the noise of the shooting forced him to shout at me.

"What is it?" I asked. Down the range, I saw Captain Barrett standing up in the jeep, scanning the line for me and Grossbart.

"My parents keep asking and asking where we're going," Fishbein said. "Everybody says the Pacific. I don't care, but my parents—if I could relieve their minds, I think I could concentrate more on my shooting."

"I don't know where, Fishbein. Try to concentrate anyway."

"Sheldon says you might be able to find out."

"I don't know a thing, Fishbein. You just take it easy, and don't let Sheldon—"

"*I'm* taking it easy, Sergeant. It's at home—"

Grossbart had finished on the line, and was dusting his fatigues with one hand. I called to him. "Grossbart, the Captain wants to see you."

He came toward us. His eyes blazed and twinkled. "Hi!"

"Don't point that goddam rifle!" I said.

"I wouldn't shoot you, Sarge." He gave me a smile as wide as a pumpkin, and turned the barrel aside.

"Damn you, Grossbart, this is no joke! Follow me."

I walked ahead of him, and had the awful suspicion that, behind me, Grossbart was *marching*, his rifle on his shoulder, as though he were a one-man detachment. At the jeep, he gave the Captain a rifle salute. "Private Sheldon Grossbart, sir."

"At ease, Grossman." The Captain sat down, slid over into the empty seat, and, crooking a finger, invited Grossbart closer.

"Bart, sir. Sheldon Gross*bart*. It's a common error." Grossbart nodded at me; *I* understood, he indicated. I looked away just as the mess truck pulled up to the range, disgorging a half-dozen K.P.s with rolled-up sleeves. The mess sergeant screamed at them while they set up the chow-line equipment.

"Grossbart, your mama wrote some congressman that we don't feed you right. Do you know that?" the Captain said.

"It was my father, sir. He wrote to Representative Franconi that my religion forbids me to eat certain foods."

"What religion is that, Grossbart?"

"Jewish."

" 'Jewish, *sir*,' " I said to Grossbart.

"Excuse me, sir. Jewish, sir."

"What have you been living on?" the Captain asked. "You've been in the Army a month already. You don't look to me like you're falling to pieces."

"I eat because I have to, sir. But Sergeant Marx will testify to the fact that I don't eat one mouthful more than I need to in order to survive."

"Is that so, Marx?" Barrett asked.

"I've never seen Grossbart eat, sir," I said.

"But you heard the rabbi," Grossbart said. "He told us what to do, and I listened."

The Captain looked at me. "Well, Marx?"

"I still don't know what he eats and doesn't eat, sir."

Grossbart raised his arms to plead with me, and it looked for a moment as though he were going to hand me his weapon to hold. "But, Sergeant—"

"Look, Grossbart, just answer the Captain's questions." I said sharply.

Barrett smiled at me, and I resented it. "All right, Grossbart," he said. "What is it you want? The little piece of paper? You want out?"

"No, sir. Only to be allowed to live as a Jew. And for the others, too."

"What others?"

"Fishbein, sir, and Halpern."

"They don't like the way we serve, either?"

"Halpern throws up, sir. I've seen it."

"I thought *you* throw up."

"Just once, sir. I didn't know the sausage was sausage."

"We'll give menus, Grossbart. We'll show training films about the food, so you can identify when we're trying to poison you."

Grossbart did not answer. The men had been organized into two long chow lines. At the tail end of one, I spotted Fishbein—or, rather, his glasses spotted me. They winked sunlight back at me. Halpern stood next to him, patting the inside of his collar with a khaki handkerchief. They moved with the line as it began to edge up toward the food. The mess sergeant was still screaming at the K.P.s. For a moment, I was actually terrified by the thought that somehow the mess sergeant was going to become involved in Grossbart's problem.

"Marx," the Captain said, "you're a Jewish fella—am I right?"

I played straight man. "Yes, sir."

"How long you been in the Army? Tell this boy."

"Three years and two months."

"A year in combat, Grossbart. Twelve goddam months in combat all through Europe. I admire this man." The Captain snapped a wrist against my chest. "Do you hear him peeping about the food? Do you? I want an answer, Grossbart. Yes or no."

"No, sir."

"And why not? He's a Jewish fella."

"Some things are more important to some Jews than other things to other Jews."

Barrett blew up. "Look, Grossbart. Marx, here, is a good man—a goddam hero. When you were in high school, Sergeant Marx was killing Germans. Who does more for the Jews—you, by throwing up over a lousy piece of sausage, a piece of first-cut meat, or Marx, by killing those Nazi bastards? If I was a Jew, Grossbart, I'd kiss this man's feet. He's a goddam hero, and *he* eats what we give him. Why do you have to cause trouble is what I want to know! What is it you're buckin' for—a discharge?"

"No, sir."

"I'm talking to a wall! Sergeant, get him out of my way." Barrett swung himself back into the driver's seat. "I'm going to see the chaplain." The engine roared, the jeep spun around in a whirl of dust, and the Captain was headed back to camp.

For a moment, Grossbart and I stood side by side, watching the jeep.

Then he looked at me and said, "I don't want to start trouble. That's the first thing they toss up to us."

When he spoke, I saw that his teeth were white and straight, and the sight of them suddenly made me understand that Grossbart actually did have parents—that once upon a time someone had taken little Sheldon to the dentist. He was their son. Despite all the talk about his parents, it was hard to believe in Grossbart as a child, an heir—as related by blood to anyone, mother, father, or, above all, to me. This realization led me to another.

"What does your father do, Grossbart?" I asked as we started to walk back toward the chow line.

"He's a tailor."

"An American?"

"Now, yes. A son in the Army," he said, jokingly.

"And your mother?" I asked.

He winked. "A *ballabusta.* She practically sleeps with a dustcloth in her hand."

"She's also an immigrant?"

"All she talks is Yiddish, still."

"And your father, too?"

"A little English. 'Clean,' 'Press,' 'Take the pants in.' That's the extent of it. But they're good to me."

"Then, Grossbart—" I reached out and stopped him. He turned toward me, and when our eyes met, his seemed to jump back, to shiver in their sockets. "Grossbart—you were the one who wrote that letter, weren't you?"

It took only a second or two for his eyes to flash happy again. "Yes." He walked on, and I kept pace. "It's what my father *would* have written if he had known how. It was his name, though. *He* signed it. He even mailed it. I sent it home. For the New York postmark."

I was astonished, and he saw it. With complete seriousness, he thrust his right arm in front of me. "Blood is blood, Sergeant," he said, pinching the blue vein in his wrist.

"What the hell *are* you trying to do, Grossbart?" I asked. "I've seen you eat. Do you know that? I told the Captain I don't know what you eat, but I've seen you eat like a hound at chow."

"We work hard, Sergeant. We're in training. For a furnace to work, you've got to feed it coal."

"Why did you say in the letter that you threw up all the time?"

"I was really talking about Mickey there. I was talking *for* him. He would never write, Sergeant, though I pleaded with him. He'll waste away to nothing if I don't help. Sergeant, I used my name—my father's name—but it's Mickey, and Fishbein, too, I'm watching out for."

"You're a regular Messiah, aren't you?"

We were at the chow line now.

"That's a good one, Sergeant," he said, smiling. "But who knows? Who can tell? Maybe you're the Messiah—a little bit. What Mickey says is the Messiah is a collective idea. He went to Yeshiva, Mickey, for a while. He says *together* we're the Messiah. Me a little bit, you a little bit. You should hear that kid talk, Sergeant, when he gets going."

"Me a little bit, you a little bit," I said. "You'd like to believe that, wouldn't you, Grossbart? That would make everything so clean for you."

"It doesn't seem too bad a thing to believe, Sergeant. It only means we should all *give* a little, is all."

I walked off to eat my rations with the other noncoms.

Two days later, a letter addressed to Captain Barrett passed over my desk. It had come through the chain of command—from the office of Congressman Franconi, where it had been received, to General Lyman, to Colonel Sousa, to Major Lamont, now to Captain Barrett. I read it over twice. It was dated May 14, the day Barrett had spoken with Grossbart on the rifle range.

Dear Congressman:

First let me thank you for your interest in behalf of my son, Private Sheldon Grossbart. Fortunately, I was able to speak with Sheldon on the phone the other night, and I think I've been able to solve our problem. He is, as I mentioned in my last letter, a very religious boy, and it was only with the greatest difficulty that I could persuade him that the religious thing to do—what God Himself would want Sheldon to do—would be to suffer the pangs of religious remorse for the good of his country and all mankind. It took some doing, Congressman, but finally he saw the light. In fact, what he said (and I wrote down the words on a scratch pad so as never to forget), what he said was "I guess you're right, Dad. So many millions of my fellow-Jews gave up their lives to the enemy, the least I can do is live for a while minus a bit of my heritage so as to help end this struggle and regain for all the children of God dignity and humanity." That, Congressman, would make any father proud.

By the way, Sheldon wanted me to know—and to pass on to you—the name of a soldier who helped him reach this decision: SERGEANT NATHAN MARX. Sergeant Marx is a combat veteran who is Sheldon's first sergeant. This man has helped Sheldon over some of the first hurdles he's had to face in the Army, and is in part responsible for Sheldon's changing his mind about the dietary laws. I know Sheldon would appreciate any recognition Marx could receive.

Thank you and good luck. I look forward to seeing your name on the next election ballot.

Respectfully,
Samuel E. Grossbart

Attached to the Grossbart communiqué was another, addressed to General Marshall Lyman, the post commander, and signed by Representative Charles E. Franconi, of the House of Representatives. The communiqué informed General Lyman that Sergeant Nathan Marx was a credit to the U.S. Army and the Jewish people.

What was Grossbart's motive in recanting? Did he feel he'd gone too far? Was the letter a strategic retreat—a crafty attempt to strengthen what he considered our alliance? Or had he actually changed his mind, via an imaginary dialogue between Grossbart *père* and Grossbart *fils*? I was puzzled, but only for a few days—that is, only until I realized that, whatever his reasons, he had actually decided to disappear from my life; he was going to allow himself to become just another trainee. I saw him at inspection, but he never winked; at chow formations, but he never flashed me a sign. On Sundays, with the other trainees, he would sit around watching the noncoms' softball team, for which I pitched, but not once did he speak an unnecessary word to me. Fishbein and Halpern retreated, too—at Grossbart's command, I was sure. Apparently he had seen that wisdom lay in turning back before he plunged over into the ugliness of privilege undeserved. Our separation allowed me to forgive him our past encounters, and, finally, to admire him for his good sense.

Meanwhile, free of Grossbart, I grew used to my job and my administrative tasks. I stepped on a scale one day, and discovered I had truly become a noncombatant; I had gained seven pounds. I found patience to get past the first three pages of a book. I thought about the future more and more, and wrote letters to girls I'd known before the war. I even got a few answers. I sent away to Columbia for a Law School catalogue. I continued to follow the war in the Pacific, but it was not my war. I thought I could see the end, and sometimes, at night, I dreamed that I was walking on the streets of Manhattan—Broadway, Third Avenue, 116th Street, where I had lived the three years I attended Columbia. I curled myself around these dreams and I began to be happy.

And then, one Saturday, when everybody was away and I was alone in the orderly room reading a month-old copy of the *Sporting News*, Grossbart reappeared.

"You a baseball fan, Sergeant?"

I looked up. "How are you?"

"Fine," Grossbart said. "They're making a soldier out of me."

"How are Fishbein and Halpern?"

"Coming along," he said. "We've got no training this afternoon. They're at the movies."

"How come you're not with them?"

"I wanted to come over and say hello."

He smiled—a shy, regular-guy smile, as though he and I well knew that our friendship drew its sustenance from unexpected visits, remembered birthdays, and borrowed lawnmowers. At first it offended me, and then the feeling was swallowed by the general uneasiness I felt at the thought that everyone on the post was locked away in a dark movie theater and I was here alone with Grossbart. I folded up my paper.

"Sergeant," he said, "I'd like to ask a favor. It is a favor, and I'm making no bones about it."

He stopped, allowing me to refuse him a hearing—which, of course, forced me into a courtesy I did not intend. "Go ahead."

"Well, actually it's two favors."

I said nothing.

"The first one's about these rumors. Everybody says we're going to the Pacific."

"As I told your friend Fishbein, I don't know," I said. "You'll just have to wait to find out. Like everybody else."

"You think there's a chance of any of us going East?"

"Germany?" I said. "Maybe."

"I meant New York."

"I don't think so, Grossbart. Offhand."

"Thanks for the information, Sergeant," he said.

"It's not information, Grossbart. Just what I surmise."

"It certainly would be good to be near home. My parents—you know." He took a step toward the door and then turned back. "Oh, the other thing. May I ask the other?"

"What is it?"

"The other thing is—I've got relatives in St. Louis, and they say they'll give me a whole Passover dinner if I can get down there. God, Sergeant, that'd mean an awful lot to me."

I stood up. "No passes during basic, Grossbart."

"But we're off from now till Monday morning, Sergeant. I could leave the post and no one would even know."

"I'd know. You'd know."

"But that's all. Just the two of us. Last night, I called my aunt, and you should have heard her. 'Come—come,' she said. 'I got gefilte fish, *chrain*—the works!' Just a day, Sergeant. I'd take the blame if anything happened."

"The Captain isn't here to sign a pass."

"You could sign."

"Look, Grossbart—"

"Sergeant, for two months, practically, I've been eating *trafe* till I want to die."

"I thought you'd made up your mind to live with it. To be minus a little bit of heritage."

He pointed a finger at me. "You!" he said. "That wasn't for you to read."

"I read it. So what?"

"That letter was addressed to a congressman."

"Grossbart, don't feed me any baloney. You *wanted* me to read it."

"Why are you persecuting me, Sergeant?"

"Are you kidding!"

"I've run into this before," he said, "but never from my own!"

"Get out of here, Grossbart! Get the hell out of my sight!"

He did not move. "Ashamed, that's what you are," he said. "So you take it out on the rest of us. They say Hitler himself was half a Jew. Hearing you, I wouldn't doubt it."

"What are you trying to do with me, Grossbart?" I asked him. "What are you after? You want me to give you special privileges, to change the food, to find out about your orders, to give you weekend passes."

"You even talk like a goy!" Grossbart shook his fist. "Is this just a weekend pass I'm asking for? Is a Seder sacred, or not?"

Seder! It suddenly occurred to me that Passover had been celebrated weeks before. I said so.

"That's right," he replied. "Who says no? A month ago—and I was in the field eating hash! And now all I ask is a simple favor. A Jewish boy I thought would understand. My aunt's willing to go out of her way—to make a Seder a month later. . . ." He turned to go, mumbling.

"Come back here!" I called. He stopped and looked at me. "Grossbart, why can't you be like the rest? Why do you have to stick out like a sore thumb?"

"Because I'm a Jew, Sergeant. I *am* different. Better, maybe not. But different."

"This is a war, Grossbart. For the time being *be* the same."

"I refuse."

"What?"

"I refuse. I can't stop being me, that's all there is to it." Tears came to his eyes. "It's a hard thing to be a Jew. But now I understand what Mickey says—it's a harder thing to stay one." He raised a hand sadly toward me. "Look at *you*."

"Stop crying!"

"Stop this, stop that, stop the other thing! *You* stop, Sergeant. Stop closing your heart to your own!" And, wiping his face with his sleeve, he ran out the door. "The least we can do for one another—the least . . ."

An hour later, looking out of the window, I saw Grossbart headed across the field. He wore a pair of starched khakis and carried a little leather ditty bag. I went out into the heat of the day. It was quiet; not a soul was in sight except, over by the mess hall, four K.P.s sitting around a pan, sloped forward from their waists, gabbing and peeling potatoes in the sun.

"Grossbart!" I called.

He looked toward me and continued walking.

"Grossbart, get over here!"

He turned and came across the field. Finally, he stood before me.

"Where are you going?" I asked.

"St. Louis. I don't care."

"You'll get caught without a pass."

"So I'll get caught without a pass."

"You'll go to the stockade."

"I'm *in* the stockade." He made an about-face and headed off.

I let him go only a step or two. "Come back here," I said, and he followed me into the office, where I typed out a pass and signed the Captain's name, and my own initials after it.

He took the pass and then, a moment later, reached out and grabbed my hand. "Sergeant, you don't know how much this means to me."

"O.K.," I said. "Don't get in any trouble."

"I wish I could show you how much this means to me."

"Don't do me any favors. Don't write any more congressmen for citations."

He smiled. "You're right. I won't. But let me do something."

"Bring me a piece of that gefilte fish. Just get out of here."

"I will!" he said. "With a slice of carrot and a little horseradish. I won't forget."

"All right. Just show your pass at the gate. And don't tell *anybody.*"

"I won't. It's a month late, but a good Yom Tov to you."

"Good Yom Tov, Grossbart," I said.

"You're a good Jew, Sergeant. You like to think you have a hard heart, but underneath you're a fine, decent man. I mean that."

Those last three words touched me more than any words from Grossbart's mouth had the right to. "All right, Grossbart," I said. "Now call me 'sir,' and get the hell out of here."

He ran out the door and was gone. I felt very pleased with myself; it was a great relief to stop fighting Grossbart, and it had cost me nothing. Barrett would never find out, and if he did, I could manage to invent some excuse. For a while, I sat at my desk, comfortable in my decision. Then the screen door flew back and Grossbart burst in again. "Sergeant!" he said. Behind him I saw Fishbein and Halpern, both in starched khakis, both carrying ditty bags like Grossbart's.

"Sergeant, I caught Mickey and Larry coming out of the movies. I almost missed them."

"Grossbart—did I say tell no one?" I said.

"But my aunt said I could bring friends. That I should, in fact."

"*I'm* the Sergeant, Grossbart—not your aunt!"

Grossbart looked at me in disbelief. He pulled Halpern up by his sleeve. "Mickey, tell the Sergeant what this would mean to you."

Halpern looked at me and, shrugging, said, "A lot."

Fishbein stepped forward without prompting. "This would mean a great deal to me and my parents, Sergeant Marx."

"No!" I shouted.

Grossbart was shaking his head. "Sergeant, I could see you denying me, but how you can deny Mickey, a Yeshiva boy—that's beyond me."

"I'm not denying Mickey anything," I said. "You just pushed a little too hard, Grossbart. *You* denied him."

"I'll give him my pass, then," Grossbart said. "I'll give him my aunt's address and a little note. At least let him go."

In a second, he had crammed the pass into Halpern's pants pocket. Halpern looked at me, and so did Fishbein. Grossbart was at the door, pushing it open. "Mickey, bring me a piece of gefilte fish, at least," he said, and then he was outside again.

The three of us looked at one another, and then I said, "Halpern, hand that pass over."

He took it from his pocket and gave it to me. Fishbein had now moved to the doorway, where he lingered. He stood there for a moment with his mouth slightly open, and then he pointed to himself. "And me?" he asked.

His utter ridiculousness exhausted me. I slumped down in my seat and felt pulses knocking at the back of my eyes. "Fishbein," I said, "you understand I'm not trying to deny you anything, don't you? If it was my

Army, I'd serve gefilte fish in the mess hall. I'd sell *kugel* in the PX, honest to God."

Halpern smiled.

"You understand, don't you, Halpern?"

"Yes, Sergeant."

"And you, Fishbein? I don't want enemies. I'm just like you—I want to serve my time and go home. I miss the same things you miss."

"Then, Sergeant," Fishbein said, "why don't you come, too?"

"Where?"

"To St. Louis. To Shelly's aunt. We'll have a regular Seder. Play hide-the-matzoh." He gave me a broad, black-toothed smile.

I saw Grossbart again, on the other side of the screen.

"Pst!" He waved a piece of paper. "Mickey, here's the address. Tell her I couldn't get away."

Halpern did not move. He looked at me, and I saw the shrug moving up his arms into his shoulders again. I took the cover off my typewriter and made out passes for him and Fishbein. "Go," I said. "The three of you."

I thought Halpern was going to kiss my hand.

That afternoon, in a bar in Joplin, I drank beer and listened with half an ear to the Cardinal game. I tried to look squarely at what I'd become involved in, and began to wonder if perhaps the struggle with Grossbart wasn't as much my fault as his. What was I that I had to *muster* generous feelings? Who was I to have been feeling so grudging, so tight-hearted? After all, I wasn't being asked to move the world. Had I a right, then, or a reason, to clamp down on Grossbart, when that meant clamping down on Halpern, too? And Fishbein—that ugly, agreeable soul? Out of the many recollections of my childhood that had tumbled over me these past few days I heard my grandmother's voice: "What are you making a *tsimmes*?" It was what she would ask my mother when, say, I had cut myself while doing something I shouldn't have done, and her daughter was busy bawling me out. I needed a hug and a kiss, and my mother would moralize. But my grandmother knew—mercy overrides justice. I should have known it, too. Who was Nathan Marx to be such a penny pincher with kindness? Surely, I thought, the Messiah himself—if He should ever come—won't niggle over nickels and dimes. God willing, he'll hug and kiss.

The next day, while I was playing softball over on the parade ground, I decided to ask Bob Wright, who was noncom in charge of Classification and Assignment, where he thought our trainees would be sent when their cycle ended, in two weeks. I asked casually, between innings, and he said, "They're pushing them all into the Pacific. Shulman cut the orders on your boys the other day."

The news shocked me, as though I were the father of Halpern, Fishbein, and Grossbart.

That night, I was just sliding into sleep when someone tapped on my door. "Who is it?" I asked.

"Sheldon."

He opened the door and came in. For a moment, I felt his presence without being able to see him. "How was it?" I asked.

He popped into sight in the near-darkness before me. "Great, Sergeant." Then he was sitting on the edge of the bed. I sat up.

"How about you?" he asked. "Have a nice weekend?"

"Yes."

"The others went to sleep." He took a deep, paternal breath. We sat silent for a while, and a homey feeling invaded my ugly little cubicle; the door was locked, the cat was out, the children were safely in bed.

"Sergeant, can I tell you something? Personal?"

I did not answer, and he seemed to know why. "Not about me. About Mickey. Sergeant, I never felt for anybody like I feel for him. Last night I heard Mickey in the bed next to me. He was crying so, it could have broken your heart. Real sobs."

"I'm sorry to hear that."

"I had to talk to him to stop him. He held my hand, Sergeant—he wouldn't let it go. He was almost hysterical. He kept saying if he only knew where we were going. Even if he knew it *was* the Pacific, that would be better than nothing. Just to know."

Long ago, someone had taught Grossbart the sad rule that only lies can get the truth. Not that I couldn't believe in the fact of Halpern's crying; his eyes *always* seemed red-rimmed. But, fact or not, it became a lie when Grossbart uttered it. He was entirely strategic. But then—it came with the force of indictment—so was I! There are strategies of aggression, but there are strategies of retreat as well. And so, recognizing that I myself had not been without craft and guile, I told him what I knew. "It *is* the Pacific."

He let out a small gasp, which was not a lie. "I'll tell him. I wish it was otherwise."

"So do I."

He jumped on my words. "You mean you think you could do something? A change, maybe?"

"No, I couldn't do a thing."

"Don't you know anybody over at C. and A.?"

"Grossbart, there's nothing I can do," I said. "If your orders are for the Pacific, then it's the Pacific."

"But Mickey—"

"Mickey, you, me—everybody, Grossbart. There's nothing to be done. Maybe the war'll end before you go. Pray for a miracle."

"But—"

"Good night, Grossbart." I settled back, and was relieved to feel the springs unbend as Grossbart rose to leave. I could see him clearly now; his jaw had dropped, and he looked like a dazed prizefighter. I noticed for the first time a little paper bag in his hand.

"Grossbart." I smiled. "My gift?"

"Oh, yes, Sergeant. Here—from all of us." He handed me the bag. "It's egg roll."

"Egg roll?" I accepted the bag and felt a damp grease spot on the bottom. I opened it, sure that Grossbart was joking.

"We thought you'd probably like it. You know—Chinese egg roll. We thought you'd probably have a taste for—"

"Your aunt served egg roll?"

"She wasn't home."

"Grossbart, she invited you. You told me she invited you and your friends."

"I know," he said. "I just reread the letter. *Next* week."

I got out of bed and walked to the window. "Grossbart," I said. But I was not calling to him.

"What?"

"What are you, Grossbart? Honest to God, what are you?"

I think it was the first time I'd asked him a question for which he didn't have an immediate answer.

"How can you do this to people?" I went on.

"Sergeant, the day away did us all a world of good. Fishbein, you should see him, he *loves* Chinese food."

"But the Seder," I said.

"We took second best, Sergeant."

Rage came charging at me. I didn't sidestep. "Grossbart, you're a liar!" I said. "You're a schemer and a crook. You've got no respect for anything. Nothing at all. Not for me, for the truth—not even for poor Halpern! You use us all—"

"Sergeant, Sergeant, I feel for Mickey. Honest to God, I do. I *love* Mickey. I try—"

"You try! You feel!" I lurched toward him and grabbed his shirt front. I shook him furiously. "Grossbart, get out! Get out and stay the hell away from me. Because if I see you, I'll make your life miserable. *You understand that?*"

"Yes."

I let him free, and when he walked from the room, I wanted to spit on the floor where he had stood. I couldn't stop the fury. It engulfed me, owned me, till it seemed I could only rid myself of it with tears or an act of violence. I snatched from the bed the bag Grossbart had given me and, with all my strength, threw it out the window. And the next morning, as the men policed the area around the barracks, I heard a great cry go up from one of the trainees, who had been anticipating only his morning handful of cigarette butts and candy wrappers. "Egg roll!" he shouted. "Holy Christ, Chinese goddam egg roll!"

A week later, when I read the orders that had come down from C. and A., I couldn't believe my eyes. Every single trainee was to be shipped to Camp Stoneman, California, and from there to the Pacific—every trainee but one. Private Sheldon Grossbart. He was to be sent to Fort Monmouth, New Jersey. I read the mimeographed sheet several times. Dee, Farrell, Fishbein, Fuselli, Fylypowicz, Glinicki, Gromke, Gucwa, Halpern, Hardy, Helebrandt, right down to Anton Zygadlo—all were to be headed West before the month was out. All except Grossbart. He had pulled a string, and I wasn't it. I lifted the phone and called C. and A.

The voice on the other end said smartly, "Corporal Shulman, sir."

"Let me speak to Sergeant Wright."

"Who is this calling, sir?"

"Sergeant Marx."

And, to my surprise, the voice said, *"Oh!"* Then, "Just a minute, Sergeant."

Shulman's *"Oh!"* stayed with me while I waited for Wright to come to the phone. Why *"Oh!"*? Who was Shulman? And then, so simply, I knew I'd discovered the string that Grossbart had pulled. In fact, I could hear Grossbart the day he'd discovered Shulman in the PX, or in the bowling alley, or maybe even at services. "Glad to meet you. Where you from? Bronx? Me, too. Do you know So-and-So? And So-and-So? Me, too! You work at C. and A.? Really? Hey, how's chances of getting East? Could you do something? Change something? Swindle, cheat, lie? We gotta help each other, you know. If the Jews in Germany . . ."

Bob Wright answered the phone. "How are you, Nate? How's the pitching arm?"

"Good. Bob, I wonder if you could do me a favor." I heard clearly my own words, and they so reminded me of Grossbart that I dropped more easily than I could have imagined into what I had planned. "This may sound crazy, Bob, but I got a kid here on orders to Monmouth who wants them changed. He had a brother killed in Europe, and he's hot to go to the Pacific. Says he'd feel like a coward if he wound up Stateside. I don't know, Bob—can anything be done? Put somebody else in the Monmouth slot?"

"Who?" he asked cagily.

"Anybody. First guy in the alphabet. I don't care. The kid just asked if something could be done."

"What's his name?"

"Grossbart, Sheldon."

Wright didn't answer.

"Yeah," I said. "He's a Jewish kid, so he thought I could help him out. You know."

"I guess I can do something," he finally said. "The Major hasn't been around here for weeks. Temporary duty to the golf course. I'll try, Nate, that's all I can say."

"I'd appreciate it, Bob. See you Sunday." And I hung up, perspiring.

The following day, the corrected orders appeared: Fishbein, Fuselli, Fylypowicz, Glinicki, Gromke, Grossbart, Gucwa, Halpern, Hardy . . . Lucky Private Harley Alton was to go to Fort Monmouth, New Jersey, where, for some reason or other, they wanted an enlisted man with infantry training.

After chow that night, I stopped back at the orderly room to straighten out the guard-duty roster. Grossbart was waiting for me. He spoke first.

"You son of a bitch!"

I sat down at my desk, and while he glared at me, I began to make the necessary alterations in the duty roster.

"What do you have against me?" he cried. "Against my family? Would it kill you for me to be near my father, God knows how many months he has left to him?"

"Why so?"

"His heart," Grossbart said. "He hasn't had enough troubles in a lifetime, you've got to add to them. I curse the day I ever met you, Marx! Shulman told me what happened over there. There's no limit to your anti-Semitism, is there? The damage you've done here isn't enough. You have to make a special phone call! You really want me dead!"

I made the last few notations in the duty roster and got up to leave. "Good night, Grossbart."

"You owe me an explanation!" He stood in my path.

"Sheldon, you're the one who owes explanations."

He scowled. "To *you*?"

"To me, I think so—yes. Mostly to Fishbein and Halpern."

"That's right, twist things around. I owe nobody nothing, I've done all I could do for them. Now I think I've got the right to watch out for myself."

"For each other we have to learn to watch out, Sheldon. You told me yourself."

"You call this watching out for me—what you did?"

"No. For all of us."

I pushed him aside and started for the door. I heard his furious breathing behind me, and it sounded like steam rushing from an engine of terrible strength.

"You'll be all right," I said from the door. And, I thought, so would Fishbein and Halpern be all right, even in the Pacific, if only Grossbart continued to see—in the obsequiousness of the one, the soft spirituality of the other—some profit for himself.

I stood outside the orderly room, and I heard Grossbart weeping behind me. Over in the barracks, in the lighted windows, I could see the boys in their T shirts sitting on their bunks talking about their orders, as they'd been doing for the past two days. With a kind of quiet nervousness, they polished shoes, shined belt buckles, squared away underwear, trying as best they could to accept their fate. Behind me, Grossbart swallowed hard, accepting his. And then, resisting with all my will an impulse to turn and seek pardon for my vindictiveness, I accepted my own.

Muriel Spark

Muriel Spark (1918–   ) was born in Edinburgh, Scotland, and began her writing career as a poet, which helped give her a sense of form, to be echoed later in her novels and short stories. As well as a sharp wit and technical virtuosity, her stories often reveal a double vision that reflects simultaneously both the comedy and horror of a simple situation. Her best-known work is probably The Prime of Miss Jean Brodie *(1961), which was later adapted as a play and as a film. Her other books include* The Go-Away Bird and Other Stories *(1958) and* The Mandelbaum Gate *(1965).* *(See page 77 of Introduction.)*

BANG-BANG YOU'RE DEAD

At that time many of the men looked like Rupert Brooke, whose portrait still hung in everyone's imagination. It was that clear-cut, "typically English" face which is seldom seen on the actual soil of England but proliferates in the African Colonies.

"I must say," said Sybil's hostess, "the men look charming.

These men were all charming, Sybil had decided at the time, until you got to know them. She sat in the dark room watching the eighteen-year-old microfilm unrolling on the screen as if the particular memory had solidified under the effect of some intense heat coming out of the projector. She told herself, I was young, I demanded nothing short of perfection. But then, she thought, that is not quite the case. But it comes to the same thing; to me, the men were not charming for long.

The first reel came to an end. Someone switched on the light. Her host picked the next film out of its tropical packing.

"It must be an interesting experience," said her hostess, "seeing yourself after all those years."

"Hasn't Sybil seen these films before?" said a latecomer.

"No, never—have you, Sybil?"

"No, never."

"If they had been my films," said her hostess, "my curiosity could not have waited eighteen years."

The Kodachrome reels had lain in their boxes in the dark of Sybil's cabin trunk. Why bother, when one's memory was clear?

"Sybil didn't know anyone who had a projector," said her hostess, "until we got ours."

"It was delightful," said the latecomer, an elderly lady, "what I saw of it. Are the others as good?"

Sybil thought for a moment. "The photography is probably good," she said. "There was a cook behind the camera."

"A cook! How priceless; whatever do you mean?" said her hostess.

"The cook-boy," said Sybil, "was trained up to use the camera."

"He managed it well," said her host, who was adjusting the new reel.

"Wonderful colours," said her hostess. "Oh, I'm so glad you dug them out. How healthy and tanned and open-necked everyone looks. And those adorable shiny natives all over the place."

The elderly lady said, "I liked the bit where you came out on the verandah in your shorts carrying the gun."

"Ready?" said Sybil's host. The new reel was fixed. "Put out the lights," he said.

It was the stoep again. Through the french windows came a dark girl in shorts followed by a frisky young Alsatian.

"Lovely dog," commented Sybil's host. "He seems to be asking Sybil for a game."

"That is someone else," Sybil said very quickly.

"The girl there, with the dog?"

"Yes, of course. Don't you see me walking across the lawn by the trees?"

"Oh, of course, of course. She did look like you, Sybil, that girl with the dog. Wasn't she like Sybil? I mean, just as she came out on the verandah."

"Yes, *I* thought it was Sybil for a moment until I saw Sybil in the background. But you can see the difference now. See, as she turns round. That girl isn't really like Sybil, it must be the shorts."

"There was a slight resemblance between us," Sybil remarked.

The projector purred on.

"Look, there's a little girl rather like you, Sybil," Sybil, walking between her mother and father, one hand in each, had already craned round. The other child, likewise being walked along, had looked back too.

The other child wore a black velour hat turned up all round, a fawn coat of covert-coating, and at her neck a narrow white ermine tie. She wore white silk gloves. Sybil was dressed identically, and though this in itself was nothing to marvel at, since numerous small girls wore this ensemble when they were walked out in the parks and public gardens of cathedral towns in 1923, it did fortify the striking resemblance in features, build, and height, between the two children. Sybil suddenly felt she was walking past her own reflection in the long looking-glass. There was her peak chin, her black bobbed hair under her hat, with its fringe almost touching her eyebrows. Her wide-spaced eyes, her nose very small like a cat's. "Stop staring, Sybil," whispered her mother. Sybil had time to snatch the gleam of white socks and black patent leather button shoes. Her own socks were white but her shoes were brown, with laces. At first she felt this one discrepancy was wrong, in the sense that it was wrong to step on one of the cracks in the pavement. Then she felt it was right that there should be a difference.

"The Colemans," Sybil's mother remarked to her father. "They keep that hotel at Hillend. The child must be about Sybil's age. Very alike, aren't they? And I suppose," she continued for Sybil's benefit, "she's a good little girl like Sybil." Quick-witted Sybil thought poorly of the last remark with its subtle counsel of perfection.

On other occasions, too, they passed the Coleman child on a Sunday walk. In summer time the children wore panama hats and tussore silk frocks discreetly adorned with drawn-thread work. Sometimes the Coleman child was accompanied by a young maid-servant in grey dress and black stockings. Sybil noted this one difference between her own entourage and the other girl's. "Don't turn round and stare," whispered her mother.

It was not till she went to school that she found Désirée Coleman to be a year older than herself. Désirée was in a higher class but sometimes, when the whole school was assembled on the lawn or in the gym, Sybil would be, for a few moments, mistaken for Désirée. In the late warm spring the classes sat in separate groups under the plane trees until, as by simultaneous instinct, the teachers would indicate time for break. The groups would mingle, and "Sybil, dear, your shoe-lace," a teacher might call out; and then, as Sybil regarded her neat-laced shoes, "Oh no, not Sybil, I mean Désirée." In the percussion band Sybil banged her triangle triumphantly when the teacher declared, "*Much* better than yesterday, Sybil." But she added, "I mean Désirée."

Only the grown-ups mistook one child for another at odd moments. None of her small companions made this mistake. After the school concert Sybil's mother said, "For a second I thought you were Désirée in the choir. It's strange you are so alike. I'm not a bit like Mrs. Coleman and your daddy doesn't resemble *him* in the least."

Sybil found Désirée unsatisfactory as a playmate. Sybil was precocious, her brain was like a blade. She had discovered that dull children were apt to be spiteful. Désirée would sit innocently cross-legged beside you at a party, watching the conjurer, then suddenly, for no apparent reason, jab at you viciously with her elbow.

By the time Sybil was eight and Désirée nine it was seldom that anyone, even strangers and new teachers, mixed them up. Sybil's nose became more sharp and pronounced while Désirée's seemed to sink into her plump cheeks like a painted-on nose. Only on a few occasions, and only on dark winter afternoons between the last of three o'clock daylight and the coming on of lights all over the school, was Sybil mistaken for Désirée.

Between Sybil's ninth year and her tenth Désirée's family came to live in her square. The residents' children were taken to the gardens of the square after school by mothers and nursemaids, and were bidden to play with each other nicely. Sybil regarded the intrusion of Désirée sulkily, and said she preferred her book. She cheered up, however, when a few weeks later the Dobell boys came to live in the square. The two Dobells had dusky-rose skins and fine dark eyes. It appeared the father was half Indian.

How Sybil adored the Dobells! They were a new type of playmate in her experience, so jumping and agile, and yet so gentle, so unusually courteous. Their dark skins were never dirty, a fact which Sybil obscurely approved. She did not then mind Désirée joining in their games; the Dobell boys were a kind of charm against despair, for they did not understand stupidity and so did not notice Désirée's.

The girl lacked mental stamina, could not keep up an imaginative game for long, was shrill and apt to kick her playmates unaccountably and on the sly; the Dobells reacted to this with a simple resignation. Perhaps the lack of opposition was the reason that Désirée continually shot Sybil dead, contrary to the rules, whenever she felt like it.

Sybil resented with the utmost passion the repeated daily massacre of herself before the time was ripe. It was useless for Jon Dobell to explain, "Not yet, Désirée. Wait, wait, Désirée. She's not to be shot down yet. She hasn't crossed the bridge yet, and you can't shoot her from there, anyway

—there's a big boulder between you and her. You have to creep round it, and Hugh has a shot at you first, and he thinks he's got you, but only your hat. And . . ."

It was no use. Each day before the game started the four sat in conference on the short dry prickly grass. The proceedings were agreed. The game was on. "Got it all clear, Désirée?" "Yes," she said, every day. Désirée shouted and got herself excited, she made foolish sounds even when supposed to be stalking the bandits through the silent forest. A few high screams and then, "Bang-bang," she yelled, aiming at Sybil, "you're dead." Sybil obediently rolled over, protesting none the less that the game had only begun, while the Dobells sighed, "Oh, *Désirée!*"

Sybil vowed to herself each night, I will do the same to her. Next time—tomorrow if it isn't raining—I will bang-bang her before she has a chance to hang her panama on the bough as a decoy. I will say bang-bang on her out of turn, and I will do her dead before her time.

But on no succeeding tomorrow did Sybil bring herself to do this. Her pride before the Dobells was more valuable than the success of the game. Instead, with her cleverness, Sybil set herself to avoid Désirée's range for as long as possible. She dodged behind the laurels and threw out a running commentary as if to a mental defective, such as, "I'm in disguise, all in green, and no one can see me among the trees." But still Désirée saw her. Désirée's eyes insisted on penetrating solid mountains. "I'm half a mile away from everyone," Sybil cried as Désirée's gun swivelled relentlessly upon her.

I shall refuse to be dead, Sybil promised herself. I'll break the rule. If it doesn't count with her why should it count with me? I won't roll over any more when she bangs you're dead to me. Next time, tomorrow if it isn't raining . . .

But Sybil simply did roll over. When Jon and Hugh Dobell called out to her that Désirée's bang-bang did not count she started hopefully to resurrect herself; but "It does count, it *does.* That's the rule," Désirée counter-screeched. And Sybil dropped back flat, knowing utterly that this was final.

And so the girl continued to deal premature death to Sybil, losing her head, but never so much that she aimed at one of the boys. For some reasons which Sybil did not consider until she was years and years older, it was always herself who had to die.

One day, when Désirée was late in arriving for play, Sybil put it to the boys that Désirée should be left out of the game in future. "She only spoils it."

"But," said Jon, "you need four people for the game."

"You need four," said Hugh.

"No, you can do it with three." As she spoke she was inventing the game with three. She explained to them what was in her mind's eye. But neither boy could grasp the idea, having got used to Bandits and Riders with two on each side. "I am the lone Rider, you see," said Sybil. "Or," she wheedled, "the cherry tree can be a Rider." She was talking to stone, inoffensive but uncomprehending. All at once she realized, without articulating the idea, that her intelligence was superior to theirs, and she felt lonely.

"Could we play rounders instead?" ventured Jon.

Sybil brought a book every day after that, and sat reading beside her mother, who was glad, on the whole, that Sybil had grown tired of rowdy games.

"They were preparing," said Sybil, "to go on a shoot."

Sybil's host was changing the reel.

"I get quite a new vision of Sybil," said her hostess, "seeing her in such a . . . such a *social* environment. Were any of these people intellectuals, Sybil?"

"No, but lots of poets."

"Oh, *no*. Did they all write poetry?"

"Quite a lot of them," said Sybil, "did."

"Who *were* they all? Who was that blond fellow who was standing by the van with you?"

"He was the manager of the estate. They grew passion fruit and manufactured the juice."

"Passion fruit—how killing. Did *he* write poetry?"

"Oh, yes."

"And who was the girl, the one I thought was you?"

"Oh, I had known her as a child and we met again in the Colony. The short man was her husband."

"And were you all off on safari that morning? I simply can't imagine you shooting anything, Sybil, somehow."

"On this occasion," said Sybil, "I didn't go. I just held the gun for effect."

Everyone laughed.

"Do you still keep up with these people? I've heard that colonials are great letter writers, it keeps them in touch with—"

"No." And she added, "Three of them are dead. The girl and her husband, and the fair fellow."

"Really? What happened to them? Don't tell me *they* were mixed up in shooting affairs."

"They were mixed up in shooting affairs," said Sybil.

"Oh, these colonials," said the elderly woman, "and their shooting affairs!"

"Number three," said Sybil's host. "Ready? Lights out, please."

"Don't get eaten by lions. I say, Sybil, don't get mixed up in a shooting affair." The party at the railway station were unaware of the noise they were making for they were inside the noise. As the time of departure drew near Donald's relatives tended to herd themselves apart while Sybil's clustered round the couple.

"Two years—it will be an interesting experience for them."

"Mind out for the shooting affairs. Don't let Donald have a gun."

There had been an outbreak of popular headlines about the shooting affairs in the Colony. Much had been blared forth about the effect, on the minds of young settlers, of the climate, the hard drinking, the shortage of white women. The Colony was a place where lovers shot husbands, or shot themselves, where husbands shot natives who spied through bedroom windows. Letters to *The Times* arrived belatedly from respectable colonists, refuting the scandals with sober statistics. The recent incidents, they said, did not represent the habits of the peaceable majority. The Governor told the press that everything had been highly exaggerated. By the time Sybil and Donald left for the Colony the music-hall comics had already exhausted the entertainment value of colonial shooting affairs.

"Don't make pets of snakes or crocs. Mind out for the lions. Don't forget to write."

It was almost a surprise to them to find that shooting affairs in the Colony were not entirely a music-hall myth. They occurred in waves. For three months at a time the gun-murders and suicides were reported weekly. The old colonists with their very blue eyes sat beside their whisky bottles and remarked that another young rotter had shot himself. Then the rains would break and the shootings would cease for a long season.

Eighteen months after their marriage Donald was mauled by a lioness and died on the long stretcher journey back to the station. He was one of a party of eight. No one could really say how it happened; it was done in a flash. The natives had lost their wits, and, instead of shooting the beast, had come calling "Ah-ah-ah," and pointing to the spot. A few strides, shouldering the grass aside, and Donald's friends got the lioness as she reared from his body.

His friends in the archaeological team to which he belonged urged Sybil to remain in the Colony for the remaining six months, and return to England with them. Still undecided, she went on a sight-seeing tour. But before their time was up the archaeologists had been recalled. War had been declared. Civilians were not permitted to leave the continent, and Sybil was caught, like Donald under the lioness.

She wished he had lived to enjoy a life of his own, as she intended to do. It was plain to her that they must have separated had he lived. There had been no disagreement but, thought Sybil, given another two years there would have been disagreements. Donald had shown signs of becoming a bore. By the last, the twenty-seventh, year of his life, his mind had ceased to enquire. Archaeology, that thrilling subject, had become Donald's job, merely. He began to talk as if all archaeological methods and theories had ceased to evolve on the day he obtained his degree; it was now only a matter of applying his knowledge to field-work for a limited period. Archaeological papers came out from England. The usual crank literature on roneo foolscap followed them from one postal address to another. "Donald, aren't you going to look through them?" Sybil said, as the journals and papers piled up. "No, really, I don't see it's necessary." It was not necessary because his future was fixed; two years in the field and then a lectureship. If it were my subject, she thought, these papers would be necessary to me. Even the crackpot ones, rightly read, would be, to me, enlarging.

Sybil lay in bed in the mornings reading the translation of Kierkegaard's *Journals*, newly arrived from England in their first, revelatory month of publication. She felt like a desert which had not realised its own aridity till the rain began to fall upon it. When Donald came home in the late afternoons she had less and less to say to him.

"There has been another shooting affair," Donald said, "across the valley. The chap came home unexpectedly and found his wife with another man. He shot them both."

"In this place, one is never far from the jungle," Sybil said.

"What are you talking about? We are eight hundred miles from the jungle."

When he had gone on his first big shoot, eight hundred miles away in the jungle, she had reflected, there is no sign of a living mind in him, it is like a landed fish which has ceased to palpitate. But, she thought, another woman would never notice it. Other women do not wish to be married to a Mind. Yet I do, she thought, and I am a freak and should not have married. In fact I am not the marrying type. Perhaps that is why he does not explore my personality, any more than he reads the journals. It might make him think, and that would be hurtful.

After his death she wished he had lived to enjoy a life of his own, whatever that might have been. She took a job in a private school for girls and cultivated a few friends for diversion until the war should be over. Charming friends need not possess minds.

Their motor launch was rocking up the Zambezi. Sybil was leaning over the rail mouthing something to a startled native in a canoe. Now Sybil was pointing across the river.

"I think I was asking him," Sybil commented to her friends in the darkness, "about the hippo. There was a school of hippo some distance away, and we wanted to see them better. But the native said we shouldn't go too near—that's why he's looking so frightened—because the hippo often upset a boat, and then the crocs quickly slither into the water. There, look! We got a long shot of the hippo—those bumps in the water, like submarines, those are the snouts of hippo."

The film rocked with the boat as it proceeded up the river. The screen went white.

"Something's happened," said Sybil's hostess.

"Put on the light," said Sybil's host. He fiddled with the projector and a young man, their lodger from upstairs, went to help him.

"I loved those tiny monkeys on the island," said her hostess. "Do hurry, Ted. What's gone wrong?"

"Shut up a minute," he said.

"Sybil, you know you haven't changed much since you were a girl."

"Thank you, Ella." I haven't changed at all so far as I still think charming friends need not possess minds.

"I expect this will revive your memories, Sybil. The details, I mean. One is bound to forget so much."

"Oh yes," Sybil said, and she added, "but I recall quite a lot of details, you know."

"Do you *really,* Sybil?"

I wish, she thought, they wouldn't cling to my least word.

The young man turned from the projector with several feet of the film-strip looped between his widespread hands. "Is the fair chap your husband, Mrs. Greeves?" he said to Sybil.

"Sybil lost her husband very early on," her hostess informed him in a low and sacred voice.

"Oh, I *am* sorry."

Sybil's hostess replenished the drinks of her three guests. Her host turned from the projector, finished his drink, and passed his glass to be refilled, all in one movement. Everything they do seems large and important, thought Sybil, but I must not let it be so. We are only looking at old films.

She overheard a sibilant "Whish-sh-sh?" from the elderly woman in which she discerned, "Who is she?"

"Sybil Greeves," her hostess breathed back, "a distant cousin of Ted's through marriage."

"Oh yes?" The low tones were puzzled as if all had not been explained.

"She's quite famous, of course."

"Oh, I didn't know that."

"Very few people know it," said Sybil's hostess with a little arrogance.

"O.K.," said Ted, "lights out."

"I must say," said his wife, "the colours are marvellous."

All the time she was in the Colony Sybil longed for the inexplicable colourings of her native land. The flamboyants were too rowdy, the birds, the native women with their heads bound in cloth of piercing pink, their blinding black skin and white teeth, the baskets full of bright tough flowers or oranges on their heads, the sight of which everyone else admired ("How I wish I could paint all this!") distressed Sybil, it bored her.

She rented a house, sharing it with a girl whose husband was fighting in the north. She was twenty-two. To safeguard her privacy absolutely, she had a plywood partition put up in the sitting-room, for it was another ten years before she had learnt those arts of leading a double life and listening to people ambiguously, which enabled her to mix without losing identity, and to listen without boredom.

On the other side of the partition Ariadne Lewis decorously entertained her friends, most of whom were men on leave. On a few occasions Sybil attended these parties, working herself, as in a frenzy of self-discipline, into a state of carnal excitement over the men. She managed to do this only by an effortful sealing-off of all her critical faculties except those which assessed a good male voice and appearance. The hangovers were frightful.

The scarcity of white girls made it easy for any one of them to keep a number of men in perpetual attendance. Ariadne had many boy friends but no love affairs. Sybil had three affairs in the space of two years, to put herself to the test. They started at private dances, in the magnolia-filled gardens that smelt like a scent factory, under the Milky Way which looked like an overcrowded jeweller's window. The affairs ended when she succumbed to one of her attacks of tropical 'flu, and lay in a twilight of the senses on a bed which had been set on the stone stoep and overhung with a white mosquito net like something bridal. With damp shaky hands she would write a final letter to the man and give it to her half-caste maid to post. He would telephone next morning, and would be put off by the house boy, who was quite intelligent.

For some years she had been thinking she was not much inclined towards sex. After the third affair, this dawned and rose within her as a whole realization, as if in the past, when she had told herself, "I am not predominantly a sexual being," or "I'm rather a frigid freak, I suppose," these were the sayings of an illiterate, never quite rational and known until now, but after the third affair the notion was so intensely conceived as to be almost new. It appalled her. She lay on the shady stoep, her fever subsiding, and examined her relations with men. She thought, what if I married again? She shivered under the hot sheet. Can it be, she thought, that I have a suppressed tendency towards women? She lay still and let the idea probe round in imagination. She surveyed, with a stony inward eye, all the women she had known, prim little academicians with cream peter-pan collars on their dresses, large dominant women, a number of beauties, conventional nitwits like Ariadne. No, really, she thought; neither men nor women. It is a not caring for sexual relations. It is not merely a lack of pleasure in sex, it is dislike of the excitement. And it is not merely dislike, it is worse, it is boredom.

She felt a lonely emotion near to guilt. The three love affairs took on heroic aspects in her mind. They were an attempt, thought Sybil, to do the normal thing. Perhaps I may try again. Perhaps, if I should meet the right man . . . But at the idea "right man" she felt a sense of intolerable desolation and could not stop shivering. She raised the mosquito net and reached for the lemon juice, splashing it jerkily into the glass. She sipped. The juice had grown warm and had been made too sweet, but she let it linger on her sore throat and peered through the net at the backs of houses and the yellow veldt beyond them.

Ariadne said one morning, "I met a girl last night, it was funny. I thought it was you at first and called over to her. But she wasn't really like you close up, it was just an impression. As a matter of fact, she knows you. I've asked her to tea. I forget her name."

"I don't," said Sybil.

But when Désirée arrived they greeted each other with exaggerated warmth, wholly felt at the time, as acquaintances do when they meet in another hemisphere. Sybil had last seen Désirée at a dance in Hampstead, and there had merely said, "Oh, hallo."

"We were at our first school together," Désirée explained to Ariadne, still holding Sybil's hand.

Already Sybil wished to withdraw. "It's strange," she remarked, "how, sooner or later, everyone in the Colony meets someone they have known, or their parents knew, at home."

Désirée and her husband, Barry Weston, were settled in a remote part of the Colony. Sybil had heard of Weston, unaware that Désirée was his wife. He was much talked of as an enterprising planter. Some years ago he had got the idea of manufacturing passion-fruit juice, had planted orchards and set up a factory. The business was now expanding wonderfully. Barry Weston also wrote poetry, a volume of which, entitled *Home Thoughts*, he had published and sold with great success within the confines of the Colony. His first wife had died of blackwater fever. On one of his visits to England he had met and married Désirée, who was twelve years his junior.

"You *must* come and see us," said Désirée to Sybil; and to Ariadne she explained again, "We were at our first little private school together." And she said, "Oh, Sybil, do you remember Trotsky? Do you remember Minnie Mouse, what a hell of a life we gave her? I shall never forget that day when . . ."

The school where Sybil taught was shortly to break up for holidays; Ariadne was to visit her husband in Cairo at that time. Sybil promised a visit to the Westons. When Désirée, beautifully dressed in linen suiting, had departed, Ariadne said, "I'm so glad you're going to stay with them. I hated the thought of your being all alone for the next few weeks."

"Do you know," Sybil said, "I don't think I shall go to stay with them after all. I'll make an excuse."

"Oh, why not? Oh, Sybil, it's such a lovely place, and it will be fun for you. He's a poet, too." Sybil could sense exasperation, could hear Ariadne telling her friends, "There's something wrong with Sybil. You never know a person till you live with them. Now Sybil will say one thing one minute, and the next . . . Something wrong with her sex-life, perhaps . . . odd . . ."

At home, thought Sybil, it would not be such a slur. Her final appeal for a permit to travel to England had just been dismissed. The environment mauled her weakness. "I think I'm going to have a cold," she said, shivering.

"Go straight to bed, dear." Ariadne called for black Elijah and bade him prepare some lemon juice. But the cold did not materialize.

She returned with 'flu, however, from her first visit to the Westons. Her 1936 Ford V8 had broken down on the road and she had waited three chilly hours before another car had appeared.

"You must get a decent car," said the chemist's wife, who came to console her. "These old crocks simply won't stand up to the roads out here."

Sybil shivered and held her peace. Nevertheless, she returned to the Westons at mid-term.

Désirée's invitations were pressing, almost desperate. Again and again Sybil went in obedience to them. The Westons were a magnetic field.

There was a routine attached to her arrival. The elegant wicker chair was always set for her in the same position on the stoep. The same cushions, it seemed, were always piled in exactly the same way.

"What will you drink, Sybil? Are you comfy there, Sybil? We're going to give you a wonderful time, Sybil." She was their little orphan, she supposed. She sat, with very dark glasses, contemplating the couple. "We've planned—haven't we, Barry?—a surprise for you, Sybil." "We've planned—haven't we, Désirée?—a marvellous trip . . . a croc hunt . . . hippo . . ."

Sybil sips her gin and lime. Facing her on the wicker sofa, Désirée and her husband sit side by side. They gaze at Sybil affectionately. "Take off your smoke glasses, Sybil, the sun's nearly gone." Sybil takes them off. The couple hold hands. They peck kisses at each other, and presently, outrageously, they are entwined in a long erotic embrace in the course of which Barry once or twice regards Sybil from the corner of his eye. Barry disengages himself and sits with his arm about his wife; she snuggles up to him. Why, thinks Sybil, is this performance being staged? "Sybil is shocked," Barry remarks. She sips her drink, and reflects that a public display between man and wife somehow is more shocking than are courting couples in parks and doorways. "We're very much in love with each other," Barry explains, squeezing his wife. And Sybil wonders what is wrong with their marriage since obviously something is wrong. The couple kiss again. Am I dreaming this? Sybil asks herself.

Even on her first visit Sybil knew definitely there was something wrong with the marriage. She thought of herself, at first, as an objective observer, and was even amused when she understood they had chosen her to be their sort of Victim of Expiation. On occasions when other guests were present she noted that the love scenes did not take place. Instead, the couple tended to snub Sybil before their friends. "Poor little Sybil, she lives all alone and is a teacher, and hasn't many friends. We have her here to stay as often as possible." The people would look uneasily at Sybil, and would smile. "But you must have *heaps* of friends," they would say politely. Sybil came to realize she was an object of the Weston's resentment, and that, nevertheless, they found her indispensable.

Ariadne returned from Cairo. "You always look washed out when you've been staying at the Westons," she told Sybil eventually. "I suppose it's due to the late parties and lots of drinks."

"I suppose so."

Désirée wrote continually. "Do come, Barry needs you. He needs your advice about some sonnets." Sybil tore up these letters quickly, but usually went. Not because her discomfort was necessary to their well-being, but because it was somehow necessary to her own. The act of visiting the Westons alleviated her sense of guilt.

I believe, she thought, they must discern my abnormality. How could they have guessed? She was always cautious when they dropped questions about her private life. But one's closest secrets have a subtle way of communicating themselves to the resentful vigilance of opposite types. I do believe, she thought, that heart speaks unto heart, and deep calleth unto deep. But rarely in clear language. There is a misunderstanding here. They imagine their demonstrations of erotic bliss will torment my frigid soul, and so far they are right. But the reason for my pain is not envy. Really, it is boredom.

Her Ford V8 rattled across county. How bored, she thought, I am going to be by their married tableau! How pleased, exultant, they will be! These thoughts consoled her, they were an offering to the gods.

"Are you comfy, Sybil?"

She sipped her gin and lime. "Yes, thanks."

His pet name for Désirée was Dearie. "Kiss me, Dearie," he said.

"There, Baddy," his wife said to Barry, snuggling close to him and squinting at Sybil.

"I say, Sybil," Barry said as he smoothed down his hair, "you ought to get married again. You're missing such a lot."

"Yes, Sybil," said Désirée, "you should either marry or enter a convent, one or the other."

"I don't see why," Sybil said, "I should fit into a tidy category."

"Well, you're neither one thing nor another—is she, honeybunch?"

True enough, thought Sybil, and that is why I'm laid out on the altar of boredom.

"Or get yourself a boy friend," said Désirée. "It would be good for you."

"You're wasting your best years," said Barry.

"Are you comfy there, Sybil? . . . We want you to enjoy yourself here. Any time you want to bring a boy friend, we're broadminded—aren't we, Baddy?"

"Kiss me, Dearie," he said.

Désirée took his handkerchief from his pocket and rubbed lipstick from his mouth. He jerked his head away and said to Sybil, "Pass your glass."

Désirée looked at her reflection in the glass of the french windows and said, "Sybil's too intellectual, that's her trouble." She patted her hair, then looked at Sybil with an old childish enmity.

After dinner Barry would read his poems. Usually, he said, "I'm not going to be an egotist tonight. I'm not going to read my poems." And usually Désirée would cry, "Oh do, Barry, do." Always, eventually, he did. "Marvellous," Désirée would comment, "wonderful." By the third night of her visits, the farcical aspect of it all would lose its fascination for Sybil, and boredom would fill her near to bursting point, like gas in a balloon. To relieve the strain, she would sigh deeply from time to time. Barry was too engrossed in his own voice to notice this, but Désirée was watching. At first Sybil worded her comments tactfully. "I think you should devote more of your time to your verses," she said. And, since he looked puzzled, added, "You owe it to poetry if you write it."

"Nonsense," said Désirée, "he often writes a marvellous sonnet before shaving in the morning."

"Sybil may be right," said Barry. "I owe poetry all the time I can give."

"Are you tired, Sybil?" said Désirée. "Why are you sighing like that; are you all right?"

Later, Sybil gave up the struggle and wearily said, "Very good," or "Nice rhythm" after each poem. And even the guilt of condoning Désirée's "marvellous . . . wonderful" was less than the guilt of her isolated mind. She did not know then that the price of allowing false opinions was the gradual loss of one's capacity for forming true ones.

Not every morning, but at least twice during each visit Sybil would wake to hear the row in progress. The nanny, who brought her early tea, made large eyes and tiptoed warily. Sybil would have her bath, splashing a lot to drown the noise of the quarrel. Downstairs, the battle of voices descended, filled every room and corridor. When, on the worst occasions, the sound of shattering glass broke through the storm, Sybil would know that Barry was smashing up Désirée's dressing table; and would wonder how Désirée always managed to replace her crystal bowls, since goods of that type were now scarce, and why she bothered to do so. Sybil would always find the two girls of Barry's former marriage standing side by side on the lawn frankly gazing up at the violent bedroom window. The nanny would cart off Désirée's baby for a far-away walk. Sybil would likewise disappear for the morning.

The first time this happened, Désirée told her later, "I'm afraid you unsettle Barry."

"What do you mean?" said Sybil.

Désirée dabbed her watery eyes and blew her nose. "Well, of *course,* it stands to reason, Sybil, you're out to attract Barry. And he's only a man. I know you do it *unconsciously,* but . . ."

"I can't stand this sort of thing. I shall leave right away," Sybil said.

"No, Sybil, no. Don't make a *thing* of it. Barry needs you. You're the only person in the Colony who can really talk to him about his poetry."

"Understand," said Sybil on that first occasion, "I am not at all interested in your husband. I think he's an all-round third-rater. That is my opinion."

Désirée looked savage. "Barry," she shouted, "has made a fortune out of passion-fruit juice in eight years. He has sold four thousand copies of *Home Thoughts* on his own initiative."

It was like a game for three players. According to the rules, she was to be in love, unconsciously, with Barry, and tortured by the contemplation of Désirée's married bliss. She felt too old to join in, just at that moment.

Barry came to her room while she was packing. "Don't go," he said. "We need you. And after all, we are only human. What's a row? These quarrels only happen in the best marriages. And I can't for the life of me think how it started."

"What a beautiful house. What a magnificent estate," said Sybil's hostess.

"Yes," said Sybil, "it was the grandest in the Colony."

"Were the owners frightfully grand?"

"Well, they were rich, of course."

"I can see that. What a beautiful interior. I adore those lovely old oil lamps. I suppose you didn't have electricity?"

"Yes, there was electric light in all the rooms. But my friends preferred the oil-lamp tradition for the dining-room. You see, it was a copy of an old Dutch house."

"Absolutely charming."

The reel came to an end. The lights went up and everyone shifted in their chairs.

"What were those large red flowers?" said the elderly lady.

"Flamboyants."

"Magnificent," said her hostess. "Don't you miss the colours, Sybil?"

"No, I don't, actually. There was too much of it for me."

"You didn't care for the bright colours?" said the young man, leaning forward eagerly.

Sybil smiled at him.

"I liked the bit where those little lizards were playing among the stones. That was an excellent shot," said her host. He was adjusting the last spool.

"I rather *liked* that handsome blond fellow," said her hostess, as if the point had been in debate. "Was he the passion-fruiter?"

"He was the manager," said Sybil.

"Oh yes, you told me. He was in a shooting affair, did you say?"

"Yes, it was unfortunate."

"Poor young man. It sounds quite a dangerous place. I suppose the sun and everything . . ."

"It was dangerous for some people. It depended."

"The blacks look happy enough. Did you have any trouble with them in those days?"

"No," said Sybil, "only with the whites."

Everyone laughed.

"Right," said her host. "Lights out, please."

Sybil soon perceived the real cause of the Westons' quarrels. It differed from their explanations: they were both, they said, so much in love, so jealous of each other's relations with the opposite sex.

"Barry was furious," said Désirée one day, "—weren't you, Barry?—because I smiled, merely smiled, at Carter."

"I'll have it out with Carter," muttered Barry. "He's always hanging round Désirée."

David Carter was their manager. Sybil was so foolish as once to say, "Oh surely David wouldn't——"

"Oh wouldn't he?" said Désirée.

"Oh wouldn't he?" said Barry.

Possibly they did not themselves know the real cause of their quarrels. These occurred on mornings when Barry had decided to lounge in bed and write poetry. Désirée, anxious that the passion-fruit business should continue to expand, longed for him to be at his office in the factory at eight o'clock each morning, by which time all other enterprising men in the Colony were at work. But Barry spoke more and more of retiring and devoting his time to his poems. When he lay abed, pen in hand, worrying a sonnet, Désirée would sulk and bang doors. The household knew that the row was on. "Quiet! Don't you see I'm trying to think," he would shout. "*I* suggest," she would reply, "you go to the library if you want to write." It was evident that her greed and his vanity, facing each other in growling antipathy, were too terrible for either to face. Instead, the names of David Carter and Sybil would fly between them, consoling them, pepping-up and propagating the myth of their mutual attraction.

"Rolling your eyes at Carter in the orchard. Don't think I didn't notice."

"Carter? That's funny. I can easily keep Carter in his place. But while we're on the subject, what about you with Sybil? You sat up late enough with her last night after I'd gone to bed."

Sometimes he not only smashed the crystal bowls, he hurled them through the window.

In the exhausted afternoon Barry would explain, "Désirée was upset—weren't you, Désirée?—because of you, Sybil. It's understandable. We shouldn't stay up late talking after Désirée has gone to bed. You're a little devil in your way, Sybil."

"Oh well," said Sybil obligingly, "that's how it is."

She became tired of the game. When, in the evenings, Barry's voice boomed forth with sonorous significance as befits a hallowed subject, she no longer thought of herself as an objective observer. She had tired of the game because she was now more than nominally committed to it. She ceased to be bored by the Westons; she began to hate them.

"What I don't understand," said Barry, "is why my poems are ignored back in England. I've sold over four thousand of the book out here. Feature articles about me have appeared in all the papers out here; remind me to show you them. But I can't get a single notice in London. When I send a poem to any of the magazines I don't even get a reply."

"They are engaged in a war," Sybil said.

"But they still publish poetry. Poetry so-called. Utter rubbish, all of it. You can't understand the stuff."

"Yours is too good for them," said Sybil. To a delicate ear her tone might have resembled the stab of a pin stuck into a waxen image.

"That's a fact, between ourselves," said Barry. "I shouldn't say it, but that's the answer."

Barry was over-weight, square and dark. His face had lines, as of anxiety or stomach trouble. David Carter, when he passed, cool and fair through the house, was quite a change.

"England is finished," said Barry. "It's degenerate."

"I wonder," said Sybil, "you have the heart to go on writing so cheerily about the English towns and countryside." Now, now, Sybil, she thought; business is business, and the nostalgic English scene is what the colonists want. This visit must be my last. I shall not come again.

"Ah, that," Barry was saying, "was the England I remember. The good old country. But now, I'm afraid, it's decadent. After the war it will be no more than . . ."

Désirée would have the servants into the drawing-room every morning to give them their orders for the day. "I believe in keeping up home standards," said Désirée, whose parents were hotel managers. Sybil was not sure where Désirée had got the idea of herding all the domestics into her presence each morning. Perhaps it was some family-prayer assembly in her ancestral memory, or possibly it had been some hotel-staff custom which prompted her to "have in the servants" and instruct them beyond their capacity. These half-domesticated peasants and erstwhile small-farmers stood, bare-footed and woolly-cropped, in clumsy postures on Désirée's carpet. In pidgin dialect which they largely failed to comprehend, she enunciated the duties of each one. Only Sybil and David Carter knew that the natives' name for Désirée was, translated, "Bad Hen." Désirée complained much about their stupidity, but she enjoyed this morning palaver as Barry relished his poetry.

"Carter writes poetry too," said Barry with a laugh one day.

Désirée shrieked. "Poetry! Oh, Barry, you can't call that stuff *poetry*."

"It is frightful," Barry said, "but the poor fellow doesn't know it."

"I should like to see it," Sybil said.

"You aren't interested in Carter by any chance, Sybil?" said Désirée.

"How do you mean?"

"Personally, I mean."

"Well, I think he's all right."

"Be honest, Sybil," said Barry. Sybil felt extremely irritated. He so often appealed for frankness in others, as if by right; was so dishonest with himself. "Be honest, Sybil—you're after David Carter."

"He's handsome," Sybil said.

"You haven't a chance," said Barry. "He's mad keen on Désirée. And anyway, Sybil, you don't want a beginner."

"You want a mature man in a good position," said Désirée. "The life you're living isn't natural for a girl. I've been noticing," she said, "you and Carter being matey together out on the farm."

Towards the end of her stay David Carter produced his verses for Sybil to read. She thought them interesting but unpractised. She told him so, and was disappointed that he did not take this as a reasonable criticism. He was very angry. "Of course," she said, "your poetry is far better than Barry's." This failed to appease David. After a while, when she was meeting him in the town where she lived, she began to praise his poems, persuading herself that he was fairly talented.

She met him whenever he could get away. She sent excuses in answer to Désirée's pressing invitations. For different reasons, both Sybil and David were anxious to keep their meetings secret from the Westons. Sybil did not want the affair mythologized and gossiped about. For David's part, he valued his job in the flourishing passion-fruit concern. He had confided to Sybil his hope, one day, to have the whole business under his control. He might even buy Barry out. "I know far more about it than he does.

He's getting more and more bound up with his poetry, and paying next to no attention to the business. I'm just waiting." He is, Sybil remarked to herself on hearing this, a true poet all right.

David reported that the quarrels between Désirée and Barry were becoming more violent, that the possibility of Barry's resigning from business to devote his time to poetry was haunting Désirée. "Why don't you come," Désirée wrote, "and talk to Barry about his poetry? Why don't you come and see us now? What have we done? Poor Sybil, all alone in the world, you ought to be married. David Carter follows me all over the place, it's most embarrassing, you know how furious Barry gets. Well, I suppose that's the cost of having a devoted husband." Perhaps, thought Sybil, she senses that David is my lover.

One day she went down with 'flu. David turned up unexpectedly and proposed marriage. He clung to her with violent, large hands. She alone, he said, understood his ambitions, his art, himself. Within a year or two they could, together, take over the passion-fruit plantation.

"Sh-sh. Ariadne will hear you." Ariadne was out, in fact. David looked at her somewhat wildly. "We must be married," he said.

Sybil's affair with David Carter was over, from her point of view, almost before it had started. She had engaged in it as an act of virtue done against the grain, and for a brief time it had absolved her from the reproach of her sexlessness.

"I'm waiting for an answer." By his tone, he seemed to suspect what the answer would be.

"Oh, David, I was just about to write to you. We really must put an end to this. As for marriage, well, I'm not cut out for it at all."

He stooped over her bed and clung to her. "You'll catch my 'flu," she said. "I'll think about it," she said, to get rid of him.

When he had gone she wrote him her letter, sipping lemon juice to ease her throat. She noticed he had brought for her, and left on the floor of the stoep, six bottles of Weston's Passion-fruit Juice. He will soon get over the affair, she thought, he has still got his obsession with the passion-fruit business.

But in response to her letter David forced his way into the house. Sybil was alarmed. None of her previous lovers had persisted in this way.

"It's your duty to marry me."

"Really, what next?"

"It's your duty to me as a man and a poet." She did not like his eyes.

"As a poet," she said, "I think you're a third-rater." She felt relieved to hear her own voice uttering the words.

He stiffened up in a comical melodramatic style, looking such a clean-cut settler with his golden hair and tropical suiting.

"David Carter," wrote Désirée, "has gone on the bottle. I think he's bats, myself. It's because I keep giving him the brush-off. Isn't it all silly? The estate will go to ruin if Barry doesn't get rid of him. Barry has sent him away on leave for a month, but if he hasn't improved on his return we shall have to make a change. When are you coming? Barry needs to talk to you."

Sybil went the following week, urged on by her old self-despising; driving her Ford V8 against the current of pleasure, yet compelled to expiate her abnormal nature by contact with the Westons' sexuality, which she knew, none the less, would bore her.

They twisted the knife within an hour of her arrival.

"Haven't you found a man yet?" said Barry.

"You ought to try a love affair," said Désirée. "We've been saying—haven't we, Barry?—you ought to, Sybil. It would be good for you. It isn't healthy, the life you lead. That's why you get 'flu so often. It's psychological."

"Come out on the lawn," Barry had said when she first arrived. "We've got the ciné camera out. Come and be filmed."

Désirée said, "Carter came back this morning."

"Oh, is he here? I thought he was away for a month."

"So did we. But he turned up this morning."

"He's moping," Barry said, "about Désirée. She snubs him so badly."

"He's psychological," said Désirée.

"I love that striped awning," said Sybil's hostess. "It puts the finishing touch on the whole scene. How carefree you all look—don't they, Ted?"

"*That* chap looks miserable," Ted observed. He referred to a shot of David Carter who had just ambled within range of the camera.

Everyone laughed, for David looked exceedingly grim.

"He was caught in an off-moment there," said Sybil's hostess. "Oh, there goes Sybil. I thought you looked a little sad just then, Sybil. There's that other girl again, and the lovely dog."

"Was this a *typical* afternoon in the Colony?" enquired the young man.

"It was and it wasn't," Sybil said.

Whenever they had the camera out life changed at the Westons. Everyone, including the children, had to look very happy. The house natives were arranged to appear in the background wearing their best whites. Sometimes Barry would have everyone dancing in a ring with the children, and the natives had to clap time.

Or, as on the last occasion, he would stage an effect of gracious living. The head cook-boy, who had a good knowledge of photography, was placed at his post.

"Ready," said Barry to the cook, "shoot."

Désirée came out, followed by the dog.

"Look frisky, Barker," said Barry. The Alsatian looked frisky.

Barry put one arm round Désirée and his other arm through Sybil's that late afternoon, walking them slowly across the camera range. He chatted with amiability and with an actor's lift of the head. He would accentuate his laughter, tossing back his head. A sound track would, however, have reproduced the words, "Smile, Sybil. Walk slowly. Look as if you're enjoying it. You'll be able to see yourself in later years, having the time of your life."

Sybil giggled.

Just then David was seen to be securing the little lake boat between the trees. "He must have come across the lake," said Barry. "I wonder if he's been drinking again?"

But David's walk was quite steady. He did not realise he was being photographed as he crossed the long lawn. He stood for a moment staring at Sybil. She said, "Oh hallo, David." He turned and walked aimlessly face-on towards the camera.

"Hold it a minute," Barry called out to the cook.

The boy obeyed at the moment David realized he had been filmed.

"O.K.," shouted Barry, when David was out of range. "Fire ahead."

It was then Barry said to Sybil, "Haven't you found a man yet . . . ?" and Désirée said, "You ought to try a love affair. . . ."

"We've made Sybil unhappy," said Désirée.

"Oh, I'm quite happy."

"Well, cheer up in front of the camera," said Barry.

The sun was setting fast, the camera was folded away, and everyone had gone to change. Sybil came down and sat on the stoep outside the open french windows of the dining-room. Presently, Désirée was indoors behind her, adjusting the oil lamps which one of the house boys had set too high. Désirée put her head round the glass door and remarked to Sybil, "That Benjamin's a fool, I shall speak to him in the morning. He simply will not take care with these lamps. One day we'll have a real smoke-out."

Sybil said, "Oh, I expect they are all so used to electricity these days. . . ."

"That's the trouble," said Désirée, and turned back into the room.

Sybil was feeling disturbed by David's presence in the place. She wondered if he would come in to dinner. Thinking of his sullen staring at her on the lawn, she felt he might make a scene. She heard a gasp from the dining-room behind her.

She looked round, but in the same second it was over. A deafening crack from the pistol and Désirée crumpled up. A movement by the inner door and David held the gun to his head. Sybil screamed, and was aware of running footsteps upstairs. The gun exploded again and David's body dropped sideways.

With Barry and the natives she went round to the dining-room. Désirée was dead. David lingered a moment enough to roll his eyes in Sybil's direction as she rose from Désirée's body. He knows, thought Sybil quite lucidly, that he got the wrong woman.

"What I can't understand," said Barry when he called on Sybil a few weeks later, "is why he did it."

"He was mad," said Sybil.

"Not all that mad," said Barry. "And everyone thinks, of course, that there was an affair between them. That's what I can't bear."

"Quite," said Sybil. "But of course he was keen on Désirée. You always said so. Those rows you used to have. . . . You always made out you were jealous of David."

"Do you know," he said, "I wasn't, really. It was a sort of . . . a sort of . . ."

"Play-act," said Sybil.

"Sort of. You see, there was nothing between them," he said, "And honestly, Carter wasn't a bit interested in Désirée. And the question is *why* he did it. I can't bear people to think . . ."

The damage to his pride, Sybil saw, outweighed his grief. The sun was setting and she rose to put on the stoep light.

"Stop!" he said. "Turn round. My God, you did look like Désirée for a moment."

"You're nervy," she said, and switched on the light.

"In some ways you *do* look a little like Désirée," he said. "In some lights," he said reflectively.

I must say something, thought Sybil, to blot this notion from his mind. I must make this occasion unmemorable, distasteful to him.

"At all events," she said, "you've still got your poetry."

"That's the great thing," he said, "I've still got that. It means everything to me, a great consolation. I'm selling up the estate and joining up. The kids are going into a convent and I'm going up north. What we need is some good war poetry. There hasn't been any war poetry."

"You'll make a better soldier," she said, "than a poet."

"What do you say?"

She repeated her words fairly slowly, and with a sense of relief, almost of absolution. The season of falsity had formed a scab, soon to fall away altogether. There is no health, she thought, for me, outside of honesty.

"You've always," he said, "thought my poetry was wonderful."

"I have said so," she said, "but it was a sort of play-act. Of course, it's only my opinion, but I think you're a third-rater poet."

"You're upset, my dear," he said.

He sent her the four reels of film from Cairo a month before he was killed in action. "It will be nice in later years," he wrote, "for you to recall those good times we used to have."

"It has been delightful," said her hostess. "You haven't changed a bit. Do you *feel* any different?"

"Well yes, I feel rather differently about everything, of course." One learns to accept oneself.

"A hundred feet of one's past life!" said the young man. "If they were mine, I'm sure I should be shattered. I should be calling 'Lights! Lights!' like Hamlet's uncle."

Sybil smiled at him. He looked back, suddenly solemn and shrewd.

"How tragic, those people being killed in shooting affairs," said the elderly woman.

"The last reel was the best," said her hostess. "The garden was entrancing. I should like to see that one again; what about you, Ted?"

"Yes, I liked those nature-study shots. I feel I missed a lot of it," said her husband.

"Hark at him—nature-study shots!"

"Well, those close-ups of tropical plants."

Everyone wanted the last one again.

"How about you, Sybil?"

Am I a woman, she thought calmly, or an intellectual monster? She was so accustomed to this question within herself that it needed no answer. She said, "Yes, I should like to see it again. It's an interesting experience."

Jorge Luis Borges

Jorge Luis Borges (1899–) was born in Buenos Aires, son to a writer. After a university education he became a leading figure in "Ultraismo," a surrealistic, imagistic literary movement, which he left in the 1930's. He taught at the University of Buenos Aires, then became Director of the National Library (he was demoted briefly to the rank of chicken inspector, by Juan Perón, the Argentine dictator who nearly eliminated constitutional liberties). Borges has taught at Harvard and lectured extensively in the United States. His short stories are difficult to describe, partly because they are hybrid forms using elements of fiction, essay, and meditation, and have given rise to the term "Borgesian." He is known for his works Ficciones *(1944),* Dream Tigers *(1960), and* A Personal Anthology *(1967).* *(See page 71 of Introduction.)*

DEUTSCHES REQUIEM

Though he slay me, yet will
I trust in him.
Job 13:15

My name is Otto Dietrich zur Linde. One of my ancestors, Christoph zur Linde, died in the cavalry charge which decided the victory of Zorndorf. My maternal great-grandfather, Ulrich Forkel, was shot in the forest of Marchenoir by franc-tireurs, late in the year 1870; my father, Captain Dietrich zur Linde, distinguished himself in the siege of Namur in 1914, and, two years later, in the crossing of the Danube.[1] As for me, I will be executed as a torturer and murderer. The tribunal acted justly; from the start I declared myself guilty. Tomorrow, when the prison clock strikes nine, I will have entered into death's realm; it is natural that I think now of my forebears, since I am so close to their shadow, since, after a fashion, I am already my ancestors.

[1] It is significant that the narrator has omitted the name of his most illustrious ancestor, the theologian and Hebraist Johannes Forkel (1799–1846), who applied the Hegelian dialectic to Christology, and whose literal version of several books of the Apocrypha merited the censure of Hengstenberg and the approval of Thilo and Gesenius. (Editor's note.)

I kept silent during the trial, which fortunately was brief; to try to justify myself at that time would have obstructed the verdict and would have seemed an act of cowardice. Now things have changed; on the eve of the execution I can speak without fear. I do not seek pardon, because I feel no guilt; but I would like to be understood. Those who care to listen to me will understand the history of Germany and the future history of the world. I know that cases like mine, which are now exceptional and astonishing, will shortly be commonplace. Tomorrow I will die, but I am a symbol of future generations.

I was born in Marienburg in 1908. Two passions, which now are almost forgotten, allowed me to bear with valor and even happiness the weight of many unhappy years: music and metaphysics. I cannot mention all my benefactors, but there are two names which I may not omit, those of Brahms and Schopenhauer. I also studied poetry; to these last I would add another immense Germanic name, William Shakespeare. Formerly I was interested in theology, but from this fantastic discipline (and from the Christian faith) I was led away by Schopenhauer, with his direct arguments; and by Shakespeare and Brahms, with the infinite variety of their worlds. He who pauses in wonder, moved with tenderness and gratitude, before any facet of the work of these auspicious creators, let him know that I also paused there, I, the abominable.

Nietzsche and Spengler entered my life about 1927. An eighteenth-century author has observed that no one wants to owe anything to his contemporaries. I, in order to free myself from an influence which I felt to be oppressive, wrote an article titled *Abrechnung mit Spengler*, in which I noted that the most unequivocal monument to those traits which the author calls Faust-like is not the miscellaneous drama of Goethe [2] but a poem written twenty centuries ago, the *De rerum natura*. I paid homage, however, to the sincerity of the philosopher of history, to his essentially German (*kerndeutsch*) and military spirit. In 1929 I entered the Party.

I will say little of my years of apprenticeship. They were more difficult for me than for others, since, although I do not lack courage, I am repelled by violence. I understood, however, that we were on the verge of a new era, and that this era, comparable to the initial epochs of Islam and Christianity, demanded a new kind of man. Individually my comrades were disgusting to me; in vain did I try to reason that we had to suppress our individuality for the lofty purpose which brought us together.

The theologians maintain that if God's attention were to wander for a single second from the right hand which traces these words, that hand would plunge into nothingness, as if fulminated by a lightless fire. No one, I say, can exist, no one can taste a glass of water or break a piece of bread, without justification. For each man that justification must be different; I awaited the inexorable war that would prove our faith. It was enough for

[2] Other nations live innocently, in themselves and for themselves, like minerals or meteors; Germany is the universal mirror which receives all, the consciousness of the world (*das Weltbewusstsein*). Goethe is the prototype of that ecumenic comprehension. I do not censure him, but I do not see in him the Faust-like man of Spengler's thesis.

me to know that I would be a soldier in its battles. At times I feared that English and Russian cowardice would betray us. But chance, or destiny, decided my future differently. On March first, 1939, at nightfall, there was a disturbance in Tilsit which was not mentioned in the newspapers; in the street behind the synagogue, my leg was pierced by two bullets and it was necessary to amputate.[3] A few days later our armies entered Bohemia. As the sirens announced their entry, I was in a quiet hospital, trying to lose and forget myself in Schopenhauer. An enormous and flaccid cat, symbol of my vain destiny, was sleeping on the window sill.

In the first volume of *Parerga und Paralipomena* I read again that everything which can happen to a man, from the instant of his birth until his death, has been preordained by him. Thus, every negligence is deliberate, every chance encounter an appointment, every humiliation a penitence, every failure a mysterious victory, every death a suicide. There is no more skillful consolation than the idea that we have chosen our own misfortunes; this individual teleology reveals a secret order and prodigiously confounds us with the divinity. What unknown intention (I questioned vainly) made me seek, that afternoon, those bullets and that mutilation? Surely not fear of war, I knew; something more profound. Finally I hit upon it. To die for a religion is easier than to live it absolutely; to battle in Ephesus against the wild beasts is not so trying (thousands of obscure martyrs did it) as to be Paul, servant of Jesus; one act is less than a man's entire life. War and glory are *facilities;* more arduous than the undertaking of Napoleon was that of Raskolnikov. On the seventh of February, 1941, I was named subdirector of the concentration camp at Tarnowitz.

The carrying out of this task was not pleasant, but I was never negligent. The coward proves his mettle under fire; the merciful, the pious, seeks his trial in jails and in the suffering of others. Essentially, Nazism is an act of morality, a purging of corrupted humanity, to dress him anew. This transformation is common in battle, amidst the clamor of the captains and the shouting; such is not the case in a wretched cell, where insidious deceitful mercy tempts us with ancient tenderness. Not in vain do I pen this word: for the superior man of Zarathustra, mercy is the greatest of sins. I almost committed it (I confess) when they sent us the eminent poet David Jerusalem from Breslau.

He was about fifty years old. Poor in the goods of this world, persecuted, denied, vituperated, he had dedicated his genius to the praise of Happiness. I recall that Albert Soergel, in his work *Dichtung der Zeit,* compared him with Whitman. The comparison is not exact. Whitman celebrates the universe in a preliminary, abstract, almost indifferent manner; Jerusalem takes joy in each thing, with a scrupulous and exact love. He never falls into the error of enumerations and catalogues. I can still repeat from memory many hexameters from that superb poem, *Tse Yang, Painter of Tigers,* which is, as it were, streaked with tigers, overburdened and criss-

[3] It has been rumored that the consequences of this wound were very serious. (Editor's note.)

crossed with transversal and silent tigers. Nor will I ever forget the soliloquy called *Rosencrantz Speaks with the Angel,* in which a sixteenth-century London moneylender vainly tries on his deathbed to vindicate his crimes, without suspecting that the secret justification of his life is that of having inspired in one of his clients (whom he has seen but once and does not remember) the character of Shylock. A man of memorable eyes, jaundiced complexion, with an almost black beard, David Jerusalem was the prototype of the Sephardic Jew, although, in fact, he belonged to the depraved and hated Ashkenazim. I was severe with him; I permitted neither my compassion nor his glory to make me relent. I had come to understand many years before that there is nothing on earth that does not contain the seed of a possible Hell; a face, a word, a compass, a cigarette advertisement, are capable of driving a person mad if he is unable to forget them. Would not a man who continually imagined the map of Hungary be mad? I decided to apply this principle to the disciplinary regimen of our camp, and . . .[4] By the end of 1942, Jerusalem had lost his reason; on March first, 1943, he managed to kill himself.[5]

I do not know whether Jerusalem understood that, if I destroyed him, it was to destroy my compassion. In my eyes he was not a man, not even a Jew; he had been transformed into a detested zone of my soul. I agonized with him, I died with him and somehow I was lost with him; therefore, I was implacable.

Meanwhile we reveled in the great days and nights of a successful war. In the very air we breathed there was a feeling not unlike love. Our hearts beat with amazement and exaltation, as if we sensed the sea nearby. Everything was new and different then, even the flavor of our dreams. (I, perhaps, was never entirely happy. But it is known that misery requires lost paradises.) Every man aspires to the fullness of life, that is, to the sum of experiences which he is capable of enjoying; nor is there a man unafraid of being cheated out of some part of his infinite patrimony. But it can be said that my generation enjoyed the extremes of experience, because first we were granted victory and later defeat.

In October or November of 1942 my brother Friedrich perished in the second battle of El Alamein, on the Egyptian sands. Months later an aerial bombardment destroyed our family's home: another, at the end of 1943, destroyed my laboratory. The Third Reich was dying, harassed by vast continents; it struggled alone against innumerable enemies. Then a singular event occurred, which only now do I believe I understand. I thought I was emptying the cup of anger, but in the dregs I encountered an unexpected flavor, the mysterious and almost terrible flavor of happiness. I essayed several explanations, but none seemed adequate. I thought: *I am*

[4] It has been necessary to omit a few lines here. (Editor's note.)

[5] We have been unable to find any reference to the name of Jerusalem, even in Soergel's work. Nor is he mentioned in the histories of German literature. Nevertheless, I do not believe that he is fictitious. Many Jewish intellectuals were tortured at Tarnowitz under orders of Otto Dietrich zur Linde; among them, the pianist Emma Rosenzweig. "David Jerusalem" is perhaps a symbol of several individuals. It is said that he died March first, 1943; on March first, 1939, the narrator was wounded in Tilsit. (Editor's note.)

pleased with defeat, because secretly I know I am guilty, and only punishment can redeem me. I thought: I am *pleased with the defeat because it is an end and I am very tired.* I thought: *I am pleased with defeat because it has occurred, because it is irrevocably united to all those events which are, which were, and which will be, because to censure or to deplore a single real occurrence is to blaspheme the universe.* I played with these explanations, until I found the true one.

It has been said that every man is born an Aristotelian or a Platonist. This is the same as saying that every abstract contention has its counterpart in the polemics of Aristotle or Plato; across the centuries and latitudes, the names, faces and dialects change but not the eternal antagonists. The history of nations also registers a secret continuity. Arminius, when he cut down the legions of Varus in a marsh, did not realize that he was a precursor of the German Empire; Luther, translator of the Bible, could not suspect that his goal was to forge a people destined to destroy the Bible for all time; Christoph zur Linde, killed by a Russian bullet in 1758, was in some way preparing the victories of 1914; Hitler believed he was fighting for *a* nation but he fought for all, even for those which he detested and attacked. It matters not that his *I* was ignorant of this fact; his blood and his will were aware of it. The world was dying of Judaism and from that sickness of Judaism, the faith of Jesus; we taught it violence and the faith of the sword. That sword is slaying us, and we are comparable to the wizard who fashioned a labyrinth and was then doomed to wander in it to the end of his days; or to David, who, judging an unknown man, condemns him to death, only to hear the revelation: *You are that man.* Many things will have to be destroyed in order to construct the New Order; now we know that Germany also was one of those things. We have given more than our lives, we have sacrificed the destiny of our beloved Fatherland. Let others curse and weep; I rejoice in the fact that our destiny completes its circle and is perfect.

An inexorable epoch is spreading over the world. We forged it, we who are already its victim. What matters if England is the hammer and we the anvil, so long as violence reigns and not servile Christian timidity? If victory and injustice and happiness are not for Germany, let them be for other nations. Let Heaven exist, even though our dwelling place is Hell.

I look at myself in the mirror to discover who I am, to discern how I will act in a few hours, when I am face to face with death. My flesh may be afraid; I am not.

Alberto Moravia

Alberto Moravia, pseudonym of Alberto Picherle (1907–), was born in Rome and had little formal education. In his early twenties he developed tuberculosis and spent two years in a sanatorium. During World War II he had several brushes with Fascist authorities, and for a while was forced to live in hiding in the mountains. His wife Else Morante is also a novelist. Psychological exploitations, particularly of sex, dominate many of his stories. His first novel, The Indifferent Ones *(1929), brought him immediate fame in Italy. His popularity in this country began in the 1950's with the first good translation of his stories. His works include* Conjugal Love *(1951) and* A Ghost at Noon *(1955). (See page 80 of Introduction.)*

HE AND I

I started talking to myself a short time after my wife had left me because, so she said, she was tired of my silence. It is true, I was silent with her, as indeed with everyone else; but I was silent because I loved her. When you love someone there is no need of words, is there? All you want is to be near the person you love, to look at her, to feel that she's there. Having been silent with her, perhaps even too much so, I became talkative with myself, as I have said, as soon as she deserted me. I am a shoemaker, and a shoemaker's job, as we all know, demands concentration, if only because working in leather is fine work and it doesn't do to make mistakes: the human foot doesn't allow for mistakes. So, when I went home in the evening, my eyes dazzled, my head ringing with the sound of hammering, my lips hurting from all the nails I shove into my mouth to damp them before driving them into the leather soles, I should have liked to find—what shall I say?—a smile, a kind word, a kiss on the forehead, a bowl of hot soup. Instead of which—nothing at all. Merely, in the darkness, the dripping sound of the drinking-water tap in the kitchen. Now silence is a lovely thing when you are in the company of a person you love and when you know that you can speak to her if you want to; but it is a torment if it is imposed upon you. And so, after my wife went back to her mother, while I got my supper ready, all alone, in the kitchen, and then, still alone, ate it very slowly, almost without knowing what I was doing, sitting at a corner of the table, I began thinking out loud.

At first the things I used to say were impersonal and were not really addressed either to myself or to anyone else. For instance, I would say: "How cold it is in this house, my goodness, how cold it is!"; or: "If it wasn't for the mice frolicking about between the ceiling and the roof, there wouldn't be a sound in this place except the tap dripping"; or again: "The bed's still unmade since this morning. Never mind, it's too late now, I'll make it to-morrow." I said these things aloud, sometimes very loudly, insignificant as they were; but it pleased me to hear my voice echoing round those three deserted rooms. Then, one day, when I was sitting as usual in the kitchen, I said: "Wine is good stuff, wine is comforting, you only need to drink a litre of wine and your troubles disappear"; and all of a sudden—how it happened, I don't know—I heard myself answering, still in a loud vioce: "Guglielmo, you're a miserable wretch and you know it. Yes, of course, wine is good stuff, but it isn't comforting. You might drink a whole demijohn but still you wouldn't forget your wife nor the fact that she's left you. Yes, wine is good, but the company of a woman who loves you is very much better." I was struck by the truth of these words, and I answered—that is, my first voice answered: "You're right. But, when all's said and done, what is there left for me now? I'm fifty, and my wife, who is twenty-five, has deserted me. Where can I find another woman who would adapt herself to living with me? There's nothing left to me now except wine—isn't that so?" Then the other voice said: "Now listen, and don't act the philosopher. You know perfectly well that you haven't given up all hope of your wife." "Who told you that?" I replied; "I *have* given up hope, I have indeed." "No, you haven't," he said; "if you had, you wouldn't burst into sobs at the sole thought of her, wherever you may happen to be, even in the lavatory or on the stairs." Well then, I now had two voices, one of which, so to speak, spoke for me, and another which spoke for someone else who was also me but at the same time wasn't. Thus it was that, without realizing it, I changed over from monologue to dialogue—that is, from talking to myself to having arguments with myself.

These arguments, moreover, were not always arguments. Sometimes we were in complete agreement, he and I. For example, in the evening, after I had drunk my litre and a half or even two litres, I would go into the bedroom and there, in front of the wardrobe mirror, would make faces, just to amuse myself. Then he would say: "Here we are again, you've been drinking. A good thing you're at home and not in the street. You've been drinking and you can't stand up straight. But aren't you ashamed, at your age?"; he would say this, however, not without a hint of complacency in his voice. We went on like this for perhaps a couple of months, more or less in agreement; until one night, when I had drunk more than usual, a whole big flask of wine, lo and behold, when I took up my position in front of the mirror and put out my tongue, I was dumbfounded to see that *he*, in the mirror, remained serious and composed, with his tongue not out and his mouth not open. Then, after looking at me lingeringly and with compassion, he said: "Guglielmo, I'm fed up with you." "Why?" I asked. "Because," he said, "instead of fighting and struggling, you're letting yourself go. You've resigned yourself to the loss of your wife, you've become a drunkard, you've even lost your love of your work." "Who says so, I should like to know?" "*I* say so. Everyone in the neighbourhood knows you drink. And people take their shoes to be re-soled elsewhere. D'you know what you are, now? Just a rag of humanity."

This made me uneasy, and I scratched my head; then I asked: "Well then, what ought I to do, according to you?" "You ought to fight and struggle and make a firm stand." "But what for?" "To get your wife home again. Seeing that, without her, your life has come to an end, try to get her back again. Aren't you the husband? Haven't you the right to have her with you? Well then, bestir yourself, go ahead and take action." "But what ought I to do?" "What ought you to do, indeed! You know perfectly well what you ought to do." "No, honestly, I don't know." Then he stared straight at me and said: "You must contrive, by fair means or foul, to make her come home." He spoke these words in a particular tone of voice which, I confess, frightened me. "By fair means I've tried," I answered, "and it was no use. By foul means I don't want even to attempt it. I don't want to do anything bad." It seemed to me I had spoken rightly, in a way that ought to convince him; but he shook his head and said threateningly: "Very well. We'll speak of this again." At the same time he vanished from the looking-glass and I was left alone.

I went to bed much worried. No sooner had I put out the light than, suddenly, his voice began speaking again in the darkness: "Now that you're calmer and no longer tipsy, I'll tell you what you must do to get your wife back again. But don't interrupt me, listen till I've finished what I have to say." I told him to continue, that I was listening; and he went on to tell me, in a joking sort of way, that I must go next morning to the shop, fetch my shoemaker's knife, then go and find my wife, hold the knife under her nose and give her this warning: "Either you come home at once or else—you see this? . . ." I replied immediately, in the darkness: "You're crazy, it's no use even talking about such a thing. I want to get my wife back, that's understood. But there's a great difference between that and threatening her with a knife. I don't in the least want to end up in prison." "No," he said, "of course you don't want to go to prison. And yet, just possibly, you might be better off in prison than you are here." "What-ever do you mean?" "I mean that in prison at least you wouldn't be alone. In fact, you have nothing to lose: either your wife comes away with you, in which case, so much the better; or else she doesn't come, you give her a touch of the knife and end up in prison, and then at any rate you'd have the company of the other prisoners." "You're mad." "I'm not mad, and you know it. You're so lonely, Guglielmo, that even the idea of prison makes your mouth water." At this point I couldn't bear it any longer and, sitting up in bed, I said with energy: "It's no use even talking about it. And now be quiet, shut that wicked mouth of yours and let me go to sleep." "I warn you that, if you don't do this, *I* shall do it." "I told you to let me sleep." "I shall do it no later than to-morrow morning." "Shut up!" "Then we're agreed." I hung out of the bed, snatched up a shoe from the floor and hurled it at him, just like that, in the dark. He must have dodged it, cunning devil that he was. I heard a crash of breaking china and realized I had hit the water-jug on the chest of drawers. Then I fell asleep.

Next morning, however, when I woke up, I was at once conscious that there was no time to lose. Of him there was no sign, in any of the three rooms. It was quite possible that, while I was lingering at home warming up some coffee, he would run off to the shop (unfortunately he had the key, I had given it to him myself), would snatch up the knife, and then—the fat would be in the fire. It made my flesh creep, on my word of honour it did, to think of what might happen. And so, without waiting for any coffee, without washing or shaving, unkempt and with hair unbrushed, I rushed out, slipping into my coat as I went downstairs. It was very early in the morning, with a heavy dew and the streets full of mist, and just a few people on their way to work, their breath hanging in little clouds in front of their mouths. My shop was in the Vicolo del Fiume, and I almost ran all the way along Via Ripetta; as I turned the corner, I saw him in the distance coming out of the shop, very stealthily, and then running off in the direction of the Tiber. "Now we're for it," I said to myself. "He's a man of his word, no doubt about it; he said he'd do it and he's doing it. And now I've got to stop him." I too hurried into the shop, I too snatched up a knife in case he should turn his fury against me, then I went into a bar close by where there was a telephone kiosk. "There's no coffee, the machine isn't working yet," called out the barman, who knew me. I shrugged my shoulders; "Never mind about the coffee," I said. To tell the truth, I was so agitated that my hands were fluttering as I turned the pages of the directory, looking for the number of the police station. At last I found it, dialled the number, a voice asked what I wanted, I explained what had happened: "You must go there at once. He's armed with a shoemaker's knife. It's a matter of life and death." The voice at the other end of the line enquired: "What's the name of this man?" I thought for a moment and then replied: "Palombini; Guglielmo Palombini," which is my own name too—one of those odd coincidences. I was assured on the telephone that they would attend to the matter as quickly as possible; and then I flew off to Piazza del Popolo, to the taxi rank: it was always possible that the police might arrive too late, and the best plan was for me to go there too. I called out the address as I jumped into the taxi, adding: "And quickly, for God's sake; it's a matter of life and death." The driver, an old man with white hair, asked what was the matter, and I told him: "A chap called Palombini, a shoemaker, has armed himself with a knife and is on his way now, in a taxi, to his wife who has left him, and he intends to kill her. . . . He's got to be stopped." "Have you informed the Police?" "Of course I have." "But how did *you* come to know about it?" "Well, Palombini and I are friends, in a way. He told me himself." The taxi-driver reflected a moment and then said: "There are plenty of people who pretend to be tough and then, when the moment comes, they go soft." "You're wrong, this man's really serious; I know him." All this time we were moving quickly through the deserted streets towards Via Giulia, where my wife was living.

The taxi stopped, I got out and paid and the driver went off; then I turned to look down the street, empty as far as the eye could reach, and saw him, the murderous ruffian, entering, at that very moment, the door of my wife's house. I recollected that my mother-in-law, a pious old bigot, always went off to church at that hour of the day; so that my wife would be alone in the flat, and in bed, into the bargain, for she was lazy and liked to sleep late into the morning. "He's chosen the right moment," I thought; "there's no denying it, he thinks of everything. . . . Now quickly, let's hurry; otherwise there's going to be bloodshed here." So I rushed in at the front door, ran upstairs four steps at a time and reached the landing just in time to see him knocking loudly at the closed door and shouting: "Gas meter, please!"—which is as good a way as any of getting a door opened to you. I drew back and, a moment later, was aware of the sound of shuffling slippers inside the flat; then the door was opened and I heard the sleepy, sing-song voice of my wife: "The meter's in the kitchen." He, as a matter of form, waited a moment, then slipped into the flat; I followed.

The corridor was in darkness; I recognized the warm, youthful smell of her body refreshed with sleep, and it made me feel faint for a moment. Walking on tiptoe, I went straight to the far end of the passage, where I knew her room to be, pushed open the door which she had left ajar when she went back to bed, and entered. The room was in darkness too, but not so much so that I was unable to distinguish the double bed and, white and full beneath the black hair spread loose over the pillow, the bare shoulders of my wife as she lay on one side, having gone back to sleep again. In truth, when I saw those shoulders, I was stricken with such a painful longing for the time when I used to see them in my own home, as I left stealthily in the morning to go to work, that I immediately forgot him and his knife, threw myself down on my knees and, seizing her hand as it lay on the coverlet, said: "My love, my darling, come back with me. Without you I can't go on living." I am sure that my wife, in such circumstances, would on this occasion have let herself be persuaded, if that vile wretch had not suddenly risen up on the other side of the bed, his hand raised holding the knife, and, shaking her by the shoulder, commanded her in a voice of terror: "You're coming back with me now; otherwise—do you see this?"

I do not intend to describe what happened after that: how I struggled with him, trying to disarm him; how my wife, screaming and upsetting things right and left, rushed half-naked across the room; and how a number of policemen suddenly burst in and jumped on me. I was careful to shout out: "Arrest him! He's dangerous. And look out for his knife!" But the policemen, possibly because I myself also had a knife in my hand, did not make such distinctions; they seized hold of me as well and hauled me bodily out of the flat and then down the stairs, while I struggled and kept repeating, with all the voice I had left: "It's *him* you must arrest, not me . . . you're making a mistake." In the street there was a great crowd. They forced me into the police van, and when I looked up, there he was, sitting handcuffed between two policemen, right opposite me, the sarcastic smile on his face seeming to say: "You see what I've done." I pointed at him and cried: "He's ruined me, that scoundrel over there . . . he's ruined me"; and then I fainted.

Now I'm in a padded cell, and they say they are keeping me under observation because they're afraid my mind has been affected by grief. I do not complain; but I feel so very alone. As for him, they took him off to the Regina Coeli prison, and thus we have been separated, he in gaol and I in an asylum. And so the only company I had has been taken away from me, and I have no one now, and I shall have to stay silent for ever.

Yukio Mishima

Yukio Mishima (1925–1970), Japanese writer, was born in Tokyo. After receiving a law degree, he worked briefly for the Japanese Government.

He began to publish in 1948, and since then his output—novels, short stories, plays, and essays—has been enormous. In 1970 he committed hara-kiri, following the failure of an attempt to overthrow Western influence in Japan and revive the old Samurai tradition. His tragic end was ironically foreshadowed in a powerful short story, "Patriotism," written a few years earlier. His works include Confessions of a Mask *(1949) and* Temple of the Golden Pavilion *(1959). (See page 69 of Introduction.)*

THE PEARL

December 10 was Mrs. Sasaki's birthday, but since it was Mrs. Sasaki's wish to celebrate the occasion with the minimum of fuss, she had invited to her house for afternoon tea only her closest friends. Assembled were Mesdames Yamamoto, Matsumura, Azuma, and Kasuga—all four being forty-three years of age, exact contemporaries of their hostess.

These ladies were thus members, as it were, of a Keep-Our-Ages-Secret Society, and could be trusted implicitly not to divulge to outsiders the number of candles on today's cake. In inviting to her birthday party only guests of this nature Mrs. Sasaki was showing her customary prudence.

On this occasion Mrs. Sasaki wore a pearl ring. Diamonds at an all-female gathering had not seemed in the best of taste. Furthermore, pearls better matched the color of the dress she was wearing on this particular day.

Shortly after the party had begun, Mrs. Sasaki was moving across for one last inspection of the cake when the pearl in her ring, already a little loose, finally fell from its socket. It seemed a most inauspicious event for this happy occasion, but it would have been no less embarrassing to have everyone aware of the misfortune, so Mrs. Sasaki simply left the pearl close by the rim of the large cake dish and resolved to do something about it later. Around the cake were set out the plates, forks, and paper napkins for herself and the four guests. It now occurred to Mrs. Sasaki that she had no wish to be seen wearing a ring with no stone while cutting this cake, and accordingly she removed the ring from her finger and very deftly, without turning around, slipped it into a recess in the wall behind her back.

Amid the general excitement of the exchange of gossip, and Mrs. Sasaki's surprise and pleasure at the thoughtful presents brought by her guests, the matter of the pearl was very quickly forgotten. Before long it was time for the customary ceremony of lighting and extinguishing the candles on the cake. Everyone crowded excitedly about the table, lending a hand in the not untroublesome task of lighting forty-three candles.

Mrs. Sasaki, with her limited lung capacity, could hardly be expected to blow out all that number at one puff, and her appearance of utter helplessness gave rise to a great deal of hilarious comment.

The procedure followed in serving the cake was that, after the first bold cut, Mrs. Sasaki carved for each guest individually a slice of whatever thickness was requested and transferred this to a small plate, which the guest then carried back with her to her own seat. With everyone stretching out hands at the same time, the crush and confusion around the table was considerable.

On top of the cake was a floral design executed in pink icing and liberally interspersed with small silver balls. These were silver-painted crystals of sugar—a common enough decoration on birthday cakes. In the struggle to secure helpings, moreover, flakes of icing, crumbs of cake, and a number of these silver balls came to be scattered all over the white tablecloth. Some of the guests gathered these stray particles between their fingers and put them on their plates. Others popped them straight into their mouths.

In time all returned to their seats and ate their portions of cake at their leisure, laughing. It was not a homemade cake, having been ordered by Mrs. Sasaki from a certain high-class confectioner's, but the guests were unanimous in praising its excellence.

Mrs. Sasaki was bathed in happiness. But suddenly, with a tinge of anxiety, she recalled the pearl she had abandoned on the table, and, rising from her chair as casually as she could, she moved across to look for it. At the spot where she was sure she had left it, the pearl was no longer to be seen.

Mrs. Sasaki abhorred losing things. At once and without thinking, right in the middle of the party, she became wholly engrossed in her search, and the tension in her manner was so obvious that it attracted everyone's attention.

"Is there something the matter?" someone asked.

"No, not at all, just a moment. . . ."

Mrs. Sasaki's reply was ambiguous, but before she had time to decide to return to her chair, first one, then another, and finally every one of her guests had risen and was turning back the tablecloth or groping about on the floor.

Mrs. Azuma, seeing this commotion, felt that the whole thing was just too deplorable for words. She was incensed at a hostess who could create such an impossible situation over the loss of a solitary pearl.

Mrs. Azuma resolved to offer herself as a sacrifice and to save the day. With a heroic smile she declared: "That's it then! It must have been a pearl I ate just now! A silver ball dropped on the tablecloth when I was given my cake, and I just picked it up and swallowed it without thinking. It *did* seem to stick in my throat a little. Had it been a diamond, now, I would naturally return it—by an operation, if necessary—but as it's a pearl I must simply beg your forgiveness."

This announcement at once resolved the company's anxieties, and it was felt, above all, that it had saved the hostess from an embarrassing predicament. No one made any attempt to investigate the truth or falsity of Mrs. Azuma's confession. Mrs. Sasaki took one of the remaining silver balls and put it in her mouth.

"Mm," she said. "Certainly tastes like a pearl, this one!"

Thus this small incident, too, was cast into the crucible of good-humored teasing, and there—amid general laughter—it melted away.

When the party was over Mrs. Azuma drove off in her two-seater sportscar, taking with her in the other seat her close friend and neighbor Mrs. Kasuga. Before two minutes had passed Mrs. Azuma said, "Own up! It was you who swallowed the pearl, wasn't it? I covered up for you, and took the blame on myself."

This unceremonious manner of speaking concealed deep affection, but, however friendly the intention may have been, to Mrs. Kasuga a wrongful accusation was a wrongful accusation. She had no recollection whatsoever of having swallowed a pearl in mistake for a sugar ball. She was—as Mrs. Azuma too must surely know—fastidious in her eating habits, and, if she so much as detected a single hair in her food, whatever she happened to be eating at the time immediately stuck in her gullet.

"Oh, really now!" protested the timid Mrs. Kasuga in a small voice, her eyes studying Mrs. Azuma's face in some puzzlement. "I just couldn't do a thing like that!"

"It's no good pretending. The moment I saw that green look on your face, I knew."

The little disturbance at the party had seemed closed by Mrs. Azuma's frank confession, but even now it had left behind it this strange awkwardness. Mrs. Kasuga, wondering how best to demonstrate her innocence, was at the same time seized by the fantasy that a solitary pearl was lodged somewhere in her intestines. It was unlikely, of course, that she should mistakenly swallow a pearl for a sugar ball, but in all that confusion of talk and laughter one had to admit that it was at least a possibility. Though she thought back over the events of the party again and again, no moment in which she might have inserted a pearl into her mouth came to mind—but, after all, if it was an unconscious act one would not expect to remember it.

Mrs. Kasuga blushed deeply as her imagination chanced upon one further aspect of the matter. It had occurred to her that when one accepted a pearl into one's system it almost certainly—its luster a trifle dimmed, perhaps, by gastric juices—re-emerged intact within a day or two.

And with this thought the design of Mrs. Azuma, too, seemed to have become transparently clear. Undoubtedly Mrs. Azuma had viewed this same prospect with embarrassment and shame, and had therefore cast her responsibility onto another, making it appear that she had considerately taken the blame to protect a friend.

Meanwhile Mrs. Yamamoto and Mrs. Matsumura, whose homes lay in a similar direction, were returning together in a taxi. Soon after the taxi had started Mrs. Matsumura opened her handbag to make a few adjustments to her make-up. She remembered that she had done nothing to her face since all that commotion at the party.

As she was removing the powder compact her attention was caught by a sudden dull gleam as something tumbled to the bottom of the bag.

Groping about with the tips of her fingers, Mrs. Matsumura retrieved the object, and saw to her amazement that it was a pearl.

Mrs. Matsumura stifled an exclamation of surprise. Recently her relationship with Mrs. Yamamoto had been far from cordial, and she had no wish to share with that lady a discovery with such awkward implications for herself.

Fortunately Mrs. Yamamoto was gazing out of the window and did not appear to have noticed her companion's momentary start of surprise.

Caught off balance by this sudden turn of events, Mrs. Matsumura did not pause to consider how the pearl had found its way into her bag, but immediately became a prisoner of her own private brand of school-captain morality. It was unlikely—she thought—that she would do a thing like this, even in a moment of abstraction. But since, by some chance, the object had found its way into her handbag, the proper course was to return it at once. If she failed to do so, it would weigh heavily upon her conscience. The fact that it was a pearl, too—an article you could neither call all that expensive nor yet all that cheap—only made her position more ambiguous.

At any rate, she was determined that her companion, Mrs. Yamamoto, should know nothing of this incomprehensible development—especially when the affair had been so nicely rounded off, thanks to the selflessness of Mrs. Azuma. Mrs. Matsumura felt she could remain in the taxi not a moment longer, and, on the pretext of remembering a promise to visit a sick relative on her way back, she made the driver set her down at once, in the middle of a quiet residential district.

Mrs. Yamamoto, left alone in the taxi, was a little surprised that her practical joke should have moved Mrs. Matsumura to such abrupt action. Having watched Mrs. Matsumura's reflection in the window just now, she had clearly seen her draw the pearl from her bag.

At the party Mrs. Yamamoto had been the very first to receive a slice of cake. Adding to her plate a silver ball which had spilled onto the table, she had returned to her seat—again before any of the others—and there had noticed that the silver ball was a pearl. At this discovery she had at once conceived a malicious plan. While all the others were preoccupied with the cake, she had quickly slipped the pearl into the handbag left on the next chair by that insufferable hypocrite Mrs. Matsumura.

Stranded in the middle of a residential district where there was little prospect of a taxi, Mrs. Matsumura fretfully gave her mind to a number of reflections on her position.

First, no matter how necessary it might be for the relief of her own conscience, it would be a shame indeed, when people had gone to such lengths to settle the affair satisfactorily, to go and stir up things all over again; and it would be even worse if in the process—because of the inexplicable nature of the circumstances—she were to direct unjust suspicions upon herself.

Secondly—notwithstanding these considerations—if she did not make haste to return the pearl now, she would forfeit her opportunity forever. Left till tomorrow (at the thought Mrs. Matsumura blushed) the returned pearl would be an object of rather disgusting speculation and doubt. Concerning this possibility Mrs. Azuma herself had dropped a hint.

It was at this point that there occurred to Mrs. Matsumura, greatly to her joy, a master scheme which would both salve her conscience and at the same time involve no risk of exposing her character to any unjust suspicion. Quickening her step, she emerged at length onto a comparatively busy thoroughfare, where she hailed a taxi and told the driver to take her quickly to a certain celebrated pearl shop on the Ginza. There she took the pearl from her bag and showed it to the attendant, asking to see a pearl of slightly larger size and clearly superior quality. Having made her purchase, she proceeded once more, by taxi, to Mrs. Sasaki's house.

Mrs. Matsumura's plan was to present this newly purchased pearl to Mrs. Sasaki, saying that she had found it in her jacket pocket. Mrs. Sasaki would accept it and later attempt to fit it into the ring. However, being a pearl of a different size, it would not fit into the ring, and Mrs. Sasaki—puzzled—would try to return it to Mrs. Matsumura, but Mrs. Matsumura would refuse to have it returned. Thereupon Mrs. Sasaki would have no choice but to reflect as follows: The woman has behaved in this way in order to protect someone else. Such being the case, it is perhaps safest simply to accept the pearl and forget the matter. Mrs. Matsumura has doubtless observed one of the three ladies in the act of stealing the pearl. But at least, of my four guests, I can now be sure that Mrs. Matsumura, if no one else, is completely without guilt. Whoever heard of a thief stealing something and then replacing it with a similar article of greater value?

By this device Mrs. Matsumura proposed to escape forever the infamy of suspicion, and equally—by a small outlay of cash—the pricks of an uneasy conscience.

To return to the other ladies. After reaching home, Mrs. Kasuga continued to feel painfully upset by Mrs. Azuma's cruel teasing. To clear herself of even a ridiculous charge like this—she knew—she must act before tomorrow or it would be too late. That is to say, in order to offer positive proof that she had not eaten the pearl it was above all necessary for the pearl itself to be somehow produced. And, briefly, if she could show the pearl to Mrs. Azuma immediately, her innocence on the gastronomic count (if not on any other) would be firmly established. But if she waited until tomorrow, even though she managed to produce the pearl, the shameful and hardly mentionable suspicion would inevitably have intervened.

The normally timid Mrs. Kasuga, inspired with the courage of impetuous action, burst from the house to which she had so recently returned, sped to a pearl shop in the Ginza, and selected and bought a pearl which, to her eye, seemed of roughly the same size as those silver balls on the cake. She then telephoned Mrs. Azuma. On returning home, she explained, she had discovered in the folds of the bow of her sash the pearl which Mrs. Sasaki had lost, but, since she felt too ashamed to return it by herself, she wondered if Mrs. Azuma would be so kind as to go with her, as soon as possible. Inwardly Mrs. Azuma considered the story a little unlikely, but since it was the request of a good friend she agreed to go.

Mrs. Sasaki accepted the pearl brought to her by Mrs. Matsumura and, puzzled at its failure to fit the ring, fell obligingly into that very train of thought for which Mrs. Matsumura had prayed; but it was a surprise to her when Mrs. Kasuga arrived about an hour later, accompanied by Mrs. Azuma, and returned another pearl.

Mrs. Sasaki hovered perilously on the brink of discussing Mrs. Matsumura's prior visit, but checked herself at the last moment and accepted the second pearl as unconcernedly as she could. She felt sure that this one at any rate would fit, and as soon as the two visitors had taken their leave she hurried to try it in the ring. But it was too small, and wobbled loosely in the socket. At this discovery Mrs. Sasaki was not so much surprised as dumbfounded.

On the way back in the car both ladies found it impossible to guess what the other might be thinking, and, though normally relaxed and loquacious in each other's company, they now lapsed into a long silence.

Mrs. Azuma, who believed she could do nothing without her own full knowledge, knew for certain that she had not swallowed the pearl herself. It was simply to save everyone from embarrassment that she had cast shame aside and made that declaration at the party—more particularly it was to save the situation for her friend, who had been fidgeting about and looking conspicuously guilty. But what was she to think now? Beneath the peculiarity of Mrs. Kasuga's whole attitude, and beneath this elaborate procedure of having herself accompany her as she returned the pearl, she sensed that there lay something much deeper. Could it be that Mrs. Azuma's intuition had touched upon a weakness in her friend's make-up which it was forbidden to touch upon, and that by thus driving her friend into a corner she had transformed an unconscious, impulsive kleptomania into a deep mental derangement beyond all cure?

Mrs. Kasuga, for her part, still retained the suspicion that Mrs. Azuma had genuinely swallowed the pearl and that her confession at the party had been the truth. If that was so, it had been unforgivable of Mrs. Azuma, when everything was smoothly settled, to tease her so cruelly on the way back from the party, shifting the guilt onto herself. As a result, timid creature that she was, she had been panic-stricken, and besides spending good money had felt obliged to act out that little play—and was it not exceedingly ill-natured of Mrs. Azuma that, even after all this, she still refused to confess it was she who had eaten the pearl? And if Mrs. Azuma's innocence was all pretense, she herself—acting her part so painstakingly—must appear in Mrs. Azuma's eyes as the most ridiculous of third-rate comedians.

To return to Mrs. Matsumura. That lady, on her way back from obliging Mrs. Sasaki to accept the pearl, was feeling now more at ease in her mind and had the notion to make a leisurely reinvestigation, detail by detail, of the events of the recent incident. When going to collect her portion of cake, she had most certainly left her handbag on the chair. Then, while eating the cake, she had made liberal use of the paper napkin—so there could have been no necessity to take a handkerchief from her bag. The more she thought about it the less she could remember having opened her bag until she touched up her face in the taxi on the way home. How was it, then, that a pearl had rolled into a handbag which was always shut?

She realized now how stupid she had been not to have remarked this simple fact before, instead of flying into a panic at the mere sight of the pearl. Having progressed this far, Mrs. Matsumura was struck by an amazing thought. Someone must purposely have placed the pearl in her bag in order to incriminate her. And of the four guests at the party the only one who would do such a thing was, without doubt, the detestable Mrs. Yamamoto. Her eyes glinting with rage, Mrs. Matsumura hurried toward the house of Mrs. Yamamoto.

From her first glimpse of Mrs. Matsumura standing in the doorway, Mrs. Yamamoto knew at once what had brought her. She had already prepared her line of defense.

However, Mrs. Matsumura's cross-examination was unexpectedly severe, and from the start it was clear that she would accept no evasions.

"It was you, I know. No one but you could do such a thing," began Mrs. Matsumura, deductively.

"Why choose me? What proof have you? If you can say a thing like that to my face, I suppose you've come with pretty conclusive proof, have you?" Mrs. Yamamoto was at first icily composed.

To this Mrs. Matsumura replied that Mrs. Azuma, having so nobly taken the blame on herself, clearly stood in an incompatible relationship with mean and despicable behavior of this nature; and as for Mrs. Kasuga, she was much too weak-kneed for such dangerous work; and that left only one person—yourself.

Mrs. Yamamoto kept silent, her mouth shut tight like a clamshell. On the table before her gleamed the pearl which Mrs. Matsumura had set there. In the excitement she had not even had time to raise a teaspoon, and the Ceylon tea she had so thoughtfully provided was beginning to get cold.

"I had no idea that you hated me so." As she said this, Mrs. Yamamoto dabbed at the corners of her eyes, but it was plain that Mrs. Matsumura's resolve not to be deceived by tears was as firm as ever.

"Well, then," Mrs. Yamamoto continued, "I shall say what I had thought I must never say. I shall mention no names, but one of the guests . . ."

"By that, I suppose, you can only mean Mrs. Azuma or Mrs. Kasuga?"

"Please, I beg at least that you allow me to omit the name. As I say, one of the guests had just opened your bag and was dropping something inside when I happened to glance in her direction. You can imagine my amazement! Even if I had felt *able* to warn you, there would have been no chance. My heart just throbbed and throbbed, and on the way back in the taxi—oh, how awful not to be able to speak even then! If we had been good friends, of course, I could have told you quite frankly, but since I knew of your apparent dislike for me . . ."

"I see. You have been very considerate, I'm sure. Which means, doesn't it, that you have now cleverly shifted the blame onto Mrs. Azuma and Mrs. Kasuga?"

"Shifted the blame! Oh, how can I get you to understand my feelings? I only wanted to avoid hurting anyone."

"Quite. But you didn't mind hurting me, did you? You might at least have mentioned this in the taxi."

"And if you had been frank with me when you found the pearl in your bag, I would probably have told you, at that moment, everything I had seen—but no, you chose to leave the taxi at once, without saying a word!"

For the first time, as she listened to this, Mrs. Matsumura was at a loss for a reply.

"Well, then. Can I get you to understand? I wanted no one to be hurt."

Mrs. Matsumura was filled with an even more intense rage.

"If you are going to tell a string of lies like that," she said, "I must ask you to repeat them, tonight if you wish, in my presence, before Mrs. Azuma and Mrs. Kasuga."

At this Mrs. Yamamoto started to weep.

"And thanks to you," she sobbed reprovingly, "all my efforts to avoid hurting anyone will have come to nothing."

It was a new experience for Mrs. Matsumura to see Mrs. Yamamoto crying, and, though she kept reminding herself not to be taken in by tears, she could not altogether dismiss the feeling that perhaps somewhere, since nothing in this affair could be proved, there might be a modicum of truth even in the assertions of Mrs. Yamamoto.

In the first place—to be a little more objective—if one accepted Mrs. Yamamoto's story as true, then her reluctance to disclose the name of the guilty party, whom she had observed in the very act, argued some refinement of character. And just as one could not say for sure that the gentle and seemingly timid Mrs. Kasuga would never be moved to an act of malice, so even the undoubtedly bad feeling between Mrs. Yamamoto and herself could, by one way of looking at things, be taken as actually lessening the likelihood of Mrs. Yamamoto's guilt. For if she were to do a thing like this, with their relationship as it was, Mrs. Yamamoto would be the first to come under suspicion.

"We have differences in our natures," Mrs. Yamamoto continued tearfully, "and I cannot deny that there are things about yourself which I dislike. But, for all that, it is really too bad that you should suspect me of such a petty trick to get the better of you. . . . Still, on thinking it over, to submit quietly to your accusations might well be the course most consistent with what I have felt in this matter all along. In this way I alone shall bear the guilt, and no other will be hurt."

After this pathetic pronouncement Mrs. Yamamoto lowered her face to the table and abandoned herself to uncontrolled weeping.

Watching her, Mrs. Matsumura came by degrees to reflect upon the impulsiveness of her own behavior. Detesting Mrs. Yamamoto as she had, there had been times in her castigation of that lady when she had allowed herself to be blinded by emotion.

When Mrs. Yamamoto raised her head again after this prolonged bout of weeping, the look of resolution on her face, somehow remote and pure, was apparent even to her visitor. Mrs. Matsumura, a little frightened, drew herself upright in her chair.

"This thing should never have been. When it is gone, everything will be as before." Speaking in riddles, Mrs. Yamamoto pushed back her disheveled hair and fixed a terrible, yet hauntingly beautiful gaze upon the top of the table. In an instant she had snatched up the pearl from before her, and, with a gesture of no ordinary resolve, tossed it into her mouth. Raising her cup by the handle, her little finger elegantly extended, she washed the pearl down her throat with one gulp of cold Ceylon tea.

Mrs. Matsumura watched in horrified fascination. The affair was over before she had time to protest. This was the first time in her life she had seen a person swallow a pearl, and there was in Mrs. Yamamoto's manner something of that desperate finality one might expect to see in a person who had just drunk poison.

However, heroic though the action was, it was above all a touching incident, and not only did Mrs. Matsumura find her anger vanished into thin air, but so impressed was she by Mrs. Yamamoto's simplicity and purity that she could only think of that lady as a saint. And now Mrs. Matsumura's eyes too began to fill with tears, and she took Mrs. Yamamoto by the hand.

"Please forgive me, please forgive me," she said. "It was wrong of me."

For a while they wept together, holding each other's hands and vowing to each other that henceforth they would be the firmest of friends.

When Mrs. Sasaki heard rumors that the relationship between Mrs. Yamamoto and Mrs. Matsumura, which had been so strained, had suddenly improved, and that Mrs. Azuma and Mrs. Kasuga, who had been such good friends, had suddenly fallen out, she was at a loss to understand the reasons and contented herself with the reflection that nothing was impossible in this world.

However, being a woman of no strong scruples, Mrs. Sasaki requested a jeweler to refashion her ring and to produce a design into which two new pearls could be set, one large and one small, and this she wore quite openly, without further mishap.

Soon she had completely forgotten the small commotion on her birthday, and when anyone asked her age she would give the same untruthful answers as ever.

LeRoi Jones

LeRoi Jones (1934–   ) was born and reared in Newark, New Jersey, where he now lives. He attended a local high school, went to Rutgers University for one year, and graduated from Howard University. He served as sergeant in the Strategic Air Command, traveling throughout the world.

Always interested in writing, he taught poetry and fiction writing at colleges in New York City. His play, Dutchman *was produced Off-Broadway in 1964 and won a theatrical award. His poetry has appeared in* Harper's, The Nation, *and other national magazines. Jones has written essays on social-cultural subjects, including several on jazz. He is deeply concerned with the development of black arts, and has worked closely with theatrical companies in local communities. He writes about black ghetto life with irony, intensity, and often with anger.* *(See page 79 of Introduction.)*

THE SCREAMERS

Lynn Hope adjusts his turban under the swishing red green yellow lights. Dots. Suede heaven raining, windows yawning cool summer air, and his musicians watch him grinning, quietly, or high with wine blotches on four dollar shirts. A yellow girl will not dance with me, nor will Teddy's people, in line to the left of the stage, readying their *Routines*. Haroldeen, the most beautiful, in her pitiful dead sweater. Make it yellow, wish it whole. Lights. Teddy, Sonny Boy, Kenney & Calvin, Scram, a few of Nat's boys jamming long washed handkerchiefs in breast pockets, pushing shirts into homemade cummerbunds, shuffling lightly for any audience.

"The Cross-Over," Deen laughing at us all. And they perform in solemn unison a social tract of love. (With no music till Lynn finishes "macking" with any big-lipped Esther screws across the stage.) White and green plaid jackets his men wear, and that twisted badge, black turban/on red string conked hair. (OPPRESSORS!) A greasy hipness, down-ness, nobody in our camp believed (having social worker mothers and postman fathers; or living squeezed in light skinned projects with adulterers and proud skinny ladies with soft voices). The theory, the spectrum, this sound baked inside their heads, and still rub sweaty against those lesser lights. Those niggers. Laundromat workers, beauticians, pregnant short haired jail bait separated all ways from "us," but in this vat we sweated gladly for each other. And rubbed. And Lynn could be a common hero, from whatever side we saw him. Knowing that energy, and its response. That drained silence we had to make with our hands, leaving actual love to Nat or Al or Scram.

He stomped his foot, and waved one hand. The other hung loosely on his horn. And their turbans wove in among those shadows. Lynn's tighter, neater, and bright gorgeous yellow stuck with a green stone. Also, those green sparkling cubes dancing off his pinkies. A-boomp bahba bahba, A-boomp bahba bahba, A-boomp bahba bahba, A-boomp bahba bahba, the turbans sway behind him. And he grins before he lifts the horn, at Deen or drunk Becky, and we search the dark for girls.

Who would I get? (Not anyone who would understand this.) Some light girl who had fallen into bad times and ill-repute for dating Bubbles. And he fixed her later with his child, now she walks Orange St. wiping chocolate from its face. A disgraced white girl who learned to calypso in vocational school. Hence, behind halting speech, a humanity as paltry as her cotton dress. (And the big hats made a line behind her, stroking their erections, hoping for photographs to take down south.) Lynn would oblige. He would make the most perverted hopes sensual and possible. Chanting at that dark crowd. Or some girl, a wino's daughter, with carefully vaselined bow legs would drape her filthy angora against the cardboard corinthian, eyeing past any greediness a white man knows, my soft tyrolean hat, pressed corduroy suit, and "B" sweater. Whatever they meant, finally to her, valuable shadows barely visible. Some stuck-up boy with "good" hair. And as a naked display of America, for I meant to her that same oppression. A stunted head of greased glass feathers, orange lips, brown pasted edge to the collar of her dying blouse. The secret perfume of poverty and ignorant desire. Arrogant too, at my disorder, which calls her smile mysterious. Turning to be eaten by the crowd. That mingled foliage of sweat and shadows: *Night Train* was what they swayed to. And smelled each other in The Grind, The Rub, The Slow Drag. From side to side, slow or jerked staccato as their wedding dictated. Big hats bent, tight skirts, and some light girls' hair swept the resin on the floor. Respectable ladies put stiff arms on your waist to keep some light between, looking nervously at an ugly friend forever at the music's edge.

I wanted girls like Erselle, whose father sang on television, but my hair was not straight enough, and my father never learned how to drink. Our house sat lonely and large on a half-Italian street, filled with important Negroes. (Though it is rumored they had a son, thin with big eyes, they killed because he was crazy.) Surrounded by the haughty daughters of depressed economic groups. They plotted in their projects for mediocrity, and the neighborhood smelled of their despair. And only the wild or the very poor thrived in Graham's or could be roused by Lynn's histories and rhythms. America had choked the rest, who could sit still for hours under popular songs, or be readied for citizenship by slightly bohemian social workers. They rivaled pure emotion with wind-up record players that pumped Jo Stafford into Home Economics rooms. And these carefully scrubbed children of my parents' friends fattened on their rhythms until they could join the Urban League or Household Finance and hound the poor for their honesty.

I was too quiet to become a murderer, and too used to extravagance for their skinny lyrics. They mentioned neither cocaine nor Bach, which was my reading, and the flaw of that society. I disappeared into the slums, and fell in love with violence, and invented for myself a mysterious economy of need. Hence, I shambled anonymously thru Lloyd's, The Nitecap, The Hi-Spot, and Graham's desiring everything I felt. In a new English overcoat and green hat, scouring that town for my peers. And they were old pinch faced whores full of snuff and weak dope, celebrity fags with radio programs, mute bass players who loved me, and built the myth of my intelligence. You see, I left America on the first fast boat.

This was Sunday night, and the Baptists were still praying in their "faboulous" churches. Though my father sat listening to the radio, or reading pulp cowboy magazines, which I take in part to be the truest legacy of my own spirit. God never had a chance. And I would be walking slowly towards The Graham, not even knowing how to smoke. Willing for any experience, any image, any further separation from where my good grades were sure to lead. Frightened of post offices, lawyer's offices, doctor's cars, the deaths of clean politicians. Or of the imaginary fat man, advertising cemeteries to his "good colored friends." Lynn's screams erased them all, and I thought myself intrepid white commando from the West. Plunged into noise and flesh, and their form become an ethic.

Now Lynn wheeled and hunched himself for another tune. Fast dancers fanned themselves. Couples who practiced during the week talked over their steps. Deen and her dancing clubs readied avant-garde routines. Now it was *Harlem Nocturne,* which I whistled loudly one Saturday in a laundromat, and the girl who stuffed in my khakis and stiff underwear asked was I a musician. I met her at Graham's that night and we waved, and I suppose she knew I loved her.

Nocturne was slow and heavy and the serious dancers loosened their ties. The slowly twisting lights made specks of human shadows, the darkness seemed to float around the hall. Any meat you clung to was yours those few minutes without interruption. The length of the music was the only form. And the idea was to press against each other hard, to rub, to shove the hips tight, and gasp at whatever passion. Professionals wore jocks against embarrassment. Amateurs, like myself, after the music stopped, put our hands quickly into our pockets, and retreated into the shadows. It was as meaningful as anything else we knew.

All extremes were popular with that crowd. The singers shouted, the musicians stomped and howled. The dancers ground each other past passion or moved so fast it blurred intelligence. We hated the popular song, and any freedman could tell you if you asked that white people danced jerkily, and were slower than our champions. One style, which developed as Italians showed up with pegs, and our own grace moved towards bellbottom pants to further complicate the cipher, was the honk. The repeated rhythmic figure, a screamed riff, pushed in its insistence past music. It was hatred and frustration, secrecy and despair. It spurted out of the diphthong culture, and reinforced the black cults of emotion. There was no compromise, no dreary sophistication, only the elegance of something that is too ugly to be described, and is diluted only at the agent's peril. All the saxophonists of that world were honkers, Illinois, Gator, Big Jay, Jug, the great sounds of our day. Ethnic historians, actors, priests of the unconscious. That stance spread like fire thru the cabarets and joints of the black cities, so that the sound itself became a basis for thought, and the innovators searched for uglier modes. Illinois would leap and twist his head, scream when he wasn't playing. Gator would strut up and down the stage, dancing for emphasis, shaking his long gassed hair in his face and coolly mopping it back. Jug, the beautiful horn, would wave back and forth so high we all envied him his connection, or he'd stomp softly to the edge of the stage whispering those raucous threats. Jay first turned the mark around, opened the way further for the completely nihilistic act. McNeeley, the first Dada coon of the age, jumped and stomped and yowled and finally sensed the only other space that form allowed. He fell first on his knees, never releasing the horn, and walked that way across the stage. We hunched together drowning any sound, relying on Jay's contorted face for evidence that there was still music, though none of us needed it now. And then he fell backwards, flat on his back, with both feet stuck up high in the air, and he kicked and thrashed and the horn spat enraged sociologies.

That was the night Hip Charlie, the Baxter Terrace Romeo, got wasted right in front of the place. Snake and four friends mashed him up and left him for the ofays to identify. Also the night I had the grey bells and sat in the Chinese restaurant all night to show them off. Jay had set a social form for the poor, just as Bird and Dizzy proposed it for the middle class. On his back screaming was the Mona Lisa with the mustache, as crude and simple. Jo Stafford could not do it. Bird took the language, and we woke up one Saturday whispering Ornithology. Blank verse.

And Newark always had a bad reputation. I mean, everybody could pop their fingers. Was hip. Had walks. Knew all about The Apple. So I suppose when the word got to Lynn what Big Jay had done, he knew all the little down cats were waiting to see him in this town. He knew he had to cook. And he blasted all night, crawled and leaped, then stood at the side of the stand, and watched us while he fixed his sky, wiped his face. Watched us to see how far he'd gone, but he was tired and we weren't, which was not where it was. The girls rocked slowly against the silence of the horns, and big hats pushed each other or made plans for murder. We had not completely come. All sufficiently eaten by Jay's memory, "on his back, kicking his feet in the air, Ga-ud Dam!" So he moved cautiously to the edge of the stage, and the gritty muslims he played with gathered close. It was some mean honking blues, and he made no attempt to hide his intentions. He was breaking bad. "Okay, baby," we all thought, "Go for yourself." I was standing at the back of the hall with one arm behind my back, so the overcoat could hang over in that casual gesture of fashion. Lynn was moving, and the camel walkers were moving in the corners. The fast dancers and practicers making the whole hall dangerous. "Off my suedes, motherfucker." Lynn was trying to move us, and even I did the one step I knew, safe at the back of the hall. The hippies ran for girls. Ugly girls danced with each other. Skippy, who ran the lights, made them move faster in that circle on the ceiling, and darkness raced around the hall. Then Lynn got his riff, that rhythmic figure we knew he would repeat, the honked note that would be his personal evaluation of the world. And he screamed it so the veins in his face stood out like neon. "Uhh, yeh, Uhh, yeh, Uhh, yeh," we all screamed to push him further. So he opened his eyes for a second, and really made his move. He looked over his shoulder at the other turbans, then marched in time with his riff, on his toes across the stage. They followed; he marched across to the other side, repeated, then finally he descended, still screaming, into the crowd, and as the sidemen followed, we made a path for them around the hall. They were strutting, and all their horns held very high, and they were only playing that one scary note. They moved near the back of the hall, chanting and swaying, and passed right in front of me. I had a little cup full of wine a murderer friend of mine made me drink, so I drank it and tossed the cup in the air, then fell in line behind the last wild horn man, strutting like the rest of them. Bubbles and Rogie followed me, and four eyed Moselle Boyd. And we strutted back and forth pumping our arms, repeating with Lynn Hope, "Yeh, Uhh, Yeh, Uhh." Then everybody fell in behind us, yelling still. There was confusion and stumbling, but there were no real fights. The thing they wanted was right there and easily accessible. No one could stop you from getting in that line. "It's too crowded. It's too many people on the line!" some people yelled. So Lynn thought further, and made to destroy the ghetto. We went out into the lobby and in perfect rhythm down the marble steps. Some musicians laughed, but Lynn and some others kept the note, till the others fell back in. Five or six hundred hopped up woogies tumbled out into Belmont Avenue. Lynn marched right in the center of the street. Sunday night traffic stopped, and honked. Big Red yelled at a bus driver, "Hey, baby, honk that horn in time or shut it off!" The bus driver cooled it. We screamed and screamed at the clear image of ourselves as we should always be. Ecstatic, completed, involved in a secret communal expression. It would be the form of the sweetest revolution, to hucklebuck into the fallen capitol, and let the oppressors lindy hop out. We marched all the way to Spruce, weaving among the stalled cars, laughing at the dazed white men who sat behind the wheels. Then Lynn turned and we strutted back towards the hall. The late show at the National was turning out, and all the big hats there jumped right in our line.

Then the Nabs came, and with them, the fire engines. What was it, a labor riot? Anarchists? A nigger strike? The paddy wagons and cruisers pulled in from both sides, and sticks and billies started flying, heavy streams of water splattering the marchers up and down the street. America's responsible immigrants were doing her light work again. The knives came out, the razors, all the Biggers who would not be bent counterattacked or came up behind the civil servants, smashing at them with coke bottles and aerials. Belmont writhed under the dead economy and splivs floated in the gutters, disappearing under cars. But for awhile, before the war had reached its peak, Lynn and his musicians, a few other fools, and I, still marched, screaming thru the maddened crowd. Onto the sidewalk, into the lobby, half-way up the stairs, then we all broke our different ways, to save whatever it was each of us thought we loved.

Abram Tertz

Abram Tertz, pseudonym for Andrei Sinyovsky (1925–   ), is a Russian writer who wrote his Ph.D. dissertation on Gorky. In 1965 he was accused of writing anti-Soviet works, and was sentenced to seven years at hard labor. A radical and avant-garde critic and teacher, he helped to rehabilitate Pasternak, support young writers, and encourage the emancipation of Russian literature from dogmatic traditions. He writes, "May the fantastic imagery of Hoffmann and Dostoevsky, of Goya, Chagall and Mayakovsky . . . and of many other realists and non-realists teach us how to be truthful with the aid of the absurd and the fantastic." His works include "On Socialist Realism" (1959), The Icicle and Other Stories *(1963), and* The Makepeace Experiment *(1965). (See page 75 of Introduction.)*

PKHENTZ

I

I met him at the laundry again today. He pretended to be completely taken up with his dirty washing and unaware of me.

First came the sheets which people here use for reasons of hygiene. Along one edge of every sheet they stitch in tiny letters the word "feet." This is by way of precaution against one's lips touching any part which the soles of one's feet may have rubbed and contaminated the night before.

Similarly a kick is considered more insulting than a blow of the hand, and not just because the foot hurts more. The distinction is probably a sign that Christianity still lives on: the foot must be wickeder than the rest of the body for the simple reason that it is farther from heaven. Only the sex organs are treated with less respect, and here there is some mystery.

Next came pillow-cases with dark impressions in the middle. Then towels, which unlike pillow-cases get dirty quicker round the edges, and, last of all, a multi-coloured bundle of crumpled personal linen.

At this point he started tossing his stuff in at such a rate that I couldn't take a good look. Either he was afraid of giving away a secret, or else he was ashamed, as people always are, to exhibit objects directly pertaining to his legs.

But it was suspicious, I thought, that he had worn his clothes so long without getting them laundered. Ordinarily hunchbacks are cleanly. They are afraid that their clothes may make them still more repulsive. But this one, surprisingly, was so slovenly that it was as if he were not a hunchback at all.

The woman who checked the laundry had seen everything. The traces left by the rarest of juices were well known to her. But even she couldn't help saying quite loudly: "What's that you're shoving under my nose, citizen? If you can't sleep properly, do your washing yourself!"

He paid his money without a word and rushed out. I didn't follow him, because I didn't want to attract anyone's attention.

At home things were as usual. The minute I got into my room Veronica appeared. She bashfully suggested that we should have supper together. It was a bit awkward for me to say no to the girl. She's the only one in the whole apartment who treats me decently. It's a pity that her sympathy is grounded only in sexual attraction. I became absolutely certain of this today.

"How's Kostritskaya?" I asked, trying to steer the conversation towards common enemies.

"Oh, Andrei Kazimirovich, she's been making threats again."

"What's wrong?"

"The same as before. Light on in the bathroom and the floor all splashed. Kostritskaya informed me that she's going to complain to the house manager."

The news infuriated me. I make less use of the plumbing than any of the others. I hardly ever go into the kitchen. Can't I make up for not using the kitchen by using the bathroom?

"Well, let her get on with it," I answered sharply. "She burns light by the kilowatt herself. And her children broke my bottle. Let the house manager come round."

But I knew very well that any appeal to the authorities to interfere would be a very risky business for me. Why draw attention to myself unnecessarily?

"Don't upset yourself, Andrei Kazimirovich," said Veronica. "I'll look after any trouble with the neighbours. Please don't upset yourself."

She put out her hand to touch my forehead, but I managed to dodge. "No, no, I'm quite well, I haven't got a temperature. Let's have supper."

Food stood on the table, steaming and evil-smelling. The sadism of cookery has always amazed me. Would-be chickens are eaten in liquid form. The innards of pigs are stuffed with their own flesh. A gut that's swallowed itself garnished with stillborn chickens. That, in fact, is what scrambled egg with sausage is.

Wheat is treated more unmercifully still: they cut it, beat it, crush it into dust.

Is this not the reason why flour and torture differ only in stress?

"Eat up now, Andrei Kazimirovich," said Veronica coaxingly. "Please don't let it worry you. I'll take the blame for everything."

What about preparing a man in the same way? Take an engineer or writer, stuff him with his own brains, place a violet in his braised nostril, and dish him up to his colleagues for dinner. Yes, the torments of Christ, Jan Hus, and Stenka Razin are a bagatelle compared with the agonies of a fish jerked out of water on a hook. They at least knew what it was all for.

"Tell me, Andrei Kazimirovich, are you very lonely," asked Veronica, coming back into the room with the teapot. While she had gone to fetch it I had emptied my plate into a sheet of newspaper.

"Did you ever have any friends,"
—she put in sugar,
—"or children,"—
another spoonful,—
"or a woman you loved?". . .
stir, stir, stir.

It was easy to see that Veronica was agitated.

"You are all the friends I need," I began cautiously. "And as for women, you can see for yourself: I'm old and hump-backed. Old and hump-backed," I repeated with ruthless insistence.

I honestly wanted to forestall a declaration of love: things were difficult enough for me without it. It wasn't worth spoiling our alliance against the spiteful neighbours by rousing this unattached girl to a keener interest in myself.

To avoid trouble I was ready to pretend to be an alcoholic. Or a criminal. Or perhaps better still a madman, or even a pederast? But I was afraid that any one of these roles would lend my person a dangerous fascination.

All I could do was to dwell on my hump, my age, my wretched salary, my humble job as a book-keeper, and all the time it took up, to insist that only a woman with a hump to match would be right for me, whereas a normal, beautiful woman needed a symmetrical man.

"No, you are too noble," Veronica decided. "You think of yourself as a cripple, and you're afraid of being a burden. Don't think it's pity on my part. It's just that I like cactuses and you are like a cactus. What a lot of them you've got growing there on your window-sill!"

Her hot fingers touched my hand. I jumped as if I'd been scalded.

"You're freezing—are you well?" asked Veronica anxiously. She was puzzled by my body temperature.

This was too much. I pleaded a migraine and asked her to leave me.

"Till tomorrow," said Veronica, waving her hand like a little girl. "And you can give me a cactus for a present tomorrow without fail."

This gentle girl talked to me in the tone of a head accountant. She declared her love for me and demanded a reward.

Didn't I read somewhere that people in love are like obedient slaves? Nothing of the kind. A man only has to fall in love to feel himself lord and master, with the right to do as he will with anyone who doesn't love him enough. How I wish that nobody loved me!

When I was alone I set about watering my cactuses from an enamel mug. I fed them slowly, my little hump-backed children, and relaxed.

It was two o'clock in the morning, when, faint from hunger, I crept on tip-toe along the dark corridor to the bathroom. But what a splendid supper I had then!

It isn't at all easy, eating only once a day.

2

That was two weeks ago. Since then Veronica has informed me that she has two beaus: a lieutenant and an actor at the Stanislavsky Theatre. But it hasn't stopped her showing her preference for me. She has threatened to shave her head so that I can't keep saying how stupid it would be to sacrifice her beauty for an old freak. Now she has got round to spying on me, lying in wait for me on the way to the bathroom.

"Cleanliness makes hunchbacks handsome"—that's my stock answer when she keeps asking why I take so many baths.

Just in case, I have started blocking up the frosted window between the bathroom and the lavatory with a piece of ply-wood. I always try the bolts before undressing. I couldn't stand the thought of somebody watching me.

Yesterday morning I wanted to fill my fountain-pen, to continue my irregular diary, so I knocked at her door. Veronica wasn't up yet. She was reading *The Three Musketeers* in bed.

Politely wishing her good morning, I said: "You'll be late for your lecture."

She closed her book. "Do you know," she said, "that the whole house thinks I'm your mistress?"

I said nothing, and then something horrible happened. Veronica, her eyes flashing, threw back the blanket, and her whole body, completely uncovered, stared up at me angrily. "Look what you've turned down, Andrei Kazimirovich!"

Fifteen years ago I came across a textbook on anatomy. I wanted to know what was what, so I studied carefully all the pictures and diagrams. Later on, I had an opportunity of watching little boys bathing in the river at the Gorky Park of Culture and Rest. But I had never before happened to see a naked woman in the flesh and at such close quarters.

It was—I repeat—horrible. I found that her whole body was of the same unnatural whiteness as her neck, face, and hands. A pair of white breasts dangled in front. At first I took them for secondary arms, amputated above the elbow. But each of them terminated in a round nipple like a bell-push.

Farther on, and right down to her legs, the whole available space was occupied by a spherical belly. That is where the food swallowed in the course of the day collects in a heap. Its lower half was overgrown with curly hair like a little head.

The problem of sex, which plays a major role in their intellectual and moral life, had long troubled me. It must be for reasons of safety that it has been wrapped from ancient times in a veil of impenetrable secrecy. Even the textbook of anatomy has nothing to say on the subject, or says it so vaguely and indirectly that no one can guess what it really means.

So now, overcoming my confusion, I decided to take advantage of the opportunity, to take a look at the place mentioned in the anatomy textbook as the site of that genital apparatus which shoots out ready-made infants like a catapult.

I caught a glimpse of something resembling a human face. Only it didn't look female to me, but more like an old man's face, unshaven and baring its teeth.

A hungry, vicious man dwelt there between her legs. He probably snored at night, and relieved his boredom with foul language. It must be this that gives rise to woman's dual nature, of which the poet Lermontov has aptly said:

> Fair as an angel of heaven,
> As a demon cruel and false.

There was no time to work the thing out, because Veronica suddenly shuddered and said:

"Come on!"

She shut her eyes and opened her mouth, like a fish pulled out of water. She thrashed about on the bed like a great white fish, helplessly, vainly, and bluish goose-pimples came out all over her body.

"Forgive me, Veronica Grigorievna," I said timidly. "Forgive me," I said, "it's time for me to go to the office."

And I tried to tread lightly and not to look back as I went away.

It was raining outside, but I was in no hurry. It was cleaning day in the department. I had escaped from Veronica, pleading my official work (the estimates, the nicotine, Head Accountant Zykov, those witless typists—all for 650 roubles a month), and now I could afford the great luxury of a walk in the open in wet weather.

I chose a leaky drain-pipe and stationed myself under the stream. It ran right down my neck, cool and delicious, and in about three minutes I was damp enough.

The people hurrying past, all of them with umbrellas and rubber soles, looked at me sideways, intrigued by my behaviour. I had to change my position, so I took a stroll through the puddles. My shoes were letting in water nicely. Down below, at least, I was enjoying myself.

"Oh, Veronica, Veronica," I repeated indignantly. "Why were you so cruel as to fall in love with me? Why weren't you just the least bit ashamed of your exterior, why did you behave with such unforgivable candour?"

Shame, after all, is man's fundamental virtue. It is a dim realization that he is irredeemably ugly, an instinctive dread of what he hides under cloth. Only shame, shame, shame can lend him a certain nobility, make him not of course more beautiful but at least more modest.

Needless to say, when I got here I followed the general fashion. You must observe the laws of the country you're compelled to live in. And anyway the constant danger of being caught, of being found out makes me force my body into this fancy-dress.

But in their place I wouldn't shed my fur coat, let alone my suit, day or night. I would find a plastic surgeon to shorten my legs and at least put a hump on my back. Hunchbacks are certainly a bit more respectable-looking than the rest of them here, though they are monsters too.

Dejectedly I made my way to Herzen Street. My hunchback lodged there in a semi-basement opposite the Conservatoire. For six weeks now I had had my eye on this gracefully vaulted person who was so unlike a human being, and reminded me somehow of my lost youth.

I had seen him three times running at the laundry and once in a flower shop, buying a cactus. I had been lucky enough to find out his address from a receipt which he had tendered to the laundress.

The time had come to dot the "i's."

I told myself that it was impossible, that they had all perished and that I was the sole survivor, like Robinson Crusoe. I myself, with my own hands, had liquidated all that was left after the crash. There were no others here besides myself.

But what if they'd sent him to look for me? And he had disguised himself, pretending to be a hunchback. . . . They hadn't forgotten me! They'd realized what had happened and mounted a search!

But how could they know? After thirty-two years. By local time, but still. Alive and well. That was not to be sneezed at.

But why here precisely? That was the question. Nobody had meant to come here. Quite a different direction. Things just don't happen like that. We missed our way. To the back of beyond. Seven and a half. Then it happened.

Perhaps it was by chance. Exactly the same error. A deviation from course and the winter timetable. The first place we came to. Do coincidences happen? Alike as two peas. Where none had set foot. It could happen, couldn't it? Disguised as a hunchback. Exactly like me. Even if there were only one, exactly like me!

The door was opened by the lady like Kostritskaya. Only his Kostritskaya was bigger and older. She exuded a smell of lilac, ten times normal strength. Perfume, that was.

"Leopold will be back soon. Come in, please."

An unseen dog was barking at the other end of the corridor. It couldn't make up its mind to spring at me. But I had had nasty experiences with animals of this kind.

"Don't worry. She doesn't bite. Niksa, tu beau, du silence!"

We wrangled politely while the animal raged, and three heads emerged from side-doors. They looked me up and down with interest and cursed the dog. The resultant din was awful.

I got through to the room, at great risk, and found there a small child armed with a sabre. When he saw us he asked for cranberries and sugar and set up a yell, wriggling and pulling faces.

"He's a sweet-tooth. Just like me," Kostritskaya explained. "Stop whining, or this man here will eat you up."

To please my hostess, I said jokingly that for soup I drank children's blood, warmed-up. The child was quiet at once. He dropped his sabre and cowered in the far corner. He didn't take his eyes off me. They were full of animal terror.

"Is he like Leopold?" the Kostritskaya asked, as though casually, but with a hoarse tenderness in her voice.

I pretended to believe the innuendo. The stale air, laced with exhalations of lilac, made me feel sick. The smell irritated my skin, and it became inflamed in several places. There was a danger that my face might come out in green spots.

But in the corridor the savage Niksa was scratching the floor with her claws, and sniffing my tracks with a noisy snuffle. The excited women lodgers, unaware of my heightened acoustic perception, were conversing in half-whispers.

"Anybody can see he's Leopold Sergeyevich's brother . . ."

"No, you're wrong, our hunchy is Pushkin's twin alongside this one."

"Hope to God I never dream of anything like that during the night . . ."

"It's unpleasant just to look at him . . ."

All this was interrupted by Leopold's arrival. I remember that I liked the way he plunged straight into his part—the classic part of the hunchback who meets a monster like himself in the presence of third parties.

"Aha, a companion in misfortune! With whom have I the honour. . . ? To what am I indebted. . . ?"

This was an imitation of a finely spun psychological spider's web, pride protected by self-mockery, shame hiding itself in buffoonery. He was mounting chairs like a horseman, gripping the seat with his legs, then jumping up and sitting down again back to front, and then, resting his head on the chair-back, pulling weird faces and continually moving his shoulders as though feeling the hump that loomed over him like a rucksack.

"Yes, yes. So you're Andrei Kazimirovich. And my name, funnily enough, is Leopold Sergeyevich. As you can see I'm a bit of a hunchback too."

I was delighted with this skilful caricature of humanity, this art which was all the more like the real thing because it was so absurd, and I acknowledged rather sadly that he was my superior at the game of living, that I lacked his ability to enter into the only form possible for us on earth . . . that of a hunchbacked monster and an injured egotist.

But business is business, and I gave him to understand that I wished to talk to him—*confidentially*.

"I don't mind going," said Kostritskaya huffily, and gave me a farewell gust of her caustic aroma as she left the room.

I revenged myself with the thought that she was saturated right through to her backbone with this smell. Even her excrement must smell of perfume, instead of boiled potatoes and home comforts, as is usually the case. She must piss pure eau-de-Cologne. In this atmosphere poor Leopold would soon start to wither away.

When we were alone, except for the petrified child sitting in the far corner with a peculiar dazed look of horror on his face, I asked him straight out:

"How long since you left?"

"Left where?" he answered evasively.

With our hostess's departure the assumed merriment had been wiped from his face. Not a trace of that clownish exhibitionism found in most hunchbacks, who are clever enough to hide their spines and proud enough not to suffer because of it. I thought that he hadn't pulled himself together yet, and that from inertia he was wearily keeping up the pretence of being something other than his true self.

"Cut it out," I said quietly. "I recognized you at first sight. You and I come from the same place. We're relatives, so to speak. PKHENTZ! PKHENTZ!" I whispered, to remind him of a name sacred to us both.

"What did you say? . . . You know, I thought there was something rather familiar about you. Where could I have seen you before?"

He rubbed his brow, frowned, twisted his lips. His face had an almost human mobility, and again I envied his extraordinarily rehearsed technique, although these cautious habits were beginning to irritate me.

"Of course!" he exclaimed, still playing the fool. "Did you work once in the Stationery Supplies network? The director there in 'forty-four was Yakov Solomonovich Zak—such a nice little Jew . . ."

"I don't know any Zak," I answered curtly. "But I know very well that you, Leopold Sergeyevich, are not Leopold Sergeyevich at all, and no hunchback, although you keep flourishing your hump all over the place. We've had enough of pretences now. After all, I'm taking just as big a risk as you are."

It was as though the devil had got into him:

"How dare you tell me who I am? Spoiling my relations with the landlady, and then insulting me as well! Go and find yourself a gorgeous woman like that," he said, "and then you can discuss my physical defects. You're more of a hunchback than I am! Do you hear? You're more disgusting. Monster! Hunchback! Wretched cripple!"

Suddenly he burst out laughing and clapped his hand to his head: "Now I remember! I've seen you at the laundry. The only resemblance between us is that we get our clothes washed in the same place."

This time I didn't doubt his sincerity. He really did think that he was Leopold Sergeyevich. He had entered too fully into his part, gone native, become human, over-adapted himself to his surroundings, surrendered to alien influences. He had forgotten his former name, betrayed his distant homeland, and unless somebody helped him he was as good as lost.

I grabbed him by his shoulders and shook him carefully. I shook him, and in a gentle, friendly way tried to get him to make an effort to remember, to return to his true self. What did he want with that Kostritskaya, who oozed such a poisonous odour? Even amongst humans copulation with animals is not respectable. And more still—betrayal of the homeland, even without malice aforethought, even out of ordinary forgetfulness . . .

"PKHENTZ! PKHENTZ!" I said over and over again, and repeated other words which I still remembered.

Suddenly an inexplicable warmth reached me through his Boston jacket. His shoulders were getting hotter and hotter, as hot as Veronica's hand, and thousands of other hot hands which I have preferred not to shake in greeting.

"Forgive me," I said, relaxing my hold. "I think there's some mistake. A regrettable misunderstanding. You see, I—how can I explain to you?—I'm subject to nervous attacks . . ."

Just then I heard a terrible row and turned round. The child was dancing about behind me, at a respectful distance, and threatening me with his sabre.

"Let Leopold alone!" he shouted. "Nasty man! Let Leopold alone! My mummy loves him. He's my daddy, he's my Leopold, not yours!"

There could be no doubt about it. I had mistaken my man. He was a normal human, the most normal of humans, hunchback or not.

3

I feel worse every day. Winter has arrived—the coldest season in this part of the world. I never put my nose out of the house.

Still, it's a sin to grumble. I retired on pension after the November holiday. I don't get much, but it's less worrying this way. How should I have managed otherwise during my last illness? I shouldn't have had the strength to dash to the office, and getting a doctor's note would have been awkward and dangerous. I wasn't going to submit to medical examination in my old age. It would have been the end of me.

Sometimes I ask myself a tricky question: why shouldn't I, after all, legalize my position? Why have I spent thirty years pretending to be somebody else, like a criminal? Andrei Kazimirovich Sushinsky. Half-Polish, half-Russian. Aged 61. Disabled. Not a Party member. Bachelor. No relatives, no children. Never been abroad. Born at Irkutsk. Father: clerk. Mother: housewife. Both died of cholera in 1901. And that's it!

But what about going to the police, apologizing, and telling the whole story simply, explaining it all just as it happened?

Well then, I'd say, it's like this. You can see for yourselves—I'm a creature from another world. Not from Africa or India, not even from Mars or one of your Venuses, but from somewhere still more remote and inaccessible. You don't even have names for such places, and if you spread out all the star maps and charts in existence before me, I honestly couldn't show you where that splendid point of light, my birthplace, has got to.

In the first place, I'm not an expert on astronomical matters. I went where I was taken. And in the second place, the picture's quite different, I can't recognize my native skies from your books and maps and things. Even now, I go out into the street at night, look up and there it is again—all wrong. I don't even know in which direction to yearn. It may be that not even my sun, let alone my earth, can be seen from here. It may be one of those on the other side of the galaxy. I can't work it out.

Please don't think that I came here with some ulterior motive. Migration of peoples, war of the worlds, and all that nonsense. I'm not a military man at all, nor a traveller, nor a scientist. Book-keeping is my profession—my profession here, that is. What I did before is best not mentioned. You wouldn't understand if I did.

In fact we had no intention of flying into space. To put it crudely we were going to a holiday resort. Then, on the way, something occurred—let's say it was a meteorite to make it easier for you—well then, we lost buoyancy and down we fell, into the unknown, for seven and a half months we went on falling—our months, mind, not yours—and by pure chance we landed up here.

When I came to and looked around—all my fellow travellers were dead. I buried them in the prescribed way, and started trying to adapt myself.

Everything around was exotic and unfathomable. A moon was burning in the sky, huge and yellow—and yet quite alone. The air was wrong, the light was wrong, and all the gravities and pressures were strange. What can I say? The most elementary pine-tree affected my other-worldly senses as a porcupine affects you.

Where could I go? I had to eat and drink. Of course, I'm not a man and not an animal; I incline more to the vegetable kingdom than to anything else you have here; but I too have my basic needs. The first thing I need is water, for want of a better form of moisture, and preferably at a certain temperature, and now and then I want the missing salts added to my water. And besides I felt a growing chill in the surrounding atmosphere. I don't have to tell you what Siberian forests are like.

There was nothing for it, I had to leave the forest. For some days past I'd been looking at people from behind bushes, sizing them up. I realized at once that they were rational creatures; but I was afraid to begin with that they might eat me. I draped myself in a bunch of rags (this was my first theft, and it was pardonable in the circumstances) and came out of the bushes with a look of friendship written all over me.

The Yakuts are a trusting and hospitable people. It was from them that I acquired the simplest human habits. Then I made my way to more civilized regions. I learnt the language, obtained an education, and taught arithmetic in a secondary school in the town of Irkutsk. I resided in the Crimea for a time, but soon left because of the climate: it's oppressively hot in summer, and not warm enough in winter, so that you still need a room with central heating, and conveniences of that sort weren't too common there in the 'twenties and cost a lot of money, more than I could manage. So I made my home in Moscow, and I've lived here ever since.

Whoever I were to tell this sad tale to, no matter how skilfully edited for the general reader, nobody would believe me, not at any price. If I could only cry as my story requires. But though I've learnt to laugh after a fashion I don't know how to weep. They'd think I was a madman, a fantasist, and what's more they might put me on trial for having a false passport, forging signatures and stamps, and other illegal activities.

And if, against all reason, they did believe me it would be worse still.

Academics from all the academies everywhere would flock in—astronomers, agronomists, physicists, economists, geologists, philologists, psychologists, biologists, microbiologists, chemists and biochemists, to study me down to the last spot on my body, omitting nothing. They would be for ever questioning, interrogating, examining, extracting.

Theses, films, and poems about me would circulate in millions of copies. Ladies would start wearing green lipstick and having their hats made to look like cactus, or failing that like rubber-plants. For years to come all hunchbacks would enjoy enormous success with women.

Motor cars would be called after my homeland, and after me hundreds of new-born infants as well as streets and dogs. I should become as famous as Lev Tolstoy, or Gulliver, or Hercules. Or Galileo Galilei.

But in spite of this universal interest in my humble person nobody would understand a thing. How could they understand me, when I myself am quite unable to express my inhuman nature in their language. I go round and round it, and try to get by with metaphors, but when it comes to the main point—I find nothing to say. I can only see a short, solid GOGRY, hear a rapid VZGLYAGU, and an indescribably beautiful PKHENTZ beams down upon my trunk. Fewer and fewer such words remain in my fading memory. I can convey their structure only approximately in the sounds of human speech. If I were surrounded by linguists asking "what do you call this?" I could only say: GOGRY TUZHEROSKIP, and hopelessly spread out my arms.

No, I'd better put up with living lonely and incognito. Given that such an odd creature has turned up, it should exist unnoticed. And die unnoticed.

Or else, when I die—and I shall die soon—they will put me in a glass jar, pickle me in alcohol, and exhibit me in a Natural History Museum. And the people filing past will shudder with horror and laugh insultingly to cheer themselves up, and thrust forward their censorious lips: "Heavens, how abnormal, what an ugly freak!"

But I'm not a freak! Just because I'm different must you immediately curse me? It's no good measuring my beauty against your own hideousness. I'm handsomer than you, and more normal. Every time I look at myself I have the evidence of my own eyes for it.

Just before I fell ill the bath was cracked. I found out about it late one evening and realized that Kostritskaya had done it to vex me. I couldn't expect any help from poor Veronica. Veronica had taken offence ever since the occasion when she offered me what was, humanly speaking, her most valuable possession, and I'd gone for a walk instead.

She has married the actor from the Stanislavsky, and sometimes the sound of her airy kisses wings to my ears through the thin wall. I was genuinely glad, for her sake, and on their wedding day I went so far as to send them an anonymous 16-rouble cake, with her initials and their monogram inscribed on it in chocolate.

But I was incredibly hungry, and Kostritskaya had damaged the bath to destroy me, and, pending repairs, the hole where the water ran out had been stopped up with a wooden bung, and the water didn't flow. So when everybody had gone to bed and I could hear an even snoring from the floor above and the floor below and all the rooms either side, I took Veronica's wash-tub off its nail in the lavatory, where it hangs with all the neighbours' tubs. It banged like thunder as I dragged it along the corridor, and somebody on the floor below stopped snoring. But I finished the job, boiled a kettle in the kitchen, drew a bucketful of cold water, carried the lot into my room, bolted the door and stuck the key in the keyhole.

What a pleasure it gave me to throw off my clothes, remove my wig, tear off my genuine India-rubber ear-shells and unbuckle the straps which constrict my back and chest. My body opened out like a potted palm brought home from the shop wrapped up. All the limbs which had grown numb in the course of the day came to tingling life.

I installed myself in the tub, seized a sponge in one hand to squeeze water over all the dry places, and held the kettle in my second hand. With my third hand I grasped a mug of cold water, added some hot to it, and tried it with my fourth and last remaining hand to see that it wasn't too hot. What comfort!

My skin freely absorbed the precious fluid pouring down on me from the enamel mug, and when the first pangs of hunger were allayed I decided to inspect myself in more detail and wash off the unhealthy slime which had seeped out of my pores and congealed in some places in dry mauve clots. True, the eyes in my hands and feet, on the crown of my head and the nape of my neck were getting appreciably dimmer, from being covered up in the day time by rough clothes and false hair. The friction of my right shoe had cost me the sight of one eye back in 1934. It wasn't easy to carry out a really thorough inspection.

But I swivelled my head, not limiting myself to a half-circle—the miserable 180 degrees allotted to the human neck—I blinked simultaneously all the eyes which were still intact, driving away fatigue and darkness, and I succeeded in viewing myself on all sides and from several different angles at once. What a fascinating sight it is, and what a pity that it is only accessible to me in the all-too-short hours of night. I only have to raise my hand and I can see myself from the ceiling, soaring and hovering over myself as it were. And at the same time with my remaining eyes I keep in view my lower parts, my back, my front, all the spreading branches of my body. If I hadn't been living in exile for thirty-two years I should probably never dream of admiring my exterior. But here I am the only example of that lost harmony and beauty which I call my homeland. What is there for me to do on this earth except delight in my person?

It doesn't matter that my rear hand is twisted by its permanent duty of representing a human lump. It doesn't matter that my fore hand is so maimed by the straps that two fingers have withered, and my old body has lost its former suppleness. I'm still beautiful for all that! Proportioned! Elegant! Despite whatever envious carpers may say.

These were my thoughts as I watered myself from the enamel mug, on the night when Kostritskaya took it into her head to murder me by means of a cracked bath. But next morning I fell ill. I must have caught cold in the tub. The worst time in my life had begun.

For a week and a half I lay on my hard couch and felt myself drying up. I hadn't the strength to go along to the kitchen for water. My body, tightly swaddled in its man-shaped sack, grew numb and inert. My desiccated skin cracked. I couldn't raise myself to slacken my wire-sharp bonds.

A week and a half went by and nobody came in.

I could imagine my neighbours joyfully ringing up the health centre when I was dead. The district medical officer would come to certify the fatal outcome, would bend over my couch, cut open my clothing, my bandages and my straps with his surgical scissors, recoil in horror and give orders for my corpse to be delivered to the biggest and best of dissecting theatres as soon as possible.

Here it came—the jar of spirit, caustic as Kostritskaya's perfume! Into the toxic bath, into a glassy tomb, into history—for the edification of posterity to the end of time they would plunge me, the monster, the greatest monster on earth.

I started groaning, quietly at first, then louder and louder, in hateful and indispensable human language. "Mama, mama, mama," I groaned, imitating the intonation of a tearful child and hoping to waken the pity of anybody who heard me. And in those two hours, while I was calling for help, I vowed that if I lived I would keep my secret to the end, and not let this last vestige of my homeland, this beautiful body, fall into the hands of my enemies for them to rend and mock.

Veronica came in. She had obviously lost weight, and her eyes, purged of love and resentment, were serene and indifferent.

"Water!" I croaked.

"If you're ill," said Veronica, "you ought to get undressed and take your temperature. I'll call the doctor. They'll bleed you."

The doctor! Bleed me! Get undressed! Next she'd be touching my forehead, which was as cool as the air in the room, and feeling for my nonexistent pulse with her red-hot fingers. But Veronica only straightened the pillow, and snatched her hand away in disgust when it came into contact with my wig. Evidently my body only revolted her, like all other humans.

"Water! Water for Christ's sake!"

"Do you want it out of the tap or boiled?"

In the end she went out and came back with a decanter. She polished a dusty tumbler with such a pensive and leisurely air that I should have thought she was taking her revenge on me if I hadn't known that she knew nothing. She said:

"You know, Andrei Kazimirovich, I really did love you. I realize that I loved you—how shall I put it—out of pity. . . . Pity for a lonely, crippled human being, if you will forgive my frankness. But I pitied you so much . . . didn't notice . . . physical blemishes. . . . To me you were the handsomest man on earth, Andrei Kazimirovich . . . the most . . . man. And when you laughed at me so cruelly . . . make an end of myself . . . loved . . . won't conceal from you . . . worthy man. . . . Fell in love again . . . even thankful now . . . fell in love . . . man . . . human . . . humanity . . . as man to man . . ."

"Veronica Grigorievna," I interrupted, unable to bear it any longer, "Please hurry. Water . . ."

"Human . . . manhu . . . hanumanu . . . Human . . ."

"Water! Water!"

Veronica filled the tumbler and suddenly raised it right to my mouth. My false teeth rattled on the glass, but I couldn't bring myself to take the liquid internally. I need watering from above, like a flower or an apple-tree, not through my mouth.

"Drink, drink!" Veronica urged me. "I thought you wanted water . . ."

I pushed her off and struggled up into a sitting position, feeling that all was lost. Water ran out of my mouth on to the couch. I managed to put out my hand and catch a few drops on my dried-up palm.

"Give me the decanter and go away," I ordered with all the firmness I could muster. "Leave me in peace! I'll drink it myself."

Slow tears trickled from Veronica's eyes.

"Why do you hate me?" she asked. "What have I done to you? You were the one who didn't want my love, who rejected my pity. . . . You're just vicious and nasty, Andrei Kazimirovich, you're a bad man."

"Veronica, if you have so much as a grain of pity left in you, go away, I beg you, I implore you, go away, leave me alone."

She went out thoroughly dejected. Then I unbuttoned my shirt and stuck the decanter inside it, neck downwards.

4

Nature is all scurry and bustle. Everything is in a fever of excitement. Leaves come out hurriedly. Sparrows sing in broken snatches. Children hurry off to their schools and technical colleges for their exams. Outside the voices of nannies are shrill and hysterical. The air has a tang in it. The Kostritskaya smell—in a low concentration—is all-pervading. Even the cactuses on my window-sill have a lemony aroma in the mornings. I mustn't forget to make Veronica a present of them before I leave.

I'm afraid my last illness has done for me. It hasn't just broken my body, it's crippled me spiritually as well. Strange desires come upon me at times. I feel an urge to go to the pictures. Or else I think I should like a game of draughts with Veronica Grigorievna's husband. He's said to be a first-class chess and draughts player.

I have re-read my notes, and am unhappy about them. The influence of an alien milieu is felt in every sentence. What good to anybody is this idle chatter in a local dialect? I mustn't forget to burn them before I leave. I've no intention of showing them to humans. And my own kind will never read them or hear anything about me. They'll never fly such an unearthly distance to this outlandish place.

It's getting harder and harder for me to recall the past. Only a few words of my native tongue have survived. I've even forgotten how to think as I used to, let alone read or write. I remember something beautiful, but what exactly I don't know.

Sometimes I fancy that I left children behind at home. Ever such bonny little cactuses. I mustn't forget to give them to Veronica. They must be quite big now. Vasya's going to school. What am I saying, school! He must be a sturdy adult. He's gone in for engineering. And Masha is married.

Lord, oh Lord! I seem to be turning into a man!

No, it wasn't for this that I stood thirty-two years of suffering, and lay on a hard couch without water last winter. The only reason I got better was so that I could go and hide in some quiet spot as soon as it got warm and die without causing a sensation. That's the only way I can preserve what is left.

Everything is ready for my departure: my ticket and seat-reservation to Irkutsk, my can for water, a decent sum of money. I've kept practically my whole pension for the winter in my savings book. I didn't spend anything on a fur coat, nor on trams or trolley-buses. I didn't go to the pictures once in all that time. And I gave up paying rent three months ago now. I've got 1,657 roubles altogether.

The day after tomorrow, when everybody's gone to bed, I shall leave the house unnoticed and take a taxi to the station. A hoot of the whistle—

and that's the last you'll see of me. Forests, forests as green as my mother's body, will take me in and hide me.

I'll get there somehow or other. For part of the way I'll hire a boat. It's about 350 kilometres. And all by river. Water right beside me. Drench myself three times a day if I want to.

There was a hole. I'll search till I find it. The hole we made when we fell. Put wood all round it. Juniper blazes up like gunpowder. I'll sit down in the hole, untie and unstrap myself and wait. Not a single human thought will I think, not a single word of alien speech will I utter.

When the first frosts begin and I see that the time is ripe—just one match will be enough. There will be nothing left of me.

But that's a long time off. There will be many warm and pleasant nights. And many stars in the summer sky. Which one of them? . . . Who knows? I will gaze at them all, together and individually, fill my eyes with gazing. One or other of them is mine.

Oh native land! PKHENTZ! GOGRY TUZHEROSKIP! I am coming back to you. GOGRY! GOGRY! GOGRY! TUZHEROSKIP! TUZHEROSKIP! BONJOUR! GUTENABEND! TUZHEROSKIP!

BU-BU-BU!

MIAOW-MIAOW!

PKHENTZ!

Donald Barthelme

Donald Barthelme (1933–) was born in Philadelphia, reared in Houston, Texas, and served in the army in Korea and Japan. While working on newspapers and magazines, Barthelme has been writing his brief, fragmentary fantasies, chiefly for The New Yorker. *His fictional world is distorted and incongruous; his language employs the noncommunicative jargon that passes for speech in some contemporary social and intellectual circles. His stories have appeared in several volumes:* Come Back, Dr. Caligari *(1964),* Unspeakable Practices, Unnatural Acts *(1968), and* City Life *(1970). (See page 71 of Introduction.)*

REPORT

Our group is against the war. But the war goes on. I was sent to Cleveland to talk to the engineers. The engineers were meeting in Cleveland. I was supposed to persuade them not to do what they are going to do. I took United's 4:45 from LaGuardia arriving in Cleveland at 6:13. Cleveland is dark blue at that hour. I went directly to the motel, where the engineers were meeting. Hundreds of engineers attended the Cleveland meeting. I noticed many fractures among the engineers, bandages, traction. I noticed what appeared to be fracture of the carpal scaphoid in six examples. I noticed numerous fractures of the humeral shaft, of the os calcis, of the pelvic girdle. I noticed a high incidence of clay-shoveller's fracture. I could not account for these fractures. The engineers were making calculations, taking measurements, sketching on the blackboard, drinking beer, throwing bread, buttonholing employers, hurling glasses into the fireplace. They were friendly.

They were friendly. They were full of love and information. The chief engineer wore shades. Patella in Monk's traction, clamshell fracture by the look of it. He was standing in a slum of beer bottles and microphone cable. "Have some of this chicken à la Isambard Kingdom Brunel the Great Ingineer," he said. "And declare who you are and what we can do for you. What is your line, distinguished guest?"

"Software," I said. "In every sense. I am here representing a small group of interested parties. We are interested in your thing, which seems to be functioning. In the midst of so much dysfunction, function is interesting. Other people's things don't seem to be working. The State Department's thing doesn't seem to be working. The U.N.'s thing doesn't seem to be working. The democratic left's thing doesn't seem to be working. Buddha's thing—"

"Ask us anything about our thing, which seems to be working," the chief engineer said. "We will open our hearts and heads to you, Software Man, because we want to be understood and loved by the great lay public, and have our marvels appreciated by that public, for which we daily unsung produce tons of new marvels each more life-enhancing than the last. Ask us anything. Do you want to know about evaporated thin-film metallurgy? Monolithic and hybrid integrated-circuit processes? The algebra of inequalities? Optimization theory? Complex high-speed microminiature closed and open loop systems? Fixed variable mathematical cost searches? Epitaxial deposition of semi-conductor materials? Gross interfaced space gropes? We also have specialists in the cuckooflower, the doctorfish, and the dumdum bullet as these relate to aspects of today's expanding technology, and they do in the damnedest ways."

I spoke to him then about the war. I said the same things people always say when they speak against the war. I said that the war was wrong. I said that large countries should not burn down small countries. I said that the government had made a series of errors. I said that these errors once small and forgivable were now immense and unforgivable. I said that the government was attempting to conceal its original errors under layers of new errors. I said that the government was sick with error, giddy with it. I said that ten thousand of our soldiers had already been killed in pursuit of the government's errors. I said that tens of thousands of the enemy's soldiers and civilians had been killed because of various errors, ours and theirs. I said that we are responsible for errors made in our name. I said that the government should not be allowed to make additional errors.

"Yes, yes," the chief engineer said, "there is doubtless much truth in what you say, but we can't possibly *lose* the war, can we? And stopping is losing, isn't it? The war regarded as a process, stopping regarded as an abort? We don't know *how* to lose a war. That skill is not among our skills. Our array smashes their array, that is what we know. That is the process. That is what is.

"But let's not have any more of this dispiriting downbeat counter-productive talk. I have a few new marvels here I'd like to discuss with you just briefly. A few new marvels that are just about ready to be gaped at by the admiring layman. Consider for instance the area of realtime online computer-controlled wish evaporation. Wish evaporation is going to be crucial in meeting the rising expectations of the world's peoples, which are as you know rising entirely too fast."

I noticed then distributed about the room a great many transverse fractures of the ulna. "The development of the pseudo-ruminant stomach for underdeveloped peoples," he went on, "is one of our interesting things you should be interested in. With the pseudo-ruminant stomach they can chew cuds, that is to say, eat grass. Blue is the most popular color worldwide and for that reason we are working with certain strains of your native Kentucky *Poa pratensis,* or bluegrass, as the staple input for the p/r stomach cycle, which would also give a shot in the arm to our balance-of-payments thing don't you know. . . ." I noticed about me then a great number of metatarsal fractures in banjo splints. "The kangaroo initiative . . . eight hundred thousand harvested last year . . . highest percentage of edible protein of any herbivore yet studied . . ."

"Have new kangaroos been planted?"

The engineer looked at me.

"I intuit your hatred and jealousy of our thing," he said. "The ineffectual always hate our thing and speak of it as anti-human, which is not at all a meaningful way to speak of our thing. Nothing mechanical is alien to me," he said (amber spots making bursts of light in his shades), "because I am human, in a sense, and if I think it up, then 'it' is human too, whatever 'it' may be. Let me tell you, Software Man, we have been damned forbearing in the matter of this little war you declare yourself to be interested in. Function is the cry, and our thing is functioning like crazy. There are things we could do that we have not done. Steps we could take that we have not taken. These steps are, regarded in a certain light, the light of our enlightened self-interest, quite justifiable steps. We could, of course, get irritated. We could, of course, *lose patience.*

"We could, of course, release thousands upon thousands of self-powered crawling-along-the-ground lengths of titanium wire eighteen inches long with a diameter of .0005 centimetres (that is to say, invisible) which, scenting an enemy, climb up his trouser leg and wrap themselves around his neck. We have developed those. They are within our capabilities. We could, of course, release in the arena of the upper air our new improved pufferfish toxin which precipitates an identity crisis. No special technical problems there. That is almost laughably easy. We could, of course, place up to two million maggots in their rice within twenty-four hours. The maggots are ready, massed in secret staging areas in Alabama. We have hypodermic darts capable of piebalding the enemy's pigmentation. We have rots, blights, and rusts capable of attacking his alphabet. Those are dandies. We have a hut-shrinking chemical which penetrates the fibres of the bamboo, causing it, the hut, to strangle its occupants. This operates only after 10 P.M., when people are sleeping. Their mathematics are at the mercy of a suppurating surd we have invented. We have a family of fishes trained to attack their fishes. We have the deadly testicle-destroying telegram. The cable-companies are coöperating. We have a green substance that, well, I'd rather not talk about. We have a secret word that, if pronounced, produces multiple fractures in all living things in an area the size of four football fields."

"That's why—"

"Yes. Some damned fool couldn't keep his mouth shut. The point is that the whole structure of enemy life is within our power to *rend, vitiate, devour,* and *crush.* But that's not the interesting thing."

"You recount these possibilities with uncommon relish."

"Yes I realize that there is too much relish here. But *you* must realize that these capabilities represent in and of themselves highly technical and complex and interesting problems and hurdles on which our boys have expended many thousands of hours of hard work and brilliance. And that the effects are often grossly exaggerated by irresponsible victims. And that the whole thing represents a fantastic series of triumphs for the multi-disciplined problem-solving team concept."

"I appreciate that."

"We *could* unleash all this technology at once. You can imagine what would happen then. But that's not the interesting thing."

"What is the interesting thing?"

"The interesting thing is that we have a *moral sense.* It is on punched cards, perhaps the most advanced and sensitive moral sense the world has ever known."

"Because it is on punched cards?"

"It considers all considerations in endless and subtle detail," he said. "It even quibbles. With this great new moral tool, how can we go wrong? I confidently predict that, although we *could* employ all this splendid new weaponry I've been telling you about, *we're not going to do it.*"

"We're not going to do it?"

I took United's 5:44 from Cleveland arriving at Newark at 7:19. New Jersey is bright pink at that hour. Living things move about the surface of New Jersey at that hour molesting each other only in traditional ways. I made my report to the group. I stressed the friendliness of the engineers. I said, It's all right. I said, We have a moral sense. I said, *We're not going to do it.* They didn't believe me.

Index